MW01595280

everycubever

A Cubrehensive guide to everyone
who wore the uniform from
1871-2018

Rick Kaempfer

ECKHARTZ
PRESS

everycubever: A Cubrehensive guide to everyone who wore the uniform from 1871-2018
Copyright © 2019 by *Rick Kaempfer*

Trade Paperback

Published in the United States by **Eckhartz Press**
Chicago, Illinois
All Rights Reserved

Cover and interior design by *Vasil Nazar*
Illustrations by *Freepik.com*

No part of this book may be used or reproduced in any manner whatsoever without written permission except in the case of brief quotations embodied in critical articles and reviews.

ISBN: 978-1-7336111-5-2

DEDICATION

To the three generations of Cubs fans in my family. To my Uncle Manny, who became a fan after immigrating here in 1957 and made me a Cubs fan in 1969, but didn't live long enough to see them win a World Series. To my sons Tommy, Johnny, and Sean who carry on the new family tradition, and my wife Bridget who converted after marriage.

And to the many Cubs players who have given me joy, sadness, anger, rage, fear, disgust, surprise, shame, pity, envy, disdain, helplessness, patience, astonishment, affirmation, and love. As a German (and a nerd), I wasn't going to naturally experience all of those emotions without your help, so thank you for making me a more well-rounded person.

INTRODUCTION

This book began as a quest. In 2008, as the Cubs were celebrating the 100th anniversary of the last time they won the World Series, I began my search for an answer. How was it possible that a franchise could go that long without winning it all? It seemed like a statistical impossibility. I figured there had to be a reason for it. I decided to leave no stone unturned in my quest. I would examine the entire history of the team looking for answers. I knew it wasn't because of that stupid goat.

During my quest I began to share my discoveries on a website and blog called Just One Bad Century www.justonebadcentury.com. At first there was an admittedly cheeky approach to the site as I looked into the dark chapters of Cubs history to see if there was a curse of some kind. I don't believe in curses, but I figured there had to be a better one than the goat. Was it because Cubs great Cap Anson erected the color barrier? No — the Cubs won it all twice after that (1907, 1908). Was it because a Lutheran seminary was torn down to build the current Wrigley Field? No, the ballpark wasn't even built by the Cubs, and let's face it, Martin Luther wasn't the cursing type. Was it the gambling Cubs that got quietly banned from baseball? No, obviously not. The White Sox won the World Series in 2005, and they actually cheated DURING the World Series in 1919.

It became obvious to me that there was no curse. So, what else could have caused it? That's when I began looking at Cubs management and ownership over the years. This is where the answer lay, and it became obvious immediately. The downturn of the franchise began when Phillip K. Wrigley took over the club after his father's death. He promised Pops he would never sell the club, but it would have been so much better for all of us if he did. Before the draft was implemented, the Cubs were among the last teams to create their own minor league system. They were also late to the game when it came to signing African-American players. Ernie Banks came a full six years after Jackie Robinson broke the color barrier. After the draft was created, they invested the least in instruction, development, and scouting. They drafted badly, and even when they got lucky, they didn't develop the talent. When the *Tribune* bought the club, they invested more money into it, but they also focused predominantly on the big league club, and not on development. That's the real reason for the drought. There was no curse. It was pure incompetence.

Of course it took me years to come up with this hypothesis. Along the way I became distracted by the great stories in Cubs history. I created features on the site that explored great Cubs nicknames, great Cubs mustaches, and great stories of Cubs lore from their winning years. I matched up the Cubs with historical events to put them into historical context. I did a feature called This Week in 1908 and This Week in 1945, to really take a deep dive into the last year the Cubs won the Series and the Pennant. And then one year, I decided to feature all the Cubs that were celebrating birthdays on that particular day. It wasn't until the year was over that something occurred to me. If I had written about every Cub celebrating a birthday every day of the year, hadn't I necessarily written about *Every Cub Ever*?

So, I went through all my archives and put them into alphabetical order. Everything I had written about every Cub was thrown into the hopper and then compared against lists of every Cub who had ever played the game. Turns out, I had missed about fifty Cubs. Some of them had been missed because nobody knew their birthdays. Some had been missed because the information about 1871-1900 was a little sketchy or hadn't yet been investigated and reported. So, I filled the holes. And I presented the list of Cubs stories on the website under the title *Every Cub Ever*. That was in 2014.

Ever since then, and especially since the Cubs won the World Series in 2016, people have been asking me why in the world I didn't convert it into a book. Well, this year I decided to listen to their advice. I went through my *Every Cub Ever* feature, and thoroughly wrote and rewrote every single entry. I double-checked the information, and I found tons of new information. Throughout it all, I wasn't really searching for stats. I was looking for stories. Sometimes all I had to go on was a box score of a game that took place over a hundred years ago. Sometimes I found way more information than I needed. I decided not to include anything that I only found from a single source unless it was a quote. All quotes are given attribution to the original source I discovered them. All stories come from multiple sources, sometimes from a dozen or more. I started doing footnotes, but soon recognized the folly in my ways. This book was already 500+ pages long. It was quickly heading toward a thousand.

Nobody wants a 1000-page book.

So, let me acknowledge the sources I used, even if I only used them once, or only used them to further understand something on background. Let's start with the big ones. Without Baseball Reference (baseball-reference.com) this book doesn't exist. That's the site where I got the birthdays that launched the quest for thousands of stories (actually 2186 stories to be exact), and that's the site where I discovered I was still missing fifty-some Cubs. The stories of the players weren't there, but the bare bones of their baseball careers were. Next up comes the incredible site Retro Sheet. They have the box scores of almost every baseball game ever played. With their help (and some newspaper archives — particularly *The Daily News* and *The Chicago Tribune*), I was able to reconstruct the stories of players who played only one inning, or one game or one week. Sometimes that was all I had. Also, the Baseball Biography Project is a great resource, especially helpful in understanding the game in the 19th century and early 20th century. They are forever publishing great stories. From the time I began profiling players in 2008 to today, they have helped me fill in the blanks for hundreds of them.

Those are the main websites I used to check and double-check my information, but many of the stories came from the thoughtful research and writing of some great authors. John Snyder's book *Cubs Journal* and Peter Golenbock's *Wrigleyville* have some incredible stories and gave me leads to research many more. The 1908 season has been chronicled well in the pages of Mike Cameron's *Public Bonehead, Private Hero*, Grant DePorter and Elliot Harris' *Hoodoo*, and David Rapp's *Tinker to Evers to Chance*. If you ever want to take a deep dive into that season, I strongly recommend all three. The 1918 season, which was controversial and fascinating, is chronicled beautifully in *Original Curse: Did the Cubs throw the 1918 World Series?* by Sean Deveney. The shootings of Billy Jurges and Eddie Waitkus have been written about dozens of times, but I particularly like *Baseball's Natural* by John Theodore and *The Showgirl and the Shortstop* by Jack Bales. If you want to find out more about either player or incident, those are great starting points. The 1945 season was captured best by Charles N. Billington in a book called *Wrigley's Last World Series*.

Here are a few others that were insightful for those years not already discussed: *Wrigley Field: The Unauthorized Biography, Chicago Cubs Yesterday & Today, Cubs by the Numbers, Essential Cubs, Baseball Babylon,* and *Harry Caray*.

The players themselves have contributed to the book by writing (or having a ghostwriter write) their autobiographies. Some great stories can be found in Cap Anson's *A Ball Player's Career: Being the Personal Reminiscences of Adrian C. Anson, The Glory of Their Times* by Lawrence Ritter (mostly about Davy Jones and his contemporaries), Leo Durocher's *Nice Guys Finish Last*, Bill Veeck's *Veeck as in Wreck*, Ron Santo's *For the Love of Ivy*, and the many books George Castle has written with Cubs of recent vintage. All of them are great.

As the media writer for the *Illinois Entertainer*, I've also been able to interview a few of the broadcasters who have covered the Cubs. The insights provided by Len Kasper, Pat Hughes, Mark Grote, Andy Masur, and Judd Sirott were incredibly helpful. I also interviewed Pat Brickhouse, widow of Jack, and she gave me great information. My publishing company Eckhartz Press has published a few great Cubs books like *Cubsessions* by Becky Sarwate Maxwell and Randy Richardson and *Best Seat in the House: Diary of a Wrigley Field Usher* by Bruce Bohrer. Both books are loaded with tales about celebrity Cubs fans and the guy who showed them their seats. In addition, I was one of the contributors to the great Cubs book *Cubbie Blues: One Hundred Years of Waiting Til Next Year*, which was edited by Donald G. Evans. Great stories of Cubs fandom in that book.

As you can tell by the wealth of resource material, this book could have been a lot longer than it is. It was very difficult to pick and choose what to describe about each player, manager, broadcaster, or owner. I focused on making sure every single person was covered, that the big highlights and most interesting moments were covered, and that I did it with respect and accuracy. I opted not to include the many celebrity Cubs fans I've interviewed because lots of them are covered in the pages of *Cubsessions,* but also because their stories will remain on my website www.justonebadcentury. com. You'll also find Cubs songs, videos, baseball cards and more there. Something had to be cut, right? Another thing I decided not to include was the stats of each player. I try to summarize where appropriate, but there are a million places to find those stats. I wanted to focus on the stories.

As you read this you may find yourself thinking, oh boy I'd like to know more about this person or that event. Hopefully my list of sources above will send you to the treasure trove that is out there awaiting you. This is just my attempt at synthesizing the stories of *EveryCubEver,* as it stands today, going into the 2019 season. Luckily for Cubs fans everywhere, new stories and new players will arise every day. That's one of the reasons we love following this team.

Heaven help us.

CHAPTER ONE

A

The starting line-up of your Chicago Cubs beginning with the letter A...

C—Jimmy Archer, Bionic Cub
1B—Cap Anson, Hall of Famer
2B—Sparky Adams, the KiKi bait
SS—Alex Arias, World Series champ (for another team)
3B—Shane Andrews, the Tokyo slugger
LF—Moises Alou, hand-pisser
CF—Richie Ashburn, Hall of Famer
RF—George Altman, the slugger
Bench—Ethan Allen, the board game creator
SP—Grover Cleveland Alexander, Hall of Famer
SP—Jake Arietta, World Series champ
RP—Ted Abernathy, the submariner
RP—Rick Aguilera, the closer

David Aardsma 1981—(Cubs 2006)
The Cubs picked up Aardsma in the trade that sent Latroy Hawkins to the Giants. He pitched out of the bullpen for the entire 2006 season and had a respectable year (3-0, 4.08 ERA, 45 appearances), but the Cubs traded him to the White Sox the following season for Neal Cotts. Aardsma didn't really find his niche in baseball until a few seasons later when the Mariners converted him to closer. Over the next two seasons he saved 69 games.

Bert Abbey 1869—1962 (Colts 1893-1894)
The pitcher was born in Vermont during the Ulysses S. Grant administration and was a teetotaler. That didn't go over so well with his Cubs (then known as the Colts) teammates. They were one of the rowdiest teams in baseball history, but Bert was a Christian gentleman. At a time of rampant racism,

Bert famously looked all the Negro porters in their eyes and tipped them into their hands instead of throwing money at their feet (which was the common practice at the time). His teammates also disliked him for that. Nevertheless, he probably would have stayed with Chicago if he had delivered on the field, and that's where Abbey fell a little short. He pitched for two seasons, won four games, and posted an ERA over five.

Ted Abernathy 1933—2004 (Cubs 1965-1966, 1969-1970)
Abernathy's delivery was memorable — he was a submariner who nearly hit the ground with his arm on every pitch. The reliever pitched for seven teams during his fourteen-year career, but probably had his best season in 1965 with the Cubs. That year he led the league in saves with 31. (He also led the league in saves with the 1967 Cincinnati Reds). By the time he returned to the Cubs in 1969, he was no longer a closer, but he remained an important part of the Cubs bullpen. Ted was traded to the Cardinals in May of 1970 and remained in the big leagues until 1972.

Cliff Aberson 1921—1973 (Cubs 1947-1949)
The local Chicago boy (Senn High School) played three seasons for the Cubs after serving in the military during the war and playing a season of pro football for the Green Bay Packers as a tailback and defensive back. He was a left fielder for the Cubs. In parts of three seasons, he hit five homers. His nickname was Kif.

Johnny Abrego 1962—(Cubs 1985)
Johnny only had one shot at the big leagues in his baseball career, and that came with the injury-depleted 1985 Cubs. The entire starting rotation from the 1984 division winners got hurt the following year, and Johnny was among the pitchers brought up to fill in. He had five starts in September and didn't impress the brass. He never got another chance. He hurt his arm in the minors and was out of baseball at the age of 24.

Jimmy Adair 1907—1982 (Cubs 1931)
He got his cup of coffee with the Cubs during the last six weeks of the 1931 season. The 24-year-old shortstop they

called "Choppy" hit .276 in 76 at-bats for the Cubs. He played another 13 seasons in the minors and never got another sniff of the big leagues.

Bobby Adams 1921–1997 (Cubs 1957-1959)

Bobby was mainly a third baseman, and he also played a little second base in his 14-year big league career, the last three of which were with the Cubs. Bobby backed up Al Dark. Adams and Dark, of course, were just keeping the position warm for the young phenom who came up their last year with the Cubs: a future Hall of Famer named Santo.

Karl Adams 1891–1967 (Cubs 1915)

They called him Rebel because he hailed from the South (Georgia). Adams pitched for the Cubs during their last season at West Side Grounds. He didn't exactly set the world on fire. His record was 1-9, and his ERA was 4.71. That stint with the Cubs was his last in the big leagues. He pitched in the minors for another ten years.

Mike Adams 1948–(Cubs 1976-1977)

Adams displayed a good combination of power and speed during his eleven minor league seasons, but never got an opportunity to display it in the big leagues. His stint with the Cubs consisted of 40 plate appearances over two years, and he barely hit over .100. He also got cups of coffee with the Twins and the A's. His father Bobby played second and third base for the Cubs in the late 1950s.

Red Adams 1921–2017 (Cubs 1946)

Adams starred for the Cubs minor league affiliate in Los Angeles while the Cubs were winning the pennant in Chicago in 1945. He won 21 games that year. The Cubs brought him up in 1946, and he ran into a buzz saw. In eight appearances Adams posted an ERA over 8. He had to settle for starring in the minor leagues after that. Adams never returned to the show. After his playing days he worked for the Dodgers as a scout and coach.

Sparky Adams 1894–1989 (Cubs 1923-1927)

His real name was Earl John Adams, and he was an energetic little guy; only 5'5. Adams spent 1923 and 1924 as the Cubs' semi-regular shortstop, but came into his own when he was switched to second base after George Grantham was traded to Pittsburgh for shortstop Rabbit Maranville. Sparky was the Cubs leadoff batter during those years and led the league in at-bats, but his real long-term value to the Cubs may have been as trade bait. Pittsburgh sent Kiki Cuyler to the Cubs for Adams and Pete Scott in 1927. Cuyler led the Cubs to two National League pennants (1929 & 1932) and is enshrined in the Hall of Fame.

Historical note: On the day that penicillin was discovered by Scottish scientist Alexander Fleming (1928), Adams was haunting his ex-Cubs teammates by scoring three runs in a 16-1 trouncing of the Cubs in Pittsburgh.

Terry Adams 1973–(Cubs 1995-1999)

Terry was a hard-throwing right-handed reliever for the Cubs in the late 90s. They thought they could make a closer out of him, but it didn't work out. He did register 18 saves in 1997, but his ERA was 4.62, and his WHIP (walks & hits per inning pitched) was an incredibly bad 1.77. Terry was traded to the Dodgers in December of 1999 for Eric Young and Ismael Valdes. A bit of Terry Adams trivia: He is one of only 13 players in big league history to have played more than 500 games and registered more walks than hits (as a batter). He had four career hits and seven career walks.

Bob Addis 1925–2016 (Cubs 1952-1953)

Bob got the most extensive playing time in his big league career with the 1952 Cubs. He was essentially a fourth outfielder filling in for Hank Sauer, Frank Baumholtz and Hal Jeffcoat. In June of 1953 he was included in the package of players sent to Pittsburgh to acquire Ralph Kiner. Pittsburgh didn't have much use for him. It turned out to be the end of the line for Bob. He played another few seasons in the minors before hanging up his spikes after the 1956 season. He passed away just a few weeks after the Cubs won the World Series in 2016.

Bob Addy 1842–1910 (White Stockings 1876)

The Canadian-born outfielder was a grizzled 34-year-old veteran when he joined the Cubs (then known as the White Stockings). He batted sixth and started in right field for the Cubs' very first game in the National League. They called him "Magnet" because of his fielding prowess. He hit .282

in his only season with Chicago. Magnet is the earliest-born Cub of all-time, beating Joe Start by about eight months. He was born only five years into the reign of Queen Victoria, and during the John Tyler administration in America.

Dewey Adkins 1918–1998 (Cubs 1949)

Dewey didn't get a lot of time in the big leagues (he pitched briefly during the war for the Senators), but his most extensive action came as a member of the Cubs in 1949. He was a right-handed pitcher and pitched mostly in relief. In 30 games (five starts) he clocked in with a 5.68 ERA. That wasn't quite good enough to extend his big league career into the 1950s. His Cubs career highlight was the day he hit his only big league home run.

Administration Cubs. There has been at least one Cub born during every presidential administration from John Tyler (10th president) through Bill Clinton (42nd president). For instance

- John Tyler—Bob Addy (earliest-born Cubs player) 1842
- James K. Polk—Oscar Bielaski (one of only two Cubs Civil War veterans) 1847
- Zachary Taylor—Jim Devlin (banned for life for gambling) 1849
- Millard Filmore—Fred Andrus (later worked as a treasurer for Albert Spalding's company) 1850
- Franklin Pierce—Charlie Waitt (2B & outfielder) 1853
- James Buchanan—Mike King Kelly (Hall of Famer) 1857
- Abraham Lincoln—John Clarkson (Hall of Famer) 1861
- Andrew Johnson—Hugh Duffy (Hall of Famer) 1866
- Ulysses S. Grant—Charles Weeghman (builder of Wrigley Field) 1874
- Rutherford B. Hayes—Harry Steinfeldt (forgotten man in Tinker/Evers/Chance

infield) 1877
- James Garfield—Johnny Evers (Hall of Famer) 1881
- Chester Arthur—Solly Hofman, Ed Reulbach, and Wildfire Schulte (1908 Cubs) 1882
- Grover Cleveland (first term)—Pat Pieper (Cubs P.A. Announcer, 'Tension please') 1886
- Benjamin Harrison—Max Flack (1918 World Series Goat) 1899
- Grover Cleveland (second term)—P.K. Wrigley (Cubs owner) 1894
- William McKinley—KiKi Cuyler (Hall of Famer) 1898
- Theodore Roosevelt—Tony Lazzeri (Hall of Famer) 1903
- William Howard Taft—Billy Herman (Hall of Famer) 1909
- Woodrow Wilson—Harry Caray (Cubs announcer) 1914
- Warren G. Harding—Ralph Kiner (Hall of Famer) 1922
- Calvin Coolidge— Sam Toothpick Jones (First African-American to pitch no-hitter) 1925
- Herbert Hoover—Ernie Banks (Mr. Cub/ Hall of Famer) 1931
- Franklin Delano Roosevelt—Billy Williams (Hall of Famer) 1938
- Harry S. Truman—Rick Reuschel (Big Daddy) 1949
- Dwight D. Eisenhower—Ryne Sandberg (Hall of Famer) 1959
- John F. Kennedy—Shawon Dunston (of Shawon-O-Meter fame) 1963
- Lyndon B. Johnson—Greg Maddux (Hall of Famer) 1966
- Richard Nixon—Len Kasper (TV-Voice of the Cubs) 1971

- Gerald Ford–Derrek Lee (Batting champion, Gold Glover) 1975
- Jimmy Carter–Kerry Wood (Kid K–20
- strikeouts) 1977
- Ronald Reagan–Carlos Zambrano (Big Z–Cubs ace) 1981
- George H.W. Bush–Anthony Rizzo (Gold Glover First Baseman) 1989 and Kris Bryant (MVP) 1992
- Bill Clinton–Kyle Schwarber (World Series Hero) 1993

Rick Aguilera 1961–(Cubs 1999-2000)

When the Cubs acquired Aguilera in May of 1999, they thought he was one of the final pieces to the puzzle. Rick had a tremendous career with the Twins — including nine seasons with double-digit saves. With the Cubs he didn't fare so well. Aguilera saved a total of 37 games over two seasons, but he also gave up 17 homers, and his ERA was pushing five. The pitcher the Cubs traded to get him, Kyle Lohse, won nearly 150 games for the Twins, Reds, Cardinals, and Brewers (and a World Series ring as a starting pitcher on the 2011 Cardinals.)

Hank Aguirre 1931–1994 (Cubs 1969-1970)

Aguirre was an All-Star with the Tigers in the early 60s and led the American League in ERA, but by the time he came to the Cubs he was strictly a reliever. His last two big league seasons were with the Cubs. He pitched pretty well in 41 games for the '69 squad, but after getting off to a slower start in 1970, he was released in early July.

Cubs players have had some great nicknames over the years. Among players starting with the letter A, you'll find nicknames like... Big George, Big Train, Bonesetter, Cap, Chief, Choppy, Kif, Magnet, The Octopus, Old Pete, Red, and Sparky.

Jack Aker 1940–(Cubs 1972-1973)

Jack was known as "Chief" and had a very solid 11-year big league career, including two with the Cubs. He was acquired from the Yankees for disappointing aging outfielder Johnny Callison. The right-handed reliever saved 29 games for the Cubs over his two years in Chicago and was released after the 1973 season. He finished his career with 129 saves. He is mentioned in Jim Bouton's classic book *Ball Four* because he was the player rep for the Seattle Pilots when Bouton pitched there.

<u>Historical note</u>: On the day Secretariat won the Triple Crown by winning the Belmont Stakes (1973), Aker was part of a Cubs bullpen implosion that gave up seven (!) runs in the ninth inning against the Reds. Aker gave up a single to Johnny Bench, a double to Dan Driessen, and a home run to Tony Perez. Reds 8-Cubs 4.

Arismendy Alcantara 1991–(Cubs 2014-2015)

Alcantara was the first of the new wave of Cubs prospects to make it up to the big leagues in the summer of 2014. He showed flashes of promise in his rookie season, but finished the year hitting only .205. Before the end of May in 2015, he was sent down to the minors to rediscover his hitting stroke. He was traded in 2016.

Dale Alderson 1918–1982 (Cubs 1943-1944)

Dale was one of the bright young pitching prospects in the Cubs minor league system. He got a cup of coffee with the team in 1943, and again in 1944, and would have had a real chance to contribute in 1945, but Uncle Sam had other ideas for Dale. He served in the military for the entire 1945 season at the Naval Training Center in San Diego, where he remained until discharged on October 19, 1945, just nine days after the Cubs lost game 7 of the World Series to the Detroit Tigers. Alderson never made it back to the big leagues again.

Vic Aldridge 1893–1973 (1917-1924)

On the day President Harding died, the Cubs beat the Boston Braves 5-1 thanks to a great pitching performance by Vic Aldridge, the #2 starter on the team (behind Grover Alexander). Aldridge went on to win 16 games for the Cubs that year. It was in the middle of a very strong three-year run with the Cubs, when he won 47 games. He was traded to the Pirates in 1925 in the trade that brought Charlie Grimm to the Cubs.

Grover Cleveland Alexander 1887–1950
(Cubs 1918-1926)

His 373 wins are the third most in baseball history. And yes, he was a Cub. He won 128 games in his years with the Cubs and had one of the best seasons in baseball history in 1920, when he led the league in wins, ERA, and strikeouts. But Alexander was troubled during his Cubs years. The only reason they got him at all was because the owner of the Phillies didn't want to get stuck paying the contract of his star pitcher (a three-time 30 game winner) if he got drafted into World War I. He did get drafted, and he came back from the war a changed man.

Old Pete, as he was known, became one of the biggest drinkers in the league during Prohibition. He showed up drunk to games. He fell asleep in the clubhouse and passed out drunk in the dugout. He smoked like a chimney before every game. He ignored his manager and openly challenged his authority. The Cubs understood up to a point. After all, the man was suffering through medical, physical, and mental problems. He was an epileptic and was prone to seizures. His arm started hurting during his Cubs career, and he had the ligament "snapped back into place" by a man named James "Bonesetter" Smith. And throughout it all he was suffering from post-traumatic stress disorder after his horrific war experience.

Somehow, against all odds, he continued to pitch well. In 1923, he pitched 305 innings and walked only 30 men. In 1924, he won his 300th game. But in 1926, after his catcher and best friend Bill Killefer went to the Cardinals, Alexander fell apart. In his last ten games with the Cubs, Old Pete showed up drunk six times and missed two games altogether. The Cubs released him and the Cardinals picked him up on waivers. Back with his best friend Killefer, he regained his pitching touch and led the Cardinals to the World Series championship, winning Game 6, and saving Game 7 of the 1926 series. Two years after his 1950 death, his story was told in the film *The Winning Team*, starring Ronald Reagan. Grover Cleveland Alexander remains the only player in baseball history to be named after a president and portrayed in a movie by a president.

<u>Historical note</u>: On the day that Warren Harding made history by being the first president to broadcast on the radio (1922), Alexander was on the mound for the Cubs. He lost the game 5-4 to the Giants.

Manny Alexander 1971– (Cubs 1997-1999)

Manny was a versatile backup infielder with the Cubs during his three years in Chicago, but he didn't hit well. The Cubs traded him to the Boston Red Sox for Damon Buford before the 2000 season. Despite a twelve-year big league career, Manny is mainly remembered for his connection to the steroids age. The year after he left the Cubs, police discovered a bottle of anabolic steroids and two hypodermic needles in a Mercedes-Benz owned by Alexander. Massachusetts State Police considered filing steroid possession charges against him, but didn't because they couldn't prove the steroids belonged to Manny. Because of that incident, Alexander's name appeared in the Mitchell Report in 2007.

Matt Alexander 1947– (Cubs 1973-1974)

Matt was an outfielder/third baseman who was known for his speed. In only 60 at-bats with the Cubs, he managed to steal ten bases. He stole nearly a hundred more before his big league career was over despite only hitting .214.

Antonio Alfonseca 1972– (Cubs 2002-2003)

He was nicknamed El Pulpo in Spanish (the Octopus) because he was born with an extra digit on his hands and feet. Antonio Alfonseca was the fireman of the year for the Marlins two seasons before he came to Chicago. The Cubs traded an unknown young pitcher named Dontrelle Willis to get him, but the Octopus really stunk up the joint in a Chicago uniform. Audible groans could be heard from the Wrigley faithful each time he walked toward the mound. He did, however, pitch well for the Cubs in the 2003 playoffs (believe it or not).

Ethan Allen 1904–1993 (Cubs 1936)

The Cubs were a strong team throughout the 1930s, including the 1936 season. They were the defending National League champions that May when they traded future Hall of Famer Chuck Klein (a relative disappointment with the Cubs) back to the Phillies for pitcher Curt Davis and a speedy left fielder near the end of his career: Ethan Allen. Allen anchored left field for the rest of the season — his last year in the majors as a regular. The lifetime .300 hitter did manage to hit .295 for the Cubs, and he stole 12 bases, but it was obvious that he wasn't in the long-term plans for the team. They sold him to the Browns after the season.

But the Ethan Allen story doesn't end there, and it doesn't end with the end of his playing days in 1938. Allen may have had a bigger impact in the world than any other member of the 1936 Cubs. (No, he wasn't the founder of Ethan Allen furniture.) Three years after he retired from baseball, former Cub Ethan Allen invented the Cadaco-Ellis board game All-Star Baseball, which remains the best-selling baseball board game of all time. Boys who grew up in the 40s, 50s, and 60s surely have fond memories of playing All-Star Baseball. The annual versions of the game were released every year between 1941 and 1993, the year Allen passed away. It wasn't discontinued until shortly thereafter because of competition from new computer games and greatly increased player licensing costs. Allen wasn't just an entrepreneur after his playing days. He also became a college baseball coach, coaching the men's varsity team at Yale University. Among his players was a skinny first baseman who would go on to become the President of the United States: George Herbert Walker Bush. He might not have had a big impact on the 1936 Cubs, but Ethan Allen made his mark on America.

Nick Allen 1888–1939 (Cubs 1916)

Allen was another catcher who played for the Cubs ever so briefly. His Cubs career lasted five games during the first year they played at Wrigley Field. Allen got on base exactly one time. He later played on the 1919 World Champion Reds: the team that won the "thrown" World Series against the White Sox. After his playing career he became a coach, scout, and mentor for several players who went on to have excellent big league careers, including Leo Durocher and Mark Koenig.

Milo Allison 1890–1957 (Cubs 1913-1914)

Milo played a grand total of three games for the Cubs over two seasons in West Side Grounds. The outfielder did manage to get a few hits and a stolen base in his extremely limited playing time. He later played for Cleveland as well. After his playing career, Milo settled in Kenosha, Wisconsin.

Albert Almora Jr. 1994–(Cubs 2016-present)

Almora made his debut during the Cubs World Series championship season, and even made the postseason roster. He was the first draft pick in the first draft conducted by the current Cubs front office, and though it took him a few years to make it to the big leagues, he was still only 22 when he wore that Cubs uniform for the first time. In 2017, Almora took a big step forward, becoming a regular part of the outfield rotation. He batted .298 in over 300 plate appearances and excelled in the postseason. He became the starting center fielder in 2018, but after a stellar first half, slumped badly in the second half of the season. He finished up at .286, with mediocre power numbers (5 HRs, 41 RBI). Albert's cousin is big leaguer Manny Machado.

Moises Alou 1966–(Cubs 2002-2004)

Moises had a borderline Hall of Fame career. He was a seven-time All-Star, a two-time Silver Slugger award winner, a World Series champion, hit over .300 for his entire 17-year career, and slugged more than 300 lifetime homers. Those numbers are very nearly HOF caliber. Unfortunately for Moises he also played in the steroids era, and he's not really remembered for his hitting at all.

Cubs fans remember Moises for two things more than anything else. First of all, he admitted that he urinated on his hands before every game to toughen his hands. That's a difficult visual to shake. But more importantly, he was in the middle of that infamous Bartman moment for the team that came only five outs away from winning the 2003 NL pennant. Moises was the one who was trying to catch the ball Bartman got his hands on, and Moises was the one who created a scene on the field, which riled up the fans and his teammates. If he had simply gone back to his position, likely nothing bad would have occurred. When ESPN produced a special on the tenth anniversary of the infamous event (in 2013), Moises also admitted that he and Aramis Ramirez decided after Game 6 to book their flights back to the Dominican because they just knew they wouldn't win Game 7. I'd like my money back for those Game 7 tickets please.

Porfi Altamirano 1952– (Cubs 1984)

He was simply the greatest Porfi to ever play in the big leagues. Altamirano pitched for the Cubs during their division-winning season of 1984 and didn't do too badly. After the season he was traded to the Yankees and never made it back to the majors again.

George Altman 1933– (Cubs 1959-1962, 1965-1967)

Big George, as he was known, had a few great seasons in the big leagues, and he was wearing a Chicago Cubs uniform when he did it. He joined Chicago after completing his military service and had an immediate impact. His two best seasons came during the ridiculous College of Coaches era, in 1961 and 1962. He clubbed 27 homers in '61 and was named to the All-Star team. He followed that up with another All-Star season in 1962, hitting 22 home runs. The Cardinals thought they were getting a star when they traded for Big George in 1963, but this trade worked out better for the Cubs. The pitchers the Cubs got in return (Larry Jackson and Lindy McDaniel) had tremendous seasons in Chicago, while George fizzled in St. Louis. He finished up his career with the Cubs, but by then he was mainly a backup.

Joe Altobelli 1932– (Cubs manager 1991)

Altobelli played big league ball with the Indians, but he achieved greater notoriety as a manager with the Giants and Orioles. He won the World Series as the manager of the Orioles in 1983. He managed exactly one game for the Cubs as their interim manager after Don Zimmer was fired in 1991, before Jim Essian was hired as his replacement. The Cubs lost.

Joey Amalfitano 1934

(Cubs player 1964-1967, Cubs manager 1979, 1981)

He not only played for the Cubs, he also managed them twice (1979, 1981) as an interim manager after Herman Franks resigned and Preston Gomez was fired. He didn't have a lot of success as a player or a manager, but he has been continually employed in baseball his entire adult life, most recently as a special assistant for player development for the San Francisco Giants.

<u>Historical note</u>: On the day that Martin Luther King Jr. was injured by a thrown rock in Chicago's Gage Park, Joey scored the game-winning run at Wrigley Field in the bottom of the 10th inning to defeat the Giants.

Vincente Amor 1932– (Cubs 1955)

Amor appeared in four games for the Cubs out of the bullpen in April of 1955. He was 22 years old at the time. They sent him back down to the minors after Vincente allowed more than two baserunners an inning. He never returned to the big leagues for the Cubs, but he did get one more cup of coffee with the Reds.

Bob Anderson 1935–2015 (Cubs 1957-1962)

Anderson was a key part of the Cubs starting rotation in the late 1950s. Among the highlights of those years: beating Don Drysdale on opening day at Wrigley Field in 1959, being on the mound that strange day when two balls were in play at one time (also in 1959), and pitching to left-handed catcher Dale Long in 1958. After the College of Coaches took over, Anderson was moved to the bullpen and wasn't nearly as effective.

<u>Historical note</u>: On the day the 50-star American flag was unveiled (after Hawaii was officially added to the union) in 1960, Anderson was on the mound at Wrigley Field against the Giants. He pitched nine innings of one-run ball and knocked in the only Cubs run, but didn't get the decision because the game was called after 14 innings because of darkness.

Brett Anderson 1988– (Cubs 2017)

Anderson began the 2017 season as the Cubs fifth starter but struggled badly. After he returned from an injury in July, the Cubs released him. He ended the season with Toronto.

Jimmy Anderson 1976– (Cubs 2004)

Jimmy pitched in the big leagues for six seasons, and during part of 2004, he pitched for the Cubs. He ended his career more than twenty games under .500, with a lifetime ERA of 5.42.

John Andre 1923–1976 (Cubs 1955)

Andre was a Filipino-American who pitched for the Cubs at the age of 32, his only season in the big leagues. In 22 appearances he posted an ERA of 5.80. In his last appearance with the Cubs, he walked the bases loaded before being yanked out of the game.

Jim Andrews 1865–1907 (Colts 1890)

Andrews was a starting outfielder for the Cubs (then known as the Colts) at the beginning of the 1890 season when they played at West Side Park, but hit only .188, and the team cut him loose. After Andrews left the team, the Cubs tore up the league. They were 29 games over .500 the rest of the season and finished in second place.

Shane Andrews 1971 – (Cubs 1999-2000)
Shane was picked up by the Cubs after the Expos released him in September of 1999. By Opening Day of 2000 (in Tokyo), he was the team's starting third baseman. It didn't work out. Before the season was over, he was sharing the job with Willie Greene. While both hitters had pop (24 combined homers), they just couldn't put the ball in play enough. Andrews hit .229 and was released after the season.

Fred Andrus 1850 – 1937 (White Stockings 1876, 1884)
Andrus was 15 years old when the Civil War ended, and played for the Cubs (then known as the White Stockings) in their first season in the National League when they still played at 23rd Street Grounds. He pitched and played outfield, but not often; a grand total of nine games. Those two years (eight years apart) were his only big league seasons. He later worked as the treasurer for his boss' (Al Spalding) sporting goods company.

Tom Angley 1904 – 1952 (Cubs 1929)
The career minor leaguer got one taste of the big-time with the Cubs for one week in 1929. He filled in for catcher Gabby Hartnett after Gabby went down with an injury. Angley managed to knock in six runs in his 16 at-bats, but was later replaced by a host of other replacement catchers. Veteran Zach Taylor eventually got the bulk of the playing time, while Angley went back to the minor leagues. The short and squat catcher (5'8", 190 lbs.) resembled Hack Wilson in his physique, but not in his results.

Cap Anson 1852 – 1922 (White Stockings 1876-1897)
He still holds Cubs career records for most hits, most runs, most doubles, most RBI, and highest batting average (with 2000 or more at-bats). Anson is quite simply the greatest player in Chicago Cubs history, and probably the most important player in 19th century baseball. Cap was 45 years old when he retired in 1897 and was famous all over the country. He toured as a Vaudeville Act, drawing big crowds wherever he went. He had business cards made up that read: "Greater Actor Than Any Ballplayer, a Greater Ballplayer Than Any Actor," according to the book *Cap Anson: The Grand Old Man of Baseball* by David Fleitz. During his retirement he was treated as royalty in Chicago. One of his biggest fans was President Warren G. Harding. Harding even invited Anson to the White House. In 1939, seventeen years after his death, Cap Anson was inducted into the Hall of Fame.

However, that's only part of Anson's legacy, and the rest of the story isn't pretty. In 1882 in a game against Toledo, Anson demanded that a player be taken out of the game because he was African-American. Five years later, Anson refused to allow his team to take the field if a black player was on the opposing team. The Giants tried to sign an African-American player, and Anson led the charge in getting the other owners to block that move and any other move that would have allowed African-Americans to play. In essence, Anson was the reason for the color line in baseball. To be fair, the ban wouldn't have happened if the other owners and players weren't also racist, but Anson was the most vocal, and he was the biggest star in the league, so nobody wanted to defy him. He hated "darkies," as he called them. He actually thought he was magnanimous toward African-Americans because he hired a "little coon who could handle a baton" (his words) to be the team mascot. As great of a player as he was, Cap Anson left a stain on this great game, a stain that wasn't erased in the league until 1947, and in Chicago until 1953.

Jimmy Archer 1883 – 1958 (Cubs 1909-1917)
He was the regular Cubs catcher from 1911 to 1917, but Jimmy Archer was much more than that. He was an early version of television's Steve Austin: the bionic Cub. During the winter of 1902, at the age of 19, Archer was working as a barrel maker in Toronto when he fell into a vat of boiling oak sap. He scalded his right arm and leg so badly that he was hospitalized for three months. Jimmy was in so much pain during his hospitalization that he begged for his arm to be amputated. But the injury had an upside that he never could have expected. As a result of the accident, the tendon in his right arm shrunk and made his right arm shorter than his left. It also made it unusually strong. Suddenly Jimmy was able to throw the baseball with incredible velocity. The catcher became famous for his arm, and he always claimed it was due to the accident.

Jimmy got his MLB start catching for the Tigers, and got some action in the World Series against the Cubs that year. He even threw out the Cubs best base stealer (Jimmy Slagle). The Cubs acquired him shortly thereafter, and Archer eventually took over the starting catching job from Johnny Kling. Jimmy was one of the best players on the Cubs during his decade in a Chicago uniform, being named to the "All American" team three years in a row (1912-1914). His throwing arm was the envy of the league. The Irish-born Archer settled in Chicago after his playing days were over and made headlines one more time before his death. On August 7, 1931, he was in the Chicago Stockyards when he saw two men dying in the cab of a truck. They were overcome with carbon monoxide gas. Archer pulled them out in time to save their lives and then administered first aid to revive them. The National Safety Council awarded him a medal for his heroism.

Jose Arcia 1943–2016 (Cubs 1968)

Jose was a 24-year-old rookie with the Cubs in 1968, and the Cuban infielder filled in at second base, shortstop, third base, left field and right field. He was considered a reliable glove man, but he only batted .190. The Padres drafted him away from the Cubs in the 1968 expansion draft, and he played two seasons with San Diego. Jose passed away in Miami as the Cubs were surging toward their first World Series in 108 years.

Alex Arias 1967–(Cubs 1992)

Arias was drafted by the Cubs and played a little shortstop for them in his rookie season in 1992, but after the season was over, he was included in the package that brought Greg Hibbard to the Cubs from the Marlins. Hibbard had one good season in Chicago, and Arias went on to become a World Series champion. In eleven seasons, Alex played for five different big league clubs.

Armistice Cubs. When Armistice Day came, ending World War I, the following Cubs had all served in the military during the war... Vic Aldridge, Grover Cleveland Alexander,

Sweetbread Bailey, Bill Bradley, Harry Chapman, Jimmy Cooney, Kiki Cuyler, Pickles Dillhoefer, Rowdy Elliot, Johnny Evers, Buck Freeman, George Grantham, Burleigh Grimes, Percy Jones, High Pockets Kelly, Pete Kilduff, Rube Kroh, Andy Lotshaw, Pat Malone, Rabbit Maranville, Johnny O'Connor, Elmer Ponder, Lance Richbourg, Dutch Ruether, Vic Saier, Johnny Schulte, Pete Scott, Earl Smith, Pete Turgeon, and Harry Weaver. Of these, the only one who passed away during the war was Harry Chapman. He died of influenza-induced pneumonia while serving stateside a few weeks before the war ended.

J. Ogden Armour 1862–1927
(Cubs minority owner 1916-1919)

Armour was Chicago's meat-packing king, the man skewered by Upton Sinclair in *The Jungle*, but he was also a big Cubs fan. He bought into the team for $50,000 and convinced a good buddy of his to do the same: William Wrigley. The year was 1916, and those men along with former Whales owner Charlie Weeghman were the saviors of the Cubs...the men who got the dreaded, hated Charles Murphy out of the game. At the time, J. Ogden Armour was one of the three richest men in Chicago.

When the stock market slumped after World War I, Armour did too, and he was forced to sell his portion of the Cubs. He was also forced out at the meat-packing business his father founded after he lost a million dollars a day for 130 days in a row. Armour saw his last Cubs game in 1923. He retired to California shortly after that. In 1927 on a trip to London, he fell ill and died. He had less than $25,000 in his personal accounts.

Jamie Arnold 1974–(Cubs 2000)

He was a first round pick of the Atlanta Braves, but Jamie Arnold never quite lived up to his billing. The Cubs got him in a trade (for Ismael Valdes) and tried him in the rotation and the bullpen, but he didn't pitch well in either role. In twelve appearances with the Cubs, he had an ERA of 6.61. He never pitched in the big leagues again. In eleven minor league seasons, Arnold was 23 games under .500.

Jake Arrieta 1986–(Cubs 2013-2017)

Arrietta was a member of Team USA in 2006 and helped them win the World University Baseball Championship before being drafted by the Orioles. He had trouble with his control and gave up a few too many long balls during his time in Baltimore, and was traded to the Cubs in 2013 along with Pedro Strop as part of the Scott Feldman trade. That turned out to be one of the best trades in Cubs history.

Jake had a breakthrough season for the Cubs in 2014, winning 10 games and posting an ERA of 2.53. In 2015, he put the Cubs on his shoulders and took them all the way to the NLCS, winning 22 games, posting an ERA of 1.77, striking out 236 batters, throwing a no-hitter, winning two playoff games (Wild Card and NLDS), and winning the Cy Young Award. In their World Series season of 2016, he wasn't quite as sharp, but he did win two crucial World Series games against the Indians. In 2017, Arrieta was once again the strongest starter in the playoffs for the Cubs after leading the team with 14 wins during the regular season. He became a free agent after the season and signed with the Phillies.

<u>Historical note:</u> On the day Donald Trump announced he was running for president (2015), Jake had one of his very few bad outings of the year. He walked six and gave up four runs, losing 6-0 to Cleveland at Wrigley Field.

Jim Asbell 1914–1967 (Cubs 1938)

They called him Big Train. Jim Asbell was a big powerful 24-year-old outfielder who had shown promise as a slugger in the minor leagues when the Cubs brought him up to the bigs during their pennant-winning season of 1938. The Cubs used him mainly as a pinch hitter. He had 33 at-bats — the only 33 at-bats of his major league career. After that he took the Big Train back to the minors. He spent a few more years in the Cardinals minor league system, but Big Train Asbell never made it back up to the big leagues again.

Jose Ascanio 1985–(Cubs 2008-2009)

Jose came to the Cubs in the trade that sent Will Ohman to the Braves. He was a power arm and the Cubs thought he would take over a late inning role in the bullpen. He wasn't that guy. Ascanio appeared in twenty games over two seasons and was traded to the Pirates for Tom Gorzelanny and John Grabow in 2009. He didn't do much for the Pirates either.

Jairo Asencio 1983–(Cubs 2012)

When he signed with the Braves, he was using a false name (Luis Valdez) and birthday, and that caused him some visa problems early in his career. Jairo pitched briefly for the Braves and the Indians, and the Cubs claimed him off waivers. He pitched exclusively out of the bullpen in 12 games for the Cubs in 2012. His ERA in 14.2 innings was 3.07. After the season, he was released.

Richie Ashburn 1927–1997 (Cubs 1960-1961)

While it was great to have the Hall of Famer Ashburn covering center field for the 1960 and 1961 Cubs, the lifetime .308 hitter was long past his prime. He put up those Hall of Fame numbers mostly for the Philadelphia Phillies. The stories about Ashburn from his early days are legendary. He loved hitting so much he slept with his Louisville Slugger when he was in slump. He was a speedy singles hitter who won two batting titles, finished second three times, and hit over .300 nine times. By the time he came to the Cubs, unfortunately, his career was declining and he no longer had the speed he exhibited early in his career. Ashburn was a five-time All-Star, but none of those appearances came with the Cubs. The Cubs let him go in the expansion draft of 1962, and he finished his career as the only All-Star on the worst team of all-time, the 1962 Mets. After his playing career ended, he became a beloved announcer for the Philadelphia Phillies. He died in 1997, two years after he was elected into baseball's Hall of Fame.

Ken Aspromonte 1931–(Cubs 1963)

Aspromonte played seven seasons in the big leagues, the highlight of which was probably his 1960 season as the starting second baseman for the Cleveland Indians. He had a good year, slugging 10 homers and batting .290. It was enough to get the attention of the Washington Senators, who selected him in the 1960 expansion draft. Aspromonte shuffled around between Washington, Cleveland, Los Angeles, and Milwaukee over the next year or so, never really claiming a full-time gig. By the time he came to the Cubs he was strictly a backup. He didn't even make it through half the season. The Cubs released him in June, and that marked the end of his big league career. Ken's brother Bob also played in the big leagues (mostly with Houston).

Paul Assenmacher 1960 — (Cubs 1989-1993)

The Cubs picked up Assenmacher towards the end of the 1989 season to help bolster their bullpen down the stretch and in the playoffs. Assenmacher didn't pitch too well for Chicago that season, but he was one of the best left-handers in baseball over the next few years. He saved 33 games and won 20 while pitching in an average of 70 games a season. After leaving the Cubs he pitched in two World Series with the Indians.

Mitch Atkins 1985 — (Cubs 2009-2010)

Mitch was a 7th round pick of the Cubs, and he got a cup of coffee with the big league club in 2009 and 2010. Unfortunately, he only pitched 12 innings and appeared in seven games. He later got another cup of coffee with the Orioles in 2011.

Toby Atwell 1924—2003 (Cubs 1952-1953)

He was an All-Star catcher with the Cubs in his rookie season of 1952, hitting .290. He would never get near that number again. Toby was one of the players sent to Pittsburgh in the trade that brought Ralph Kiner to the Cubs in 1953, and he remained with the Pirates for the next four seasons.

Earl Averill 1931—2015 (Cubs 1959-1960)

His father was a Hall of Famer with Cleveland, but Earl Jr. wasn't quite the player his father was. He had decent pop in his bat (11 homers with the Cubs), but he struggled to hit for average. He hit .233 and .237 with the Cubs. He also played for the Indians, White Sox, Angels, and Phillies. His best season was probably 1961 (with the Angels), when he hit 21 homers. He also reached base 17 consecutive times — still a major league record.

Alex Avila 1987 — (Cubs 2017-present)

Avila was traded to the Cubs by his own father, the GM of the Detroit Tigers. The nine-year veteran catcher filled an important role on the Cubs during their stretch run. He replaced the injured Willson Contreras and had some key hits while Contreras recovered.

Bobby Ayala 1969 — (Cubs 1999)

Ayala was a big league reliever for eight years and had a couple of very good seasons with Seattle. He was their closer and saved 56 games for them. When the Cubs got him in 1999 he was toast. His last appearance in a big league uniform came with the Cubs on October 2, 1999.

Manny Aybar 1972 — (Cubs 2001)

Aybar pitched in the big leagues for eight seasons, but he never achieved any kind of lasting success. In his one season with the Cubs his ERA was 6.35. He gave up five homers in only 22 innings. Manny's lifetime ERA was 5.11.

> ***Additional Entries...***If you check out the Every Cub Ever feature at www.justonebadcentury. com, you'll find several additional entries, including celebrity Cubs fans, writers, and bloggers. Under the letter A, you'll find poet Franklin P. Adams (the immortalizer of Tinker, Evers & Chance), and political writer Jonathan Alter, a lifelong Cubs fanatic.

CHAPTER TWO

B

The starting lineup of your Chicago Cubs beginning with the letter B...

C–Michael Barrett, the AJ puncher
1B–Ernie Banks, Mr. Cub
2B–Ross Barnes, the .400 hitter
SS–Javy Baez, World Series Champ
3B–Kris Bryant, MVP
LF–Steve Bilko, the slugging inspiration
CF–Frankie Baumholtz, "You got it"
RF–Lou Brock, Hall of Famer
Bench–Bill Buckner, Batting Champ
Bench– Glenn Beckert, All-Star
SP–Mordecai Brown, Hall of Famer
SP–Hank Borowy, '45 MVP
SP–Mark Baldwin, 30-game winner
SP–Hiram Bithorn, Puerto Rican Pioneer
RP–Rod Beck, the Shooter
RP–Joe Borowski, '03 Closer

Fred Baczewski 1926–1976 (Cubs 1953)

Fred made the Cubs out of spring training in 1953 but was traded to the Reds in June for Bubba Church. Fred was a left-handed pitcher. Can you guess what his nickname was? That's right, they called him Lefty.

Ed Baecht 1907–1957 (Cubs 1931-1932)

Baecht was a pitcher who made it up to the Cubs for a brief stint in 1931. That was a year of great turmoil in the Cubs clubhouse. The manager (Rogers Hornsby) and slugger (Hack Wilson) were hardly on speaking terms. Baecht kept his head down and pitched fairly well in 22 games. Ed's problem was his command. His lifetime WHIP (Walks+Hits per Innings Pitched) was an astounding 1.73.

Javier Baez 1992 – (Cubs 2014-Present)

Baez was the 9th overall pick of the 2011 draft: the last first round pick of the Jim Hendry era. At each level of the minors, Baez was a superstar. He joined the Cubs in August 2014 and hit a game-winning homer in his first game. He hit nine homers for the season, but he also struck out in more than 40% of his at-bats and batted .169. In 2015 he wasn't brought up to the big leagues until the end of the season, but he performed much better, playing second base primarily, but Cubs fans began to get a taste of what was to come. In the 2015 playoffs, Baez hit a homer to help beat the Cardinals. Baez really became a stud in 2016. He hit 15 homers and stole 15 bases all while playing incredible jaw-dropping defense at multiple positions in the infield. By the time the playoffs arrived, Javy was the everyday second baseman. He responded by winning the NLCS MVP award. In 2017, Baez hit 23 homers and knocked in 75 runs. But it was his 2018 season which proved to be his best. Javy hit 40 doubles, 34 homers, stole 21 bases, clubbed nine triples, and led the Cubs with 111 RBI. Despite the Cubs' early elimination in the playoffs, Baez was a finalist for NL MVP.

Ed Bailey 1931–2007 (Cubs 1965)

Ed was one of the best catchers in the National League in the late 50s and early 60s. He was a five-time All-Star and a World Series hero during his time with the Cincinnati Reds and San Francisco Giants. One of his personal highlights during those years was when he caught his brother Jim (a pitcher for the Reds in 1959). The Cubs acquired him along with Harvey Kuehnn and Bob Hendley in 1965. He was near the end of his career when he came to the Cubs, but he still played well. He was clearly the best catcher on that 1965 team. The Cubs acquired Randy Hundley the following year, which made Ed expendable. He finished his career with the Angels.

Sweetbread Bailey 1895–1939 (Cubs 1919-1921)

His real name is Abraham Lincoln Bailey because he shares a birthday with the famous president. What is the origin of his nickname? Well, sweetbread is defined as "the thymus or, sometimes, the pancreas of a young animal (usually a calf or lamb) used for food," and though the origins of Bailey's nickname have been lost to time, historians think it may have come from Bailey's tendency to swerve his pitches right into the batter's sweetbread. He hit seven batters there. The Cubs signed him in 1917, but before he joined the team he served in the military with the 72nd field artillery. He was a reliever for the Cubs, winning four games and saving none. That was the extent of his big league career. After a few more seasons in the minors, he returned to his hometown of Joliet, and that's where he died of pituitary cancer in 1939 at the way-too-young age of 44.

Historical note: On the day the Treaty of Versailles was signed (1919), officially ending World War I, Bailey was on the mound for the Cubs (in relief of Lefty Tyler). He beat the Cardinals 6-5 despite giving up a homer to Hall of Famer Rogers Hornsby.

Dusty Baker 1949 – (Cubs manager 2003-2006)

His managing stint with the Cubs began in a promising fashion. He led the team to their first playoff appearance in five years, and then led them to their first playoff series win in 95 years. But he will forever be associated with their epic collapse in the 2003 NLCS. His critics claimed he should have gone out to calm down Mark Prior, who completely fell apart after the Bartman incident and ensuing error by Alex Gonzalez. Dusty was also blamed by many fans for overusing Prior and Wood, which they felt led to the two pitchers developing arm problems. By the time 2006 rolled along, Baker was incredibly unpopular in Chicago. After he was fired, Baker claimed that a fan somehow got into the dugout overnight and left an excrement deposit on the dugout step Dusty liked to occupy.

Historical note: On the day the movie *Caddyshack* was released (1980), Dusty got the game-winning hit in the bottom of the ninth to defeat Bruce Sutter and the Cubs 7-6 in Dodgers Stadium.

Gene Baker 1925 – 1999 (Cubs 1953-1957)

After Jackie Robinson finally broke the color barrier in 1947, Cubs owner Phillip Wrigley still didn't sign a black player for several more years. Wrigley was afraid of signing black players because his fan base was almost totally white and he worried how they would react. It wasn't until the end of the 1953 season that Gene Baker was finally called up. He was 28 years old and had hit well in the minor leagues, but the Cubs hadn't called him up earlier despite having no one

better on the major league roster. They were 40 games out of first place. Ernie Banks was signed shortly thereafter from the Kansas City Monarchs. They signed Ernie strictly because they needed another black player to room with Baker. If they didn't have Baker, they wouldn't have signed Banks. Banks just happened to play in a game first and is therefore remembered as the first black player in Cubs history, but Baker was also on the roster at the same time. His best season with the Cubs was in 1955, when he was named to the All-Star team. Baker was later traded to the Pirates and won a World Series ring with them in 1960. Gene later broke a few color barriers with Pittsburgh. He became the first black manager in organized baseball in 1961 (Batavia Pirates), and the first black coach in 1962 (Triple A). He finished his baseball career as a scout.

Historical note: On the day Disneyland opened in California (1955), Baker had one of his biggest days with the bat. He and Ernie Banks combined for nine runs knocked in, but the Cubs still lost the game 11-10 to the Phillies.

Jeff Baker 1981 – (Cubs 2009-2012)

The Cubs got Baker from the Rockies to back up second baseman Mike Fontenot, and he got significant playing time in that capacity his first years with the team. He flirted with the starting job a few times, but never really seemed to claim the position. The Cubs traded him to the Tigers during the 2012 season.

Historical note: On the day the BP oil rig exploded in the Gulf of Mexico (2010), Baker hit the game-winning homer in a 4-3 win over the Reds in Cincinnati.

John Baker 1981 – (Cubs 2014)

The highlight of Baker's Cubs career was when he came in to pitch a scoreless inning during an extra inning game. That was mainly memorable because Baker was a catcher. As the backup to Wellington Castillo, he hit only .192. He was granted free agency after the season.

Scott Baker 1981 – (Cubs 2013)

Baker was a former 15-game winner coming off arm surgery when the Cubs signed him. He rehabbed for an entire year on the Cubs' dime and came back at the end of the year for three appearances. The Cubs wanted to re-sign him, but Baker opted to go to Texas instead. In 2014 he pitched mainly out of the bullpen for Texas.

Tom Baker 1934–1980 (Cubs 1963)

Baker was a left-handed pitcher who got a cup of coffee with the Cubs in 1963, pitching mainly out of the bullpen (although he did have one start). In ten appearances he posted a very respectable 3.00 ERA. Unfortunately for Baker, he was a 29-year-old rookie, and there isn't a lot of call for 30-year-old pitchers with limited big league experience. He pitched a few more years in the minors before hanging up his spikes for good.

Paul Bako 1972– (Cubs 2003-2004)

Bako was the backup catcher for the Cubs during their division-winning 2003 season. In the NLCS that year he got quite a bit of playing time thanks to his left-handed bat, and hit .250 in 17 plate appearances. He also caught for the Tigers, Astros, Marlins, Braves, Brewers, Dodgers, Royals, Orioles, Reds, and Phillies in his twelve-year big league career.

Mark Baldwin 1863–1929 (White Stockings 1887-1888)

Baldwin won 31 games over two seasons with the Cubs (then known as the White Stockings), but really came into his own after leaving the team. He started more than 50 games a season over the next four years, leading the league in innings pitched. One year he threw over 500 innings, struck out 368 men, walked 274, and threw 83 wild pitches. Those are the kind of numbers the game will never see again. Baldwin's nickname was Fido.

Jay Baller 1960– (Cubs 1985-1987)

He pitched out of the Cubs bullpen for three seasons ('85-'87) and got progressively worse each season (3.46 ERA, 5.37 ERA, 6.35 ERA). After the '87 season, the Cubs sent him packing. He later had a cup of coffee with the Royals and the Phillies.

Tony Balsamo 1937– (Cubs 1962)

Balsamo's only big league season was with the woeful 1962 Cubs. That team was among the three or four worst teams in Cubs history, despite the presence of four Hall of Famers on the roster (Banks, Williams, Santo, and Lou Brock). Tony was a right-handed reliever who pitched in 18 games the first few months of the season. He didn't fare too well. His ERA was 6.44.

Ernie Banks 1931–2015 (Cubs 1953-1971)

Ernie is not only a Hall of Famer, he's the first African-American player to ever play for the Chicago Cubs. The way he became a Cub is almost a fluke. At the end of the 1953 season, Gene Baker was called up to be the first African-American Cubs player. Ernie was signed shortly thereafter from the Kansas City Monarchs. They signed Ernie strictly because they needed another black player to room with Baker. They honestly had no idea what they were getting in Banks. One of the Cubs coaches, Ray Blades, gave Ernie a book called *How to play baseball* even though he had hit .380 for the Monarchs. Banks only got in the lineup first because Baker was hurt (he got into a game three days later). At the time, inserting Banks into the lineup was a very controversial move, because shortstop was considered a thinking man's position, and Banks was the first African-American in major league history to play shortstop on a regular basis. Needless to say, it worked out just fine.

Why do they call Ernie Banks Mr. Cub? Ernie is among the top 5 all-time Cubs in games played (1st), at-bats (1st), hits (2nd), runs (5th), doubles (3rd), home runs (2nd), and RBI (2nd). Unfortunately he also played in more losses than any other player in baseball history. In a little known bit of trivia, he also was the first African-American manager. When manager Whitey Lockman was kicked out of a game on May 8, 1973, Ernie was the acting manager for one inning. Frank Robinson became the first full-time African-American manager just a few months later. Banks was elected to the Hall of Fame in 1977, and in 2008 Ernie became a part of Wrigley Field when the club unveiled his statue. It stands right in front of the main gate at Addison and Clark. Countless Cubs fans take pictures in front of it every year.

Historical note: On the day the Supreme Court ruled segregation in public schools illegal (1954), Ernie tripled and knocked in two runs for the Cubs in a 10-6 win over the Pirates in Pittsburgh.

Willie Banks 1969 – (Cubs 1994-1995)

Willie was a World Champion with the 1991 Twins and was brought to Chicago by his old general manager Andy McPhail, but Banks didn't pitch well in Chicago. His two seasons with the Cubs were the strike years of 1994 and 1995. Before the strike he was hit hard as a starter. After the strike he was hit hard as a reliever. The Cubs traded him to the Dodgers in June of 1995.

Steve Barber 1938 – 2007 (1970)

Barber was a two-time All-Star pitcher for the Orioles in the 1960s. He was also a 20-game winner. But by the time he arrived in Chicago, Barber had endured less successful stints with both the Yankees and the Seattle Pilots. He was signed as a free agent by the Cubs in April of 1970 and was released by the end of June. His ERA in only five appearances (all in relief) was 9.63. After leaving the Cubs, Barber managed to stay in the big leagues until 1974, pitching in relief for the Braves, Angels, and Giants.

Turner Barber 1893 – 1968 (Cubs 1917-1922)

Barber played six seasons in Chicago during the first few years in the new ballpark now known as Wrigley Field. He was a backup outfielder and first baseman for most of that time (including the pennant-winning season of 1918), but he did finally claim a starting outfield spot during the 1921 season. Unfortunately for Turner, he didn't really have the power necessary to keep a corner outfield job. He hit only one homer. The Cubs decided his .314 average wasn't enough to let him keep the spot. Barber played in the minor leagues until 1930.

Bret Barberie 1967 – (Cubs 1996)

Barberie was a backup infielder for Montreal, Florida, and Baltimore before coming to the Cubs in 1996. He didn't last the year in Chicago. By June he was sent back to Iowa, never to return to the big leagues.

Richie Barker 1972 – (Cubs 1999)

He was a 37th round draft choice of the Cubs who eventually made it all the way up to the big leagues for a cup of coffee in 1999. The right-hander appeared in five games early in that season and posted an ERA of 7.20 (probably in honor of the radio home of the Cubs at the time, 720 AM, WGN).

Ross Barnes 1850 – 1915 (White Stockings 1876-1877)

Barnes was an integral member of that first National League Cubs team (then known as the White Stockings). He was one of three players brought over from Boston by Al Spalding to stock that original National League team. Barnes was already a four-time champion in the National Association in Boston.

As the leadoff man, he was the first Cub to ever hit in a National League game. In 1876 he won the first ever NL batting title, hitting .429, and hit the first ever homer in National League history on May 2, 1876. That year he also had the best OBP (.462), the best slugging percentage (.590), the best OPS (1.052), the most total bases (190), the most doubles (21), triples (14), walks (20), singles (102), and had the best fielding percentage of any 2B in the league. Not too shabby. But Barnes got sick the following season (they called it ague, which was a fever of some sort), and he lost his explosiveness and strength. He was merely ordinary after that. Ross still finished his nine-year career with a lifetime average of .360.

Darwin Barney 1985 – (Cubs 2011-2014)

Barney was the starting second baseman for the Cubs for three seasons, and performed pretty well the first two of those. In his rookie season he hit .276 and finished seventh in the Rookie of the Year voting thanks to his excellent glove work. His second season, he won a Gold Glove. Unfortunately for Darwin, his hitting started to slide. By his third season at second base he hit only .208. The Cubs traded him to the Dodgers in 2014.

Cuno Barragan 1932 – (Cubs 1961-1963)

Cuno Barragan's real name, by the way, was Facundo Anthony Barragan. On September 1st, 1961, the Cubs catcher became one of the few players in baseball history to hit a home run in his first major league at-bat. He did it at Wrigley Field in front of 5427 fans against the San Francisco Giants in a 4-3 12-inning loss. The pitcher was Dick LeMay, who later became his teammate. Among the Cubs starters that day: center fielder Richie Ashburn, second baseman Don Zimmer, shortstop Ernie Banks, and a couple youngsters by the names of Williams and Santo. That home run turned out to be the only home run he would hit in the majors. He hung around with the Cubs for two more seasons as a backup catcher and got a total of 163 at-bats before being traded to the Dodgers along with pitcher Jim Brewer in exchange for pitcher Dick Scott. Cuno never played in the majors again.

Bob Barrett 1899–1982 (Cubs 1923-1925)

Barrett was mainly a backup infielder in his three seasons with the Cubs, and he wasn't a particularly big man. He stood at 5'11" and weighed 175 pounds, but his teammates all called him Jumbo. He may have been nicknamed after the grocery chain Holland & Barrett, which sold a Jumbo Roll.

Dick Barrett 1906–1966 (Cubs 1943)

His nickname was "Kewpie Dick" because he resembled a Kewpie doll. Dick was a right-handed pitcher. The 37-year-old appeared in fifteen games for the Cubs during the war year of 1943, and didn't win a single game. He had been a big league pitcher in the early 1930s and thought it would be a good time to make a comeback because so many players were in the military service. Barrett did get four more big league seasons thanks to the war, but even with slightly inferior competition, he had a rough go of it. His career record is 23 games below .500, and he lost 20 games in one season with the Phillies in 1945.

Michael Barrett 1976–(Cubs 2004-2007)

Barrett was the starting catcher for the Cubs for several seasons. He hit the ball well, clubbing 16 homers and knocking in more than 60 runs every year in Chicago, but he also had his difficulties defensively. Barrett is remembered most for three events. 1) He suffered a gruesome twisted testicles injury that made every man in Chicago grimace. 2) He and Carlos Zambrano got into a fistfight in the dugout/clubhouse, leading to a Barrett black eye. And most importantly, 3) He earned the applause and respect of everyone in baseball when he punched taunting White Sox catcher A.J. Pierzynski in the face.

Shad Barry 1878–1936 (Cubs 1904-1905)

Barry was a super-utility man for the Cubs, playing every position except pitcher and catcher. He stole 17 bases over two seasons. He also played for Philadelphia, Cincinnati, Boston, St. Louis, and the Giants over a ten-year big league career.

Dick Bartell 1907–1995 (Cubs 1939)

Acquired in a trade with the Giants (for, among others, starting shortstop Billy Jurges and outfielder Frank Demaree), Dick was the starting shortstop for the Cubs in 1939. Bartell's 1939 season started off badly in spring training when he made a blimp joke to a chubby sportswriter for the *Chicago Tribune* (Ed Burns). Imagine Bartell's surprise when he discovered the Chicago media was a little more sensitive than New York's, and Burns just happened to be the official scorer for the Cubs. Bartell hit only .238 for the Cubs after hitting over .300 seven times in the seasons before he joined the team. He also recorded the worst fielding percentage of his career. Did the angry official scorer have any impact on that? Possibly. Ironically, Bartell was born in Chicago, and the worst season of his career was with the Cubs. The Cubs traded him after the season to the Tigers. He was Detroit's starting shortstop in the 1940 World Series.

Vince Barton 1908–1973 (Cubs 1931-1932)

Vince was a Canadian who played outfield for the Cubs in the early 30s. As a rookie on the Rogers Hornsby-managed team in 1931, he hit 13 homers in a part-time role.

Cliff Bartosh 1979–(Cubs 2005)

Bartosh was acquired from the Indians just before the 2005 season began, and the lefty made nineteen appearances before being sent to the minor leagues. That ended up being his final season in baseball.

> *Basketball Cubs...*The following Cubs all also played basketball at a very high level. Frank Baumholtz (Cleveland Rebels), Chuck Connors (Boston Celtics), Dick Groat (Fort Wayne Pistons), Fergie Jenkins (Harlem Globetrotters), Kenny Lofton (University of Arizona), Irv Noren (Chicago American Gears), Robin Roberts (Michigan State University), and Tim Stoddard (North Carolina State)

Anthony Bass 1987–(Cubs 2018)

The journeyman reliever had made stops in San Diego, Texas, and Houston before arriving in Chicago. He appeared in 16 games during the summer of 2018 in a fill-in role, and posted a 2.93 ERA. He was granted free agency after the season.

Charlie Bastian 1858–1943 (White Stockings 1889)

Charlie was a backup infielder for the Cubs (then known as the White Stockings) in 1889. He wasn't on the roster because of his hitting ability. In 180 plate appearances, Charlie hit only .135. After the season, he joined some of his fellow teammates when they jumped to the upstart Players' League.

Johnny Bates 1882–1949 (Cubs 1914)

Johnny had over a thousand big league hits, including a homer in his first big league at-bat (for Boston), but only one of those hits came in a Cubs uniform. The outfielder only played a month or so with the Cubs. Earlier in his career, Bates had a knack for getting on base. He had four different seasons with an on-base percentage above .400.

Miguel Batista 1971– (Cubs 1997)

Miguel was a member of that horrible '97 Cubs team (losers of their first 14 games), and he didn't pitch particularly well either (5.70 ERA), but he did serve a very important role. He was the trade bait that convinced the Montreal Expos to trade Henry Rodriguez to the Cubs. Henry was a key part of the Cubs 1998 playoff team and helped stabilize a position (left field) that had fielded eleven different Opening Day starters in the previous eleven seasons. Batista pitched for 18 seasons in the big leagues with the Pirates, Marlins, Expos, Royals, Blue Jays, Mariners, Nationals, Mets, Braves, and the 2001 World Champion Arizona Diamondbacks.

Russ Bauers 1914–1995 (Cubs 1946)

Bauers was a big right-handed pitcher who had his best seasons with Pittsburgh before the war. He pitched mostly in relief with the Cubs in 1946 after a five-year absence from the big leagues. He won two games and saved another. The Cubs sent him back to the minors the following year, and he re-emerged for one final big league season with the St. Louis Browns in 1950.

Frank Baumann 1933– (Cubs 1965)

Baumann had already pitched in the big leagues for ten years when he arrived on the north side of Chicago. He had a few very good years for the White Sox in the early 60s (leading the league in ERA), but by 1965, he was nearing the end of the line. He only made four appearances for the Cubs and was hit pretty hard. The Cubs cut him loose in May, and his major league career was over.

Frank Baumholtz 1918–1997 (Cubs 1949, 1951-1955)

Frank was the starting center fielder with the Cubs, and he had his work cut out for him during most of those years. Left fielder Ralph Kiner combined with the equally slow Hank Sauer in right, so the Cubs outfield might have been the worst fielding outfield the Cubs ever had. Kiner joked that both he and Sauer used to scream "You got it, Frankie" every time the ball was hit in the air. Frankie was also a pretty good hitter. In 1952 his .325 average was second in the league.

Jose Bautista 1964– (Cubs 1993-1994)

Not to be confused with the former Blue Jays slugger Jose Bautista, this Jose Bautista was a relief pitcher from the Dominican Republic. He had a great season with the Cubs in 1993, going 10-3, with a 2.82 ERA, and another good year in the strike-shortened 1994 season, but though he remained in the big leagues a few more seasons (with the Giants, Tigers, and Cardinals), he never again achieved the success that he had with the Cubs.

Mike Baxter 1984– (Cubs 2015)

Baxter was a journeyman outfielder/first baseman who got a little bit of playing time when Cubs outfielders were injured during the summer of 2015. He previously played for the Padres, Mets, and Dodgers.

Don Baylor 1949–2017 (Cubs manager 2000-2002)

Baylor was a great player for the Orioles, A's, Angels, Yankees, and Twins during his playing career — an All-Star, MVP, and World Series champ — but never played for the Cubs. He managed them at the turn of the 21st century. Despite being previously named NL manager of the year (with the Rockies), Baylor only had one winning season (2001) in Chicago, and was fired with the Cubs mired in fifth place in 2002. He passed away after a long struggle with cancer during the 2017 season.

Tommy Beals 1850−1915 (White Stockings 1880)

Beals had played pro ball in the days before the National League (in the National Association), but his only year in the NL came with the Cubs (then known as the White Stockings) in 1880. He was already 30 years old at the time and hadn't played professionally in five years. It showed. Tommy hit .152 in 13 games. That 1880 team won 21 games in a row.

Dave Beard 1959−(Cubs 1985)

Dave was one of the many arms that made it through the walking wounded Cubs pitching staff of 1985. The 6′5 former Oakland reliever didn't fare well in Chicago. In nine games he posted an ERA of 6.39. He didn't make it back up to the big leagues until 1989 (with the Tigers).

Ginger Beaumont 1876−1956 (Cubs 1910)

Beaumont was a great hitter. The center fielder's lifetime average was .311, and that included a batting title with the 1902 Pirates. His last season in the big leagues was as a member of the pennant-winning 1910 Cubs. The 33-year-old hit .267 in 76 games for the team that year and batted three times in the 1910 World Series. He walked once and scored a run in that series. After it was over, so was his big league career.

Clyde Beck 1900−1988 (Cubs 1926-1930)

Clyde was a backup infielder for the Cubs for most of his five-year Cubs career. He started nearly 90 games for them in the 1928 season, and then went back to the bench for the pennant-winning 1929 season. The highlight of his career was probably May 12, 1930. The Cubs hit four homers in the seventh inning that day and were only the second team in history to do it. Clyde Beck hit the record-tying HR. The Cubs shipped him off to Cincinnati after the season, and that's where he played his final year in the big leagues. His nickname was Jersey. He passed away just a few weeks before the first night game at Wrigley Field.

Rod Beck 1968−2007 (Cubs 1998-1999)

They called him "The Shooter" because he was like a gunslinger out there, and he didn't waste any of his bullets. Rod Beck was the Cubs closer during the Wild Card season of 1998, saving 51 games in truly scary fashion. By the time he arrived with the Cubs, he was throwing junk — his fastball was in the mid-80s at the very best — but he somehow still got the outs. Without him, they wouldn't have made the playoffs that year. Cubs fans embraced him and his blue collar attitude. But after more arm problems the following year, he was traded to the Boston Red Sox. He managed to stay in the majors until 2004, and had a few more good seasons in Boston and San Diego, but he died tragically in 2007 from an apparent drug overdose. He was only 38 years old.

Historical note: On the day the Starr Report was released by Independent Prosecutor Kenneth Starr (1998) implicating President Clinton in several crimes, Beck saved a game for Kerry Wood and the Cubs in Arizona.

Heinz Becker 1915−1991 (Cubs 1943-1946)

Becker had problems with his feet during his playing career, which is how he got the nickname Bunions. Born in Berlin, Germany in the midst of World War I, Becker got his chance to play in the big leagues because so many players were World War II draftees. Bunions spent most of his short career as a backup, but he did help the Cubs win the National League Pennant in 1945. He played in three games of the World Series against the Detroit Tigers, singling and walking in three at-bats. The Cubs traded him to the Indians the following spring.

Glenn Beckert 1940−(Cubs 1965-1973)

Glenn was a 4-time All-Star, a Gold Glove second baseman (1968), and for four seasons in a row, the toughest man to strike out in all of baseball. In 1971 he hit .342. Another season (1968), he led the league in runs scored. His scrappy play and willingness to do whatever it took to get on base is the reason he became a favorite of his manager, Leo Durocher. In his book *Nice Guys Finish Last*, Durocher, a man who rarely praised his players, said this about his second baseman: "I got a guy over here, Beckert, bustin' his rear end. He works on his hitting. He works on his fielding. He works on all of his weaknesses. He's made himself into a hell of a player." That's probably why Cubs fans loved him too.

Historical note: On the day the infamous 1968 Democratic Convention opened in Chicago, Beckert got the only hit for the Cubs in a 3-0 loss against Gaylord Perry and the Giants.

Fred Beebe 1879–1957 (Cubs 1906)

Beebe was a local Chicago boy, having attended Hyde Park High School and the University of Illinois. The right-handed pitcher was off to a good start in his rookie season of 1906, going 6-1 with a 2.70 ERA, when the Cubs traded him to St. Louis for their former ace Jack Taylor. Despite a lifetime ERA of only 2.86, Beebe finished his career nearly 20 games under .500.

Dallas Beeler 1989– (Cubs 2014-2015)

Beeler was called up for two emergency starts in 2014 and pitched well, although he lost both games. He got three emergency starts in 2015 and it went significantly worse. His ERA was a gaudy 9.42.

Jeff Beliveau 1987– (Cubs 2012)

He pitched out of the bullpen for the Cubs in the 2012 season but couldn't overcome his command issues. He walked twelve and gave up five homers in only 17 innings pitched. Jeff was released after the season and later pitched for Tampa, Toronto, and Cleveland.

George Bell 1959– (Cubs 1991)

Bell was a three-time All-Star and former MVP when the Cubs signed him to a big free agent contract before the 1991 season. He had a good year with the Cubs, slugging 25 homers and hitting .285, but his long-term value to the Cubs came during the following offseason. The Cubs traded Bell across town to the White Sox for a young outfielder named Sammy Sosa. Bell contributed to the White Sox division-winning team of 1993, but Sosa went on to hit more homers in a Cubs uniform than any other player in history.

Les Bell 1901–1985 (Cubs 1930-1931)

Bell and Woody English shared the third base position for two seasons. Despite having a few big years with the Cardinals and Braves before coming to Chicago, Bell didn't hit that well in the hitters years of 1930 and 1931. That '31 season proved to be his last in the big leagues.

Mark Bellhorn 1974– (Cubs 2002-2003)

Bellhorn was a utility man for the Cubs playoff team of 2003, and was lucky enough to be part of ending a couple of curses. Unfortunately, it wasn't with the Cubs. In 2004, he was a key member of the Red Sox team that won the first World Series for Boston in 86 years. That team had three ex-Cubs, which also helped disprove the ridiculous ex-Cubs curse theory of Mike Royko. (The 2001 Diamondbacks team was the first team to disprove it.)

Francis Beltran 1979– (Cubs 2002-2004)

Not to be confused with slugging outfielder Carlos Beltran (no relation), this Beltran was sent to the mound from the Cubs bullpen. He was mostly ineffective in his two years with the Cubs, and later experienced serious arm problems while pitching for the Expos and Tigers.

Alan Benes 1972– (Cubs 2002-2003)

His brother Andy was already a star MLB pitcher when Alan came to the big leagues. Alan had a few good years with the Cardinals before hurting his arm. He was never quite the same after that, including his two seasons with the Cubs.

Butch Benton 1957– (Cubs 1982)

Butch was a first round draft choice of the Mets, but never blossomed into the starting catcher they envisioned he would be. The Cubs took a flyer on him after the Mets gave up on him, and he did get up to the big leagues for a very brief cup of coffee in 1982. He appeared in four games and hit .143. After the season the Cubs traded him to the Expos for future White Sox manager Jerry Manuel, who never played a game for Chicago.

Jason Bere 1971– (Cubs 2001-2002)

Bere came up as a rookie with the White Sox and made an immediate impact, winning 12 games and pitching in the ALCS in 1993. He was runner-up for Rookie of the Year. The following year was even better, as Bere became an All-Star. Unfortunately for the fireballer, he developed arm problems after that and struggled mightily. His one-year resurgence came in his first year with the Cubs. He won 11 games and looked like he might be back. He wasn't. His last year in Chicago was so bad, it was one for the ages. He went 1-10 with an ERA of 5.67.

Justin Berg 1984 – (Cubs 2009-2011)

Berg was a reliever who pitched for the Cubs for parts of three seasons. His most extended time with the club was in 2010. That season he appeared in 41 games, but he struggled with his control, and his ERA was north of five. Berg got one more brief taste the following year, but hasn't been back up in the big leagues since.

Jason Berken 1983 – (Cubs 2012)

The Cubs picked up the right-handed starter from the Orioles at the end of the 2012 season. He failed to win any of his four starts with the Cubs. Nevertheless they gave him a shot to make the club in spring training of 2013. Jason was among the final cuts. He hasn't pitched in the big leagues since.

Jittery Joe Berry 1904 – 1958 (Cubs 1942)

Jittery Joe was a fidgety right-hander with a herky-jerky delivery who spent 18 years in the minors before debuting with the Cubs as a 37-year-old rookie. Jittery Joe didn't do much for the Cubs (2 innings pitched, gave up 7 hits), so they traded him to the A's, where he had two good seasons during the war years of 1944 and 1945 (as a 39- and 40-year-old). He was a very thin man, tipping the scales at no more than 135 pounds. How thin was he? He was once blown off the mound by a gust of wind, which caused him to balk, and cost his team the game. Joe passed away in car accident in California.

Quinton Berry 1984 – (Cubs 2015)

Berry was picked up off waivers at the end of August, and the outfielder was a part of the 2015 postseason roster as a potential pinch runner. He had never been thrown trying to steal in 25 stolen base attempts, but with the Cubs he was thrown out for the first time. Before joining the Cubs, Berry played for the Tigers, Orioles, and Red Sox.

Damon Berryhill 1963 – (Cubs 1987-1991)

Berryhill was the primary catcher for the surprising 1989 Cubs team that won their division, the Boys of Zimmer. He shared the position with fellow young catcher Joe Girardi. He was known for his toughness behind the plate and his clutch hitting, but he also proved to be injury-prone. He missed that 1989 playoff series because of an injury. After a few more seasons of waiting for Berryhill to stay healthy for an entire season, he was traded to the Braves in the deal that brought Turk Wendell to Chicago. He played in the World Series for the 1992 Braves.

Dick Bertell 1935 – 1999 (Cubs 1960-1964, 1967)

Bertell was a catcher for the Cubs during the College of Coaches era. He was in the starting lineup the day the Beatles played in Chicago for the very first time. Over his seven-year big league career, Bertell hit ten homers and batted .250.

Historical note: On the day that Marilyn Monroe was found dead in Los Angeles (1962), Dick was the hitting star in a Cubs victory against the Dodgers on the other side of town.

> Cubs players have had some great nicknames over the years. Among players starting with the letter B, you'll find nicknames like Buckshot, Bunions, Buttons, Chief, Duke of Tralee, Dusty, Dutch, Fido, Footsie, Gnat, Good Kid, Grin, Jersey, Jittery Joe, Jumbo, Kewpie Dick, Kitty, Lefty, Mr. Cub, Mississippi Mudcat, Sheriff, The Shooter, Smoky, Sweetbread, Three Finger, Trolley Line, and You-Got-It-Frankie.

Oscar Bielaski 1847 – 1911 (White Stockings 1875-1876)

Oscar was the right fielder of the Cubs (then known as the White Stockings) the season before the National League was founded, and also played with them in the National League's first season (1876). Bielaski's lifetime batting average was .240. His baseball career might not have amounted to much, but he holds a special distinction among players that have worn the Chicago uniform. A decade before joining the team, Oscar served in the 11th Calvary Regiment of New York in 1864. That's right, Oscar was a Civil War veteran. He is buried in Arlington Cemetery in Washington. Shortly after he died in 1911, his nephew Alexander was named the director of the FBI. Oscar's father was also a Captain in the Civil War and died in action.

Mike Bielecki 1959 – (Cubs 1988-1991)

There was no way the Cubs could have anticipated Bielecki was going to be an 18-game winner in 1989. He had won 12 total games in his previous five big league seasons. Something just clicked that division-winning year. Bielecki not only won 18 games, he pitched four complete games, three shutouts, and posted a sparkling 3.14 ERA. He started the only game the Cubs won in the NLCS that year. He came back down to earth the following season, but in 1991 he did it again, winning 13 games. The Cubs traded him to the Braves at the end of the season, giving Bielecki his only shot at the World Series. He pitched two perfect innings in the 1996 World Series.

Larry Biittner 1945 – (Cubs 1977-1980)

Of all the Cubs players in history with two consecutive "i's" in their last name, Larry Biittner was the greatest of them all. Unfortunately, he cost the Cubs a perennial power hitter, Andre Thornton. (Let's not quibble that a 1B who hit over 250 home runs was too high a price to pay). As a regular who split time between 1B and LF, Biittner did manage to hit .298 with 12 homers in 1977, but after that season he was mostly an extra outfielder. He never had as many as 350 at-bats in his other Cubs seasons, and after 1980, the Cubs let him go. Still, when he was batting, he remains the only Cubs batter who ever heard "good eye, good eye" and wondered if someone was making fun of the spelling of hiis name.

<u>Historical note:</u> On the day the movie *The Blues Brothers* was released (1980), Biittner hit the game-winning sacrifice fly for the Cubs in Atlanta to beat the Braves 4-2.

Steve Bilko 1928 – 1978 (Cubs 1954-1957)

When he arrived from the St. Louis Cardinals on April 30, 1954, Bilko looked like a ferocious slugger. He was 6'1" and weighed anywhere from 230 to 260 pounds, and most of it was solid muscle, but he didn't do much for the Cubs in 1954. They gave him 92 at-bats with the big club before sending him down to the minors. At the time, the Cubs minor league team was in Los Angeles, California, and that's where Bilko became a cult hero. In three minor league seasons for the minor league LA Angels, Bilko hit .330 and slugged 148 home runs. He became a huge box office attraction and got the attention of Hollywood. One Hollywood star, Phil Silvers, even named a television sitcom character after him. The name Bilko is now most associated with that memorable character in *The Phil Silvers Show*, but to Cubs fans, Bilko

was just another player who could do well at the minor league level, but never in the big leagues. They traded him to the Cincinnati Reds after the 1957 season.

Doug Bird 1950 – (Cubs 1981-1982)

Bird was an important part of the Kansas City bullpen throughout most of the 1970s, but when he was acquired by the Cubs (from the Yankees) in 1981, Cubs brass thought he would make a better starter. They were wrong. He started 45 games for the Cubs in 1981 and 1982, and allowed more home runs than any other pitcher in baseball (31). While it's true they gave up their best pitcher (Rick Reuschel) to acquire Bird, they gained something that Reuschel never would have been able to provide. A world-class mustache.

Bill Bishop 1864 – 1932 (White Stockings 1889)

Bishop appeared in two games for Chicago in September of 1889 and was rocked for 13 runs in only three innings. He somehow recorded saves in both appearances, a mathematical anomaly that can only be explained by Stephen Hawking. Two weeks after his last appearance, the states of Washington, Montana, North Dakota, and South Dakota were granted statehood.

Hiram Bithorn 1916 – 1951 (Cubs 1942-1946)

Bithorn was from Puerto Rico, the first Puerto Rican to ever play major league baseball. Known for his high leg kick, he had one great season with the Cubs in 1943, winning 18 games with seven shutouts, and an ERA of 2.60. Unfortunately, he was drafted into the military during World War II, and after he returned from the Navy he had gained 45 pounds. Bithorn tried to pitch for the Cubs in 1946 but didn't have anything left in the tank. The two-year layoff was too much to overcome. His life took a tragic turn while he was trying to make a comeback in the Mexican League. On New Year's Day in 1952, he was shot to death by a policeman in Mexico, in what is still considered a mysterious case. Bithorn is still a hero in Puerto Rico. The baseball stadium in San Juan is named Hiram Bithorn Stadium.

<u>Historical note:</u> On the day American troops landed in Sicily (1943), Hiram was on the mound for the Cubs. He pitched a complete game victory against the Giants at the Polo Grounds.

Earl Blackburn 1892–1966 (Cubs 1917)

Earl was a catcher who played in two games for the Cubs in July of 1917. They were the last two games of his five-year big league career. Before coming to the Cubs, Earl was a backup catcher for Boston, Cincinnati, and Pittsburgh.

Tim Blackwell 1952– (Cubs 1978-1980)

With Blackwell on the roster from 1978-1980, the Cubs knew that they had someone who could hit against both lefties and righties (he was a switch hitter), and if necessary, he could also be an emergency understudy for any Wyatt Earp movie being filmed in the ballpark. He sported a 19th century-worthy bushy mustache. Unfortunately for the Cubs, Blackwell wasn't much of a hitter (he hit .223, .164, .272, and .234 in his four seasons), and he made quite a few errors in the one season he played the most (1980).

Rick Bladt 1946–(Cubs 1969)

The Cubs were looking for a center fielder the whole year in 1969, and Rick was one of the guys brought up to play there. They hoped to catch lightning in a bottle. They didn't. Rick only hit .154 and was sent back down to the minors. He didn't make it back up to the big leagues until 1975 (with the Yankees).

Footsie Blair 1900–1982 (Cubs 1929-1931)

His real name was Clarence Vick Blair, and he was primarily a backup second baseman (he also backed up 1B and 3B) with the Cubs from 1929-1931. In 1930, he became the regular second baseman after Rogers Hornsby broke his ankle. That 1930 team had five future Hall of Famers on the roster, but choked away the pennant in the closing weeks of the season. Clarence played his entire major league career with the Cubs (only three seasons), and he wasn't a great player, but he'll always be remembered for his great nickname. His teammates dubbed him Footsie because he was the only soccer star to make the majors, and he pioneered the "intentional boot" play, where he kicked grounders to proper base.

Sheriff Blake 1899–1982 (Cubs 1924-1931)

Sheriff was a pretty common nickname before the war — there have been 13 baseball players who went by the name, but Cubs pitcher Sheriff Blake was the best. His real name was John Frederick Blake, and he was a pretty good starting pitcher for the Cubs, winning over 80 games with the team. In 1928, he led the league in shutouts, but he was also a little wild (he led the league in walks too). Blake pitched in relief during the 1929 World Series against the A's…and unfortunately for him, he was the second (of three) pitchers in the seventh inning of the infamous 10-9 game where the Cubs blew an eight-run lead. Blake was the losing pitcher of that game.

<u>Historical note</u>: On the day the radio show Amos & Andy debuted on the NBC Network (in Chicago), Blake was on the mound for the Cubs, shutting out the Brooklyn Robins 3-0.

Andres Blanco 1984–(Cubs 2009)

Blanco was a backup infielder for the Royals before joining the Cubs. He got quite a bit of playing time with the Cubs, filling in for the oft-injured Aramis Ramirez. The Cubs traded him to the Rangers during spring training of 2010, and he played the next two seasons for Texas.

Henry Blanco 1971–(Cubs 2005-2008)

Affectionately called Hank White by the Cubs broadcasters (Blanco means White), Blanco was a backup catcher for the Cubs for two of their playoff years (2007-2008). The veteran served as a stabilizing force for the pitching staff and also provided a little pop off the bench. He hit 15 homers in his time with the Cubs. Blanco was mentioned by his Braves/Cubs teammate Greg Maddux in his Hall of Fame induction speech in 2014. In 2015, the Cubs added him to their coaching staff.

Kevin Blankenship 1963–(Cubs 1988-1990)

Blankenship was acquired in the trade that sent fan favorite Jody Davis packing in 1988. He pitched a total of 23 innings over three seasons with the Cubs. Blankenship was technically a member of the division-winning 1989 Cubs, although he only pitched 5 1/3 innings for them that season.

Jeff Blauser 1965–(Cubs 1998-1999)

Blauser was a stud for Atlanta, but definitely not for the Cubs. Stuart Shea, author of *Wrigley Field: The Long Life and Contentious Times of the Friendly Confines* identifies Blauser as one of his 10 Cubs to Forget. He was injured frequently, didn't hit well, and became a clubhouse problem. When his time with the Cubs ended, no one else wanted him.

Cy Block 1919–2004 (Cubs 1942-1946)

Cy played briefly for the Cubs during the 1942 season, but Uncle Sam stole him before the 1943 season began. Block returned to the roster before the end of the 1945 season, in September, just a few weeks before the World Series. He didn't get a chance to bat in the Series, but he did come in as a defensive replacement. (Cy played 2B and 3B). The Cubs sent him to the minors for the 1946 season when all of their wartime players returned, but in September Cy got one more shot at the bigs, his final four major league games. After his playing career was over, he became a successful businessman and philanthropist. Block died in September 2004 in the midst of that season's notorious Cubs collapse.

Randy Bobb 1948–1982 (Cubs 1968)

Randy got exactly one hit in the big leagues on August 21, 1968, a single against pitcher Ron Reed. He got into three more games in September the following season (during the epic 1969 collapse), and was traded to the Mets before the 1970 season for veteran catcher J.C. Martin. He never made it back to the show. He was 21 years old at the time. Randy Bobb died in a car accident in 1982.

John Boccabella 1941–(Cubs 1963-1968)

Boccabella was considered one of the brightest prospects in the Cubs organization. He was so highly touted that Cubs manager Leo Durocher couldn't wait to play him at first base and send Ernie Banks out to pasture. In the only season Boccabella got over 200 plate appearances with the Cubs, however, he hit only .228. The Cubs left him unprotected in the 1968 expansion draft, and he was chosen by the Expos. His playing time increased in Montreal. In 1973 he became the team's starting catcher. He was later replaced by a gentleman named Gary Carter.

Brian Bogusevic 1984–(Cubs 2013)

He was drafted as a pitcher by the Astros, but converted to outfield. The Cubs signed him as a free agent before the 2013 season, and Brian would have had a decent chance to log significant playing time on that team, but he kept getting hurt. After the season he was traded to the Marlins for Justin Ruggiano.

Jim Bolger 1932–(Cubs 1955-1959)

Bolger backed up all three outfield positions for the Cubs in the late 50s. His best season was 1957, when he got the most extensive playing time of his career. He hit .275 in 273 at-bats and knocked in 33 runs. He also played for the Reds, Indians, and A's in his big league career. His nickname was Dutch.

Bobby Bonds 1946–2003 (Cubs 1981)

Bobby Bonds was one of the most exciting players of his era. Unfortunately, his era came long before he became a member of the Chicago Cubs. He was already 36 years old when the Cubs got him from the Rangers in June of 1981, and he was nowhere near the dynamic superstar he was with the Giants, Yankees, and Angels. In his first game with the Cubs he broke a finger trying to catch a fly ball and didn't even get up to bat. He did eventually get over a hundred at-bats with the Cubs in the last season of his career, but he looked lost in the outfield. It was difficult to watch because this once-electrifying outfielder was obviously no longer a major league player. He couldn't field anymore, and he also couldn't hit. Of his 332 career home runs, only six came for the Cubs. Of his 461 career stolen bases, only five came for the Cubs. He struck out 44 times in 163 at-bats, and batted .215. Although Bonds was a borderline Hall of Famer, he never got the number of votes needed to make it. Certainly his last season with the Cubs didn't leave a good taste in the mouths of HOF voters.

Julio Bonetti 1911–1952 (Cubs 1940)

Julio was one of the rare big leaguers who was born in Italy. He pitched briefly for the Browns before coming to the Cubs and didn't get much of a shot with Chicago. He only pitched in one game before he was shipped out. Bonetti was later quietly banned from the game for associating with gamblers.

Bill Bonham 1948–(Cubs 1971-1977)

Bonham won 53 games for the Cubs during his time in Chicago, and even showed some flashes of promise. Unfortunately, he also once lost 22 games in a season (1974), and led the league in earned runs allowed in 1975. On July

31, 1974, Bonham became one of the few pitchers to strike out four men in one inning. His catcher dropped the third strike against Expos pitcher Mike Torrez, allowing Torrez to get on base, but Bill then struck out Ron Hunt, Tom Foli, and Willie Davis. A few years later Bonham was traded to the Reds for Bill Caudill and Woody Fryman. Bonham pitched in the big leagues until 1980. He is third on the Cubs all-time list for most balks.

Historical note: On the day the first of three impeachment charges was recommended against President Nixon by Congress (1974), Bonham lost a 3-2 heartbreaker to the Cardinals at Wrigley Field. Billy Williams knocked in both runs for the Cubs.

Emilio Bonifacio 1985 – (Cubs 2014)

The veteran utility man was brought in to lead off and play center field for the Cubs, and he got off to a good start before getting injured. After he came back from injury, he wasn't quite as effective. By the time he was traded to the Braves at the trading deadline, his average was down to .279.

Zeke Bonura 1908 – 1987 (Cubs 1940)

Bonura was a track and field star as a teen, setting a record for the javelin throw. Zeke started off his baseball career with a bang too, averaging 20 homers and 100+ RBIs four seasons in a row for the White Sox. After going to the Senators and Giants, Bonura returned to Chicago to play for the Cubs in 1940. He no longer had it, hitting only four homers and driving in 20 over the last few months of the season. During the war he served in Algeria and helped organize a baseball league there for soldiers. Zeke Bonura is in the Italian-American Sports Hall of Fame.

Julio Borbon 1986 – (Cubs 2013)

He stole 19 bases in only 46 games as a rookie with the Rangers in 2009, and it appeared he was going to be a big star. But Borbon was undisciplined at the plate and couldn't get on base enough to take advantage of his speed. The Cubs claimed him off waivers in 2013 and he had a few good moments, but he was abruptly released in August when he angered manager Dale Sveum with a boneheaded play on the base paths.

George Borchers 1869 – 1938 (White Stockings 1888)

George was a pitcher for the Cubs (then known as the White Stockings) for one season (1888), and went 4-4 in ten starts for the second place finishers. His teammates called him Chief, which would leave you to believe he had some American Indian blood in him. However, he's not listed on the Baseball Almanac list of Native American players.

Rich Bordi 1959 – (Cubs 1983-1984)

Bordi was an important part of the bullpen during the division-winning season of 1984. He started, pitched middle relief, was a setup man, and even closed a few times. The 6'7 Bordi was traded after the season to the New York Yankees and pitched in the big leagues for another four seasons.

Bob Borkowski 1926 – 2017 (Cubs 1950-1951)

The son of a Cubs scout was an umpire during an Army pickup game during the war and called his dad after he saw Borkowski play. Bob played quite a bit as a reserve outfielder in his rookie season of 1950, and was traded to the Reds along with Smoky Burgess in 1951. The Cubs lived to regret that trade, although not necessarily because of Bob. He never really blossomed into a starting player. Smoky Burgess, on the other hand, played in the big leagues until the late 60s.

Steve Boros 1936 – 2010 (Cubs 1963)

The Cubs acquired Boros from the Tigers (for Bob Anderson) before the 1963 season. He was a third baseman, and the Cubs had a young star named Ron Santo manning the position, so Boros didn't get a lot of playing time. The Cubs sold him to the Reds the following year. After his playing career Boros became a statistical guru and scout. He managed the A's and Padres and worked in the front office and scouted for the Tigers and Dodgers.

Joe Borowski 1971 – (Cubs 2001-2005)

Joe was the ultimate blue collar player — a New Jersey kid who got into the big leagues thanks to his hard work and moxie. In 2003 he fell into the closer role and kept the job the rest of the season. His 33 saves were key to winning the division that year. Joe hurt his arm the following year, however, and struggled over his last few seasons in Chicago. Borowski had one more turn as a closer a few years later. He saved 36 games for the Marlins in 2006 and 45 games for the Indians in 2007. Joe's luck ran out the next year…his last one in the big leagues.

Hank Borowy 1916–2004 (Cubs 1945-1948)

He had won 17, 14, and 15 games in his three previous seasons with Yankees, and had already won 10 games in 1945 when the Cubs acquired Hank. Borowy was 29 years old and in the prime of his career. People thought the Yankees had lost their minds. After Borowy joined the Cubs he became even better. For the rest of 1945 he was absolutely unhittable. He went 11-2 the rest of 1945, with an ERA of 2.13. He also shut out the Tigers in Game 1 of the 1945 World Series, and won Game 6 with a heroic effort in relief. Don't ask what happened in Game 7, when he volunteered to start despite pitching several innings the day before. Let's just say he didn't pull a Josh Beckett. After 1945, when all the players returned from the war, Borowy was exposed as an average pitcher, so maybe the Yankees knew what they were doing after all. By the time he left the Cubs after the 1948 season, he was only two games over .500 for the team (36-34), which means he went 25-32 after his amazing 1945 season.

J.C. Boscan 1979– (Cubs 2013)

The Venezuelan catcher played in the minor leagues for 18 seasons, but he did get a few tastes of action in the big leagues with the Braves and the Cubs. He caught six games for the Cubs in 2013.

Shawn Boskie 1967– (Cubs 1990-1994)

Boskie was a first round draft pick by the Cubs (10th overall) and pitched in the big leagues for nine years, but never really reached the stardom that was predicted for him. He showed flashes, but didn't really contribute significantly out of the rotation or the bullpen. His lifetime ERA was over five.

Thad Bosley 1956– (Cubs 1983-1986)

Bosley was a fourth outfielder for the Cubs, and a clutch pinch hitter. One year he hit .328 in that limited role. Unfortunately for the Cubs, when they used him as a pinch hitter during the 1984 playoffs, he struck out both times. Bosley was also a member of a funk band along with fellow ex-Cub Lenny Randle. After his playing career he went into coaching, becoming the head coach of a small college in Nebraska.

David Bote 1993– (Cubs 2018-present)

Bote was called up to fill in for Kris Bryant during Bryant's injury-plagued 2018 season. At first he took the league by storm, getting clutch hits and making great plays at third. By the end of the season, the pitchers had caught up to him, and he ended the season at .239. On the other hand, he will always be remembered for one incredible summer day, when he hit a walk-off grand slam homer in the bottom of the ninth against the Nationals to beat them 4-3.

Derek Botelho 1956– (Cubs 1985)

Derek was called up during the 1985 season when all five Cubs starters spent time on the disabled list. He made seven starts at the end of the season and went 1-3, with a 5.12 ERA. He never pitched in the big leagues again. Botelho pitched in the minor league system of Kansas City, Cincinnati, and St. Louis before hanging up his spikes for good after the 1988 season. He has worked as a minor league pitching coach ever since.

John Bottarini 1908–1976 (Cubs 1937)

Bottarini was a minor league catcher for a whopping 18 seasons, and a big leaguer for one. He was 29 years old when he served as a backup for Gabby Hartnett during the 1937 season. He appeared in 26 games and hit one homer.

Kent Bottenfield 1968– (Cubs 1996-1997)

Kent pitched for eight different clubs in his nine-year big league career, switching between the starting rotation and the bullpen. With the Cubs he was a reliever, and appeared in 112 games over two seasons. Two years later the Cardinals put him in the starting rotation, and Bottenfield responded with an 18-win season and an All-Star appearance.

Historical note: On the day the first sheep was cloned in England (1996), Bottenfield was on the mound for the Cubs. He was one of three pitchers (Steve Trachsel, Randy Myers) who combined to four-hit the Reds. The Cubs somehow still lost the game 3-0.

Ed Bouchee 1933–2013 (Cubs 1960-1961)

Bouchee had a couple of decent years with the Phillies in the 1950s, but he was also arrested and pled guilty to exposing himself to young girls. He was still on probation when the Cubs inexplicably traded for him in 1960. They thought they didn't have a first baseman on their roster, but discovered in 1961 that there was someone named Ernie Banks who could play the position. Bouchee's time in Chicago was uneventful. He hit 17 homers over two seasons and was left unprotected in the 1962 expansion draft. The Mets took him and he played on the worst team in history that year.

Lou Boudreau 1917–2001 (Cubs manager 1960, Cubs announcer 1958-1987)

Lou had a Hall of Fame playing career with the Cleveland Indians, winning the World Series as a player/manager in 1948 (the last time Cleveland won it), but he spent many more years in his hometown of Chicago, covering the Chicago Cubs. Lou's only season wearing a Cubs uniform was 1960. He took over the managing job from Charlie Grimm and led the team to a 7th place finish, 29 games under .500. After the season he asked for his radio job back, and was replaced as manager by the ridiculous College of Coaches experiment. A whole generation of Cubs fans grew up listening to Lou on the radio. His interviews with Cubs manager Leo Durocher were the stuff of legend. Because of Durocher's unique personality, the show (Durocher in the Dugout) was often entertaining. Lou passed away in 2001 at the age of 84. His nickname was Good Kid.

Pat Bourque 1947–(Cubs 1971-1973)

The 33rd round draft choice, and 770th overall pick in 1969, was a long shot to make it to the big leagues (to say the least), but the first baseman managed to slug his way to the big club in 1971. Once he got up to the big leagues, Bourque could never quite find a full-time slot. He did hang on for a few years as a reserve for the Cubs, A's, and Twins. His best season was 1973 when he combined to hit 9 homers for the Cubs and the A's.

Larry Bowa 1945–(Cubs 1982-1985)

Bowa was known as "Gnat" because he was one of the peskiest little players of his era. The All-Star Gold Glove shortstop had his best years with the Phillies, including the year they won the World Series in 1980. When Dallas Green came over from Philadelphia to run the Cubs in 1982, he immediately

traded for his former team's leader. The idea was for Bowa to groom the young superstar in training (Shawon Dunston), work with the young infielder that was thrown in on the deal (Ryne Sandberg), and provide some veteran leadership. Bowa did the second two pretty well. He formed an excellent double play combination with Sandberg, and he did help lead the Cubs to their division championship in 1984. On the other hand, the following season the shortstop position was handed over to Dunston, and Bowa's fiery competitiveness had a hard time dealing with that. They released him in August of that year. Bowa later managed in the big leagues for the Padres and the Phillies.

Michael Bowden 1986–(Cubs 2012-2013)

The Cubs acquired Bowden in the deal that sent Marlon Byrd to the Red Sox. Bowden was a local boy who grew up in nearby Aurora. He became a valuable member of the bullpen for two seasons, appearing in 64 games. After the 2013 season, Bowden left via free agency and signed a contract to pitch in Japan.

Rob Bowen 1981–(Cubs 2007)

The Cubs got him from the Padres in the Michael Barrett trade in June of 2007, and Bowen was expected to become their regular catcher. After going 2 for 31, the Cubs traded him to the A's a month later for Jason Kendall.

Micah Bowie 1974–(Cubs 1999)

Bowie was one of the highly touted pitching prospects the Cubs got in a trade with the Atlanta Braves (for Terry Mulholland and Jose Hernandez), but they quickly discovered that he wasn't much of a pitcher. Bowie was absolutely torched in eleven starts. His ERA was 9.96. He gave up 73 hits (including eight homers) and 30 walks in only 47 innings pitched. The Cubs released him after he had similar results in the minors the next few seasons. Bowie did eventually come back and pitch in the big leagues for the A's, Nationals, and Rockies.

Bill Bowman 1867–1944 (Colts 1891)

Bill was a 24-year-old catcher in his one big league season (1891). Though he was considered good defensively, he hit only .089 in more than 50 at-bats. That season he and his teammates played some of their games at South Side Park, which was almost exactly on the same spot the White Sox play on today.

Bob Bowman 1910–1972 (Cubs 1942)

Bowman pitched in exactly one game as a Cub. It happened on May 25, 1942: a Monday afternoon game at Wrigley Field. Bowman came in to pitch the top of the ninth in a blowout 10-2 loss to the Cardinals. He gave up one hit and no runs. Johnny Schmitz was the loser that day, failing to record a single out in the first inning.

Bill Bradley 1878–1954 (Orphans 1899-1900)

Chicago signed him as a shortstop, but he made eight errors in his first five games, so they moved him over to 3B. At first that wasn't much better. He set a record for most errors in a double-header with six. When his career ended 14 years later, he was considered one of the top third basemen in baseball history. His best day in a Cubs uniform came during a double-header in September. Bradley went 7 for 10, with a double and a homer. He jumped to the American League in a contract dispute in 1901 (urged to do so by another ex-Chicago star (Clark Griffith), and over the next three seasons he was in the top ten in batting average, runs, hits, doubles, triples, homers, and slugging percentage. He was also the best fielding third baseman in the league. How much was the difference between the Cubs offer in 1901 and the offer from Cleveland? $3100. Doesn't sound like much, but it was 3/4 of his yearly salary.

George Bradley 1852–1931 (White Stockings 1877)

One of the Chicago players who was named after a president (George Washington), Bradley pitched for the Cubs (then known as the White Stockings) in their second National League season. His most memorable game was in June, when Al Spalding got hit in the torso in the first inning with a liner (off the bat of a former teammate Bob Addy) and had to be replaced. Bradley came in for the star pitcher and won the game. That season Bradley won 18 games…but he also lost 23, and led the league in earned runs allowed. His nickname was Grin. Before coming to the Cubs he pitched the first no hitter in big league history when he was with St. Louis.

Historical note: On the day that Billy the Kid killed his

first victim (1877), Bradley was on the mound for Chicago in a 12-6 victory over St. Louis.

Milton Bradley 1978– (Cubs 2009)

It's not that Milton Bradley wasn't a good player. He was an All-Star and led the entire American League in on-base percentage with a .436 on-base percentage the year before he joined the Cubs. But Milton was troubled, and his time in Chicago was a mess. He was suspended in the first week of the season for bumping an umpire. He later threw a ball into the stands thinking it was the third out…allowing two runs to score. He got into a near-fight with manager Lou Piniella in the dugout. In September he ripped the organization and said "I can see why they've gone a hundred years without winning." The Cubs suspended him for the rest of the season and traded him to the Mariners for Carlos Silva in the off-season.

Michael Brady 1854–? (1875 White Stockings)

Brady played in only one game for the Cubs (known as the White Stockings at that time), and it came the year before the National League was founded. The date was 9/22/1875. Spike, as he was known, went 1-4 and played in the outfield. Very little else is known about him, including if he was right-handed or left-handed or when/if he died. Perhaps there is a 165-year-old man wandering the hills.

Mike Brannock 1851–1881 (1871, 1875 White Stockings)

Mike was only 19 years old when he made his debut as a third baseman. In his two short stints in two different seasons (he attended Notre Dame University in between), Brannock only managed two hits and two stolen bases and finished his career with a lifetime average of .087. The 1871 team was disbanded after the Great Chicago fire destroyed their ballpark on Michigan Avenue and Randolph. Chicago didn't have a baseball team in 1872 and 1873 as the city was busy rebuilding itself. Brannock lived through that, but he didn't live to see the turn of the century. He passed away in 1881 at the age of 29.

Kitty Bransfield 1875–1947 (1911 Cubs)

Kitty Bransfield played for the Cubs in his last season in the big leagues. He was a great first baseman for the Pirates before coming to the Cubs, and they called him Kitty there. The reason for the nickname, according to the Baseball Biography Project: "His original nickname was 'Kid,' but a reporter with bad hearing heard it as "Kitty" and the name stuck."

Danny Breeden 1942–(Cubs 1971)

Danny and his brother Hal both played for the Cubs. Danny was a backup catcher who got limited opportunities behind starter Randy Hundley, but one of those games just happened to be a no-hitter. Breeden caught Ken Holtzman's no-hitter against the Reds on June 3, 1971.

Hal Breeden 1944–(Cubs 1971)

Hal got his start with the Cubs in 1971 — the same year his brother Danny was on the Cubs roster. Breeden was mainly a first baseman, and got very few chances in Chicago. He later played more extensively for the Montreal Expos.

Thom Brennaman 1963–(Cubs announcer 1990-1995)

Brennaman worked in the Cubs broadcast booth during the early 90s alongside the likes of Harry Caray and Steve Stone, but he left to pursue a career with the network. He is now one of the top announcers for Fox in both baseball and football. His father Marty is the Hall of Fame Reds announcer who famously called Cubs fans the most obnoxious fans in baseball.

William Brennan 1963–(Cubs 1993)

Obviously he's not the movie, television, and recording star from a bygone age, he's a pitcher. In 1993 he got a cup of coffee with the Cubs, and pitched respectably in his eight appearances. Trouble was, he was already 30 years old. His appearance on October 2, 1993 was his final one in the big leagues. He pitched two innings against the Padres and gave up a homer to Melvin Nieves.

Bob Brenly 1954–(Cubs announcer 2005-2012)

He was a former big league ballplayer (Giants, Blue Jays) and World Series-winning manager (Diamondbacks) before joining the Cubs television booth. Brenly and Len Kasper formed a great team during their years together. Brenly was known for his tough criticism of certain players (especially Alfonso Soriano), and he and Kasper often also riffed about rock and roll (and even played together on stage at the House of Blues every year before the Cubs convention). He left the Cubs booth after the 2012 season when the Arizona Diamondbacks offered him a chance to broadcast the games of the team he took to the championship.

Roger Bresnahan 1879–1944 (Cubs 1913-1915)

Roger Bresnahan was a proud Irishman. So proud, in fact, that he told everyone that he was actually born in the Irish city of Tralee. That led to the nickname, the Duke of Tralee. Turns out, he wasn't from Ireland at all. He was born and raised in Toledo, Ohio. But Bresnahan was one of the all-time great catchers. He was Christy Mathewson's catcher with the New York Giants, and was involved in that infamous Merkle Boner game in 1908. It wasn't until his last three years in the big leagues that he came to Chicago. He wasn't the same player by then, but was still revered for his smarts and moxie. So much so, the Cubs eventually hired him to manage the team. He was their player/manager for the 1915 season and led them to a fourth place finish. That was the final season in West Side Grounds. The next year the Cubs moved into what is now known as Wrigley Field. He was inducted into the Hall of Fame in 1945, just a few months after his death.

Duke Brett 1900–1974 (Cubs 1924-1925)

Duke pitched two seasons for the Cubs, appearing a grand total of eleven big league games. The Virginia native went 1-1, with a 3.97 ERA. After his playing career ended, Duke was a minor league manager for more than twenty years.

Jim Brewer 1937–1987 (Cubs 1960-1963)

Jim Brewer was a rookie pitcher for an unbelievably bad Cubs team in 1960. He was a little bit wild, and was having trouble controlling his pitches, and on one very unfortunate August day (8/4/60), he threw a fastball behind Cincinnati Reds infielder Billy Martin's head (yes, that Billy Martin). Martin didn't do anything immediately. Instead he waited for the next pitch and "accidentally" lost control of his bat, which went sailing right at Brewer. Brewer stepped down from the mound and said: "You little dago son of a bitch." That led Martin to charge the mound. It wasn't a lengthy fight, but

Martin did get one good punch into Brewer's face, shattering his cheekbone and putting him in the hospital for two weeks. Brewer later sued Martin for a million dollars. Martin was suspended and fined, and the lawsuit went all the way to a jury trial. Jim Brewer was awarded $10,000. It took Billy Martin several years to pay it off. The Cubs traded Brewer in 1963 to the Dodgers (for Dick Scott), and he later pitched in three World Series for them.

Charlie Brewster 1916–2000 (Cubs 1944)

Charlie played 17 seasons in the minors, but also got a few tastes of the big-time, including a ten-game stint with the Cubs in 1944. The shortstop hit .250 as the replacement for Lennie Merullo, and then was shipped back down to the minors.

Jack Brickhouse 1916–1998 (Cubs announcer from the 1940s until 1981)

Jack was the man that had to describe the play-by-play of a Cubs team that went twenty seasons in a row without being in the upper division. In 1949, there were three television stations covering the Cubs. Whispering Joe Wilson on WBKB-TV, Jack Brickhouse on WGN, and Rogers Hornsby on WENR. (WGN didn't get exclusive rights until 1952). There were afternoons when those stations were the only three television stations on the air in Chicago, and the Cubs were broadcast on all three. The Cubs lost the first game broadcast on all three channels, 1-0. On July 23rd, 1962, Jack Brickhouse and the Cubs made television history. Their game against the Philadelphia Phillies in Wrigley Field was beamed into Europe by the Telstar, the first communications satellite. This was the first live sporting event from America ever beamed into Europe. The Cubs lost 5-3. At first only the home games were broadcast on television. It wasn't until 1958 that a road game was, and only five road games were televised each year until 1967. Beginning in 1968, however, the Cubs expanded the schedule to include all home games, and most of the Cubs road games. The White Sox made a fatal mistake that same season. They moved away from WGN to WFLD, a station with a much worse signal. In so doing, they also lost Jack Brickhouse (who did both teams on WGN). It was the beginning of the end of their dominance in Chicago (1951-1967). The Cubs have been Chicago's #1 team ever since. And

it's due, in no small part, to the power of television. Television showed off the beauty of Wrigley Field, and Jack managed to weave tales that captured the imagination of the viewers. (It certainly wasn't the team playing on that field.) Even when the team was terrible, Jack was always able to find the bright spots. He won the Ford Frick award in 1983, inducting him into the Scribes & Mikemen section of Baseball's Hall of Fame. Jack also did the Bears games on the radio for many years (with Irv Kupcinet) and is a member of the Radio Hall of Fame as well.

Al Bridwell 1884–1969 (Cubs 1913)

Al played very briefly for the Cubs, but he had a long career with the Giants before that, and was involved in the most controversial moment in Giants and Cubs history. Bridwell hit the ball that led to the famous Merkle boner.

Buttons Briggs 1875–1911 (Colts/Orphans 1896-1898, Cubs 1904-1905)

Buttons was a pitcher who had a pretty good rookie season for Chicago in 1896, and then struggled for several years. In one two-game stretch in 1897, he gave up 32 runs against Washington. Between 1899 and 1903 he wasn't even in the big leagues, but when he got his second chance in 1904, he responded with 19 wins and a 2.05 ERA. Buttons won 8 more games in 1905. After that season, Briggs was part of the trade bait used to lure Jimmy Sheckard from Brooklyn. That turned out to be a great trade for Chicago. Sheckard was a key contributor to the Cubs dynasty of 1906-1910. Buttons never pitched for Brooklyn.

Historical note: On the day the United States declared war against Spain (1898), beginning the Spanish-American War, Briggs was on the mound for Chicago. He beat Cincinnati 7-4.

Dan Briggs 1952– (Cubs 1982)

The Cubs acquired the first baseman/outfielder from the Expos before the 1982 season, but he didn't have much of an impact. He played his final big league game in a Cubs uniform in July of that year. Briggs finished his seven-season big league career as a .195 hitter.

John Briggs 1934–2018 (Cubs 1956-1958)

John was a right-handed pitcher for the Cubs who saw limited duty over three seasons in the 1950s. His best year was '58 when he won 5 games in 17 starts. Briggs passed away on Christmas Day in 2018.

Harry Bright 1929–2000 (Cubs 1965)

The Cubs always liked Harry Bright. He was in their farm system three different times. Bright made it to the big leagues with the Pirates in 1958. He was with the Pirates the year they won the World Series, the starting first baseman for the Senators in 1962, and made the postseason roster for the 1963 Yankees (striking out in both World Series at-bats), but he didn't make it to the big leagues with the team that owned him three times in his youth, the Cubs, until his last season as a player. The 35-year-old was strictly a pinch hitter in Chicago and batted .280.

Jim Brillheart 1903–1972 (Cubs 1927)

Brillheart was a 30-year veteran of professional baseball (1921-1951), but only had occasional tastes of the big-time. One of those came with the Cubs in 1927. The lefty won 4 games in 12 starts and posted an ERA of 4.31. His last taste of the big leagues came with the 1931 Boston Red Sox. He was 48 years old when he finally hung up his spikes in 1951.

Leon Brinkopf 1926–1998 (Cubs 1952)

Leon started the season with the Cubs in 1952 as a backup infielder (shortstop) and pinch hitter. He only lasted until May 5th. After the game that day, Leon was sent back to the minor leagues, never to return. He had a couple of excellent seasons in the minors with the Cubs minor league team in Los Angeles, but wasn't given another chance at the big-time.

Pete Broberg 1950 (Cubs 1977)

Pete was a first round pick of the Washington Senators in 1971, but could never quite harness his control. He led the American league in hit batsmen in two different seasons before the Cubs acquired him. Broberg pitched only 36 innings for the Cubs in 1977. He was a little wild for the Cubs too (18 walks in 36 innings) and a little hittable (eight home runs allowed in 36 innings). The Cubs traded him to the A's the following year, Broberg's last season in the majors.

Lou Brock 1939– (Cubs 1961-1964)

It's not that the Cubs didn't realize they had a good potential player on their hands. It's just that they didn't know how to develop him. Brock came up through the Cubs system during their ill-fated College of Coaches era. Every few weeks Lou was getting different directions. When they traded him in 1964 for a former 20-game winner, there wasn't much of an uproar in Chicago, but the Cubs players knew their team was making a big mistake. Lou Brock was a six-time All-Star for the Cardinals, led the league in runs scored (twice), doubles, triples, and stolen bases (eight times). He hit over .300 eight times. He retired as the all-time career leader in stolen bases. And most importantly, he retired as a two-time World Series champion. In his first year of eligibility, Lou Brock was elected into baseball's Hall of Fame. He has more career hits than any other player born in Arkansas.

Tarrik Brock 1973– (Cubs 2000)

Brock broke camp with the Cubs in 2000 and remained with the big league club until the end of April. He only saw limited action in the outfield, getting two hits in 12 at-bats. The speedy outfielder also stole a base. It was his only stint in the big leagues after a 13-year minor league career. Nevertheless, he remains the all-time greatest Tarrik to ever play for the Cubs.

Ernie Broglio 1935– (Cubs 1964-1967)

It's too bad that Broglio's name has become a punchline. He was actually a pretty good pitcher before the Cubs traded Lou Brock to get him. Broglio was a former 20 game winner and was coming off an 18-win year, but he was not happy to be traded to the Cubs. He never liked the day games because he felt the batters could see the ball better, and though he didn't tell anyone, he was beginning to get arm problems. He won four games with the Cubs the second half of 1964, but his elbow blew up on him, and he won only three more games over the next two full years.

Historical note: On the day the U.S. Supreme Court established Miranda Rights (1966), Broglio and the Cubs were crushed by the Giants 8-0. Willie McCovey homered.

Herman Bronkie 1884–1968 (Cubs 1914)

Herman played with the Cubs during a season they were only

the third most popular professional baseball team in Chicago (behind the White Sox and the Federals). Dutch, as he was called by his teammates, ended his Cubs career with a 1.000 batting average, a 2.000 slugging percentage, and 3.000 OPS. Care to guess how that happened? He batted only once and hit a double. (He also drove in a run and scored one).

Mandy Brooks 1897–1976 (Cubs 1925-1926)

He was a 27-year-old rookie when he came to Chicago in May of 1925, but he was the team's starting center fielder for the rest of the year. Brooks had a good year too, hitting .281 with 14 homers and 72 RBI. But Joe McCarthy took over the Cubs the following year, and Riggs Stephenson and Hack Wilson were brought aboard — a major upgrade in the outfield. Brooks hung on as a sub for the first half of the 1926 season, but was gone by the end of June. He played six more years in the minors before officially hanging up his spikes and returning to his native Wisconsin.

Historical note: On the day 200,000 KKK members marched in Washington in 1925, Brooks got one of only three hits in a 3-0 shutout loss to the Phillies at Cubs Park (Wrigley).

Jim Brosnan 1929–2014 (Cubs 1954-1958)

Brosnan helped set a record on April 24, 1957. The Cubs were playing the Reds in Cincinnati on a cold day in front of only 7212 fans at Crosley Field. Moe Drabowsky, Jackie Collum, and Jim combined to walk nine batters in one inning. By the time the inning was over, a one-run lead had turned into a six-run deficit. In one inning the Reds managed to score seven runs on one hit, thanks to a still-record nine walks in one inning. Ironically, Brosnan later became the closer for the Cincinnati Reds and led to them to the 1961 World Series.

*Brother Cubs...*The following brothers all played for the Cubs, although not necessarily at the same time...Danny & Hal Breeden, Kid & Lew Camp, Larry & Mike Corcoran, Sammy & Solly Drake, Scott & Jerry Hairston, Jiggs & Tom Parrott, Corey & Eric Patterson, Paul & Rick Reuschel, Ed & Hank Sauer, and Jim & Wayne Tyrone.

Brant Brown 1971– (Cubs 1996-1998, 2001)

Brant Brown had good pop in his bat and played well in his time with the Cubs. He also paid big dividends for the team because trading him to the Pirates brought 20-game winner Jon Lieber in return. But Brant Brown will always be known for an error he committed during the Cubs playoff push in 1998. The date was September 23, and the Cubs were poised to win a game against the Brewers. They had a two-run lead with the bases loaded when a routine fly ball was hit to Brown that should have been the last out of the game. He dropped the ball, and Cubs radio announcer Ron Santo famously screamed "OH NO!" The Cubs lost that game, so the moment had that certain Cubs doom feel to it. But the Cubs won a one-game playoff game at the end of the season, and still managed to get the Wild Card in 1998. Brown came back to the Cubs a few years later for his final big league season.

Joe Brown 1859–1888 (White Stockings 1884)

Brown came to Chicago during a rare Cubs down season in the 1880s. The team was already out of it when he arrived in August of that year, but the Cubs (then known as the White Stockings) got their money's worth out of him. He pitched (going 4-2), played first base, outfield, and catcher. The team still played at Lakefront Park that year, located at the corner of Michigan Avenue and Randolph Street. That was the last year they played there. The following season the Cubs went to West Side Park, and Joe Brown went to Baltimore.

Jophery Brown 1945–2014 (Cubs 1968)

The story of Jophery Brown's Cubs career is a short one. He pitched exactly two innings of one game on a Saturday afternoon, September 21, 1968, at Forbes Field in Pittsburgh. Joe Niekro started that game for the Cubs against the Pirates, but he simply didn't have it. He gave up four runs in the fourth inning, so Cubs manager Leo Durocher sent Brown out to start the 5th inning. He faced Maury Wills, Freddie Patek, Matty Alou, Roberto Clemente, and Don Clendenon. Not too shabby. If you mention the name Clendenon to Brown today, it would probably still elicit a groan from him, because Clendenon singled to left, driving in Maury Wills. That run turned out to be the only one given up by Jophery Brown in his big league career. Brown pitched one more year in the minors after that, developed arm trouble, and retired from the game at the ripe old age of 24.

But Jophery Brown certainly didn't go quietly. Even during his minor league career he had dabbled in Hollywood, working as a stuntman for the television series *I Spy* (starring Bill Cosby). When his baseball career was officially over, he returned to Hollywood and was soon working steadily. Among his 117 feature films and television shows, Jophery Brown has done stunts for *Live and Let Die, Papillion, Smokey and the Bandit, Convoy, Foul Play, The Blues Brothers, Vacation, Scarface, To Live and Die in LA, Die Hard, Speed, Get Shorty* and all three *Lethal Weapon* movies.

Jumbo Brown 1907–1966 (Cubs 1925)

When Brown came up with the Cubs as a rookie, he immediately set a record. He was the heaviest player to ever play in the big leagues at that time, tipping the scales at 295 pounds. He may be remembered for his size, but Jumbo was actually a trailblazer in the big leagues. He was one of the first pitchers who was kept on a roster strictly as a relief pitcher. In the first three and last four seasons of his big league career, he didn't start a single game.

Lew Brown 1858–1889 (White Stockings 1879)

Brown was a catcher and considered a troublemaker. After he left Chicago he was suspended for an entire season for general insubordination. One night, at the age of 30, he was wrestling with a friend and twisted his knee. He went into the hospital for treatment, contracted pneumonia, and never came again. The January 23, 1889 issue of *Sporting Life* had his obituary and praised his catching abilities during an age when the catchers didn't wear any equipment (including mitts) or padding.

Mordecai Brown 1876–1948 (Cubs 1904-1912, 1916)

He was born in 1876, the same year the Cubs played their very first season in the National League. Three Finger probably owns one of the best nicknames in baseball history, and he earned it the hard way. As a seven-year-old boy, Mordecai caught his right hand in a corn grinder on his uncle's farm. They needed to amputate almost the entire index finger, and the middle finger was mangled and left crooked. His little finger was also stubbed. When he learned to add spin to the ball by releasing it off his stub, he became a pitcher. When

he started to have success, the newspapers called him Three Finger for obvious reasons. Three Finger is one of the greatest pitchers to ever wear a Cubs uniform. In ten years with the Cubs, he won 188 games, including 29 games in 1908 and 27 games in 1909. He led the league in wins, ERA, shutouts, and even saves (in four different years). He also pitched in four World Series for the Cubs. In seven World Series starts, he won five (five complete games), and three of those were shutouts. That, sadly, is probably a Cubs record that will never be broken. Three Finger was inducted into the Hall of Fame in 1949: one year after his death. His 1.80 career Cubs ERA and 48 shutouts are both the best in franchise history.

<u>Historical note:</u> On the day that Mark Twain died (1910), Brown was on the hill for the Cubs. He beat the Reds 6-1 at West Side Grounds.

Ray Brown 1889–1955 (Cubs 1909)

Ray was only 20 years old when he got his cup of coffee with the Cubs, the tenth youngest player in league history at that point. He pitched exactly one game, on September 29, 1909 against the Phillies at West Side Grounds. Brown threw a five-hit complete game victory, but somehow never pitched in the big leagues again. After a few more seasons in the minors, he hung up his spikes at the tender age of 24.

Roosevelt Brown 1975– (Cubs 1999-2002)

Roosevelt was on the Cubs for three seasons strictly as a backup outfielder and pinch hitter, and he showed flashes of promise. They finally played him more extensively in the 2002 season to see what he could do (as an injury replacement for Moises Alou), and Brown didn't seize the opportunity. In over 200 plate appearances, he batted only .211. The Cubs released him after the season, and he never made it back up to the big leagues.

Tommy Brown 1927– (Cubs 1952-1953)

They called him "Buckshot" because the shortstop sprayed hits all over the field. He was acquired from the Phillies during the 1952 season and hit incredibly well for the Cubs the rest of that year (.320 average). The following season, however, he had a much tougher time (.196 average). That turned out to be his last season in the big leagues. The Cubs had another shortstop who could handle the job. His name was Ernie Banks. Brown remains the youngest non-pitcher to ever play in the big leagues. He came up during wartime (1944) to play with the Brooklyn Dodgers at the age of 16.

Byron Browne 1942 – (Cubs 1965-1967)

Byron was the starting left fielder for the Cubs during the 1966 season and clubbed 16 homers, but he also led the league in strikeouts. He was traded to the Cardinals in 1968 and was later involved in the infamous Curt Flood/Dick Allen trade which led to Flood challenging baseball's reserve clause. He finished his career with the Phillies.

George Browne 1876 – 1920 (Cubs 1909)

George was a solid major leaguer for 12 seasons (Phillies, Giants, Braves, Senators, White Sox, and Dodgers), but only played a portion of one of those seasons with the Cubs. He was a right fielder.

Mike Brumley 1963 – (Cubs 1987)

Mike was acquired in the Eckersley for Buckner trade. He was a backup infielder who got quite a bit of playing time with the Cubs in his rookie season of 1987. The Cubs traded him to the Padres in the Goose Gossage trade (along with Keith Moreland), and Brumley went on to play seven more seasons in the big leagues with the Tigers, Mariners, Red Sox, A's, and Astros. Brumley was never a star, but how many people can say they were involved in trades with two Hall of Famers?

Warren Brusstar 1952 – (Cubs 1983-1985)

Warren pitched out of the bullpen for the Cubs for three seasons. His first two were excellent, and his third one was so bad it became the last season of his big league career. He also played for the Phillies and the White Sox before joining the Cubs.

Clay Bryant 1911 – 1999 (Cubs 1935-1940)

Bryant was a journeyman pitcher for the Cubs until he suddenly blossomed and won 19 games out of nowhere in 1938. He pitched well in the World Series that year against the Yankees, at least for 4 innings, before losing Game 3, 5-2. The Cubs were eventually swept in the series. Unfortunately for Bryant, he came crashing back to earth pretty quickly. He had arm problems in 1939 and missed most of the year.

When he started out the 1940 season with arm problems (elbow) again, Cubs owner PK Wrigley suspended him indefinitely without pay. Bryant wanted to go to LA to have his arm treated, but he couldn't afford to do it without a steady paycheck, so he protested the suspension to Commissioner Landis. Landis sided with Wrigley, and Wrigley refused to buckle on the suspension. He did, however, find a way to help Bryant without losing face. Wrigley eventually paid Bryant's wife $50 a week for 4 weeks to accompany him to Los Angeles. Clay Bryant got his treatment, but it didn't help. He never made it back to the majors.

Historical note: On the day the book *Gone with the Wind* was released (1936), Bryant was on the mound for the Cubs and took the loss against the Pirates at Wrigley Field.

Don Bryant 1941 – 2015 (Cubs 1966)

Bryant was a backup catcher for the Cubs in 1966, who didn't get a lot of playing time behind starter Randy Hundley. He later got a shot as the backup catcher for the Astros. After his playing days, he coached for the Boston Red Sox.

Kris Bryant 1992 – (Cubs 2015-present)

After being drafted #2 overall and leading the minor leagues in home runs, the third baseman arrived in Chicago in April as one of the most hyped rookies in history. He clearly lived up to the hype, hitting 26 homers, driving in 99 runs, and winning the Rookie of the Year award. Then Bryant got even better. In 2016 he was simply the best player in the National League. He didn't just hit 39 homers — he crushed them. They bounced off the video board. He also led the league in runs scored, but he did something even more important than that. He led the Cubs to the World Series. As fate would have it, Bryant even recorded the final out on a slow roller to third. It is a moment that will be remembered as the greatest moment in Cubs history. That smile on his face as he threw the ball to Anthony Rizzo across the diamond will never be forgotten. After the season he was named the MVP. His 2017 season was down by Bryant's standards, but he still scored 111 runs, hit 29 homers, and hit .295. In 2018 Kris struggled through shoulder injuries and didn't live up to his potential, but after that 2016 season, Cubs fans were inclined to forgive him.

Historical note: On the day Pope Francis visited America for the first time (2015), Bryant was the hitting star for the

Cubs in a 4-0 win over the Brewers. Kris homered, doubled, and knocked in three of the runs.

Tod Brynan 1863–1925 (White Stockings 1888)

Brynan pitched for the Cubs (then known as the White Stockings) as the fifth or six starter (on a fill-in basis) during the 1888 season for manager Cap Anson. He won two games. He later had a very brief (and incredibly unsuccessful) stint with Boston.

Jake Buchanan 1989–(Cubs 2016)

Jake pitched briefly for the Astros before being acquired by the Cubs. He spent nearly all of the 2016 season with Iowa, but was called up in September when the rosters were expanded and appeared in two games. He pitched for the Reds in 2017.

Bill Buckner 1949–(Cubs 1977-1984)

In his first season with the Cubs in 1977, Bill Buckner hit a respectable .284, but Billy Buck went on to have a great Cubs career, capped off by a batting title in 1980. In his seven-plus seasons with the Cubs, Buckner never hit less than .280. When the Cubs traded him early in 1984, it was only because they had another player to take his place at first base… Leon Durham. Durham and Buckner, of course, share a common fate. Both of their outstanding careers will always be remembered for one little ball that went through their legs at the worst possible time.

Steve Buechele 1961–(Cubs 1992-1995)

Steve was supposed to be the elusive player who would finally solidify the third base position — which had remained a trouble spot since the departure of Ron Santo twenty years earlier. He didn't exactly replace Santo in the hearts and minds of Cubs fans, but he did perform respectably. In 1993, he slugged fifteen homers, and followed that up with 14 during the strike year of 1994. It was pretty obvious, however, that he was slowing down. After the strike was resolved the following season, the Cubs released him. Buechele finished his career where he began — with the Texas Rangers. Steve Buechele trivia: his college roommate was John Elway.

Art Bues 1888–1954 (Cubs 1914)

Art may have had a slight advantage when he made it up to the big leagues in 1913 to play for Boston. The manager of the team was his uncle, Gentleman George Stallings. But he made it on his own in Chicago the following year. On a team that featured the last two members of the Cubs dynasty (Wildfire Schulte and Heinie Zimmerman), Bues backed up third base and got 45 at-bats. Unfortunately for Art, not many people saw him play. 1914 was a year when the crosstown Chi-Feds outdrew the Cubs because of their brand new ballpark (now known as Wrigley Field). Bues wasn't around anymore when the Cubs moved their games there in 1916.

Damon Buford 1970–(Cubs 2000-2001)

The son of Orioles great Don Buford played nine seasons in the big leagues, including the last two of his career with the Cubs. In 2000 he got the most extended shot of playing time in his entire career. In over 550 plate appearances, he batted .251 with 15 homers. After a tough start in 2001, the Cubs released him in May. He never played in the big leagues again.

Bob Buhl 1928–2001 (Cubs 1962-1966)

Pitchers are not supposed to be great hitters, but Bob Buhl took that concept to a whole different level. His record-setting streak began in 1961, when he was still with the Milwaukee Braves. That year he got a whopping 4 hits in 60 at-bats and struck out 30 times. But he really took it up a notch when he joined the Cubs in 1962. That year he went the entire season without getting a single hit. He was 0-70 and struck out 36 times. He didn't get another hit until May 8, 1963, when he slapped a single off Pirates pitcher Al McBean, who probably was razzed about it by his teammates the rest of his career. Buhl's record still stands today: 88 consecutive at-bats without getting a hit. Luckily for Buhl, he was a pretty good pitcher. He pitched in the big leagues for 15 seasons and won 15 or more games five times, including once with the incredibly lousy 1964 Cubs. Buhl even managed to do something completely foreign to his Cubs teammates. He won a World Series ring (with the 1957 Milwaukee Braves).

Scott Bullett 1968–(Cubs 1995-1996)

Bullett was a reserve outfielder for the Cubs for two seasons. He served mainly as a backup to Luis Gonzalez and Brian McRae, but he appeared in over 100 games two years in a row. It was his last taste of the big leagues. He had previously played for the Pittsburgh Pirates.

Jim Bullinger 1965–(Cubs 1992-1996)

On the first pitch of his first big league at-bat, Bullinger hit a home run, an incredible accomplishment for any player, let alone a pitcher. Jim was in and out of the Cubs rotation for a few seasons. His career year came in 1995, when he won 12 games with an ERA of 4.14. He finished his career pitching for the Expos and Mariners.

Freddie Burdette 1936–2010 (Cubs 1962-1964)

Burdette was a right-handed reliever who pitched for the Cubs in the early 60s. He wasn't exactly known for his command. In his 34.1 big league innings, he walked twice as many men (20) as he struck out (10). His only career win was saved by the man the Cubs acquired for Lou Brock…Ernie Broglio.

Lew Burdette 1926–2007 (Cubs 1964-1965)

He was a well-known spitballer. Red Smith of *The New York Times* said that he needed three columns for his statistics: wins, losses, and relative humidity. Nevertheless, he won over 200 games in his career, was a three-time All-Star, and pitched his team to a World Series title, but of course, that team was not the Chicago Cubs — it was the Milwaukee Braves. By the time he came to the Cubs, Burdette was 37 years old, and his career was pretty much over. He won 9 games for the Cubs in two seasons, and his ERA was over five.

Historical note: On the day the Republicans nominated Barry Goldwater to take on President Lyndon Johnson (1964), Burdette hit the game-winning homer for the Cubs against the Mets at Wrigley Field.

Smoky Burgess 1927–1991 (Cubs 1949-1951)

His real name was Forrest Harrill Burgess, but no one called him that. He was Smoky Burgess, a five-time National League All-Star. He was a very good catcher, but he became even better known as one of the best pinch hitters of his era. He retired with a record 507 pinch at-bats. Only Lenny Harris, Mark Sweeney, and Manny Mota have more than Burgess's 145 pinch hits. Unfortunately, none of that happened with the Cubs because they traded him after his second season in the majors (1951) for little-remembered Johnny Pramesa

and Bob Usher. If he had stayed with the Cubs, he could have been their starting catcher for a decade. (Pramesa played 22 games for the Cubs, Usher played one.) Smoky always said that his most satisfying pinch hit was his home run off Cubs pitcher Sam Jones with two games left in the 1956 season. The Reds, his team at the time, were going for the record — most home runs by a team in a season. The record was 221, and when Smokey came up to bat, the Reds had 220. Smoky ended his career as a pinch hitter for the White Sox — and played until he was 40 years old.

Historical note: On the day Senator McCarthy was chastised by Joseph Nye Welch ("Have you no sense of decency, Sir?") in 1954, Smoky helped the Phillies beat the Cubs with a late hit.

Leo Burke 1934–(Cubs 1963-1965)

The Cubs acquired the utility man from the Cardinals in exchange for relief pitcher Barney Schultz. Barney became a key member of the 1964 Cardinals bullpen, and Leo stuck with the Cubs for several seasons as a jack of all trades. He played some infield, some outfield, and pinch hit for the Cubs. 1964 was his best season in the big leagues, when he got up to bat more than a hundred times for the only time in his career. He knocked in 14 runs and hit .262.

Alex Burnett 1987–(Cubs 2013)

Burnett appeared in exactly one game for the Cubs on May 29, 2013. He pitched the ninth inning against the White Sox at Wrigley Field that day, and allowed only one hit, a single by Jeff Keppinger. The Cubs won the game 9-3. Burnett previously pitched for the Twins and Orioles.

Jeromy Burnitz 1969– (Cubs 2005)

Burnitz was a big slugger for the Brewers and the Rockies, and for one brief season, he knocked the ball out of Wrigley on behalf of the Cubs. He hit 24 homers and knocked in 87 runs, but his career was winding down. The Cubs allowed him to leave via free agency after the season, and he only played one more year in the big leagues. In his career Burnitz hit over 300 home runs.

Historical note: On the day Hurricane Katrina hit New Orleans (2005), Burnitz slugged two homers for the Cubs in a game against the Dodgers. The Dodgers still won 9-5.

Tom Burns 1857–1902 (White Stockings/Colts 1880-1891, manager 1898-1899)

Tom was an infielder on one of the most dominant teams in baseball history. From 1880 (his rookie season) until 1886 they won the National League championship five times. During that 1886 season he was attacked by an angry mob in Detroit and hurt his thumb fighting them off. But that was nothing compared to what he had to fight off during his time in Chicago.

Burns survived two massive purges of players. When all of the drinkers were sent away by Al Spalding after the 1886 season, Burns remained. In 1890, after a full-fledged player revolt, only three players remained — Cap Anson, Bill Hutchison, and the survivor, Tom Burns. Other than the three oldtimers, the players who played for Chicago in 1890 were so young that the newspapers started calling the team the Colts. Burns probably had the best season of his career during that 1890 Colts season. He knocked in a career-high 86 runs and stole 44 bases. He later came back to manage the Cubs (then known as the Orphans) for two seasons after Cap Anson was let go.

Ray Burris 1950–(Cubs 1973-1979)

Ray anchored the Cubs rotation in the mid-70s, twice winning 15 games in a season ('75 & '76). Unfortunately for Ray, expectations were very high for him. He arrived on the Cubs just as Fergie Jenkins was departing, and the team hoped that Burris could step into that role. Turns out there was only one Fergie. The Cubs traded Burris to the Yankees in 1979 for reliever Dick Tidrow. Ray had a very respectable 15-year big league career. He won over a hundred games for the Cubs, Yankees, Mets, Expos, A's, Brewers, and Cardinals. In 1981 he pitched in the NLCS for the Montreal Expos. He shut out the Dodgers in Game 2 of that series, before losing a pitcher's duel to Fernando Valenzuela in the deciding Game 5. Burris is currently a pitching coach in the Phillies organization.

<u>Historical note</u>: On the day Americans evacuated their last troops out of Saigon (1975), Ray was on the mound for the Cubs at Wrigley Field. He beat the Mets 7-4.

John Burrows 1913–1987 (Cubs 1943-1944)

Burrows was a wartime player for the Cubs. The 30-year-old pitcher appeared in 23 games for the Cubs in 1943, but by 1944 he was getting hit very hard and went back down to the minors. He pitched in the minor leagues until 1949.

Ellis Burton 1936–2013 (Cubs 1963-1965)

Burton was an outfielder for the Cubs and had a few decent years filled with clutch hits and homers. The problem with Ellis is that he couldn't put the bat on the ball consistently enough. His career average was a woeful .216. His teammates called him Bones.

Dick Burwell 1940–(Cubs 1960-1961)

Dick got two very short cups of coffee with the Cubs in September of 1960 and 1961. In those two Septembers he pitched in a total of five games, and was hit pretty hard. He walked eleven batters in just over 13 innings of work and gave up two homers. Both of those homers were given up in his first (and only) big league start against the Cincinnati Reds at Crosley Field. Although he didn't get a lot of time in the big leagues, he did manage to pitch against some Hall of Famers including Frank Robinson in his 1960 debut, and Willie Mays & Orlando Cepeda in his 1961 finale. He was only 21 years old but never made it back to the big leagues. After four more years in the minors, he hung it up at the age of 25.

Guy Bush 1901–1985 (Cubs 1923-1934)

The Mississippi Mudcat got his nickname because he came from Mississippi and had a very strange delivery. Bush won 150+ games for the Cubs, as a starter and reliever (he led the league in relief wins 4 times). Some of those were key games in Cubs history. On May 4, 1927 he pitched 18 innings in one game, when the Cubs beat the Braves 7-2. He started and won Game 3 of the 1929 World Series against the A's, giving up only one run. He also pitched Game 1 of the 1932 series against the Yankees, but this time the results weren't quite as good. He was shelled for eight earned runs in less than six innings. One last notation on Bush's career highlights: He was the last pitcher to give up a home run to Babe Ruth. He did that as a member of the Pirates in 1935.

<u>Historical note</u>: On the day the gangsters Bonnie & Clyde were gunned down (1934), Bush was on the mound for the Cubs. He lost that one to the Giants, 5-2.

Eddie Butler 1991– (Cubs 2017-2018)
The Cubs acquired the former first round pick of the Rockies during the 2017 season and he filled the fifth starter role during the summer. Butler had good moments and bad, and the Cubs eventually felt it was necessary to acquire another starting pitcher. For the season Butler was 4-3, with 3.95 ERA. In the 2018 season he made the club out of spring training and pitched well until he was injured. The Cubs eventually included Butler in the package that brought Cole Hamels from the Rangers.

Johnny Butler 1893–1967 (Cubs 1928)
They called him Trolley Line, and Johnny more than likely acquired his nickname thanks to the town of Butler, Pennsylvania, which featured a well-known Trolley line (the Butler Short Line). Butler didn't have much power (3 career home runs), and he didn't hit that well (career .252 hitter), but he was a pretty good glove man in the infield, and he was versatile. Trolley Line Butler played 3B/SS for 1928 Cubs. He stayed in the big leagues for four seasons — two years with Brooklyn before joining the Cubs, and one season with the Cardinals in 1929. By the turn of the decade, the Trolley Line was shut down.

John Buzhardt 1936–2008 (Cubs 1958-1959)
Buzhardt burst onto the scene in September of 1958 and immediately made his presence known. In his first two big league starts he beat Sandy Koufax and Don Drysdale. The following year he tossed a one-hitter for the Cubs before developing elbow problems. The Cubs traded him to the Phillies (along with Alvin Dark and Jim Woods) for future Hall of Famer Richie Ashburn. Ashburn had a few more seasons in the tank. Buzhardt had a decade. He pitched for the Phillies, White Sox, Orioles, and Astros before hanging up his spikes following the 1968 season. He never quite lived up to his early promise. His final record was 25 games under .500, although he had a very respectable 3.66 lifetime ERA.

Freddie Bynum 1980– (Cubs 2006)
The Cubs acquired Freddie just before the 2006 season began, and he got the most extensive playing time of his big league career during Dusty Baker's last season in Chicago. Bynum played all three outfield positions and second base. He hit four homers and stole eight bases. The Cubs traded him to the Orioles the following spring for pitcher Kevin Hart.

Marlon Byrd 1977– (Cubs 2010-2012)
Byrd was signed as a free agent by the Cubs after a stellar run in Texas. In his first year with the Cubs he was an All-Star, and hit .293 with 66 RBI. The center fielder's output went down a bit the following year. He also sustained a truly scary injury that year when he was hit in the face with a pitch from Red Sox fireballer Alfredo Aceves at Fenway Park. He had to be helped off the field, and was out of the lineup for quite a while. When he returned he wore a newly designed batting helmet that shielded his cheek. The Cubs traded Byrd to Boston (for Michael Bowden) in 2012.

*Additional Entries...*If you check out the Every Cub Ever feature at www.justonebadcentury.com, you'll find several additional entries, including celebrity Cubs fans, writers, and bloggers. Under the letter B, you'll find some great ones, including the Belushi Brothers (John & Jim), MadTV's Ike Barinholtz, 1930s movie star Joe E. Brown, Happy Days dad Tom Bosely, race car driver Kurt Busch, Tarzan writer Edgar Rice Burroughs, radio disc jockey Lin Brehmer, and Cubs author/usher Bruce Bohrer. All are HUGE Cubs fans.

CHAPTER THREE

C

The starting lineup of your Chicago Cubs beginning with the letter C...

C – Willson Contreras, World Series Champ
1B – Frank Chance, the Peerless Leader
2B – Starlin Castro, the kid
SS – Jimmy Cooney, Unassisted Triple Play
3B – Ron Cey, the Penguin
LF – Joe Carter, World Series Hero
CF – Kiki Cuyler, Hall of Famer
RF – Jose Cardenal, the afro
Bench – Phil Cavaretta, MVP
Bench – Chuck Connors, the Rifleman
SP – John Clarkson, Hall of Famer
SP – Larry Corcoran, 40-game winner
RP – Aroldis Chapman, the closer

Alberto Cabrera 1988 – (Cubs 2012-2013)

The young Dominican pitched out of the Cubs bullpen for parts of two seasons. He appeared in 32 games and posted an ERA of 5.20. He hasn't made it back to the big leagues since. His brother Mauricio pitched briefly for the Atlanta Braves.

Trevor Cahill 1988 – (Cubs 2015-2016)

The former 18-game winner with Oakland was down on his luck when the Cubs took a flyer on him towards the end of the 2015 season. They put Cahill in the bullpen, and he rebounded with a tremendous performance. Even during the 2015 playoffs, Trevor was a key contributor out of the pen. The Cubs outbid Pittsburgh to re-sign him after the season. In 2016, he suffered through injuries and wasn't able to repeat his 2015 effectiveness.

Miguel Cairo 1974 – (Cubs 1997, 2001)

Miguel had a very impressive 17-year big league career. He played for ten different teams, including six playoff teams,

and amassed nearly 4000 at-bats. Two of his 17 seasons were played in Chicago. He backed up Ryne Sandberg during the Hall of Famer's final season, and then played a bigger role during his second stint with the Cubs, backing up second base, shortstop, and third base. The closest he came to playing in the World Series was with the 2004 New York Yankees. That's the team that had a 3-game lead to the Red Sox in the ALCS before blowing the series.

Marty Callaghan 1900 – 1975 (Cubs 1922-1923)

The backup outfielder only had limited playing time with the Cubs in his two seasons in Chicago, but one of those days was the highest scoring game in baseball history. He set a big league record in that game (shared by a few others) when he batted three times in one inning on August 25, 1922. He had two singles and a strikeout during the fourth inning of a 26-23 win against the Phillies.

Jimmy Callahan 1874 – 1934 (Orphans/Colts 1897-1900)

The newspapers at the time liked to call him by his childhood nickname Nixey. He was mainly a pitcher, and a good one at that, but he could also hit, and he had blinding speed, so the Cubs (then known as the Colts and Orphans) found ways to get him on the field even on days he wasn't pitching. He played a little outfield and a little third base. On the mound, though, is where Jimmy Callahan really made his mark. When Jimmy went out there to pitch, the Cubs knew he was going to finish what he started. Out of 116 starts, 113 of them were complete games. One of the most memorable probably came on July 4th, 1900. The Cubs drew a big crowd that day for Independence Day, and hundreds of fans arrived with guns. They shot off their guns in celebration when Nixey and Chicago won the game 5-4. When the American League was founded he jumped across town with Clark Griffith and finished his career with the White Sox. While pitching for the White Sox, Callahan hurled the first no-hitter in American League history. Jimmy still holds two Cubs records that will never be broken. On September 6, 1900, he allowed 25 hits and 20 runs in one game.

Johnny Callison 1939 – 2006 (Cubs 1970-1971)

The Cubs acquired him in November of 1969, in a trade

that they hoped would put them over the top. They traded pitcher Dick Selma (who had been a favorite of the Bleacher Bums because of his cheerleading routine from the bullpen) and a young prospect to the Phillies for the former All-Star outfielder. Unfortunately for the Cubs, that young prospect turned out to be Oscar Gamble. Gamble was only 19 years old at the time, but he had already gotten a taste of the majors with the Cubs. How did that trade turn out? Gamble played in the majors until 1985, hitting 200 home runs. Callison had one semi-decent year in Chicago, then was done. Needless to say, he wasn't the final piece to take them over the top.

Historical note: On the day that Martin Luther King delivered his "I Have a Dream" speech in Washington, Callison (then a Phillie) got the game-winning homer to defeat the Cubs in Chicago.

Dick Calmus 1944–(1967 Cubs)

Dick Calmus got into 21 games with the 1963 Dodgers but didn't get back up to the big leagues until September 2, 1967. He was the starting pitcher for the Cubs that day in the second game of a double-header against the Mets at Wrigley Field. The Cubs spotted him a 4-1 lead, but Calmus couldn't hold it. He gave up two home runs to the Mets second baseman Jerry Bucheck, and was pulled in the fifth inning. It was his last big league appearance. He was 23 years old.

Dolph Camilli 1907–1997 (Cubs 1933-1934)

After Cubs owner William Wrigley and team president Bill Veeck Sr. died, the club was handed to an inexperienced fish wholesaler named William Walker. He traded Dolph to the Phillies for Don Hurst. Camilli went on to hit over 200 home runs, made two All-Star teams, and led the 1941 Brooklyn Dodgers to the World Series. He won the MVP that year too. Cubs fans might have been forgiven if they found themselves rooting for the Brooklyn Dodgers in the 1941 World Series. Seven ex-Cubs led that Brooklyn team to the National League pennant. Dolph Camilli played first base. Billy Herman played second. Augie Galan was an outfielder. Kirby Higbe won 22 games. Hugh Casey won 14 games. Larry French pitched valuable innings out of the bullpen, and Babe Phelps was a backup catcher.

Kid Camp 1869–1895 (Colts 1894)

They called him Kid because his big brother Lew was also on the team. Kid was a pitcher. He started two games for the Cubs (then known as the Colts) and completed both of those games, but he was hit pretty hard. He gave up more than two runners an inning and registered an ERA of 6.55. He previously had a cup of coffee with the Pirates. He died in 1895 before the season began. Kid was only 25.

Lew Camp 1868–1948 (Colts 1893-1894)

Lew was a backup infielder for two seasons with the Cubs (then known as the Colts), and hit two homers in limited play. His real name was Robert Plantagenet Llewallen Camp. Pretty smart to convert that mouthful to Lew. He and his brother were both part of the team when their stadium West Side Grounds burned down during a game. Cause of the fire was probably a cigar stub.

Shawn Camp 1975–(Cubs 2012-2013)

Camp didn't pitch in every game for the Cubs in 2012 — it only seemed like it. He did lead the league in appearances with 80. And while he started off strong, that wear and tear eventually caught up with him. By the end of the season he was getting knocked around regularly, and the following season it was worse. When the Cubs released him in July of 2013, his ERA was north of seven.

Tony Campana 1986–(Cubs 2011-2012)

The speedy Campana was a big hit with Cubs fans because of the excitement he stirred every time he reached base. In limited opportunities, he stole 24 and 30 bases in his two years with the Cubs. He also once hit an inside-the-park home run — the only homer in his entire career (minor and major leagues). Unfortunately for Tony, he couldn't steal first, and he didn't take walks. He was released before the 2013 season and signed with the Diamondbacks.

Bill Campbell 1948–(Cubs 1982-1983)

Like anyone with the last name of Campbell, Bill was tagged with the nickname of Soup pretty early on in his career. He was an excellent relief pitcher for the Twins and Red Sox, playing in an All-Star game as a representative of the Red Sox in 1977. With the Cubs, Soup led the league in appearances in 1982, but slumped a bit in 1983. Nevertheless, he played an important role in the Cubs 1984 division championship because he was part of the trade that brought Gary Matthews and Bob Dernier to the Cubs.

Gilly Campbell 1908–1973 (Cubs 1933)
Gilly was a catcher and had a cup of coffee as Gabby Hartnett's backup during the 1933 season. He hit .280 in that limited capacity, and helped handle a pitching staff that included big-time pitching stars like Lon Warneke, Guy Bush, Charlie Root, and Pat Malone (all of them double-digit winners that year). The following season he was sold to Cincinnati. Gilly was a big leaguer until 1938.

Joe Campbell 1944– (Cubs 1967)
Joe was serving in the U.S. Marines when the Cubs took him from the Mets in the Rule V Draft. He finally arrived on May 3rd, and played his first and only game in the big leagues. He went 0 for 3 and struck out all three times. The Cubs returned him to the Mets after the game and he never made it back up the majors. In that one game, however, Campbell can say that he was in the same lineup as three Hall of Famers (Banks, Santo, and Williams), and that the other lineup included Felipe Alou, Joe Torre, Rico Carty, and one of the best hitters of all-time, Hank Aaron.

Mike Campbell 1964– (Cubs 1996)
After stops in Seattle, Texas, and San Diego, Campbell came to the Cubs in 1996 and had his best season in the big leagues. He went 3-1 with a 4.46 ERA. He went to Japan after that and developed shoulder problems. Campbell's claim to fame was being part of the trade that brought Randy Johnson to the Mariners. He and Mark Langston went to the Expos in exchange for the future 300-game winner.

Ron Campbell 1940– (Cubs 1964-66)
Ron was mainly a backup infielder for the Cubs, but he did get one shot in the starting lineup. In September of 1964, he was the team's starting second baseman. He hit fairly well (.272) and had several clutch hits (including six doubles, a triple, and a homer), but when 1965 began, the Cubs had a new second baseman in the starting lineup — Glenn Beckert. Campbell got a few tastes of the big leagues in '65 and '66,

but he didn't do as well. He played three more seasons in the minors after that, and retired from the game after the 1970 season at the age of 30.

Vin Campbell 1888–1969 (Cubs 1908)
He got his cup of coffee with the Cubs in their most momentous year, 1908. He got his chance only because the Cubs were decimated with injuries. Outfielder Jimmy Sheckard was out with an eye injury, reserve infielder Heinie Zimmerman was out because he was beaten up by his teammates for causing Sheckard's eye injury, backup catcher Pat Moran was spiked, starting pitcher Chick Fraser was hit in his pitching hand with a line drive, starter Orval Overall had a bad back, and a flu bug was sidelining utility man Solly Hofman, reserve Del Howard, and most importantly, first baseman Frank Chance & second baseman Johnny Evers. Campbell got only one at-bat on June 6, 1908. Campbell played six seasons in the big leagues after that (for other teams) and retired as a .310 hitter.

Jim Canavan 1866–1949 (Colts 1892)
Canavan was the starting second baseman for most of the 1892 season, but he had a hard time with the bat. He only hit .166 in 487 plate appearances — among the worst performances in Cubs history. He finished his career with Cincinnati.

Jeimer Candelario 1993– (Cubs 2016-2017)
The third baseman had a great season with Triple A Iowa in 2016, and when the Cubs suffered a few injuries, he briefly had a run with the parent club. In eleven at-bats he only recorded one hit. He had another brief call up in 2017, but with no real place to play on the big league club, he was the centerpiece of a trade that brought Justin Wilson and Alex Avila to the Cubs at the trade deadline. In 2018, he hit 19 homers for the Tigers.

Chris Cannizzaro 1938–2016 (Cubs 1971)
Chris had been the starting catcher for the Padres before coming to the Cubs. Chicago acquired him because catcher Randy Hundley had gone down with an injury. Cannizzaro got extensive playing time during that 1971 season and caught Cy Young winner Fergie Jenkins, but his hitting was

atrocious. In nearly 200 at-bats, he hit a mere .213. The Cubs let him go after the season and he finished his career as the backup catcher in Los Angeles.

Mike Capel 1961 – (Cubs 1988)

The Cubs brought up the University of Texas product in 1988, and he appeared in 21 games for the team that year. After spending the 1989 season in the minors, he was released. Capel did make it back up to the big leagues with the Brewers in 1990, but he posted an almost unbelievable ERA of 135.00.

Doug Capilla 1952 – (1979-1981 Cubs)

He was a big part of the Cubs bullpen in his seasons with the Cubs, but he had control issues. In his six-year big league career (which included time with the Cardinals and Reds), he walked nearly as many men as he struck out.

Victor Caratini 1993 – (Cubs 2017-present)

The Cubs acquired Victor at the trade deadline in 2014 for Emilio Bonafacio and James Russell. The switch-hitting catcher was brought up to the big league club in 2017 when Miguel Montero was released and became a reliable bat off the bench during the stretch run. During the 2018 season Victor served as the main backup to Willson Contreras.

Chip Caray 1965 – (Cubs announcer 1998-2004)

He was hired to work alongside his grandfather in the booth, but before Chip broadcast his first Cubs game, Harry Caray passed away. Chip was paired with Steve Stone for seven seasons and provided solid if unspectacular coverage of the team. He wasn't asked back after a controversy erupted at the end of the 2004 season between players and the broadcasters — and Steve Stone followed him out of the booth. Chip now does Atlanta Braves games, just as his father did before him.

Harry Caray 1914 – 1998 (Cubs announcer 1982-1997)

Harry was more than just the announcer for the Cubs. He was the symbol of the team during his time on the North Side. He had some great moments in the division-winning year of 1984, but Cubs fans truly got a taste of what it would be like without him when he had a stroke in 1987 and had to miss some time. When Harry Caray finally returned to the broadcast booth in May of 1987, it was a big deal across the country. He had been out of commission for the first month of the year, and WGN's Superstation trumpeted his return across the nation. It seemed that every baseball fan in America was tuning in that day Harry returned. It also happened to be in an era when the President of the United States was a big Cubs fan, and he even called into the booth to wish Harry well. Most people would have been thrilled, but Harry took the phone call in stride, even when President Reagan said: "I just wanted to welcome you back. The Cubs need you, the baseball world needs you, and the country needs you. You're great for baseball." President Reagan went on to talk about Nancy, and Chicago, and his broadcasting days. Harry didn't really seem to be paying attention to what the President said. Instead, he cut him off by saying "Mr. President, Bob Denier just singled and I've got to let you go." Then he hung up on the President. How many people can say they have done that? Obviously, Ronald Reagan didn't take it personally. The following season he came to Wrigley Field and did an inning with Harry in the booth. Harry passed away in February of 1998. He was replaced in the Cubs broadcast booth by his grandson Chip.

Jose Cardenal 1943 – (Cubs 1972-1977)

Jose Cardenal was one of the most colorful players to wear a Cubs uniform. With his gigantic afro, his hat tucked into his back pocket, and his crouched batting stance and running style, he was easy to spot. But he was also an interesting guy, prone to some rather unusual on- and off-the-field incidents. A lot has been made of his embarrassing injuries (covered later in this book), but he also once caused the injury of the Cubs best pitcher in a very unusual way. Jose was trying to steal home, and Fergie was at-bat and didn't know Jose was coming. Cardenal ran right into his star pitcher, knocking him out of the game. His big off-field controversy came in 1975 when he was charged with resisting arrest after a confrontation with police at O'Hare. Jose was being picked up by his wife, and when he saw her arguing with a cop, he grabbed the cop's nightstick and hit him with it. (He later filed a $750,000 lawsuit against the city — charging police brutality — and it was settled out of court.)

He may have been mercurial, but Jose Cardenal was a crowd favorite throughout his Cubs years. Though he played for other teams in other towns and coached for other teams in other towns, he always considered Chicago his American home.

Historical note: On the day the Watergate burglars were arrested (1972), Jose was the hitting star for the Cubs in a 7-2 win over the Dodgers at Wrigley Field. Jose homered off Al Downing, who would give up Hank Aaron's record-breaking 715th homer a few years later.

Adrian Cardenas 1987– (Cubs 2012)

The Cubs acquired Cardenas from the Oakland organization, and he served as a pinch hitter and occasional spot starter in the infield during his one season in the big leagues. The highlight of that year was probably the hit he got to break up A.J. Burnett's no-hitter in the 8th inning. Before the 2013 season, Cardenas abruptly retired at the age of 24. He is now pursuing a career as a writer.

Don Cardwell 1935–2008 (Cubs 1960-1962)

The Cubs acquired Cardwell from the Phillies in exchange for second baseman Tony Taylor. Taylor went on to play big league ball for 16 more seasons, but initially, it looked like a steal for the Cubs. On May 15, 1960, in his first start in a Cubs uniform, Don Cardwell pitched a no-hitter. He won 15 games for the Cubs the following year, but fell off in 1962 and was traded to the Pirates after the season. In return the Cubs got future 20-game winner Larry Jackson (among others). Jackson was later the key part of the trade that allowed the Cubs to acquire Ferguson Jenkins. After leaving Chicago, Cardwell pitched for the 1969 Mets team that broke his former team's heart.

Historical note: The day of his no-hitter with the Cubs (1960) was the same day the Soviets launched Sputnik 4.

Esmailin Caridad 1983– (Cubs 2009-2010)

The Dominican pitched out of the Cubs bullpen during parts of two seasons with mixed results. He pitched pretty well in 2009, but was lit up in 2010. He remains, however, the greatest Esmailin in Cubs history. He pitched in the minors and the Mexican League until 2017.

Tex Carleton 1906–1977 (Cubs 1935-1938)

Tex Carleton got his nickname because he hailed from Comanche, Texas and attended Texas Christian University.

His real name was James. He pitched for two Cubs pennant winners (1935 and 1938) and had a pretty good run for the team, averaging about 13 wins a season in his four years in Chicago. He pitched eight shutouts for the Cubs, but he was also known for his wildness. In his only start in the 1935 series, he walked seven men and lost to the Tigers. He had an even worse 1938 series. He faced three batters, gave up a hit, two walks, two earned runs, two wild pitches, and didn't retire anyone, officially ending the series with an ERA of infinity. The Cubs got rid of him after that series, and he resurfaced in Brooklyn for one more year in 1940. That season he threw a no-hitter for the Dodgers.

Historical note: On the day of the 1936 Summer Olympics Opening Ceremony in Berlin (with Adolf Hitler in the viewing booth), Carleton was on the mound for the Cubs. He tossed an 11-inning complete game 1-0 shutout against Boston.

Don Carlsen 1926–2002 (Cubs 1948)

He was just a 21-year-old rookie when he got his shot with the Cubs in 1948. He didn't exactly seize the opportunity. Carlsen pitched one inning, gave up five earned runs, and was sent back down to the minors. He later re-emerged in the big leagues with the Pirates.

Hal Carlson 1892–1930 (Cubs 1927-1930)

Hal Carlson was a veteran starting pitcher acquired by the Cubs in 1927 from the Pittsburgh Pirates. He pitched for them for several seasons and didn't make much of an impact. Hal was never one of their best starters, but he was valuable enough to make the postseason roster in 1929, and did make two appearances in the World Series. In 1930, the Cubs had an offense that would have made any pitcher happy to take the mound on their behalf. Carlson was in great spirits. He won four of his first six starts, and was pitching well. Unfortunately, one night in late May, the 38-year-old started having horrible stomach cramps. He had been suffering from ulcers for a couple of years, so he wasn't too worried about it at first. But when the pain got worse, he called teammates Riggs Stephenson, Kiki Cuyler, and Cliff Heathcote asking them to come to his apartment and help. When they saw what kind of pain he was suffering, his teammates called the team doctor, but it was too late. By the time the doctor arrived at the apartment, there wasn't anything he could do. Carlson died that night of a stomach hemorrhage. The Cubs dedicated the season to their fallen comrade.

Bill Carney 1874–1938 (Cubs 1904)

The career minor leaguer was brought up to play in a double-header on August 24, 1904. He played in right field and went 0 for 7 with four strikeouts. He was 30 years old at the time. He played another seven years in the minors after his brief cup of coffee with the Cubs.

Bob Carpenter 1917–2005 (Cubs 1947)

He was a local Chicago boy (Parker High School) who pitched for the Giants before and after the war before finally getting his shot at pitching for his hometown Cubs as a 29-year-old in 1947. Carpenter appeared in only four games, and posted an ERA of 4.91. It was the last stop of his big league career.

Chris Carpenter 1985– (Cubs 2011)

Not to be confused with the great Chris Carpenter who pitched for the Cardinals, this Chris Carpenter was a reliever. The tall right-hander showed some promise in his rookie season with the Cubs (2.79 ERA), but was traded to the Red Sox during spring training in 2012, and developed arm problems shortly after the trade. He hasn't pitched in the big leagues since.

Cliff Carroll 1859–1923 (Colts 1890-1891)

Cliff was already a champion when he came to Chicago (he won the 1884 World Series with Providence), and the left fielder became a key member of the team. He led the league in at-bats in his first year with the Cubs (then known as the Colts). By the way, the official records say Cliff Carroll hit 31 career homers. That's only because of a rule that no longer exists. By today's rules, he would have hit 32. In 1890 he broke up a ninth inning tie with a two-run walk-off homer. He only got credit for a double because the run scoring before him actually won the game.

Al Carson 1882–1962 (Cubs 1910)

The 1910 Cubs went to the World Series, but Al only pitched for them twice during the regular season: May 6 and May 12. The right-hander held his own. He pitched two games

for his hometown Cubs, with an ERA of 4.05. His nickname was Soldier.

Joe Carter 1960– (Cubs 1983)

The Cubs had the second pick in the 1981 draft, and for once, they didn't blow it. They chose Joe Carter. Carter would go on to be a five-time All-Star, hit nearly 400 career homers, steal more 200 career bases, and hit a walk-off home run to win the World Series. He did all of this, of course, for other teams. The Cubs traded Carter to the Indians in 1984. He was the key to the Rick Sutcliffe trade. In fairness to the Cubs, that trade did secure a division championship in 1984 (and 1989). Carter's career totals on the Cubs (all in 1983) are as follows: one double, one triple, one RBI, one stolen base, and a .176 batting average in 51 at-bats. His career did come full circle, however. He made the last out in the 1998 one-game playoff against the Cubs at Wrigley Field, a popup to Mark Grace. That was the last at-bat of his career. Carter later also spent an unsuccessful year as a Cubs broadcaster.

Paul Carter 1894–1984 (Cubs 1916-1920)

Carter pitched for the Cubs in their first five seasons at Wrigley Field. His ERA was always solid. In 1916 and 1917 he was a spot starter, but in his final three seasons, including the pennant-winning year of 1918, he pitched exclusively out of the bullpen. In five years he won 18 games and saved 7, with an ERA of 3.32. His nickname was Nick. He passed away three weeks before Steve Garvey stabbed Cubs Nation in the heart.

Rico Carty 1939– (Cubs 1973)

Rico Carty was a great hitter with the Atlanta Braves. He was an All-Star, won a batting title, had a cool nickname ("Beeg Boy"), and had an incredible on-base percentage one year (.454). Unfortunately, he hurt his knee, and by the time he came to the Cubs just a few years later, he couldn't really play the outfield anymore. He was a Cub for exactly 30 days. They sold him to the A's in September. Of course, 1973 was also the year the DH rule was instituted by the AL. Carty had a second career as a DH, hitting 90 of his 204 career homers in the last five years of his career. He finished with a lifetime average of .299.

Bob Caruthers 1864–1911 (1893 Colts)

The very fashionable "Parisian Bob" was a great pitcher (two-time 40-game winner), but unfortunately that was for other teams. When he came to Chicago he only played a handful of games in the outfield. He is considered one of the best players of the 19th century. Parisian Bob has the best winning percentage of any pitcher from that era, and the third best in history.

Doc Casey 1870–1936 (Cubs 1903-1905)

Casey was the switch-hitting third baseman who played alongside Tinker, Evers, and Chance in their formative years. By 1905, however, he was starting to lose his skills, and the Cubs traded him to Brooklyn while he still had some value. The player they got in return, outfielder Jimmy Sheckard, became a key member of the Cubs dynasty (1906-1910).

Hugh Casey 1913–1951 (Cubs 1935)

Hugh T. Casey pitched 13 games for the Cubs during their NL Pennant-winning season of 1935, then spent the next four years in the minors. In the minors they tried to get him to harness his wildness to no avail. The Cubs shipped him off to Brooklyn, and he eventually made it back to the big leagues with the Dodgers. Casey even won 15 games for them in 1939 — and made the All-Star team. But the war came along shortly thereafter and Uncle Sam came calling. Casey served in the military during the war, and when he returned, they converted him into a reliever in 1946. That's where he got his nickname "Fireman." On July 3, 1951, less than two years after his last appearance in the majors, he committed suicide following years of heavy drinking and womanizing. He was just 37 years old.

Andrew Cashner 1986– (Cubs 2010-2011)

Cashner was a Cubs first round pick in 2008, and came up to the big club just two years later. He appeared in 53 games as a reliever and showed flashes of brilliance, mixed with a few really bad appearances. There was little doubt, however, that he was a key piece of their pitching future. That is, until the new brain trust came aboard, led by Theo Epstein. They traded him to San Diego shortly after they took the reins, and that was a trade few Cubs fans will regret. In return for Cashner, the Cubs got Anthony Rizzo.

Larry Casian 1965– (Cubs 1995-1997)

The reliever had two pretty good seasons as a situational lefty for the Cubs in the mid-90s, posting ERAs under two in both of those seasons. After he got off to a rough start in 1997, he was released and finished his career with the White Sox.

John Cassidy 1855–1891 (White Stockings 1878)

Cassidy had pitched a little bit for other teams before coming to Chicago, but the Cubs (then known as the White Stockings) used him mainly as an outfielder. He didn't have a great season, and moved on after the season. Cassidy died just a few years after his baseball career ended at the age of 36.

Frank Castillo 1969–2013 (Cubs 1991-1997)

Castillo had a couple of very productive seasons as a starting pitcher for the Cubs. He was never blessed with a blazing fastball, but Castillo utilized a devastating change-up. His best season was 1995, when he won 11 games for the Cubs and posted a sparkling 3.21 ERA. On September 25th of that year, he was only one strike away from throwing a no-hitter against the Cardinals at Wrigley Field. Bernard Gilkey tripled to ruin the day. Castillo was working as a minor league pitching instructor for the Cubs when he drowned while boating with his family in Arizona. He was only 44 years old.

Lendy Castillo 1989– (Cubs 2012)

Castillo was a Rule V pick from the Phillies, and he pitched with the Cubs for part of the 2012 season, but was hit hard in limited action. In 13 appearances, his ERA was 7.88. He spent the entire 2013 season pitching in the lower minor leagues for the Cubs (Kane County and Daytona). The Phillies filed a grievance with the league because the Cubs didn't keep Castillo on their big league roster long enough, and won the grievance. That cost the Cubs a chance to make a Rule V pick in 2014.

Welington Castillo 1987– (Cubs 2010-2014)

The young Dominican was the starting catcher for the Cubs from 2012-2014. He showed some glimpses of power, but he mainly started for the Cubs for his defensive abilities. He led NL catchers in errors in 2013, but he also threw out 28 baserunners trying to steal — second best in the league. The

Cubs traded him early in the 2014 season after signing free agents Miguel Montero and David Ross.

Starlin Castro 1990– (Cubs 2010-2015)

The Dominican shortstop burst onto the scene as the youngest player in the big leagues (age 20) in 2010 and was an immediate smash. He hit .300 as a rookie, became an All-Star, led the league in hits in his second year, and improved his power numbers and made the All-Star team again in his third year. But in 2013, the train went off the tracks. The Cubs tried to tinker with his approach at the plate to get him to take more pitches, and Castro suddenly looked lost. His play at shortstop, which had already been inconsistent, got worse. Then in 2014, he suddenly rediscovered his hitting stroke, and once again was named to the All-Star team. His 2015 season was a microcosm of his Cubs career. His first half was so terrible, he was replaced as the starting shortstop. After being moved to second base, he hit over .400 during August. The roller coaster ride finally came to end when the Cubs traded him to the Yankees after the 2015 season.

Bill Caudill 1956– (Cubs 1979-1981)

The Cubs were mesmerized by Bill Caudill's strikeout potential. He came up through the system as a starting pitcher and never seemed able to put it all together. In his rookie season of 1979 he won only one of his twelve starts. It wasn't until they moved him into the bullpen that they saw a glimmer of what he could be. He had a great 1980 setting up for Bruce Sutter (2.19 ERA), but the following year they moved him back into the starting rotation. It was a disaster. Needless to say, the Cubs gave up on him. They dumped him off in a trade for Pat Tabler. Another very bad trade for the Cubs. Tabler didn't do much of anything in his time in Chicago, but Bill Caudill became an All-Star closer in the American League. The Seattle Mariners wisely put him back in the bullpen, and he saved over 100 games the next four seasons.

Historical note: On the day the Monty Python movie *The Life of Brian* was released (1979), Caudill got the start for the Cubs against the Padres at Wrigley. The Cubs won 9-6 but Caudill didn't factor in the win. Two future Cy Young winners relieved him that day, Willie Hernandez and Bruce Sutter.

Phil Cavarretta 1916–2010 (Cubs 1934-1954)

Philabuck, as he was known, had a tremendous career for the Chicago Cubs. The local Chicago boy (Lane Tech High School) wore a Cubs uniform for twenty seasons, including the last few when he was a player/manager. Phil was Mr. Cub before Ernie Banks. He was the heart and soul of the pennant-winning Cubs team in 1945, a year he won a batting title and the MVP, and hit over .400 in the World Series. That was his 3rd World Series for the Cubs — he had been an integral member of the 1935 and 1938 teams as well. Unfortunately, his great Cubs career didn't end well. He was the Cubs manager in the spring of 1954, when he was called into Phillip Wrigley's office. The boss asked him what he thought of that year's prospects. Speaking honestly, Phil told him he only liked a few players on the team, including rookie shortstop Ernie Banks, and said he was still upset about the trades which had depleted his roster (like trading Andy Pafko and Johnny Schmitz to the Dodgers for four stiffs). Wrigley responded by firing him…during spring training. He and the Cubs never made amends. Cavarretta passed away in 2010 at the age of 94.

Art Ceccarelli 1930–2012 (Cubs 1959-1960)

The Korean War veteran pitched in parts of five big league seasons, but his best season came with the Cubs in 1959. That season he went 5-5, hurling four complete games and two shutouts. Unfortunately for Art, he was nearly 30 years old at the time, and when he got off to a slow start the following season, the Cubs released him. He pitched in the minors a few more years, but never made it back up to the big leagues.

Ronny Cedeno 1983– (Cubs 2005-2008)

Ronny filled in nicely for Nomar Garciaparra when he was called up as a rookie, and got the starting job the following season, but he couldn't get on base. He managed only 17 walks in over 500 at-bats in 2006, the worst ratio in the entire league. He managed to stay in the big leagues thanks to his glove.

Ron Cey 1948– (Cubs 1983-1986)

Ron Cey earned his nickname because of the way he waddled when he walked. One look at his stocky build, short legs, and choppy running style was all it took to see that "The

Penguin" was a perfect nickname. Cey was one of the first "star" players (not affiliated with the Phillies) acquired by Dallas Green. He was a 6-time All-Star and a World Series MVP with the Los Angeles Dodgers. (The Cubs got him for Vance Lovelace and Dan Cataline, which has to qualify as a rare good trade.) When Cey joined the Cubs they offered him an incentive they've probably never offered since…a bonus for increased attendance. That little clause paid off nicely for the Penguin. Even though Cey was definitely on the downside of his career, he had a few good years left in him. He hit 25 HR and 97 RBI (which led the team) in the Cubs playoff year of '84. He also hit a home run in the '84 NLCS. Unfortunately, in that series another former Dodger stuck a dagger in the heart of Cubs fans everywhere.

Cliff Chambers 1922–2012 (Cubs 1948)
Cliff got his big league start with the Cubs in 1948, but had a pretty rough season (2 wins, 9 losses, and a 4.43 ERA). The Cubs traded him to Pittsburgh after the season, and he had a few solid seasons with the Pirates. On May 6, 1951 he pitched a no-hitter against the Boston Braves.

Frank Chance 1876–1924 (Cubs 1898-1912)
His real name was Frank Chance, but even his teammates called him "The Peerless Leader." (Sometimes they just shortened it to "PL"). He was the undisputed leader of the best Cubs team in history, the Cubs of the '00s. With the Peerless Leader at the helm, they won four pennants and two World Series titles. He allowed the boys to have their fun (he usually bought drinks and played cards with them), but in exchange he expected them to shut down the festivities at midnight the night before games, and to play their hardest during the games. He led by example. Anyone who wondered how to perform merely needed to watch the way Chance fiercely defended his turf and teammates. He was known as a brawler, and he was so unafraid in the batter's box he was beaned more times than any player of his era, and more times than any other Cubs player in history. (Complications from those beanings eventually ended his career, and probably shortened his life).

Chance was a fierce competitor. James J. Corbett, heavyweight champ, called him "one of the best amateur fighters I've ever seen." One time he provoked a riot by punching out Giants pitcher Joe McGinnity at the Polo Grounds. Another time he threw a bottle into the stands at fans in Brooklyn. Chance and his double play mates (Tinker and Evers) were inducted into baseball's Hall of Fame in 1946. Unfortunately for Frank, he had already been dead for 22 years.

Aroldis Chapman 1988– (Cubs 2016)
Chapman was acquired mid-season by the Cubs, and it cost them a pretty penny to acquire him. Four top prospects, including the Cubs top prospect (shortstop Gleyber Torres) went to the Yankees in the deal. But Chapman became the final piece to the World Series puzzle. He was dominant as the Cubs closer, saving 16 games with a 1.01 ERA in the regular season before saving four more in the playoffs — including one in the World Series. Though he left the Cubs after the season as a free agent, he will always be remembered for his performances down the stretch (including, unfortunately for him, the homer he gave up in the bottom of the 8th in Game 7). He is the only pitcher in Cubs history to regularly throw the ball over 100 miles an hour.

Harry Chapman 1885–1918 (Cubs 1912)
His debut game in the big leagues on October 6, 1912, was also the last game of the season for the Cubs. The catcher caught Larry Cheney, went 1 for 4 with an RBI and a stolen base, and the Cubs won the game 4-3 over St. Louis at West Side Grounds. It was his only game in a Cubs uniform. Harry later caught for Cincinnati and St. Louis. He died in 1918 while serving in the U.S. Army (of influenza-induced pneumonia).

Jaye Chapman 1987– (Cubs 2012)
He appeared in 14 games in 2002 and had a 3.75 ERA, but he walked 10 in only 12 innings of work. The Cubs got him in the trade that also brought Arodys Vizcaino from the Braves for Reed Johnson, Paul Maholm, and cash. But after getting crushed in Iowa during the 2013 season, he was let go by the Cubs. He's now back in the Braves organization.

Tyler Chatwood 1990– (Cubs 2018-present)
Chatwood was signed before the 2018 season to be the Cubs fifth starter. Although he managed to find a way to pitch

out of trouble at first, his staggering walk totals eventually caught up to him. In 103 innings pitched, he walked 95 men. By the end of the season he was no longer in the rotation.

Jesse Chavez 1983 – (Cubs 2018)

The Cubs acquired the well-traveled Chavez from the Rangers just before the trade deadline in July, and Jesse became one of the most important relievers for the team down the stretch. He appeared in 32 games and posted an incredible 1.15 ERA. The Cubs were his ninth team in the big leagues (Pirates, Braves, Royals, Blue Jays, A's, Dodgers, Angels, Rangers).

Virgil Cheeves 1901 – 1979 (Cubs 1920-1923)

Cheeves was part-Cherokee, and in the politically incorrect 1920s, his teammates nicknamed him "Chief." To be fair, nearly every Native American to ever play the game was given the same nickname. Virgil's best season was 1922, when he won 12 games and posted an ERA of 4.09.

Historical note: On the day comedian Fatty Arbuckle was accused of murder in the death of actress Virginia Rappe (1921), Cheeves lost to the Cardinals 4-3. The game was called after the fifth inning because of darkness.

Larry Cheney 1886 – 1969 (Cubs 1911-1915)

Cheney was a great pitcher for the Cubs, winning twenty games or more three seasons in a row. In his first big league start at the end of 1911 he got hit with a line drive that broke his fingers. When the fingers recovered he couldn't grip the ball the same way anymore. The way he had to grip the ball after the injury involved digging his fingernails into the ball. Cheney accidentally discovered the knuckleball. As a rookie in 1912 he led the league with 26 wins. The following season the Cubs began using him as a closer too. He saved 11 games in 1913 and led the league in appearances. He logged over 300 innings three seasons in a row. If Cheney had a weakness as a pitcher, it was that he didn't field his position well. He led the league's pitchers in errors four times. He also led the league in wild pitches six times. The year after he left the Cubs, Cheney got his only shot at the World Series. He and his Brooklyn teammates lost the 1916 series to Babe Ruth and the Boston Red Sox.

Historical notes: On the day the Titanic sunk (1915),

Cheney was on the mound for the Cubs. The Cardinals beat him that day 4-2.

Rocky Cherry 1979 – (Cubs 2007)

Blessed with one of the great names in baseball history, Cherry was a journeyman pitcher who pitched out of the bullpen for the Cubs during their playoff year of 2007. Unfortunately for Rocky, he wasn't around anymore when the team made it to the playoffs. He was traded in August for Steve Trachsel.

Scott Chiasson 1977 – (Cubs 2001-2002)

Chiasson was mainly a minor league pitcher, toiling in the minors for 13 seasons. But he did get a few tastes of the big-time with the Cubs at the end of the 2001 season and beginning of the 2002 season. In ten overall appearances, the right-handed reliever posted an ERA of 11.12. He gave up four homers in only 11 innings pitched.

Chicago Cubs... It's one thing to play for the Cubs. It's another thing to *be* a Chicago (born) Cub. Here are some of them... Cliff Aberson, Dick Bartell, Bill Bowman, Ray Brown, Phil Cavarretta, Len Church, Phil Collins, Harry Croft, Jim Fanning, John Felske, Cliff Floyd, Chick Fraser, Ed Gasfield, Emil Geiss, Charlie Guth, Alan Hargesheimer, Roy Henshaw, Fred Holmes, Marty Honan, Garry Jestadt, Abe Johnson, Don Johnson, Tony Kaufmann, Ray King, Emil Kush, Freddie Lindstrom, Hank Miklos, George Moriarty, Tony Murray, Pet O'Brien, Johnny Ostrowski, Dave Otto, Don Pall, Eric Pappas, Chick Pedro, George Piktusis, Paddy Quinn, Laurie Reis, Germany Schaefer, Milt Scott, Rick Stelmaszek, Tuffy Stewart, Charlie Wiedemeyer, Ed Winceniak, Marvell Wynne, and Bob Zick.

Cupid Childs 1867 – 1912 (Orphans 1900-1901)

Cupid was a very tough out. The second baseman retired with a lifetime on-base percentage of .416, which was tremendous even for his era. He had a great career for Cleveland, but was coming off a bout of malaria when he signed with the Cubs (then known as the Orphans), and it affected his hand-eye coordination. He was never quite the same player again. On the other hand, that hand-eye coordination didn't seem affected the day he got into a fist fight with the Pirates manager Fred Clarke. It was in public at a train station. Childs was said to have been the instigator. After his playing days, Cupid Childs did something that a lot of unskilled laborers did — he went to work in the coal business. He died at the age of 45 in his native Baltimore.

Pete Childs 1871–1922 (Orphans 1901)

Pete was the starting second baseman the second half of the season with the 1901 Cubs (then known as the Orphans), replacing Cupid Childs (no relation). He hit only .229 and was released.

Bob Chipman 1918–1973 (Cubs 1944-1949)

The Cubs traded their young second baseman Eddie Stanky for Chipman, who was really just a journeyman pitcher. Stanky went on to play in three World Series, was named to three All-Star teams, led the league in on-base percentage twice, and most famously started the ninth-inning rally that culminated in Bobby Thomson's pennant-winning home run. Chipman pitched for the Cubs for five seasons, never winning more than nine games.

Harry Chiti 1932–2002 (Cubs 1950-1956)

Harry was a backup catcher for the Cubs during most of his time in Chicago. He missed two full seasons (1953-1954) because he was serving in the military. Harry's best season was 1955, when he hit 11 homers and caught over 100 games. He later also caught for Kansas City, Detroit, and the Mets (in their inaugural season). In 1962 Harry was traded for himself. The Indians traded him to the Mets for a player to be named later, and that player ended up being himself.

Hee Seop Choi 1979–(Cubs 2002-2003)

The Cubs were convinced he was their first baseman of the future. Choi was an impressive physical specimen, 6'5, 230 pounds, and displayed tremendous power in the minor leagues. He hit 26 homers and drove in 97 runs at Triple-A Iowa in 2002, and was the Opening Day first baseman at Wrigley Field in 2003. He was off to a decent start but suffered a concussion when he crashed into Kerry Wood while chasing

a pop fly in June of that year. The Cubs went on to the playoffs, but Choi was not a part of that run. He never reclaimed his starting job. Choi was traded before the 2004 season to the Florida Marlins for Derrek Lee.

Steve Christmas 1957–(Cubs 1986)

The journeyman backup catcher got into a grand total of three games for the Cubs at the beginning of the 1986 season. He got one hit in nine at-bats before being sent down to the minors, never to return.

Loyd Christopher 1919–1991 (Cubs 1945)

Loyd got exactly one at-bat for the Cubs during their 1945 pennant-winning season. He was claimed off waivers from the Red Sox that year. Christopher spent most of his career in the minor leagues, where he hit .283 over 16 seasons. He also had a cup of coffee with the White Sox in 1947.

Bubba Church 1924–2001 (Cubs 1953-1955)

Church was a Southern boy through and through — born in Birmingham, attended school at LSU and Mississippi State — so it was only natural that his teammates called him Bubba. Bubba burst onto the scene with a 15-win season for the Phillies in 1951, but he never came close to repeating that performance. He was hit in the face with a batted ball (off the bat of Ted Kluszewski), had some arm problems, and struggled the rest of his career. As a Cub, he was knocked around pretty hard. In just over 120 innings over three seasons, the right-handed swingman gave up 25 home runs.

Len Church 1942–1988 (Cubs 1966)

Church pitched in the Cubs minor league system for nearly a decade, but the Lane Tech grad got only one cup of coffee with the big club in August and September of 1966. Church pitched out of the bullpen for the last place team, and it didn't go well. In six innings, he walked seven men and gave up a long ball. His final big league ERA was 7.50.

John Churry 1900–1970 (Cubs 1924-1927)

Churry was with the Cubs for four full seasons but only appeared in 12 games during that time. He was the third-string catcher behind Gabby Hartnett and Bob O'Farrell (and later Mike Gonzalez).

> Cubs players have had some great nicknames over the years. Among players starting with the letter C, you'll find nicknames like Beeg Boy, Bunk, Chief, Count, Cupid, Dad, Doc, Fiddler, Fidgety Phil, Fireman, Hooks, Kid, Kiki, King, Nixey, Pancho, Parisian Bob, Penguin, Peerless Leader, Philabuck, Red, Rifleman, Ripper, Scoops, Soup, Tex, and Wildfire.

Steve Cishek 1986– (Cubs 2018-present)

The veteran reliever with the rubber arm came to the Cubs after stints with Miami, Seattle, St. Louis, and Tampa. He led the team in relief appearances in 2018 with 80, but that might have been a bit too many appearances. After being unhittable for most of the year, he began to be knocked around a bit in the season's closing days. Nevertheless he ended the year with a sterling 2.18 ERA, with four wins and four saves.

Dad Clark 1873–1956 (Orphans 1902)

Clark was a left-handed first baseman who got a cup of coffee with the 1902 Cubs (then known as the Orphans). He didn't hit well (.186 in 48 plate appearances), so he returned to his native West Coast for the rest of his career. He played in the minor leagues out there for the next decade.

Dave Clark 1962– (Cubs 1990, 1997)

Clark was a fourth outfielder for the Cubs during two different stints. The first time he shared left field with Dwight Smith. The second time he backed up both Doug Glanville and Sammy Sosa. Clark was a pretty good hitter (he hit .300 in his second stint with the Cubs), but he never really nailed down a full-time job in the big leagues. Nevertheless, he managed to play for 13 seasons, mostly with Pittsburgh. Clark is the only Cubs player in history born in the same town as Elvis Presley: Tupelo, Mississippi.

Mark Clark 1968– (Cubs 1997-1998)

Clark was acquired along with Lance Johnson during the woeful 1997 Cubs season in exchange for Brian MacRae, Mel Rojas, and Turk Wendell. It actually turned out to be a good trade for the Cubs because both Clark and Johnson were key contributors during the playoff year of 1998. Clark started Game 1 of the NLDS against John Smoltz and the Atlanta Braves. He pitched a solid game, but the bullpen exploded after he left the game in the seventh inning. The Braves won 7-1. Mark finished his big league career with the Rangers.

Dad Clarke 1865–1911
(1888 White Stockings)

Not to be confused with the other Dad Clark who played a decade later, this Clarke (with an e at the end) was a pitcher who eventually pitched seven years in the big leagues, but his stay in Chicago lasted only two games at the age of 23. Clark hit a player in the head with his first big league pitch and knocked him out of the game.

Henry Clarke 1875–1950 (Orphans 1898)

Clarke had two short cups of coffee in the big leagues while he was on summer break from college. He attended both the University of Chicago and the University of Michigan, and eventually became an attorney, but on July 5th, 1898, he got a chance to start a game for the Cubs (then known as the Orphans), filling in for the injured future Hall of Famer Clark Griffith. He pitched a complete game, gave up two earned runs and eight hits, and won the game.

Sumpter Clarke 1897–1962 (Cubs 1920)

If you want to go back in time to see Clarke play for the Cubs, simply set the wayback machine to September 27, 1920. It was his only game in a Cubs uniform. The outfielder went 1 for 3 against Cardinals pitcher Ferdie Schupp in a 16-1 Cubs loss at Wrigley Field (then known as Cubs Park). Clarke's brother Rufe also played in the big leagues briefly with the Detroit Tigers.

Tommy Clarke 1888–1945 (Cubs 1918)

Clarke had a nine-year run as the catcher of the Reds before coming to Chicago. To say his playing time in Chicago was brief would be an understatement. He only got in one game (defensively) for the Cubs in 1918, but didn't get an at-bat. It came on August 21, 1918. Tommy replaced backup catcher

Bob O'Farrell and caught the last few pitches of Lefty Tyler's 17th win of the season.

John Clarkson 1861–1909
(White Stockings 1884-1887)

John Clarkson would have won several Cy Young Awards if he wasn't a contemporary of Young. He started 70(!) games for the Cubs in 1885 and won 53(!) of them, easily the most in the league. 10 of those wins were shutouts. In 1887 he led the league in wins and strikeouts while starting 60 games. Those two seasons were definitely worthy of the award. The rest of his career wasn't so bad either. He finished with 328 career wins. In 1963, 54 years after his death, John Clarkson was inducted into baseball's Hall of Fame.

Historical note: On the day that former President Ulysses S. Grant died (1885), Clarkson and the White Stockings won the game 12-2.

Fritz Clausen 1869–1960 (Colts 1893-1894)

Fritz pitched well during his first season with the Cubs (then known as the Colts), but when he got off to a slow start in 1894 (a really slow start — 14.54 ERA), the Cubs pulled the plug. He later got up to the big leagues with Louisville, but didn't have much more luck with them. If it bothered him, Fritz didn't show it. He was 90 years old when he passed away in 1960.

Clem Clemens 1886–1967 (Cubs 1916)

Clemens was known as the Count. He got his start with the Chi-Feds in the very first season at what is now Wrigley Field. The backup catcher was considered valuable enough to remain with the team when the Cubs took over the ballpark in 1916. He got 15 at-bats for the Cubs and zero hits.

Doug Clemens 1939– (Cubs 1964-1965)

Clemens got the biggest chance of his big league career with the 1965 Cubs. As the fourth outfielder for the Cubs that year, he got over 300 plate appearances for the first time in his career. Unfortunately for Clemens, he hit only .221, with four homers. The Cubs traded him to the Phillies for Wes Covington in the off-season.

Matt Clement 1974– (Cubs 2002-2004)

Clement was an excellent starting pitcher during his three years as a Cub. He inspired a fan craze with his soul patch tuft of hair, and people began to wear fake ones on the days he started. In 2003 he was a 14-game winner. Unfortunately for Cubs fans, he wasn't used in Game 7 of the NLCS against the Marlins. Manager Dusty Baker opted to go with bad relievers like Dave Veres instead of the fully rested and ready-to-go Clement, because he was saving Matt for a World Series game that never happened.

Steve Clevenger 1986– (Cubs 2011-2013)

Steve was the team's backup catcher at the beginning of the 2012 season and got off to a hot start. He was hitting .500 with 5 doubles (a few of them game-winners) when he got hurt at the end of April. He came back later in the season, but the magic was gone. He ended the year hitting only .201. The Cubs included him in the Scott Feldman trade to the Orioles, which brought Jake Arietta and Pedro Strop to the Cubs. In 2016, as a member of the Mariners, during the hotly contested presidential campaign, he engaged in a series of racist Tweets, which caused him to be suspended for the rest of the season.

Ty Cline 1939– (Cubs 1966)

Cline was a journeyman outfielder who played 12 seasons in the big leagues for seven different teams, including the Cubs at the beginning of the 1966 season. He was sold to the Braves in July of that season.

Gene Clines 1946– (Cubs 1977-1979)

Clines was an excellent hitter, hitting .334 for the 1972 Pirates. But Gene was never too slick with the glove, and that hampered his playing time. When he joined the Cubs he was more or less a fourth outfielder. He hit well (.293 his first season), but never got more than 250 at-bats. The Cubs turned out to be his last big league team. After his playing career, Clines became a well-respected hitting coach — even logging some time on the staff of the Chicago Cubs.

Historical note: On the day Elvis Presley died in Memphis, Clines got the game-winning hit for the Cubs in the bottom of the 15th inning to defeat the Pittsburgh Pirates at Wrigley Field.

Billy Clingman 1869–1958 (Orphans 1900)

He was the backup shortstop during his one year with the Cubs (then known as the Orphans), but he also saw action with Cincinnati, Pittsburgh, Louisville, Washington, and Cleveland in his ten-year big league career.

Otis Clymer 1876–1926 (Cubs 1913)

Otis played six years in the majors, including part of the 1913 season for the Cubs. He hit .229 as a backup outfielder in Chicago, his last gasp as a big leaguer. Earlier in his career he hit for the cycle (in 1908). After his career, he became a car dealer.

Andy Coakley 1882–1963 (Cubs 1908-1909)

He only played one month with the Cubs during their championship year, but he did make three crucial starts during that month (September), winning 2 games, and finishing with an ERA of 0.89. With the Reds before he came to the Cubs on 9/2, he was 8-18, with a 1.86 ERA. Andy only had two more starts in his major league career, one the following year with the Cubs (he got rocked), and one in 1911 with the Highlanders (Yankees). He ended his career as a three-time World Series champ (A's in '02 and '05, and Cubs '08), and is 20th on the Major League Baseball all-time ERA list (2.35).

Buck Coats 1982– (Cubs 2006)

Coats got a cup of coffee with the Cubs in August of 2006. He hit his only career home run during that time. Buck was an outfielder who was used primarily as a pinch hitter. Coats was one of those outfielders who hit well, but not well enough. He had some power, but not enough. The Cubs traded him to the Reds in 2007 for reliever Marcos Mateo. He later played briefly for the Reds and the Blue Jays.

Kevin Coffman 1965– (Cubs 1990)

The Cubs got him in the Jody Davis trade, and things never really worked out in Chicago. His 11.26 ERA in 18.2 innings pretty much sums it up.

Dick Cogan 1871–1948 (Orphans 1899)

Cogan started exactly five games for the Cubs (then known as the Orphans) in the last year of the 19th century, but he completed all five of those starts. He won 2 games and posted an ERA of 4.30. Among his teammates that year, future Hall of Famers Frank Chance and Clark Griffith.

Frank Coggins 1944–1994 (Cubs 1972)

Frank appeared in six games for the Cubs in 1972. In his last appearance with the Cubs (and in the big leagues) on July 30, 1972, he came in during the 8th inning to pinch hit for catcher Ken Rudolph. Coggins managed to coax a walk. He scored the tying run on a Glenn Beckert double, and Jim Hickman scored behind him for the winner, as the Cubs beat the Cardinals 5-4.

Chris Coghlan 1985– (Cubs 2014-2016)

Coghlan was the Rookie of the Year for the Marlins in 2009 when he hit .321, but he suffered through a series of injuries over the next few years. In 2014 with the Cubs, he finally got another chance to start, and he responded with a great season. He had a .352 OBP, hit 9 homers, stole 7 bags, and clubbed 43 extra base hits. In some ways, his 2015 season was even better. For a time, he was serving as the #3 hitter in the lineup and starting every day at second base. Despite setting career records for homers (16) and stolen bases (11), he slumped badly at the end of the year and lost his starting job. During the 2015 playoffs, he served mainly as a pinch hitter. The Cubs traded Chris to the A's after the season, but reacquired him in 2016, and he once again served an important role. Coghlan appeared in four of the seven World Series games. He was granted free agency after the series.

Hy Cohen 1931– (Cubs 1955)

The big right-hander (6'5 , 220 lbs.) pitched in exactly seven games for them in 1955, between April and June. He was 24 years old at the time. He got his first action on April 17, 1955 when the Cubs starting pitcher Harry Perkowski couldn't record an out in the first inning. Cohen pitched seven innings of relief to save the bullpen that day. But he was hit hard. He gave up 13 hits and 7 earned runs against the Cardinals. Ken Boyer doubled. Stan Musial tripled. Wally Moon homered. It was ugly. The final score was 14-1. In his final game on June 2nd, he entered under similar circumstances in the second inning, and got hit hard again — this time by the Phillies. Hy never made it back to the big leagues. He pitched three more seasons in the minors before hanging up his spikes.

Phil Coke 1982 – (Cubs 2015)

The Cubs picked up the left-handed reliever late in spring training in 2015 as a free agent. Coke had previously pitched for the Yankees and the Tigers and had appeared in a World Series for each team. His 2009 Yankees won the championship, and his 2012 Tigers lost to the Giants. His Cubs career lasted almost exactly one month. He was designated for assignment in May.

Jim Colborn 1946 – (Cubs 1969-1971)

Colborn couldn't crack the Cubs rotation during his formative big league years, but he broke out in a big way when he arrived in Milwaukee. In 1973 he was an All-Star, won 20 games, and had a sparkling 3.18 ERA. Colborn could never quite recreate that success, but he did win another 50+ games, including 18 with the 1977 Kansas City Royals. Cubs fans shouldn't be too upset about Colborn's success. The player the Cubs acquired in exchange for Colborn was fan favorite Jose Cardenal.

Dave Cole 1930 – 2011 (Cubs 1954)

Cole was a right-handed starting pitcher the Cubs acquired from the Braves for Roy Smalley. He started 14 games for the 1954 Cubs, but was hit pretty hard. His 5.36 ERA was very high for that era. He also walked almost twice as many men as he struck out (62/37) — a recipe for disaster. The Cubs sold him to the Phillies the following spring training.

King Cole 1886 – 1916 (Cubs 1909-1912)

His real name was Leonard Leslie Cole. He started his baseball career as a pitcher with the Cubs in 1909. By 1910, he was the ace of the staff. He led the National League that season with a record of 20-4 and helped win a National League Pennant for the Cubs. His 20-4 record is the best winning percentage (.866) for a Cubs pitcher in the twentieth century. He was immortalized as "King" Cole by Ring Lardner, who no doubt got it from the children's nursery rhyme 'Old King Cole.' King Cole didn't stay with the Cubs very long. He won 18 games for them in 1911, and was traded (along with fan favorite Solly Hofman) to the Pirates for Tommy Leach early in the 1912 season. He later landed in the American League, where Cole gave up Babe Ruth's first ever hit in the majors (a double on October 2, 1914). But this King Cole would not live to be a merry old soul. In 1915, he contracted a disease that knocked him out of baseball. Some sources say it was malaria, others say tuberculosis, and still others speculate it was syphilis, but whatever the disease, it took Cole's life. He died on January 6th, 1916, a few months shy of his 30th birthday.

Casey Coleman 1987 – (2010-2012)

The son of former big league pitcher Joe Coleman (who also pitched briefly for the Cubs in 1976) and grandson of former big league pitcher Joe Coleman (an All-Star with the Athletics in the 40s), Casey was a starting pitcher for the Cubs for several seasons. He mostly bounced between Iowa and the Cubs, serving as a sixth starter when needed or filling in for injured members of the starting rotation. He won 7 games over three seasons.

Joe Coleman 1947 – (Cubs 1976)

He pitched in the big leagues for 15 seasons and won 142 games, but only 2 of those came for the Cubs. His father (also named Joe) pitched ten years in the big leagues too, and his son Casey made it to the show as well (with the Cubs).

Bill Collins 1882 – 1961 (Cubs 1911)

Bill was acquired in the trade that sent Johnny Kling to Boston in 1911. Collins didn't get many opportunities with the Cubs. The outfielder was mainly a defensive replacement. He only batted three times wearing a Cubs uniform.

Bob Collins 1909 – 1969 (Cubs 1940)

Born in Pittsburgh the year after the Cubs won the championship, Rip Collins, as he was known, was a not-so-youthful 30 years old when he got his first chance at the big leagues. He was one of three catchers who backed up starter Al Todd. His .208 average didn't exactly wow his manager — one of the other backup catchers — Gabby Hartnett. Collins later got a very brief cup of coffee with the 1944 Yankees and that was the extent of his big league career.

Dan Collins 1854 – 1883 (White Stockings 1874)

Dan played three different positions in his very short stint in Chicago. He pitched two games and appeared in three games, and only got one hit. Dan later played for Louisville. He died in his hometown of New Orleans at the tender age of 29.

Marla Collins (Cubs ball girl 1980s)

Her name was Marla Collins. While it's true that Marla was a ball girl, she wasn't exactly a kid. She was "all grown up in all the right places," as Cubs broadcaster Harry Caray used to say. She dressed in a skimpy Cubs outfit and ran the balls out to the umpire, and Harry talked about her quite a bit. The cameramen at WGN also were known to focus their cameras on Marla more than they did for a typical ball girl. The result was that Marla became one of the most popular attractions in Wrigley. At the peak of her popularity, she was so famous that she got her own shoe contract. But in 1986, Marla's 15 minutes of fame came to a crashing end. The Cubs discovered that their innocent young ball girl Marla (whom Harry and the WGN cameramen had turned into a sex object for several seasons) had posed nude for Playboy. The Cubs were shocked (SHOCKED!) and fired her immediately. She appeared in the September issue of Playboy, but she never again appeared in her cute little outfit on her cute little metal folding chair at Wrigley Field.

Fidgety Phil Collins 1901–1948 (Cubs 1923)

He was a local Chicago boy, and he got his nickname because he constantly fidgeted on the mound, fingering the rosin bag, tugging at his trousers, and tramping around the mound. He got his start with the Cubs in 1923, and pitched exactly one game. He started the game, lasted five innings, and got the win. Unfortunately for Phil, he never pitched another game for his hometown team. Fidgety Phil fidgeted around the minor leagues for six years after that, and didn't re-emerge in the big leagues until 1929. He eventually became the ace of the worst team in the league (the Philadelphia Phillies) and even won 16 games for them in 1930, but he always stunk against the Cubs. In 1930, he gave up five home runs and nine runs to the Cubs in two innings.

Ripper Collins 1904–1970 (Cubs 1937-1938)

His real name was James Anthony Collins, but everyone called him Rip or Ripper. He said he got his nickname when, as a boy, he hit the team's only ball and snagged it on a fence nail, ripping its cover. Collins was a star with the Cardinals,

and to be fair, he got off to a good start with the Cubs too. Ripper was an All-Star for the Cubs in '37, and played on the pennant winner in 1938, but he hit only .133 in the Series, and with Phil Cavarretta on the team, Collins was no longer wanted or needed. The Cubs released him before the 1939 season…on his 35th birthday.

Historical note: On the day the Hindenburg exploded in 1937, Collins got one of his most dramatic hits for the Cubs. He knocked in the game winner in a 1-0 win against the Phillies.

Jackie Collum 1927–2009 (Cubs 1957)

Jackie was part of the worst single inning in Cubs history… an inning in which Cubs pitchers gave up a record 9 walks. He came into the game after Moe Drabowsky walked the first four batters of the inning. Collum walked three more batters, before being relieved by Jim Brosnan, who walked the final two of the inning. Jackie was traded a few months later to the Brooklyn Dodgers for Don Elston: a rare good trade for the Cubs. Elston anchored the Cubs bullpen for the next seven seasons, and Collum only pitched a few more games in the majors after the trade.

Tyler Colvin 1985–(Cubs 2009-2011)

Colvin was a first round pick for the Cubs in 2006, and made it up to the big leagues just a few years later. He got extensive playing time for the Cubs in 2010 and hit 20 homers, but his season ended in a very scary way. He was a runner on third base when a jagged piece of a broken bat flew in the air and stabbed him in the chest. He had to miss the rest of the year. The following year, Colvin never quite got in the flow of things. He hit only .150 and was sent back to the minors. When the Epstein era began in 2012, Colvin was traded to the Rockies (along with DJ Lemahieu) for Ian Stewart.

Jorge Comellas 1916–2001 (Cubs 1945)

They called Jorge "Pancho" after the character in *The Cisco Kid*, a story by O'Henry. It was turned into a popular radio program in the 1940s, about a Mexican crime fighter in the Wild West and his trusty sidekick Pancho. At the end of each episode, Cisco would say "Oh Pancho" and Pancho would reply "Oh Cisco." Jorge Comellas wasn't Mexican, but in the politically incorrect 40s, he was close enough. He was a pitcher the Cubs signed out of Havana, Cuba, and they had high hopes he could contribute in the 1945 season because he won 18 games with a 2.44 ERA for their minor league club in Los Angeles in 1944. Unfortunately, Comellas didn't win a single game for the Cubs in seven appearances, and was hit pretty hard. At the end of May they sent him back to the minors, from which he never returned. His short stint on the 1945 Cubs comprises his entire major league career.

Historical note: On the day that Adolf Hitler married Eva Braun in a bunker beneath Berlin, Jorge was on the mound for the Cubs. The Cubs lost 5-4 to the Phillies.

Clint Compton 1950–(Cubs 1972)

Clint was a left-handed reliever who pitched in exactly one game for the Cubs. It came on October 3, 1972. Clint relieved Larry Gura. In two innings he walked two, and gave up two hits and two earned runs. The Cubs lost 11-1 to the Phillies. It was his only appearance in the big leagues, but Clint can always say that he faced two Hall of Famers in that game: Steve Carlton and Mike Schmidt. Carlton grounded out to first and Schmidt singled to right.

Gerardo Concepción 1992–(Cubs 2016)

The Cuban-born Concepción worked his way through the Cubs minor league system beginning in 2012, but didn't get his shot in the big leagues until a one-week stint at the end of June during the Cubs World Series year. He pitched OK in the big leagues, but was sent back down before July. His AAA season with Iowa went very badly after that. He finished the year with an ERA over seven.

Bunk Congalton 1875–1937 (Cubs 1902)

He was 27 years old when he finally made the show in 1902 and the outfielder hit .239 in his one season in Chicago. He later had a few better seasons with Cleveland. He died in 1937 at the age of 62 after suffering a heart attack as a spectator at a Cleveland Indians game.

Fritzie Connally 1958–(Cubs 1983)

Fritz is one of eight players in big league history named Fritz. He got ten at-bats for the Cubs in 1983 and got one hit. There's an outside chance that the name Fritz will make a comeback, but until it does, Connally will remain the final big league Fritz. He was a third baseman.

Terry Connell 1855–1924 (White Stockings 1874)

He was part of the first team to play in Chicago after the Great Chicago Fire. On June 20, 1874, Terry Connell played in his only big league game. He was only 19 years old at the time. The catcher went 0 for 4. After his playing career he became an umpire, and later a policeman.

Jim Connor 1863–1950 (Orphans 1897-1898)

Not to be confused with tennis star Jimmy Connors, this Jim (not Jimmy) Connor (no s) played three seasons with the Cubs (then known as the Orphans). He hit .291 in 1897 and was rewarded with more playing time in 1898 (505 at-bats), but slumped to .226. He hit only .205 in his last season, 1899.

Billy Connors 1941–2018 (Cubs 1966, Cubs pitching coach 1982-1986, 1992-1993)

Billy Connors was a highly touted pitcher in the Cubs system, who never quite made it. He did pitch in 11 games for the Cubs in 1966, and later also got a cup of coffee with the New York Mets, but his pitching career was over by 1968. After his playing days, he became a well-respected pitching coach. He oversaw the Cubs staff that led the Cubs to the playoffs in 1984, but when they were injured the next few years, Dallas Green decided to pull the plug on Billy. He did it while Connors was in the hospital recovering from hip replacement surgery. Connors was later the pitching coach for Royals, Mariners, and Yankees. His last job in baseball was working in the front office for the New York Yankees.

Chuck Connors 1921–1992 (Cubs 1951)

The physically imposing 6'5" Connors played first base for the Cubs in 1951 and hit a whopping two home runs in 200 at-bats, not exactly the kind of power you want from a big first baseman. That performance earned him a trip back to the minors. Luckily for him, the Cubs minor league team at the time was in Los Angeles. While he was playing in the Cubs minor league system he got a bit part in the movie *Pat & Mike* (starring Spencer Tracy — 1952). That led him to quit baseball for good and become a full-time actor. By 1958, he was starring in *The Rifleman*, which aired until 1963.

He also starred in *Old Yeller*, *Soylent Green*, and *Roots*, and is arguably the greatest Cubs actor of all-time (other than Sammy Sosa during his "corked bat" press conference).

Willson Contreras 1992 – (Cubs 2016-present)

Willson began the championship season as the Cubs top prospect, but he wasn't brought up to the big leagues until one of the other catchers was injured. He started off with a bang, hitting a homer on the first pitch he ever saw in the bigs. Contreras didn't slow down from there. His energy was contagious, and before the season was over he was the team's starting catcher. The rookie catcher hit over .600 in the NLDS, slugged a homer in the NLCS, and knocked in a run in the World Series-clinching Game 7. In 2017 Contreras was the starting catcher all season. Most of the time he batted in the clean-up spot. He hit 21 homers and knocked in 74 runs despite missing an entire month with an injury. He was voted the starting catcher in the 2018 All-Star Game, but the big second half the fans expected never materialized. Willson ended the year with only 10 homers and a .249 batting average.

Jim Cook 1879 – 1949 (Cubs 1908)

The University of Illinois product got one shot in the big leagues with the 1903 Cubs, and it didn't work out too well. He hit only .154 in his two weeks with the Cubs. After that he played nine seasons in the minors.

Ron Coomer 1966 – (Cubs 2001, Cubs announcer 2014-present)

Coomer was brought in as a free agent as a 34-year-old in 2001. He played third base and first base for the Cubs, but didn't quite live up to his former All-Star status. The Cubs let him go after the year and he finished his big league career with the Yankees and Dodgers. Ron was named the radio color commentator for Cubs games in 2014 and has been working alongside Pat Hughes ever since.

Jimmy Cooney 1865 – 1903 (Colts 1890-1892)

One of two Jimmy Cooney's to play for Chicago. This Jimmy Cooney is not the one that recorded an unassisted triple play in the 1920s. This Jimmy Cooney was his dad. He was also a shortstop, but he played in the 1890s. In his rookie season of 1890 he led the league in plate appearances and fielding

percentage. His success dwindled every year after that. By the time he left Chicago in 1892, he was hitting only .171.

Jimmy "Scoops" Cooney 1894 – 1991 (Cubs 1926-1927)

Cooney was already 32 years old when he joined the Cubs in 1926, but he had only played parts of four major league seasons (two with the Cardinals, one each with the Red Sox and Giants). But the Cubs had no one else to play shortstop when they acquired him, so he was given the full-time job. During that 1926 season, he hit only .251, his on-base percentage was a woeful .288, and he had a whopping 24 extra base hits in more than 500 at-bats. Still, his glove kept him in the lineup. The following season (1927) he was still the starting shortstop when that glove made major league history. On May 30, 1927, in the fourth inning of a game against the Pirates, Cooney caught Paul Waner's liner, stepped on second to double Lloyd Waner, and tagged Clyde Barnhart coming down from first, to record an unassisted triple play. No other National Leaguer would do it for the next 65 years. In 1992, future Cub Mickey Morandini finally broke the streak by recording an unassisted triple play for the Philadelphia Phillies. How did the Cubs reward Cooney for his miraculous play? They traded him to the Pirates eight days later. Jimmy's dad also played for the Cubs, and his brother Johnny played in the big leagues for 20 years in Boston, Brooklyn, and New York.

Mort Cooper 1913 – 1958 (Cubs 1949)

He was a four-time All-Star and former NL MVP (Cardinals 1942) before he came to the Cubs, but he clearly had nothing left in the tank in Chicago. He pitched exactly once for the Cubs on May 7, 1949. He faced three batters in the fourth inning that day (in relief of Bob Rush). He walked the first batter, Pee Wee Reese. He then threw a wild pitch to Gene Hermanski, before eventually giving up a single to him. His last batter was Duke Snider, and the Duke took him out of the ballpark. Mort was yanked and never pitched again. Despite a very good MLB career (128 wins, 33 shutouts, and a 2.97 lifetime ERA), Cooper's final ERA with the Cubs was infinity.

Walker Cooper 1915 – 1991 (Cubs 1954-1955)

He played 17 seasons in the big leagues, caught two no-hitters, made eight All-Star teams, and was a World Series champ…before he came to the Cubs. His best years were with the Cardinals and the Giants.

Wilbur Cooper 1892–1973 (Cubs 1925-1926)

Cooper is one of the most successful left-handed pitchers in baseball history. He was a four-time 20-game winner, and won over 200 games in his big league career. The Cubs got him along with Charlie Grimm and Rabbit Maranville after the 1924 season. He had just won 20 games for the Pirates, and was not happy to be traded to the Cubs. He felt the Pirates were on the verge of winning it all, and he was right. The trade robbed him of his only chance to pitch in the World Series. (The Pirates won it all in 1925). His time in Chicago was disappointing. He went 12-14 for the last place 1925 Cubs, and was released in June of the following year. At that time he had the career record for most innings pitched and games started as a left-handed pitcher, records that have since been broken.

Larry Corcoran 1859–1991 (White Stockings 1880-1885)

In 1880 and 1881, Larry Corcoran was clearly the best pitcher in all of baseball. He was ambidextrous — he once pitched both left-handed and right-handed in a game. But the diminutive Corcoran (only 5'3 , 127 pounds) dominated the rest of the National League. In 1880, his rookie season, he won a whopping 43 games and led the league in strikeouts with 268, while registering a 1.95 ERA. The next season he was even better. His 31 wins led the league. Corcoran would have won the Cy Young Award if it existed yet. (Young wouldn't pitch in the majors until 1890). Larry was great the next three years too (winning 27, 34, and 35 games respectively), but he was no longer quite as dominant as he was those first two years. During his time in Chicago, Corcoran threw three no-hitters, which would remain the record for most no-hitters until 1965 (when Sandy Koufax pitched his fourth… and it was against the Cubs). Corcoran died at the age of 32 of Bright's Disease.

Historical note: On the day future president Harry Truman was born (1884), Corcoran was the winning pitcher for Chicago.

Mike Corcoran 1858–1927 (White Stockings 1884)

Mike was the older brother of fellow Cubs pitcher Larry Corcoran (a 30-game winner), and somehow found his way to the mound on July 15, 1884. He pitched exactly one big league game: a complete game 16-hitter, in which the opponents (Detroit) scored an astounding 10 unearned runs. The Cubs (then known as the White Stockings) lost the game 14-0. Larry pitched the day before and the day after with much better results. Mike never pitched again.

Manny Corpas 1982– (Cubs 2012)

Manny was the closer for the only Rockies team to ever go to the World Series (2007), but the young Panamanian developed arm problems after that. When the Cubs took a flyer on him in 2012, he was coming off arm surgery. He did appear in 48 games for the Cubs that season, but he was largely ineffective. His ERA was over 5. After the season, he went back to the Rockies.

Red Corriden 1887–1959 (Cubs player 1913-1915, Cubs coach 1930s)

John "Red" Corriden was a controversial pickup by the Cubs in 1913. At that time, the shortstop and third baseman was probably best known for the way he helped Nap Lajoie win the batting title in 1910 over the universally hated Ty Cobb. Corriden played back on purpose and allowed Nap to get enough bunt singles to win the title. He was mainly a backup as a player for the Cubs, but he returned to the team during their heyday in the 1930s as a coach. He was on the staff of the teams that went to the 1932, 1935, and 1938 World Series. Red later managed the White Sox. How much of a baseball man was he? He died at the age of 72 while watching a crucial Milwaukee Braves — LA Dodgers game on television at the end of the 1959 season. Red got his nickname the same way every other player named Red got his. He was a redhead.

Frank Corridon 1880–1941 (Cubs 1904)

Frank is known as the father of the spitball. He is said to have invented the pitch that was eventually outlawed by baseball in 1920. Unfortunately for Frank, it didn't help him too much. He was sickly and developed arm problems. He won 70 games in his five-year big league career. The first five wins came for the 1904 Chicago Cubs. His nickname was "The

Fiddler" because of the way he fiddled with the ball — not because he could play the violin.

Historical note: On the day the first ice cream cone was unveiled in St. Louis (1904), Corridon was on the mound for the Cubs. He beat the Pirates 3-2 in 10 innings.

Jim Cosman 1943–2013 (Cubs 1970)

Though Cosman is listed as a "Rookie Star" on his Topps baseball card, he pitched briefly for the Cardinals in 1966 and 1967 before coming to the Cubs. The big right-hander (6'5) had control problems throughout his pitching career. With the Cardinals he walked 24 men in 31 innings in 1967. He didn't make it back to the majors until the Cubs gave him a shot three seasons later. The date was April 30, 1970, and the Cubs were facing the Atlanta Braves. Chicago was already down 6-2 when Cosman came in to start the seventh inning. The first batter he faced was Hank Aaron and Aaron took him deep. Cosman didn't make it out of the inning, and never pitched in another big league game. After leaving baseball he became a successful executive in the waste management business. He passed away in January of 2013.

Dick Cotter 1889–1945 (Cubs 1912)

The Cubs acquired Dick before the 1912 season for Peaches Graham. Cotter played catcher for the Cubs in their old home field West Side Grounds. In his one season in Chicago, he appeared in 26 games and batted .278.

Hooks Cotter 1900–1955 (Cubs 1922-1924)

He only had one AB in 1922 (and hit a double), but he had an extended look in 1924 at first base, and hit .261 filling in for injured Cubs first baseman Ray Grimes.

Henry Cotto 1961–(Cubs 1984)

He was only with the Cubs for one season, but he was a key sub on that team. He got a hit in his only at-bat in the NLCS, but he was used often as a defensive replacement in the outfield. It was Henry who watched that home run by Steve Garvey sail over his head and into the stands in Game 4. Henry played nine more years in the big leagues with the Yankees, Mariners, and Marlins.

Ensign Cottrell 1888–1947 (Cubs 1912)

Ensign wasn't his rank in the Navy, it was his given first name. The Hoosick (NY) native pitched one game for the 1912 Cubs. That team still had eight players from the last World Series champion, but several of them were near the end of the line, including Frank Chance. Cottrell had a strange big league career. He pitched only one game for the Pirates, two for the A's, one for the Braves (during their miracle year), and seven for the Yankees. 12 games for five different teams in 5 big league seasons.

Neal Cotts 1980–(Cubs 2007-2009)

Cotts was a key member of the White Sox bullpen during their World Series year (2005), but he wasn't the same pitcher with the Cubs. He was used most often during 2008, mainly against left-handed batters. After he left the Cubs in 2009, he didn't make it back up to the big leagues until 2013 (with the Rangers).

Roscoe Coughlin 1868–1951 (Colts 1890)

Roscoe's ten-year baseball career was spent mostly in the minor leagues, but he did get a few tastes of the big-time, including part of the 1890 season with Chicago. The Cubs (then known as the Colts) discovered him in the California leagues and added the right-hander to the staff at the beginning of the season. He started ten games and completed all of them, but he didn't wow anyone. The Colts released him in June. He got one more shot the following year with the New York Giants, but that was the extent of his big league career. He later fought in the Spanish-American War.

Wes Covington 1932–2011 (Cubs 1966)

Covington roamed the same outfield as Hank Aaron in Milwaukee for several years, including a few years Wes posted some pretty strong numbers (over 20 homers twice). He was part of the Milwaukee Braves team that won the World Series in 1957, and hit .330 the following year. In the early to mid-60s he also had three good years for the Phillies. But by the time he arrived in Chicago, he was considered strictly a pinch hitter. He started the 1966 season with the Cubs, but after going 1 for 11, they gave up on him and released him. Covington resurfaced with the Dodgers, and his last big league at-bat came in the 1966 World Series. There was no joy in Mudville. The mighty Wes struck out.

Billy Cowan 1938 – (Cubs 1963-1964)

The mid-60s Cubs had several players who whiffed more than they made contact. In 1964, Billy Cowan was the Cubs regular center fielder. Cowan had some pop in his bat — he hit 19 homers that year — but he also had a habit of swinging and missing. In more than 400 at-bats that season, Cowan struck out 128 times while managing to get only 120 hits. He also led all National League center fielders in errors that season. The Cubs traded him to the Mets for George Altman before the 1965 season.

Larry Cox 1947–1990 (Cubs 1978)

One of the three catchers for the 1978 Cubs, Larry Cox hit .281 in just over a hundred at-bats. In a combined 450 at-bats, starter Dave Rader and his backups Larry Cox and Tim Blackwell managed to hit only five home runs. After his playing career ended, Cox coached for the Cubs. He was on the coaching staff of the division-winning 1989 Cubs. Unfortunately, he died of a heart attack after the season at the very young age of 42.

Harry Craft 1915–1995 (Cubs manager/College of Coaches 1961)

Harry was a center fielder nicknamed "Wildfire" for the Reds during his playing days (late 1930s — early 1940s) before going into coaching. He was Mickey Mantle's first coach in the minor leagues. He became a big league coach with Lou Boudreau on the Kansas City A's, and eventually replaced Lou as the manager when he was fired. Lou is also responsible for bringing Harry to the Cubs when he was their manager in 1960. But in 1961, Cubs owner P.K. Wrigley decided to go with the strange coach-by-committee approach known as the College of Coaches. Harry was asked to stay on as one of those coaches. Each of them got a chance to manage the team for a few weeks. Harry got two different stints that season. The Cubs went a combined 7-9 in games managed by Harry Craft. When the expansion Houston Colt 45s asked him to manage their team in 1962, Harry jumped at the chance. In their inaugural season under Harry's direction, the Colt 45s finished ahead of the Cubs.

Doug Creek 1969 – (Cubs 1999)

He had already pitched for the Cardinals and Giants and was coming off a season in Japan when the Cubs signed him before the 1999 season. He didn't make the club coming out of spring training, but after a decent half season in Iowa, the Cubs brought him up in June. It didn't work out. After six appearances and a 10.50 ERA, he was sent back to Iowa. They released him in September of that year. Creek later pitched for the Rays, Mariners, Blue Jays, and Tigers until 2005.

Chuck Crim 1961 – (Cubs 1994)

Crim was a right-handed reliever who pitched for the Cubs during the strike-shortened 1994 season. He picked up two saves that year — his final season in the big leagues. He previously had pitched for the Brewers and the Angels.

Harry Croft 1875–1933 (Orphans 1901)

Croft started three games for the Cubs (then known as the Orphans) in September of 1901. He batted twelve times, got four hits (all singles), and drove in four runs. He played a few more seasons in the minors after that, before retiring to his hometown of Chicago. He passed away in 1933 in Oak Park.

George Crosby 1857–1913 (White Stockings 1884)

How obscure was George Crosby? There's no record of whether he was right-handed or left-handed. The only thing we know about him is that he was born in Idaho. George was a pitcher who appeared in 3 games. All of them were complete games and he won one of them.

Ken Crosby 1947 – (Cubs 1975-1976)

The Canadian right-hander pitched parts of two seasons with the Cubs at the end of 1975 and the beginning of 1976. In '75, it went pretty well. He posted an ERA of 3.24 in nine appearances, despite having some control issues. The Cubs figured he could contribute to the team the next year as well. Bad call. He was lit up in 1976 to the tune of 12.00 ERA, and was sent back down to the minors never to return.

Jeff Cross 1918–1997 (Cubs 1948)

Cross played shortstop and third base in sixteen games. It was his last year in the big leagues. His most productive baseball years were spent serving the country in the United States Navy during the war. Jeff kept his fingers in the game, though. In 1950 he coached a team to the Little League World Series.

Hector Cruz 1953 – (Cubs 1978,1981-1982)

Heity, as he was called by his teammates, came from a baseball family. His older brother Jose was a star for the Astros, his cousin Tommy got a cup of coffee with the White Sox, and his nephew Jose Jr. had a 12-year big league career. Hector had a few good years with the Cardinals in the mid-70s, but by the time he came to Chicago, he was a mainly a backup. His best year in Chicago was probably 1981 when he hit seven homers. When Cruz was inducted into the Caribbean Baseball Hall of Fame in 2007, he was working as a mailman on the north side of Chicago.

Juan Cruz 1978 – (Cubs 2001-2003)

Cruz came up in the wave of good young arms in the first few years of the century, along with Carlos Zambrano and Mark Prior. Many scouts thought Cruz might be the best of all of them. He wasn't very good for the Cubs, but he did have a very solid 12-year big league career. Cruz pitched for the Braves, A's, Diamondbacks, Royals, Rays, and Pirates (mostly out of the bullpen), and posted a 4.05 career ERA. He pitched for the Cubs in the 2003 playoffs and against the Cubs in the 2007 playoffs (as a member of the Diamondbacks). He still shares the Cubs record for most consecutive strikeouts. In 2003 he struck out eight men in a row.

Cuban Cubs. The following Cubs were all born in Cuba...Jose Cardenal, Aroldis Chapman, Gerardo Concepción, Jorge Comellas, Tony Fossas, Mike Gonzalez, Leonys Martin, Rey Ordonez, Reggie Otero, Rafael Palmeiro, Chick Pedroes, Freddy Rodriguez, Jorge Soler, Tony Taylor, and Oscar Zamora.

Dick Culler 1915–1964 (Cubs 1948)

He was a slick-fielding infielder for eight big league seasons, but just one with the Cubs. He was primarily a backup in Chicago: his second to last season in the bigs.

Ray Culp 1941 – (Cubs 1967)

Ray Culp was already a two-time 14-game winner when the Cubs acquired him before the 1967 season, and they gave up former 20-game winner Dick Ellsworth to get him from the Phillies. But in his only season with Chicago, Culp was mediocre, managing only 8 wins. He also didn't hit it off with the manager of the team. Leo Durocher felt he couldn't trust Culp to be a big contributor, so the Cubs shipped him off the Boston Red Sox after the 1967 season in exchange for minor league outfielder Bill Schlessinger. This turned out to be one of the worst trades of the Durocher era. Schlessinger never played in a single game for the Cubs, while Ray Culp became one of the best pitchers in the American League. He won 16 games in 1968, 17 games in 1969, 17 games in 1970, and 14 games in 1971. During those same years, the Cubs always seemed to be one starting pitcher short of competing for a title.

Historical note: On the day the Beatles released *Sgt. Pepper*, Ray was on the mound for the Cubs. The Cubs lost the game in the bottom of the 9th when Bill Hands walked in the winning run.

Will Cunnane 1974 – (Cubs 2002)

Will had already pitched in the big leagues for five years (with the Padres and Brewers) before joining the Cubs in 2002. He pitched out of the bullpen and didn't have a tremendous amount of success in Chicago. The following year, as a member of the Atlanta Braves, he pitched against the Cubs in the National League Divisional Series. At the time, it was the only playoff series the Cubs had won since 1908.

Bert Cunningham 1865–1952 (Orphans 1901-1902)

He was small even by 19th century standards (5'6), but he pitched in the big leagues for 12 years. The last stop of his career was Chicago. He was not exactly overpowering. Bert only struck out nine batters in 73 innings pitched for the Cubs (then known as the Orphans).

Doc Curley 1874–1920 (Orphans 1899)

Curly was a backup second baseman to Barry McCormick and only appeared in ten games. His big league career didn't make it into the next century. That was his only season. His best hit was a triple.

Clarence Currie 1878–1941 (Cubs 1903)

The last six big league appearances of the Canadian pitcher's career came in a Cubs uniform. He started three games and completed two of them. He also recorded a save. But the well-stocked Cubs pitching staff didn't have any room for him in 1904. Currie went back to Canada and pitched there.

Cliff Curtis 1881–1943 (Cubs 1911)

Cliff was a very mediocre pitcher about a hundred years ago. One year with the Boston Braves he had an incredible record of 6 wins and 24 losses. During that season he set a record with 23 consecutive losses. That record was later broken by future Cub Anthony Young. Curtis still has the record for most consecutive starts without a win (28), although that was tied by future Cub Matt Keough. With the Cubs Cliff was 1-2, with a 3.86 ERA.

Jack Curtis 1937– (Cubs 1961-1962)

He was in the Cubs starting rotation in 1961 but was hit pretty hard, giving up 23 homers and finishing with 4.89 ERA. They traded him to Milwaukee for Bob Buhl in 1962.

Jack Cusick 1928–1989 (Cubs 1951)

Cusick made it up to the big leagues with the Cubs in 1951 at the age of 23. The shortstop backed up Roy Smalley, but his batting average was about the same as his weight (.177), and he didn't last long. After the season the Cubs traded Jack to the Boston Braves for outfielder Bob Addis. Cusick played one more season with the Braves. When no one offered him a big league job after the 1952 season, Cusick retired at the age of 24.

Ned Cuthbert 1845–1905 (White Stockings 1874)

Ned played left field for the White Stockings in 1874. That was the first team to play in Chicago after the Great Chicago Fire. He was one of the veterans on the team, a ripe old man of 29. He later managed St. Louis to a 5th place finish. If you count the years pre-1871, he played baseball for 19 years.

Kiki Cuyler 1898–1950 (Cubs 1928-1935)

His real name is Hazen Shirley Cuyler. Cuyler was called "Cuy" by his school teammates. It was while winning the MVP title of the Southern Association with Nashville in 1923 that he acquired the Kiki nickname. Fans heard the players shout for him to take the ball when he rushed in on a short fly. The shortstop would yell, "Cuy," and the second baseman would echo the call. In the press box the writers turned this into "Kiki." (It's the long "i" sound, although it doesn't look like it.) Kiki was a great player. He led the league in stolen bases four times, runs twice, doubles once, and had an incredible lifetime batting average of .321 (although he never won a batting title — he finished in the top ten five times). He was part of the Cubs pennant winners of 1929 and 1932, although his teammates didn't like him much. They thought he was a bit of a fancy lad because he used to put suntan powder on his face. Kiki Cuyler was elected into the Hall of Fame by the veterans committee in 1968, eighteen years after his death. His .325 career Cubs batting average is the fifth best in Cubs history.

Mike Cvengros 1900–1970 (Cubs 1929)

He was a left-handed reliever for the pennant-winning 1929 Cubs. Mike appeared in 32 games, and in a big year for hitting, he gave up his fair share of hits. On the other hand, Cvengros won five games and saved another. It was the last stop of his big league career. He had previously pitched for the Pirates (pennant winners in '27), the White Sox, and the Giants.

Additional Entries...If you check out the Every Cub Ever feature at www. justonebadcentury.com, you'll find several additional entries, including celebrity Cubs fans, writers, and bloggers. Under the letter C, you'll discover former First Lady and Presidential Candidate Hillary Clinton, movie star John Cusack, and rock star Billy Corgan (all huge fans), plus Cubs authors Mike Cameron and George Castle, and Cubs songwriter Terry Cashman. There's also an entry about a Cub that never made it to the bigs – Beanball Ben Christenson.

Chapter Four

D

The starting lineup of your Chicago Cubs starting with the letter D...

C – Jody Davis, All-Star
1B – Leon Durham, the Bull
2B – Paddy Driscoll, NFL Hall of Famer
SS – Shawon Dunston, Shawon-O-Meter
3B – Bad Bill Dahlen, the Anger Management Issue
LF – Abner Dalrymple, 5-time champ
CF – Hugh Duffy, Hall of Famer
RF – Andre Dawson, Hall of Famer
Bench – Frank Demaree, All-Star
SP – Dizzy Dean, Hall of Famer
SP – Moe Drabowsky, the Polish Prince
RP – Ryan Dempster, the Jokester

Bad Bill Dahlen 1870–1950 (1891-1898 Colts/Orphans)

Bill Dahlen played shortstop and third base in Chicago for most of the 1890s. They called him "Bad Bill" because he had a violent temper and was a ferocious competitor. He is considered by some baseball experts to be one of the greatest players still excluded from the Hall of Fame. He certainly has the credentials. He once had a 42-game hitting streak, he hit over .350 twice, he had the record for games played when he retired, and still holds the record for total chances as an infielder. He was a great hitter, a great fielder, and he had a great nickname.

Babe Dahlgren 1912–1996 (Cubs 1941-1942)

This Babe will always be remembered as the player who took Lou Gehrig's place when the Iron Man's long streak finally ended in 1939. In 1941, rumors made their way around the league that Dahlgren had smoked marijuana. He demanded a drug test, and became the first big league player to have

one. (He was clean.) The Cubs picked up the ex-Yankee during the 1941 season and he had an immediate impact, slugging 16 homers and driving in 59 runs the rest of the season. When the Cubs got wind that Babe was going to be drafted the following year, they sold him to the Browns. Dahlgren never did have to serve in the military and wound up becoming an All-Star with the Philadelphia Phillies.

Con Daily 1864–1928 (Colts 1896)

Daily was born before Abraham Lincoln was re-elected. Con (short for Cornelius) was a catcher, outfielder, and first baseman and had a good big league career before he came to Chicago as a 32-year-old. He hit .074 in nine games for the Cubs (then known as the Colts), and that was it for his days in the big leagues. His brother Ed played in the majors too.

Dom Dallessandro 1913–1988 (Cubs 1940-1947)

His real name was Nicholas Dominic Dallessandro, but he went by his middle name Dom. Despite the sound of it, his teammates didn't call him Dim Dom because he was stupid. It was because of his diminutive height. He was only 5'6. Dim Dom played outfield for some pretty mediocre Cubs teams in the early 40s, and had one good season in 1944 (hitting .304). Unfortunately for Dom, his timing wasn't the best. After his best season, he was called into the military in early 1945 and missed the only Cubs World Series of the decade. He did return to play a few more seasons for the Cubs, but was shipped out to the minor league team in Los Angeles after the 1947 season. Dim Dom finished his professional baseball career there.

Abner Dalrymple 1857–1939 (White Stockings 1879-1886)

Dalrymple was the starting left fielder for the Cubs (then known as the White Stockings) when they dominated the National League in the 1880s. They won five championships during his seven years. Unfortunately, team owner Al Spalding didn't like the way they did it. They were known as a bunch of rowdy hell-raisers and drinkers. After the 1886 championship season, Spalding dismantled the team, sending all the drinkers (including Abner) to other teams. They didn't win another championship until 1907. Abner finished his career in Pittsburgh.

Tom Daly 1866–1938 (White Stockings 1887-1888)

His nickname was Tido, and he was a utility man during his time in Chicago, playing every position on the field except pitcher and third base. He managed to parlay that utility role into a 17-season big league career. His brother Joe also played.

Tom Daly 1891–1946 (Cubs 1918-1921)

Not to be confused with 19th century Tom Daly, 20th century Tom Daly (no relation) was a big Canadian backup catcher for the Cubs for four seasons. His best season was probably 1920 when he hit over .300 in nearly 100 plate appearances. After Tom's playing career he coached for the Red Sox.

Kal Daniels 1963– (Cubs 1992)

Daniels was a slugger with the Reds and the Dodgers (over 100 career homers) and had good speed, but he was at the tail end of his career when he came to the Cubs. In 1989 he had knee surgery, and he was never the same player after that. Daniels hit his final four big league homers wearing a Cubs uniform. He was released after the season and retired.

Alvin Dark 1922–2014 (1958-1959 Cubs)

Dark had his best years with the Giants in New York (including the World Series champs of 1954). Dark didn't have the prototypical corner infielder power — he was more of a contact hitter (.289 career average) — but the former Rookie of the Year had a great 14-year big league career. He was in his late 30s by the time he came to Chicago, but as a member of the Cubs he was involved in one of the strangest plays in baseball history. It happened on June 30, 1959, when two balls were accidentally put in play at the same time. It involved a bat boy, the field announcer Pat Pieper, catcher Sammy Taylor, pitcher Bob Anderson, Ernie Banks, Bobby Thomson, Stan Musial, and Alvin. The umpires eventually sorted out the situation and called Stan Musial out. It's the only time in recorded baseball history this happened. After his playing days, Dark managed in the big leagues for many years, leading the Giants to the NL Pennant (1962) and the Oakland A's to the World Series title (1974).

Dell Darling 1861–1904 (White Stockings 1887-1889)

Darling was a backup catcher for the Cubs (then known as the White Stockings) for a few seasons, but he bolted in the player revolt of 1890 along with many other players on his team. He later played for St. Louis. His most memorable moment in Chicago might have been the day he started a fist-fight at home plate during the first inning of a game against Indianapolis.

Yu Darvish 1987– (Cubs 2018-present)

The Cubs signed Darvish to a huge 6-year contract before the 2018 season. He was coming off a World Series appearance with the Dodgers. But he started off slow in Chicago, and it got worse from there. By the end of the season it was announced that he would be undergoing arm surgery. The Cubs paid $25 million for 8 starts, 1 win, and an ERA of 4.95.

Bobby Darwin 1943– (Cubs 1977)

To say that Darwin was a free swinger is to understate the case. He led the AL in strikeouts three seasons in a row when he was with the Twins (1972-1974). The outfielder's stay in Chicago was very short. In 1977 he got exactly twelve at-bats.

Doug Dascenzo 1964– (Cubs 1988-1992)

Dascenzo was one of the best fielding outfielders in the National League during his time with the Cubs. He started his career with a then-record of 241 consecutive games without an error. Doug was an extra outfielder during the exciting Boys of Zimmer division champion season of 1989. He never really managed to claim a full-time starting position because his hitting was a little weak. His best hitting season with the Cubs was 1992, when he hit .255. While he was with the Cubs, he also pitched when they ran out of pitchers at the end of blowouts. He appeared in four games and didn't allow a single run. Dascenzo returned to the Cubs as part of the coaching staff for the 2015 season.

Bill Davidson 1887–1954 (Cubs 1909)

He was a 22-year-old center fielder when he came up with the Cubs at the very end of the 1909 season. Davidson played in only two games, but he opened some eyes because of his speed. Brooklyn traded for him the following season (along with Happy Smith and Tony Smith), and let him play every day in 1910. Davidson responded by stealing 27 bases. He would have had more if he didn't have such a difficult time getting on base. By 1911 his big league career was over, doomed by a lifetime batting average of .235.

Brock Davis 1943 – (Cubs 1970-1971)

Brock was a talented and speedy player who got the bulk of playing time for the 1971 Cubs in center field. Unfortunately for him, he never quite figured out how to translate his speed onto the basepaths, and he had no power at all. He stole zero bases and hit zero homers, and after the season the Cubs traded for Rick Monday to replace him. Davis was sent to Milwaukee in the package that brought Jose Cardenal to the Cubs.

Curt Davis 1903 – 1965 (Cubs 1936-1937)

The Cubs were the defending National League champions when they traded future Hall of Famer Chuck Klein (a relative disappointment with the Cubs) back to the Phillies for Davis and a speedy left fielder near the end of his career: Ethan Allen. Davis was known as Coonskin, and he pitched for the Cubs for two seasons. Curt was an All-Star in his first season with the Cubs and then won 10 games the following year (1937). The Cubs traded him to the Cardinals in 1938 for Dizzy Dean. How many players can say they were traded for Hall of Famers twice? It sounded like a good deal for the Cubs at the time, but the Cardinals surely got the better of the deal. Davis went on to win 100 more games (including 22 one year with the Cards), while Dean won only 22 more games in his entire career. Davis later pitched for Brooklyn during the war years and became buddies with an author who lived near the Dodgers' spring facility in Cuba…Ernest Hemingway.

Doug Davis 1975 – (Cubs 2011)

The Cubs always had a hard time beating the soft-tossing lefty when he pitched for Milwaukee and Arizona, so they took a flyer on him when he became available in 2011. They gave him nine starts, and he went 1-7 with a 6.50 ERA. That was the end of his big league career.

Jim Davis 1924 – 1995 (Cubs 1954-1956)

The lefty started and relieved for the Cubs, posting four complete games, nine saves, and 23 wins over three seasons. Davis was a junkballer, who threw everything from a screwball to a knuckler. In his last season with the team, he struck out four batters in one inning, making him one of only a handful of players to ever accomplish that feat. The Cubs traded him to the Cardinals after the 1956 season along with Hobie Landrith, Sam Toothpick Jones, and Eddie Miksus. This Jim Davis is no relation to the Jim Davis who draws the Garfield comic strip.

Jody Davis 1956 – (Cubs 1981-1988)

Jody was an outstanding player for the Cubs during the 1980s: a two-time All-Star and Gold Glover. But even though he hit over 120 homers in his Cubs career (including six seasons in a row with double-digit homers), he was really made famous by Harry Caray, who used to sing the following to the tune of "Davy Crockett" every time Jody did something notable… "Jody. Jody Davis. Catcher without a fear." Jody was also part of the singing Cubs that came out with a country song in 1984. That song was called "Men in Blue." Jody still holds the Cubs record for most runs scored in a game with five.

Ron Davis 1955 – (Cubs 1986-1987)

Davis was an All-Star reliever who saved more than a hundred games in his career, but none of those saves came with the Cubs. By the time Davis put on the Cubs uniform, his career was on the decline. He gave up eleven homers in only fifty innings, and was released. His son Ike currently plays in the big leagues.

Steve Davis 1953 – (Cubs 1979)

Davis appeared in three games for the Cubs as a September call-up in 1979. He played second base and third base, and didn't record a single big league hit. He did, however, knock in one run with a groundout. Dave Kingman scored that run.

Taylor Davis 1989 – (Cubs 2017-2018)

The Cubs rewarded their longtime farmhand with a call up to the big league club during September of the 2017 season. He got 13 at-bats in limited action and didn't make the postseason roster. He spent 2018 at Triple A also, and got another six plate appearances with the big league club in September.

Tommy Davis 1939 – (Cubs 1970 & 1972)

Tommy Davis had an outstanding eighteen-year big league career. He was a two-time All-Star, two-time batting champ, and won a World Series ring with the Dodgers, but his two stints with the Cubs were short and uneventful. By the time he came to Chicago, Tommy was no longer the dynamic outfielder he had been earlier in his career. When the Cubs traded him to the Orioles in 1972, it led to his final career resurgence…as one of the very first designated hitters. Davis amassed over 2000 career hits and his lifetime batting average was a very impressive .294.

Wade Davis 1982 – (Cubs 2017)

The Cubs acquired the closer from Kansas City for Jorge Soler before the 2017 season, and the veteran reliever had the best season of his career. He saved 32 games in 33 chances, struck out 79 batters in 58 innings, and was the lone Cubs representative in the 2017 All-Star game. By the end of the season, however, Davis was pitching on fumes. He performed heroically in the NLDS against the Nationals, but had very little left in the tank during the 2017 NLCS. He did save their only win of the series, but he wasn't the same pitcher that he was during the regular season. After the season ended, Davis became a free agent and signed with Colorado.

Andre Dawson 1954 – (Cubs 1987-1992)

Andre Dawson was a fan favorite with the Cubs from 1987-1992. Warren Cromartie, one of Andre's teammates with the Expos, explained Andre's nickname in his autobiography: "Andre's nickname was the 'Hawk' because his facial features resembled a hawk's. He had a body like one, too."

The Cubs only got him because the owners were colluding to keep salaries down before the 1987 season, and Dawson said he would play for the Cubs for any amount they wanted to give him. After playing on the unforgiving turf in Montreal, he was desperate to play on the natural grass of Wrigley Field. The Cubs got him for the bargain basement price of $500,000 (he later recovered the salary he should have earned when the Players Association won a significant judgment against the owners for collusion.) Andre was MVP that year for a last-place team: the first player ever to accomplish that feat. Andre was also an important part of the Cubs team that went to the playoffs in 1989. Unfortunately for him and his teammates, Dawson was hurt at the end of that year and had a horrendous playoff series, hitting only .105, and striking out six times.

On May 22, 1990, he set a major league record for intentional walks received in one game when he got five in a 16-inning contest. Dawson tied for the NL league in intentional walks that year with 21 — half his walk total for the year. At the end of the 1990 season he stole his 300th base, making him a member of the exclusive 300/300 club. His stats are comparable to guys like Billy Williams and Al Kaline, and he absolutely deserves to be in the Hall of Fame. Dawson was inducted into the hall in 2010. He ended his career with more hits than any other player born in Florida.

Historical note: On the day of the Chernobyl disaster in Ukraine (1986), Andre was the hitting star for the Expos and helped beat his future Cubs team 4-2 in Wrigley Field.

Boots Day 1947 – (Cubs 1970)

If he had gone by his given name of Charles Day instead of using his childhood nickname, we probably wouldn't remember the month-and-a-half that he was a member of the Cubs during the 1970 season. Boots wasn't exactly one of the all-time great players, but he did kick around the majors for six seasons. The Cubs acquired him for pitcher Rich Nye, but he couldn't crack the lineup often enough. They traded him just a month into the season to the Montreal Expos for backup catcher Jack Hiatt. Boots had a grand total of eight at-bats for the Cubs and got two hits.

Brian Dayett 1957 – (Cubs 1985-1987)

The Cubs got Brian from the Yankees (for Henry Cotto) the December after their famous 1984 playoff collapse. He started out in the minors, but got a taste of big league action in September of 1985 and 1986. Dayett's big chance with the Cubs came in 1987. That year he shared the left field job with Rafael Palmeiro. Palmeiro eventually beat him out, leading Dayett to take his talents to Japan. He never played in the majors again.

Charlie Deal 1891 – 1979 (Cubs 1916-1921)

Charlie was the starting third baseman for the Cubs for five seasons, including their pennant-winning season of 1918. He wasn't a great hitter (lifetime average .257) and he didn't have a lot of power (only 11 career homers), but he was a gamer who knew how to handle the bat. One year he led the league in sacrifices. Charlie also played an important role in the shortest game in Cubs history (played on September 21, 1919). With Grover Cleveland on the mound, Charlie knocked in two runs in the 6th with a double, and another in the 8th with a ground out, and Alexander did the rest. The game was finished in less than one hour (58 minutes). That record has a very good chance of never being broken.

Historical note: On the day the U.S. began drafting soldiers into World War I (1918), Deal scored the only run in a 3-1 loss to the Phillies.

Dizzy Dean 1910–1974 (Cubs 1938-1941)

He was colorful, exciting, cocky, and the best pitcher in baseball. Unfortunately, that last description only applied to his years before he joined the Cubs in 1938. His best years were with the Cardinals, where he led the league in strikeouts four times, wins twice (including 30 wins one year), innings pitched three times, complete games three times, and even saves once. In 1934, he won the Most Valuable Player award when he led the Cardinals to the World Championship. During those years he was undoubtedly the cockiest player in the game. He suffered an arm injury, however, and by the time Cubs owner P.K. Wrigley ordered his scouts to acquire Dean at any cost, he was just an ordinary pitcher. They signed him for $185,000 in 1938, which was a huge contract for the time. Dean helped the Cubs win the 1938 National League pennant, and pitched pretty well in Game 2 of the World Series before losing to the New York Yankees in what became known as "Ol' Diz's Last Stand." After that, he was done. He tried to pitch for the Cubs until 1941, but he just couldn't do it anymore. He retired after that season. That's when he started his second popular career: radio broadcaster. Dizzy's malapropisms were legendary, and fans loved it. In 1950 he began doing baseball's Game of the Week on national television. He remained in sportscasting for more than 20 years.

Wayland Dean 1902–1930 (Cubs 1927)

Wayland Dean was one of those tragic stories that pepper baseball history. He was deeply troubled; a chronic alcoholic who suffered from depression. But he had a live fastball and

made his way up to the majors in 1924 with the New York Giants. The Giants under John McGraw were known to take chances on troubled players. McGraw didn't care what his players did off the field, only on it. Unfortunately for Dean, he could never harness his fastball. He was as wild on the mound as he was in the speakeasies at night. He did pitch for the Giants in the 1924 World Series (a loss to the Senators) and won ten games in 1925, but they could no longer tolerate his off-the-field antics, and sent him packing to the Phillies in 1926. It didn't take the Phillies long to figure out what they had, and they sent him to the Cubs in 1927. When Dean arrived in Chicago, he told the team he had a sore arm. He pitched in a total of two games for the team before disappearing during a trip to New York. He went on a drinking binge, was released by the Cubs, and was dead three years later at the age of 28.

George Decker 1866–1909 (Colts 1892-1897)

Decker was nicknamed Gentleman George. He was the steady understudy to Cap Anson at first base (and eventually succeeded him there), but he was also a jack-of-all-trades utility man, helping out the team wherever and whenever they needed him. One time they really needed him was the day West Side Grounds burned down in 1894. Decker and his teammates Walt Wilmot and Jimmy Ryan saved a bunch of lives that day by breaking down the fence with their baseball bats. The fence had been built to keep unruly fans off the field. Unfortunately, his story doesn't end well. Decker reportedly went insane in 1900. By 1909, Gentleman George was dead at the age of 43.

Joe Decker 1947–2003 (Cubs 1969-1971)

Decker was considered one of the Cubs best prospects when they brought him up during the September collapse of 1969. He pitched well that season, so they thought he would be ready to assume the role of fifth starter in 1970. He started 17 games and won only two. He did eventually win 16 games in a season, but that was after the Cubs traded him to the Twins (along with Bill Hands) for reliever Dave LaRoche. Decker passed away after hitting his head during a fall at his home.

David DeJesus 1979–(Cubs 2012-2013)

DeJesus was signed as a free agent in the fall of 2011. The

veteran outfielder was considered a placeholder until some of the young talent came up through the system. He played hard in Chicago and became a fan favorite. He was an above-average defender at all three outfield positions, and had a good on-base percentage as a hitter. The Cubs traded him to the Nationals in the fall of 2013. After his playing career he went into broadcasting, working as an in-studio analyst for Cubs games. His wife Kim was once a contestant on *The Amazing Race*.

Iván de Jesus 1953 – (Cubs 1977-1981)

The Cubs made a rare good trade after the 1976 season when they sent Rick Monday to the Dodgers for Bill Buckner and a little known prospect named Iván de Jesus. Iván had a few very good years with the Cubs, especially in the field. In his first season in Chicago he made 595 assists, which is still the fifth best season in baseball history for a shortstop. He could hit a little too...at least in his first few seasons. He even scored more than a hundred runs during the 1978 season, which led the league that year. But his 1981 season is among the worst in history. He hit only .194 in over 400 at-bats and drove in only 13 runs. The Cubs traded him after the year. It was probably their best trade in history, because in return for their .194 hitting shortstop the Cubs got a future Hall of Famer (Ryne Sandberg) and a gritty veteran starting shortstop (Larry Bowa) to keep the position warm until their star minor leaguer Shawon Dunston was ready to play in the big leagues.

Jim Delahanty 1879 – 1953 (Cubs 1901)

The infielder played his rookie season for the Cubs, batting .190 in 70 plate appearances. The Cubs let him go after the year, but Delahanty managed to play another 12 seasons in the big leagues for the Giants, Braves, Reds, Browns, Senators, and Tigers. Along the way he certainly learned how to hit. In 1911 with the Tigers, Jim hit .339 with 94 RBI. Four of his brothers also played in the big leagues: Ed (a Hall of Famer who played for the Phillies), Frank (who was nicknamed Pudgie), Joe (who played for the Cardinals), and Tom (who played for four different teams). All of the brothers were infielders except for Pudgie. Jim was the second youngest brother.

Jorge De LaRosa 1981 – (Cubs 2018)

The Cubs picked up Jorge from the waiver wire in August of 2018 because they needed some help in the bullpen. The crafty 15-year veteran provided much-needed help in his 17 appearances for the Cubs. He was released after the season.

Bobby Del Greco 1933 – (Cubs 1957)

Del Greco was a well-traveled veteran. During his nine-year big league career, he played for six different teams. One of those teams (for a portion of the 1957 season) was the Cubs. Del Greco was mainly a center fielder who was known for his ability to cover a lot of ground. He wasn't much of a hitter (career .229 average), however, so he never really managed to claim a full-time job. With the Cubs he only got into twenty games and hit .200 before the Cubs traded him to the Yankees in September. The Yankees used him to fill in for Mickey Mantle late in games, so the Mick could rest those ailing knees.

Fred Demarais 1866 – 1919 (Colts 1890)

The French-Canadian pitched in one game at the big league level, and it happened on July 26, 1890. The Cubs (then known as the Colts) were playing at home against Brooklyn. Chicago lost the game 10-4, but Demarais pitched two scoreless innings.

Al Demaree 1884 – 1962 (Cubs 1917)

Not to be confused with Cubs outfielder Frank Demaree (no relation), this Demaree was a right-handed starting pitcher for the Cubs. He was a 19-game winner with the Phillies when Chicago acquired him 1917 (in exchange for Jimmy Lavender), but he got off to a slow start with the Cubs and was traded to the Giants before the season was over. While he was still playing he became a cartoonist. The Sporting News printed a bunch of his cartoons, and that's what he did for a career after his playing career ended.

Frank Demaree 1910 – 1958 (Cubs 1932-1938)

Frank had a very unusual upbringing. He grew up in California to deaf-mute parents, but he managed to thrive in both school and athletics. Demaree became an important cog for a very strong Cubs team in the 1930s. The outfielder appeared in three World Series ('32, '35, & '38), and two

All-Star games ('36 & '37). Demaree was a very good hitter. He came exactly one hit short of hitting .300 for his career, and his best seasons were with the Cubs. He batted .350 in 1936, and knocked in over a hundred runs in 1937. The Cubs traded him to the Giants after a disappointing 1938. He played another six seasons in the big leagues but never again put up the kind of numbers he did in Chicago.

Harry DeMiller 1867–1928 (Colts 1892)

Harry was a left-handed pitcher who got two starts for the Cubs (then known as the Colts) in the summer of 1892. He won one and lost one and posted an ERA of 6.38.

Gene DeMontreville 1873–1935 (Orphans 1899)

The Cubs (then known as the Orphans) got him in the Bad Bill Dahlen trade with the Orioles, and DeMontreville had big shoes to fill. Luckily, he came to Chicago with some credentials on his resume, including a 36-game hitting streak. Apparently the Cubs were not satisfied with the infielder's performance, however, because he was traded back to the Orioles just a few months later. Turns out that Gene was a bit of a drinker and a brawler. Gene's brother Lee also played in the big leagues, for the St. Louis Cardinals. Gene died in a fire in Memphis.

Ryan Dempster 1977– (Cubs 2004-2012)

Dempster was one of the most popular Cubs during his time in Chicago. He had a soft touch with the fans and really seemed to embrace the idea of being a Cub. When the Cubs signed him he was coming off arm surgery. The longtime starting pitcher was used out of the bullpen while his arm recovered. For a few years, Dempster was a respectable closer. He saved 85 games between 2005 — 2007. The following year he was put back into the rotation and responded with the best season of his career. Dempster was 17-8, with an ERA under three, and was named to the All-Star team. Unfortunately, he also started Game 1 of the NLDS playoffs, and the nerves seemed to get to him. Dempster walked the bases loaded and gave up a grand slam to Dodgers first baseman James Loney, and the Cubs never recovered.

In 2012 Dempster was traded to the Rangers for promising prospects Christian Villanueva and Kyle Hendricks. In 2013 he won his first World Series as a member of the Boston Red Sox. He is now officially retired as a player and working for the Cubs. Only Kerry Wood has a better strikeouts-to-nine-innings rate in Cubs history.

Chris Denorfia 1980– (Cubs 2015)

Denorfia was a ten-year veteran when he signed with the Cubs before the 2015 season, having previously roamed the outfield for the Reds, Padres, A's, and Mariners. The right-handed batter was considered mainly a platoon player or fourth outfielder at this stage of his career, and that's the role he served with the Cubs. He did have a few glorious moments, however. In the last home game of the regular season, he hit a dramatic extra-inning walk-off home run to break a 0-0 tie against the eventual World Champion Royals. Denorfia left via free agency after the season.

Roger Denzer 1871–1949 (Colts 1897)

Denzer had one of the greatest nicknames of all-time. His teammates called him "Peaceful Valley." That nickname wasn't given to him because he had a Zen-like approach to the game. He merely resembled the lead actor in a Broadway play named *Peaceful Valley*. Denzer was a right-handed pitcher for the Cubs (then known as the Colts) for one season and compiled a 2-8 record with a 5.13 ERA. He later also pitched for the Giants and the White Sox. Roger actually got the first official win in Chicago White Sox franchise history.

Bob Dernier 1957– (Cubs 1984-1987)

Bobby was the lead-off man for the 1984 Cubs — the first Cubs team to make the playoffs in 39 years. He and #2 hitter Ryne Sandberg were dubbed the Daily Double by Cubs announcer Harry Caray. Both Dernier and Sandberg got on base a lot, played great defense up the middle (Dernier was the Gold Glove-winning center fielder, Sandberg the Gold Glove-winning second baseman), and stole bases (Bobby had 44 in '84, Ryno had 32). Unfortunately injuries got the best of Bobby. He missed a lot of time over the next few seasons, and the Cubs eventually traded him back to the Phillies. Bobby played two more years in Philadelphia before calling it a career. Dernier now works in the front office for the Cubs.

Mark DeRosa 1975– (Cubs 2007-2008)

DeRosa played 16 seasons in the bigs, the best two of which

were with the Cubs. He was an important part of the first back-to-back playoff teams for the Cubs in a century. DeRosa played wherever the Cubs needed him (OF, 1B, 2B, SS, 3B), and seemed to get all the clutch hits. He can't even be blamed for the collapse in both of those playoff series because he hit over .300 each time, although he did make a key error in Game 2 of the 2008 NLDS. The Cubs traded him after the season for pitcher Chris Archer. Before retiring, DeRosa won a World Series ring as a member of the 2010 San Francisco Giants.

Claud Derrick 1886–1974 (Cubs 1914)

Deek, as he was known by his teammates, was a utility infielder for most of his big league career. His final season in the majors was with the Cubs. He hit .219. Deek played in the minors for another seven seasons before hanging up his spikes at the age of 35.

Paul Derringer 1906–1987 (Cubs 1943-1945)

To say that Derringer was a colorful personality is to understate the case. He got into quite a bit of trouble in the years before he joined the Cubs. He once woke up from an operation in a hospital recovery room, swung at a nurse, and knocked her out cold. Another time (in 1936), he got drunk and walked into the wrong party in a Philadelphia hotel. Derringer attacked an envoy of New York Mayor LaGuardia, who was there meeting with the Secretary of War, and put him in the hospital for eight weeks. His fighting wasn't confined to off the field, either. In 1939, Derringer and Dizzy Dean got into a fistfight on the field *before* a game at Crosley Field. They wrestled each other to the ground right on home plate and exchanged punches before being separated by teammates. Despite his anger management problems, Derringer won over 200 games in his career, was an All-Star, and has the distinction of winning the first night game in baseball history (for the Reds in 1935).

Unfortunately, he only pitched for the Cubs the last three seasons of his career. His very last game in the majors was the last World Series game in Cubs history for 71 years. He came in to relieve Hank Borowy in the first inning of Game 7 against the Detroit Tigers. Derringer pitched 1 2/3 innings, walked five, gave up two hits and three earned runs. In 1946, while pitching in the minors for Indianapolis, Derringer

tried to bean Jackie Robinson on two different occasions. The second time he narrowly missed Robinson's head — and Jackie hit a triple on the following pitch. After that, Derringer told Branch Rickey that Robinson "will do."

Jim Deshaies 1960–(Cubs announcer 2013-present)

Deshaies replaced Bob Brenly in the Cubs broadcast booth, and has developed a pretty good chemistry with play by play man Len Kasper. Before coming to Chicago, Deshaies was a big league pitcher (1984-1995) for the Astros, Padres, Twins, Giants, and Phillies, and a long-time announcer for the Houston Astros.

Delino Deshields 1969–(Cubs 2001-2002)

Delino DeShields had a very respectable big league career. He finished second in the Rookie of the Year voting with the Expos in 1990, and had two great years with Montreal after that. They were so good, in fact, the Dodgers traded Pedro Martinez to get him. Whoops. Delino's game was speed. He stole 463 bases in 13 big league seasons. Unfortunately, by the time Delino came to the Cubs, he was at the end of his career. Only 22 of those steals came in a Cubs uniform. Deshields ended his career as the all-time hits leader among players born in Delaware. Delino's son Delino Jr. is currently in the big leagues.

Tom Dettore 1947–(Cubs 1974-1976)

Detorre started and relieved for the Cubs in the mid-70s with varying degrees of success. In 1974 he managed to post an ERA of 4.18 while appearing in 16 games. That was by far the best season of his big league career. He has remained active in baseball as a minor league pitching coach.

Jim Devlin 1849–1883 (White Stockings 1875)

Devlin only won seven games for the Cubs (then known as the White Stockings) in 1875. He went to Louisville after his stay in Chicago and became a two-time 30-game winner. Unfortunately for Jim, his career ended abruptly after the 1877 season in Louisville. Devlin and a few of his teammates were caught throwing games for gamblers, and were banned from baseball for life. He died of tuberculosis at the age of 34.

Blake DeWitt 1985 – (Cubs 2010-2012)

The Cubs got DeWitt from the Dodgers in the trade that sent fan favorites Ted Lilly and Ryan Theriot to Los Angeles. Blake was the Dodgers' starting second baseman at the time. DeWitt played second base and third and had a couple of good stretches with Chicago, but they let him go after the 2012 season. He finished his career with the Atlanta Braves.

Charlie Dexter 1876 – 1934 (Orphans 1900-1902)

Charlie played three seasons in Chicago as a catcher/infielder/outfielder. He played everywhere on the field for the Cubs (then known as the Orphans) except shortstop and pitcher. His best season was 1901 when he drove in 66 runs and stole 22 bases. His average dropped to .227 the following year, however, and the Cubs cut him loose. In 1903 Charlie was at the Iroquois Theater in Chicago when a fire broke out. That fire killed over 600 people, but not Charlie. He and another former Cub John Houseman were credited with kicking down a door and saving a number of people that horrible day.

> Cubs players have had some great nicknames over the years. Among players starting with the letter D, you'll find nicknames like Babe, Bad Bill, Boots, Bridget, Bull, Coonskin, Cozy, Deek, Dim Dom, Dirty Jack, Dizzy, Doc, Gentleman George, Hawk, Kid, Laughing Larry, Leo the Lip, Monk, Peaceful Valley, Pickles, Red, Shufflin Phil, Tido, and Toothpick Sam.

Thomas Diamond 1983 – (Cubs 2010)

Diamond was a first round pick of the Texas Rangers in 2004, but he was a 27-year-old journeyman by the time he came to Chicago. The Cubs gave him his only shot at the big leagues. Diamond wasn't quite up to the task. He started a few games and came out of the bullpen a few times, but he didn't succeed in either role (6.83 ERA). When he also got lit up in Triple A the following season, the Cubs cut him loose.

Mike Diaz 1960 – (Cubs 1983)

Diaz only played six games for the Cubs in September of 1983 (backing up Jody Davis). The following spring training he was part of the trade that brought Bobby Dernier and Gary Matthews to the Cubs. He later went to Japan and played there for a few years. Diaz did something in Japan that foreigners are almost never allowed to do: he played catcher. He was the first foreigner in twelve years to do so.

Lance Dickson 1969 – (Cubs 1990)

The Cubs picked Lance one pick before Rondell White in the first round of the draft in 1990. Dickson tore up the minor leagues, and made his big league debut in September of that year. It didn't go well. Lance was rocked hard in his three September starts — which turned out to be the only three appearances of his big league career. The following year he suffered a stress fracture, and then he hurt his arm. By 1995, Dickson was out of baseball.

> **Died while they were Cubs...**Lots of Cubs have died young, but the following Cubs all died *while* they were Cubs...Hal Carlson (stomach hemorrhage), Jim Doyle (appendicitis), Ken Hubbs (plane crash), Jim Korwin (tuberculosis), Steve Macko (cancer), and Jiggs Parrot (tuberculosis).

Mike Difelice 1969 – (Cubs 2004)

Difelice was a well-traveled backup catcher, logging big league time with the Cardinals, Rays, Diamondbacks, Royals, Tigers, and Mets in addition to the Cubs. He was with the Cubs for the shortest amount of time. He went 0 for 3 in 2004, and caught parts of four games in September of that season, the month of their infamous collapse. After his playing career, he became a minor league manager.

Steve Dillard 1951 – (Cubs 1979-1981)

Dillard may have only been a backup infielder for the Cubs from 1979-1981, and he may have only hit .225 and .218 in two of those years, but Steve Dillard's mustache didn't take a back seat to anyone. He once pulled the hidden ball trick by hiding it in his mustache. Not really, but he could have. His mustache was that spectacular. Dillard also played for the Red Sox, White Sox, and Tigers in his 8-year big league career.

Historical note: On the day the US military failed in their effort to rescue the hostages in Iran (1980), Dillard got the game-winning hit to beat the Pirates 5-3 at Wrigley Field. He was pinch-hitting for Rick Reuschel.

Pickles Dillhoefer 1894–1923 (Cubs 1917)

His name was William Martin Dillhoefer, but everyone called him Pickles. During his rookie season in 1917 (his only season with the Cubs), he was the third-string catcher behind Art Wilson and Rowdy Elliot. It's safe to say that he wasn't going to challenge Ty Cobb in the batter's box. Pickles only batted .126 that year, and the Cubs finished 5th out of eight teams. Pickles was a throw-in to the trade that brought Grover Cleveland Alexander to the Cubs in 1918, and he played for the Phillies and Cardinals the next four seasons. His best year was probably 1920, when he batted a whopping .263 in 200+ at-bats. Unfortunately, tragedy struck just as he was experiencing his greatest happiness. Pickles died at the young age of 27 from typhoid fever on February 23, 1922, just a few weeks after his wedding. He left behind a young bride, a colorful personality, and one of the best nicknames in baseball history. When the Sporting News did an article in 2001 about the best nicknames of all time, Pickles was named #1.

Miguel Dilone 1954– (Cubs 1979)

Dilone was a speedster. In the year before he joined the Cubs, Miguel stole 50 bases for Oakland despite getting less than 300 plate appearances. He stole 15 bases for the Cubs in only 38 plate appearances in 1979. The year after he left Chicago he stole 61 bases and hit .340 for Cleveland. Unfortunately for Dilone, that season was a complete fluke. His lifetime batting average was .265 thanks to that one year, but in ten of his twelve big league seasons he couldn't crack .235.

Frank DiPino 1956– (Cubs 1986-1988)

The Cubs got DiPino in a trade with the Astros for aging speedster Davey Lopes. Ironically, DiPino looked even older. The prematurely gray reliever was called upon quite often during his time with the Cubs. In two and a half years he appeared in over 150 games for Chicago. He won seven games, saved 10, and gave up 20 homers. A little known tidbit about Frank: He was the loser of the game played on the day Geraldo opened Al Capone's vault.

Alec Distaso 1948–2009 (Cubs 1969)

In 1967, the Chicago Cubs had the first pick in the amateur draft. Most of the teams in the league agreed the top two picks were outfielder Ken Singleton and catcher Carlton Fisk. The Cubs disagreed with most teams. They chose a pitcher instead; an 18-year-old high schooler from California. His name was Al Distaso. The Cubs considered him the second coming of Don Drysdale. He didn't have Drysdale's size or fastball, but he did resemble him physically. And at first, he showed some promise. In his first two minor league seasons he struck out 225 in just over 300 innings. But he also hurt his elbow, and by the time spring training rolled around in 1969, he wasn't the same pitcher. Leo Durocher took a chance he could rediscover the magic and named him the 10th man on the pitching staff going into the season. Al debuted on April 20th against the Expos and pitched two scoreless innings. He came in again on April 22nd, but this time he wasn't facing the Expos. He was facing the fearsome Pittsburgh Pirates. Richie Hebner, Matty Alou, Roberto Clemente, and Willie Stargell all got hits against Al in what turned out to be his final major league appearance. He was sent down to the minors after that and never returned. But Al found a higher calling after leaving baseball for good in 1970. He became a police officer; a decorated homicide detective in the roughest neighborhood of Los Angeles. Al retired from the force in 1994, and as a gift for the other guys in his unit, he presented all of them with a copy of his 1969 Cubs Rookie card.

John Dobbs 1875–1934 (Cubs 1902-1903)

Dobbs hit over .300 as the Cubs starting center fielder the last half of the 1902 season, but when he slumped at the beginning of 1903, they cut him loose. He later played with Brooklyn. After his playing career ended Dobbs went into coaching. He managed in the minor leagues until the year before his death.

Jess Dobernic 1917–1998 (Cubs 1948-1949)

Like many of his contemporaries, Jess lost a few key years of his baseball career to the war. It took him two full seasons to return to big league form, but he finally joined the Cubs in 1948. He had an excellent season that year, pitching in 54 games. He won seven games, saved another, and posted a very respectable ERA of 3.15. The next season was a different story, unfortunately. Jess was rocked in his four appearances and was traded to the Reds.

Cozy Dolan 1872–1907 (Orphans 1900-1901)

Cozy was actually named Patrick Henry Dolan after the founding father, and became one of two Cozy Dolans to play in the big leagues (no relation). He played for the Cubs at the turn of the century. The outfielder/first baseman was sold to Brooklyn during the 1901 season, and had significantly more success with the Superbas (as they were known at the time). In spring training of 1907 he got sick and died of typhoid fever.

John Dolan 1867–1948 (Colts 1895)

Dolan started exactly two games for the Cubs (then known as the Colts) in September of 1895. He lost one and had a no-decision in his other outing. That was the end of his big league career. He previously pitched for Cincinnati, Columbus, Washington, and St. Louis.

Tom Dolan 1855–1913 (White Stockings 1879)

He got his first taste of the big leagues in Chicago (4 at-bats in 1979), but later played seven big league seasons elsewhere. His best season was with St. Louis in 1883, when he hit his only career home run. Tom was mainly a catcher.

Rafael Dolis 1988– (Cubs 2011-2013)

Dolis pitched parts of three seasons with the Cubs with limited success. The Cubs allowed him to leave via free agency after the 2013 season. After a few years in the minors with the Tigers organization, Dolis made the move to Japan, and has been pitching there ever since.

Dominican Cubs. The following Cubs were all born in the Dominican Republic…Arismendy Alcantara, Manny Alexander, Antonio Alfonseca, Manny Aybar, Miguel Batista, George Bell, Francis Beltran, Emilio Bonifacio, Alberto Cabrera, Esmailin Caridad, Lendy Castillo, Wellington Castillo, Starlin Castro, Miguel Dilone, Rafael Dolis, Jesus Figueroa, Felix Heredia, Junior Lake, Carlos Marmol, Sandy Martinez, Juan Mateo, Roberto Novoa, Jose Nunez, Ramon Ortiz, Carlos Pena, Aramis Ramirez, Fernando Rodney, Henry Rodriguez, Randy Rosario, Alfonso Soriano, Rafael Soriano, Sammy Sosa, Pedro Strop, Julian Tavarez, Amaury Telemaco, Jose Veras, Carlos Villanueva, Aroyds Vizcaino, Jose Vizcaino, Luis Vizcaino, and Enrique Wilson.

Tim Donahue 1870–1902 (Orphans/Colts 1895-1900)

His teammates may have nicknamed him Bridget, but Donahue was one of the toughest men in the league when he played for the Cubs (then known as the Orphans and Colts). He was so tough, he once caught an entire game with two splints on broken fingers. Donahue was known as a good catcher (he caught Walter Thornton's no-hitter in 1898), but a weak hitter. He was quick to anger and fought with opponents and teammates regularly. His time with the club ended in 1900, and Tim's departure was not a classy one. Here's an excerpt from a note he wrote to his teammates when he was let go (as reported by the *Baseball Biography Project*): "Former Comrades: Ye called me knocker, and ye did well to call me such. Upon the West Side grounds I made you look like soiled deuces in a clean deck. I beat you all in batting, fielding, and baserunning. None of you had any edge on me. I was too good for you." Donahue also owned a saloon and was a successful gambler during his time with Chicago, and became a wealthy man. Unfortunately for him, he contracted Addison's Disease and died at the age of 32.

Ed Donnelly 1932–1994 (Cubs 1959)

In his only shot at the big leagues, Ed appeared in 9 games for the Cubs. He had trouble with his command, walking 10 and giving up 18 hits in 14 innings. His grandson Jarred Cosart is currently pitching in the big leagues.

Frank Donnelly 1869–1953 (Colts 1893-1894)

How long ago did Frank Donnelly pitch for the Cubs (then known as the Colts)? There is no record of whether he was a right-hander or a lefty. What is known is that he wasn't very good. In eight appearances his ERA was over six

Mickey Doolin 1880–1951 (Cubs 1916)

Doc, as he was known, was part of the first Cubs team to play at Wrigley Field. The previous season Doolin had also called the ballpark home — as a member of the Federal League Whales. When team owner Charles Weeghman merged the Whales/Cubs teams, he cherry-picked the best of each club to form the 1916 Cubs. Mickey was 36 years old, but he had established a reputation as a slick -ielding shortstop (mostly with the Phillies). He led the league in assists six times, double plays seven times, and fielding percentage twice. Mickey's glove is what kept him in the big leagues for 13 years, but it didn't keep him on the Cubs roster the entire 1916 season. They released him in June.

Brian Dorsett 1961–(Cubs 1996)

The backup catcher played for six different teams in his big league career, the last of which was the Cubs in 1996. After his playing career ended, he moved back home to Terre Haute, Indiana and opened up a car dealership.

Herm Doscher 1852–1934 (White Stockings 1879)

Herm was born a month after Franklin Pierce was elected president. The youngster from New York grew up to be a big league third baseman. He played in three games for the 1879 White Stockings and managed only one hit in eleven at-bats. Don't judge him too harshly for that. He was actually a member of the opposing team (Troy) and was lent to Chicago because the Cubs didn't have enough healthy players. He also played for Brooklyn, Washington, and Cleveland. His son Jack became a big leaguer too — the very first second generation big leaguer in history.

Jack Doscher 1880–1971 (Cubs 1903)

Doscher was a pitcher in the big leagues for five seasons, yet he only managed to win two games. Neither of those came for the Cubs. He pitched in exactly one game for Chicago, on July 2, 1903. He started the game for the Cubs that day and was knocked out of the game in the fourth inning. His father Herm also played for Chicago.

Félix Doubront 1987–(Cubs 2014)

The Venezuelan lefty was an important part of the Red Sox pitching staff that won the 2013 World Series, but he got off to a rough start in 2014 and was acquired by the Cubs. In limited action at the end of the 2014 season, he pitched fairly well for the Cubs (3.98 ERA), but he didn't make the roster out of spring training in 2015, and was released.

Phil Douglas 1890–1952 (Cubs 1915-1919)

They called him "Shufflin' Phil" Douglas because he sort of shuffled his feet when he walked, but he was one of the best pitchers on the Cubs. Phil was a starter in their 1918 pennant-winning rotation. Unfortunately, Douglas was also a notorious drunk. The Cubs manager at the time was Fred Mitchell, who actually had a soft spot for him. "There's no harm in the fellow," he said in 1919, "it's just that I never knew where the hell he was or if he was fit for work." His drinking was so bad that the Cubs shipped him off to the New York Giants. There he would disappear for days at a time, and people were constantly sent to his hotel room to wake him or sober him up. Shufflin' Phil's story doesn't end well. After Douglas was caught sending a letter to an ex-teammate (Les Mann) offering to "not show up" in exchange for some money, Commissioner Landis banned him for life. He applied for reinstatement many times, and was turned down every time. Phil Douglas never pitched another game in the big leagues.

Taylor Douthit 1901–1986 (Cubs 1933)

Taylor was the starting center fielder for the 1926 St Louis Cardinals championship team, and had a few very good seasons in St. Louis, hitting over .300 and playing an outstanding center field. He still holds the record for best range factor for a center fielder, and he also set the record for most outfield putouts in a season in 1928. But by the time he came to Chicago in 1933, he was strictly an extra outfielder. The Cubs were the last stop on his baseball tour. Taylor ended his career as .291 lifetime hitter.

Dave Dowling 1942–(Cubs 1966)

Dowling pitched in one game for the Cubs. He started the game on September 22nd of that year and got a complete game victory. He gave up two runs in the first to the Reds, and shut them out the rest of the way. Among the Reds in the lineup that day: Pete Rose. Rose went 1-4 with a single. Among the Cubs who played behind Dowling that day: Hall of Famers Billy Williams, Ron Santo, and Ernie Banks. They combined to score four runs and provide the margin of victory.

Tom Downey 1884–1961 (Cubs 1912)

Tom had a six-year big league career, and Chicago was the last National League stop for the infielder. He later played two more seasons in the upstart Federal League with Buffalo. During his years in Cincinnati he was known as a bit of a butcher in the field. In 1909 he led the league with 62 errors.

Red Downs 1883–1939 (Cubs 1912)

He was already well-known to the Cubs when he joined the team in 1912. Downs had been on the Detroit Tigers team the Cubs beat in both the 1907 and 1908 World Series. Red was a pretty slick fielder, so the Cubs brought him in to back up a few other slick fielders, future Hall of Famers Johnny Evers and Joe Tinker. But after the 1912 season was over, so was his major league career. He played six more seasons in the minor leagues out west, but never quite made it back to the show.

After he retired Red became a hero to the old-timers because he founded the Professional Ballplayers of America, which was an organization dedicated to helping retired ballplayers that had fallen on hard times, either through illness or poverty or both. He ran the organization himself until 1925. But when the Great Depression hit, Red became one of those needy ex-ballplayers himself. He started drinking heavily, couldn't find a job, and then he became desperate. In 1932, Red and a friend, armed with pistols, entered the jewelry store in Los Angeles' swanky Biltmore Hotel and made off with $52,000 in merchandise. It didn't take the police too long to find him. A week later he was captured and arrested. The former major leaguer received a sentence of 5 years-to-life for that armed robbery.

Downs was a model citizen in prison, organizing the prison baseball team, and because he was promised a job by his uncle in Iowa, he was released on probation three and a half years later. Unfortunately, after he was released, Red slowly drank himself to death. He died of cirrhosis of the liver just three years later.

Scott Downs 1976–(Cubs 2000)

Scott wasn't considered a great prospect during his time in Chicago, so the Cubs were excited that they could get Rondell White in exchange for him in 2000. They had no way of knowing that Downs would still be pitching in the league fourteen years later. He was a steady and reliable lefty out of the bullpen for the Expos, Angels, Blue Jays, Braves, White Sox, and Royals until 2014.

Jack Doyle 1869–1958 (Cubs 1901)

Doyle was born in Ireland, and in 1901, the Cubs acquired the catcher/infielder/outfielder known as Dirty Jack. Why did they call him Dirty Jack? Because he was a gritty rugged baserunner who always got his uniform dirty. He was known as someone who always played the game hard. Doyle only played one season with the Cubs (then known as the Orphans), but his big league career lasted 17 years. In over 6000 career at-bats, Dirty Jack only struck out 281 times.

Jim Doyle 1881–1912 (Cubs 1911)

Jim was the starting third baseman for the Cubs the year after they appeared in the 1910 World Series (versus the Philadelphia A's). He hit .282, knocked in 62 runs, and stole 19 bases. His future looked bright, but in February of 1912, he had horrible pain in his stomach. Before he could make it to the hospital, his appendix burst, killing him at the age of 30.

Larry Doyle 1886–1994 (Cubs 1916-1917)

The Cubs acquired "Laughing Larry" at the end of their first season at Wrigley. Doyle was widely respected and admired in the league. The second baseman had been the captain of the Giants, and had both speed and power for the era. The Cubs got him for Heinie Zimmerman and inserted him right into their starting lineup. Doyle was excited to be playing alongside his old Giants teammate Fred Merkle (the Cubs first baseman.) Even though Doyle had just won the batting title for New York, he didn't hit well in Chicago, batting only .254. The Cubs traded him back to the Giants before the 1918 season for Lefty Tyler. Tyler was a key starter for the Cubs in that pennant-winning season. Doyle retired soon after returning to New York. He ended his career with a .290 lifetime average in 14 big league seasons.

Moe Drabowsky 1935–2006 (Cubs 1956-1960)

Moe was born in Poland and was a hot young gun pitcher for the Cubs in the late 50s. His best season with the Cubs was probably 1957, when he won 13 games as a 22-year-old for a very bad Cubs team. He never lived up to that in the following years, so the Cubs eventually gave up on him. He later pitched for the Braves, Athletics, and Reds in the early 60s, but really found a home in Baltimore. Moe became a key part of the bullpen for two World Series champions Orioles teams in 1966 and 1970. He beat Don Drysdale to win Game 1 of the 1966 World Series. Moe ended up pitching 17 years in the big leagues. <u>Historical note:</u> On the day Jerry Lee Lewis announced he had married his 13-year-old cousin (1958), Moe was on the mound for the Cubs. The Cubs beat the Phillies 7-4.

Sammy Drake 1934–2010 (Cubs 1960-1961)

Drake was a speedster who used mainly as a pinch runner by the Cubs in parts of two seasons. Unfortunately for Drake, he wasn't much of a hitter. He only got one hit as a Cub. Sammy's time with the Cubs came just a few years after his big brother Solly wore a Cubs uniform.

Solly Drake 1930– (Cubs 1956)

Solly got a lot of time in center field for the 1956 Cubs. He showed some speed on the base paths (nine stolen bases), and played decently defensively, but didn't really hit enough to keep his spot in the lineup. Drake later played for the Dodgers and Phillies. Both of his career homers were hit while wearing a Cubs uniform. Solly's brother Sammy played for the Cubs too.

Paddy Driscoll 1895–1968 (Cubs 1917)

Paddy Driscoll is an NFL Hall of Famer, but he also got a cup of coffee in Major League Baseball thanks to the Cubs. In 1917, the team's second season at what is now known as Wrigley, he played in 13 games and got 32 at-bats. Unfortunately, he only managed three hits. Among the games he played in was the famous double no-hitter on May 2, 1917, featuring Hippo Vaughn and Fred Toney. Fellow NFL Hall of Famer Jim Thorpe played in that game too (as a Red).

Dick Drott 1936–1985 (Cubs 1957-1961)

Drott burst onto the scene as a 20-year-old in a way that was eerily similar to a certain kid pitcher who arrived in Chicago in 1998. He struck out batters with abandon, was given a great nickname (Hummer), and finished third in the Rookie of the Year voting, with a record of 15-11. Like Kerry Wood, he also blew out his arm. Unfortunately for Drott, the medical profession wasn't nearly as advanced in 1957 as it was thirty years later. Drott never reclaimed that former glory. Over the next six years he won fewer games combined than he did in his rookie season. By the time he was 26, his career was over.

Monk Dubiel 1918–1969 (Cubs 1949-1952)

After the 1948 season the Cubs decided they needed to boost their pitching staff, so they traded their popular first baseman Eddie Waitkus to the Phillies for two aging starting pitchers (Dutch Leonard and Monk Dubiel). Eddie Waitkus was shot by a deranged fan in his first trip back to Chicago. Monk won a total of 14 games in his four seasons with the Cubs.

Jason Dubois 1979– (Cubs 2004-2005)

Jason showed lots of power potential, and hit nine homers in limited at-bats with the Cubs in 2004. Unfortunately, he also struck out quite a bit (74 Ks in 187 ABs). The Cubs gave up on him in 2005 and traded him to the Indians for Jody Gerut. DuBois played in the minors until 2010 before finally calling it quits.

Jimmy Dudley 1909–1999
(Cubs announcer 1938-1941)

Dudley was a radio announcer for the Cubs before the war, but when World War II broke out, he enlisted and served in the military. After the war ended he returned to broadcasting, but this time with the Cleveland Indians. He remained there for the next twenty years, was given the Ford Frick award, and inducted into the "Scribes and Mikemen" section of baseball's Hall of Fame.

Brian Duensing 1983– (Cubs 2017-2018)

After a successful career as a reliever in Minnesota and Baltimore, Duensing joined the Cubs bullpen in 2017 and became a key left-hander for the team. He made 68 appearances and posted a 2.74 ERA. His 2018 season, however, went as badly as the previous season went well. He developed arm problems, posted a 7.65 ERA, and spend a good portion of the season on the DL.

Ed Duffy 1844–1888 (White Stockings 1871)

Ed was known as a bit of a shady character. He was well-known for hanging around with gamblers, and was banned from baseball before the National Association began playing in 1871. He was reinstated for one year, and played for the White Stockings in their first official year. The Irish-born shortstop hit .231 in the only season he was allowed to play. Ed was in the lineup in the last game played at Lakefront Park before the Great Chicago Fire. Chicago didn't field a baseball team again until 1874.

Hugh Duffy 1866–1954 (White Stockings 1888-1889)

Duffy was a little guy (only 5'7), but he was a great hitter. Sir Hugh, as he was known, was coming off a great season (12 HR, 89 RBI, .312 average) when he joined the player revolt and fled to the Players' League. When he returned to the National League, it wasn't with Chicago. He played the rest of his career in Boston, where he was one of the best hitters in all of baseball. Duffy had over 100 RBI seven seasons in a row, led the league in homers twice, won two batting titles, stole 574 bases, and won a Triple Crown. His lifetime batting average was .326. Duffy was elected into the Hall of Fame in 1945.

Nick Dumovich 1902–1978 (Cubs 1923)

Dumovich was just a 21-year-old kid when he got his chance, but in his only season in the bigs, the young pitcher was hit hard and didn't have good control. Dumovich pitched in the minors for ten seasons.

Courtney Duncan 1974–(Cubs 2001-2002)

Duncan was a right-handed reliever who initially experienced some success when he first came up to the big leagues with the Cubs. Unfortunately, the hitters in the National League eventually caught up with him. In his rookie season he appeared in 36 games and posted a 3-3 record, but by the end of the season his ERA had climbed over 5. He got another short taste the following season, but that was the extent of his big league career.

Jim Dunegan 1947–2014 (Cubs 1970)

Dunegan was a high draft choice of the Cubs (2nd round, 1967) who pitched in seven games for the Cubs in 1970. The converted outfielder had all sorts of control issues. Dunegan walked 13 batters in 13 innings and gave up two long balls. In six minor league seasons he never managed to harness his control, so he didn't get another shot at the big leagues.

Sam Dungan 1866–1939 (Orphans/Colts 1892-1894, 1900)

Dungan was an outfielder/first baseman who got quite a bit of playing time in Chicago during his three years in a Cubs (then known as the Colts and Orphans) uniform. He was known as one of the toughest men in the league to strike out. He finished in the top ten in that category in three different seasons. His lifetime batting average was over .300.

Ron Dunn 1950–(Cubs 1974-1975)

Dunn was a backup infielder for the Cubs for two seasons. He had a total 112 at-bats and hit 3 homers. After the Cubs sent him back down to the minors, he played one more season for them at AAA before deciding to call it quits. He was only 26 at the time.

Shawon Dunston 1963–(Cubs 1985-1995, 1997)

Dunston was the first overall pick in the 1982 amateur draft and had one of the greatest arms of any shortstop in baseball history. He was also a fan favorite (fans kept track of his batting average with the Shawon-O-Meter), and had a successful 17-year major league career. Although he didn't have a "first pick in the draft" kind of career, Dunston was a two-time All-Star with the Cubs (1988 and 1990). He finally got a chance to play in the World Series in his final big league season in 2002 (with the Giants). That team, led by Dusty Baker, choked away the championship to the Angels in the closing innings of Game 6, and then lost decisively in Game 7. (An eerie preview of what awaited the Cubs the following year.) Shawon's son later played in the Cubs minor league system.

Historical note: On the day that Mikhail Gorbachev was arrested by Soviet hard liners (1991), Shawon knocked in Ryne Sandberg with the winning run to defeat the Phillies at Wrigley Field.

Todd Dunwoody 1975 – (Cubs 2001)

Todd was one of the top prospects in baseball coming up in the Marlins organization, but he lacked the plate discipline to stay in the starting lineup. After a fairly uneventful rookie season in Florida, he bounced around to the Royals, and then to the Cubs. In the 2001 season, Dunwoody backed up all three Cubs outfielders (Gary Matthews Jr, Sammy Sosa, and Rondell White), but he hit only .213 and was allowed to leave via free agency after the season.

Kid Durbin 1886 – 1943 (Cubs 1907-1908)

They called him Kid because he was only 20 when he joined the Cubs. Frank Chance used him as a pitcher and an outfielder, although he didn't give him much playing time in either spot. Durbin only played in 25 games over two seasons, but was a member of the first two World Series champion teams in Cubs history. He became a baker after his playing career ended.

Leon Durham 1957 – (Cubs 1981-1988)

Of course, his real name was Leon, but it was hard to be named Durham without getting the nickname Bull. No Cubs fan will ever forget him. Durham had a pretty good career with the Cubs, making the All-Star team twice, hitting more than 20 homers five times, and stealing more than twenty bases twice, but he will also be remembered for Game 5 of the 1984 NLCS. The Cubs were eight outs away from going to the World Series, leading the game 3-2. A ground ball by Tim Flannery went through Leon's legs and opened the floodgates. The Padres scored three more times, including two runs on a fluke double that should have been a double-play, but took a weird hop over Ryne Sandberg's head instead. A whole new generation of Cubs fans built up scar tissue that remains inside their bodies today.

Historical note: On the day the 1984 Olympic Games began in Los Angeles, Leon was the hitting star for the Cubs in an 11-4 win over the Mets at Shea Stadium. The Cubs scored eight runs in one inning.

Leo Durocher 1905 – 1991 (Cubs manager 1965-1972)

How did people really feel about Leo Durocher? A quote from Jack Brickhouse: "In the early days Leo was an SOB, but a sharp SOB. By the time he finished in Chicago he was just an old SOB." Suffice it to say, Leo was not beloved. When he was a player, he once gave Babe Ruth a black eye. He was such a taunter that he was thrown at by Cubs pitchers…while he was in the dugout. And he didn't suddenly become Mr. Nice Guy when he became the Cubs manager. He punished players that beat him at Gin Rummy (especially Ken Holtzman). He once ripped the phone out of the dugout in Houston and threw it onto the field because he was upset at a scoreboard cartoon (1965). He set up a folding chair in the dugout in 1967 so his buddy Frank Sinatra could watch the game from there. His third base coach walked out on him in the middle of a game (Pete Reiser). He left the team in June 1969 for his bachelor party, and blew off two more games to visit his new wife's (Lynne Walker Goldblatt) kids in Wisconsin. Leo was fired in July of '72. He was fired for the same reason he was fired everywhere else he had ever worked. He couldn't zip his ever-famous lip. If ever a person deserved a nickname, it was Leo 'The Lip' Durocher.

Frank Dwyer 1868 – 1943
(White Stockings 1888-1889)

Dwyer won 16 games at the tender age of 21 with the Cubs (then known as the White Stockings) in 1889, but he joined the player revolt and followed several teammates to join the new league founded by the players in 1890. When the league folded, Dwyer came back to the majors (1892) and joined St. Louis. He stayed in the big leagues until 1899 and won 177 career games.

*Additional Entries…*If you check out the Every Cub Ever feature at www. justonebadcentury.com, you'll find several additional entries, including celebrity Cubs fans, writers, and bloggers. Under the letter D, you'll discover arch-criminal John Dillinger, comedian Tom Dreesen, and restauranteur Grant DePorter. All are HUGE Cubs fans. There's also a heartbreaking story about a Hall of Famer (beginning with the letter D) who was offered to the Cubs first — and the Cubs turned him down — something Marilyn Monroe did not do.

CHAPTER FIVE

E

The starting lineup for your Chicago Cubs beginning with the letter E...

C—Rowdy Elliot, the Drinker
1B—Wild Bill Everitt, .300 hitter
2B—Johnny Evers, Hall of Famer
SS—Lee Elia, Potty Mouth
3B—Woody English, All-Star
LF—Hank Edwards, .300 hitter
CF—Dave Eggler, Look Out for that Train
RF—Jim Edmonds, the Enemy
Bench—Pete Elko, Picolo Pete
SP—Dennis Eckersley, Hall of Famer
SP—Dick Ellsworth, All-Star
RP—Dick Elston, All-Star

Don Eaddy 1934–2008 (Cubs 1959)

Eaddy was a great athlete. He starred in three different sports at the University of Michigan (baseball, football, and basketball). The Cubs signed him just before he was drafted by Uncle Sam (and served in the Air Force for three years). When he finally returned to baseball, the Cubs brought him up to the big leagues to use him as a pinch runner. He got into fifteen games in that capacity, but only one game as a position player. On August 1, 1959, Eaddy came in to play third base. Two balls were hit to him and he made an error on one of them. He also got his only big league at-bat in that game. He struck out. They never let him hit or field again. After his baseball career, he became a franchisee for Burger King.

Bill Eagan 1869–1906 (Colts 1893)

He was known as "Bad Bill" and it appears there was good reason for that. Bad Bill wasn't so much known for his hitting or fielding (he hit .263 for the 1893 Cubs — then known as the Colts). He was known for his bad behavior and drinking. A few years after he left the Cubs (when he was playing with Pittsburgh), he threatened to murder his wife and blow his own brains out. The police got to him before he could do it and sent him off to an asylum. Bad Bill died at the age of 35.

Howard Earl 1869–1916 (Colts 1890)

They called him "Slim Jim" because he was a tall and lanky infielder. Slim Jim played first, second, and third base for the second place team. Hall of Famer Cap Anson was his manager during his only year in Chicago. Earl played only one more big league season, but stayed in baseball for another 22 years, mainly as a minor league player/manager.

Arnold Early 1933–1999 (Cubs 1966)

Early was a lefty reliever for the Cubs in 1966. He appeared in 223 games in his big league career, and all but ten of those were from the bullpen. With the Cubs, Early posted a 3.57 ERA in 13 appearances. He previously pitched for the Red Sox, and finished his career with the Astros.

Mal Eason 1879–1970 (Orphans 1900-1902)

They called him "Kid" because he was only 21 when he came up to the Cubs (then known as the Orphans) in 1900. He pitched a complete game on the last game of the season that year, so the team thought they had a pitcher. Not so much. The following season he started 25 games and lost 17 of them. Eason was released early in the 1902 season. Kid eventually pitched for Boston, Detroit, and Brooklyn, but his lifetime record was more than 30 games under .500. He became an umpire and umped in the big leagues until 1917.

Roy Easterwood 1915–1984 (Cubs 1944)

It's safe to say that Roy wouldn't have made it to the big leagues if it wasn't for World War II. He played fifteen seasons in the minors, but his only big league stop was with the Cubs during the war season of 1944. Even on a war-depleted roster, Roy didn't get much playing time. His teammates called him Shag.

Rawly Eastwick 1950– (Cubs 1981)

Rawly was the shutdown closer for the Big Red Machine team that won two World Series for Cincinnati (1975-1976). By the time he came to Chicago five years later, he was a shell of his former self. He actually pitched fairly well (2.28 ERA in

43 innings), but the Cubs released him just before the 1982 season and nobody gave Eastwick another chance.

Historical note: On the day the first Space Shuttle was launched (1981), Eastwick blew the save for the Cubs.

Vallie Eaves 1911–1960 (Cubs 1941-1942)

Vallie was part Cherokee Indian, so naturally his teammates called him "Chief". Eaves was a pitcher. In 1941, he completed four of his seven starts and posted a respectable 3.53 ERA. It was really his last hurrah in the big leagues. He appeared in two more games in 1942, but the rest of his career was spent in the minor leagues. Eaves was 46 years old when he retired from baseball in 1957.

Angel Echevarria 1971–(Cubs 2002)

By the time Angel arrived in Chicago, the first baseman was already 31 years old. He had a few cups of coffee with Colorado and Milwaukee before playing for the Cubs. Angel hit pretty well (a career-high .306) and drove in some big runs (21 RBI), but was never given another shot at the big-time.

Dennis Eckersley 1954–(Cubs 1984-1986)

Dennis was a 2-time All-Star as a starting pitcher, and a 4-time All-Star as a relief pitcher in 24 big league seasons. He was one of the rare pitchers who was a superstar in both roles. Eck won 20 games in a season and threw a no-hitter as a starting pitcher, and then as a reliever won a Cy Young, an MVP, and a World Series title while saving an astounding 390 games in eleven seasons.

As you might have guessed, very little of that happened in Chicago. He was acquired by the Cubs from the Red Sox in exchange for Bill Buckner and contributed greatly to their 1984 division-winning club. The next two seasons were a nightmare, however. He later admitted he was struggling mightily with an alcohol problem at the time. In 1986, he managed to win only 6 games in 32 starts for the Cubs. Of course, he rediscovered his magic touch as soon as he was traded to Oakland for four minor leaguers who never made it to the show. Dennis got sober and became one of the greatest closers of all-time. Eckersley was inducted into the Hall of Fame in 2004.

Charlie Eden 1855–1920 (White Stockings 1882)

He was a backup outfielder in Chicago for one season and later also played in Cleveland (where he led the league in doubles) and Pittsburgh. In his four-year big league career, he hit a grand total of four homers. None of those were for Chicago.

Tom Edens 1961–(Cubs 1995)

Edens had already pitched for the Mets, Brewers, Twins, Astros, and Phillies before he arrived in Chicago. He only appeared in five games for the Cubs, the last five of his big league career. His last appearance came in a 11-1 loss to the Cardinals on May 10, 1995. After the Cubs sent him down to the minors, he stuck it out for one more year before hanging up his spikes at the age of 35.

Jim Edmonds 1970–(Cubs 2008)

Edmonds was an eight-time Gold Glover and four-time All-Star with the Angels and Cardinals before coming to the Cubs from the Padres in the middle of the 2008 season. He had been a hated rival while a member of the World Series champion Cardinals, but Cubs fans warmed to Edmonds pretty quickly. He slugged 19 homers, many of them dramatic, and played a great center field. That turned out to be the last hurrah of Jimmy Baseball's career. The Cubs opted not to re-sign him after the playoff collapse that year, and Edmonds finished his career with the Brewers and Reds in 2010.

Bruce Edwards 1923–1975 (Cubs 1951-1954)

Edwards was a two-time All-Star catcher with the Dodgers who had appeared in two World Series when the Cubs acquired him, but he would never live down how he came to Chicago. He was part of the trade that sent Andy Pafko to Brooklyn. Edwards (nicknamed "Bull") played parts of three seasons with the Cubs, and really had more value as a pinch hitter than he had as a catcher. He hit .363 as a pinch hitter his first year with the Cubs. Among his career highlights: Bruce was the starting catcher in Jackie Robinson's first game in the big leagues.

Historical note: On the day that Adlai Stevenson was nominated to run against Dwight D. Eisenhower during the 1952 Democratic National Convention in Chicago, Bruce hit his only home run of the season for the Cubs.

Carl Edwards Jr. 1991 – (Cubs 2015-present)

The string bean slinger, as he is also known, was the key acquisition in the trade that sent Matt Garza to the Rangers. The Cubs also acquired Justin Grimm, Mike Olt, and Neil Ramirez in the deal, but Edwards was the top pitching prospect. He was brought up to the big league club toward the end of the 2015 season so he could get a taste of the winning atmosphere. He performed well in a relief role (4 Ks in 4 innings), but didn't make the postseason roster. In 2016, however, Edwards became a crucial cog in the bullpen. Manager Joe Madden used him in more and more high pressure situations and Carl responded. He was on the mound in the 9th inning of the 7th game of the World Series, a moment he will surely never forget. In 2017, he became the primary set-up man for the Cubs and pitched well for most of the year, but during the playoffs the wheels came off. Edwards couldn't find the plate and finished the NLDS with an ERA of 23.14. His 2018 was remarkably similar to 2017; flashes of brilliance followed by inexplicable ineffectiveness.

Hank Edwards 1919 – 1988 (Cubs 1949-1950)

Edwards was a backup outfielder who provided some pop off the bench. In 1950 he hit .364 in limited opportunities and slugged seven homers. The Cubs traded him to the Dodgers for Dee Fondy and a little-known first baseman named Chuck Connors — who would go on to become a television star.

Dave Eggler 1849 – 1902 (White Stockings 1877)

Eggler was not a home run hitter (he didn't hit a single one in 11 big league seasons). The center fielder hit .265 in his one year with the Cubs (then known as the White Stockings). He died in 1902 in Buffalo, New York, when he was hit by a train.

> Cubs players have had some great nicknames over the years. Among players starting with the letter E, you'll find nicknames like Bad Bill, Bull, Chief, Crab, Jimmy Baseball, Kid, Lief, Picolo Pete, Rowdy, Slim Jim, Tub, and Wild Bill.

Ed Eiteljorge 1871 – 1942 (Colts 1890)

Ed was born in Berlin, Germany, but came to America as a boy. When he joined the Cubs (then known as the Colts), he was still only 18. If you want to see Ed pitch in a Chicago uniform, set the wayback machine to May 2, 1890. He pitched two innings and gave up seven runs. He never pitched for Chicago again.

Lee Elia 1937 – (Cubs player 1968, Cubs manager 1982-1983)

Elia was a big league shortstop who got a cup of coffee as a player with the Cubs in 1968. He got 3 hits in 17 at-bats. The following spring he was traded to the Yankees for Nate Oliver. Cubs fans don't remember Lee for his playing days, however. They remember him for his stint as Cubs manager. Elia was the first manager brought in by Dallas Green after he was named general manager. That Cubs team didn't have a ton of talent, and Elia got a bit frustrated by the impatience of the fans. It blew up on him on that infamous day in April of 1983. His expletive-filled rant, recorded by WLS-AM sports reporter Les Grobstein, is the stuff of legend. *(Listen to a version of it on the Just One Bad Century website.)*

Pete Elko 1918 – 1993 (Cubs 1943-1944)

Piccolo Pete, as he was known, was a wartime player for the Cubs. Pete backed up Cubs legend Stan Hack at third base two different seasons, and got a grand total of 56 big league plate appearances. Unfortunately for him, he managed only one extra base hit (a double). Piccolo Pete wasn't quite good enough to make the 1945 pennant-winning roster, and once the veterans all returned from military service, he knew his days in baseball were numbered. He nevertheless plugged away at it in the minor leagues until 1950.

Allen Elliott 1897 – 1979 (Cubs 1923-1924)

The first baseman was called Ace by his teammates. He backed up the oft-injured Ray Grimes, and got quite a bit of playing time (especially in 1923) as a result. His stint with the Cubs was his only taste of the big leagues.

Carter Elliott 1893 – 1959 (Cubs 1921)

Elliott was called up in September of 1921 and handed the starting shortstop job because starter Charlie Hollocher was ailing. Elliott hit .250 and played a respectable shortstop, but it apparently wasn't good enough. He never got another shot at the big leagues.

Rowdy Elliot 1890–1934 (Cubs 1916-1918)

His real name was Harold Elliot, but his teammates called him Rowdy. The reason for his nickname has been lost to time, but when you hear Rowdy Elliot's story, you can probably make an educated guess. He was a catcher for the Cubs from 1916 to 1918. His first year with the Cubs was the first year they played in what is now known as Wrigley Field. Rowdy was one of eight catchers to play for the Cubs that year. The 1916 group includes Nick Allen (four games), Jimmy Archer (61 games), Clem Clemens (nine), Rowdy Elliot (18), Bill Fischer (56), Bucky O'Connor (one), Bob O'Farrell (one), and Art Wilson (34). His Cubs career ended in May of 1918, when he suddenly left the team and enlisted in the Navy to fight in World War I. Rowdy played one more big league season after the war (with Brooklyn), and he bounced around in the minors after that until 1929. Five years later Rowdy was dead. He fell from an apartment window and died from the injuries. Though the rumor was never confirmed, it's been reported that Rowdy was drunk at the time of his death. A collection was taken up by friends to keep Rowdy Elliott, who was penniless, from being buried in a potter's field.

Jim Ellis 1945–(Cubs 1967)

Jim was a promising young starter in the Cubs minor league system. They promoted him to the big club at the end of the 1967 season when he was 22 years old. Ellis only got into eight games, but showed enough promise to attract the attention of the Dodgers. They traded for him (along with Ted Savage) after the season in return for Jim Hickman and Phil Regan — one of the best trades in Cubs history. Ellis got one last cup of coffee with the Cardinals in 1969, and was out of baseball by 1971.

Dick Ellsworth 1940–(Cubs 1958-1966)

Ellsworth experienced the highest highs and the lowest lows during his Cubs career. The left-hander won 20 games one year (one of only six lefties to lead the team in wins since World War II), and lost 22 games another year. He made the All-Star team, but finished that season with a sub .500 record. He pitched for the Cubs during their darkest days (two 100-loss seasons), and was traded (for Ray Culp in 1967) right before they got good. But he also won more than a hundred games in a very solid thirteen-year big league career. His career record may have been under .500, but Hall of Famer Willie McCovey once told the Sporting News: "Don't let Dick's won-and-lost record fool you. It's misleading. He's tough on any hitter."

Bob Elson 1904–1981 (Cubs announcer 1928-1941)

Elson was mainly known for broadcasting White Sox games (which he did until 1970), but he also broadcast Cubs home games for many years during the radio era. Elson famously recruited Jack Brickhouse to join the broadcast team. He was inducted into the "Scribes & Mikemen" section of baseball's Hall of Fame as the winner of the Ford C. Frick award in 1979.

Don Elston 1929–1995 (Cubs 1953, 1957-1964)

Elston's career really took off when he was converted into a reliever in 1958. In his first two seasons in the pen he led the league in appearances. In 1959 he was recognized for his stellar relieving by being named to the All-Star team. He got the save in the National League's 5-4 victory. After pitching more than just about any other pitcher in the league for five solid years, however, Elston began to run out of gas in 1964. His ERA rose above five for the season. During spring training of 1965, the Cubs and Elston finally parted ways.

Historical note: On the day Yuri Gagarin became the first man in orbit (1961), Elston got the save for the Cubs in a 3-2 against the Phillies.

*Embarrassing Cubs Injuries...*Over the years the Cubs have had many embarrassing injuries...Sammy Sosa injured himself sneezing. Randy Veres hurt his hand pounding on the wall of his hotel room, trying to get the people next door to make less noise. Ryan Dempster injured his toe jumping over the railing to celebrate a victory. Kerry Wood once slipped and fell in a hot tub. Mike Morgan fell on a wet step near his pool. Pitcher Mike Harkey got injured doing handstands in the outfield. Jose Cardenal declared himself unfit to play because crickets in his hotel room had kept him awake all night. Another time, Jose said that he couldn't play because his eyelid was stuck open. That's right, stuck open, not closed. Brandon Morrow hurt his back taking off his pants. Mike Remlinger hurt his hand on his La-Z-Boy chair. Kyle Farnsworth hurt his leg kicking an electric fan.

Mario Encarnacion 1975 – (Cubs 2002)

The outfielder got to bat exactly nine times in a Cubs uniform. He didn't get a single hit. The Dominican played nine seasons in the minors, mostly in the Oakland A's organization.

Steve Engel 1961 – (Cubs 1985)

The lefty started eight games for the injury-riddled Cubs of 1985. He wasn't really up to the task. Engel posted a 1-5 record with a 5.57 ERA. That was his only stint in the big leagues.

Woody English 1906 – 1997 (Cubs 1927-1936)

Woody was an All-Star shortstop for the Cubs, but he also played quite a bit at third base. He was part of three Cubs pennant-winning teams (1929, 1932, and 1935). Woody would have had a chance to be a hero in Game 6 of the 1935 series, but he and his buddies on the Cubs bench razzed the umpire so loudly that the entire bench was kicked out of the game. Instead of Woody going up to pinch hit in the 9th, with the winning run on third base, Charlie Grimm had to let his pitcher Larry French bat. French stranded Stan Hack on third and gave up the series-winning run in the bottom of the inning. English was traded to Brooklyn in 1937 and finished his career with the Dodgers.

Al Epperly 1918 – 2003 (Cubs 1938)

Epperly was the youngest player in the majors when he was called up by the 1938 Cubs. He was like a babe in a tub. That's why his teammates nicknamed him Tub. Epperly pitched only 27 innings for the team, but the Cubs still had high hopes for his future. Unfortunately for Tub, he didn't make the team the following year, and languished in the minors several more years before being drafted into the service during the war. In what can only be described as a Hollywood ending, Tub made it back to the big leagues five years after the war ended. Brooklyn called him up in 1950, at the age of 32. Epperly got to pitch in the big leagues one last time, making five appearances for the Dodgers.

Theo Epstein 1973 – (Cubs President of Baseball Operations 2011-Present)

When Epstein took over control of the Cubs baseball operations, they were a team in disarray. The minor league system was considered one of the worst in the league, and the big league club's roster was full of bloated veteran contracts. He told Cubs fans that it would take a while, and he certainly wasn't lying about that. After several last place finishes, the Cubs finally emerged from the darkness in 2015, in no small part due to the work of Theo Epstein. Before coming to the Cubs, of course, Theo led the Boston Red Sox to two World Series titles. His grandfather Phillip G. Epstein won an Academy Award for co-writing the screenplay for "Casablanca", widely regarded by screenwriters as the best screenplay ever written. But when Theo wrote the script for the Cubs World Series championship in 2016, he surpassed his grandfather's incredible accomplishment and ensured a future place for himself in the Baseball Hall of Fame.

Paul Erickson 1915 – 2002 (Cubs 1941-1948)

Erickson pitched for the Cubs throughout the war, including their pennant-winning season of 1945. In fact, he (or Hy Vandenberg) probably should have started Game 7 of that series. Cubs manager Charlie Grimm went with his ace Hank Borowy on short rest (very short rest — one day), and the Cubs got killed in that final game. His teammates called Erickson Lil Abner after the comic strip character. One of the least proud moments of his career came in Jackie Robinson's first game against the Cubs. Erickson was one of the Cubs pitchers who threw at Robinson — but he was the only one who threw at his head.

Historical note: On the day the Marshall Plan was unveiled to rebuild Europe (1947), Erickson tossed a three-hit complete game to defeat the Giants at Wrigley Field.

Frank Ernaga 1930 – 2018 (Cubs 1957-1958)

Ernaga did a good job as a pinch hitter for the Cubs in 1957. In his very first game he hit a homer and a triple against Warren Spahn. For the season Frank hit .314 with seven extra base hits (out of 11 hits) and drove in seven runs. The following year he couldn't repeat that success and was sent back down to the minors where he finished his career.

Dick Errickson 1912–1999 (Cubs 1942)

Errickson was a relief pitcher. It should come as no surprise that Errickson was nicknamed "Lief" by his teammates. He pitched his final game in the big leagues as a Cub. In the first game of a double-header against his former team the Boston Braves on September 13, 1942, he was lit up for five hits and three runs in an 11-6 loss.

Jim Essian 1951–(Cubs manager 1991)

Essian was named Cubs manager midway through the 1991 season, replacing Don Zimmer who had led the Cubs to the division championship in 1989. Essian didn't fare so well. Even though he was considered an up-and-coming managerial candidate at age 40, his Cubs didn't respond to him at all. They finished four games under .500 and Essian was sent packing after the season. He never managed in the big leagues again.

Shawn Estes 1973–(Cubs 2003)

He was the fifth starter on a Cubs team that also sent Wood, Prior, Zambrano, and Clement to the mound. Estes was clearly the weak link. Dusty Baker remembered him fondly for his 19-win All-Star season with the Giants (Dusty was his manager), so he kept sending him out there every five days, and Estes kept getting rocked. His ERA in 28 starts was 5.83. The Cubs unloaded him after the season and he won 15 games for the Rockies in 2004. Shawn's claim to fame (other than his incredible 1997 season) happened on May 24, 2000. He became the first Giants pitcher to hit a grand slam home run.

Chuck Estrada 1938–(Cubs 1966)

Estrada pitched for the Orioles for several seasons before coming to the Cubs, leading the American League in wins as an All-Star rookie in 1960, and in losses in 1962. He got one start with the Cubs in 1966 and didn't make it out of the first inning. His final Cubs ERA after pitching out of the bullpen the rest of the season was 7.30.

Uel Eubanks 1903–1954 (Cubs 1922)

Uel's cup of coffee was both empty and full. In his one month on the Cubs, he pitched 1.2 innings and got exactly one at-bat. In that one at-bat, he got a hit, so his lifetime average is 1.000. But he was rocked hard on the mound. His final ERA is 27.00. Eubanks was in the minors for six seasons after his little nibble of the big leagues, but he never got another shot at the big-time.

Bill Everitt 1868–1938 (Colts/Orphans 1895-1900)

They called him "Wild Bill" and he played third base for his first few years with the Cubs (then known as the Colts) until switching over to first base for his final three years with the team. Wild Bill was an excellent hitter (.317 lifetime average) with excellent speed (179 stolen bases in six years). In 1901 he jumped to the upstart American League, and finished his career with Washington.

Johnny Evers 1881–1947 (Cubs 1902-1913, Cubs manager 1913)

Johnny Evers was the starting second baseman for the greatest Cubs team of all-time, the 1906-1910 dynasty. He got his nickname, the Crab, for the way he sidled up to grounders, but he lived up to his nickname in another way. Evers was only 120 pounds, but he was known as tough and humorless. For instance, he didn't talk to the other half of his double play combination, shortstop Joe Tinker, for many years. According to Evers, Tinker started the fight in 1907 by throwing a ball too hard at Evers, breaking his finger. Then he laughed… which is, of course, unforgivable. The two didn't talk, other than what they needed to say on the field, for over thirty years. First baseman/manager Frank Chance also didn't like to listen to Evers' constant bitching. He once considered moving him to the outfield just so he didn't have to hear him in his one good ear. The umpires didn't like him either. He must have set the record for ejections after arguments with umpires. But Johnny Evers was a great fielder, a sparkplug on the offense, and despite his grumpy disposition, deserves his status as a member of baseball's Hall of Fame.

Scott Eyre 1972–(Cubs 2006-2008)

Eyre was a veteran bullpen guy when he came to the Cubs as a 34-year-old in 2006. He pitched quite a lot in his first season, but fell out of favor quickly when Lou Piniella became the team's manager the following season. It got so bad at one point that Lou honestly couldn't even remember Eyre's first name. The Cubs traded him to the Phillies in 2008, and Eyre had the last laugh. He and his Phillies teammates won the World Series.

*Additional Entries...*If you check out the Every Cub Ever feature at www. justonebadcentury.com, you'll find several additional entries, including celebrity Cubs fans, writers, and bloggers. Under the letter E, you'll find out more about our publisher Eckhartz Press, which has published several great Cubs books, including this one, Cubs blogger Mark Edwards, and Cubs author/ Chicago Literary Hall of Fame Founder Donald G. Evans. There's also a great feature about The Evil Eye that P.K. Wrigley hired to psych out opponents in the late 1930s.

CHAPTER SIX

F

The starting lineup for your Chicago Cubs beginning with the letter F...

C – Silver Flint, No-Hitter Catcher
1B – Jimmie Foxx, Hall of Famer
2B – Mike Fontenot, Fan Favorite
SS – Lonnie Frey, World Series Champ
3B – Carmen Fanzone, the Trumpet
RF – Max Flack, World Series Goat
CF – Dexter Fowler, World Series Champ
LF – Cliff Floyd, All-Star
Bench – Dee Fondy, .300 Hitter
Bench – Kosuke Fukudome, Japanese Savior
SP – Chick Fraser, World Series Champ
SP – Larry French, Bear Owner
SP – Bill Faul, Coo-Coo for Coco Puffs
SP – Jocko Flynn, 20-game Winner
RP – Kyle Farnsworth, Fighter

Jim Fanning 1927–2015 (Cubs 1954-1957)

Fanning was a minor league catcher who occasionally came up to the big club for a cup of coffee. All 64 of his games as a big league player came with the Cubs. But after his playing career ended, Fanning went on to have a very successful career working for the Montreal Expos. As the Expos GM, he traded for Rusty Staub and drafted Gary Carter and Andre Dawson. As the team's manager, he led the Expos to their only playoff appearance in 1981. And finally, as the scouting and player development director, he developed the likes of Randy Johnson, Larry Walker, and Andres Gallarraga. Not bad for a Cubs catcher with a lifetime batting average of .170.

Carmen Fanzone 1943– (Cubs 1971-1974)

Although he played 2B and 3B and was one of the players who wore #23 like Ryne Sandberg, Carmen's similarities with the Future Hall of Famer ended there. Fanzone was probably better known for his musical abilities and his incredible mustache than he was for the .190 he hit backing up Bill Madlock in 1974. He played four seasons for the Cubs as a backup infielder (1971-1974), and he played the trumpet so well the Cubs asked him to perform the National Anthem. After his playing career ended, he pursued his musical dreams and played the jazz flugelhorn. Despite rumors to the contrary (Wikipedia!), Fanzone never played with the Tonight Show band. He did hang out with them, though. For many years after his playing days, he also participated in Randy Hundley's fantasy camp in Arizona.

Kyle Farnsworth 1976– (Cubs 1999-2004)

Farnsworth had a great arm. He routinely threw the ball in the upper 90s, and the Cubs hoped he would develop into a closer. It just never seemed to happen. Part of the reason was that Farnsworth had the reputation of being a bit of a flake (he once was injured kicking an electric fan in the Cubs dugout) and a bit of a headhunter (he started more than one bench-clearing brawl, including one where he tackled the opposing pitcher and threw him to the ground). He also was part of the implosion of 2003. In that series his ERA was over 10, and he pitched in five of the seven games in the NLCS. Farnsworth went on to pitch ten more years in the big leagues after he left the Cubs, including stints with the Braves, Tigers, Yankees, Royals, Rays, and Pirates. His best season was 2011 when he saved 25 games for Tampa Bay. He still shares a Cubs record for consecutive strikeouts. He struck out eight men in a row in 2001.

Historical note: On the day the Anthrax mail attacks began (2001), Kyle gave up three runs in the bottom of the ninth to lose to the Reds in Cincinnati.

Doc Farrell 1901–1966 (Cubs 1930)

Doc had a long and successful big league career. The middle infielder played for the Cardinals, Giants, Yankees, and Red Sox in addition to the 1930 Cubs. That 1930 Cubs team blew the pennant in the last few weeks of the season, costing future Hall of Fame manager Joe McCarthy his job.

Duke Farrell 1866–1925
(White Stockings 1888-1889)

Duke came up with Cubs (then known as the White Stockings). He was known as a snappy dresser who enjoyed a good night out on the town, but he also could hit the baseball. Farrell had some power, hitting eleven homers in one of his Chicago seasons — a very high total for that time. Duke left the team during the player revolt of 1890 and had his greatest success in subsequent stints with Boston and Washington. One year with Boston he led the league in homers (12). The catcher/third baseman/outfielder played 18 seasons in the big leagues. He later also coached for the Yankees, Red Sox, and Braves.

Luke Farrell 1991–(Cubs 2018)

The son of former big league manager John Farrell got a cup of coffee with the Cubs in the summer of 2018 after he was released by the Cincinnati Reds. Luke started two games and relieved in 18 others, and posted an ERA over five. The Cubs released him in early September and he was picked up by the Angels.

Jeff Fassero 1963–(Cubs 2001-2002)

He was a very good starting pitcher before he came to the Cubs, but during his year and a half in Chicago he was strictly a reliever. His first year he saved twelve games and appeared in eighty for a pretty good Cubs team. His second year wasn't nearly as successful, and he was traded to St. Louis in August. Fassero was a big leaguer for sixteen years.

Darcy Fast 1947–(Cubs 1968)

Darcy was a hard throwing lefty in the Cubs bullpen in the late 1960s, but only had a cup of coffee with the big league team in 1968. In eight appearances covering ten innings, he struck out ten batters…but he also walked eight. He never returned to the big leagues after that. Darcy has written a book about his life, called *The Missing Cub*. Fast is now a pastor.

Father & Son Cubs. There have been eight father/son teams to play for the Chicago Cubs over the years…Bobby/Mike Adams, Joe/ Casey Coleman, Jimmy/Jimmy Scoops Cooney, Herm/Jack Doscher — the first father/son big leaguers ever, Randy/Todd Hundley, Marty/ Matt Keough, Gary/Gary Jr. Mathews, and Chris/Justin Speier.

Bill Faul 1940–2002 (Cubs 1965-1966)

Some players are known as characters. Some are known as eccentrics. Still others seem to have come from another planet. Bill Faul was one of *those* guys…and he wasn't even a lefty…or a Californian. Faul pitched for the Cubs in 1965 and 1966. It's safe to say that he had a quirk or two. He claimed that he could hypnotize himself before games. He had been a Karate instructor in the Air Force, and his hands and feet were both considered registered weapons. He talked to his arm. He allegedly swallowed live toads (to get "extra hop" on his fastball) and ripped the heads off parakeets with his teeth. He once held a guy off a fourth floor balcony by his shoes. Faul also insisted on wearing #13.

But as wild and unpredictable as Faul was, he was cool as a cucumber on the field. He had to be awakened in the clubhouse only thirty minutes before his first major league start. Faul shook out the cobwebs, grabbed the ball, warmed up, and pitched a three-hitter. Faul always seemed to be in the middle of the excitement. He was one of only a handful of pitchers to be involved in fielding a triple play, and one of only two major league pitchers in history to have three triple plays in one season while he was on the mound.

Unfortunately for Faul, the league figured him out in 1966. When his ERA climbed over five, he was sent down to the minors and never returned to the Cubs. He kicked around the minor leagues for a few seasons before turning up for a cup of coffee with the Giants in 1970. Bill Faul died in 2002, at the age of 62.

Historical note: On the day Bob Dylan went electric and stunned the audience at the Newport Folk Festival (1965), Faul was on the mound for the Cubs, three-hitting the Pirates.

Vern Fear 1924–1976 (Cubs 1952)

Fear was blessed with one of the great names in baseball history. Unfortunately, his pitching did not strike fear in the heart of big league hitters. He pitched in four games for the Cubs, the entire extent of his big league career. In his first appearance with the Cubs he faced four Dodgers: Duke Snider, Andy Pafko, Roy Campanella, and Gil Hodges. He gave up three singles and a homer (to Snider) and was pulled out of the game with an ERA of infinity.

Tim Federowicz 1987–(Cubs 2016)

Federowicz played in parts of four seasons for the Dodgers before joining the Cubs. The catcher got a brief taste of a World Championship season when he was called up due to an injury. He played in 17 games and hit .194. After the season ended, Federowicz was granted free agency.

Federal League Cubs...When the Cubs first moved into what is now known as Wrigley Field (then Weeghman Park), they essentially merged with the former 1915 Federal League Whales team owned by Charles Weeghman. Several of the players from that Whales team played on the Cubs during the 1916 season. They were...Mordecai Brown, Clem Clemons, Mickey Doolin, William Fischer, Max Flack, Claude Hendrix, Les Mann, George McConnell, Charlie Pechous, Mike Prendergast, Joe Tinker, Art Wilson, Rollie Zeider, and Dutch Zwilling.

Marv Felderman 1915–2000 (Cubs 1942)

He got exactly six at-bats in the big leagues, and all of them came for the Cubs during the war year of 1942. The backup catcher got one hit. It was his only career big league hit. His nickname was Coonie. Coonie played in the minor leagues until 1951.

Scott Feldman 1983–(Cubs 2013)

Feldman was one of the "flip-able" players brought in during the Epstein regime to garner prospects in return, and it worked like a charm. He was traded to the Orioles in July 2013, in exchange for pitchers Jake Arietta and Pedro Strop, an unbelievable steal for Chicago. Feldman has the distinction of having the most wins in a season by a Jewish pitcher (17 in 2009) since Steve Stone in 1980.

John Felske 1942–(Cubs 1968)

Felske appeared in four games as a Cub in 1968 as a catcher. He got a grand total of two at-bats and didn't record a hit. The following year he was taken in the expansion draft. He later managed in the minors, coached in the big leagues, and even briefly served as the general manager for the Philadelphia Phillies.

Bob Ferguson 1845–1894 (White Stockings 1878)

Ferguson was the player/manager of Chicago for one season, and was known for his ferocious temper. He was a great player, he hit .351 in his only season with the White Stockings, but was fired because owner Al Spalding considered him tactless and brutish. Ferguson also had one of the greatest nicknames of all time: Death To Flying Things. After his playing career he became an umpire.

Charlie Ferguson 1875–1931 (Orphans 1901)

Charlie pitched exactly two innings for the Cubs (then known as the Orphans) on September 20, 1901, during a double-header against the Boston Braves. He walked two and gave up a hit, but didn't allow any runs to score, meaning his lifetime ERA was a perfect 0. After his one shot of big league glory, he went back to the minors the following season and pitched there until 1909. Even though he only spent one day as a big leaguer, he could always say that he played alongside two Hall of Famers. Rube Waddell and Frank Chance were both on his team. He later became an umpire. Ferguson drowned on a fishing trip in Whitefish Bay.

Felix Fermin 1963–(Cubs 1996)

Felix played ten big league seasons, including several years with Cleveland when he was the team's starting shortstop. By the time he arrived in Chicago, it was the tail end of his career. He had already been cut by the Yankees and the Mariners in 1996 when the Cubs took a flyer on him. Fermin was done. He batted only .125 in 11 games, and never appeared in the major leagues again. Although, to be fair, Felix was always more known for his fielding than his hitting. In over 3000 big league plate appearances, Fermin hit only 4 homers.

Frank Fernandez 1943–(Cubs 1971-1972)

Frank was a catcher for the Cubs and a few other teams in

his big league career, and while he was never good enough to play regularly, he does have a few very odd records. For instance, he has the most homers for a player with a career average below .200 (39), and he had more walks in his big league career than hits, and he had more than a hundred of each (164 walks, 145 hits).

Cubs players have had some great nicknames over the years. Among players starting with the letter F, you'll find nicknames like Beast, Buck, Bud, Buster, Cherokee, Coonie, Dibbie, Death to Flying Things, Doc, Duke, Fordham Flash, Jocko, Lefty, Mechanic, Moonlight Ace, Suds, and Tito.

Jesus Figueroa 1957–(Cubs 1980)

The Dominican outfielder played for the Cubs one year, his only season in the big leagues. The Cubs used him mainly as a pinch hitter that season. He was a contact hitter with a good eye, but didn't really have the power necessary to stick in the majors as a corner outfielder. The Cubs traded him after the season (along with Jerry Martin) to the Giants, and he couldn't crack the roster there. The Giants had a stacked outfield that included Larry Herndon, Jack Clark, Bill North, and Jeff Leonard.

Tom Filer 1956–(Cubs 1982)

Filer was a right-handed starting pitcher who debuted in the big leagues with the Cubs in 1982. In eight starts he only won once. He later pitched for the Blue Jays, Brewers, and Mets.

William Fischer 1891–1945 (Cubs 1916)

Fischer was a backup catcher for the Cubs in their first year at what is now known as Wrigley Field. He had been part of the Federal League Whales the previous year, so he already had some experience playing in the ballpark. In fact, in the first ever Cubs game at Wrigley (Opening Day 1916), Fischer was the hitting star, going 4 for 5 and scoring two runs in a dramatic 7-6 come from behind walk-off win. Unfortunately, Fischer hit only .196 for the Cubs the rest of that year and was traded to the Pirates. Also included in that trade was one of the last remaining members of the Cubs dynasty — Frank Schulte.

Bob Fisher 1886–1963 (Cubs 1914-1915)

After Joe Tinker jumped to the Federal League, Fisher became the everyday shortstop for the Cubs in their last season at West Side Grounds. He was known for his bat control. In 1915 he led the entire league in sacrifice hits with 42, and batted .285. As good as he was with the bat, however, he was a terrible baserunner. Fisher was thrown out trying to steal 20 times that season, and was successful only 9 times. When the Cubs and Feds merged in 1916, Fisher was not asked to come along. He finished his career with the Reds and Cardinals.

Cherokee Fisher 1844–1912 (White Stockings 1877)

Fisher was a heavy drinker and a very good pitcher who played in exactly one game for the White Stockings in 1877. The former pitcher took a stab at third base and went 0 for 4. He never pitched for Chicago. Fisher is listed as the 38th player in big league history because he was there from the very beginning in 1871 with Rockford. While he was still a pitcher he won the ERA title twice (in the National Association), and also has the distinction of giving up the first homer in National League history — to future teammate Ross Barnes.

Howard Fitzgerald 1902–1959 (Cubs 1922, 1924)

Fitzgerald is one of the few people nicknamed "Lefty" who wasn't a pitcher. He was an outfielder. Unfortunately for Howard, he didn't have a lot of power for a corner outfielder. In 150 career plate appearances, he hit exactly zero home runs. Lefty spent most of his baseball career in the minor leagues. He hung up his spikes after the 1933 season. Fitzgerald died in an automobile accident in Texas at the age of 56.

Max Flack 1890–1975 (Cubs 1916-1922)

Max has the distinction of playing in the very first game in Weeghman Park history as a member of the Chi-Feds, and then playing in the very first game the Cubs played in the same ballpark (as a Cub). He was their star right fielder during that time. During their pennant-winning season of 1918, he led the league's outfielders in fielding percentage, putouts, double plays, and assists. He also, unfortunately, dropped an easy fly ball in the 1918 World Series. The Cubs were leading the game 1-0 at the time, and the dropped fly ball allowed the Red Sox to score two runs and win the game

2-1. Whenever someone accuses the Cubs of throwing that series (entire books have been written on the subject), this is one of those plays that is discussed. In 1922, Max was traded to the Cardinals for Cliff Heathcote in the middle of a double-header. The two men just changed uniforms and dugouts.

Historical note: On the day of terrible race riots in Chicago (38 killed, 500 injured) in 1919, Flack hit the game-winning homer to help the Cubs beat the Cardinals 4-0.

John Flavin 1942– (Cubs 1964)

Flavin showed some promise in the Reds minor league system, so the Cubs thought they were getting a pretty good pitcher when they claimed him. He was only 22 years old and was coming off a 12-2 season at Triple A. Unfortunately, it didn't work out for Flavin in Chicago. He appeared in five games, and had a 13.50 ERA in 4.2 innings.

Bill Fleming 1913–2006 (Cubs 1942-1944, 1946)

Fleming pitched for the Cubs during the war, and had a very respectable season in 1944. He won nine games and posted a 3.13 ERA. He would have been a key part of the pitching staff in 1945, but Uncle Sam had other ideas. Fleming was serving in the military while the Cubs made it all the way to the 1945 World Series. He pitched for the Cubs again in 1946, but it didn't go well. That was his last year in the big leagues.

Scott Fletcher 1958– (Cubs 1981-1982)

Fletcher was actually traded for his fellow birthday boy Steve Trout. He was just a young prospect with the Cubs who never would have gotten much playing time (a youngster named Ryne Sandberg was rated slightly higher), but Fletcher blossomed with the White Sox. He shared the second base job on their 1983 playoff team, and went on to have a very respectable 15-year big league career with the White Sox, Rangers, Brewers, Red Sox, and Tigers. He was also part of the trade that brought Sammy Sosa from Texas to the White Sox.

Sliver Flint 1855–1892 (White Stockings 1879-1889)

Flint was a catcher on those early Cubs (then known as White Stockings) championship teams of the 1880s, and he also was the player/manager briefly in his first season with the club. Flint was a tough cookie who played hard on and off

the field. On the field he caught the first four no-hitters in franchise history (three by Larry Corcoran, and one by HOFer John Clarkson). Off the field, he enjoyed his beverages. Flint died of tuberculosis in 1892 at the age of 36, only two years after his playing career ended.

Jesse Flores 1914–1991 (Cubs 1942)

The first Mexican-born pitcher in big league history made his debut with the Cubs during the war. He only pitched in four games and posted an ERA of 3.38 before the Cubs sent him down for more seasoning. He later pitched for the A's and the Indians. After his playing career, Jesse became one of the best scouts in baseball. His signings for the Minnesota Twins included Bert Blyleven, Lyman Bostock, Bill Campbell, Rick Dempsey, and Jesse Orosco.

Dylan Floro 1990– (Cubs 2017)

The Cubs gave a shot to the former Tampa Rays reliever in 2017, but it didn't work out. In just over nine innings pitched, Dylan gave up seven earned runs. He was released in August. He has since pitched for the Reds and the Dodgers.

Cliff Floyd 1972– (Cubs 2007)

The local Chicago boy didn't get to play for his hometown team until his 15th big league season. He was only two years removed from hitting 30+ homers for the Mets, but Cliff didn't quite reach those heights with the Cubs. He started most of the season in right field and hit .284 with nine homers. Nevertheless, Cliff had a tremendous big league career. Floyd was an All-Star, a World Series champ, and led four different teams to the playoffs, including the 2007 Cubs. In his 17-year big league career, Cliff Floyd hit 233 homers.

John Fluhrer 1894–1946 (Cubs 1915)

The outfielder played briefly for the Cubs in their last season at West Side Grounds, including one game under the pseudonym William G. Morris. It was his only time in the big leagues.

George Flynn 1871–1901 (Colts 1896)

Dibby, as he was known, got his only taste of the big leagues for the 1896 Cubs (then known as the Colts). The Chicago-born outfielder stole twelve bases and hit .255 in just over a hundred at-bats. Five years after his baseball career ended, Flynn died at the age of 30.

Jocko Flynn 1864–1907 (White Stockings 1886-1887)

Jocko pitched only one season with the Cubs (then known as the White Stockings) in 1886 and won 23 games, but he was a small man (5'6 , 143 pounds) with a very large appetite for booze. He blew out his arm and became a full-fledged alcoholic. Jocko died shortly after his 43rd birthday. He still holds the record for most wins by a pitcher who only pitched one season in the big leagues (23).

    <u>Historical note:</u> On the day of the Haymarket Riots in Chicago, Jocko was on the mound. The White Stockings lost the game In 11 innings against St. Louis.

Gene Fodge 1931–2010 (Cubs 1958)

Fodge had one of the great nicknames in the league. His teammates called him Suds. Suds was with the Cubs for the first four months of the 1958 season, serving as a swing starter and reliever. After the South Bend native was sent back down to the minors in July, the 27-year-old right-hander decided the time was right to call it a career. He resided in Mishawaka, Indiana until his death in 2010.

Tom Foley 1844–1896 (White Stockings 1871)

A member of the first official Chicago team (in the National Association), Foley played outfield, catcher, and second base. That puts in an exclusive club — players who played for Chicago before the Great Chicago Fire. It was his only season in the big leagues. If you ever see a picture of him, prepare to be freaked out. He was a dead ringer for Edgar Allan Poe.

Will Foley 1855–1916 (White Stockings 1875)

Will played third base for the White Stockings the season before they joined the National League. He got into exactly three games, and went 3 for 12. Foley later played in the National League for Cincinnati, Milwaukee, and Detroit.

Dee Fondy 1924–1999 (Cubs 1951-1957)

Fondy was the starting first baseman for the Cubs for most of the 1950s. His best seasons were in 1953 (when he hit .309 and clubbed 18 homers) and 1955 (when he hit 17 homers). After the 1957 season he was sent to Pittsburgh along with

color-barrier-breaking teammate Gene Baker for Dale Long and Lee Walls.

Lew Fonseca 1899–1989 (Cubs announcer 1930s)

In 12 big league seasons he played first base, second base, and left field for the Reds, Phillies, Indians, and White Sox. As a manager, he led the White Sox to one of their worst seasons of all time in 1932. They finished that year 49-102. After his playing/managing career ended, Lew settled in Chicago and became one of the early radio announcers for the Chicago Cubs. Lew Fonseca is buried in the same cemetery (All Saints in Des Plaines) as another famous Cubs announcer, Harry Caray.

Mike Fontenot 1980– (Cubs 2005-2010)

Fontenot was acquired in the trade that sent Sammy Sosa to the Orioles. He quickly became a fan favorite. Cubs fans loved the way the little Fontenot (5'9 , 165 lbs.) delivered clutch hits with surprising pop. In their exciting 2008 season, Fontenot hit .305 for the Cubs and slugged nine homers, while forming a double play combination with his college teammate Ryan Theriot. Mike slumped a bit in 2009, and was traded to the Giants in 2010. That turned out to be a good trade for Fontenot — the 2010 Giants won the World Series.

Ray Fontenot 1957– (Cubs 1985-1986)

Fontenot was acquired by the Cubs just after their close call in the 1984 playoffs. Fontenot couldn't crack the starting rotation on his merits, but when everyone started getting hurt, he got the call. In 1985 he started 23 games, won 6 and lost 10, and posted an ERA of 4.36. He was traded to the Twins in the middle of '86.

> Football Cubs...The following Cubs were also tremendous football players...Cliff Alberson (Green Bay Packers), Paddy Driscoll (NFL Hall of Famer), Don Eaddy (University of Michigan), Bob Garbark (All-American at Allegheny), John Herrnstein (University of Michigan), Chick King (All-American in high school), Carl Lundgren (University of Illinois), Ray Mack (drafted by the Bears), Harry McChesney

(Pittsburgh Stars), Lloyd Merriman (Stanford), Keith Moreland (University of Texas), Jeff Samardzija (Notre Dame), Bull Smith (Canton Bulldogs), Matt Szczur (Villanova), Rube Waddell (Philadelphia Athletics football), and Cy Williams (Notre Dame).

Barry Foote 1952– (Cubs 1979-1981)

Barry Foote hit sixteen home runs as the Cubs every-day catcher in 1979, but he didn't have a great relationship with Cubs manager Herman Franks. When Franks (a World War II vet) resigned at the end of the 1979 season, he specifically called out Foote (along with Ted Sizemore, Bill Buckner, and Mike Vail) as a whiner. The Cubs traded Foote to the Yankees in 1981. After his playing career, Barry remained in baseball as a major and minor league coach for the Yankees, Blue Jays, White Sox, and Mets.

Davy Force 1849–1918 (White Stockings 1874)

Force played fifteen years in the big leagues, and one of those seasons was in Chicago. Davy went where the money was — he played for nine different teams. Wee Davy, or Tom Thumb as he was called, played 2B, SS, and 3B and was considered one of the best in the league. He was only 5'4", among the shortest players in Cubs history. Force also indirectly caused the National League to be formed. His contractual dispute was such a headache for the previous league (the NA), future Hall of Famer William Hulbert organized a new league so that he didn't have to abide by the findings. The Cubs still play in that league today.

Tony Fossas 1957– (Cubs 1998)

Fossas was a journeyman reliever (known as "The Mechanic") who was 31 years old when he made it up the big leagues. He pitched for the Rangers, Brewers, Cardinals, and Mariners before coming to fix the Cubs bullpen in the summer of 1998. In four innings he walked six men, and gave up eight hits and four runs. He wasn't allowed to work in the bullpen anymore after that. The Cubs moved on to a different mechanic.

Elmer Foster 1861–1946 (Colts 1890-1891)

Foster was a backup outfielder with the Cubs (then known as the Colts) in the early 1890s. In his first season in Chicago he was a big help off the bench. He slugged five homers and stole 18 bases in only 27 games. Unfortunately for Elmer, he fell out of favor with the Cubs brass early the following season and was released. It was his last shot at the big leagues.

Kevin Foster 1969–2008 (Cubs 1994-1998)

Kevin Foster was born and raised in the Chicago area, so it was a dream come true when he came to the Cubs in 1994. He had his ups (a 12-win season in '95 and a 10-win season in '97), and downs (trouble giving up the long ball) with his hometown team, but Foster was a popular player because of his positive attitude and his happy-go-lucky charm. After he hurt his arm in 1997, he was essentially done in the big leagues outside of a brief stint with the Rangers in 2001. In 2008 he was working as a truck driver when he was diagnosed with renal cell carcinoma, a very powerful cancer. He died only six months later at the age of 39.

Dexter Fowler 1986– (Cubs 2015-2016)

Dexter was acquired before the 2015 season from the Houston Astros in exchange for pitcher Dan Straily and infielder Luis Valbuena, and he paid immediate dividends for his new team. The Cubs put him at the top of their order and started him in center field. In that role, he posted a .346 on-base percentage, scored over a hundred runs, played a pretty good center field, and got clutch hits all season long, including two big home runs in the playoffs (versus Pittsburgh and St. Louis). His 17 homers were a career high, and Fowler had been a regular in the big leagues since 2009. After the season it looked like he would leave via free agency, but the Cubs surprised everyone by signing Dexter late during spring season. He was brought out on the practice field in his street clothes to surprise his teammates, and they were overjoyed to welcome him back. Dexter had another great season in 2016, and served as the leadoff man for the World Champion Cubs. He posted a .393 on-base percentage, was named to the All-Star team, and led off Game 7 of the World Series with a home run. He signed with the Cardinals as a free agent after the season.

Chad Fox 1970–(Cubs 2005-2009)

Fox had a pretty good career as a reliever in Milwaukee before he came to the Cubs, but he spent most of his time in Chicago rehabbing from injuries. He missed the entire 2006 and 2007 seasons, and when he pitched in 2009 he suffered a gruesome injury — it looked like his arm was just dangling. His ERA that season was 135.00. That was the end of the line for Fox.

Charlie Fox 1921–2004 (Cubs manager 1983)

Fox never played for the Cubs (he was a Giant), but he did get the call from general manager Dallas Green to manage the Cubs at the tail end of the 1983 season after Lee "it's a playground for the c*********" Elia was fired. The Cubs went 17-22 under his tutelage on their way to a 5th place finish. The following season Jim Frey was at the helm, and the Cubs came ever so close to winning the NL pennant.

Jake Fox 1982–(Cubs 2007-2009)

Fox had big-time power, but he didn't play any defensive position well. The University of Michigan Wolverine played 1B, 3B, C, RF, and LF for the Cubs. They were desperate to find a spot for him in the lineup because of his power. In 2009, he got his most extended time in the lineup and he hit 11 homers, many of them dramatic. Jake hit over 20 homers in ten of his eleven minor league seasons. Fox later played with the Orioles and A's.

Bill Foxen 1879–1937 (Cubs 1910-1911)

The Cubs acquired Foxen during the pennant-winning season of 1910. He only got in two games for the Cubs that season (and was rocked), so Foxen wasn't on the postseason roster. In 1911 he appeared in his last 3 MLB games. He was 1-1 for the Cubs, with a 2.08 ERA in 13 innings. He walked 12 in those 13 innings — a major reason why he didn't stick in the big leagues.

Jimmie Foxx 1907–1967 (Cubs 1942, 1944)

Jimmie was nicknamed the Beast because of his imposing physical presence. Foxx is one of the all-time greatest sluggers: a two-time World Series champ, a three-time MVP, winner of two batting titles. Foxx led the league in home runs four times, RBI three times (despite playing at the same time as Ruth and Gehrig), and hit 534 career home runs. Unfortunately for Cubs fans, only three of those home runs came with the Cubs, who picked him up one year after his last good season. He hit .190 with the team in 225 at-bats, and was released in 1944. He later managed one of the women's teams during the war and was the inspiration for the character played by Tom Hanks in *A League of Their Own*.

Ken Frailing 1948–(Cubs 1974-1976)

Ken was part of the Ron Santo trade with the White Sox (along with Steve Stone and Steve Swisher). He was mainly used as a swing man, switching between the bullpen and starting. He did pitch one complete game for the Cubs, although it certainly wasn't your typical complete game. He gave up 15 hits.

Andy Frain 1904–1964
(Cubs usher/security 1928-1964)

In 1928 Wrigley Field was known as a place where ushers would take bribes to allow people into the good seats. Andy Frain pitched the Cubs owner to let him do security to clean up the problem. Frain offered to give back Mr. Wrigley's money if he wasn't completely satisfied with his performance. Wrigley was so impressed, he hired Frain to run the entire show and gave him $5000 for uniforms. Those uniforms became his company's trademark. In the 1930s, 40s, and 50s, the Notre Dame blue and gold Andy Frain uniforms were on hand at every major sporting event in Chicago, including football, baseball, and hockey games. They also kept the peace at political conventions, the Kentucky Derby, and more. Frain had a few tips he told his staff. Some of them might not exactly stand the test of time. For instance, he never trusted a man with a mustache, or a man who carried an umbrella. Shady characters. He insisted his own men were tall — because six-footers intimidated. Also, the only color that mattered to him was the color of the customer's ticket. Frain's men became such an institution that ushers at Wrigley Field were simply called "Andy Frains" for many years. Andy died in 1964. His sons carried on the company until 1982.

Ossie France 1858–1947 (Colts 1890)

If you want to travel back in time to watch France pitch in the big leagues, set the wayback machine to July 14, 1890, and go to Brooklyn. He pitched two innings for the Cubs (then known as the Colts) and gave up three runs in a 10-3 loss. It was his only appearance in the big leagues. And yes, this only Cub named France pitched his only game on Bastille Day.

Matt Franco 1969 – (Cubs 1995)

Franco came up with the Cubs and got his first taste of the big leagues in 1995, appearing in 16 games. He was traded to the Mets the following year, where he put together a pretty good career as a backup outfielder and pinch hitter. Matt was very good in that pinch-hitting role for the Mets and Braves, before finishing his career as a full-time player in Japan.

Terry Francona 1959 – (Cubs 1986)

Francona was nicknamed Tito because his father Tito was a big leaguer too. Terry wasn't quite as good as his dad, but he managed to play ten seasons with the Expos, Cubs, Reds, Indians, and Brewers. He was a first baseman/outfielder who mainly served as a backup, but in his limited at-bats the lefty could hit. He hit .346 and .321 in two seasons with the Expos. With the Cubs he hit only .250 backing up Gary Mathews, Bobby Dernier, and Keith Moreland. Of course, after his playing career was over, Francona became a manager. He will always be remembered in Boston for ending their 86-year curse when he led the team to the 2004 World Series title. He won another in 2007. He was also at the helm of the Cleveland Indians when the Chicago Cubs won their first World Series in 108 years.

Historical note: On the day of the Live Aid concert (1985), Francona had the winning hit against Steve Trout as the Expos beat the Cubs.

Seth Frankoff 1988 – (Cubs 2017)

Seth was 28 years old when he made his big league debut with the Cubs in June of 2017. He came into a tie game against the Rockies and proceeded to give up a single to the pitcher and a homer to Charlie Blackmon, and took the loss. He never pitched for the Cubs again.

Herman Franks 1914 – 2009 (Cubs manager 1977-1979, GM 1982)

Franks was grizzled old catcher — a World War II veteran

— a no-nonsense kind of guy. The Cubs club he managed did not fit that same description unfortunately. They got off to a good start in his first season (1977) only to completely fall apart at the end of the season (to finish at .500). They had moments in the next two seasons as well, but they never put it together. Franks became so disgusted with the players that he actually resigned. He said he couldn't stand the roster of cry-babies.

Chick Fraser 1873 – 1940 (Cubs 1907-1909)

Chick was the old-timer on the pitching staff of the first two Cubs World Series champion teams. He turned 35 during the 1908 season. He once no-hit the Cubs (1903) while pitching for the Phillies. Fraser was a headhunter and is still 5th on the all-time hit batsmen list behind Walter Johnson, Eddie Plank, Randy Johnson, and Joe McGinnity. Fraser was summarily fired from the team in 1909 by Frank Chance, after Chance sent him home to Chicago to get his arm ready for a series. When Frank discovered Chick hadn't shown up at the ballpark at all, that was the end of his big league career.

George Frazier 1954 – (Cubs 1984-1985)

Not to be confused with the former Heavyweight Champion of the world, this George Frazier was a pretty good reliever in the big leagues who came to the Cubs as part of the Rick Sutcliffe trade. He made over 400 appearances in his 10-year career, with stops in St. Louis, New York, Cleveland, Minnesota and, of course, Chicago. George was an important part of the Cubs bullpen during their division-winning 1984 season, and even appeared in the NLCS that year. After a much rougher 1985, the Cubs traded him to the Twins, where he finished his career.

Ryan Freel 1976 – 2012 (Cubs 2009)

Freel's stay in Chicago was very brief. The Cubs were one of three teams he played for in 2009. He only managed four hits in a Cubs uniform after being acquired from the Orioles in May of that year. By early July he was gone. Freel was known as a bit of a flake. When he was with the Reds in 2006, he admitted that he often spoke to an imaginary voice in his head named "Farney". His eccentricities were accepted by his teammates, however, because Freel was a take-no-prisoners rub-some-dirt-in-it kind of player who would do absolutely anything to help his team. Because of that, he suffered a series of concussions. In December of 2012, just a few years after retiring from baseball, Freel took his own life. His family had his brain examined after his suicide, and doctors found that he had been suffering from chronic traumatic encephalopathy — brought on by the many concussions.

Buck Freeman 1896–1953 (Cubs 1921-1922)

Freeman was part of the starting rotation of the Cubs in 1921 as a rookie, alongside the likes of Hall of Famer Grover Cleveland Alexander. Buck didn't impress. He won 9 games, but he only struck out 42 batters in 177 innings. He got one more shot the following year and was hit hard. That was the end of his big league career.

Hersh Freeman 1928–2004 (Cubs 1958)

Freeman's nickname was Buster. Unfortunately for the Cubs, that nickname may have described what he could do to close games when he came in from the bullpen. He had been a pretty solid reliever for the Reds (he won 14 and saved 18 in 1956) and the Cubs thought he was worth the gamble when they traded Turk Lown for him in the middle of the '58 season, but in 13 innings for the Cubs he gave up 23 hits and 12 runs and never pitched in the big leagues again. Turk Lown, by the way, was traded by the Reds to the White Sox, and became a key member of their 1959 pennant-winning pitching staff.

Mark Freeman 1930–2006 (Cubs 1960)

The 29-year-old got the most extended shot of his career with the Lou Boudreau-managed Cubs of 1960. He appeared in 30 games and posted an ERA of 5.63. It was also his last chance in the big leagues. The big right-hander (6'4) hung up his spikes after the Cubs cut him loose following the season. Freeman passed away in 2006.

Mike Freeman 1987– (Cubs 2017-2018)

After having an embarrassment of riches in infield prospects for several years, and trading many of them away, the Cubs found themselves shorthanded in August of 2017 when Addison Russell suffered an injury. They signed Freeman off waivers from the Dodgers and he did get significant playing time during that month. Unfortunately for Mike, he and

his Cubs teammates were eliminated from the playoffs by his former Dodgers teammates in the NLCS. Freeman spent the entire 2018 season in the minors, but did return for one plate appearance in September. He sacrificed, which didn't technically count as an at-bat.

George Freese 1926–2014 (Cubs 1961)

Bud, as he was called by his teammates, was 34 years old when he got his ever-so-brief shot in a Cubs uniform. He been in the minor leagues for most of his career, but did get brief tastes of the big-time with the Tigers in 1953 and the Pirates in 1955. His seven at-bat stint with the Cubs wasn't the end of the line for Bud either. He played another three seasons in the minors, before finally retiring in 1964 at the age of 37. The third baseman hit 198 career homers. Only three of those came in the big leagues. He coached for the Cubs after his playing career ended.

Howard Freigau 1902–1932 (Cubs 1925-1927)

The Cubs acquired Freigau from the Cardinals in the deal that sent catcher Bob O'Farrell to St. Louis. Ty, as his teammates called him, started at third base for the Cubs for two seasons. In his first year in Chicago, he hit over .300. He slumped in his second year, and was replaced at the third base in 1927. He later played for Brooklyn and Boston. Howard died in 1932 when he dove into a shallow swimming pool and broke his neck.

Historical note: On the day both Marilyn Monroe and Andy Griffith were born, Howard scored the winning run for the Cubs in a dramatic 10-9 win over the Cardinals at Cubs Park (Wrigley).

Larry French 1907–1987 (Cubs 1935-1941)

French was one of the most memorable characters to wear a Cubs uniform. He was a hero off the field (after leaving baseball, he participated in the invasion of Normandy as a landing craft material officer), but on the field it was a slightly different story. French started a World Series game for the Cubs in 1935 (losing it in the bottom of the ninth), and appeared in the 1938 World Series as a reliever, but that season he also made history. Larry became the only pitcher with a losing record in Major League history to lose as many as 19 games for a pennant winner. He went 10-19 on a team that was 89-63, personally accounting for nearly 1/3 of the team's losses. That's a pretty staggering total. Despite this "achievement," French was very popular with the fans and his teammates. Again, it was the off-the-field stories that fueled his popularity. In 1938, he made news when he bought a live bear cub from a fan for $10. Larry learned a valuable lesson that summer…keeping a live bear cub isn't as easy as it sounds. After the cub tore up his apartment, French somehow managed to convince his teammate Ripper Collins to take the bear off his hands. Collins learned the same valuable lesson. After a similar unpleasant experience, he donated the cub to a conservation camp in New York. Despite his record-setting season of 1938, Larry French was a pretty good starting pitcher during his Major League career. He won 18 games for the Pirates twice, and had two good years with the Cubs in 1935 and 1936, winning 17 and 18 games respectively. He finished his Major League career with 197 wins and a 3.44 ERA, and went to his grave (in 1987) without ever again owning a live bear cub.

Historical note: On the day the Germans invaded Poland in World War II (1939), French was on the mound for the Cubs, beating the Brooklyn Dodgers.

Jim Frey 1931– (Cubs manager 1984-1986, GM 1988-1991)

Frey came to Chicago after taking the Royals to the World Series in his previous job and nearly did the impossible with the Cubs. In his first season as their manager he led the Cubs to their first-ever division championship (and first playoff appearance in 39 years). As we all know, the Cubs came within a few outs of going to the 1984 World Series. It fell apart fast. By 1986, Frey was gone. In 1988, however, Frey was brought in to replace Dallas Green as the team's general manager. He and his old pal Don Zimmer managed to win another divisional championship ('89), but Frey had a tendency to prefer veterans to prospects, and it took many years for the Cubs minor league system to recover after he left the team.

Lonny Frey 1910–2009 (Cubs 1937, 1947)

Frey was a second baseman/shortstop who played for the Cubs in two different seasons ten years apart. Between those two seasons he was a three time All-Star and a World Series champ with the Reds. After he left the Cubs the second time

he won another World Series…as a member of the New York Yankees. In 20 World Series at-bats, Lonny got zero hits. His nickname was Junior.

Bernie Friberg 1899–1958 (Cubs 1919-1920, 1922-1925)

Bernie was the starting third baseman for the Cubs in 1923 and 1924 and hit quite well. In '23 he drove in 88 runs and batted .318. He drove in another 82 runs the following season. Unfortunately, Bernie was also one of the worst fielding third sackers in the league, finishing the top five in errors both seasons. The Cubs cut him loose in 1925, and the Phillies picked him up and converted him into a utility man. Bernie spent eight seasons in Philadelphia, playing every position on the field except pitcher and catcher.

Danny Friend 1873–1942 (Colts/Orphans 1895-1898)

Friend was a left-handed pitcher in the 1890s as the team transitioned from a veteran-dominated All-Star club into a younger team (hence the nicknames Colts and Orphans). At the age of 24, Danny won 18 games for Chicago in 1896. He was the Opening Day starter for the team that year, one of their youngest Opening Day starters ever. He led the league in one category that season — he hit 39(!) batters.

Historical note: On the day the U.S. Supreme Court reaffirmed the Jim Crow laws in the south as legal (1896), Friend and his teammates lost a 7-0 shutout to the Giants.

Owen Friend 1927–2007 (Cubs 1955-1956)

Owen played five seasons in the big leagues during the 1950s, the last two of which were with the Cubs. The backup infielder got a grand total of twelve trips to the plate in those two seasons, and struck out five times. Red, as he was called by his teammates, went on to play in the minor leagues until 1964.

Frankie Frisch 1898–1973 (Cubs manager 1949-1951)

Frankie Frisch was nicknamed the Fordham Flash because he attended Fordham and he was a big base stealer during his playing career (1919-1937). Frisch is a Hall of Famer as a player, and a World Series champ as a player/manager with the St. Louis Cardinals in 1934 (he also won 3 other series as a player). But the Fordham Flash had no chance as a manager of the simply terrible late 40s, early 50s Cubs. He was warned not to take the job by everyone before it was offered, but he took it anyway, and crashed and burned. His teams finished 8th, 7th, and 8th. He was fired after he was caught reading a novel in the dugout DURING a game. It turned out to be his last managing job.

Woody Fryman 1940–2011 (Cubs 1978)

Fryman was already in his 12th season in the big leagues (and had been a two-time All-Star) when he arrived in Chicago. The Cubs acquired him for starting pitcher Bill Bonham. Woody got off to a slow start with the Cubs, and by June they figured he was washed up at age 38. They traded him to the Montreal Expos, and wouldn't you know it, Fryman pitched another six seasons. In his career, Woody played 18 seasons, won 141 games, and fielded his position about as well as it could be fielded. He had three seasons with no errors at all, and his lifetime fielding percentage of .988 is the sixth best in history. After his playing career, Woody retired to his native Kentucky and passed away in 2011.

Oscar Fuhr 1893–1975 (Cubs 1921)

Fuhr made the Cubs out of spring training in 1921. The lefty looked like he had the goods. *The Sporting News* thought he would be the next Grover Cleveland Alexander. He wasn't. He pitched exactly one game for the Cubs and was rocked. He gave up eleven hits and nine runs in only four innings, and was sent to the minors after the game. Fuhr later pitched for the Red Sox (with similar results)

Kyuji Fujikawa 1980– (Cubs 2013)

Fujikawa was brought in from the Japanese league to be the Cubs closer. He had incredible success in Japan, saving 220 games for Hanshin. Unfortunately for Kyuji and the Cubs, he developed arm problems early in his first season in Chicago. He has only pitched in a handful of games since.

Kosuke Fukudome 1977– (2008-2011)

When Kosuke arrived in 2008, he was hailed as the savior. The Cubs had outbid several other teams also trying to sign the Japanese League batting champion. At first, he looked pretty good. Kosuke homered on Opening Day to tie up the game in the bottom of the ninth, hordes of Japanese media members followed him wherever he went, and Fukudome was named to the All-Star team. After that, reality set in. Kosuke couldn't handle the outside pitch and would corkscrew himself into the ground trying to reach it. He completely disappeared in the 2008 playoffs, going 1 for 10. Fukudome averaged about 10 homers and 40 RBI in his time with the Cubs, and never hit better than .263.

Sam Fuld 1981– (Cubs 2007-2010)

Sam was a crowd favorite in his limited playing time with the Cubs, mainly because of his take-no-prisoners style of outfield defense. The fans loved the way he flung himself toward the ball. He wasn't a bad hitter either. In his longest stretch of playing time in 2009, Fuld hit .299. It was enough to attract the attention of the Rays, who asked for Sam to be included in the trade package that brought Matt Garza to the Cubs. Fuld has since also played for Oakland and Minnesota. He has stolen more than 20 bases in a season twice since he left Chicago.

Fred Fussell 1895–1966 (Cubs 1922-1923)

Fussell may not have been a great big leaguer with the Cubs (4-6 with an ERA over five), but he had one of the all-time great nicknames. His teammates called him "Moonlight Ace" because he once threw a no-hitter at night in the minor leagues.

Mike Fyhrie 1969– (Cubs 2001)

Mike appeared in 15 games for the Cubs in 2001, but was traded to Oakland midseason that year. He pitched for four different teams (Mets, Angels, Cubs, A's) in his five-year career, and also pitched a season in both Japan and Korea.

*Additional Entries...*If you check out the Every Cub Ever feature at www. justonebadcentury.com, you'll find several additional entries, including celebrity Cubs fans, writers, and bloggers. Under the letter F, you'll discover actors Dennis Farina and Dennis Franz (both huge Cubs fans), plus Cubs blogger Neil Finnell, and Cubs songwriter Johnny Frigo.

CHAPTER SEVEN

G

The starting lineup for your Chicago Cubs beginning with the letter G...

C—Joe Garagiola, Hall of Famer (as a broadcaster)
1B—Mark Grace, 90s Hits Leader
2B—Mark Grudzielanek, 2003 Cub
SS—Nomar Garciaparra, Injured Soccer Husband
3B—Gary Gaetti, One Season Wonder
LF—Luis Gonzalez, World Series champ (for another team)
CF—Augie Galan, All-Star
RF— George Gore, Piano Legs
Bench— Oscar Gambel, Rookie Afro
Bench—Charlie Grimm, Jolly Cholly
Bench—Ray Grimes, Rookie Phenom
SP—Clark Griffith, the Old Fox
SP—Burleigh Grimes, Hall of Famer
RP—Tom Gordon, the Flash
RP—Goose Gossage, Hall of Famer

Gabe Gabler 1930–2014 (Cubs 1958)

Gabler was a power hitter during his 11-year minor league career, but he only got one shot at the big-time with the 1958 Cubs. He was used as a pinch hitter three times. His first time up he struck out in the 10th inning of a game in Philadelphia. The Cubs won it later that inning. His second shot came in the seventh inning of a game at Wrigley Field against the Dodgers. Gabe struck out. And in his final at-bat in the big leagues (also against the Dodgers at Wrigley), Gabe was brought in as a pinch hitter in the bottom of the ninth against former Cub Johnny Klippstein. There was no joy in Wrigley, as the mighty Gabler struck out again.

Len Gabrielson 1940–(Cubs 1964-1965)

Gabrielson had one of the best seasons of his nine-year career with the Cubs in 1964. After Lou Brock was traded in June of that season, Len became the team's starting right fielder. It was just a tiny bit of a downgrade for the Cubs. Brock hit .348 for the Cardinals (and led them to the World Series), and Gabrielson hit .246 for the Cubs (and led them to 8th place). Len's father (also named Len) was a big leaguer too. He played for the Phillies in 1939.

Gary Gaetti 1958–(Cubs 1998-1999)

The Cubs acquired the former World Series champ (Twins) for the stretch run in 1998. Gaetti came through with clutch hit after clutch hit. In only 27 games he hit 8 homers and batted .320. Unfortunately, he disappeared in the playoffs against the Braves. The Cubs gave him a shot to be their third baseman the following year too, but the lightning had been let out of the bottle. The 40-year-old was out of gas. He hit only .204 in over 300 plate appearances in 1999.

Phil Gagliano 1941–2016 (Cubs 1970)

Gagliano played 12 seasons in the big leagues (including 1970 with the Cubs), but he never claimed a starting job in all that time. The infielder played a little first, second, and third base for Chicago in 26 games, and hit .150. He passed away in 2016, one month after the Cubs ended the 108-year drought. His brother Ralph also played briefly for the Yankees.

Augie Galan 1912–1993 (Cubs 1934-1941)

Augie was the leadoff man on the Cubs team that set the all-time record by winning 21 games in a row in 1935. He was the hottest hitter of all the Cubs during the streak. Augie hit 5 of his 12 home runs that season and batted an astounding .358 to finish the season at .314. There were only two games he didn't reach base. But after carrying the team on his back to win the pennant, Galan didn't have a good World Series against the Tigers. He hit only .160. In 1936, Augie was an All-Star. In 1937, he led the league in stolen bases, and in 1938 he was a part of the pennant winners as well. But despite his many heroics in a Cubs uniform, the Cubs traded Augie to the Dodgers in 1941. Galan still had plenty left in the tank. He played another eight seasons of big league ball for the Dodgers, Reds, Giants, and A's.

Sean Gallagher 1985– (Cubs 2007)

Gallagher was brought up for a trial with the Cubs as a 21-year-old rookie, and was hit pretty hard. In 14.2 innings he gave up 14 runs and walked 12. The Cubs threw him in the deal for Rich Harden (along with future All-Star Josh Donaldson) in 2009. Gallagher later pitched for the A's, Padres, and Pirates.

Oscar Gamble 1949–2018 (Cubs 1969)

Gamble was only 19 years old when he was included in the trade for Johnny Callison. How did that trade turn out for the Cubs? Gamble played in the majors until 1985, and hit 200 home runs. Of those 200 home runs, only one of them came for the Cubs (in his rookie season of 1969). Gamble starred for the Indians, White Sox (their Southside Hit Men year of 1977), Padres, and Rangers, and went on to play in the World Series for the Yankees. Gamble hit .358 for them in 1979. Oscar was well-known for his incredible afro. Imagine if the Cubs had kept him and he and Jose Cardenal shared corner outfield spots. That would have been the best fro-outfield in baseball history.

Bill Gannon 1873–1927 (Orphans 1901)

Gannon was a career minor leaguer who got one cup of coffee in the big leagues in 1901. He was a 28-year-old rookie outfielder who filled in for future Hall of Famer Frank Chance (who hadn't yet been moved to first base). Gannon went back to the minors after the season, and played baseball until 1907. His story does not have a happy ending, however. In 1927, Bill Gannon committed suicide in Fort Worth, Texas.

John Ganzel 1874–1959 (Orphans 1900)

Ganzel was a first baseman on the 1900 Cubs (then known as the Orphans). He hit .275 and drove 32 runs, but was better known for his glove work. He later played for the Giants, Yankees (where he hit the first HR in franchise history), and Reds. His brother Charlie and nephew Babe also both played big league ball. After his playing days, he became a big league manager with the Reds.

Joe Garagiola 1926–2016 (Cubs 1953-1954)

Joe was a backup catcher for most of his nine-year big league career, and that's the role he served in Chicago. His big claim to fame with the Cubs was catching all nine innings of a game in what was at the time the hottest day in Chicago history, June 20, 1953. Despite the 104 degree heat, 17,000+ fans came out to Wrigley Field to see the Cubs lose to the Dodgers 5-3. Of course, Joe became much more famous after his playing career as a sportscaster and television personality. He is in the "Scribes & Mikemen" section of baseball's Hall of Fame because of his legendary broadcasting career. He passed away in 2016.

Bob Garbark 1909–1990 (Cubs 1937-1939)

Garbark was a backup catcher in the big leagues for seven seasons, three of which were with the Cubs. Of course, he was backing up Hall of Famer Gabby Hartnett at the time, so Bob didn't get a lot of playing time. He appeared in 48 games over three seasons, and didn't get a single extra base hit. He later played for the A's and the Red Sox. Bob was also an All-American football player in college.

Rich Garces 1971– (Cubs 1995)

Rich only pitched for the Cubs for two months in 1995. He appeared in seven games and posted a 3.27 ERA. Garces was nicknamed "El Guapo" by former teammate Mike Maddux because he looked like the villain in the movie *The Three Amigos*. After he left the Cubs he became a pretty good reliever for the Red Sox. He pitched in the big leagues until 2002.

Jaime Garcia 1986– (Cubs 2018)

The Cubs probably figured that Garcia was worth a flyer when he was released by the Blue Jays in August of 2018. They signed the 4-time 10-game-plus winner for the remainder of the season. Garcia appeared in eight games and posted a 4.70 ERA.

Nomar Garciaparra 1973– (Cubs 2004-2005)

The Red Sox shocked the world when they traded their five-time All-Star and two-time batting champion to the Cubs as part of a four-team trade in 2004. It seemed like the Cubs made a great trade. They gave up their shortstop that had made a critical error the year before (Alex Gonzalez) and a few other minor prospects, for one of the best hitters in the American League. Red Sox nation was very upset by the trade (made by Theo Epstein, by the way), and Chicago gave Nomar a standing ovation his first time up to bat. His wife (Mia Hamm) became a regular at Wrigley Field that summer. So what happened? The Red Sox won the World Series. And the Cubs? They blew a big lead in the closing week of the season to miss the playoffs completely. The following season Nomar suffered a horrible injury (tearing his groin) and missed most of the year. Despite a very warm welcome and a fan base that was rooting for him, it never worked out for Nomar in Chicago. In 2006, he signed as a free agent with the Dodgers, where he had his final All-Star season.

Jim Gardner 1874–1905 (Orphans 1902)

The 28-year-old was only given three starts. He completed two of them. Those were the last two appearances of his big league career. He also played in the field earlier in his career (2B, 3B, OF) for Pittsburgh. Gardner's last game in Chicago was the same week future mayor Richard J. Daley was born.

Rob Gardner 1944–(Cubs 1967)

Gardner was a lefty reliever who pitched for seven different teams in his eight-year big league career. One of those teams was the 1967 Cubs. Gardner appeared in 18 games and posted an ERA of 3.98. The Cubs traded him to the Indians after the season. He also pitched for the Mets, Yankees, A's, and Brewers.

Daniel Garibay 1973–(Cubs 2000)

Garibay was born and raised in Mexico, and didn't get his first shot at Major League Baseball until he was 27 years old. The Cubs used him as a spot starter and a reliever, and he didn't do well in either role. He went 2-8 with an ERA over six.

Mike Garman 1949–(Cubs 1976)

Garman was the third overall pick in the 1967 draft by the Red Sox (right before John Matlack). He was acquired by the Cubs from the Cardinals for Don Kessinger after the 1975 season, and spent one full season in the Cubs bullpen. Garman had a few good years in the big leagues,

including the year before (10 saves) and year after (12 saves) his time with the Cubs, but he couldn't hack it in Chicago. He appeared in 47 games, and his ERA hovered around five. He was part of the package (along with Rick Monday) that brought Bill Buckner and Iván de Jesus to Chicago from Los Angeles.

Adrian Garrett 1943–(Cubs 1970, 1973-1975)

Garrett was primarily used as a pinch hitter because he had a lot of power. He hit 280 homers in the minors, 102 in Japan and four with the Cubs. His little brother Wayne was a member of the 1969 Miracle Mets.

Cecil Garriot 1916–1990 (Cubs 1946)

Cecil's only shot in the big leagues came as a September call-up for the Cubs in 1946. He batted six times — always as a pinch hitter — and didn't get a hit. He was hit by a pitch in one of those at-bats, however, and scored his only big league run. Cecil played 16 seasons in the minors. He served in the Army during World War II.

Ned Garvin 1874–1908 (Orphans 1899-1900)

Ned pitched for seven seasons in the big leagues, including the Cubs (then known as the Orphans) at the turn of the 20th century. His two seasons in Chicago were probably the best of his career, even though he finished with a losing record. Garvin isn't remembered for his baseball play as much as his off-field troubles. He was a violent man. Ned shot a saloon keeper, was implicated in the attempted murder of a black man in a barber shop, attacked an insurance salesman, and was kicked out of the National League for attacking the team's traveling secretary. He died of tuberculosis at the age of 34. His nickname was the Navasota Tarantula, because he hailed from Navasota, Texas.

Matt Garza 1983–(Cubs 2011-2013)

Garza was a stud starting pitcher who had pitched a no-hitter and led his Tampa Rays to the World Series before he joined the Cubs. Matt was acquired for several prospects prior to the 2011 season, including Chris Archer (who has turned out to be a very good pitcher) and Sam Fuld. Unfortunately, Garza never could put it together for Chicago. He had flashes of brilliance, and rashes of arm injuries. He was 6-1 in 2013 when the Cubs traded him to the Rangers for four prospects in 2013. Two of those prospects played for the Cubs in 2014 and 2015: Mike Olt and Neil Ramirez. The other two pitched even longer in the Cubs bullpen: Justin Grimm and Carl Edwards Jr.

Charlie Gassaway 1918–1992 (Cubs 1944)

They called him the Sheriff. Charlie pitched for the Cubs during the war season of 1944, and it didn't go well. In two appearances covering 11.2 innings, he allowed a massive 30 baserunners. He later pitched for the A's and Indians.

Ed Gastfield 1865–1899 (White Stockings 1885)

Ed was only 19 years old when he played for the Cubs (then known as the White Stockings) on July 11, 1885. The team was on its way to a championship, and Ed was a one-day replacement at catcher. He went 0 for 3. The following season he played in the minors up in Wisconsin, but his baseball career was essentially over by time he was 21. Ed didn't live to see the turn of the century. He died in Chicago in 1899 at the age of 34.

Joey Gathright 1981–(Cubs 2009)

Gathright was a speedster who stole nearly 80 bases in the five seasons before coming to the Cubs (in limited playing time). With the Cubs his playing time was even more limited. They just couldn't find a spot to play him, so they traded him to the Orioles for Ryan Freel in May of 2009.

John Gaub 1985–(Cubs 2011)

The Cubs picked up John in the Mark DeRosa trade to the Indians on New Year's Eve 2008 (along with pitcher Chris Archer and Jeff Stevens). Gaub was a major leaguer for exactly two weeks in September of 2011. He pitched out of the bullpen for the Cubs as a situational lefty. In four appearances he pitched a total of 2.2 innings and gave up two runs. By 2013 he was out of baseball and studying for his business degree.

Chad Gaudin 1983–(Cubs 2008)

The Cubs acquired Chad in the trade that brought Rich Harden to the team in July of 2008 (for Matt Murton and Eric Patterson). While Harden showed flashes of brilliance, Gaudin did not. He was hit hard, and hit often. His ERA with Chicago was 6.26. The Cubs released him the following April thinking his career was done, but Gaudin surprised everyone. He has since pitched for the Padres, A's, Nationals, Marlins, Giants, and Yankees. That 2009 Yankees team won the World Series.

Chippy Gaw 1892–1968 (Cubs 1920)

One of the greatest names in baseball history — Chippy Gaw — pitched only briefly for the Cubs. After logging nearly ten years in the minors, he got into six big league games in 1920, mainly as a reliever. In his last Major League appearance on July 4, 1920, he came in to relieve Cubs great Hippo Vaughn. He pitched a third of an inning and didn't allow a run. He pitched a few more years in the minors before hanging up his spikes for good in 1922. After his playing career was over, Chippy went into coaching…hockey. He was the head hockey coach at both Princeton and Dartmouth, and later also coached Boston University's baseball team. His real first name, by the way, was George.

Historical note: On the day Warren Harding was named the Republican nominee for U.S. President (1920) in Chicago's Blackstone Hotel, Chippy came in to pitch seven-plus innings after starter Speed Martin couldn't get out of the first inning. Cubs lost 8-3 to the Pirates.

Dave Geisel 1955–(Cubs 1978-1981)

Geisel pitched for the Cubs for three seasons, and later also pitched for the Blue Jays and Mariners. In seven big league seasons, the lefty reliever won five and saved five games.

Emil Geiss 1867–1911 (White Stockings 1887)

Emil was a 20-year-old Chicago boy who got exactly one big league start, and that came for his beloved hometown Cubs (then known as the White Stockings) on May 18, 1887. He took the mound against the Washington Nationals (that's what they were called in the 1880s) in Washington. Young Emil went the distance, but he gave up 17 hits and 11 runs, and the White Stockings lost the game 11-4. Emil knocked around the minors a few years after that, but never got another shot at the big-time. He passed away in Chicago in 1911 at the way-too-young age of 44.

Greek George 1912–1999 (Cubs 1941)

His real first name was Charles, but the Greek-American was called Greek his whole career. The backup catcher played one season for the Cubs in 1941. He also played for the Indians, Dodgers, and Athletics in his big league career. His big league career ended a bit prematurely in 1945 when he was with the Athletics. He punched an umpire, and never played in the big leagues again.

Dave Gerard 1936–2001 (Cubs 1962)

Gerard was a right-handed reliever, and he pitched for the Cubs during the 1962 season. In 39 appearances, he saved three games and won two more for one of the worst Cubs teams of all-time. That was his only season in the big leagues. The Cubs traded him to Houston after the season. He pitched in the minors for Houston and Pittsburgh for nearly ten years before hanging up his spikes.

George Gerberman 1942–(Cubs 1962)

George got exactly one big league start, and it came for the Cubs on September 23rd. The location was the Polo Grounds, and the opponent was the worst team in big league history, the 1962 New York Mets. Gerberman lasted into the sixth inning and got a no-decision, although the Cubs eventually lost their 100th game of the season in the ninth. George walked five batters, but gave up only three hits. One of those hits was a home run by former Cub Frank Thomas. Gerberman's only strikeout victim was future Cub Jim Hickman. George was only 20 years old at the time, but he never got another chance in the big leagues. He remained in the minors until 1968.

> ***German Cubs.*** Cubs throw the best Oktoberfest parties. All of these Cubs were born in Germany...Heinz Becker (Berlin), Ed Eiteljorge (Berlin), Edwin Jackson (Neu-Ulm), Jack Katoll (unknown town), Marty Krug (Koblenz), Craig Lefferts (Munich), Joe Miller (unknown town), Fritz Mollwitz (Coberg), Will Ohman (Frankfurt), Dave Pavlas (Frankfurt), Skel Roach (Danzig), and Reggie Richter (Dusseldorf).

Justin Germano 1982–(Cubs 2012)

The Cubs picked up Germano from the Red Sox organization during the summer of 2012 and he was given a chance to make the rotation. He started twelve games and went 2-10 with a 6.75 ERA. Needless to say, he didn't make it. The Cubs let him go after the season and he since pitched for Toronto and Texas.

Gonzalez Germen 1987–(Cubs 2015)

The Cubs picked up Germen when the Rangers waived him in January of 2015. They saw the Dominican reliever as a promising prospect, but after getting knocked around a few times, he was designated for assignment in early May. Germen had previously had a cup of coffee with the Mets in 2013 and 2014 and threw smoke. Early season injuries to Cubs relievers brought him to the big leagues with the Cubs in April. He was released in July and finished the season with the Colorado Rockies.

Dick Gernert 1928–2017 (Cubs 1960)

He was the nephew of fellow Cub Dim Dom Dallessandro. Gernert had a few good years with the Red Sox before coming to the Cubs. The outfielder/first baseman had 100 career homers on his resume when he arrived at Wrigley Field. Unfortunately for the Cubs, he didn't hit any for the Cubs in 96 at-bats, and was sold by August of 1960. His final career homer came the following year for the Tigers. Gernert later worked in the front office for the Mets and Rangers.

Jody Gerut 1977–(Cubs 2005)

The Cubs acquired the local boy (Willowbrook) from the Indians midseason. He was one of seven or eight players to get a shot at the left field job. One of those left fielders (Jason Dubois) was the player traded to Cleveland for Gerut. In his first 14 at-bats, Jody got one hit (an .071 average), and was shipped off to Pittsburgh for another possibility — Matt Lawton. Jody also played for the Padres and Brewers before hanging it up after the 2010 season.

Doc Gessler 1880–1924 (Cubs 1906)

Everyone called him Doc, but the already-nicknamed youngster was also called Brownie. The Cubs acquired him to be a backup outfielder/first baseman in 1906, and he became part of the all-time winningest team in history. He even got a few at-bats in the 1906 World Series against the White Sox. Unfortunately for Doc, he was traded in 1907 in a bizarre revenge trade. Cubs player/manager Frank Chance was so ticked off at Reds pitcher Jack Harper for beaning him so many times, he acquired him just to punish him. Doc is the man he had to give up to get Harper. Harper was sent to the end of the bench with the Cubs, and was never allowed to pitch — effectively ending his career. Doc played five years in the big leagues for Boston and Pittsburgh.

Cubs players have had some great nicknames over the years. Among players starting with the letter G, you'll find nicknames like Brownie, Chippy, Doc, El Guapo, Flash, Gee Gee, Gonzo, Goose, Greek, Jolly Cholly, Lefty, Lucky, Old Fox, Ol' Mate, Ol' Stubblebeard, Patcheye, Peaches, Piano Legs, and Sheriff.

George Gibson 1880–1967 (Cubs manager 1925)

As a player, George was a World Series-winning catcher for the Pittsburgh Pirates, and his nickname was Moon. As a manager he was brought in to replace the highly volatile Rabbit Maranville on the Cubs. Gibson had a slightly different style than the hyperactive shortstop with a flask in his uniform, but it didn't work much better with the 1925 Cubs. That team still managed to finish in last place for the first time in franchise history. As we all know, it wasn't the last time. Gibson went on to manage the Pirates.

Robert Gibson 1869–1949 (Colts 1890)

Don't let anyone tell you that Bob Gibson never pitched for the Cubs. Robert Gibson did indeed pitch for Chicago. In 1890, the team was still known as the Colts, and the 20-year-old Gibson pitched a complete game on August 7th. It was his only appearance in a Chicago uniform.

Norm Gigon 1938–2013 (Cubs 1967)

Norm was a utility man for the Cubs in 1967. He played second base, third base, and outfield. On April 23, he hit the only home run of his big league career. It came off Pirates starting pitcher (and future Cub) Juan Pizarro in a 7-3 Cubs (Fergie Jenkins) win.

Charlie Gilbert 1919–1983 (Cubs 1941-1946)

It wasn't Charlie's fault that he was part of the trade that sent fan favorite Billy Herman to the Dodgers in 1941. But Cub fans never let him forget it. While Herman was leading the Dodgers to the World Series, Charlie was hitting a whopping .184. Charlie's time with the Cubs was interrupted by his military service in World War II. He missed their entire pennant-winning season of 1945.

Johnny Gill 1905–1984 (Cubs 1935-1936)

His teammates called him "Patcheye." Johnny didn't wear a patch over his eye, although he must have at least once, because the nickname "Patcheye" stuck with him throughout his career. He was a minor league lifer, playing more than 23 seasons. He was one of those players that would be considered a 4A player today — too good for the minors (lifetime average over .320, with nearly 300 homers), but just not quite good enough for the big leagues. Gill got a few cups of coffee in the show before coming to the Cubs in their pennant-winning season of 1935 (in 1927 and 1928 with Cleveland, and 1931 and 1934 with the Senators), but he never had more than 69 at-bats in a season. He got a whopping three at-bats in 1935 for the Cubs. Patcheye stayed with the team as a backup outfielder in 1936 (backing up Augie Galan, Frank Demaree, Ethan Allen) and got the longest look of his big league career that season. He made the most of it, hitting 7 homers in only 174 at-bats. Unfortunately for Gill, that turned out to be the swan song of his major league career. Johnny Gill didn't even make it back to the bigs during the war era, though he was playing in the minors that whole time (in Portland). He retired as a player (from the minors) after the 1947 season, and then managed the minor league team in his hometown of Nashville, Tennessee.

Cole Gillespie 1984– (Cubs 2013)

The Cubs took a flyer on this outfielder after he was waived by the Giants. He appeared in 25 games, but didn't really show the Cubs that he was worth keeping on the roster. After the season he was given his release. He has since played for Toronto and Seattle.

Paul Gillespie 1920–1970 (Cubs 1942-1945)

He was a big strong boy, just off a two-year stint in the Coast

Guard, when he rejoined the Cubs as their only left-handed hitting catcher in 1944. He was a real contributor during their pennant-winning season of 1945. At 6'3, 195 pounds, Paul was an imposing figure in the batter's box. He hit .288 and knocked in 25 runs in 75 games, and even got a shot at playing in the World Series (he went 0 for 6), but he never played in the big leagues again.

Historical note: On the day Americans dropped the atom bomb on Nagasaki (1945), Gillespie had one of his best days at the plate, knocking in two runs in a loss to Boston.

Henry Gilroy 1852-1907 (White Stockings 1874)

Henry played catcher and right field for the club two years before Chicago joined the National League. He only got into eight games, and had a total of eight hits.

Chris Gimenez 1982–(Cubs 2018)

Chris was signed because he was Yu Darvish's catcher in LA, but Yu never really pitched in 2018, which immediately diminished his usefulness. Gimenez was the backup catcher for a month or two, but when he relayed Darvish's fears that Chicago didn't love him, he was released shortly thereafter.

Joe Girardi 1964–(1989-1992, 2000-2002)

Girardi was a rookie catcher on the Cubs team that surprised everyone and won their division in 1989. Even in his younger days he was seen as a calm force on the team. The Northwestern Grad (and Peoria native) seemed to really enjoy playing in his home state. But the Cubs left him unprotected in the 1993 expansion draft, and Joe was drafted by the Rockies. He didn't really make a name for himself, however, until he joined the Yankees in 1996. Girardi was the starting catcher of the team that won the World Series in 1996 and in 1998, and backed up Jorge Posada for the 1999 World Series champs. The following year Joe returned to the Cubs and made his first All-Star team. All of the players looked up to him, and he became the spokesperson for a team that featured the likes of Sammy Sosa. When Darryl Kile of the Cardinals died tragically in 2002 (the night before a Cubs-Cards game), it was Joe who stepped to the microphone to pay tribute to Kile in front of the Wrigley Field crowd. Girardi has since become a big league manager and won another World Series title in that role with the Yankees in 2009.

Historical note: On the day Iraq invaded Kuwait, which eventually led to American involvement in the Gulf War (1990), Girardi had a great day at the plate for the Cubs. He was 3 for 5, but the Cubs still lost 8-5 to Pittsburgh.

Dave Giusti 1939–(Cubs 1977)

Giusti won 100 games and saved 145 more in his outstanding career, including 30 in his All-star 1971 season, when he led the Pirates to the World Series. By the time he came to the Cubs, however, he was a whisper of what he once was. He did get one save in 20 appearances, but his ERA was two and a half runs higher than his career average. It was the last gasp of his big league career.

Lucky Glade 1876–1934 (Orphans 1902)

Glade had one start for the Cubs (then known as the Orphans) in 1902, and gave up eight runs in eight innings and took the loss. He got his nickname "Lucky" when he was with the St. Louis Browns in 1905. That year he made 32 starts and won only six of them. His final record that season was 6-25, despite having an ERA of only 2.81. Lucky never worried about it too much. He was a wealthy man from a wealthy family and he only played when he felt like it.

Doug Glanville 1970–(Cubs 1996-1997, 2003)

Glanville was a first round draft choice by the Cubs, and had a very respectable nine-year big league career. In his rookie season with the Cubs, he hit .300 and stole 19 bases. The Cubs took a big chance by trading him after the season to Phillies for Mickey Morandini. This is one of those trades that worked out for both teams. Morandini was a key member of the Cubs 1998 playoff team, while Glanville starred for the Phillies. He was an outstanding outfielder, and in 1999 he hit .325 and stole 34 bases. Towards the end of his career, Glanville was reacquired by Chicago for the stretch run of their 2003 playoff season. He had a few key hits, including a pinch hit RBI triple in the 2003 NLCS. He is now a broadcaster and a writer. He has written for the *New York Times* and the *Atlantic*, and is the author of T*he Game From Where I Stand* (2010).

Jim Gleeson 1912–1996 (Cubs 1939-1940)

The Cubs were reigning NL Champs when Gleeson joined

the team is (his teammates nicknamed him "Gee Gee"). Gleason got quite a bit of playing time in the outfield during his time in Chicago, including his best season in the big leagues, 1940. That year he was the team's starting center fielder and hit over .300. The Cubs traded him after the season and he finished his playing career in Cincinnati. Gee Gee later coached and scouted for several teams including the Yankees, and was the first base coach for the Yanks when they won the 1964 World Series.

Bob Glenalvin 1867–1944 (White Stockings 1890-1893)

Bob was the backup second baseman for the Cubs (then known as the White Stockings) in two different seasons, 1890 and 1893. In between those two years he played minor league ball in Los Angeles. After his playing days, he became a manager. Bob was the first-ever manager of the Detroit Tigers.

Ed Glenn 1875–1911 (Orphans 1902)

Glenn played in two games for the Cubs (then known as the Orphans) as a shortstop in June of 1902. He only reached base once (on a walk). It was his last shot at the big leagues. He was only 36 when he died after falling into a railroad pit.

John Glenn 1850–1888 (White Stockings 1876-1877)

Glenn was with the Cubs (then known as the White Stockings) before they joined the National League, and for the first two seasons in the NL. He was an outfielder/first baseman. Glenn hit zero homers in four seasons in Chicago. In 1888, just 11 seasons after he stopped playing big league baseball, Glenn died at the age of 38. He was shot by a policeman during an attempting lynching. Glenn was accused of raping a 12-year-old girl.

Ross Gload 1976– (Cubs 2000)

Ross was a power hitting 1B/OF the Cubs acquired from the Marlins for Henry Rodriguez. He only got one chance to show his power in the big leagues for the Cubs, and the sample size was probably a little too small. In just over 30 at-bats, he managed only one home run. The Rockies got him from the Cubs the following year, but Gload didn't really put it together until he joined the White Sox. In 2005 he was part of that White Sox championship team. Gload eventually put

together a very respectable 10-year big league career, which also included two playoff appearances for the Phillies (in 2010 and 2011).

Al Glossop 1914–1991 (Cubs 1946)

Al was a backup infielder for the Phillies, Dodgers, Giants, and Boston before coming to the Cubs in 1946. He got his only shot at starting in the big leagues during the war year of 1942. Unfortunately for Glossup, he hit only .225 for the Phillies that year and never got another chance. He was drafted into the Navy after that year and spent 1944 and 1945 in the Pacific. His stint with the Cubs in 1946 was his final gasp in the big leagues. In fourteen plate appearances as a Cub, he didn't get a single hit.

John Goetz 1937–2008 (Cubs 1960)

The 22-year-old broke camp with the Cubs in April of 1960, but didn't last long. By May he was back in the minors. Those four appearances he had for the Cubs in 1960 were the only ones of his career. He spent 11 seasons in the minor leagues.

Mike Golden 1851–1929 (White Stockings 1875)

Golden was born during the Millard Fillmore presidency, and started 14 games for the Cubs (then known as the White Stockings) the year before they officially joined the National League. His record was 6-7. As was common practice in those days, Mike also played in the outfield for another 27 games.

Historical note: On the day former president Andrew Johnson died (1875), Golden was on the mound for the White Stockings. Chicago lost the game 15-3.

Fred Goldsmith 1856–1939 (White Stockings 1880-1884)

Goldsmith was a great pitcher for the Cubs (then known as the White Stockings) during their early National League dynasty. He won 20 or more games four years in a row. Many baseball historians credit Fred as the inventor of the curveball. He is the first known person to have given a public demonstration of it (way back in 1870), and when he died, several baseball broadcasters and writers eulogized him as the "father of the curveball." Unfortunately for Goldsmith's legacy, another man was inducted into the Baseball Hall of Fame for that very thing — Goldsmith's old rival Candy Cummings.

Historical note: On the day President Garfield was shot by Charles Guiteau (1881), Goldsmith was on the mound. The White Stockings won the game 10-5 against Troy.

Walt Golvin 1894–1973 (Cubs 1922)

He got his cup of coffee with the Cubs early in the 1922 season as a 28-year-old rookie. The first baseman got two at-bats and didn't reach base either time. He played another three years in the minors after that, and retired for good at the age of 31.

Leo Gomez 1966–(Cubs 1996)

Leo was the starting third baseman for the Cubs in 1996. He hit 17 homers and played a respectable third base, but he swung and missed (94 strikeouts) more often than he swung and hit (86 hits). After the season the Cubs let him go. Before coming to the Cubs, Leo played five seasons with the Orioles.

Preston Gomez 1923–2009 (Cubs manager 1980)

Two days before Pope John Paul II landed in Chicago in 1979, the Cubs announced the name of their new manager: Preston Gomez. Gomez' track record included one of the worst winning percentages in baseball history (.392). He had managed for the Padres and the Astros and was a colossal failure both times. Needless to say the same thing happened with the Cubs. He didn't make it through the entire 1980 season before he was fired. The Cubs were 39-51 at the time.

Alberto Gonzalez 1983–(Cubs 2013)

Alberto began the 2013 season with the Cubs as a backup infielder, but was traded to the Yankees in May. He's currently in the San Diego Padres organization.

Alex Gonzalez 1973–(Cubs 2002-2004)

Gonzalez was the starting shortstop with the Cubs during his years in Chicago and had more than his share of big games. His game-winning homers were the stuff of legend. But despite the good moments, he'll always be remembered for muffing an easy double play ball immediately after the infamous Steve Bartman moment in the 2003 playoffs. If he had made that play, the Cubs almost certainly would have made it to the 2003 World Series. In fairness to Gonzalez, they might not have even been in that spot if not for his

hitting heroics. In that NLCS series he hit three homers and drove in seven runs.

Geremi Gonzalez 1975–2008 (Cubs 1997-1998)

When he pitched for the Cubs, his first name was incorrectly spelled Jeremi. He didn't bother to correct the record until later in his career. Gonzalez won 11 games for the Cubs as a rookie, and it looked like they had a rotation mainstay. It didn't quite turn out that way. He never regained the form of his rookie season. He later pitched for the Rays, Red Sox, Mets, and Brewers. Gonzalez died suddenly at the age of 33, when he was hit by lightning and killed in his native Venezuela (2008).

Luis Gonzalez 1967–(Cubs 1995-1996)

Luis Gonzalez obviously got his nickname from his last name, because he already had it when he was on the Cubs, and he obviously didn't hit like a Gonzo in Chicago (22 home runs in his 1 ½ years with the team). It's not as if Gonzo's Cubs career was a total flop, however. He was acquired mid-season in 1995 (along with catcher Scott Servais), and helped lead the team to a surprising third place finish that strike-shortened season. In 1996, he had a very solid season (15 HR, 79 RBI, .271 Ave), but because he was a corner outfielder, the Cubs felt they needed more power out of that position and allowed him to leave via free agency. Ironically, Gonzo discovered his power stroke very soon after leaving Chicago. He hit 23 HRs for the Tigers in 1998, and then really blossomed in 2001, when he hit 57 home runs and finished 3rd in the MVP voting. He also got the game-winning hit in Game 7 of the World Series that year. Still, Gonzo enjoyed his time in Chicago immensely. One of his most treasured possessions is a ball thrown to him before he filed for free agency in 1997, signed by Wrigley Field's bleachers bums.

Mike Gonzalez 1890–1977 (Cubs 1925-1929)

The Cuban catcher was a trailblazer in baseball. He was the first Latin-American to ever play for the Cubs. The 35-year-old veteran provided some stability backing up young stud catcher Gabby Hartnett. Mike (real name Miguel) got his only World Series at-bat with the Cubs in 1929. Before coming to the Cubs, he also caught for the Braves, Reds, Cardinals, and Giants. He played in the big leagues for twenty years and coached and scouted many more after his playing career ended. He is said to have coined the term "Good field, no hit" when he was a scout.

Raul Gonzalez 1973 – (Cubs 2000)

The Puerto Rican outfielder made his big league debut in a Cubs uniform in May of 2000, but he only got two at-bats with the Cubs and struck out both times. He later played for the Reds, Mets, and Indians.

Wilbur Good 1885 – 1963 (Cubs 1911-1915)

Wilbur came to the Cubs in the trade that sent popular catcher Johnny Kling to Boston. His nickname was "Lefty" and he played for the Cubs in the years after their dynasty (1906-1910) and before their move to Wrigley Field (1916). Good was a backup outfielder his first few years in Chicago (he hit the first pinch hit HR in Cubs history in 1913), before being given the full-time right field job in 1914. Wilbur responded by stealing more than 30 bases and hitting .272. Those numbers went down the following year, and when the Cubs moved across town to Wrigley Field (then known as Weeghman Park), Wilbur was not invited to join them. He was sold to the Phillies. Good holds the distinction of being the very last player to hit a homer at West Side Grounds. It came on September 29, 1915 in a 5-4 victory over the Braves. Think of Wilbur on Groundhog Day. He's the only Cub ever born in Punxatawney, Pennsylvania.

Ival Goodman 1908 – 1984 (Cubs 1943-1944)

He was known as "Goodie" or "Ol' Mate" and was a two-time All-Star who hit 30 homers one season for the Reds. He also led them to a 1940 World Series title. By the time he was roaming the Wrigley Field outfield during the war, Goodie was no longer that goodie. He was strictly a fourth outfielder for the Cubs. His power was completely gone. In two full seasons, he hit four homers.

Curtis Goodwin 1972 – (Cubs 1999)

Curtis was with the Cubs the first few months of the 1999 season. The speedy center fielder hit .242 in 175 plate appearances, but was put on waivers in August of that year. He previously had two good 20+ stolen base seasons with the Orioles and the Reds. 1999 was his last season in the big leagues.

Tom Goodwin – (Cubs 2003-2004)

Goodwin was a speedster for the Dodgers, Royals, Rockies, Rangers, and Giants before joining the Cubs at age 34. His speed wasn't quite what it once was, but Goodwin was nevertheless an important outfield reserve during the division-winning 2003 season. He stole 24 of 369 career stolen bases with the Cubs. When the Cubs released him after the 2004 season, his playing career was over. He remains in baseball as a coach.

Mike Gordon 1953 – 2014 (Cubs 1977-1978)

Gordon came up with the Cubs a few times as an emergency catcher, but he only got into twelve games over two seasons. Gordon came up to bat 35 times and only got two hits. He passed away in 2014 after a long bout with leukemia.

Tom Gordon 1967 – (Cubs 2001-2002)

Flash, as he was known, had a stellar big league career as a starter and a reliever. He was predominantly a starter for the Royals at the beginning of his career, including six seasons with double-digit wins. The Red Sox converted him into a closer and he responded with an All-Star season and a league-leading 46 saves. Unfortunately, Gordon blew out his arm. When the Cubs acquired him as a free agent, it had been more than a year since he pitched. He repeated the Boston experience. His first year with the Cubs, Gordon was excellent. He saved 27 games. The following year he hurt his arm again. When the Cubs traded him to the Astros they thought he was pretty much finished. He wasn't. Flash pitched another six seasons for the White Sox, Yankees, Phillies, and Diamondbacks. His son Dee is an All-Star second baseman/outfielder.

George Gore 1854 – 1933 (White Stockings 1879-1886)

Gore had one of the greatest nicknames of all-time: they called him Piano Legs. George was the center fielder for the Cubs (then known as the White Stockings) during the team's longest period of excellence. During Gore's eight seasons, the team won the championship four times, including three years in a row (1880-1882). Piano Legs won a batting title (1880), hit over .300 six times, led the league in runs twice (1881-1882), and walks three times ('82, '84, '86), and still holds the club record for most steals in a game (7). But George was also known as a big drinker and hellraiser off the field, and ran into constant conflict with team manager/captain Cap Anson. After the 1886 season, when some of the "drunks" on the team didn't play up to their abilities in the World Series against St. Louis, Gore was shipped off to New York. (The others soon followed.) In Anson's book (which came out in 1900), he said that he saw Gore years later, and that his life had been ruined by "wine and women."

Terrance Gore 1991 – (Cubs 2018)
Gore set a career high in 2018 for at-bats (5) and hits (1 — his first) in a season, because he is mainly a base stealer. He got on base six times and stole six bases.

Hank Gornicki 1911 – 1996 (Cubs 1941)
Hank was acquired from the Cardinals. The Cubs pitched him in one game in 1941, didn't like what they saw, voided the deal, and sent him back to the Cardinals. The Pirates later gave him a longer shot in the big leagues, but his stint with that team was interrupted by his service in the war.

Johnny Goryl 1933 – (Cubs 1957-1959)
Johnny was a backup infielder (2B, 3B) for the Cubs in the late 50s. He got the most playing time in the 1958 season, when he hit four homers and hit .242 in over 200 at-bats. He later also played for the Minnesota Twins. After his playing career, he coached and managed for Minnesota, and worked in the front office for the Indians.

Tom Gorzelanny 1982 – (Cubs 2009-2010)
The homegrown pitcher (Marist High School) was acquired by the Cubs in the summer of 2009 when their starting rotation suffered a few injuries. He had pitched for the Pirates the previous 4 1/2 seasons, and had been a bit of a Cubs-killer. When he put on the Cubs uniform he had a few good outings, but never approached the success he had with Pittsburgh. The Cubs traded him to the Washington Nationals after the 2010 season.

Goose Gossage 1951 – (Cubs 1988)
He was so universally referred to by his nickname when he arrived in Chicago in 1988, even the baseball card makers (Fleer) didn't bother using his real first name anymore. (It was Rich.) Unfortunately for the Cubs, Rich got richer pitching for the Cubs only after his best days were behind him. He was signed to be the closer, but didn't quite have the stuff needed for the role. He managed only 13 saves (including the 300th of his career) in what turned out to be his last season as a full-time closer. The Cubs released him before the 1989 season. In 2008, Goose Gossage was inducted into baseball's Hall of Fame.

Billy Grabarkewitz 1946 – (Cubs 1974)
By the time the Cubs acquired the former All-Star second baseman in 1974, he was strictly a backup. He played for the Cubs part of the 1974 season. He was an All-Star with the Dodgers and also played for the Angels, Phillies, and A's.

John Grabow 1978 – (Cubs 2009-2011)
Grabow was a very effective left-handed reliever with the Pirates for several seasons, so the Cubs went out and got him via trade (along with Tom Gorzelany). As soon as he arrived in Chicago, however, Grabow started to get knocked around. He developed arm problems, and missed a good chunk of the 2010 season. His last year in the big leagues was with the Cubs in 2011. In retrospect, that wasn't a very good trade for the Cubs. They sent a few prospects to Pittsburgh in that deal, including future All-Star Josh Harrison.

Earl Grace 1907 – 1980 (Cubs 1929-1931)
Earl was a catcher who got a cup of coffee with the Cubs in two different seasons — 1929 and 1931. He was traded to the Pirates early in 1931 for fellow backup catcher Rollie Hemsley. Earl's best season was 1932 when he hit eight homers for the Pirates. Grace remained in the big leagues until 1937.

Mark Grace 1964 – (Cubs 1988-2000)
They called him Amazing Grace, after the song, and because of his amazing glove work around first base. Mark Grace anchored first for the Cubs for more than a decade and became one of Wrigley Field's fan favorites. He won four Gold Gloves, hit .300 nine times, led the league in doubles and at-bats per strikeout, and had more hits than any other player in the 1990s. He also saved his best for the most important

moments. In the 1989 NLCS vs. the Giants, Grace was on fire, hitting .647 and driving in eight runs. He also became a World Series champion…although sadly, after he left the Cubs. In the 2001 World Series, Grace hit a home run for the Diamondbacks, and later had a key at-bat in the ninth inning of the clinching game 7 in Arizona. After his playing career ended, he made a seamless transition to the broadcasting business. Unfortunately for Mark, that career ended when he was arrested and convicted of driving under the influence of alcohol.

Historical note: On the day the nation stood transfixed watching the slow-speed chase of OJ Simpson (1994), Grace knocked in the only Cubs run in a 6-1 loss against the Giants in Candlestick Park.

Peaches Graham 1877–1939 (Cubs 1903, 1911)

Peaches had two different stints with the Cubs. The first one was ever so brief. He pitched in one game in 1903, and got knocked around (nine hits, six runs). After spending five years in the minors, he re-emerged in the big leagues as a catcher in Boston. He had three-plus productive seasons there with the Braves before the Cubs reacquired him for Johnny Kling in June of 1911. Peaches was the main backup catcher (to Jimmy Archer) the rest of the season. His son Jack later played in the big leagues too (for the Dodgers, Giants, and Browns).

Alex Grammas 1926–(Cubs 1962-1963)

Grammas was a big league infielder for ten years, the last year and half of which were with the Cubs. He came to the Cubs (along with Don Landrum) from the Cardinals in the midst of the College of Coaches fiasco. The veteran glove man backed up young Cubs studs Ken Hubbs, Andre Rodgers, and Ron Santo. After his playing career he became a big league manager for the Pirates and Brewers.

Hank Grampp 1903–1986 (Cubs 1927-1929)

Grampp had a really unusual big league career. He was on the team's big league roster for three years and literally pitched every single day —but only because the team used him as their daily batting practice pitcher. Over those three seasons he appeared in only three big league games, and was rocked pretty badly. But what would you expect? He had

already thrown thousands of innings. Grampp wore his Cubs uniform for the final time during the 1929 World Series. He didn't appear in any of those games, but he was there throwing batting practice. Years later he was hired by the team as a scout.

Tom Grant 1957–(Cubs 1983)

Grant spent the entirety of his very brief big league career with the Cubs. The outfielder batted 20 times and got 3 hits. One of them was a double. In the last game of the 1983 season, in his last at-bat in the big leagues, Grant knocked in both of his career RBI. The Cubs still lost 9-6.

George Grantham 1900–1954 (Cubs 1923-1924)

In his two years as the Cubs starting 2B (1923, 1924), George led the league in strikeouts both years. He also led the league in being caught stealing. The Cubs traded him to the Pirates in the deal that brought Charlie Grimm to Chicago. Grantham had a good run in Pittsburgh. In his first season there he helped lead the team to a World Series title. He played with Pittsburgh for seven seasons before ending his career with the Reds and Giants.

Joe Graves 1906–1980 (Cubs 1926)

Joe played exactly one day in the big leagues, and it was for the Cubs on September 26, 1926, the last day of the season. He played third base in the first game of a double-header against Brooklyn and got one at-bat against Dazzy Vance (he didn't get on base). He started the second game of the double-header and went 0 for 4. The Cubs lost both games. His middle name was Ebenezer.

Jeff Gray 1981–(Cubs 2010)

The Cubs acquired him from the A's in the trade that sent Jake Fox and Aaron Miles to the A's. Gray appeared in 7 games for the Cubs in middle relief and didn't fare well. He allowed 17 baserunners in only nine innings pitched. He was released after the season. Gray later pitched for the White Sox, Mariners, and Twins.

Dallas Green 1934–2017 (Cubs GM 1982-1987)

Dallas Green may have been a pretty good judge of talent (he brought Maddux, Palmeiro, Sandberg, Dawson, Grace,

Smith, Moyer, Dunston, Sutcliffe, et al to the team), and he may have been gotten the Cubs as close to the World Series as anyone else did before Epstein, but he was also known for his prickly personality — not exactly the kind of personality you look for in a general manager. As a matter of fact, he had a ruthless streak. When he fired Billy Connors, a former Cubs pitcher and a widely respected pitching coach (after the 1986 season), he did it while Connors was in the hospital recovering from hip replacement surgery. According to the book *Cubs Journal*, Green pulled up to the hospital, left the car running, went up to Connors' room and fired him, and then came back down to his car and drove away. Dallas Green resigned just over a year later, on October 29, 1987. He might have been difficult to deal with, but there's no question that Green was one of the best general managers in Cubs history. In his post-baseball life, Dallas suffered an unspeakable tragedy. His granddaughter was one of the victims in the shooting spree that also injured congresswoman Gabrielle Giffords. Green passed away in March of 2017, just a few months after the Cubs finally did win it all.

Danny Green 1876–1914 (Orphans 1898-1902)

Green was a good hitting outfielder who always seemed to find a way to get on base. His lifetime on-base percentage was .359. After hitting .313 and stealing 31 bases for the 1902 Cubs (then known as the Orphans), he jumped to the upstart American League team across town — the White Sox. His last year in the big leagues was 1905 — the year before the Cubs-White Sox World Series.

Adam Greenberg 1981– (Cubs 2005)

His Cubs career was undeniably unique. On July 9, 2005, the Chicago Cubs called him up to the big leagues. They were in Miami facing the Florida Marlins. Greenberg's entire family flew down to Florida from Connecticut to watch his first major league series. They could barely contain their excitement in the 7th inning of the game, when Adam was called on to pinch hit for Cubs pitcher Will Ohman. The pitcher was Valerio De Los Santos, a left-hander. Here's the way *New York Times* reporter Ira Berkow described the only pitch of Greenberg's major league career: "No one imagined that the very first pitch the left-handed Greenberg faced in the major leagues would be a fastball that would crack him

squarely in the head, smashing against his helmet and the part of his neck just under his right ear, making a sound so loud that it stunned the crowd of almost 23,000." Greenberg had to be removed from the game and was placed on the disabled list after the game. He never returned to the Cubs, and never returned to the majors until the Marlins gave him one at-bat at the end of the 2012 season as a publicity stunt. He struck out.

Willie Greene 1971– (Cubs 2000)

Greene was a former first round pick. He was signed as a free agent after having a couple of pretty good power years as the third baseman for the Reds. Willie's issue was his inability to make contact. He did slug ten homers for the 2000 Cubs, but he also hit only .201. It was the last stop of his big league career.

Kevin Gregg 1976– (Cubs 2009, 2013)

Gregg was signed as a free agent by the Cubs in two different seasons to help stabilize the back end of the bullpen. In 2009 he was brought in to replace Kerry Wood, and in 2013 he was brought in to replace Carlos Marmol. And though he saved 56 games for the Cubs in those two seasons, and his numbers were respectable, he isn't remembered by Cubs fans as a great closer. Those 19 homers he gave up always seemed to happen at the worst possible times.

Lee Gregory 1938– (Cubs 1964)

The Cubs acquired Gregory just before the 1964 season, and he got a cup of coffee in the big leagues that season. He pitched in eleven games, and registered a 3.50 ERA. He had a horrendous season in the minors the next year (1-9, 5.61 ERA), however, and the Cubs released him. Gregory never returned to the big leagues.

Ben Grieve 1976– (Cubs 2004-2005)

Grieve is the son of a big leaguer — his father Tom played for the Texas Rangers. Ben got a great start to his own baseball career when he won the Rookie of the Year award in 1998 with the Oakland A's, but by the time he came to the Cubs he was a fourth outfielder. He played sparingly for the Cubs in that role. Chicago was the last stop in his big league career.

Hank Griffin 1886–1950 (Cubs 1911)

Pepper Griffin, as he was known, pitched in exactly one game for the Cubs in 1911. Actually he only pitched one inning. To say it didn't go well is probably a kind way of saying it. He walked three men and gave up a homer. He later had a cup of coffee with the Boston Braves and it didn't go much better there.

Mike Griffin 1957– (Cubs 1981)

Griffin was a spot starter for the truly awful 1981 Cubs. He started nine games for them during that strike-shortened season and went 2-5, with a 4.50 ERA. He also pitched for the Yankees, Padres, Orioles, and Reds. After his playing career he went into coaching and is currently a minor league pitching coach.

Clark Griffith 1869–1955 (1893-1900)

They called him the Old Fox, but when he was with the Cubs (then known as the White Stockings), he wasn't old yet. He had his best years wearing the uniform of Chicago's National League ball club. Clark Griffith joined what was to become known as the Cubs the same year as the Columbian Exposition (1893). Beginning in 1894 he won 20 games for the Cubs six years in a row, a feat that wouldn't be repeated by a Cub until Fergie Jenkins did it. Griffith was fearless on the mound. He still holds the Cubs franchise record for batters beaned (116).

Griffith went on to manage in the American League for twenty years, including twelve years as a player/manager. He led the White Sox to the American League pennant in 1901, and spent the last nine years of his career managing the Washington Senators. Griffith became the owner of the Senators in 1920, and ran the club until his death in 1955. The highlight of those years was probably the 1924 World Series, won by the Senators over the New York Giants. (President Calvin Coolidge attended that series.) He became such an institution in Washington that the stadium was named after him.

Griffith was elected into the Baseball Hall of Fame in 1946. His son, Calvin Griffith, took over the team after his father's death and moved the Senators to Minnesota in 1961, where they still play today as the Minnesota Twins.

Coleman Griffith 1893–1966 (Cubs psychologist 1938)

In 1938, University of Illinois psychologist Coleman Griffith was asked by PK Wrigley to do a complete psychological analysis of the Cubs for a project he called "Experimental Laboratories of the Chicago National League Ball Club." Naturally, his first target was manager Charlie Grimm. "Jolly Cholly" wasn't exactly receptive. When Grimm was replaced in July by player/manager Gabby Hartnett, a man later declared as the winner of the "Drizzlepus Derby" as grumpiest manager in baseball by one Chicago paper, Griffith could have folded up his tent and quit, but he didn't. He wrote a paper explaining "pepper" to the future Hall of Famer. He pointed out in another paper that there was no such thing as "instinct." Somehow, and this is also going to be a big shock, his information was not exactly embraced by the players. The 1938 Cubs were a veteran team (average age: nearly 30). With future Hall of Famers like Dizzy Dean and Tony Lazzeri on the roster, they were not the prototypical audience for experimental psychological research. Griffith also didn't help his cause with his analysis of the players. For instance, he used a very complex statistical model to show that Phil Cavarretta should be traded because he would never amount to anything. People made fun of Wrigley for using Griffith that year, but on the other hand, the Cubs did go to the World Series in 1938. Wrigley really wanted him to come back full-time for the 1939 season, but Griffith wanted to spend more time with his family in Urbana.

The "headshrinker" who tells the players in the book/movie *The Natural* that "losing is a disease" was surely inspired by Griffith. Ironically, as widely mocked as this idea was in 1938, every big league team today has a psychologist on staff. And every big league club uses statistical analysis to assess their players.

Frank Griffith 1872–1908 (Colts 1892)

If you want to travel back in time to see Griffith pitch for the Cubs (then known as the Colts), set the wayback machine for August 13, 1892. That was his only appearance for the team. The Northwestern University product started and was knocked out of the game after only four innings. He gave up six walks and three hits (including a homer) and finished with an ERA of 11.25. He later pitched a bit for Cleveland, and brought his lifetime ERA closer to ten.

Tommy Griffith 1889–1967 (Cubs 1925)

Griffith played 13 seasons in the big leagues (mostly for Boston, Cincinnati, and Brooklyn), the last of which was with the Cubs. The right fielder hit .285. When the season ended, Griffith hung up his spikes for good. The highlight of his career was probably playing for Brooklyn in the 1920 World Series. The Indians won the series that year, but Tommy batted third in the lineup and started in right field for Brooklyn.

Denver Grigsby 1901–1973 (Cubs 1923-1925)

Grigsby's best season was 1924 when he was the team's starting left fielder. He hit .299 and played a very solid left field, leading the league in fielding percentage, assists, and double plays. But Denver didn't really have the power to play a corner outfield position, and Cliff Heathcote was manning center field, so he went back to the bench in 1925. It was his last season in the big leagues. His name (Denver), by the way, was not a nickname. It was his given name.

Burleigh Grimes 1893–1985 (Cubs 1932-1933)

Grimes never shaved on days he pitched, because the slippery elm he chewed to increase saliva irritated his skin, so he always had stubble on his face when he took the mound. That led to his nickname, Ol' Stubblebeard. He wasn't just known for his stubble, he was also known as one of the toughest competitors to ever take the mound. His scowl would have made Randy Johnson's look like a smiley face, and when it was time to give someone an intentional walk, he was known to throw four pitches near the batter's head. Grimes is a Hall of Famer, but certainly not for his one and half years with the Cubs (1932-1933). He was a five-time 20-game winner, but only went 9-17 for the Cubs. Ol' Stubblebeard was the last legal spitball pitcher in the majors. When he retired, so did that pitch. (Wink, wink. Right, Gaylord Perry?)

Ray Grimes 1893–1953 (Cubs 1922-1925)

Ray Grimes was an instant phenom for the Cubs when he joined them for his rookie season of 1922. He was an absolute RBI machine, one of the great clutch hitters of his era. During that season he set a record that still stands today when he got an RBI in seventeen consecutive games. During that streak he was so "in the zone" that he was unconscious. In 66 at-bats, he had 28 hits, including eight doubles, two triples, three homers, and 27 RBI. The Cubs thought they had a first baseman that would hold down the position for a decade. Unfortunately for Ray and the Cubs, his sophomore season was an entirely different experience. In May of 1923, he badly dislocated his back sliding into second base: a very serious injury. Instead of taking the time to recuperate, he rushed back onto the field a few weeks later and re-injured himself. That put him out for two months. It was an injury he couldn't quite shake. The following season he started off well too, but was re-injured in June, and by July 8th of the following year, the Cubs decided they didn't need him anymore. By then they had another first baseman (Harry Cotter). Ray Grimes — their great hope of only a few years earlier — was released. In his four seasons in Chicago he hit .321, .354, .329, and .299. He re-surfaced briefly in 1926 on the Phillies, and could still hit (.297), but his back simply wouldn't allow him to play on a regular basis. Ray Grimes became another "what could have been" story in a long line of them for the Chicago Cubs.

Charlie Grimm 1898–1983 (Cubs player 1925-1936, Cubs manager 1932-1938, 1944-1949, 1960)

They called Charlie Grimm "Jolly Cholly" because he was a fun-loving guy who always seemed to be happy during his 20 seasons as a player. He played the banjo to loosen up the team on long train rides, and was a constant chatterbox on the field. He was so beloved by his teammates that Phillip K. Wrigley named him to manage the team while he was still a player (Charlie played first base). His laidback and tolerant approach seemed to coax great performances from mediocre teammates and legendary performances from great players. Taking over the team from the despised disciplinarian Rogers Hornsby in 1932, Charlie led the team to the pennant that season. He was also the manager of the 1935 pennant winners and the last Chicago team to win the National League — the 1945 Cubs. After he stepped down as a manager, he remained in the Cubs front office in one capacity or another for the rest of his life. He was such an important part of Cubs lore that his wife was allowed to spread his ashes in Wrigley when he died in 1983.

Historical note: On the day the 1932 Democratic Convention began in Chicago (which nominated FDR for the first time), Charlie slammed a homer to help beat the Reds 7-0 at Wrigley Field.

Justin Grimm 1988– (Cubs 2013-2017)

Grimm was acquired in the trade that sent Matt Garza to the Texas Rangers. Grimm was a fairly solid (if inconsistent) reliever for the Cubs during his five seasons in Chicago after having a rougher go of it as a starter for Texas. He also helped out the Cubs by being the official designated Catcher-of-the-Ceremonial-First-Pitch. The Cubs released him during spring training in 2018.

Historical note: On the day the US reestablished relations with Cuba (2015), Grimm was the losing pitcher for the Cubs after giving up the go-ahead homer to Jay Bruce in Cincinnati.

Greg Gross 1952– (Cubs 1977-1978)

Greg was a slap-hitting outfielder (zero home runs in about 1500 at-bats) for the Astros (in their rainbow pajama uniform era) when the Cubs acquired him before the 1977 season. The Cubs made a run at the division title before fading at the end of the year, and Gross was a key member of that team as a fourth outfielder. He hit .322 in over 200 at-bats. He even discovered a semi-power stroke, hitting six of his career home runs (he only hit 7 in 17 big league seasons) in a Cubs uniform. After his playing career he went into coaching with the Phillies and Diamondback organizations.

Mark Grote 1972– (Cubs announcer 2015-2017)

Grote did the radio pre- and post-game shows for the Cubs for three seasons, and also filled in during the games occasionally. In 2015, I interviewed him about what that was like. "There's about five hours of prep that goes into a baseball game," Grote admitted. "You're in the clubhouse four hours before the game starts — talking to players, trying to get interviews, and it's not always easy to get exactly what you want when you go into a clubhouse. There are some days when the player that you would like to speak to is not interested in speaking for whatever reason. It's not like I can just go in there and say 'we want him, him, and him,'

and they give them to us. We have to work for it too." After the 2017 season he and Zach Zaidman switched roles, with Grote going to cover the Bears, and Zaidman taking Grote's spot in the radio booth.

Ernie Groth 1884–1950 (Cubs 1904)

The 19-year-old Groth pitched in three games for the Cubs in 1904. He started (and completed) two of those game, and saved the third one, and then never pitched in the big leagues again. The Wisconsin boy was nicknamed "Dango."

Mark Grudzielanek 1970– (Cubs 2003-2004)

Mark was an All-Star early in his career with the Expos and a Gold Glover at second base for the Royals late in his career, but he also made several other big league stops along the way, including Los Angeles, St. Louis, Cleveland, and of course, the Cubs. He was acquired in an excellent trade from the Dodgers that also brought Eric Karros to the team in exchange for Cubs albatross Todd Hundley. The two ex-Dodgers were key members of the Cubs team that won the division in 2003. Grudzielanek had one of the best seasons of his career, hitting .314 and providing veteran leadership to a team that came only five outs away from the World Series. The following season he got hurt, and left in free agency before the 2005 season.

Marv Gudat 1903–1954 (Cubs 1932)

Marv was a backup outfielder/first baseman for the pennant-winning 1932 Cubs. He appeared in sixty games that year, and was part of the postseason roster. Gudat got two at-bats in the 1932 World Series against the Yankees. His last big league at-bat was a pop out to shortstop in Game 3. After the series he went out west and played another 13 seasons in the minors.

Matt Guerrier 1978– (Cubs 2013)

The Cubs acquired the veteran reliever from the Dodgers in 2013 (for Carlos Marmol), and he pitched quite well for them out of the bullpen. In fifteen appearances, his ERA was only 2.13. But just when he was becoming a key part of the bullpen, Matt hurt his arm, ending his season, and his stint with the Cubs. In his eleven-year big league career he also pitched for the Twins.

Ad Gumbert 1868–1925 (White Stockings 1888-1889, 1991-1992)

Gumbert was a starting pitcher, and a fairly good one for his time. In his fourth and final season with the Cubs he won 22 games, but he also gave up a whopping 399 hits and walked over a hundred men in 382 innings. He later also pitched for Pittsburgh, Brooklyn, and Philadelphia. His brother and nephew both also played in the big leagues.

Dave Gumpert 1958– (Cubs 1985-1986)

Gumpert had his best season as a pro with the Cubs in 1986. He appeared in 38 games out of the bullpen, won two games, and saved two. The following year the Cubs traded him (along with Thad Bosley) to the Royals for catcher Jim Sundberg.

Larry Gura 1947– (Cubs 1970-1973, 1985)

Gura didn't pitch too much for the team that drafted him. He appeared in a total of 54 games over four seasons (mostly out of the bullpen). The Cubs traded him for pitcher Mike Paul. Paul had very little left in the tank. Gura, on the other hand, was just getting started. He became an All-Star and two-time 18-game winner for the Kansas City Royals. Gura pitched in the World Series for the Royals in 1980, but was released before they returned to the World Series in 1985. Which team picked Gura up to finish his career? The Cubs. He went 0-3 with an 8.31 ERA in his final stint with the team in 1985. Overall, only three of Larry's 126 career wins came with the Cubs.

Frank Gustine 1920–1991 (Cubs 1949)

Frank was coming off three consecutive All-Star seasons when he arrived in Chicago in December of 1948. The Hoopeston, Illinois native was probably excited to be playing for the Cubs after spending the previous ten seasons with the Pirates. (His roommate on the road with the Pirates was Hall of Famer Ralph Kiner). Unfortunately, it didn't quite work out for Frank in Chicago. He split time at third base with Bob Ramazzotti, and neither of them hit well. Gustine hit only .226, and was released before the season was over. He resurfaced briefly with the St. Louis Browns the following season, but that was the end of his big league career.

Charlie Guth 1856–1883 (White Stockings 1880)

Guth played exactly one game with the Cubs (then known as the White Stockings) on September 30, 1880. He was a semi-pro pitcher in the area, and the two pitchers on the White Stockings (Larry Corcoran and Fred Goldsmith) were sick — so Charlie was called in to take the mound. It was his only game in the big leagues. He tossed a complete game victory, allowing twelve hits and five earned runs. Charlie tragically passed away in the summer of 1883 at the age of 27.

Mark Guthrie 1965– (Cubs 1999-2000, 2003)

Guthrie had two stints with the Cubs. In his first one, he arrived from Boston in exchange for Cubs fan favorite Rod Beck. In the middle of the next year he was traded for another fan favorite, Davey Martinez. Guthrie was a decent left-handed reliever, but never exactly a fan favorite. In his return to the Cubs in 2003, however, he was excellent all season. He appeared in 65 games as a lefty specialist, and posted a sparking 2.95 ERA. Unfortunately, he also lost Game 1 of the NLCS in Wrigley Field against the Marlins. Dusty Baker brought him in because lefties were coming up, but Jack McKeon outsmarted him, and brought in righty Mike Lowell to pinch hit. Lowell homered to win the game. Guthrie made one more appearance in the series: mop up duty in the Cubs victory in Game 2. That was his last appearance in the big leagues.

Ricky Gutierrez 1970– (Cubs 2000-2001)

Gutierrez was known to Cubs fans before he came to Chicago as the guy who got the only hit (a ball that should have been called an error) in Kerry Wood's 20-strikeout game. Ricky had two very solid seasons at shortstop for the Cubs at the turn of the century. He was a very unselfish player, leading the league in sacrifices both years. Ricky's big league career ended in style. He was part of the 2004 Boston Red Sox team that broke Boston's curse, along with former Cubs teammates Bill Mueller and Mark Bellhorn.

Angel Guzman 1981– (Cubs 2006-2009)

Angel was one of the young stud pitchers who came up to the big leagues for the Cubs in the first decade of this century (along with Prior, Zambrano, and Cruz). Some scouts thought Guzman had the greatest upside of any of them, but he hurt his arm, and though he tried to come back multiple times, he was never the same.

Jose Guzman 1963 – (Cubs 1993-1994)

The Cubs signed Guzman as a free agent after a few successful seasons with the Texas Rangers. He was supposed to be the pitcher that helped Cubs fans forget Greg Maddux because GM Larry Himes signed Guzman instead of re-signing Maddux. Needless to say, this was a horrible, horrible, (did we say horrible yet?) decision. Although, to be fair, Guzman looked good at first. On April 6, 1993, he came just one out away from throwing a no-hitter. Otis Nixon broke it up with a single. Guzman won 12 games in 1993 (while Maddux won the Cy Young with Atlanta), and then developed arm problems. 1994 was his last year in the big leagues. After his playing career ended he became a Spanish-language broadcaster for the Texas Rangers.

*Additional Entries...*If you check out the Every Cub Ever feature at www. justonebadcentury.com, you'll find several additional entries, including celebrity Cubs fans, writers, and bloggers. Under the letter G, you'll discover Comedian Jeff Garlin, Cardinal Francis George, broadcaster Bryant Gumbel, Cubs songwriter Steve Goodman, and Cubs author/tweeter Jimmy Greenfield.

CHAPTER EIGHT

H

The starting lineup of your Chicago Cubs starting with the letter H...

C – Gabby Hartnett, Homer in the Gloamin
1B – Jim Hickman, All-Star
2B – Rogers Hornsby, Best Right-Handed Hitter Ever
SS – Charlie Hollocher, Troubled Stomach
3B – Stan Hack, 4-World Series Cub
LF – Babe Herman, Wrong Babe
CF – Solly Hofman, 1908 Cub
RF – Billy Hatcher, World Series MVP (for another team)
Bench – Billy Herman, Hall of Famer
Bench – Randy Hundley, the Rebel
Bench – Ken Hubbs, Gold Glover
SP – Ken Holtzman, 2 No-Hitters
SP – Wild Bill Hutchinson, 40-game winner
SP – Kyle Hendricks, World Series Champ
SP – Bill Hands, 20-game Winner
SP – Burt Hooton, Rookie No-Hitter
RP – Willie Hernandez, Cy Young Winner (for another team)

Eddie Haas 1935 (Cubs 1957)

Eddie Haas went 5 for 26 as a September backup outfielder for the 1957 Cubs. He knocked in 4 runs. He got two more brief shots with the Milwaukee Braves before he went into coaching. In 1985 Haas was given a shot to manage the Atlanta Braves. The Braves were 21 games under .500 when he was fired in the midst of his first and last season as a big league manager. His cousins Phil & Gene Roof were both big leaguers too.

Stan Hack 1909 – 1979 (Cubs 1932-1947)

Smiling Stan Hack played his entire career for the Cubs , anchoring four World Series teams (and hitting .348 in those series), and a few not-so-good teams. He also managed the team for a while, and throughout his many years in a Cubs uniform, was known for having a smile on his face. The person that noticed Stan's perpetual smile was none other than Bill Veeck, Jr. Veeck was only 21 when he came up with a Stan Hack promotion for the Cubs in 1935. Fans were given mirrors labeled "Smile with Stan" with Hack's face on the reverse side. Unfortunately for Veeck, the fans used the mirrors to reflect sunlight into the eyes of opposing batters. The umpires threatened to forfeit the game if they didn't stop, and the league banned any future promotions involving mirrors. Smilin' Stan was the National League's best third baseman in the late 1930s and early 1940s. The leadoff hitter batted .301 lifetime, scored 100 runs seven times, led the league in hits and stolen bases twice, and was a four-time All-Star. His .394 career on-base percentage was the highest by a 20th-century third baseman until Wade Boggs exceeded it in the late 1980s, and remained the best in the National League until 2001. Smilin' Stan died in 1979. He still holds the Cubs all-time record for most career walks (1092).

Warren Hacker 1924 – 2002 (Cubs 1948-1956)

Hacker was a starting pitcher for the Cubs in the 1950s, and had a few pretty good seasons for less than stellar teams. In 1952 he went 15-9 with a sparkling 2.58 ERA. He tossed 12 complete games and five shutouts that season. Hacker had a few more double-digit win seasons in 1953 and 1955, but he also gave up a ton of homers. In only 140 starts, he gave up 156 long balls. Hacker was traded to the Reds (along with Dick Hoak) in 1956.

Historical note: On the day the CIA helped install the Shah of Iran (1953), Hacker was on the mound for the Cubs. He beat the Cardinals 5-3 in St. Louis.

Casey Hageman 1887 – 1964 (Cubs 1914)

Casey was not a typical pitcher in many ways. When he was a minor league pitcher in 1909, he killed a batter with a pitch. He never totally got over that. He was also a rebel. In 1912 he was sent to the minor leagues by the Red Sox, and he refused to go. That led to an early challenge of baseball's reserve clause and made him an undesirable, despite his great promise. The Cubs gave him another shot in 1914 when they still played at West Side Grounds. He won one game and saved another, and pitched respectably for the club. But there was another way that Casey was far from a typical relief pitcher. He batted 15 times, and his average was an astounding .467. After the season he and the Cubs couldn't come to an agreement on a contract, and he quit big league baseball for good at age 27.

Rip Hagerman 1886–1930 (Cubs 1909)

His real name was Zerah Zequiel Hagerman, but his Cubs teammates opted to reject that mouthful and call him Rip. Rip pitched very well for the Cubs during his only year in Chicago. His 1.82 ERA in 79 innings pitched were a real help to the team that year. He later pitched for Cleveland with less success. He was only 43 years old when he died in 1930.

Jerry Hairston Jr. 1976– (Cubs 2005-2006)

Hairston's claim to fame in Chicago will always be that he was the player the Cubs got in exchange for Sammy Sosa. He had a decent if unspectacular debut season with the Cubs as a jack-of-all-trades utility man, but the following year the Cubs were desperate for power, so they traded Hairston to the Texas Rangers for Phil Nevin. Jerry was named as a PED user by the Mitchell Report, a charge he vehemently denied. Hairston got his first and only World Series ring as part of the 2009 Yankees championship team. Jerry's uncle John and brother Scott also played for the Cubs.

John Hairston 1944– (Cubs 1969)

Five Hairstons played big league baseball in Chicago. John's father (Sam) and brother (Jerry) played for the White Sox, and his nephews (Jerry Jr. & Scott) later followed in his Cubs footsteps. Johnny Hairston has the distinction of being the first-ever second-generation African-American big leaguer. He was a September call-up during the infamous 1969 Cubs collapse. He got into four games as a catcher, left-fielder, and pinch hitter. His only hit came on September 18, 1969 — a squib single against Phillies pitcher Grant Jackson.

Scott Hairston 1980– (Cubs 2013)

His grandfather Sam was a big leaguer, so was his father Jerry

Sr., and his brother Jerry Jr. Scott probably had the most power of any of them. He had a few very good power seasons for the Padres (17 HRs twice) and Mets (20 homers). But he was supposed to platoon in right field with Nate Schierholtz for the Cubs in 2013, and it didn't work out too well. Scott only hit .172 before being traded to the Washington Nationals.

Hall of Fame Cubs...The following players, managers, or executives spent at least a part of their career with the Cubs, and are enshrined in baseball's Hall of Fame...Grover Cleveland Alexander, Cap Anson, Richie Ashburn, Ernie Banks, Roger Bresnahan, Lou Boudreau, Lou Brock, Mordecai Brown, Frank Chance, John Clarkson, KiKi Cuyler, Andre Dawson, Dizzy Dean, Leo Durocher, Hugh Duffy, Dennis Eckersley, Johnny Evers, Frankie Frisch, Jimmie Foxx, Goose Gossage, Clark Griffith, Burleigh Grimes, Gabby Hartnett, Billy Herman, Rogers Hornsby, William Hulbert, Monte Irvin, Fergie Jenkins, George Kelly, King Kelly, Ralph Kiner, Chuck Klein, Tony LaRussa, Tony Lazzeri, Freddie Lindstrom, Joe McCarthy, Greg Maddux, Rabbit Maranville, Hank O'Day, Robin Roberts, Ryne Sandberg, Ron Santo, Frank Selee, Al Spalding, Bruce Sutter, Joe Tinker, Rube Waddell, Deacon White, Hoyt Wilhelm, Billy Williams, and Hack Wilson.

Drew Hall 1963– (Cubs 1986-1988)

For the most part, Dallas Green did a very good job drafting during his time at the helm of the Cubs, but in 1984 he spent the third overall pick on pitcher Drew Hall. (Mark McGwire was picked a few picks later). Hall had an electric arm but was never able to harness it. His time with the Cubs was memorable for how badly it went. He was hit hard, was wild in the strike zone, and after three seasons was shipped off to Texas along with two other projects that had slightly better careers (Rafael Palmeiro and Jamie Moyer). Hall pitched his last pitch in the big leagues at the age of 27.

Jimmy Hall 1938– (Cubs 1969-1970)

Hall's career started out well with the Minnesota Twins. He

was All-Star in 1964, and got to replace Mickey Mantle in center field that game. In 1965, he made the All-Star team again, but when the Twins went to the World Series, he spent most of it on the bench. By then his inability to hit lefties had been exposed, and a little-known lefty named Koufax started three games for the Dodgers in that series. By the time the Cubs got him in 1969 to help with their playoff push, the pitchers had caught up to him. He hit less than .200 and was shipped off to Atlanta in June of 1970.

Mel Hall 1960 – (Cubs 1981-1984)

Hall really burst onto the scene during the 1983 season. After getting a taste of the big leagues at the end of the '81 and '82 seasons, he won a job in 1983, and responded with a great year. Mel slugged 17 homers, hit .283 in just over 400 at-bats, and finished third in the Rookie of the Year voting. He was in the Opening Day lineup in 1984 too, and was on his way to a decent (if unspectacular) year when he was called into the manager's office on June 13th. That's when he found out he had been traded to the Cleveland Indians along with Joe Carter for pitcher Rick Sutcliffe. Sutcliffe led the Cubs to the playoffs, and Hall had three good, but not great seasons with the Indians, before being traded to the Yankees. Before his career was over, Hall had clubbed 134 homers in 13 big league seasons, and another 64 in Japan. But that's only the baseball part of the Mel Hall story. There is a much darker side to Hall as well. After his baseball career ended, Hall was convicted of being a sexual predator, and was sentenced to 45 years in prison.

Jimmy Hallinan 1849–1879 (White Stockings 1877-1878)

The Irish-born Hallinan came to the Cubs (then known as the White Stockings) when his previous team the Reds ran into financial difficulty. Hallinan was a pretty good hitter, but Chicago had trouble finding places for him to play on the field because he was a terrible fielder. In his career he made 161 errors in only 111 games. In the middle of the 1878 season he had to quit because he became ill. The following year he died at the age of 30, from what was then described as "inflammation of the bowels" likely due to excessive drinking.

Halloween Cubs...If you want to dress up like a Cub for Halloween, which one would be the most appropriate choice? Go back the mid-50s and dress up like Cubs outfielder/first baseman Bob Speake. Why him? His nickname was Spook.

Cole Hamels 1983 – (Cubs 2018-Present)

The Cubs picked up the former World Series MVP (for the Phillies), and the last pitcher to no-hit them (July 2015), at the trading deadline in 2018. Hamels pitched like he had been doused in the fountain of youth. After struggling in Texas, Hamels dominated in his 12 starts with the Cubs. He had a 2.38 ERA, struck out 72 in 74 innings, and was the team's best pitcher down the stretch. He pitched so well, the Cubs picked up his option for 2019. Cole Hamels trivia: His wife Heidi was once a contestant on the show *Survivor*.

Milo Hamilton 1927–2015 (Cubs announcer 1955-1957, 1980-1982)

Milo is a Ford C. Frick Award winner in the "Scribes and Mikemen" section of baseball's Hall of Fame. As a young broadcaster he worked for the Cubs alongside Vince Lloyd, but was moved out of the booth when Lou Boudreau became available. He went on to broadcast for many other teams including the White Sox, Braves, and Pirates. (Milo, of course, is most famous for his call of Hank Aaron's 715th home run.)

He came back to the Cubs in 1980, and at first enjoyed it. He was promised Brickhouse's job when Jack retired, but when that time actually came, Harry Caray was brought in instead. Milo couldn't stand Harry Caray, and especially didn't like the way Harry broadcasted. In his autobiography, he wrote; "He rode the managers, he rode the players, it didn't matter. He treated everyone the same way. In short, he was a miserable human being." Milo offered another example of that in his book. When Milo was hospitalized for leukemia in 1982, Harry responded on the air that he "Couldn't understand how a guy can take time off during the season. Unlike some other broadcasters I know, I've never missed a game." Milo left town, landed in Houston, and broadcast games there until his retirement in 2012.

Steve Hamilton 1934–1997 (Cubs 1972)

Hamilton was a 37-year-old 12-year veteran (Indians, Senators, Yankees, White Sox, Giants) when the Cubs acquired the lefty reliever in 1972. He appeared in the final 22 games of his big league career for the Cubs that year, posting a 4.76 ERA as a situational lefty. Hamilton retired after the season. His nickname was Gomer.

Jason Hammel 1982–(Cubs 2014-2016)

Hammel was signed as a free agent by the Cubs prior to the 2014 season and responded with the best year of his career. He was 8-5 with 2.98 ERA when the Cubs traded him along with Jeff Samardzija to the Oakland A's in July. He didn't pitch as well in Oakland, and became a free agent again, so the Cubs signed him again. In 2015 Hammel had a great first half, but slumped after the All-Star break, and really struggled in the playoffs. His 2016 season was much better. Hammel won 15 games, but was hurt toward the end of the year, and was kept off the postseason roster. The Cubs granted him free agency after the World Series. He signed with Kansas City.

Ralph Hamner 1916–2001 (Cubs 1947-1949)

Hamner came up to the big leagues after the war, but because of the interruption in his playing time, he was already 29 years old. They called him Bruz. He had flashes of brilliance, pitching seven complete games, but in 220 career innings, Bruz allowed an astounding 368 baserunners.

Justin Hancock 1990–(Cubs 2018)

Hancock was acquired in a trade with the Padres for Matt Szczur in 2017, and made his big league debut as a 27-year-old in May of 2018. He pitched well in limited duty (10 appearances) for the Cubs.

Bill Hands 1940–2017 (Cubs 1966-1972)

Bill Hands was nicknamed "Froggy" because his style was reminiscent of Don Larsen, who was with the Cubs at the end of his illustrious career, and the beginning of Hands' career. Larsen was nicknamed Froggy, so Hands was given the nickname too. Hands became a 20-game winner in 1969 and helped the Cubs to a second-place finish behind the Mets. He won another 18 games for the Cubs in 1970, and on August 3, 1972, he had his best performance as a Cub, beating the Montreal Expos 3-0. With Hands one out away from a no-hitter, Ken Singleton hit a little ground ball toward second base, and Hands tried to catch it. It went off his glove and away from second baseman Paul Popovich, ending the no-hitter.

The Cubs traded him after the 1972 season to the Minnesota Twins for Dave LaRoche. After pitching for two seasons with the Minnesota Twins, and one more with the Rangers, Hands retired after the 1975 season. After his baseball career, he moved to rural New York and bought a gas station.

Historical note: On the day four student protestors were killed by National Guard troops at Kent State University, Bill was on the mound for the Cubs against the Astros. He didn't fare well. The Cubs lost 7-2 to *Ball Four* author Jim Bouton.

Chris Haney 1968–(Cubs 1998)

Haney was a left-handed pitcher who managed to pitch for five different teams (Expos, Royals, Indians, Red Sox, Cubs) over an eleven-year big league career despite posting a career ERA over five. He appeared in five games for the Cubs, covering five innings, and managed to give up two homers. His ERA in Chicago was 7.20.

Fred Haney 1896–1977 (Cubs 1927)

Haney had three at-bats in four games with the Cubs in 1927, and didn't get on base. As a manager, he led the Milwaukee Braves to two World Series in a row, winning it all in 1957, and losing to the Yankees in 1958. Despite his championship, he wasn't considered a great manager. Baseball historian/statistician Bill James says that Haney had one of the worst seasons as a manager in baseball history in 1959. The stacked Braves lost the NL to the vastly inferior Los Angeles Dodgers, largely (according to James) because of Haney's mistakes.

Todd Haney 1965–(Cubs 1994-1996)

Haney was a backup infielder for the Cubs in the mid-90s, mostly backing up Ryne Sandberg and Steve Buechele. He was one of three Todds on the 1995 Cubs, along with Todd Pratt and Todd Zeile, one of the most Todd-heavy teams in Cubs history.

Frank Hankinson 1856—1911
(White Stockings 1878-1879)

Frank played in the big leagues for ten years, the first two of which were in Chicago. Over the course of his career he played every position except catcher. The Cubs (then known as the White Stockings) had him pitch and play third base and outfield. As a pitcher he won 15 games for the team in 1879 and didn't allow a single home run in over 230 innings. As a batter, he finished tied for fifth in the league in homers. He hit one.

Historical note: On the day the White Stockings visited Cleveland and saw electric street lights for the very first time, Hankinson was on the mound for Chicago. He lost the game 10-7.

Bill Hanlon 1876—1905 (Cubs 1903)

Big Bill played one year in the big leagues. His role with the Cubs was backing up first baseman Frank Chance. He hit .095 in limited chances. He passed away just two years after his last big league game.

Dave Hansen 1968—(Cubs 1997)

Hansen was one of the best pinch hitters of his generation. He played one full season for the Cubs in 1997, but that turned out to be a rather unpleasant experience. After being on a perpetual winner in Los Angeles, the 0-14 start the Cubs had in 1997 must have scarred him. After the season he left the country and played in Japan for a year. He returned to play another seven big league seasons. In spring training of 2005, the Cubs signed him again. They cut him the day before the season began, and he finished his career with the Seattle Mariners.

Ollie Hanson 1896—1951 (Cubs 1921)

Ollie got a very brief shot with the Cubs in 1921. Very brief. Eight days, to be precise. In those eight days he was the starting pitcher twice. In his first start on April 27, 1921 at Redland Field, he pitched pretty well against Cincinnati. He went the distance and gave up only two runs in a 2-1 loss. His second start was his only one at Wrigley Field (then known as Cubs Park). He gave up five earned runs in one inning and was yanked out of the game. Ollie never made it back to the big leagues.

Ed Hanyzewski 1920—1991 (Cubs 1942-1946)

Ed was a Notre Dame product who pitched for the Cubs during the war years. His best season was 1943 when he won 8 games with a 2.56 ERA. Unfortunately for Ed, he didn't get much of an opportunity during the pennant season of 1945. He only appeared in two games, and wasn't on the postseason roster.

Ian Happ 1994—(Cubs 2017-present)

Happ was an invaluable member of the Cubs right out of the box. The former first rounder came up to the big league club during the 2017 season and hit 24 homers, drove in 68 runs, stole 8 bases, and played five positions (2B, 3B, RF, CF, LF). He earned the lead-off job out of spring training in 2018 and led off the season with a homer — but it went downhill from there. Happ did manage to hit 15 homers and play well defensively in the outfield, but his strikeouts spiked and his batting average dipped to .233.

Bill Harbridge 1855—1924 (White Stockings 1878-1879)

They called him Yaller Bill, and during the 1878 season he was the main catcher for the Cubs (then known as the White Stockings). Unfortunately for his teammates, Yaller Bill wasn't so great at that position. He lead the league with 56 passed balls. The following year they moved him to the outfield, and that turned out to be his last season with Chicago. He also played for Hartford, Troy, and Philadelphia.

Rich Harden 1981—(Cubs 2008-2009)

The Cubs knew they were getting a fragile but talented pitcher from the A's during their division-winning season of 2008, but gambled that he could help. When he got on the mound, he did. Harden had a 5-1 record after being acquired, but he wasn't available to pitch every five days, and in his one start of the playoffs against the Dodgers he was hit pretty hard. Unfortunately for the Cubs, they included a future All-Star and potential MVP in the deal to acquire Harden. In addition to Matt Murton and Eric Patterson, the A's received third baseman Josh Donaldson. Harden won 9 games in 2009, but it was clear his arm wouldn't hold up, and he was allowed to leave via free agency after the season. Donaldson became a star in Oakland a few years later.

Lou Hardie 1864—1929 (White Stockings 1886)

Hardie played catcher, infield, and outfield for the 1886 champs. It was his only season in Chicago. He also played for Philadelphia, Boston, and Baltimore in his big league career.

Bud Hardin 1922—1997 (Cubs 1952)

A veteran of World War II, Hardin made the club out of spring training as a 29-year-old rookie 2B/SS. He backed up Roy Smalley and Eddie Miksis for a few weeks before being sent back down the minors. Hardin appeared in a grand total of three Cubs games, and registered one hit. He played in the minors until he was 35 years old.

Jason Hardtke 1971—(Cubs 1998)

Hardtke got a cup of coffee with the Cubs during their playoff season of 1998. He played a little third base and outfield during his brief stay, and hit .238. Before coming to the Cubs, he got a similarly brief shot with the Mets. Most of his career was spent in the minors. He also played one season in Japan.

Alex Hardy 1876—1940 (Cubs 1902-1903)

Hardy was a Canadian-born pitcher who started seven games over two seasons for the Cubs more than a hundred years ago. He went 3-3, with a 4.34 ERA. Of the seven games he started, he completed five of them. After his playing career ended, he moved back home to his native Ontario.

Jack Hardy 1877—1921 (Cubs 1907)

One of the most obscure members of the first World Series champion Cubs team (1907), Hardy played in exactly one game for Chicago. The catcher went 1 for 4, with a single and a strikeout. He got a few more cups of coffee in the big leagues with Cleveland (his hometown team) and the Washington Senators, but played the majority of his time in the minor leagues. His longest stint was with Montreal. Hardy died in 1921 at the age of 44.

Dan Haren 1980—(Cubs 2015)

The Cubs picked up the 3-time All-Star and 150-game winner at the trading deadline, and Haren took a spot in the rotation for the rest of the season. In his eleven starts he posted a respectable 4-2 record with a 4.01 ERA. After the Cubs were eliminated from the playoffs, Haren announced his retirement.

Alan Hargesheimer 1954—(Cubs 1983)

Alan was a Chicago boy who bounced around the big leagues with stops at Kansas City and San Francisco, but he also got to pitch for his hometown Cubs in five games during the 1983 season. The right-handed reliever gave up four earned runs in his four innings pitched to finish his Cubs career with an ERA of nine. After his playing career he became an MLB scout for several teams, including the Padres, Rockies, and Tigers.

Bubbles Hargrave 1892—1969 (Cubs 1913-1915)

His real name was Eugene Hargrave, but everyone called him Bubbles because he stuttered every time he said a word that started with the letter "B". As much as Bubbles hated his nickname, he must have known that it could have been worse. His younger brother also played in the majors, and his nickname was Pinky. Bubbles was a catcher for the Cubs from 1913-1915, but didn't get a lot of playing time because the two catchers ahead of him, Roger Bresnahan and Jimmy Archer, were both All-Star caliber players. The Cubs released him after the 1915 season, and he didn't make it back to the majors until 1920 (with the Reds), but when he got another chance, he took full advantage of it. In 1926, he became the first full-time catcher to win the batting title when he hit .353 for the Reds.

Mike Harkey 1966—(Cubs 1988-1993)

Mike Harkey was a first round pick of the Cubs who had a very promising 1990 season, winning 12 games. The following year he was goofing around in the outfield before the game doing handsprings and cartwheels. He landed wrong, tore up his knee, and was never the same pitcher. He did manage to win 10 games in his final season with the Cubs, but that was accompanied by a 5.26 ERA. He went into coaching after his playing days, and currently serves on the New York Yankees staff.

Dick Harley 1872—1952 (Cubs 1903)

Harley was a starting outfielder for the Cubs in 1903, but he simply didn't hit. In over 450 plate appearances, he managed only ten extra base hits, with a batting average of .231. Dick had some speed (27 stolen bases that season), but not enough to keep his job. He never played in the big leagues again. After his playing days, he became a college coach, including stints at Villanova, Penn State, and Pitt.

Jack Harper 1878–1950 (Cubs 1906)

Harper may be the greatest example of "what goes around, comes around" in baseball history. In 1904 when he was a pitcher with the Reds, Harper beaned Cubs first baseman Frank Chance several times. One time he knocked him out cold. Chance didn't get mad, he got even. By 1906 Chance was calling the shots for the Cubs. He contacted the Reds to see if they would be interested in trading Harper. Sure enough…they traded him to Chance. Frank let him start one game, pulled him in the first inning, and let him fester on the bench for the rest of the year. Harper never pitched in the big leagues again.

Ray Harrell 1912–1984 (Cubs 1939)

The Cubs got Harrell in the off-season after their World Series loss to the Yankees, and had high hopes for him. Ray pitched horribly (8.31 ERA) however, so they included him in the trade that brought Claude Passeau to the Cubs. That turned out to be a great trade for Chicago as Passeau anchored their rotation for several years, including their 1945 pennant season.

Brendan Harris 1980–(Cubs 2004)

Harris made his big league debut for the Cubs on July 6th of 2004, but before the month was over he was involved in a big trade. Harris was one of the players in the Nomar Garciaparra trade. Harris was a utility infielder in the big leagues for eight seasons with the Expos, Nationals, Reds, Rays, Twins, and Angels.

Lenny Harris 1964–(Cubs 2003)

Lenny holds the all-time record for most pinch hits in a career (with 212). He was part of the Cubs team that won the division in 2003, although he had been let go by the time the playoffs began. Lennie also played for the Reds, Dodgers, Mets, Rockies, Diamondbacks, Brewers, and Marlins. After his playing days he became a hitting coach.

Vic Harris 1950–(Cubs 1974-1975)

Harris can always say that he was traded for Hall of Famer Ferguson Jenkins. It's true, he was the throw in to the trade that brought Bill Madlock to Chicago. The Cubs had high hopes for Harris and handed the second base job to him at the beginning of the 1974 season, but he just couldn't hit, and was sent down to the minors. He hit .179 for the Cubs in 1975, and that was all she wrote for Vic. He was traded to the Cardinals for another infielder who couldn't hit — Mick Kelleher.

James Hart 1855-1919 (Cubs owner 1902-1905)

Hart became the president of the Cubs (then known as the White Stockings) in 1892. He purchased the Cubs from Albert Spalding in 1902. Spalding had owned the team for twenty years. Hart's stay at the helm wasn't nearly as long. After the 1905 season he sold the team to a group of investors led by Charles Murphy. Among the financiers for Murphy was Charles Taft, the brother of the future president of the United States.

Kevin Hart 1982–(Cubs 2007-2009)

Kevin had flashes of effectiveness out of the bullpen for the Cubs for a few seasons, including the playoff years of 2007 and 2008. He even made the 2007 postseason roster as a 24-year-old rookie. The Cubs traded him to the Pirates midway through the 2009 season in a trade they clearly regret. It wasn't because Kevin turned out to have such a good Pirates career (he didn't — after 2009 he never appeared in the big leagues again). It's because the prospect thrown in to the deal (Josh Harrison) has gone on to become an All-Star. In return the Cubs got two pitchers who didn't do much with the club — Tom Gorzelanny and John Grabow.

Chuck Hartenstein 1942–(Cubs 1966-1968)

His real name was Charles Oscar Hartenstein, but he got the nickname Twiggy because he was so thin. At 5'11, 165 pounds, he looked like he was barely capable of pitching, let alone intimidating the opponent. Twiggy pitched for the Cubs from 1966 to 1968. He did fairly well in 1967, winning nine games and saving ten. After a less productive 1968, the Cubs traded him to the Pirates for Manny Jimenez, an outfielder who only batted six more times in his major league career. Twiggy pitched two more seasons in the National League, then re-emerged in 1977 for one final season with the expansion Toronto Blue Jays.

Gabby Hartnett 1900–1972 (Cubs 1922-1940)

Gabby was one of the greatest Cubs of all-time. His real name was Charles Leo Hartnett. No surprise where that nickname came from, he was known as someone who was "constantly talking" when he was catching. Gabby was the National League's catcher in the first six All-Star games. He played in four World Series for the Cubs, as a backup catcher/pinch hitter in 1929, the starting catcher in '32 and '35 (he won the MVP that year), and in 1938, his "Homer in the Gloamin" won the pennant for the Cubs. He was also the manager of that team. As a player he was beloved. As a manager, he was hated. His nickname as the manager was "Drizzlepuss" or "Old Tomato Face". He left the Cubs after 1940 and his last year was spent as a player/manager for the New York Giants. Gabby is buried in All Saints Cemetery in Des Plaines, the same cemetery as Harry Caray.

Historical note: On the day that future president George Herbert Walker Bush was born in 1924, Gabby was the hitting star for the Cubs, knocking in three runs in a 9-5 victory over the Braves.

Topsy Hartsel 1874–1944 (Orphans 1901)

Topsy set a record while playing for the Cubs (then known as the Orphans). On September 10, 1901, he set the record for putouts by a left fielder in a nine-inning game: 11 against Brooklyn. The next season he went to the Philadelphia A's and led the American League in stolen bases and runs scored. He became a star in Philly, one of the most feared baserunners in the league. He was a two-time World Series champ, including one year against his former teammates the Cubs (1910).

Jeff Hartsock 1966–(Cubs 1992)

Jeff came to the Cubs in a trade from the Dodgers for fellow reliever Steve Wilson. Wilson pitched well for the Dodgers, but Hartsock only made four appearances in September of 1992. They were the only four appearances of his big league career. He pitched seven seasons in the minors.

Zaza Harvey 1879–1954 (Orphans 1900)

He only got three at-bats for Chicago, but later got a little more playing time in Cleveland. Zaza was an outfielder. His real first name was Ervin.

Ron Hassey 1953–(Cubs 1984)

Hassey had a long and successful career as a backup catcher (14 seasons in the big leagues). He came to the Cubs along with Rick Sutcliffe in the trade that sent Joe Carter and Mel Hall to the Indians. Hassey didn't get a lot of playing time backing up Jody Davis, but he was a part of the team that won the division. The Cubs traded him to the Yankees after the 1984 season. Ron has one truly unique item on his resume: Hassey caught two perfect games — one in each league. He was behind the plate for Len Barker's in Cleveland, and Dennis Martinez' in Montreal. After his playing career, he coached, managed, and scouted for several teams including Arizona, Colorado, and St. Louis.

Scott Hastings 1847–1907 (White Stockings 1875)

Hastings was born during the James K. Polk administration. He was the regular catcher for the 1875 White Stockings, but only hit .254. He was dumped and replaced by future Hall of Famer Deacon White.

Billy Hatcher 1960–(Cubs 1984-1985)

Hatcher was a bright young prospect in the Cubs system that came up at a time the Cubs outfield was crowded with veterans. He was traded to Houston, and it didn't take long for the Cubs to realize they made a mistake. Billy Hatcher turned out to be a postseason juggernaut after he left the Cubs. He led the 1986 Astros to the NLCS and hit a dramatic homer in the bottom of the 14th inning of Game 6 to tie the game against the Mets. But he will always be remembered for his performance in the 1990 World Series. Hatcher hit an incredible .750 for the series (9 for 15) and helped lead the underdog Reds to a sweep of the heavily favored Oakland A's.

Joe Hatten 1916–1988 (Cubs 1951-1952)

He served in the military during World War II, and didn't make his big league debut until he was nearly 30 years old. He had a couple of good seasons with Brooklyn (including World Series seasons 1947 and 1949) before being included in that incredibly unfortunate (for the Cubs) deal that sent Andy Pafko to the Dodgers. Hatten won six games over two seasons as a spot starter in Chicago, and didn't do well. After his time with the Cubs was over, he pitched another eight seasons in the minors before hanging up his spikes for good at the age of 43.

Grady Hatton 1922–2013 (Cubs 1960)

Hatton was an All-Star second baseman, and a rare breed for his era — an infielder with power. Naturally all of that occurred before he came to the Cubs. He was 37 years old when he joined Chicago for the last 28 at-bats of his career. He also played for the Reds, Red Sox, White Sox, Cardinals, and Orioles.

LaTroy Hawkins 1972–(Cubs 2004)

The Cubs signed LaTroy to be their closer after Joe Borowski went down with an arm injury. Hawkins, a local kid from Gary, Indiana, had pitched incredibly well with the Twins the previous few seasons. He had some good moments with the Cubs too, but he also had some very bad moments. He saved 25 games, but he blew consecutive saves down the stretch at the worst possible time. The Cubs had a playoff spot in their hands and LaTroy blew it. Hawkins gave up ten homers that year — a very big number for a closer. The Cubs shipped him off to the Giants in 2005. Latroy later led the 2007 Rockies to the World Series. He also pitched for the Orioles, Yankees, Astros, Brewers, Angels, Mets, and Rockies again. His final appearance of the 2014 season was the 1000th appearance of his big league career.

Jack Hayden 1880–1942 (Cubs 1908)

Hayden was part of the 1908 Cubs team that won the World Series, but he didn't play much. He hit .200 in eleven games, and played right field. He filled in when the Cubs were suffering a rash of injuries to their key players.

Bill Hayes 1957–(Cubs 1980-1981)

In 1978 Tom Brunansky was taken right after the Cubs picked Bill Hayes. Brunansky led his team to the World Series. Hayes got nine big league at-bats. The catcher got two hits and struck out three times. Like many other Cubs named Bill, his nickname was Wild Bill. Hayes went into coaching after his playing career ended, and served on the big league staffs of the Rockies and Giants. With the Giants he won three World Series titles as their bullpen coach. He also managed in the minors for the Cubs for six years.

Egyptian Healy 1866–1899 (1889 White Stockings)

They called him Egyptian because he hailed from Cairo...

Illinois. His real first name was John. Healy was a pitcher in the 1880s and early 1890s, and not a very good one at that. Although he lasted eight big league seasons, he once lost an amazing 29 games in a single season. For his career he was 58 games under .500. In his one season in Chicago, Egyptian was 1-4 in five starts for a third place club. Healy was only 32 years old when he died of consumption in St. Louis.

Bill Heath 1939–(Cubs 1969)

Bill Heath was a backup catcher for the Cubs in 1969, and with less than 200 career at-bats, certainly qualifies as a cup of coffee. But his big league story has a very dramatic ending. Heath was catching on August 19, 1969. If you're a real stats geek, you may remember that Ken Holtzman threw a no-hitter for the Cubs that day. Even though Heath started the game, he wasn't around for that dramatic last out. Early in the game he was hit by a foul tip and broke his hand. Gene Oliver finished the game at catcher, and Heath was placed on the DL. He never played in the majors again. Ironically, Ken Holtzman's second no-hitter for the Cubs (June 3, 1971), also was caught by a cup-of-coffee backup catcher who rarely played (Danny Breeden). After his playing days, Heath suffered an unspeakable tragedy. His wife and daughter were murdered in 1975, during a home invasion.

Cliff Heathcote 1898–1939 (Cubs 1922-1930)

He became a Cub in 1922 when he was traded to the team between games of a double-header with the Cardinals. The Cardinals got Max Flack in return, and both players played for both teams that day. Cliff was an excellent defensive outfielder and played with the Cubs until 1930. On 8/25/22 he was part of the highest scoring game in baseball history. He reached base seven times during that 26-23 win. Cliff died tragically at the way-too-young age of 40 in 1939 from a pulmonary embolism.

*Heaviest Cub...*There have been a few big boys to suit up in Cubs blue over the years, but one Cub stands out. They didn't call him Jumbo Brown for nothing. The right-handed pitcher tipped the scales at 295 pounds when he debuted as an 18-year-old in 1925.

Richie Hebner 1947–(Cubs 1984-1985)

Richie Hebner was famous for working as a gravedigger at a cemetery run by his father during the off-season, and that's where the nickname "The Gravedigger" originated. He played the last two seasons of his career with the Cubs (84-85), mainly as a pinch hitter, but got several key hits during the Cubs division-winning season of 1984. In his years with the Pirates, Phillies, and Cubs, he played in the NLCS eight times, and won it only once (1971 Pirates). He played 18 seasons in the big leagues, and hit over 200 home runs, but only five of them came with the Cubs.

Mike Hechinger 1890–1967 (Cubs 1912-1913)

He had a cup of coffee with his hometown Chicago Cubs at the tail end of the 1912 season and the beginning of 1913, but the backup catcher got only five at-bats, and didn't manage to get a hit. He finished his career with Brooklyn.

Jim Hegan 1920–1984 (Cubs 1960)

Hegan was a five-time All-Star catcher for the Cleveland Indians, including their World Series championship year of 1948. Shanty, as he was nicknamed, was never a great hitter (lifetime .228 in 17 big league seasons), but he was one of the best defensive catchers of his era. He played his final season in the big leagues in Chicago for his old Indians manager, Lou Boudreau. The 39-year-old was one of eight catchers for the Cubs that year. After his playing career ended, Hegan went into coaching and scouting for the New York Yankees, mentoring the likes of Thurman Munson and Rick Dempsey. Hegan's son Mike also played in the big leagues and was himself an All-Star first baseman for the Seattle Pilots.

Aaron Heilman 1978–(Cubs 2009)

Heilman was a steady reliever who made nearly 500 career relief appearances, including 70 with the Cubs in 2009. Chicago acquired him for Ronnie Cedeno that year, and although Heilman gave up his fair share of long balls and walks, he was trotted out to the mound on a regular basis by manager Lou Piniella. Heilman also pitched for the Mets and Diamondbacks in his nine-year big league career.

Al Heist 1927–2006 (Cubs 1960-1961)

Heist was with the Cubs during the ill-fated College of Coaches era. One of those coaches in 1961 apparently liked him, because he got the bulk of playing time at center field during the 1961 season. Heist batted .255 with 7 homers. The Cubs left him unprotected in the 1962 expansion draft, and Houston picked him up. He didn't play much with the Colt 45s in 1962, but that team actually finished higher in the standings than the 1962 Cubs. Al worked as a scout after his playing days, for the Astros, Cubs, Giants, and Padres.

Rollie Hemsley 1907–1972 (Cubs 1931-1932)

Rollie was the backup catcher on the Cubs in 1931 and 1932, but he didn't get along with manager Rogers Hornsby. Although Hornsby was a degenerate gambler, he was also a teetotaler that really cracked down on the team drinkers. Offenders included just about everyone on the team, particularly their best pitcher (Pat Malone), and their backup catcher, Rollie. Hemsley didn't play often because he was Gabby Hartnett's backup and Hartnett played every day, so Rollie often hung out in the illegal speakeasies with his teammates without fear of playing with a hangover. In the 1932 season, the team finally couldn't take any more of Hornsby, and lobbied the young owner of the team (PK Wrigley) to fire him. They got their wish, and everybody's best pal, first baseman Charlie Grimm was named the player-manager. Wrigley took a chance on Grimm — but not before he got Grimm's word that he would make sure the players stayed out of trouble. The first meeting after he was named manager, the new manager told his team to please play it straight for a little while, ending his speech with; "Fellas, we got a darn good chance to win this thing. Everybody take good care of yourselves." That same night, Rollie Hemsley had to be bailed out of jail after he went out and got drunk. Mr. Wrigley and Charlie Grimm were not amused. The Cubs traded Rollie to the Reds after the World Series that year (he batted three times in the 1932 series and struck out all three times). Hemsley went on to have a pretty darn good major league career with the Browns, Phillies, Indians, and Yankees, making the All-Star team five times. But Charlie Grimm never forgot that first night he was the manager of the Cubs, when a backup catcher almost ended his managing career the same day it began.

Ken Henderson 1946 – (Cubs 1979-1980)

Henderson was an acrobatic outfielder who was beloved on the south side of Chicago during his days with the White Sox (1973-1975), but by the time he returned to Chicago in a Cubs uniform, he was running out of gas. He filled in at all three outfield positions for the Cubs, but he only hit .235 and .195 in his two seasons on the north side. They were the final two seasons of his career.

Steve Henderson 1952 – (Cubs 1981-1982)

The Cubs got Henderson from the Mets in the trade that sent Dave Kingman back to New York. Truth be told, the Cubs would have taken a bag of balls for Kingman by that point because he had so thoroughly worn out his welcome. Henderson was much better than that, but he never quite lived up to his potential. Scouts saw him as a can't-miss power hitter (he had earlier been part of the trade that sent Tom Seaver to the Reds), but he never hit more than twelve homers in a season. He hit only seven in Chicago over two full seasons. After the 1982 season the Cubs traded him to the Mariners for Rich Bordi.

Bob Hendley 1939 – (Cubs 1965-1967)

Hendley only won 10 games in his two and a half seasons with the Cubs, but he had a few moments of shining glory. His most memorable game in a Cubs uniform came on September 9th, 1965 at Dodgers Stadium. The Dodgers scored without the benefit of a hit in the 5th inning, and Hendley didn't give up a hit until the 7th inning. That harmless double was the only hit he allowed all game. It was a truly incredible pitching performance by Hendley, but it wasn't good enough. The other pitcher was just a little more incredible. His name was Sandy Koufax, and all he did was pitch a perfect game.

Harvey Hendrick 1897 – 1941 (Cubs 1933)

Gink, as he was known to his teammates, was a utility man in the big leagues for eleven seasons, including one year with the Cubs. He backed up defensively-challenged outfielders Babe Herman and Riggs Stephenson and third baseman Woody English. Gink's story does not end well. Just a few years after his playing career ended, he shot himself to death at the age of 43.

Elrod Hendricks 1940 – 2005 (Cubs 1972)

He was the starting catcher for three consecutive Baltimore Orioles World Series teams, including the 1970 World Series champions. But by 1972, he had fallen out of favor in Baltimore, so they traded Elrod to the Cubs for Tommy Davis. Davis played incredibly well for Orioles, and Hendricks didn't do much for the Cubs, so the Cubs traded Elrod back to the Orioles in 1973. Hendricks played in another ALCS for the Orioles in 1974. Elrod is still on the post-1900 Cubs record books, however. On September 16, 1972, he walked five times in one game. Only one other Cubs player did that in the 20th century (Andre Dawson in 1990).

Jack Hendricks 1875 – 1943 (Orphans 1902)

His lifetime average as a Cub (then known as the Orphans) is one of the best in club history…he hit .571 for the team. Unfortunately, he only got seven at-bats. He got another shot with the Senators the following season for one of the more unusual reasons in baseball history. He replaced Ed Delahanty, who fell to his death over Niagara Falls (after being kicked off a train for threatening passengers with a straight razor). After his playing career ended, Hendricks went into coaching. Jack managed the Reds and the Cardinals, although he never finished better than 2nd place.

Kyle Hendricks 1989 – (Cubs 2014-present)

The Cubs acquired Hendricks in the trade that sent Ryan Dempster to the Texas Rangers. The youngster quickly worked his way through the Cubs minor league system, and made his debut in 2014. He was outstanding as a rookie, going 7-2 with a 2.46 ERA in 13 starts. Hendricks finished in seventh in the Rookie of the Year voting despite not being called up to the big leagues until July. In 2015, he was a member of the rotation for the entire season, and posted a record of 8-7, with a 3.95 ERA, in 32 starts. But in 2016, Hendricks became a star. He led the league in ERA, won 16 games, won the clinching game that brought the Cubs to their first World Series since 1945, and started Game 7 of the World Series. He finished third in the Cy Young voting. An injury in 2017 slowed his progress, but Kyle still managed to win a crucial Game 1 vs. the Nationals in the NLDS. In 2018 it appeared he was having an off-year, but when the dust settled he had won 14 games, posted a 3.44 ERA, and pitched just shy of 200 innings.

Claude Hendrix 1889−1944 (Cubs 1916-1920)

Claude Hendrix may be one of the most important figures in early Wrigley Field history. He started the very first game played in the ballpark (as a member of the Chi Feds), and the very first game the Cubs played there. On the other hand, his career ended with a gigantic asterisk. Team president Bill Veeck got a telegram before a game in August of 1920, saying that there had been an unusual amount of betting against the Cubs. The starting pitcher that day, Claude Hendrix, reportedly bet $5000 himself. The Cubs didn't let him start the game. Grover Cleveland Alexander started instead (and was offered a $500 bonus if he won the game) — but the Cubs still lost 3-0. Though he had no proof it was true, Veeck ruled that the spitballer Hendrix couldn't play for the Cubs the rest of the season. (History fails to note that Hendrix was running out of gas at the time anyway). Veeck also reported the incident to Judge Kennesaw Landis. In Judge Landis' autobiography, he admitted that he quietly banned Hendrix for life. No public announcements were made. While Hendrix suffered greatly for his role in this case, he didn't suffer as badly as the team across town. The investigation into this game didn't turn up anything against Hendrix, but it did turn up a much bigger scandal: The Chicago White Sox had fixed the 1919 World Series. The Sox were acquitted in court, but banned for life by baseball anyway. Unlike Hendrix, they will forever be branded as the most notorious cheaters in baseball history.

Jim Hendry 1955−(Cubs GM 2002-2011)

Hendry did some good work when he was scouting director of the Cubs in the late 90s. For a few years the Cubs farm system consistently provided the team with good arms, including the likes of Kerry Wood, Mark Prior, and Carlos Zambrano. As a GM he had a few good moments (trading for Aramis Ramirez) and a few clunkers (signing Todd Hundley), but perhaps his biggest sin is that he let the farm system atrophy. When he left after the 2011 season, the cupboard was nearly bare.

George Hennessey 1907−1988 (Cubs 1945)

Because of the travel restrictions placed on baseball during World War II, the Cubs played their spring training in French Lick, Indiana. On March 3rd, 1945, when they gathered at Chicago's Dearborn train station to board the train to camp, Hennessy was one of only six players on that train. He was a 37-year-old minor leaguer at the time. That perseverance eventually paid off, because George did get into two games for the Cubs during that pennant-winning season. His nickname was "Three Star" after the famous brandy (at the time) Hennessey's 3 Star.

Bill Henry 1927−2014 (Cubs 1958-1959)

Bill led the league in appearances in his second and final season with the Cubs. He served as their closer in 1959, winning 9 games, and saving 12. After the season ended, Henry was traded (along with Lou Jackson and Lee Walls) to the Reds for slugging third baseman/first baseman Frank Thomas. Henry became an All-Star with the Reds, and saved more than 60 games over the next few seasons. He pitched in the big leagues until 1969 (at the age of 42).

Roy Henshaw 1911−1993 (Cubs 1933-1936)

Roy Henshaw was not a big man. The University of Chicago product was no taller than 5'8" and didn't weigh a pound over 155. But he was also one of the best starting pitchers on the 1935 Cubs team that would win the National League pennant before losing to the Detroit Tigers in the World Series. Henshaw had a sterling 13-5 record, and for one glorious day — June 28, 1935 — he thought he was perfect. He didn't get flustered in the 6th inning when Pirates pitcher Mace Brown hit a ball that Cubs center fielder Freddie Lindstrom camped under, had two hands on, and dropped. Everyone in the crowd and both dugouts assumed the play had been ruled an error. They had no way of knowing, because in those days the scoreboard didn't record that information (scoring decisions or the number of hits allowed), and the public address announcer was still using a giant megaphone, and that was only used to announce who was batting or who was pitching. So when the game ended, everyone thought Henshaw had thrown a no-hitter. The crowd erupted and the players swarmed their hero on the mound. It wasn't until after the game, in the clubhouse, that they discovered the sad news. The ball hit by the Pittsburgh pitcher had been ruled a hit. Henshaw had only thrown a one-hitter. But it was still the best game of his career.

Felix Heredia 1985 – (Cubs 1998-2001)

Felix was picked up for the playoff drive of 1998. He had been a part of the '97 champion Marlins team and was an important part of their bullpen, but he didn't pitch well for the Cubs. He had a very high ERA for a reliever, but the lefty got plenty of opportunities over the next few years. The Cubs finally gave up on him in 2001. His nickname was "El Gato Flaco," which is Spanish for "Skinny Cat."

Babe Herman 1903 – 1987 (Cubs 1933-1934)

That's right, "Babe" played for the Cubs. Unfortunately, it wasn't THE Babe. His real name was Floyd Caves Herman, and his manager in the minors called him "Babe" after he got a hit in his first at-bat. Babe Ruth was playing then, and the manager said, "You're my babe." The name stuck. He was always a good hitter (he finished his career with a .324 average), but his fielding was notoriously bad. He led the league in errors two years in a row, playing outfield and first base. One of his former Brooklyn teammates liked to joke that the only reason Babe wore a glove was because it was the custom. As bad as he was in the field, his baserunning was even worse. His most legendary baserunning error was one for the ages. He accomplished something that was almost impossible...he doubled into a double play. Babe was tagged out at third base when he was the third one to arrive at the base.

Billy Herman 1909 – 1992 (Cubs 1931-1941)

He was named William Jennings Bryan Herman after the famed orator, and this Billy had an incredible big league career. He was a 10-time All-Star in 15 big league seasons (and his first two years, the All-Star game hadn't been invented yet). He was considered the best hit and run man to ever play the game. His lifetime batting average was .304. He led the league in hits, doubles, triples, and sacrifices, but he was even better known for his glove. In his 15 years as a second baseman he led the league in putouts seven times, not to mention leading the league in assists, fielding percentage, and range. And he was elected into baseball's Hall of Fame in 1975. But sadly, Herman didn't spend his entire career with the Cubs. The team somehow traded him to the Dodgers in 1941. Leo Durocher, the Dodgers manager at the time, tells how this happened in his book *Nice Guys Finish Last*. He

was traded to the Dodgers at four in the morning. According to Durocher, who got this information directly from his GM (MacPhail), the trade was made during a night of drinking. MacPhail was invited to the suite of the Cubs GM Jim Gallagher when the Cubs were in New York. MacPhail was a well-known drunk, but he figured out pretty quickly that Gallagher and manager Jimmy Wilson were trying to get him drunk to talk trade. So, instead of drinking the brandy, MacPhail only pretended to drink it while he was actually pouring it out in flower pots, toilet bowls, and wherever else he could. Meanwhile, every time the Cubs poured MacPhail a drink, they also poured themselves one. Instead of getting him drunk, they got themselves drunk. By 4 AM MacPhail had acquired the best second baseman in baseball in exchange for a backup outfielder and a utility infielder. The deal was put in writing on the back of an envelope. And yes, MacPhail's grandson later became the president and general manager of the Cubs: the infamous Andy MacPhail.

Billy Herman still holds the Cubs record for most hits on Opening Day. He got five in 1936.

Chad Hermansen 1977 – (Cubs 2002)

Hermansen was acquired from the Pittsburgh Pirates for outfielder Darren Lewis. He didn't get a lot of playing time with the Cubs (35 games), but he did play enough to catch the eye of the Dodgers. Hermansen was included in the Todd Hundley trade, which brought Eric Karros and Mark Grudzielanek from the Dodgers to the Cubs.

Gene Hermanski 1920 – 2010 (Cubs 1951-1953)

During his time with the Dodgers, Gene was one of the first players to accept Jackie Robinson as a teammate. He once joked that all of the Dodgers should wear the number 42 so that snipers didn't know which one was Jackie. Hermanski came to the Cubs from the Dodgers in one of the most lopsided trades in team history along with light-hitting shortstop Eddie Miksis, Bruce Edwards, and Joe Hatten in exchange for the most popular player on the Cubs (Andy Pafko), one of their best starting pitchers (Johnny Schmitz), catcher Rube Walker, and Wayne Terwilliger. The trade was so lopsided fans thought that Cubs GM Wid Matthews, a former Branch Rickey protégé, was still on Rickey's payroll. The Dodgers won the pennant in 1952 with those players while the Cubs finished 19 1/2 games behind them. Hermanski was mainly the fourth outfielder in Chicago during his time with the Cubs.

Chico Hernandez 1916–1986 (Cubs 1942-1943)

His teammates called him "Chico" and in 1942 he and Cubs pitcher Hi Bithorn formed the very first all-Latin battery in big league history. Chico was from Cuba. Bithorn was from Puerto Rico.

Jose Hernandez 1969–(Cubs 1994-1999, 2003)

Hernandez was a long-time mainstay on the Cubs during the slugging Sammy Sosa era, and Jose fit right in. He was an oddity in that he was a swing-for-the-fences shortstop, but he did club 71 homers as a Cub. He also struck out 504 times. Jose was a good glove man too — playing every position in the infield, and occasionally even in the outfield. He was picked up by the Cubs again at the tail end of the 2003 season, although he didn't make the postseason roster. Between his two stints with the Cubs, Jose was an All-Star with Milwaukee — and led the league in strikeouts twice.

Ramon Hernandez 1940–2009 (Cubs 1968, 1976-1977)

Ramon was known for his herky-jerky deceptive delivery that worked like a charm while he was a member of the Pittsburgh Pirates, but not so much as a member of the Cubs. His lifetime ERA was 3.03, but those very good stats (including 46 career saves) mainly benefited our divisional rival Pittsburgh. In his two stints with the Cubs (1968 and 1976-77), Ramon pitched a grand total of 18 innings. In those 18 innings, he gave up 16 earned runs. But in a Cubs locker room stuffed to the gills with quality mustaches, the stash on the face of Ramon Hernandez took second place to no one.

Willie Hernandez 1954–(Cubs 1977-1983)

Willie was a pretty good relief pitcher for the Cubs in the late 70s and early 80s, pitching in over 50 games during five of his six Cubs seasons. The Cubs traded him to the Phillies for Dick Ruthven in 1983. Ruthven won a total of 22 games for the Cubs in four mediocre seasons. Hernandez went on to pitch in the World Series for the Phillies in 1983. He also won

the MVP and Cy Young after leading the 1984 Detroit Tigers to the World Series championship.

Tom Hernon 1866–1902 (Colts 1897)

Tom spent most of his career in the minor leagues, but did get a brief cup of coffee with the Cubs (then known as the Colts) at the end of the 1897 season. He was 30 years old at the time — and didn't quite seize the day. In his four games in the lineup as the team's left fielder, Hernon hit only .063. He died of Bright's Disease in 1902 at the age of 35.

Jonathan Herrera 1984–(Cubs 2015)

With the youngest infield in the league in 2015, the Cubs needed a veteran backup, so they signed Herrera as a free agent. He had previously served as a backup infielder (2B, SS, 3B) for the Rockies and Red Sox. Herrera had several clutch hits during the season, and played an excellent 2B and 3B, but with the emergence of Javy Baez and Addison Russell, his playing time diminished significantly. He didn't make the postseason roster.

Leroy Herrmann 1906–1972 (Cubs 1932-1933)

Herrmann pitched in relief for the pennant-winning 1932 Cubs, but didn't make it on the postseason roster. Leroy pitched in 16 games over his two Cubs seasons, earning two wins and a save, but struggling mightily with big league hitters. His lifetime ERA is over six. He later also pitched for the Reds.

John Herrnstein 1938–2017 (Cubs 1966)

After starring in two sports in college (University of Michigan), Herrnstein was drafted by the Phillies. The Cubs got him in the deal that also sent Fergie Jenkins to Chicago. Herrnstein was a power hitter in the minor leagues, but in his one extended big league opportunity (with the Phillies in 1964), he didn't really produce. The Cubs were one of the three teams John played for in 1966. In seventeen at-bats with Chicago he managed three hits. All three were singles.

Buck Herzog 1885–1953 (Cubs 1919-1920)

Herzog had a very good 13-year big league career with the Giants (four pennant winners), Braves, Reds, and Cubs, but in Chicago he will always be remembered for the way his career ended. Team president Bill Veeck got a telegram before a game in August of 1920, saying that there had been an unusual amount of betting against the Cubs. The starting pitcher that day, Claude Hendrix, reportedly bet $5000 himself. Veeck reported the incident to Judge Kennesaw Landis. In Judge Landis' autobiography, he admitted that he quietly banned Hendrix for life. No public announcements were made. The other implicated Cubs player was Buck Herzog. Buck was also quietly shoved out of baseball by Landis. After the season he was attacked by a fan who called him a crook. During the melee, a friend of the fan stabbed Herzog three times (he recovered from his injuries).

Jason Heyward 1989 – (Cubs 2016-present)

When the Cubs signed the 3-time Gold Glover to an eight-year contract after the 2015 season, Cubs fans were beyond excited. St. Louis Cardinals fans (where he had played the previous season) didn't feel the same way. But he had a rough first season in a Cubs uniform, hitting only .230 and driving in a measly 49 runs. On the other hand, he is credited with firing up his teammates with a crucial pep talk during a rain delay in the 7th game of the World Series. Heyward also won a Gold Glove for his incredible defensive skills in right field. His hitting improved a bit in 2017, but once again it was his steady glove that made him valuable. He won another Gold Glove in 2017. Jason had his best offensive season with the Cubs in 2018 (hitting .270), and had some incredible clutch hits, including a dramatic walk-off grand slam. On the other hand he still only managed 8 homers for the year. Not the kind of output you expect from the highest paid player on the team.

> Cubs players have had some great nicknames over the years. Among players starting with the letter H, you'll find nicknames like Babe, Bubbles, Buck, Bud, Chico, Circus Solly, Coldwater Jim, Egyptian, Froggy, Gabby, Gink, Gravedigger, J-Hey, Long Tom, Mr. Chips, Rebel, Rip, Shanty, Shakes, Skinny Cat, Smilin' Stan, Topsy, Trader, Twiggy, Wild Bill, and Yaller Bill.

Jack Hiatt 1942 – (Cubs 1970)

Hiatt was a backup catcher for the Cubs in 1970, getting pretty extensive at-bats during a year Cubs starter Randy Hundley was sidelined. He hit .242 in that role. It was his only season in Chicago. He previously served as a backup catcher in San Francisco, Los Angeles, and Montreal, and finished up his career with the Houston Astros. The Cubs acquired him from Montreal for Boots Day. After his playing career he managed in the minor leagues for the Cubs many years, and later became the director of player development for the Giants.

Greg Hibbard 1964 – (Cubs 1993)

Hibbard was drafted away from the White Sox by the Marlins in the 1992 expansion draft, who promptly turned around and traded the left-hander to the Cubs before the 1993 season. Greg had the best season of his career with the Cubs, winning 15 games and posting an ERA under four. He signed a big free agent deal with the Mariners the next year, but blew out his arm early in the year and never pitched in the big leagues again.

John Hibbard 1864 – 1937 (White Stockings 1884)

Hibbard was a local Chicago boy who got two starts for the Cubs (then known as the White Stockings) in the summer of 1884. He completed both games, and one of them was a shutout. But Hibbard went to the University of Michigan in the fall of that year, and his big league baseball career ended. He became a successful engineer and businessman, and served for a time as the commissioner of the National Metal Trades Association.

Bryan Hickerson 1963 – (Cubs 1995)

The Cubs used Hickerson quite a bit during the first half of the 1995 season (38 appearances), but he was rocked hard. By the time they dumped him off to the Rockies in July, Hickerson's ERA was 6.82. After his career, he worked for a baseball ministry, which spread the love of Jesus and baseball at the same time. He has also traveled to several war zones to preach and to feed our soldiers.

Eddie Hickey 1872 – 1941 (Orphans 1901)

Hickey was a backup third baseman for the 1901 Cubs (then known as the Orphans). Among his teammates on that team

— future Hall of Famers Frank Chance and Rube Waddell. He hit .162 in his limited shot at the big-time. The rest of his 14-year baseball career was spent in the minor leagues.

Jim Hickman 1937–2016 (Cubs 1969-1973)

After eight forgettable seasons with three different teams, Jim Hickman was magically transformed from a perennial struggler to a powerful slugger. In 1970 at the age of 33, "Gentleman Jim" somehow batted .315, with 32 home runs, 115 runs batted in, and 102 runs scored for the Chicago Cubs. Not bad for a player whose previous career bests were a .257 average, 21 homers, 57 RBI, and 54 runs scored. He also drove in a hard-charging Pete Rose with a 12th inning single in that season's All-Star Game (probably the most famous moment in All-Star Game history). When asked to explain his surprising turnabout, Hickman replied, "I really don't know. If I knew, I'd tell you." His manager Leo Durocher loved him because he was a gentleman (hence the nickname) and because he would defend the boss against what Durocher considered the "trouble-making" faction of Milt Pappas and Joe Pepitone. Hickman passed away on June 25, 2016 during the Cubs World Championship year.

Kirby Higbe 1915–1985 (Cubs 1937-1939)

Higbe didn't get a lot of playing time with the Cubs in parts of three seasons in Chicago, including the 1938 pennant-winning year. The Cubs used him primarily out of the bullpen. They traded him in the 1939 season, and Higbe later became a two-time All-Star and 20-game winner with the Brooklyn Dodgers. He didn't respond well to the arrival of Jackie Robinson in 1947, however, and was shipped off to Pittsburgh. Thanks to the movie *42*, he'll forever be remembered as a villain. It's probably a pretty accurate portrayal of Higbe, who grew up in South Carolina, and claimed to have developed his throwing arm by throwing rocks at black people.

Irv Higginbotham 1882–1959 (Cubs 1909)

Higginbotham was an effective relief pitcher for the Cubs (2.19 ERA) in his final big league season (1909). Unfortunately for Irv, his timing was less than ideal. If he had arrived in any other year that half-decade he would have been part of a pennant-winning team. The 1909 crew fell just a little short.

After his playing career he became a house painter.

Dick Higham 1851–1905 (White Stockings 1875)

Born during the reign of Queen Victoria in Ipswich, England, Dick came to America as a young lad and picked up the sport pretty fast. He was only 19 years old when he made his big league debut, and 24 when he played for Chicago in 1875. The second baseman/catcher/outfielder also played for the New York Mutuals in 1875. Dick's story, however, does not have a happy baseball ending. He became an umpire after he quit as a player, and was banned for life by the league after it was discovered he was fixing games with a gambler. He's the only umpire ever to be banned for that.

Bobby Hill 1978– (Cubs 2002-2003)

Hill was supposed to be the Cubs second baseman of the future. Cubs brass considered him to be their top prospect. He got significant playing time during the 2002 season, and showed enough promise to convince the Pittsburgh Pirates to trade their young third baseman Aramis Ramirez to the Cubs. That turned out to be a great trade for Chicago. Hill only played part of one season for the Pirates before disappearing into their minor league system. Ramirez anchored the hot corner for the Cubs for the better part of a decade.

Glenallen Hill 1965– (Cubs 1993-1994, 1998-2000)

The bulging biceps and nasty scowl on Hill's face may have come from artificial sources (as the Mitchell Report intimated in 2007), but he will always be remembered for a home run he hit on May 11, 2000. That day Hill became the only player in history to hit a homer onto the rooftop of the building across the street. It was a monumental blast, estimated at well over 500 feet.

Koyie Hill 1979– (Cubs 2007-2011, 2012)

Koyie was a backup catcher for most of his time in a Cubs uniform, but he's not really remembered for anything he did behind the plate or with the bat. He's remembered for a horrific injury he was able to overcome. He was using a table saw and his hand got caught in the blade, severing his thumb and damaging his fingers. Somehow he was miraculously able to continue playing baseball. One other bit of Koyie Hill trivia: he was the catcher who went in the game to replace

Michael Barrett after Barrett and Carlos Zambrano got into a fistfight during a game on June 1, 2007.

Rich Hill 1980 – (Cubs 2005-2008)
When he was a young left-hander coming up through the Cubs organization, the team really thought they had something special. Hill was tall (6'5) and commanding on the mound, and he threw a wicked curveball. In 2007, that took him a long way. He struck out 183 batters in 195 innings and won 11 games for the division-winning Cubs. But the following year he couldn't find the strike zone. The Cubs gave up on him and sold him to the Orioles before the 2009 season. He managed to stay in the big leagues as a specialty lefty reliever for several season In 2013 with the Indians, he pitched in 63 games, but didn't even register 40 innings pitched. But Rich was put back into the starting rotation by the Oakland A's in 2016 and after experiencing a resurgence was traded to the Dodgers. He shut out the eventual World Champion Chicago Cubs in the NLDS for the Dodgers, and has been an elite starter in the big leagues ever since.

R.E. Hillebrand (Orphans 1902)
His first name has been lost to time, and virtually nothing is known about the man who was listed as "Hillebrand" and played right field for the Cubs on August 29, 1902. We don't know if he batted right-handed or left. We don't know when he was born or where. We just know he went 0 for 4 with a walk (and a run scored) in a 9-3 win over the first place Pirates in Pittsburgh. He was let go after the game. The newspapers described him as a kid who looked really nervous.

Frank Hiller 1920 – 1987 (Cubs 1950-1951)
One of the many Cubs nicknamed "Dutch" (because of his German heritage), Hiller was a right-handed swing starter. He had a very good year in 1950, going 12-5 with a 3.53 ERA. The following year was the opposite (6-12, 4.84 ERA), so the Cubs traded him to the Reds for Willie Ramsell. Hiller lacked a strikeout pitch, which was his Achilles heel as a reliever. In over 533 innings pitched, he only struck out 197 batters.

Dave Hillman 1927– (Cubs 1955-1959)
Hillman appeared in over a hundred games for the Cubs in

the 1950s. The right-hander worked both as a starter and reliever, and had a respectable ERA, but he had the propensity to give up the long ball. After the 1959 season Hillman was traded to the Red Sox. He spent two years in Boston — the last season of Ted Williams' career, and the first of Carl Yastremski's.

Larry Himes 1940 – (Cubs GM 1992-1994)
Yes, he traded for Sammy Sosa, but Larry Himes will always be remembered for letting Hall of Famer Greg Maddux go for no good reason. When he signed Jose Guzman, he said it would make up for the loss of the best pitcher of his generation. Um…not so much. Himes was also known for his prickly and harsh personality. He instituted nitpicky rules like dress codes for players and no beer allowed in the clubhouse, which needless to say, didn't win him any friends on the team. Cubs players, managers, and fans couldn't stand him, and when he left, everyone cheered. In his years with the Cubs, they finished 4th, 4th, and 5th.

Vedie Himsl 1917 – 2004 (Cubs manager 1961)
Vedie was one of the coaches during the College of Coaches era, and had three stints during the 1961 season at the helm of the team. The combined record was 10-21. By 1962 he was out of the coaching rotation.

Paul Hines 1855 – 1935 (White Stockings 1875-1877)
Hines played in the very first game the Cubs (then known as the White Stockings) played as a member of the National League. In those days before mitts, when the mound was closer, and the rules hadn't been quite been nailed down yet, Hines was a center fielder, first baseman, and second baseman. In that first NL season, he led the league in doubles. He left Chicago after the 1877 season and promptly won the Triple Crown for Providence. Hines played 20 seasons in the big leagues, and is considered one of the best players of his era.

Alex Hinshaw 1982 – (Cubs 2012)
Hinshaw pitched in only two games for the Cubs, and the last one was bad enough to keep him out of the big leagues ever since. He faced five batters, and all five of them reached base. Actually, three of them only briefly did, as they touched every

base on their home run trots. (Aramis Ramirez, Ryan Braun, and Corey Hart)

Gene Hiser 1948– (Cubs 1971-1975)

Hiser was a first round pick of the Cubs in 1970, and quickly made it up to the big leagues, but he never really broke through. It was hard getting playing time in the Cubs outfield with the likes of Rick Monday, Jose Cardenal, and Billy Williams on the roster. He served mainly as a pinch hitter and extra outfielder for a few seasons, finishing with a career batting average of .202. He remains in the Chicago area and is very active working with Cubs-related charities.

Don Hoak 1928–1969 (Cubs 1956)

He was a Marine and a boxer before he came to baseball, so it's no wonder his teammates called him Tiger. Before he made it to the big leagues, Hoak played in Cuba for a part of a season and faced future dictator Fidel Castro in a game. He was a World Series champ with the Dodgers in 1955, and shared third base with an aging Jackie Robinson that season, so the Cubs were excited to get him (along with Russ Meyer and Walt Moryn) a few weeks after the series ended. Unfortunately, he had a terrible season in Chicago in 1956. He set a Cubs record when he struck out six times in one game. In over 400 at-bats, he hit only .215, so the Cubs got rid of him. Of course, after he left the Cubs, he immediately became an All-Star (in 1957). Then, in 1960, he finished 2nd in the MVP voting and led the Pittsburgh Pirates to the World Series championship. Hoak died of a heart attack while chasing his brother-in-law's stolen car.

Glen Hobbie 1936–2013 (Cubs 1957-1964)

Hobbie was part of the Cubs rotation in the late 50s and early 60s: one of the worst stretches in Cubs history. Hobbie's lifetime record was nearly twenty games under .500, and he lost twenty games in one season (1960), but he did have some moments of brilliance in a Cubs uniform. He threw eleven shutouts for the Cubs, and won 16 games in two different seasons. He worked for the Roller Derby Association after he retired from baseball.

Historical note: On the day that U2 Pilot Gary Powers was shot down over the Soviet Union (1960), Hobbie was on the mound for the Cubs. He defeated the Cardinals 5-4 in St. Louis.

Charlie Hodes 1848–1875 (White Stockings 1871)

A member of the very first official Chicago team (National Association) before the National League was even formed, Charlie was a catcher, center fielder, and third baseman on the last team to play in Chicago before the Great Chicago Fire. His baseball career ended when he contracted tuberculosis. Charlie was only 26 when he died in 1875.

Russ Hodges 1910–1971 (Cubs announcer 1935-1938)

Hodges was a Cubs radio announcer during two of their pennant seasons ('35 & '38), but then moved on to New York. He is best remembered for his call on Bobby Thomson's home run that won the pennant for the Giants: "The Giants win the pennant! The Giants win the pennant! The Giants win the pennant!" He is in the "Scribes & Mikemen" section of baseball's Hall of Fame as a winner of the Ford C. Frick award.

Billy Hoeft 1932–2010 (Cubs 1965-1966)

Billy was a former All-Star pitcher when he came to the Cubs (he had won 20 games in a season for the Tigers). However, by the time he put on his Cubs uniform, he was no longer pitching at that level. He was used mostly in relief by Chicago, and pitched quite well: a 2.81 ERA. It didn't last, unfortunately, and Billy was let go before the end of the 1966 season. One of Billy's claims to fame is that he gave up the first home run of Harmon Killebrew's career.

Guy Hoffman 1956– (Cubs 1986)

Guy was a left-handed swing starter for the Cubs in 1986 and posted respectable, if unspectacular numbers. He was 6-2, with a 3.86 ERA. The Cubs traded him to the Reds the following year and Hoffman had his best season in the big leagues. He won 9 games in 22 starts for the 1987 Reds. That was his last good year. By 1988 he was out of the big leagues. He signed in Japan, and finished his career there.

Larry Hoffman 1878–1948 (Orphans 1901)

The native Chicagoan got one small taste of the big-time with his hometown Cubs (then known as the Orphans) in 1901. He hit over .300 in 25 plate appearances, but spent the rest of his baseball career (which lasted another ten years) in the minors. Hoffman played second and third base.

Micah Hoffpauir 1980 – (Cubs 2008-2010)

The big first baseman was considered one of those 4A players — too good for AAA, but not quite big league material. He got his longest shot in 2009 with the Cubs and hit 10 homers in only 239 at-bats. After he spent the 2010 season mainly in Iowa, Hoffpauir went to Japan.

Solly Hofman 1882 – 1956 (Cubs 1904-1912, 1916)

His nickname was Circus Solly, and he played for the Cubs during their most dominant era, and was a key member of four World Series teams. At first he was a utility man, but by the time his Cubs tenure was through, he was their full-time center fielder. Circus Solly was only a lifetime .269 hitter, but in the World Series he took his game up a notch. He hit .298 in 57 World Series at-bats, and made some spectacular plays in the outfield. His most famous moment in a Cubs uniform, however, occurred during the infamous Merkle Boner game in 1908. When that game supposedly ended, the ball was in Circus Solly's hands. Johnny Evers called for it, but when Hofman threw it, it sailed over Evers' head. Evers did finally get his hands on the ball, and touched second base. That resulted in the force-out that cost the Giants the pennant. Circus Solly played for the Cubs from 1904-1912, and then returned to finish his career with them in their first season at what is now known as Wrigley Field in 1916.

Brad Hogg 1889 – 1935 (Cubs 1915)

Hogg pitched in two games for the Cubs during their last season in West Side Grounds, including a complete game shutout. He finished up his career in Philadelphia with the Phillies in 1919.

John Holland 1910 – 1979 (Cubs GM 1957-1975)

Holland oversaw the resurgence of the Cubs in the 1960s and 1970s. He acquired Ferguson Jenkins, Glenn Beckert, Jim Hickman, and Randy Hundley, and signed or drafted the likes of Ron Santo, Billy Williams, and Don Kessinger. On the other hand, he also traded Lou Brock. You can't win 'em all. As a matter of fact, he never won a single time. In all of his years at the helm of the Cubs, they never made the playoffs a single time.

Todd Hollandsworth 1973 – (Cubs 2004-2005)

Hollandsworth was the 1996 Rookie of the Year for the Dodgers, and was part of that 2003 Florida Marlins team that broke the hearts of Cubs fans in the playoffs, but he was mostly a fourth outfielder for the Cubs in his time here. He hit a few dramatic homers and contributed to the team in both of his seasons in Chicago, but the Cubs traded him for a pair of minor leaguers once they determined they were out of the pennant race in 2005. Hollandsworth later worked in the Comcast studios doing pre- and post-game analysis during the Cubs television broadcasts.

Ed Holley 1899 – 1986 (Cubs 1928)

Holley was a reliever for the Cubs in his rookie season of 1928. He appeared in 13 games and registered a 3.77 ERA. After leaving the Cubs he became a 13-game winner for Philadelphia in 1933 — clearly the best season of his big league career.

Jesse Hollins 1970 – 2009 (Cubs 1992)

He made four appearances for the Cubs out of the bullpen after being called up in September, and was hit hard. Jesse hurt his arm the next season and never made it back to the big leagues. On July 9, 2009, Jessie passed away at the age of 39. His body was found floating in a lake, apparently the victim of a fishing accident.

John Hollison 1870 – 1969 (Colts 1892)

His nickname was Swede. He pitched in only one game for the Cubs (then known as the Colts) on August 13, 1892 — a 6-2 loss to the first place Cleveland Spiders. He relieved HOFer Clark Griffith, pitching four innings, and giving up one run — a home run. When he died on August 19, 1969 (the day of Ken Holtzman's no-hitter), he was 99 years old. At that time, the oldest living big league player.

Charlie Hollocher 1896 – 1940 (Cubs 1918-1924)

Charlie's life was a series of very high highs and very low lows. He was one of the greatest hitters on the Cubs in his seven seasons in the big leagues. He led the 1918 team to the pennant, and led the league in hits. In 1922, he only struck out four times in 509 at-bats, still the best ratio in Cubs history. In two different seasons he was in the top ten in hitting, and he anchored the team's defense at shortstop. He seemed destined to have a Hall of Fame career. But Charlie was a very troubled man. In 1923 he developed a strange stomach problem. In August of that season, he left a note for his manager one day, saying he was going to quit for the year. He was convinced that baseball was making him sick. This is what his letter said, according John Snyder's *Cubs Journal*: "Feeling pretty rotten so made up my mind to go home and take a rest and forget baseball for the rest of the year. No hard feelings, just don't feel like baseball for the rest of the year."

He wrote that note on the day President Warren Harding died, so it didn't get much attention in the Chicago press. The Cubs simply described his problem as "nervousness," and vowed he would return the following season. It seemed like everything was fine when he came back the next year, but he couldn't shake the stomach problems. He saw dozens of doctors and specialists, but no one could figure out what he had. After the 1924 season, at the ridiculously young age of 28, he retired...with a lifetime average of .304.

When his playing days were over, he dropped out of public view and drifted from job to job, but Hollocher continued to suffer mightily, both physically and mentally, most likely from clinical depression. His return to baseball was rumored nearly every year, but the demons that ended his playing career eventually ended his life. In 1940, at the age of 44, he bought a shotgun and shot himself.

*Hollywood & the Cubs...*The Cubs had one of the strongest connections to Hollywood of any MLB team. The Cubs became the first team to go out West (their minor league team played in Los Angeles, and the big league team trained in Catalina Island). Minor league Cubs like Chuck Connors *(The Rifleman)*, Steve Bilko (inspired Phil Silvers), and Jophery Brown (stunt man/Cubs pitcher) directly affected the industry. A Cubs announcer (Ronald Reagan) did a film test while covering the team in spring training, and later played a Cub in the movies (Grover Cleveland Alexander). Joe E. Brown, a huge star in the 1930s, befriended Cubs players and was inspired to make two movies featuring a

Cubs player as the main character. Movies like *Rookie of the Year, The Natural, Takin' Care of Business, 42, The Babe Ruth Story, Ferris Buehler's Day Off, The Blues Brothers, The Break-Up* and *A League of Their Own* all have scenes that take place at Wrigley Field. Television shows like *The Bob Newhart Show* and *Punky Brewster* did entire episodes about the Cubs. Very few teams have had that many connections to Hollywood.

Billy Holm 1912–1977 (Cubs 1943-1944)

The local Chicago boy got his shot with his hometown Cubs during the war. He was in his 30s when he broke in to the big leagues. Billy was a decent catcher, but unfortunately Holm simply couldn't hit big league pitching, even wartime big league pitching. In two seasons in Chicago he hit .067 and .136, respectively.

Fred Holmes 1878–1956 (Cubs 1904)

Holmes played exactly one game for his hometown Cubs on April 24, 1904. He was the catcher for Three Finger Mordecai Brown against St. Louis at West Side Grounds. Fred went 1 for 3 with a double and a run scored.

Ken Holtzman 1945– (Cubs 1966-1971)

He would become one of the rarest animals on the North American continent...a quality homegrown Chicago Cubs starting pitcher. But Holtzman was the real deal. He went 9-0 for the Cubs while serving in the National Guard in 1967, and when his military service was over, he followed that up with back-to-back 17-win seasons in 1969 and 1970. Holtzman also pitched a no-hitter in each of those seasons. When he had an off-year in 1971, and started arguing with Leo Durocher (who allegedly was mad because Holtzman beat him at gin rummy), he was shipped off to Oakland in the trade that brought Rick Monday to the Cubs. In four seasons with Oakland he won an astounding 77 games, was named an All-Star twice, became a three-time World Series champ, won four games in those World Series, and even hit a home run. He returned to the Cubs in 1978 for the last two seasons of a very impressive career.

Historical note: On the day the Woodstock Festival opened in New York, Holtzman was outdueled by Hall of Famer Juan Marichal in a 3-0 loss to the Giants. Kenny threw his first no-hitter in his very next start.

Marty Honan 1869–1908 (Colts 1890-1891)

Honan appeared in parts of two seasons for the Cubs (then known as the Colts), but just barely. The backup catcher played in one 1890 game, and five in 1891. He got two hits including a triple, and drove in four runs. He also committed two errors. Honan died during the last Cubs championship season of the 20th century in 1908 at the age of 39.

Burt Hooton 1950–(Cubs 1971-1975)

Hooton got off to an incredible start in his big league career. He came up at the end of the 1971 season and had three tremendous starts (2-0, two complete games, one shutout, 22 Ks in 21 innings). In fact, he was so good, the Cubs felt they could afford to trade Ken Holtzman in the offseason. It sure looked good early when Hooton used his incredible knuckle-curve to pitch a no-hitter in his fourth career start. In fact, he pitched well the entire 1972 season, despite going only 11-14. But Hooton slumped a bit in 1973 and 1974, and in the early part of 1975, the Cubs shipped him off to the Dodgers for Geoff Zahn and Eddie Solomon. That turned out to be a terrible trade for Chicago. Hooton was still young and only needed a little guidance, something he got in Los Angeles. He won 18 games for the Dodgers that year, went on to pitch another eleven seasons, became an All-Star, a World Series champ, and a runner-up for the Cy Young Award. Don't ask what the players the Cubs got in return for him did.

Historical note: On the day Elvis Presley performed at the Chicago Stadium in Chicago in 1972, Hooton pitched a shutout against the Dodgers at Wrigley Field.

Trader Horne 1899–1983 (Cubs 1929)

His real name was Berlyn Dale Horne and he was a right-handed reliever for the 1929 pennant-winning Cubs. The nickname came from real-life trader and adventurer Alfred Aloysius "Trader" Horn, who was famous at the time for his safaris in Africa. Trader Horne the pitcher was a 30-year-old rookie finally living his dream on that great 1929 Cubs team. Cubs owner William Wrigley had a soft spot for this 10-year

minor league veteran. Unfortunately for Horn, he simply couldn't find home plate. He gave up 21 walks and 24 hits in 23 innings. By the time the Cubs made it to the World Series against the A's that year, Trader had pitched in his final major league game.

Rogers Hornsby 1897–1963 (Cubs 1929-1932)

It's hard to imagine that one of the greatest players in history was not popular in Chicago — but Hornsby clearly was not. Hornsby had one great season for the Cubs, their World Series year of 1929, and he became the manager at the very end of the following year. Despite managing a notoriously rowdy team, he ruled with an iron fist. He didn't just ban drinking (which, of course, was illegal at the time), he banned reading, movies, soda pop, smoking, and eating in the clubhouse. He was so hated by his players that when the 1932 team won the pennant (after he was fired), the players voted to give him zero cents of a playoff share, even though he had been with the team for 4 months.

Their hatred of him went much deeper than his strict rules. He was in deep debt to many of the players on the team. The Commissioner of Baseball, Judge Kennesaw Mountain Landis, became so alarmed by the reports he was getting about Hornsby, that he sent letters warning the team and the players about him. He also sent one to the NL President demanding any and all information he had about Hornsby's gambling. Hornsby was defiant about it until the very end: "Gambling's legal," he would say. He never bet on baseball, only the horses. Probably influenced by Hornsby's star power, Landis chose not to punish him. But his letters to the club led to an internal Cubs investigation. Team owner William Wrigley and team president William Veeck discovered that Hornsby had borrowed $11,000 from his own players. That's when they fired him and replaced him with Charlie Grimm. Grimm led the 1932 team to the World Series. Hornsby never experienced the playoffs again.

Later in life he was hired by Wrigley's son Phillip to become the team's first minor league batting instructor. The same prickly personality and inability to understand why people couldn't naturally hit as well as he did, however, made him as lousy at that job as he was as a manager. As a player Rogers Hornsby had very few peers. His lifetime batting average is .358. He hit .400 three different times. He narrowly missed it a fourth time (.397). He won two MVP awards, two triple crowns, and seven batting titles. And he did all that while gambling away nearly every dime he earned.

Tim Hosley 1947–2014 (Cubs 1975-1976)

Hosley was a backup catcher in his nine-year big league career, and his best season in baseball was with the 1975 Cubs. (His Oakland A's teams in 1973 and 1974 won the World Series, but Tim wasn't on the post-season roster). With the Cubs he backed up Steve Swisher and George Mitterwald, got over a hundred at-bats, and hit six homers. The Cubs let him go early in the 1976 season, and he returned to the Oakland As.

John Houseman 1870–1922 (Colts 1894)

He was the first big leaguer born in the Netherlands. (Not the actor who did the Smith Barney commercials in the 70s and 80s.) Houseman's baseball career was uneventful, the utility man played only two big league seasons. But during the famous Iroquois Theater fire, Houseman distinguished himself along with fellow ballplayer Charlie Dexter by breaking down a door and rescuing several patrons. Over 600 people died in that fire.

Tyler Houston 1971– (Cubs 1996-1999)

He was a catcher and first baseman with a little pop in his bat, but could never claim a starting position. Houston was part of the 1997 Cubs team that started the season 0-14. He later played for the Indians, Brewers, Dodgers, and Phillies.

Del Howard 1877–1956 (Cubs 1907-1908)

On Christmas Eve 1877, a boy named George Elmer Howard was born in Kenney, Illinois. During his childhood everyone began calling him Del. Good Ol' Del became a big league ballplayer with the Chicago Cubs. He was a backup outfielder, first baseman, and second baseman on the first Cubs teams to win the World Series, the 1907 and 1908 Cubs. Del Howard only hit two homers in his two seasons in Chicago, but he also won two rings.

Cal Howe 1924–2008 (Cubs 1952)

If you want to travel back in time to watch Cal pitch, set the wayback machine for September 26, 1952. It was his only appearance in the big leagues, and it happened in St. Louis' Sportsman's Park. Cal pitched the final two innings of a 10-3 Cubs loss. Even though he only pitched in that one game, he did face and retire two Hall of Famers (Red Schoendienst & Stan Musial) and the son of another (Dick Sisler, George Sisler's son). Howe didn't give up a hit, and finished his big league career with a perfect 0.00 ERA.

Jay Howell 1955– (Cubs 1981)

Howell went 2-0 for the Cubs during the strike-shortened 1981 season, but they traded him in the off-season to the Yankees for Pat Tabler. Howell went on to become a three-time All-Star closer and World Series champion. Tabler was included in the package that brought Steve Trout to the Cubs the following season.

Bob Howry 1973– (Cubs 2006-2008, 2010)

Howry was signed as a free agent after proving he was over arm problems with a solid season in Cleveland. He had previously pitched for the White Sox and served as their closer. With the Cubs, he was a key member of their bullpen his first two seasons, and even pitched in the 2007 playoffs. But in 2008 he began to get hit pretty hard. He still appeared in over 70 games, but he gave up 90 hits, including 13 homers — a very large number for a reliever. The Cubs let him go after the season. Howry pitched for the Giants and Diamondbacks the next two seasons, but when he was waived by Arizona, the Cubs gave him one last shot. His final pitches in the big leagues came for the Cubs. As of Opening Day 2019, Bob is the last player in the big leagues to go by the name Bob.

Jed Hoyer 1973– (Cubs GM 2011-Present)

Hoyer was brought in to be the general manager of the Cubs by his former colleague at the Red Sox, Theo Epstein. Hoyer came aboard after a successful stint as GM for the San Diego Padres. One of his first trades as the Cubs GM was acquiring a player he had drafted in Boston and traded for in San Diego — first baseman Anthony Rizzo. He has since acquired several top level prospects in trade deadline deals, and helped lead the Cubs out of their long darkness. Theo gets all the credit, but Jed is his essential partner

Mike Hubbard 1971– (Cubs 1995-1997)

Mike was the Cubs backup catcher behind Scott Servais for three seasons in the 90s. He also served as a backup for Montreal, Texas, and Atlanta.

Trenidad Hubbard 1964– (Cubs 2003)

He was born in Chicago, went to Southern Illinois University, and got to fulfill a childhood dream by playing in the big leagues in his hometown. His last 16 big league at-bats were for the Cubs. He went 4 for 16 with 2 RBI in July of 2003 before being returned to the minors. In his career he also played for the Giants, Rockies, Indians, Dodgers, Braves, Orioles, Royals, and Padres.

Ken Hubbs 1941–1964 (Cubs 1961-1963)

He wasn't even 20 when he debuted for the Cubs in September of 1961, but he made enough of an impact to be named the starting second baseman in 1962. It was a rough year for the Cubs (they finished with their worst record ever — behind even the expansion Houston Colt 45s, and ahead of only the worst team of all-time, the '62 Mets), but it was a breakout year for Ken Hubbs. He won a Gold Glove for his play at second base and was named the Rookie of the Year. One of the roughest transitions for Hubbs had been the travel schedule. He was terrified of flying. *(His roommate Ron Santo vividly describes the sheer terror Hubbs felt every time the Cubs had to fly in his autobiography "For the Love of Ivy," a book we highly recommend)*. Instead of letting it get the best of him, Hubbs tackled it head-on and learned how to fly himself. The technique worked. He purchased an airplane (a Cessna 172) in November of 1963, and got his pilot's license in late January of 1964. By learning how to fly, he had conquered his fear. On February 13th, he took his life-long pal Larry Doyle up in the plane from their hometown in California to Provo, Utah, to visit Doyle's wife. On the way home, however, he made the mistake of taking off in a snowstorm. Ken Hubbs and Larry Doyle died when they crashed into a lake just five miles from the airport. Their bodies weren't found until two days later. Hubbs was only 22 years old.

Johnny Hudson 1912–1970 (Cubs 1941)

Hudson was a backup infielder who played seven seasons in the big leagues, but remained in the game for the rest of his life (mostly as a scout for the Giants). He was dubbed "Mr. Chips" by Dodgers broadcaster Red Smith because the movie *Mr. Chips* was popular at the time, and Johnny always seemed to come through when the chips were down. He came to the Cubs in the historically bad trade that sent Hall of Famer Billy Herman to the Dodgers. Hudson didn't do much in Chicago. He hit .202, while Herman led the Dodgers to the pennant.

Jim Hughes 1923–2001 (Cubs 1956)

Jim was a career-long relief pitcher in a day when such a thing wasn't nearly as common as it is today. Before coming to the Cubs, Hughes led the league in saves with the Brooklyn Dodgers. His 1956 Cubs team may have featured a burgeoning superstar in Ernie Banks, but their pitching staff was atrocious, including Hughes. He clearly no longer had whatever he had in Brooklyn. The Cubs finished in last place that year, while his former Brooklyn team finished in first.

Joe Hughes 1880–1951 (Orphans 1902)

Hughes played in exactly one game, on August 30, 1902 in Pittsburgh. He played right field and got three at-bats (no hits) that day. The Orphans (Cubs) lost in the bottom of the 12th inning, 3-2. Rumor has it that the Orphans were racked with injuries, and Hughes was just a guy that somebody knew who could fill in that day. The fact that he never played again does lend credence to that rumor.

Pat Hughes 1956– (Cubs announcer 1996-present)

Pat has been the radio play by play for the Cubs for more than 20 years, and before that he worked in Milwaukee on Brewers broadcasts with Bob Uecker. I interviewed him once and asked him to compare and contrast Bob Uecker and Ron Santo. This is what he said: "In some ways the two of them are similar: They're among the most popular figures in the history of their respective cities, they're both ex-players, although granted, a slightly different caliber — Ron was a great player and Uecker was more of a mediocre one. But I consider myself incredibly fortunate to have worked with both of them. In addition, I worked with Harry Caray for two years and did Marquette basketball with Al McGuire. Those are some larger-than-life personalities. I'm lucky to have known and worked with all of them." Pat will also be in the Hall of Fame someday.

Roy Hughes 1911–1995 (Cubs 1944-1945)

Roy was a member of the pennant-winning 1945 Cubs and got quite a bit of playing time in the 1945 World Series (starting six of the seven games at shortstop) after serving mainly as the utility infielder during the regular season. He also played for the Indians, Browns, and Phillies in his nine-year big league career.

Terry Hughes 1949–(Cubs 1970)

Hughes is a great example of the Cubs drafting prowess in the first twenty years of the amateur draft. The Cubs took Terry with the second overall pick in 1967. They could have had future All-Stars Jon Matlack, John Mayberry, or Ted Simmons instead. It's not like those guys were surprises. All of them were chosen in the top ten picks, and all of them eventually played in the World Series. Hughes played in two games with the Cubs in September of 1970. The third baseman went 1 for 3, including 0 for 2 in his debut, a 17-2 shellacking of the Phillies at Wrigley Field. He later got a cup of coffee with Red Sox as a late inning defensive replacement for Rico Petrocelli at third base.

Tom Hughes 1878–1956 (Orphans 1900-1901)

Long Tom Hughes was in the starting rotation the first two seasons of the 20th century. He pitched over 300 innings during the 1901 season and struck out 225 batters (leading the league in Ks/9 innings), but his record was woeful. He was 10-23 that season, his last with the Cubs (then known as the Orphans). After the 1901 season, he jumped to the upstart American League and eventually became a 20-game winner with the 1903 Red Sox. Long Tom was a bit of a tough luck pitcher. Despite a career ERA of only 3.09 over 13 seasons, he was 42 games under .500. His brother Ed was a big leaguer too (with the White Sox).

James Hughey 1869–1945 (Colts 1893)

They called him Coldwater Jim because he came from Coldwater, Michigan. Jim was also cold as ice on the mound. In seven big league seasons he was more than 50 games under .500. For the Cubs (then known as the Colts) he was 0-1 with an 11.00 ERA.

William Hulbert 1832–1882 (White Stockings President, Founder of National League)

William was born during the Andrew Jackson presidency. Hulbert became the president of the White Stockings after the Chicago Fire, and signed a bunch of players against league rules. Anticipating that he would get in trouble for that, he worked behind the scenes with fellow owners to form a new league the next season. The National League officially began play in 1876, and Hulbert was not punished. He became the president of the National League the following season and served in that role until his death in 1882. Among his accomplishments was ridding the league of the rampant gambling that had been such a big problem in the National Association. His gravestone in Graceland Cemetery looks like a baseball. He is a member of baseball's Hall of Fame.

Bob Humphreys 1935–(Cubs 1965)

He was coming off a World Series appearance with the Cardinals when the Cubs acquired him in 1965. Humphreys was known for his strange pendulum-style windup which he referred to as the rocking chair. Bob pitched well for the Cubs, winning 2 games in 41 appearances out of the bullpen. But Humphreys wasn't a fan of all the day games the Cubs played and asked out of Chicago. The Cubs obliged, sending him to the Washington Senators after the season.

Bert Humphries 1880–1945 (Cubs 1913-1915)

Bert was an important part of the Cubs pitching staff during the last few years they played at West Side Grounds. In 1913, he had a tremendous year, going 16-4, with a 2.69 ERA. In 1915, Bert was part of history. He got off to a bad start and was replaced by Zip Zabel. Zabel went on to pitch 18 1/3 innings of relief — a record that will never be broken. When the Cubs moved to their new ballpark in 1916, Bert was not asked to come along. He never pitched in the big leagues again.

Randy Hundley 1942–(Cubs 1966-1973, 1976-1977)

Randy was a good ol' boy from Martinsville, Virginia who talked with a Southern accent, and also had a fierce competitiveness. So naturally, his teammates called him Rebel. During his stellar Cubs career he was an All-Star and Gold Glove winner (in an era that Johnny Bench also played in the NL), and in 1968 set a record that will probably never be broken. He caught 160 games for the Cubs that year — an astonishing achievement. Unfortunately, he was never really the same after that year. The Cubs traded him to the Twins in 1974 (for George Mitterwald), and he played one season for both the Twins and the Padres before ending his career back in Chicago right where it began. (His son Todd also later caught for the Cubs.) After his playing career was over Randy created the first Cubs fantasy camp, a program that still runs to this day.

Historical note: On the day that Bobby Darin performed his final concert in Las Vegas (1973), Randy got the game-winning hit in the Astrodome for the Cubs.

Todd Hundley 1969–(Cubs 2001-2002)

This seemed like a no-brainer free agent signing. The slugging son of Cubs icon Randy Hundley, returning to the ballpark of his youth to relive the glories of his father. Well, it didn't quite turn out that way. His time with the Cubs was an unhappy one for both player and team. He was booed mercilessly by Cubs fans because he hit only .187 in his first year with the team, and .211 the following year. In 2001 he struck out 89 times in only 246 at-bats. Hundley was plagued with injuries too. But he did have one shining moment in a Cubs uniform when he homered to beat the hated crosstown White Sox.

Herb Hunter 1895–1970 (Cubs 1916-1917)

The young infielder only got into a handful of games with the Cubs during the first two seasons they played at what is now known as Wrigley Field. He was part of the trade that shipped Heinie Zimmerman out of town. Unfortunately, he never got a hit in a Cubs uniform. Hunter served in the Navy during World War I. He later played for the Red Sox and Phillies.

Tommy Hunter 1986–(Cubs 2015)

The right-handed reliever and former closer was acquired from the Orioles at the trading deadline (for Junior Lake) to bolster the Cubs bullpen down the stretch. Unfortunately, Hunter never really found his rhythm. He gave up four long balls in only 15.2 innings and posted an ERA over five. After the season he was permitted to leave via free agency.

Walt Huntzinger 1899–1981 (Cubs 1926)

His nickname was "Shakes" and he pitched for the Cubs at the end of the 1926 season. Shakes pitched very well out of the bullpen, but after the season was over, he went back to the minor leagues and never returned to the big leagues. Before playing baseball, he was a college basketball coach in Pennsylvania.

Don Hurst 1905–1952 (Cubs 1934)

Hurst was a feared slugger in his day, leading the league in RBI, and slugging more than 100 homers. Unfortunately, his day was before he came to Chicago. Those gaudy stats were accumulated in Philadelphia, in a ballpark that was a bandbox for left-handed hitters. To get Hurst, the Cubs gave up their own young slugging first baseman, Dolph Camilli. Camilli became an All-Star and an MVP. Hurst hit three homers in a Cubs uniform and was out of the game the following year. The trade remains among the most lopsided trades in Cubs history…and that's saying something.

Jeff Huson 1964–(Cubs 2000)

Huson managed to stay in the big leagues for twelve seasons, largely thanks to his reliable glove. The backup infielder (2B, SS, 3B) played for the Expos, Rangers, Orioles, Brewers, Mariners, Angels, and Cubs in parts of three different decades. The Cubs were his last stop. Among his career highlights: playing in Cal Ripken's record setting game in 1995, and Nolan Ryan's 7th no-hitter.

Ed Hutchinson 1867–1934 (Colts 1890)

He was only 1 for 17 with Chicago. That one hit was a double. He never played for another big league team. He later became a manager in the minor leagues.

Wild Bill Hutchinson 1859–1926 (White Stockings/ Colts 1889-1895)

The Yale man was born the year before Abraham Lincoln was first elected, and didn't pitch for Chicago until he was 29 years old. Wild Bill had his season to remember in 1892. He led the league in wins the previous 2 seasons as well (with 44 and 41), but in 1892, Hutchinson had the whole package. He started 70(!) games, completed 67 of those, and led the league in wins (36) and strikeouts (314). During the three years of 1890-1892, he pitched nearly 1800 innings, far and away the highest total in the league. Of course the rules were quite different in his era, but he was still one of the best pitchers in the league. He has more complete games than any other pitcher in franchise history. Unfortunately, he also still holds the Cubs record for most career losses (158), walks (1109), and wild pitches (120).

Historical note: On the day Lizzie Borden's parents were found dead, Wild Bill was on the mound for Chicago. He took the loss in a 6-1 game against St. Louis.

Herb Hutson 1949 – (Cubs 1974)

Hutson was a right-handed pitcher for the Cubs for a few different stints during the 1974 season. He had been a lifetime starting pitcher that the Cubs tried to use out of the bullpen. He had limited success (3.45 ERA in 20 appearances) and went back to the minors for the 1975 season. After that year, he hung up his baseball spikes at the age of 26.

*Additional Entries...*If you check out the Every Cub Ever feature at www. justonebadcentury.com, you'll find several additional entries, including celebrity Cubs fans, writers, and bloggers. Under the letter H, you'll find author Ernest Hemingway, Bears founder George Halas, comedian Bonnie Hunt, and filmmaker John Hughes (all Cubs fans), plus Cubs writer/website The Heckler.

CHAPTER NINE

I

The starting lineup for your Chicago Cubs beginning with the letter I...

C – Pitchback machine with Strike Zone
1B – Pitchers-hand out
2B – Frank Isbell, the Bald Eagle
SS – Cesar Izturis, the Gold Glover
3B – Charlie Irwin, the Error Machine
LF – Monte Irvin, the Hall of Famer
CF/RF – Automatic Outs
SP – Blaise Ilsley, the 30-year-old Rookie

Blaise Ilsley 1964 – (Cubs 1994)

Blaise pitched for the Cubs during the strike season of 1994. He was a 30-year-old rookie who had bounced around the minor leagues, and it didn't go well with the Cubs. In ten appearances he registered an ERA of 7.80. After his playing days, he went into coaching, and continues to coach in the St. Louis organization.

*Irish Cubs...*The following Cubs were all born in Ireland...Jimmy Archer, Jack Doyle, Ed Duffy, Fergy Malone, Tom Needham, Johnny O'Connor, Jack O'Neill, Bill Sullivan, and John Tener.

Monte Irvin 1919 – 2016 (Cubs 1956)

Irvin was a star in the Negro Leagues and didn't make his debut in the majors until at the age of 30. But even though he only played a few big league seasons and hit only 99 career homers, he was inducted into the Hall of Fame in 1973. He had a few great seasons with the Giants, leading them to the National League pennant in 1951 and the World Series championship in 1954. When the Cubs got him in 1956, he was already 37 years old. His power stroke was diminished, but he was still the best left fielder in the league.

In his last big league season he led the National League in fielding percentage and range. When he died in 2016 he was the oldest living major leaguer.

Two of the great Cubs nicknames are in this chapter. Monty Irvin was nicknamed "Mr. Murder" for the way he murdered the baseball. Frank Isbell was prematurely bald and was a little sensitive about it, so naturally his teammates called him "The Bald Eagle".

Charlie Irwin 1869 – 1925 (Colts 1893-1895)

The team was still known as the Colts when Charlie manned third base and shortstop for Chicago. In 1894 he had a great season with the bat (100 runs batted in), but he was also the worst infielder in all of baseball. That season he committed 91 (91!) errors. He later played for the Reds and Brooklyn during a pretty respectable 10-year big league career, and he settled in Chicago after his playing days were over. That's where he was hit by a bus and killed in 1925.

Frank Isbell 1875 – 1941 (Orphans 1898)

He was known as the Bald Eagle. Isbell got his start with the Cubs (then known as the Orphans), but his best years were with the White Sox. He was the starting second baseman on the 1906 White Sox team that beat the Cubs in the World Series. The Bald Eagle could fly. He stole over 250 bases in his career, only three of which were for the Cubs.

Cesar Izturis 1980 – (Cubs 2006-2007)

He will always be remembered by Cubs fans as the player the Cubs got in return for Greg Maddux. Cesar was a slick-fielding shortstop, but his stay in Chicago was a relatively short and unhappy one. All told he was with the Cubs for about one calendar year before they shipped him off to Pittsburgh. Nevertheless, Izturis has enjoyed a long and productive big league career. He played for nine different teams in 13 seasons and was an All-Star and Gold-Glove winner.

Additional Entries... If you check out the Every Cub Ever feature at www.justonebadcentury. com, you'll find several additional entries, including celebrity Cubs fans, writers, and bloggers. Under the letter I, you'll discover Cubs songwriters the Ides of March, celebrity chef Stephanie Izard (a HUGE Cubs fan) and Cubs blogger/author Kelly Ignarski.

CHAPTER TEN

J

The starting lineup for your Chicago Cubs beginning with the letter J...

C—Cliff Johnson, Aging Slugger
1B— Jay Johnstone, Wacky Prankster
2B—Don Johnson, '45 All-Star
SS—Billy Jurges, Shooting Victim
3B—Randy Jackson, Handsome Ransom
LF—Charley Jones, Home Run Champ
CF—Lance Johnson, One Dog
RF—Darrin Jackson, "He was a Cub?"
Bench—Howard Johnson, Hotel Namesake
Bench—Lou Johnson, Perfect Game Run Scorer
SP—Ferguson Jenkins, Hall of Famer
SP—Larry Jackson, 24-Game Winner
SP—Toothpick Sam Jones, No-Hitter
RP—Hal Jeffcoat, Converted Outfielder

Austin Jackson 1987—(Cubs 2015)

Jackson had been a great player for the Tigers and Mariners, so Cubs nation was excited when Austin was acquired in late August to augment the Cubs outfield heading into the playoffs. When Jorge Soler went down with an injury, Jackson got quite a bit of playing time. Unfortunately, he never really found his groove in a Cubs uniform. In 79 at-bats, he hit only .236. Jackson did provide a steady glove in the outfield, however, and because of that got playing time in all three postseason series. He was granted his free agency after the season.

Brett Jackson 1988—(Cubs 2012)

Jackson was the top prospect in the Cubs system for several years. He seemingly had it all: power, speed, and great defense in center field. Unfortunately, Jackson was always prone to striking out. He struck out a lot in the minors, and he never found a way to overcome it. He got his one shot at the big leagues in 2012, when the Cubs handed him the center field job. In 120 at-bats, he struck out 59 times. That's the single worst strikeout ratio in baseball history. He hasn't made it back up to the big leagues since.

Damian Jackson 1973—(Cubs 2004)

The Cubs signed Damian at the end of spring training when he was waived by the Rockies and gave him a shot to backup second baseman Mark Grudzielanek. Jackson hit only .067 in his two months with the Cubs. They traded him to the Royals at the end of May. He didn't show it with the Cubs, but Jackson had a productive eleven-year big league career.

Danny Jackson 1962—(Cubs 1991-1992)

Danny was a very good starting pitcher. In fact, he was a two-time All-Star. Unfortunately for the Cubs, those two All-Star seasons happened before and after his Cubs year. His time in Chicago was a disaster. He was 5-14 with an ERA over five.

Darrin Jackson 1963—(Cubs 1985-1989)

Jackson is well known to White Sox fans as their radio announcer ("DJ"), but he got his big league start playing outfield for the Chicago Cubs. DJ was one of their top prospects, a second round draft choice, who played in the big leagues at ripe old age of 21. In 1988 he had his best season with the Cubs, playing in 100 games and hitting .266 with 6 homers and 20 RBI. But in the middle of the division-winning season of 1989, the Cubs traded him to the Padres (along with Calvin Schiraldi) for Marvell Wynne and Luis Salazar. DJ went on to play 12 seasons in the big leagues for the Padres, Mets, White Sox, Twins, and Brewers. He was having a career season with the 1994 White Sox (hitting .312) when baseball went on strike.

Edwin Jackson 1983—(Cubs 2013-2015)

Jackson was the first free agent signed by the Theo Epstein regime (4 year, $40 million), and let's just say they don't exactly advertise that on their business cards. Edwin came to Chicago with decent credentials. He had pitched a no-hitter, and appeared in two World Series and one All-Star game, but it didn't worked out for Edwin with the Cubs. In 2013 he lost a whopping 18 games, and finished with an ERA of nearly five. In 2014, he was worse. He did play a part in setting a record with the Cubs, however. He and Michael Bowden combined to throw five wild pitches in one inning. In his last season with the Cubs (2015), he pitched exclusively out of the bullpen. The Cubs released him at the end of July, and he finished the year with the Atlanta Braves. He has since gone on to pitch for Miami, San Diego, Washington, Baltimore, and Oakland.

Larry Jackson 1931−1990 (Cubs 1963-1966)

Larry was already a 3-time All-Star when the Cubs acquired him from the Cardinals before the 1963 season (in the Don Cardwell trade), and he paid immediate dividends. In his first season with the Cubs he was an All-Star again, winning 14 games. But it's his 1964 season that will be remembered. That year he put it all together and had one of the best years in Cubs history. Jackson led the league in wins with 24 (on a terrible, terrible Cubs team), and finished second in the Cy Young voting to Dean Chance, who won 20 games for the Angels. Jackson would have won the NL Cy Young Award, but at the time only one was given out in all of baseball. He tailed off a little during the 1965 season, but Larry Jackson may have done his greatest service to the Chicago Cubs in the early part of 1966. He was the player the Phillies acquired in the famous trade that brought Ferguson Jenkins to the Cubs.

Historical note: On the day that Michael Jackson was born in Gary, Indiana, Larry Jackson (then a Cardinal) beat the Cubs in St. Louis.

Lou Jackson 1935−1969 (Cubs 1958-1959)

The Grambling product was a backup outfielder for the Cubs during two brief cups of coffee in the late 50s. He hit his only big league homer in a Cubs uniform. He later got one more brief taste of the big leagues with the 1964 Baltimore Orioles. Jackson went to Japan after his stint in Baltimore and had some success there, but one day when he was batting, he collapsed at the plate. He died the following year of pancreatitis, at the age of 33.

Randy Jackson 1926−(Cubs 1950-1955, 1959)

His real first name was Ransom, and gosh darn it, he was kind of handsome, so his teammates began calling him Handsome Ransom (His teammates thought he looked like

Gregory Peck). "Handsome Ransom" Jackson was one of the best players on the Cubs in the early 50s — a National League All-Star third-baseman in 1954 and 1955. He hit 19, 19, and 21 homers in 1953-55 (his three seasons on the Cubs), and was a pretty good fielder too. (In 1955 he led NL third basemen in double plays.) His greatest day in a Cubs uniform was April 17, 1954 against St. Louis. Jackson had four hits — including a home run that hit an apartment building on Waveland Avenue. With the wind blowing out at Wrigley Field, the Cubs beat the Cardinals 23-13 in a National League record (at the time) three hour and 43 minute game. The two teams combined for 35 hits — including five homers. The Dodgers traded Walt Moryn, Don Hoak, and Russ Meyer to the Cubs for Jackson and pitcher Don Elston after the 1955 season with the expectation that the slugger would succeed Jackie Robinson at third base. Unfortunately for Jackson and the Dodgers, he suffered a serious knee injury in 1957, and Handsome Ransom never played regularly again.

Historical note: On the day that Julius and Ethel Rosenberg were executed (1953), Jackson hit a grand slam for the Cubs in an 11-8 victory over the Dodgers.

Elmer Jacobs 1892−1958 (Cubs 1924-1925)

Jacobs was a right-handed journeyman pitcher who lasted nine seasons in the big leagues, including two with the Cubs. He was a part of the rotation in 1924, and won 11 games. The following season he was used mostly as a reliever, and didn't have as much success. Jacobs also pitched for the White Sox, Phillies, Pirates, and Cardinals.

Mike Jacobs 1877−1949 (Orphans 1902)

Jacobs was a shortstop who played for the Cubs (then known as the Orphans) for exactly one week in July of 1902. The 24-year-old hit .211 in 19 plate appearances. He never played in the big leagues again. Jacobs was a native of Louisville.

Ray Jacobs 1902−1952 (Cubs 1928)

Ray played exactly two games in the big leagues and both of them were with the Cubs in 1928. In his first game, at Wrigley Field on April 20th, he pinch hit late in the game for Cubs first baseman Joe Kelly. He struck out. His second (and last) at-bat came a few weeks later at Forbes Field in Pittsburgh. Once again he came in as a pinch hitter, this time for Cubs pitcher

Percy Jones — who had been getting rocked. Jacobs made another out, and never got another chance. Despite only playing in two games (both Cubs losses), he played alongside and against several Hall of Famers. His Cubs teammates at the time included Kiki Cuyler and Hack Wilson. The Pirates team he played against sported three Hall of Famers in their lineup that day, brothers Paul and Lloyd Waner, and Pie Traynor.

Tony Jacobs 1925–1980 (Cubs 1948)

Jacobs made only two appearances in the big leagues, and they came almost seven years apart. His debut came with the Cubs in September of 1948. He pitched two innings and gave up three hits, including a home run to future Cub Gene Hermanski, in a 8-1 loss to the Dodgers in Brooklyn. He did manage to retire two Hall of Famers that day: Pee Wee Reese (strikeout) and Jackie Robinson (groundout). Seven seasons later he made the Opening Day roster of the Cardinals and pitched against the Cubs. This time he was hit pretty hard. Ernie Banks and Randy Jackson both had two hits. One of Jackson's hits was a homer. That was the last Tony Jacobs ever saw of big league baseball. He pitched twelve seasons in the minors.

Merwin Jacobson 1894–1978 (Cubs 1916)

Merwin had one of the strangest big league careers you'll ever see. He played sparingly for the Giants in 1915, and the Cubs in 1916 (their first season at what is now known as Wrigley Field), but then went down to the minors and played there for ten long years. He got one more shot in the majors with the Brooklyn Dodgers in 1926 and got his first significant playing time as the team's fourth outfielder. He was not a power hitter. Of his 76 career hits (71 of which were for the Dodgers), he only got 11 extra base hits (nine doubles and two triples).

Jake Jaeckel 1942–(Cubs 1964)

His real first name was Paul, but his teammates called him Jake. Jaeckel got a cup of coffee as a September call-up for the last place 1964 Cubs. He pitched two scoreless innings in his debut, retiring the likes of Sandy Alomar, Matty Alou, Rico Carty, and Joe Torre. In his second appearance, he won the game as the Cubs rallied in the bottom of the 9th at Wrigley

to beat the Dodgers 4-3. In his third appearance he picked up the save in another 4-3 win against the Dodgers, striking out Willie Crawford to win the game. His last game with the Cubs was at Candlestick Park in San Francisco. He pitched two more scoreless innings, retiring Orlando Cepeda and Jose Cardenal, among others. Though he was lights out in the big leagues, Jaeckel never got another chance. He spent the next three seasons in the minors before hanging up his spikes at the ripe old age of 26.

Joe Jaeger 1895–1963 (Cubs 1920)

His teammates called him Zip. Zip played in exactly two games with the Cubs. The team brought him in to help out in the bullpen on days they had double-headers. The first time he came in was on July 28, 1920. He relieved Hippo Vaughn and gave up two runs on three hits in an 8-4 loss. His final game on the Cubs (and in the majors) was on September 6th of that year. He didn't have good control. He walked three, gave up three hits and four earned runs. His final ERA was 12.00.

Art Jahn 1895–1948 (Cubs 1925)

Art was called up as 29-year-old rookie in the middle of the 1925 season and was handed the starting left field job. He performed admirably — hitting .301 and fielding the position well. Unfortunately, he had no power at all (zero homers) and little speed (two stolen bases), and the Cubs had lots of options that were more traditionally equipped to play corner outfield. It took Art three more seasons to make it back up to the big leagues, but he did eventually play for the Giants and the Phillies.

Cleo James 1940– (Cubs 1970-1973)

James was one of the parade of center fielders who came through Chicago in the years before Rick Monday stabilized the position. James had decent speed and hit .287 one year (1971), but he didn't have the complete package. His last gasp in the majors was with the 1973 Cubs. By then he was 33 years old. He played another season in the minors before retiring.

Rick James 1947–(Cubs 1967)

No record of whether or not this Rick James was super-freaky, but he was a highly touted prospect. The Cubs had the sixth pick in the very first amateur draft (1965) and chose pitcher Rick James. He only pitched three big league games. His ERA was 13.50 in those games. The player chosen right after him was future All-Star catcher Ray Fosse. Not a good start for the Cubs in the draft era.

Jon Jay 1985 – (Cubs 2017)

The Cubs probably didn't expect Jay to be their steadiest leadoff man in 2017, but that's what the veteran free agent signing became. Jay played all three outfield positions, hit .296, had a .374 OBP, and made the pitcher work hard in every at-bat. He became a free agent after the 2017 season. The well-traveled veteran has also played for St. Louis, Kansas City, San Diego, Arizona, and the White Sox.

Hal Jeffcoat 1924 – 2007 (Cubs 1948-1955)

Jeffcoat came up to the big leagues as a center fielder. He had good years and bad years with the bat, but he always had a great arm. In 1954 the Cubs converted him into a relief pitcher. He did very well in that role. In two seasons out of the Cubs bullpen, he appeared in 108 games. He won 13 games and saved 13. The Cubs traded him to the Reds in 1956. In his first month with the Reds, Jeffcoat beaned Don Zimmer of the Dodgers, ending his season. Zimmer later had to have a plate put in his head because of that beaning.

Frank Jelincich 1917 – 1992 (Cubs 1941)

Jelly, as he was known to his teammates, spent most of his baseball career in the minors. His career lasted from 1937-1950, but he only got eight big league at-bats. They came for the Cubs in September of 1941. He got one hit, and knocked in two runs. Three months later Pearl Harbor was bombed, and Jelly found himself serving Uncle Sam. He never made it back up to the big leagues after his return.

Ferguson Jenkins 1942 – (Cubs 1966-1973, 1982-1983)

Fergie might be the best pitcher to ever wear a Chicago Cubs uniform. He led the league in wins twice, fewest walks per nine innings five times, and complete games nine times, and did it while being so cool, his nickname was "Fly." Fergie's streak of six straight seasons with 20 or more wins (1967-1972) is the longest streak in the major leagues since Warren Spahn did it between 1956 and 1961. And he did it despite not having the best of luck. You've heard the expression "it's better to be lucky than good"? Well in 1968, Fergie Jenkins was good…but he certainly wasn't lucky. He won 20 games, but he also lost 15 games that year. It was the way he lost the games that were unlucky. Five times that season he lost 1-0 games. Not many pitchers in baseball history can say that they pitched in nine different games in one season that their own team was shut out — but that happened to Fergie in 1968. And 1968 wasn't the only year he had that kind of luck. In his Hall of Fame career, Fergie Jenkins lost 45 games in which his team didn't score a run. 45! No wonder he was voted into the Hall of Fame despite not reaching that magical win total of 300. Jenkins had 284 career wins, but if the Cubs had come through for him with a run in only half of his 1-0 losses, he would have easily surpassed 300 wins. Fergie's secret was his incredible control. There are only four pitchers in big league history with more than 3000 strikeouts and less than a thousand walks. Greg Maddux (who also wore #31 with the Cubs), Curt Schilling, Pedro Martinez, and Ferguson Jenkins. He richly deserves his status as a Hall of Famer. Fergie remains the Cubs all-time leading strikeout pitcher (2038 in a Cubs uniform).

Historical note: On the day Disneyworld opened in Florida (1971), Fergie had just completed his Cy Young season. He won his 24th game of the year against former Cub Bill Stoneman and the Expos.

Doug Jennings 1964 – (Cubs 1993)

Jennings was a backup outfielder with Oakland for four seasons before coming to Chicago. The Cubs used Jennings as a pinch hitter and occasional first baseman. He was fairly effective in that role, hitting .250 with two homers. It was his last season in the big leagues. His next stop was Japan.

Robin Jennings 1972 – (Cubs 1996-1999)

Jennings holds the distinction of being the only person born in Singapore to play Major League Baseball. Unfortunately for Robin, he didn't play much. In parts of three seasons with the Cubs, he never had more than 62 at-bats, and didn't tally a single home run. He later got similar tastes of the big-time with Oakland, Colorado, and Cincinnati.

Garry Jestadt 1947– (Cubs 1971)

Jestadt was an infielder (2B, 3B), but his career with the Cubs was incredibly short. At the beginning of the 1971 season he was on the roster long enough to log a total of three at-bats (no hits), and play three total innings in the field (at 3B, spelling Ron Santo). The Cubs traded him in May of that year to the San Diego Padres. In San Diego he got the most extensive playing time of his big league career.

Cubs players have had some great nicknames over the years. Among players starting with the letter J, you'll find nicknames like Available, Baby, Fly, Footer, Handsome Ransom, Jelly, Kangaroo, One Dog, Pep, Slick, and Zip.

*Jewish Cubs...*There have been quite a few Jewish Cubs over the years including...Cy Block, Hy Cohen, Scott Feldman, Sam Fuld, John Grabow, Adam Greenberg, Ken Holtzman, Ryan Kalish, Johnny Kling, Johnny Klippstein, Andrew Lorraine, Jason Marquis, Ed Mayer, Levi Meyerle, Dave Roberts, Art Shamsky, and Steve Stone.

Manny Jimenez 1938–2017 (Cubs 1969)

Jimenez was in his seventh big league season when he came to the Cubs. The 30-year-old outfielder was used strictly as a pinch hitter. He came up six times, struck out twice, got one hit, and was released. He never played in the big leagues again. Don't blame Manny for the collapse of 1969. His last game was in May. Manny's brother Elvio played for the Yankees.

Joa the Cub (Cubs mascot 1916)

In 1916 Cubs minority owner J. Ogden Armour (the sausage king) donated a mascot to the Cubs. A juvenile black bear. The bear was named "Joa" after Armour's initials, and the team built him a den (actually a cage) at Addison Street and Sheffield Avenue. It was the first year the Cubs played at what was then known as Cubs Park. Joa debuted on June 20, 1916,

for a Cubs-Reds game. (It was rained out.) Joa lived there for most of that 1916 season, but by September the club realized he was more trouble than he was worth, and sold him to the Lincoln Park Zoo for twenty bucks.

Abe Johnson (Colts 1893)

Abe was an obscure pitcher who pitched exactly one inning for the Cubs on July 16, 1893. There is no record of his birthdate or whether he was a righty or a lefty, but we do know that he gave up four earned runs in his one inning of big league ball, and finished with a 36.00 ERA.

Ben Johnson 1931– (Cubs 1959-1960)

Johnson was basically a career minor leaguer. He played sixteen years in the minors and only had two small cups of coffee with the Cubs. He pitched well as a 28-year-old rookie in September of '59, which led to a more extended shot the following season. He pitched out of the bullpen for seventeen games and registered an ERA of nearly 5. His big league career never made it into his 30s.

Bill Johnson 1960–2018 (Cubs 1983-1984)

He was acquired along with Dick Ruthven for Willie Hernandez (a terrible trade in retrospect) from the Philadelphia Phillies. Johnson was a September call-up for the Cubs in both the 1983 and 1984 seasons, but didn't get a lot of opportunities to pitch. He appeared in 14 games and posted a 3.57 ERA. Hernandez went on to win the Cy Young Award.

Cliff Johnson 1947– (Cubs 1980)

Johnson was a slugging catcher who hit nearly 200 career homers. Ten of those came with the Cubs in the second half of the 1980 season. The Cubs were very bad that year, but Johnson's dramatic homers helped brighten a dark summer. After leaving the Cubs he became what he probably should have been all along — a designated hitter with the A's, Blue Jays, and Rangers.

Davey Johnson 1943– (Cubs 1978)

Davey Johnson had a very distinguished playing career before he became a manager. He was a four-time All-Star, three time Gold Glove second baseman, two-time World Series champ, and once hit 43 homers in a season, but by the time he came to the Cubs, those days were in his rearview mirror. The Cubs got him from the Phillies in August of 1978, and he played with them for the last few months of his big league career. Johnson went into coaching shortly thereafter and has since won six divisional championships and a World Series title (with the 1986 Mets) as a manager.

Don Johnson 1911–2000 (Cubs 1943-1948)

Johnson was the starting second baseman for the pennant-winning Cubs team in 1945. He was an energetic infielder, and his teammates called him "Pep." Johnson was a young phenom in the minor league system, and the Cubs thought so highly of his eventual development, they traded their Hall of Fame second sacker Billy Herman. Then, they traded the other second baseman on their team, future All-Star Eddie Stanky, and gave the job to Johnson. In 1944, Johnson was an All-Star himself, leading all 2B with 71 RBI. He also, unfortunately, committed 44 errors. Johnson had another All-Star season with the bat in 1945, hitting .302, but after the players returned from the war in 1946, he was exposed as a liability. Johnson became a non-factor in 1947 and 1948 (his last season in the big leagues) while Eddie Stanky led two different teams to the NL pennant. Some Don Johnson trivia: His father Ernie also had a Chicago connection. He was signed by the Chicago White Sox to replace banned shortstop Swede Risberg after the Black Sox scandal, and remained in the big leagues for ten years. In 1925, exactly twenty years before his son would play in the World Series, Ernie Johnson played in the World Series for the New York Yankees.

Footer Johnson 1932– (Cubs 1958)

His real name was Richard Allen Johnson, but everyone called him Footer or Treads because he was fast. Footer was known for his speed in the minor leagues and at Duke University (he was there the same time as Dick Groat), but he didn't make much of an impact in his very short major league career. In 1958, Footer got a grand total of five at-bats in eight games (his other three appearances were as a pinch runner), but never got a hit. He did, however, score one run when he pinch ran for Cubs catcher Sammy Taylor during a double-header on June 22nd. He was knocked in by another obscure Cub… future manager Chuck Tanner.

Howard Johnson 1960– (Cubs 1995)

His parents obviously had a sense of humor, because they named their son Howard, the same name as a famous hotel and restaurant chain. His nickname naturally ended up being the same thing as the restaurant's nickname (HoJo), but he had the last laugh. Howard Johnson became a big leaguer. He was a great player in his day with the Mets (over 200 homers and stolen bases), but by the time he joined the Cubs in 1995, he was 35. It was his last season in the majors, and he only hit .195.

Ken Johnson 1933–2015 (Cubs 1969)

Johnson only pitched the final two months of the 1969 season for the Cubs. When he joined the team they were riding high, with a big lead over the Mets. Six weeks later the season was over and the Cubs were eight games behind the Mets. It's probably unfair to say that Johnson was a bad luck charm, but his previous claim to fame makes you wonder. In 1964 while pitching for the Houston Colt 45s, he pitched a nine-inning no-hitter…and lost the game 1-0.

Lance Johnson 1963– (Cubs 1997-1999)

Johnson had a very impressive 14-year big league career that included playoff appearances with the Cardinals (1987) White Sox (1993), and Cubs (1998), and an All-Star appearance as a member of the Mets (1996). He was a speedy center fielder who hit for average (lifetime .291), hit lots of triples (he led the league five times), and stole base (327 lifetime). With the Cubs playoff team of 1998, he was the leadoff man to a lineup that featured the likes of Sammy Sosa, Mark Grace, and Henry Rodriguez. Unfortunately, he managed only two hits in that playoff series. Lance left the Cubs after an injury-plagued 1999, and finished his career with the Yankees. His nickname was One Dog, because he wore #1. (Nickname courtesy of Hawk Harrelson)

Lou Johnson 1934– (Cubs 1960, 1968)

His nickname was Sweet Lou or Slick. Lou played for the Cubs in two different seasons, his rookie year and his second to last season in the big leagues, and neither of those seasons were particularly remarkable. Lou is probably better remembered for what he did against the Cubs, when he was on the Dodgers. He scored the only run in Sandy Koufax's perfect game against the Cubs. The score was 0-0 in the bottom of the fifth and neither pitcher had allowed a single baserunner. That ended when Cubs pitcher Bob Hendley walked Lou to lead off the inning. He was bunted to second base by Ron Fairly, and stole third, scoring on Chris Krug's errant throw to Ron Santo. The Dodgers had scored without the benefit of a hit. The Dodgers later got exactly one hit, a harmless double, but it didn't factor in the scoring.

Pierce Johnson 1991–(Cubs 2017)

The former first round draft choice finally made the big leagues for the Cubs in the summer of 2017, but only pitched in one game. The Cubs made three errors in his only inning pitched. He was waived in September. He was picked in the same first round as Albert Almora Jr. and Addison Russell.

Reed Johnson 1976–(Cubs 2008-2009, 2011-2012)

Johnson was a fan favorite during his time with the Cubs. He made highlight-reel catches in center field (including one he smashed into the wall in Washington), and delivered clutch hits time after time. Reed hit over .300 in three of his four Cubs seasons. He was traded to Atlanta during the stretch run of the 2012 season. He retired after the 2015 season after a successful 13-year big league career with Toronto, Los Angeles, Atlanta, Miami, Washington, and the Cubs.

Historical note: On the day Michael Phelps won his record-setting 8th Olympic Gold Medal in Beijing (2008), Johnson knocked in three runs during an eight-run inning to defeat the Marlins 9-2 in Miami.

Jimmy Johnston 1889–1967 (Cubs 1914)

Johnston had an outstanding 13-year big league career. He played for the Cubs in 1914 and served as a utility man, but Johnston really blossomed after leaving Chicago. He led Brooklyn to two World Series and finished in the top ten in hits, runs, and stolen bases four times. His career batting average was an impressive .294. He played every position in the field except pitcher and catcher.

Jay Johnstone 1945–(Cubs 1982-1984)

Johnstone had a tremendously successful big league career. He played 20 years in the majors and won two World Championships (1978 Yankees and 1981 Dodgers). His best

seasons were probably with the Philadelphia Phillies teams in the mid-70s. By the time he came to the Cubs in 1982, he was more of a part-time player, but Johnstone was still productive. He was also the life of the party. His teammates loved him because he was such a jokester.

Roy Joiner 1906–1989 (Cubs 1934-1935)

Joiner pitched in twenty-two games for some very good Cubs teams, but didn't fare too well. His lifetime ERA was 5.28. His nickname was Pop.

Eric Jokisch 1989–(Cubs 2014)

Eric threw a no-hitter for the Cubs in the minor leagues in 2013, so expectations were high when Jokisch was called up to the Cubs in September of 2014. He pitched well in limited action, appearing in four games, including one start, and posting a 1.88 ERA. The Northwestern product never made it up to the big leagues again. He bounced around the minors for the A's, Rangers, and Marlins, before signing a contract to pitch in Korea.

Charley Jones 1852–1911 (White Stockings 1877)

When Jones retired from baseball in 1888, he was the all-time home run champion with 56 homers. By the turn of the century he wasn't even in the top ten. Jones, who was nicknamed Baby, didn't hit any of those homers for the Cubs (then known as the White Stockings). Chicago was just a temporary stop for the notorious troublemaker (he only played two games) before he returned to the Reds. Baby could have hit a few more homers. He was banned from baseball for two seasons in the middle of his career (1881-1882).

Clarence Jones 1941–(Cubs 1967-1968)

Clarence backed up the corner outfielders (Billy Williams and Ted Savage) and first baseman (Ernie Banks) during the 1967 season, but despite performing pretty well in that role, he wasn't a part of the Cubs future plans. He played sparingly in 1968, and was traded to the Reds (along with Bill Plummer) in 1969 for Ted Abernathy.

Davy Jones 1880–1972 (Orphans/Cubs 1902-1904)

Nicknamed "Kangaroo" by his teammates, Jones was one of the colorful characters of his era. His best season with the

Cubs was 1903 when he hit .282 and drove in 62 runs as the starting center fielder. The rest of his Cubs career, he was plagued with injuries and illnesses. He contracted typhoid one year and broke his leg another year. After leaving Chicago he played for the Tigers against the Cubs in the 1907 and 1908 World Series. His last game as a big leaguer was one of the most unusual finales of all-time. He was attending the game as a fan in 1918 when his old teammates asked him to come out and play. So he did. The ball is in the baseball Hall of Fame. It says: "Last ball used in game at Navin Field in last game of season, 1918, caught by Davy Jones. Hit by Shano Collins of the Chicago White Sox. Season ending on Labor Day on account of War."

Doug Jones 1957– (Cubs 1996)

Jones was the rarest type of closer imaginable — he threw junk. Jones never had a blazing fastball, but he somehow managed to save over 300 games in an 18-year big league career. The Cubs signed him as a free agent before the 1996 season, but something happened to Jones in a Cubs uniform. He had the worst ERA of his career and managed only two saves before the Cubs cut him loose. Of course, he was far from done. The very next year he saved over 30 games for Milwaukee.

Jacque Jones 1975– (Cubs 2006-2007)

Jones had a very respectable ten-year big league career. He hit more than 150 homers, stole over 80 bases, and played a very good right field. He signed a three-year contract as a free agent with the Cubs in 2006, and his first year was actually quite good. He hit 27 homers with a .285 average. But Dusty Baker was fired after that season, and Jones had a big problem with that. He asked to be traded. The Cubs obliged him in 2007, and his career was over shortly thereafter. Jones never connected with Chicago fans.

Percy Jones 1899–1979 (Cubs 1920-1922, 1925-1928)

Percy was a fifth starter/spot starter for the Cubs during his time in Chicago. He had two double-digit win seasons (1926, 1928), but was included in the trade that brought Rogers Hornsby to the Cubs just before the Cubs made it to the World Series in 1929. One of Percy's roommates with the Cubs was the hard-drinking Pat Malone. They didn't get along. Jones insisted on getting a new roommate after Malone trapped some pigeons on a hotel ledge and put them in Jones' bed as he slept.

Sam Jones 1925–1971 (Cubs 1955-1956)

The first African-American to ever pitch for the Cubs. Sam Jones was called "Toothpick" because he always had a toothpick in his mouth, even when he was pitching. Jones was great and not-so-great for the Cubs during his two years. He was the first African-American to pitch a no-hitter in the majors (which he did in front of a whopping 2918 fans on May 12, 1955), but he also lost twenty games that year, and had the single wildest season in Cubs history. He walked 185 batters in 242 innings, nearly 7 walks per nine innings. The next year he walked 115, and he was traded shortly after that year. He later became a twenty game winner and All-Star for the San Francisco Giants.

<u>Historical note</u>: On the day that Emmet Till was murdered in Mississippi, Sam was on the mound for the Cubs, defeating the Pirates in Pittsburgh. He was one of only three African-Americans on the Cubs roster at that time (Banks and Baker were the other two).

Sheldon Jones 1922–1991 (Cubs 1953)

His real name was Sheldon, but he got his nickname "Available" from a character in the Lil Abner comic strip. "Available Jones" was always available to his friends "fo' a price, natcherly". The Cubs' Available Jones lived up to the nickname for slightly different reasons than the Li'l Abner character. He was a pitcher who was always "available" to start or relieve for the Giants, and did both well, but by the time the Cubs got him, well…let's just say he was available. He pitched only one year for the Cubs (1953), almost exclusively in relief, and after the season his 5.40 ERA was "available" once again to anyone who wanted him. No one did.

Claude Jonnard 1897–1959 (Cubs 1929)

Claude had a couple of good seasons as a reliever with the Giants before coming to the Cubs, but let's just say that the stock market isn't the only thing that crashed in 1929. Jonnard pitched in twelve games for the Cubs that summer and was pounded. He allowed 52 baserunners in 27 innings and that wasn't going to do on a team that was headed to the World Series. They released him in July. His brother Bubber (yes Bubber) was also a big leaguer for four big league teams, including the White Sox.

Billy Jurges 1908–1997 (Cubs 1931-1938, 1946-1947)

He was known as a fiery, ill-tempered, good fielding, weak-hitting shortstop for the Cubs, but he was also one of the team leaders during the best decade of the Cubs bad century (they were in the World Series in '32, '35, and '38). Stories of Jurges' on-the-field skirmishes were legendary. In 1933 he threw two balls into the Phillies dugout, which led to a benches-clearing brawl. In 1935, he got into a fist-fight with his teammate Walter Stephenson…over the Civil War. In 1936, he punched Gilly Campbell of the Reds in the face after a hard slide into second base. In 1937, he got into a lengthy dirt-kicking fracas with an umpire.

But truth be known, he and his teammates were happy he was around for those games, because his life very nearly ended in 1932. Billy Jurges will always be remembered for what happened on July 6, 1932. He was living at the Hotel Carlos at 3834 N. Sheffield Ave (now known as the Sheffield House Hotel), and so was a girl he had "seen" a few times — Violet Valli. She called Jurges on the telephone, and asked if she could see him. Before leaving her room, she wrote a suicide note saying that she was sorry for killing Billy Jurges and herself, but she had no choice because their "beautiful love had been broken up" by his teammates Kiki Cuyler and Lew Steadman. Jurges later said he had no idea what she meant by that.

Jurges let Violet into his room, but when he saw she had a gun, he grabbed at it and took a bullet in the hand and another through the ribs. Despite the injuries, he managed to get the gun away from her, and prevented her from killing herself. Then, after he recovered from the shooting, he refused to testify against her in court. The case was dismissed. Valli used her notoriety as part of her act (she was a dancer), and signed a contract to sing in local nightclubs and theaters. She was billed as "Violet (What I did for love) Valli, the Most Talked About Girl In Chicago."

Amazingly, Jurges wasn't hurt too seriously. He returned to the Cubs before the end of the season, and hit .364 in the World Series against the Yankees. He was traded to the Giants after the 1938 season, and was named to the All-Star team with the Giants the next two years. After his playing career was over, Jurges became a big league manager. As a manager, he is probably best remembered as being the manager of the Boston Red Sox the year they became the last team in baseball to break the color barrier. In his last season with the Red Sox, they finished in seventh place. He died in 1997 in Clearwater, Florida at the age of 88.

Historical note: On the day Wrong Way Corrigan accidentally landed his plane in Ireland instead of California (1938), Jurges scored the walk-off winning run in a dramatic 7-6 win against Boston at Wrigley Field.

*Additional Entries...*If you check out the Every Cub Ever feature at www.justonebadcentury.com, you'll find several additional entries, including celebrity Cubs fans, writers, and bloggers. Under the letter J, you'll discover legendary Chicago broadcaster Walter Jacobson.

K

The Starting Lineup for your Chicago Cubs starting with the letter K...

C−King Kelly, Casey at the Bat
1B−High Pockets Kelly, Hall of Famer
2B−Jerry Kindall, Bonus Baby
SS−Don Kessinger, All-Star
3B− Mark Koenig, Babe Ruth Inspirer (playing out of position)
LF−Ralph Kiner, Hall of Famer
CF−Chuck Klein, Hall of Famer
RF−Dave Kingman, Grumpy Slugger
Bench−Bill Killefer, the Reindeer
Bench−Johnny Kling, 1908 Cub
SP− Rube Kroh, Puncher Heard Round the World
SP−Mike Krukow, the Polish Prince
RP−Darold Knowles, Man We Got For Billy Williams

Mike Kahoe 1873−1949 (Orphans 1901-1902, Cubs 1907)

Kahoe was a jack of all trades. He played mostly catcher (one of the few who wore shin guards in his day), but also got time at every infield position during his Chicago years. He skipped out of town in 1902 and joined the American League (St. Louis Browns). His big league career lasted eleven seasons. Kahoe came back to the Cubs in 1907 for a very brief stint during their first World Series championship year, but by the time the season ended, he was on Washington's roster.

Al Kaiser 1886−1969 (Cubs 1911)

Kaiser had one of the great nicknames — they called him Deerfoot. The outfielder reached base fewer than thirty times with the Cubs, but he still managed to steal six bases.

Unfortunately, he couldn't steal first base. His career batting average was only .216. He later played for the Boston Braves, and finished his career in the Federal League.

Don Kaiser 1935− (Cubs 1955-1957)

His real first name was Clyde, he went by Don, and everyone called him Tiger. Unlike another well-known Tiger today, Chicago's Tiger was not controversial. Don Kaiser was a bonus baby pitcher the Cubs signed in 1955 with high hopes. That '55 Cubs team was as bad as any of Chicago's incredibly woeful 1950s bunch, so they brought Tiger right up to the bigs and put him in the bullpen. He performed well enough to get a shot at the starting rotation the next year, and the tall (6'5") right-hander from Oklahoma was 6-15 as a member of the Cubs rotation in '56 and '57. He was dealt to the Braves after the '57 season. Tiger couldn't crack that loaded NL champion team squad the next spring, however, and never made it back to the big leagues again.

Historical note: On the day President Eisenhower had to call in the National Guard to allow nine black students to enter a formerly all-white school in Little Rock, Kaiser was on the mound for the Cubs. He lost a heartbreaker 4-3 to the Reds in Cincinnati.

Ryan Kalish 1988− (Cubs 2014, 2016)

Kalish came up through the Red Sox system, and was signed as a free agent by his former bosses Theo Epstein and Jed Hoyer. With the Cubs he showed great hustle and determination, but he hit only .248 in 57 games. He signed with the Blue Jays after the season. The Cubs brought him back in 2016 and he played with the big league club for about a week in May. He had a few big hits, but the stacked roster didn't have a permanent place for Kalish. He was granted his free agency after the season again.

John Kane 1882−1934 (Cubs 1909-1910)

Kane was a utility infielder for the Cubs team that was renowned for their defense. He backed up both Tinker and Evers. In 1910 Kane was on the postseason roster for the Cubs, and batted twice (without a hit) in the 1910 World Series. Kane died in an automobile accident at the age of 51.

Matt Karchner 1967 – (Cubs 1998-2000)

Acquired in one of those classic terrible Cubs trades (for farmhand Jon Garland), Karchner was brought in to help out the struggling bullpen in 1998. The former White Sox closer was lit up the rest of that year, and hurt his arm the following season. Meanwhile, Jon Garland went on to win more than 10 games six years in a row (including two 18-win seasons) for the White Sox. Among Garland's exploits, starting Game 3 of the 2005 World Series (an eventual win for the Sox).

Eric Karros 1967 – (Cubs 2003)

Karros only played with the Cubs for one year, but it was quite a year — the year the Cubs were within five outs of going to the World Series. When he wasn't playing in the games, Karros was filming the historic moments from inside the Cubs dugout. The former Rookie of the Year with the Dodgers played pretty well in his only Cubs season. He hit 12 homers while splitting time at first base with midseason acquisition Randall Simon.

Len Kasper 1971 – (Cubs announcer 2005-present)

Len has been the TV play-by-play man for the Cubs since 2005. He replaced Chip Caray. Len does a great job on the broadcasts, often spicing them up by appealing to the stats geeks (with an occasional SABR-metric) and the rock and roll generation (with music references). He also hosts an occasional rock and roll show on WXRT radio. When Bob Brenley was his color man, Len & Bob would even rock out every year the night before the Cubs Convention.

Jack Katoll 1872 – 1955 (1888-1889 Orphans)

Known as "Big Jack" or "Katy", Katoll was one of several Cubs (then known as Orphans) players to be born in Germany. He started four games for Chicago over two seasons, and threw three complete games. He later also pitched for the White Sox and Baltimore. After his playing career he settled in the Chicago area.

Tony Kaufmann 1900 – 1982 (Cubs 1920-1927)

Kaufmann was a local Chicago boy who made it to the big leagues with his hometown Cubs at the young age of 20. After a few years of bullpen work and spot starting, Tony claimed a spot in the rotation in 1923 and began a string of three excellent seasons. He won 14, 16, and 13 games those three years — pitching as the third starter in a rotation that also included an aging Grover Cleveland Alexander (he was 14 years older than Tony). Kaufmann was traded to the Phillies in 1927, and finished his career (in 1935) with the St. Louis Cardinals. After his playing days were over, Tony relocated back to his hometown. He passed away in Elgin in 1982.

Historical note: On the day Charles Lindbergh departed for Europe aboard the Spirit of St. Louis (1927), Kaufmann was on the mound for the Cubs. Tony was also the hitting star that day as the Cubs beat Brooklyn 7-5.

Munenori Kawasaki 1981 – (Cubs 2016)

The energetic Japanese infielder was 35 years old when the Cubs signed him to help provide backup infield help. Kawasaki had a great career in Japan, and was coming off a solid season with the Blue Jays. He made the Cubs roster out of spring training, but spent most of the season with Iowa. He returned after the rosters expanded in September. Kawasaki was a popular teammate thanks to his enthusiasm. The Cubs granted him free agency after the season.

Teddy Kearns 1900 – 1949 (Cubs 1924-1925)

Teddy only played in seven games for the Cubs over two seasons. In parts of three big league seasons (one with Philadelphia), Teddy got exactly one extra base hit. It was a triple. He was a first baseman.

Chick Keating 1891 – 1959 (Cubs 1913-1915)

Keating played 14 years of minor league ball, but did have two brief tastes of the big-time. Chick was a backup infielder for the Cubs during their last three seasons at West Side Grounds. He didn't get many opportunities, probably because he was definitely a liability as a batter. In 43 at-bats, he only managed to scratch out four hits (a double and three singles). Eleven years after his Cubs stint, he returned to the big leagues for a cup of coffee with the Phillies.

Vic Keen 1899 – 1976 (Cubs 1921-1925)

Keen was the fifth starter and swingman on a Cubs staff that also featured Hall of Famer Grover Cleveland Alexander. He won 12 games in that capacity in 1923. In '24, they moved him into the rotation full-time and Vic responded with his best big league season. He and another Vic, Vic Aldridge, each won 15 games that year. The Cubs traded him to the Cardinals in 1925 for slick-fielding shortstop Jimmy Cooney.

George Keerl 1847–1923 (White Stockings 1875)

George was a second baseman for the White Stockings, but didn't get a lot of playing time. He only appeared in six games, and came up to bat 23 times. He managed only three singles.

John Kelleher 1893–1960 (Cubs 1921-1923)

Kelleher was a backup infielder for the Cubs for three seasons, filling in at every infield position. He got a lot of playing time too, because two of the infielders from that era (Grimes and Hollocher) were oft-injured. Luckily for the Cubs, Kelleher was also a good hitter. He hit over .300 two of his three years. After his playing career, he became a college coach, first for Harvard, and later for Brown.

Mick Kelleher 1947– (Cubs 1976-1980)

In more than 1000 at-bats, covering 11 major league seasons (including five with the Cubs), Kelleher never hit a home run. He was the starting second baseman for the Cubs in 1976 but batted only .228. That led the Cubs to acquire Manny Trillo to cover the position the following year. Kelleher remained with Chicago in a mainly backup role for another four seasons. After his playing career he coached for the Yankees, Pirates, and Tigers.

Historical note: On July 4, 1976, America's Bicentennial, Mick had his best day at the plate for the Cubs. He was 3 for 3 in a 4-2 victory against the Mets.

Frank Kellert 1924–1976 (Cubs 1956)

Kellert was a first baseman who only got a brief taste of the big leagues in the 1950s. He got cups of coffee with the Browns, Orioles, and Dodgers, before he came to Chicago. With the Dodgers he was part of the Boys of Summer who won the World Series. Frank even got three at-bats and one hit in that series. The Cubs gave him his most extended playing time of his career the following year. In 129 at-bats he hit four homers and knocked in 17 runs, but he hit only .186. That was it for the big leagues. Kellert spent the rest of his career in the minors, before hanging up his spikes for good in 1959.

Bob Kelly 1927– (Cubs 1951-1953)

Kelly was a right-handed pitcher who came up with the Cubs and pitched as a swing-starter for two seasons, and part of a third. The Cubs traded him to the Reds in the middle of the 1953 season for Bubba Church. Kelly couldn't have been thrilled with the trade. He was sent to the minors shortly after arriving in Cincinnati and didn't return to the big leagues until five years later.

George Kelly 1895–1984 (Cubs 1930)

Kelly was a member of the legendary 1930 Cubs team that blew the pennant in the last few days of the season. Tall for his time (6'4), Kelly was nicknamed Highpockets and Long George by the press; but to his teammates he was Kell, a reserved and even-tempered Derrek Lee-type, and one of the best fielding first basemen of all time. He is a Hall of Famer, although not because of his year with the Cubs. Like many of the Hall of Famers who wore a Cubs uniform, he only wore it after his glory years. He was in his 15th big league season. Kelly hit .331 in 39 games for the Cubs. He isn't considered a Hall of Famer by many baseball experts, including Bill James, who calls him "the worst player in the Hall of Fame." He was elected into the Hall by a veterans committee consisting of ex-teammates (with the Giants).

Joe Kelly 1886–1977 (Cubs 1916)

Kelly was a backup outfielder for the Cubs during their first year in Wrigley Field. He played all three outfield positions and hit .254. He had good speed, but no power. His career totals tell the story: 66 stolen bases, 6 homers. Kelly also played for the Boston Braves and Pittsburgh Pirates, but the bulk of his career was spent in the minors. He played an incredible 23 seasons in the minor leagues.

Joe Kelly 1900–1967 (Cubs 1926-1928)

Kelly actually played for the Cubs in 1926 and 1928, and was in the minors In 1927. In '26 he hit .334 in 176 at-bats as a corner outfielder, backing up two even better hitters Riggs Stephenson and Hack Wilson. Most of his at-bats in 1928 came at the end of the season when the Cubs were already out of it

Mike Kelly 1857–1894 (White Stockings 1880-1886)

King Kelly was famous for his running and hitting (he invented or at least perfected the hit and run), and he was said to have inspired the poem "Casey at the Bat," but he was also considered a big fat cheater. If the umpire wasn't looking, he would run from first to third by running across the diamond over the pitcher's mound. He once came into the game in the middle of a play (from a drunken stupor on the bench) and announced "Kelly, Now Catching" so that he could take the throw and tag out the runner at home plate. (A rule was instituted after that banning something that nobody assumed needed to be spelled out — No mid-play substitutions). They even wrote a song about him called "Slide Kelly Slide."

But that's not what he was remembered for. Mike King Kelly was also a notorious drunk. Cap Anson hired a Pinkerton to keep an eye on him. One time the game had to be held up because Kelly was getting drunk with some fans in the box seats. Of course it caught up to him. The White Stockings (now known as the Cubs) got rid of him by selling him to Boston for $10,000 (which was a ton of money in those days). In Boston, the drinking took its toll. He had to be sobered up before every game in a Turkish bath. He lasted until 1893, but the last few years he was just a shell of the player he once was…and he wasn't even that old. He drank himself to death the following year at the age of 36. 5000 fans came to see him at his funeral. King Kelly was elected into the Baseball Hall of Fame in 1945.

David Kelton 1979–(Cubs 2003-2004)

David was a second round pick of the Cubs, but he never really developed into the offensive force they projected. The outfielder had respectable, if not outstanding numbers in the minors, but only got two brief shots with the big club. One time he was called up when Sammy Sosa was put on the disabled list for injuring himself sneezing. In 22 at-bats over two seasons, he got three hits. Kelton went into coaching after his playing days.

Jason Kendall 1974–(Cubs 2007)

The Cubs knew they weren't getting the same caliber of player that had been named to three All-Star teams and was second all-time in stolen bases by a catcher. Kendall had really lost all the pop in his bat when the Cubs acquired him for the 2007 playoff push. He did start at catcher for the team the rest of the year, and in the playoffs, but the Cubs looked elsewhere for a catcher the following season.

Bob Kennedy 1920–2005 (Cubs "Head Coach" 1963-1965, Cubs GM 1977-1981)

Kennedy was a very good big league player. He played 16 seasons in the majors (ten of those seasons were with the White Sox) and would have had a few more if the war hadn't interrupted his playing career. The native Chicagoan was brought in to save the Cubs from their preposterous College of Coaches experiment. Although, P.K. Wrigley wasn't quite ready to admit defeat about this plan — he still didn't refer to Kennedy as a manager, only as the head coach. In his first year at the helm of the Cubs, Kennedy led them to their best season in years. The team finished over .500 — although that still placed them in the bottom half of the division. Nevertheless, with a good nucleus of players like Banks, Santo, Williams, and Brock, things looked like they were going in the right direction. The next year they regressed a bit (and traded Lou Brock), and by mid-1965, Kennedy was replaced by Lou Klein. In 1977, Wrigley brought Kennedy back, this time as the General Manager of the team. He held that position for 4 1/2 years before being replaced by Dallas Green. His best draft choice as the GM was probably Joe Carter. Of course, that pick was only made possible by the team's horrendous play the year before (Carter was second overall pick). Kennedy's son Terry was also a big league player. He was the starting catcher on the 1984 Padres team that broke the hearts of Cub fans everywhere.

Junior Kennedy 1950–(Cubs 1982-1983)

Kennedy was a utility infielder in the big leagues for seven seasons, the last two of which were with the Cubs. He actually got a substantial amount of playing time in his first season in Chicago, getting over 240 at-bats. Unfortunately for Junior, he didn't take advantage of the situation, batting only .219. After his playing career, Kennedy coached in the Cubs farm system.

Snapper Kennedy 1878–1945 (Orphans 1902)

Kennedy had one of the all-time great names, but he only

played in one big league baseball game. That came with the Cubs (then known as the Orphans) on May 1, 1902. He played center field and batted five times in a scoreless 12-inning game at West Side Grounds that was called because of darkness. Snapper didn't reach base.

Ted Kennedy 1865–1907 (White Stockings 1885)

He was signed by Chicago in June of 1885 because they were down to one pitcher (John Clarkson) and Kennedy had been doing some incredible things on a team in Keokuk. He pitched nine games for Chicago (and won 7 of them), but developed an arm injury, and was released in September. After his playing days he worked for Al Spalding's sporting goods company, and invented the catcher's mitt. No record of whether or not he ever visited Chappaquiddick.

Historical note: On the day the unassembled Statue of Liberty arrived on a freighter from France (1885), Kennedy was on the mound for Chicago. They beat Buffalo that day 9-8.

Marty Keough 1934–(Cubs 1966)

Marty is the patriarch of a baseball family — his little brother Joe and his son Matt both also played big league baseball. Marty had an eleven-year career as a big league outfielder, even though he didn't get many chances to crack the starting lineup. He played for the Red Sox, Senators, Indians, Reds, and Braves before finishing his career with the Cubs. He may not have been a star, but he played alongside a who's who of his era: HOFers Ted Williams (Red Sox), Frank Robinson (Reds), Tony Perez (Reds), Hank Aaron (Braves), Phil Niekro (Braves), Ernie Banks (Cubs), Ron Santo (Cubs), Billy Williams (Cubs), and Fergie Jenkins (Cubs). He remained in the game after his playing career ended, working as a scout for the Padres, Dodgers, and the Cardinals.

Matt Keough 1955–(Cubs 1986)

Matt's father Marty played for the Cubs when Matt was 11 years old. Matt got off to a good start in his own big league career. He was an All-Star in his second year, but soon developed arm problems. After that, Keough managed to hang on in the big leagues for another six years despite having very little success. One of those years (1986) was with the Cubs. He was 2-2 with a 4.97 ERA when the Cubs released him in June.

Mel Kerr 1903–1980 (Cubs 1925)

Kerr is one of only two Manitobans to play in the big leagues — but his time was incredibly brief. His entire career can be described as follows: He came in as a pinch runner for Tommy Griffith, who had gotten a single as a pinch hitter. Kerr scored a run, but it was too little too late, and the Cubs lost 8-6 to Boston.

Don Kessinger 1942–(Cubs 1964-1975)

Kessinger had a brilliant career with the Cubs, holding down the starting shortstop position for over a decade during the Cubs resurgence of the late 60s/early 70s. Kessinger was an All-Star five years in a row (68-72) and a two-time Gold Glover. He and Glenn Beckert formed the Cubs double play combination for nine seasons. Kessinger was known as a fine glove man, and though he was probably miscast as a leadoff man on a team that didn't really have a better alternative, he was also a tough out. He scored a lot of runs with the likes of Banks, Williams, and Santo hitting behind him. He was up to bat when the infamous black cat crossed Ron Santo's path in the on-deck circle in 1969. When Kessinger was traded away in 1975, he was the last player from that fondly recalled era. He later played for the Cardinals and White Sox, and even managed the Sox.

Historical note: On the day Jim Morrison died in a bathtub in Paris (1971), Kessinger hit one of his two homers that season.

Cubs players have had some great nicknames over the years. Among players starting with the letter K, you'll find nicknames like Clouting Kraut, Dutch, High Pockets, Hoosier Hammer, Katy, King, Matches, Noisy, Polish Prince, Reindeer, Rube, Slim, Snapper, and Tiger.

Brooks Kieschnick 1972– (Cubs 1996-1997)

Kieschnick was a great college hitter even though his primary position was pitcher. The Cubs liked him so much they drafted him with the tenth overall pick and converted him into an outfielder. He was considered their top prospect, and eventually made it up to the big league club. But Brooks was not an everyday player. He struck out too much, and he had a hard time in the field. The Cubs left him unprotected in the expansion draft of 1997 and Tampa picked him. Kieschnick eventually made it back up to the show with the Brewers who used him as a pitcher and pinch hitter. He is the only player in history to hit a homer as a pitcher, designated hitter, and pinch hitter in the same season.

Pete Kilduff 1893–1930 (Cubs 1917-1919)

Pete was an infielder (mainly second base) for the Cubs during the first few years at their new ballpark (Wrigley Field). He was on the pennant-winning team of 1918, but didn't appear in the World Series against the Red Sox. A few years later he got his only taste of the World Series as a part of the Brooklyn Robins. His claim to fame is being one of the three outs of an unassisted triple play. Pete was hired to be the manager of the minor league San Francisco Seals in 1930, but fate intervened. He died of an appendicitis attack before the season started. He was only 36 years old.

Paul Kilgus 1962– (Cubs 1989)

He was part of the trade that brought Mitch Williams to the Cubs (at great cost — Rafael Palmeiro and Jamie Moyer went to the Rangers). Kilgus and Williams both contributed during the Cubs division-winning season of 1989. Kilgus threw three shutout innings in the series against the Giants, one of the few Cubs pitchers who pitched well. Even Greg Maddux was lit up by the white-hot Will Clark.

Bill Killefer 1887–1960 (Cubs 1918-1921, Cubs manager 1921-1925)

Bill Killefer was nicknamed Reindeer for his lumbering running style. Reindeer was a catcher and he ran like one. But he wasn't just any catcher. Killefer was the personal catcher for Grover Cleveland Alexander, and he was the only one who could handle him on and off the field. Bill caught him with the Phillies, and for the first four years Alexander was with the Cubs, and managed him after that (with the Cubs), but when he was fired by the Cubs, Alexander fell apart. Some of the most legendary stories of Alexander's drinking occurred during the days that Reindeer wasn't around. When Alexander was reunited with Killefer in St. Louis (where Reindeer Bill was a coach), he immediately

regained his touch, and added a few more great seasons to one of the greatest pitching careers of all-time.

Frank Killen 1870–1939 (Orphans 1900)

Killen was a two-time 30-game winner for Pittsburgh before he came to the Cubs (then known as the Orphans). Chicago was the last stop of his excellent career, but Killen was pretty much done. He had pitched 2500 innings in his previous nine big league seasons. With the Cubs he was 3-3. His nickname was Lefty.

Matt Kilroy 1866–1940 (Orphans 1898)

Kilroy set a record early in his career that will likely never be broken. He pitched 589 innings in one season for Baltimore. He also won 46 games that year. By the time he came to the Cubs (then known as the Orphans), he had logged 2300 innings in his nine year career. He completed ten of his eleven starts and won 6 games in the last season of his career. His teammates called him Matches. After his playing career he owned a tavern in Philadelphia.

Newt Kimball 1915–2001 (Cubs 1937-1938)

Newt had a cup of coffee with the Cubs in both 1937 and 1938, and it didn't go well either time. He was rocked hard, registering ERAs of 10.80 and 9.00. However, after spending a few more seasons in the minors, he stuck in the majors for the first few years of the 1940s (with the Dodgers, Cardinals, and Phillies). After his playing days were over he became a minor league manager in Las Vegas.

Bruce Kimm 1951– (Cubs player 1979, Cubs manager 2002)

Kimm was a big league catcher, but other than his first season in the big leagues when he was the personal catcher for Mark Fidrych in Detroit, and his last one in 1980 with the White Sox, he didn't get a lot of playing time. His Cubs playing career lasted exactly nine games. He went 1 for 11. Kimm is probably better remembered for his stint as manager of the Cubs. He took over the job from Don Baylor after Baylor was fired. When the season was over, Kimm was replaced by Dusty Baker.

Jerry Kindall 1935–2017 (Cubs 1956-1961)

The Cubs signed Jerry (nicknamed Slim) as a Bonus Baby, but he never quite made the impact they anticipated. His best season with the Cubs was 1961. He hit .242 that year. Jerry played on the Cubs for parts of five seasons, and later played with the Indians and Twins, but the second baseman holds a career record that nobody wants. Of all the players since 1920 with more than 2000 career at-bats, Jerry has the lowest batting average (.213). On the other hand, after his big league career, he became a college coach at the University of Arizona and had a tremendous career. He won three College World Series titles and was inducted into the American Baseball Coaches Association Hall of Fame.

Ralph Kiner 1922–2014 (Cubs 1953-1954)

He was one of the most feared sluggers in the league when he played for the Pirates, but by the time the Cubs got him (1953), he was not the same player. He led the league in home runs all seven seasons with the Pirates, and though he did have a decent power season with the Cubs in 1953 (making the All-Star team), he was so slow by then, he could barely field his position. Combined with the equally slow Hank Sauer in the other corner, the Cubs outfield during those two seasons might have been the worst fielding outfield the Cubs ever had. Kiner joked that both he and Sauer used to scream "You got it, Frankie" every time the ball was hit in the air. Frankie Baumholtz was the center fielder on that team. After the 1954 season Kiner was traded to the Indians for Sam Jones, who went on to pitch a no-hitter for the Cubs in 1955. Ralph Kiner is a proud member of baseball's Hall of Fame, but when you look at his plaque, don't expect to see him wearing a Cubs hat.

Historical note: On the day that John F. Kennedy married Jackie (1953), Kiner slammed a homer off fellow Hall of Famer Hoyt Wilhelm to win the game for the Cubs.

Chick King 1930–2012 (Cubs 1958-1959)

The center fielder was mainly a career minor leaguer who got an occasional taste of the show for the Tigers, Cardinals, and Cubs. Over five seasons, he had only 76 career big league plate appearances. He was a .280 hitter in his eleven years of minor league ball. King was an All-American football player in high school.

Jim King 1932–2015 (Cubs 1955-1956)

King broke into the big leagues with the Cubs and got significant playing time in right field for two seasons. He hit 26 homers for the Cubs and was traded to the Cardinals in 1957 for Bobby Del Greco. King played eleven seasons in the big leagues, including five full seasons as a starter with the Washington Senators. (He hit for the cycle with the Senators on 5/26/64). He also played for the White Sox, Indians, and Giants, including the very first West Coast home game for the Giants in 1958.

Marshall King 1849–1911 (White Stockings 1871)

Marshall played with the very first official Chicago professional team (National Association) as a center fielder, catcher, and shortstop. He hit two homers. That was the last Chicago team before the Great Chicago Fire. King was no longer a big leaguer by the time the National League was founded in 1876.

Ray King 1974– (Cubs 1999)

King got his start with the Cubs, but the left-handed reliever pitched another nine years after he left them. Ray got around. He was a Brewer (twice), Brave, Cardinal, Rockie, and a National (twice). In 593 career appearances he never started a game.

Dave Kingman 1948– (Cubs 1978-1980)

Kingman hit more homers than any Sagittarius in history (442). All the elements were in place for a wonderful long term-marriage between the Cubs and Dave Kingman. He was a prodigious slugger; his home runs were already the stuff of legend. The Cubs were having trouble drawing fans, and he was the kind of player that brought people to the ballpark. In addition to that, he was a local boy (Prospect High School) returning to play in front of his hometown fans. He even lived up to his billing at first, slugging home runs onto Waveland Avenue with regularity. Yet, by the time Kingman left Chicago, he might have been one of the most hated players in Cubs history. How did things go so horribly wrong? His first year with the Cubs (1978) he hit 28 homers, and some of them were dramatic, but his personality was already rubbing people the wrong way. His 1979 season was one of the best in Cubs history (he hit 48 homers), so his teammates and fans looked the other way as he said and did things that irritated one and all. It wasn't until 1980 that things really got ugly, and they got ugly in a hurry. He threw a bucket of ice water on a reporter. He didn't show up for a game. He hurt his shoulder, and missed two months, including Dave Kingman Day at the ballpark. (He was in town, just didn't bother showing up.) *Chicago Sun-Times* columnist Mike Royko hated Kingman so much, he temporarily became a White Sox fan after a lifetime supporting the Cubs. Royko called him Ding Dong.

In the off-season the Cubs did what they had to do; they traded Kingman back to the Mets. After news of Kingman's trade became public, his teammates all expressed relief that he was gone. Royko even became a Cubs fan again. And though Dave Kingman continued to slug homers (he hit another 172 in his career), and retired with the most career homers of any player not in the Hall of Fame, he never even got a sniff from Hall of Fame voters. It's hard to get votes from baseball writers when you're remembered for throwing ice cold water at one of their colleagues.

Historical note: On the day that CNN debuted in Atlanta (1980), Kingman scored the winning run for the Cubs against the Phillies.

Brandon Kintzler 1984– (Cubs 2018-present)

The Cubs thought they were getting an important bullpen cog when they acquired Kintzler from the Nationals. Unfortunately, the former Twins closer was a shell of his former self. In 25 appearances he was hit hard and finished with a Cubs ERA of 7.00.

Walt Kinzie 1858–1909 (White Stockings 1884)

Kinzie was a backup infielder for the 1884 Cubs (then known as the White Stockings). He had an uneventful big league career and finished with a .132 lifetime batting average. After his career ended, he settled in Chicago, and when he died in 1909, he was buried in Graceland Cemetery. At the time, the cemetery was just a few blocks away from a Lutheran Seminary. That seminary's former location now houses Wrigley Field.

Jim Kirby 1923–2009 (Cubs 1949)

Kirby's big league career lasted exactly twelve days. He celebrated his 26th birthday as a big leaguer with the Cubs. During those twelve days in May of 1949, Kirby got into three games. He went 1 for 2 in those limited opportunities, giving him a .500 career batting average. His only hit was a single against Reds pitcher Buddy Lively on May 13, 1949. The Cubs lost that game 7-0. Kirby played in the minor leagues until 1958.

Chris Kitsos 1928–2004 (Cubs 1954)

Some players have a cup of coffee in the show. Chris Kitsos only got a sip. He was a switch-hitting shortstop, but he languished in the minor leagues until April 21, 1954. On that day he finally got the call from the big club and was inserted as a defensive replacement for shortstop Eddie Miksis in the bottom of the eighth inning against the Braves in Milwaukee. Two of the Braves batters hit grounders to him, and he retired them both, including future Hall of Famer Warren Spahn. But he didn't get a chance to bat in the top of the ninth inning, and he never appeared in another big league game. Kitsos played in the minor leagues until 1959.

Malachi Kittridge 1869 (Colts 1890-1897)

When your given name is Malachi, you're bound to acquire a nickname. Kittridge went by his middle name instead; the equally unwieldly Jedediah. Kittridge was the starting catcher for the Cubs (then known as the Colts) for much of the 1890s. He didn't hit well (except for the fluky .315 he hit in 1894), but he was a solid defensive catcher. After leaving Chicago, he also caught for Louisville, Washington, Boston, and Cleveland before finally hanging up his spikes in 1906.

Chuck Klein 1904–1958 (Cubs 1934-1935)

Chuck Klein had two great nicknames: "The Hoosier Hammer" and "The Clouting Kraut." The Hoosier part of his nickname came from his Indiana roots, and the Kraut part, of course, came from his German heritage. Needless to say, the hammer and clouting parts of those nicknames were inspired by his propensity to hit home runs. The Cubs got the big slugger just after he won the Triple Crown, the first time anyone had ever traded a Triple Crown winner. The Phillies obviously recognized that his stats were padded by playing in a ballpark with a ridiculously short right field porch. Once he joined the Cubs, he suffered a series of injuries. He drove in only 80 and 73 runs in his years spent with the Cubbies. On the other hand, Klein did help Chicago to a World Series in 1935, and hit .333 in that Series (the Cubs lost in six games to the Tigers). After he was traded back to the Phillies, he hit four home runs in his first game back. Ah, there's nothing like a short right field porch. Chuck Klein was inducted into baseball's Hall of Fame in 1980, 22 years after his death.

Lou Klein 1918–1976
(Cubs manager 1961-1962, 1965)

He played five years in the big leagues (mostly with the Cardinals), but he also got a chance to manage the Cubs. Lou was part of the rotation of coaches in the College of Coaches in 1961 and 1962. In that capacity he was 17-23, which wasn't too bad for the Cubs of that era. He later got a chance to finish out the 1965 season as the Cubs manager, and finished ten games under .500. After the season he was replaced by Leo Durocher.

Johnny Kling 1875–1947 (Cubs 1900-1911)

Kling was one of the best catchers in baseball; a grizzled veteran who was so good defensively, he caused former catcher Frank Chance to move positions (to first base). Hall of Fame pitcher Mordecai "Three Finger" Brown often said that his secret weapon was Johnny Kling. Kling (nicknamed "Noisy" and "The Jew") was loved by his teammates because of his gritty attitude, loved by the umpires because he didn't swear, smoke, or drink, and loved by the fans. He was the starting catcher for all four pennant-winning teams in the first decade of last century (1906, 1907, 1908, 1910), and the pitchers claimed that his absence, and his absence alone, was the only reason the Cubs didn't win five pennants in a row. Kling sat out the 1909 season to pursue and win the World Pockets Billiard Championship. After a salary dispute, the Cubs traded him in 1911.

Johnny Klippstein 1927–2003 (Cubs 1950-1954)

Klippstein was a swing starter/reliever in his days with the Cubs. He has the distinction of winning the game at Wrigley Field on the same day and in the same town (July 1952 in Chicago) General Dwight D. Eisenhower was nominated to be president by the Republican Party. He beat the Brooklyn Dodgers that day. He later won the World Series as a member

of the 1959 Los Angeles Dodgers (beating the Chicago White Sox). In his 18-year big league career, Johnny won 101 games, and saved 66 more.

Joe Klugmann 1895–1951 (Cubs 1921-1922)

Klugmann played in the minors for many years, but only had a few opportunities in the big leagues. He got his first shot with the Cubs in 1921. He was 26 years old at the time. In his two seasons in Chicago he only got into eight games. Klugmann later played for the Dodgers and Indians. He became a manager after his playing career was over.

Joe Kmak 1963–(Cubs 1985)

Joe was a high school teammate of Barry Bonds, and eventually made it to the big leagues as a backup catcher. He had 53 at-bats for the 1995 Cubs and hit .245. After his baseball career he went into teaching. He teaches high school calculus and trigonometry.

Otto Knabe 1884–1961 (Cubs 1916)

The incredibly German-sounding Otto Knabe was, of course, nicknamed Dutch. (That was common in those days — Dutch was an Americanized version of "Deutsch"). He had a very good eleven-year big league career mostly as a second baseman. Dutch was renowned for his ability to handle the bat. He led the league in sacrifice hits four different times. By the time he joined the Cubs for their first season in Wrigley Field in 1916, he was coming off a stint as a player/manager in the Federal League. The Cubs traded the last link to their championship teams — Frank Schulte — to the Pirates to acquire Otto, and used him as a utility man. He saw time at 2B, SS, 3B, and RF, and retired from baseball after the season.

Pete Knisely 1887–1948 (Cubs 1913-1915)

Knisely played outfield and second base for the Cubs. In 1915 he got his most extended playing time and drove in 17 runs, by far the best of his career. That was also his last season in the big leagues. He played another eight years in the minors.

Darold Knowles 1941–(1975-1976)

After being acquired in the trade of Cubs icon Billy Williams, Knowles became a mentor for a young Bruce Sutter in the bullpen for the Cubs. Knowles had been a key member of the bullpen for the Oakland A's dynasty in the early 70s, but when he pitched for the Cubs in 1975, his command suddenly disappeared and he was lit up like a Christmas tree (5.81 ERA). Darold had a much better season in 1976, but during the off-season he was traded to the Texas Rangers for Gene Clines.

Mark Koenig 1904–1993 (Cubs 1932)

The ex-Yankee Mark Koenig replaced Cubs shortstop Billy Jurges after Jurges was shot by a fan. Despite hitting .353 during the season and saving the hides of the Cubs, the players voted not to give him a full World Series share. This really angered the Yankees, especially their emotional leader Babe Ruth. It was one of the reasons he wanted to beat the Cubs so badly in that 1932 World Series…and he did. Koenig played one more year for the Cubs in 1933, before finishing his career with the Reds and Giants.

Elmer Koestner 1885–1959 (Cubs 1914)

Elmer was a pitcher for several big league teams (including Cleveland and Cincinnati), but he also pitched for the Cubs briefly in 1914 at West Side Grounds. The ballpark was falling apart that year and more fans were going to see the Federal League Whales in what is now known as Wrigley Field. Elmer appeared in only four games before the Cubs cut him loose. His nickname was Bob.

Cal Koonce 1940–1993 (Cubs 1962-1967)

Cal won ten games for the Cubs as a rookie in 1962, and that's saying something. That team won only 59 games all season. Over the next few seasons he started and relieved for the Cubs, never really achieving excellence in either role. His main problem was command of the strike zone. He won 29 games and saved 4 in his six years with the Cubs. He was traded to the Mets in 1967 and became a key part of the bullpen of the Mets team that broke the Cubs' hearts in 1969.

Historical note: On the day Medicare began in America (1966), Cal was one of the four Cubs pitchers who got rocked by the Phillies in a 7-0 loss in Philadelphia.

*Korean War Veterans…*The following Cubs served in the military during the Korean War… Ted Abernathy, Ken Aspromonte, Ed Bailey, Ernie Banks, Cuno Barragan, Frank Baumann, Ed Bouchee, Leon Brinkopf, Jim Brosnan, Bob Buhl, Hy Cohen, Wes Covington, Larry French, Dick Groat, Footer Johnson, Bob Kennedy, Don Larsen, Lloyd Merriman, Mel Roach, Paul Schramka, Curt Simmons, Bob Speake, Sammy Taylor, Vito Valentinetti, and Pete Whisenant.

John Koronka 1980– (Cubs 2005)

Koronka came up from Iowa in 2005 and filled in for injured Cubs starters. It didn't go well. He had a 7.47 ERA. He later pitched for the Rangers and the Marlins, and also spent a year in Japan. After his playing career, the Cubs hired him as a scout.

Jim Korwan 1874–1899 (Colts 1897)

The tall lanky left-hander was known to his teammates as Long Jim. He only started four games for the Cubs (then known as the Colts), but three of them were complete games. His control was the issue. He walked 28 men in those 34 innings. Among his teammates were future Hall of Famers Cap Anson and Clark Griffith. Long Jim died of tuberculosis at the age of 25, just six months before the turn of the century.

Fabian Kowalik 1908–1954 (Cubs 1935-1936)

Kowalik was a converted infielder who became a relief pitcher. He pitched for the Cubs in 1935 and 1936, and even made the postseason roster in 1935. Fabian pitched 4 1/3 innings in game 2 of the 1935 World Series against the Tigers, giving up only one run in relief of Charlie Root. The Cubs lost the game 8-3 (in Detroit). In 1936 he was traded to the Phillies along with Hall of Famer Chuck Klein for outfielder Ethan Allen and pitcher Curt Davis.

Joe Kraemer 1964– (Cubs 1989-1990)

Kraemer was brought up for one spot start near the end of the division-winning season of 1989, and then made the team the following year. The lefty pitched in eighteen games out of the bullpen before being sent back down to the minor leagues for good. His lifetime ERA was 6.91.

Historical note: On the day the Hubble Telescope was sent into orbit (1990), Kraemer was one of three Cubs pitchers getting rocked. The other two were Greg Maddux and Jeff Pico. The Cubs lost 13-3 to San Diego.

Randy Kramer 1960– (Cubs 1990)

Kramer spent exactly one month in a Cubs uniform, September of 1990. He appeared in ten games for the Cubs, including two starts. The right-hander had a respectable ERA (just a shade under 4), but he gave up three homers and walked twelve men in only 20 innings. The Cubs released him after the season. Kramer also pitched for the Pirates and Mariners.

Ken Kravec 1951– (Cubs 1981-1982)

Kravec had been a 15-game winner for the White Sox just a few years before he was acquired by the Cubs in a rare crosstown trade (for Dennis Lamp). This one worked out for the Cubs, but not in the way you might expect. Kravec was terrible as a Cubs pitcher, going 2-7 in two full seasons, with an ERA over five. However, after his playing career ended, Ken went to work for the Cubs as a scout. He's been a valuable member of their front office staff.

Historical note: On the day Sandra Day O'Connor was approved as the first female Supreme Court Justice (1981), Kravec was on the mound for the Cubs. He lost a 2-0 heartbreaker to the Cardinals at Wrigley Field.

Mike Kreevich 1908–1994 (Cubs 1931)

Kreevich was a short guy (only 5'7") but no one would ever accuse him of being small. The former coal miner was strong as a bull. The Cubs were the first team that gave the center fielder a chance, but he only got into a handful of games for them in 1931. He didn't really blossom until later in his career. He became an All-Star with the White Sox in 1938, and also played with the Browns, A's, and Senators.

Mickey Kreitner 1922–2003 (Cubs 1943-1944)

Mickey was just a 20-year-old kid when he came up the Cubs in the war year of 1943. The catcher didn't get a lot of playing time with the Cubs that year, but did get into 39 games in 1944. Unfortunately for Mickey, he spent the entire pennant-winning 1945 season in the minors. He hung his up spikes when all the players who had been serving in the military returned from the war.

Jim Kremmel 1948–2012 (Cubs 1974)

He was the ninth overall pick of the draft in 1971, but by December of 1973, he came to the Cubs as the player to be named later in the Ron Santo trade with the White Sox. Kremmel appeared in 23 games for the Cubs in 1974, his most extended time in the majors. His lifetime ERA was a disappointing 6.08.

Bill Krieg 1859–1930 (White Stockings 1885)

He played one game with Chicago, got three at-bats, struck out twice, and made two errors as a catcher. But Krieg was a great minor league hitter. He had a lifetime batting average of .335 in the minors and played until he was 42 years old.

Gus Krock 1866–1905 (White Stockings 1888-1889)

Gus was a shooting star. Krock won 25 games for the Cubs in 1888 as a 22 year old rookie (7th best in the league), and was 8th in the league in strikeouts with 161. Unfortunately he also gave up 20 homers, second worst in baseball. He started the next season with the Cubs too (then known as the White Stockings), before being shipped off to Indianapolis mid-season. By 1890 he was out of baseball. Krock was only 38 when he died in 1905.

Rube Kroh 1886–1944 (Cubs 1908-1910)

His real name was Floyd Kroh, but Rube was a common nickname in the first half of last century, indicating that the player was a country boy. Rube Kroh certainly fit that description. He grew up in a small town in New York named Friendship. Kroh's first season with the Cubs was 1908, which was, needless to say, a very memorable year. He also played a bit part in the most important play of that season. He may have led the Cubs to the World Series without throwing a single pitch. Instead, it was a single punch. During the melee in the "Merkle Boner" game on September 23, 1908, while the Giants fans stormed the field before the umpire had called the game over, it was Rube Kroh that "forcibly retrieved" the ball from a Giants fan, and threw it in to Johnny Evers. Evers stepped on second base, and the Cubs won the game because the "winning run" didn't count. Fred Merkle hadn't yet stepped on second. The game ended in a tie, and the Cubs went on to win the pennant. Kroh also happened to be a good pitcher, but on that Cubs team, he wasn't good enough to get on the mound very often. In three seasons during the Cubs dynasty years, he won 14 games. They let him go after the 1910 season.

Chris Krug 1939 – (Cubs 1965-1966)

Krug split the catching job with Vic Roznovsky in 1965, and the pair were probably the worst catcher tandem in all of baseball. Krug hit .201. The Cubs went out and got Randy Hundley from the Giants the following season, and Krug stayed on the team during Hundley's rookie season. He later also played for Padres.

Gene Krug 1955 – (Cubs 1981)

To say the 29th round draft choice was a long shot to make it is an understatement, but Krug managed to defy the odds, and was called up to the show. His big league career consisted of exactly seven games in the 1981 (strike) season. He went 2 for 5 at the plate (both singles), giving him a lifetime big league average of .400.

Marty Krug 1888 – 1966 (Cubs 1922)

Krug was a German immigrant who came to this country as a child. He was a pretty good hitter, but was such a bad fielder that it kept him out of the big leagues for most of his baseball career. He came up for a cup of coffee in 1912, and didn't return for an entire decade. The Cubs gave him lots of playing time in 1922 because they wanted his bat in the lineup. The infielder hit .276 and drove in 60 runs in 127 games. He also committed 21 errors, third worst total in the league. After his playing career, Krug went into coaching and scouting. He famously missed badly on one prospect. A kid he called "too fragile" eventually made it to the big leagues and did OK for himself. His name was Ted Williams.

Mike Krukow 1952 – (Cubs 1976-1981)

Mike Krukow shares a nickname with singer Bobby Vinton (The Polish Prince), but Mike Krukow was not known for botching the National Anthem. He was known for his stellar career as a starting pitcher for the Cubs, the Phillies, and the Giants. He never quite managed to harness his wild streak while he was a Cub, so they traded him to the Phillies as part of the deal that brought Keith Moreland to the Cubs. Krukow didn't really flourish until joining the Giants. He put

it all together in the 1986 season, winning 20 games. He also pitched in the NLCS for the Giants the following year, beating the St. Louis Cardinals in his only start. After retirement, the Polish Prince became a broadcaster for the San Francisco Giants, and he remains in that job today.

Harvey Kuenn 1930 – 1988 (Cubs 1965-1966)

Harvey came up as a shortstop and had a tremendous start to his career with the Tigers. He was the Rookie of the Year in 1953, and appeared in eight straight All-Star games. By the time he came to the Cubs in the mid-60s, he was at the tail end of his career. By then he was a part-time outfielder. The Cubs traded him to the Phillies at the beginning of the 1966 season and Kuenn finished his career in Philadelphia. His career batting average was .303 and he only struck out only 404 times in over 7600 big league plate appearances. After his playing days were over, Harvey went into managing. He'll always be remembered in Milwaukee for leading the Brewers to an American League pennant.

Historical note: On the day the Watts Riots began in Los Angeles (1965), Kuenn had one of his best days on the Cubs, scoring two big runs in a 7-3 win against the Reds.

Jeff Kunkel 1962 – (Cubs 1992)

Kunkel was a successful utility man for the Rangers for several years. He played every position except catcher (including pitcher). The Cubs gave him his last shot in the big leagues when he was 30 years old in 1992. He had missed the entire 1991 season because of an injury. Kunkel didn't have much left in the tank. He hit .138 in 29 at-bats.

Emil Kush 1916 – 1969 (Cubs 1941-1942, 1946-1949)

Emil was born in Chicago during the Cubs' first season at Wrigley Field, and was a Chicago boy through and through. He played his entire big league career with the Cubs, and died a few months after they broke our hearts in 1969. The right-handed pitcher was a valuable member of the bullpen in the years after the war. Unfortunately for him, he missed the World Series season of 1945 because he was serving in the US Navy.

Additional Entries... If you check out the Every Cub Ever feature at www.justonebadcentury.com, you'll find several additional entries, including celebrity Cubs fans, writers, and bloggers. Under the letter K, you'll discover your humble author and WGN-TV's Bill Kissinger.

CHAPTER TWELVE

L

The Starting Lineup for your Chicago Cubs starting with the letter L...

C–Dale Long, Left-Handed Catcher
1B–Derrek Lee, Batting Champ
2B–Tony LaRussa, Hall of Famer (as manager)
SS–Tony Lazzeri, Hall of Famer (as Yankee)
3B– Freddie Lindstrom, Hall of Famer (Chicago Boy)
LF–Bill Lange, Little Eva
CF–Kenny Lofton, Lead Off Man
RF–Peanuts Lowrey, Child Actor
Bench– Vance Law, '89 Cub
Bench–Pete LaCock, Game Show Son
SP–Jon Lester, World Series Hero
SP–Bill Lee, the General
SP–Jimmy Lavender, No-Hitter
SP–Ted Lilly, Presidential Namesake
RP–Turk Lown, One That Got Away

Rene Lachemann 1945–(Cubs manager 2002)

Lachemann was a backup catcher in his playing days (mostly for the Kansas City A's) before becoming a big league manager in some pretty challenging situations. He managed the Mariners during their early years, the Brewers during their 20-year under .500 streak, and the Marlins during their early years. He never finished better than 4th place. With the Cubs he managed exactly one game. He took the reins after Don Baylor was fired, before Bruce Kimm arrived in Chicago to manage the rest of the season. The Cubs lost the game.

John Lackey 1978–(Cubs 2016-2017)

After the 2015 season the Cubs realized they needed one more big starter to take them to the next level. Lackey was

signed to a free agent contract to fill that role. The 2-time World Series champ (with Angels and Red Sox) was exactly the veteran presence the Cubs were looking for — he won 11 games, posted a solid 3.35 ERA, and held down a spot in the postseason rotation (although he didn't win any of those games). He is now a 3-time World Series champ. Lackey finished his Cubs career in 2017. He went 12-12 and gave up a league-leading 36 homers. While he didn't make the NLDS roster against the Nationals, Lackey did pitch in three games in the NLCS (all in relief). He was lit up. His worst moment (9.82 ERA) was in Game 2 when he gave up the game-winning walk-off homer in the bottom of the ninth.

Pete Lacock 1952–(Cubs 1975-1976)

Pete was mainly a backup first baseman/outfielder for two seasons. He had a little pop in his bat (14 homers), but his average was low. The Cubs traded him to the Royals after the 1976 season, and he played a more significant role on that team. For one thing, he began hitting for average, including a season over .300. For another, he got to play in three ALCS with Kansas City.

Two bits of trivia about Pete LaCock. His father was the host of Hollywood Squares — Peter Marshall. He also once walked into P.K. Wrigley's office at the Wrigley building because he wanted to see if he really existed or not.

Doyle Lade 1921–2000 (Cubs 1946-1950)

The Cubs got him from the White Sox during the 1946 season, and Doyle stayed with the Cubs the rest of the decade. His best season was 1947. He won 11 games and posted a 3.94 ERA pitching for a less-than-stellar Cubs team. After that season, he was mostly used as a spot starter until his release in spring training 1951. Lade was a farm boy from Nebraska, and his teammates called him Porky.

Bryan LaHair 1982–(Cubs 2011-2012)

LaHair was a slugger in the minor leagues, and then stormed out of the box in the beginning of the 2012 season for the Cubs. He was among the league leaders in homers for the first few months and made the All-Star team. Then...reality set in. At the end of the year he still had 16 homers. By the next season he was in Japan.

Junior Lake 1990 – (Cubs 2013-2015)

Lake wasn't considered one of the best prospects in the talented Cubs minor league system, but he forced his way up to the Cubs with his performance. He made a big splash in the big leagues in his first season, hitting .284. 2014 was a different story — as Lake struggled mightily — and struck out a lot. In July of 2015 the Cubs traded him to the Orioles for reliever Tommy Hunter.

Steve Lake 1957 – (Cubs 1983-1986, 1993)

Steve spent eleven years in the big leagues as a backup catcher, beginning and ending his career with the Cubs. He was known as a great defensive catcher. Lake ranks ninth on the all-time list for percentage of baserunners thrown out trying to steal. But Steve also wasn't much of a hitter. In nearly 1200 lifetime at-bats, he hit only eighteen homers, and batted only .237. Probably the highlight of his career came in 1987 as a member of the St. Louis Cardinals. He got the start behind the plate in the deciding Game 7 of the World Series versus the Twins. The Twins won the game, but Lake played well. He went 1 for 3, drove in a run, and threw out Kirby Puckett trying to steal third base.

Blake Lalli 1983 – (Cubs 2012)

Lalli made a very brief stop in Chicago. He went 2 for 15 for the Cubs in May of 2012, with 2 RBI. His first at-bat was in a Cubs/Sox game (won by the Sox). He grounded out to the shortstop in the ninth inning for the second to last out of the game. The catcher/first baseman moved on to the Diamondbacks organization after his time with the Cubs.

Jack Lamabe 1936 – 2007 (Cubs 1968)

The Cubs were the last stop of the big league tour for Jack. The right-hander pitched seven seasons for seven teams in the bigs, and won a World Series with the 1967 Cardinals. With the 1968 Cubs, he appeared in 42 games, and posted an ERA of 4.30. The Cubs included him in the trade with the Expos (along with Adolpho Phillips) that brought Paul Popovich to Chicago, but Lamabe never pitched for Montreal. After his playing career he went into coaching, including a stint as head coach at LSU.

Pete Lamer 1873 – 1931 (Orphans 1902)

His real first name was Pierre, and he played only two games for the Cubs (then known as the Orphans) in September of 1902. The catcher got nine trips to the plate, and singled twice.

Dennis Lamp 1952 – (Cubs 1977-1981)

His major league debut came late in the 1977 season, when he was called up to help out the fading Cubs team that had started so strong that season. Judging by his 6.30 ERA, he wasn't quite ready for prime time. Lamp was a member of the starting rotation the next few years, and even won 11 games in 1979 (a year in which he also gave up Lou Brock's 3000th hit), but sadly, it wasn't until he was traded to the White Sox in 1981 that somebody figured out his rubber arm belonged in the bullpen. He may have given up Cal Ripken Jr.'s first career hit pitching in that role, but that's also where he made his mark in the big leagues. He was a key member of the 1983 White Sox playoff team, and later pitched in the playoffs for the Blue Jays and the Red Sox.

Historical note: On the day the movie *Animal House* was released (1978), Lamp shut out the Giants at Candlestick Park for a 1-0 Cubs win.

Les Lancaster 1963 – (Cubs 1987-1991)

Lancaster was an integral member of the bullpen for the 1989 division winners. He had a pretty good career with the Cubs, winning 34 games and saving 22 in five seasons with Chicago. After his playing days were over, he went into coaching, and continues to coach in the minor leagues. His name appears only once on the Cubs all-time career pitching lists. Only two Cubs pitchers in history balked more batters than Les. He is tied for third on the list with Bill Bonham and Fergie Jenkins (14 balks). Needless to say, he achieved that landmark in far fewer innings pitched.

Hobie Landrith 1930 – (Cubs 1956)

Hobie was a catcher who lasted fourteen seasons in the big leagues, including 1956 with the Cubs. That season Hobie got over 300 at-bats for the only time in his career, but he didn't take advantage of the opportunity. He led all big league catchers in errors, and only hit .221. The Cubs traded him to the Cardinals after the season. He also played for the

Reds, Giants, Mets, Orioles, and Senators. After his playing career he went to work for Volkswagen.

Bill Landrum 1957– (Cubs 1988)

The Cubs got Landrum from Cincinnati in a trade for infielder Luis Quinones. He had been a pretty effective reliever for the Reds, but didn't do much in a Cubs uniform. They let him go after the season, and Landrum signed with the Pirates. The Pirates made him their closer and he saved 56 games for them over the next three years.

Ced Landrum 1963– (Cubs 1991)

Landrum was a speedster. The outfielder appeared in 56 games but only got 99 plate appearances because he was used mainly as a pinch runner. Landrum stole 27 bases for the Cubs that year. If he ever figured out a way to steal first base, he would have been a keeper. He batted only .233. He later had a cup of coffee with the Mets.

Don Landrum 1936–2003 (Cubs 1962-1965)

Landrum was mostly a backup outfielder during his big league career, but he did get some extensive playing time with the Cubs in his final season with the club. Unfortunately, he only hit .226. But he served the Cubs well because he was included in a trade (along with Lindy McDaniel) that brought two important players to Chicago — Randy Hundley and Bill Hands. That remains one of the best trades the Cubs ever made. Landrum also played for the Phillies and Cardinals.

Historical note: On the day the Voting Rights Act was signed by President Johnson (1965), Landrum hit a 3-run homer to help the Cubs beat the Mets 4-3 at Shea Stadium.

Walt Lanfranconi 1916–1986 (Cubs 1941)

The small (5'7') right-handed pitcher only got a cup of coffee with the Cubs in September of 1941 (two appearances) before being drafted into the military. He spent the rest of the war working for Uncle Sam. Lanfranconi never pitched for the Cubs again, but he did get one more cup of coffee with the Braves in 1947.

Bill Lange 1871–1950 (Colts/Orphans 1893-1899)

Bill Lange was one of the star players for the 1890s Cubs/Colts. A flashy charismatic outfielder that played with grace, he was just as well-known for his fancy dance moves off the field. They called him "Little Eva" because of his dancing prowess. So how is it that you may never have heard of Little Eva? Because, at the age of 28, while still at the peak of his career, he abruptly retired. Little Eva had met an extremely wealthy girl, and the girl's father, who controlled the purse strings, would not allow his daughter to marry a ballplayer. In those days ballplayers were held in low regard by proper society. So, Little Eva retired for his sugar mama. Unfortunately for him, the marriage ended in divorce, just like his baseball career. Bill Lange has the 4th highest Cubs career batting average of all-time (.330), was a 6-time .300 hitter, a 5-time 80-RBI man, and the fastest player on the Cubs. In his last season he stole 41 bases. But even though he also stole a girl's heart, she jumped out of her crouch in time to throw out the last few productive years of his potential career.

Terry Larkin 1856–1894 (White Stockings 1878-1879)

Larkin pitched over a thousand innings and won 60 games in just two seasons with the Cubs (then known as the White Stockings). He was in the top five in the league in wins both seasons, and in the top six in innings pitched, and his team finished in 4th place both years. Not surprisingly, by 1880 he didn't have anything left in the tank. He tried to pitch for Troy but he was lit up. Larkin was a very troubled man in the years after his baseball career ended and clearly suffered from mental illness. He threatened to shoot his dad. He actually did shoot his wife, and tried to kill himself. He challenged someone to a duel. Larkin was eventually committed to a mental institution. While he was in there, he slit his own throat and killed himself. Terry Larkin was only 38 years old.

Dave LaRoche 1947– (Cubs 1973-1974)

He was supposed to be the closer for the Cubs when they acquired him from the Twins before the 1973 season (for Bill Hands and Joe Decker), but LaRoche couldn't do the job. His ERAs were 5.80 and 4.79 in his two seasons with the Cubs. Of course he managed to rediscover his touch after leaving Chicago. In the next five years he saved 90 games, pitched in the All-Star game for Cleveland in 1976 and 1977, and the playoffs in 1979 for the Angels. His sons Adam and Andy both played major league ball.

Vic LaRose 1944–2011 (Cubs 1968)

Vic was the starting second baseman on the Cubs AAA team for the entire 1968 season, and was called up in September to get a taste of the big leagues. He backed up Glenn Beckert and Don Kessinger for a few weeks, and got into four games. That was the extent of his cup of coffee. Vic never got another chance. In three big league plate appearances, he didn't get a hit.

Don Larsen 1929– (Cubs 1967)

When the MLB channel debuted, the first full game they showed was the only perfect game in World Series history. Everyone remembers that game, pitched by the immortal Don Larsen. Not many Cubs fans realize that the same Don Larsen also pitched for the Cubs. Even though the two-time World Series champ hadn't pitched in the majors at all in 1966, the Cubs signed him for the 1967 season. Larsen pitched a total of four innings for the Cubs, the last four innings of his major league career. His ERA was 9.00. The MLB channel won't be showing those four innings any time soon.

Dan Larson 1954– (Cubs 1982)

Larson was one of the Phillies brought over by Dallas Green after becoming general manager of the Cubs. He came over in the Keith Moreland/Dickie Noles for Mike Krukow trade. Unlike his fellow ex-Phillies, Larson didn't have much success with the Cubs. He began the 1982 season with the team, went 0-4 with a 5.62 ERA, and was shipped out by July 1st. Chicago was the last stop of his big league career. (He had also pitched for Houston before joining the Phillies)

Tony LaRussa 1944– (Cubs 1973)

On April 6, 1973, the Cubs won the opener 3-2 over the Expos in the bottom of the ninth because the best relief pitcher in baseball, Mike Marshall, walked in two runs. The winning run was scored by Tony LaRussa in his only game as a Cub. He came in as a pinch runner for Ron Santo. Of course after his unexceptional playing career (he only had a total of 203 plate appearances in parts of six big league seasons), LaRussa became a Hall of Fame manager, winning the World Series with both the Oakland A's and St. Louis Cardinals.

Al Lary 1928–2001 (Cubs 1954, 1962)

Lary was a pitcher in the Cubs system for twelve seasons and won over 100 games in the minor leagues, but he only had two very brief cups of coffee with the big league club. The first came in 1954. He made his big league debut as a pinch runner in a blowout loss to the Milwaukee Braves, running for the incredibly slow Hank Sauer. He later made one start as a pitcher, in the second-to-last game of the season (against the Reds), but didn't get a decision in the Cubs win. Lary didn't return to the mound in the big leagues until 8 years later. In 1962 he was brought up and made 15 appearances as a 33-year-old, mostly out of the bullpen. He didn't fare well. His ERA was over seven.

Albert Lasker 1880–1952 (Cubs owner 1910s/1920s)

Lasker was an advertising pioneer, a minority and majority owner of the Cubs (the one who convinced Weeghman to buy the Cubs, and William Wrigley to take it over a few years later), and he also played an important role in the presidency of Warren G. Harding. In 1920, Harding was nominated by Republican party leaders in a smoke-filled Chicago hotel room: Suite 4046 on the 13th floor of the Blackstone Hotel. Albert Lasker was one of those Republican operatives who helped Harding secure the nomination in that smoke-filled room. Unfortunately he also introduced Harding to another Cubs minority owner, Harry Sinclair. Sinclair was later a key figure in the Teapot Dome Scandal that forever tarnished Harding's legacy. Lasker was considered an advertising genius, and the firm he founded was sold to three gentlemen who renamed it after themselves: Foote, Cone, and Belding.

Tommy La Stella 1989– (Cubs 2015-2018)

The Cubs front office really saw something in La Stella because they traded one of their prized pitching prospects (Vizcaino) to the Braves to acquire him. La Stella was given the second base job on Opening Day, but was injured and missed most of the season. When he returned to action, he became a valuable bat and reliable glove off the bench. He served in that role for most of the 2016 season as well, but when the Cubs faced a roster crunch, they sent Tommy to the minors. He did not respond well. For several weeks he refused to report to Iowa. He eventually did come back, and made it back up to the big leagues to help the Cubs down the stretch.

In 2017 he remained with the big league club for most of the season, but 2018 was his best year with the Cubs. He led the National League in pinch hits, and played well as a spot starter for Kris Bryant. The Cubs traded him after the season.

Chuck Lauer 1865–1915 (Colts 1890)

Chuck was playing in the Central Interstate League, which featured teams from Illinois and Indiana, when he was snapped up for a short stay in Chicago. He played two games at catcher, made three errors, and was promptly returned to the Central Interstate League.

Jimmy Lavender 1874–1960 (Cubs 1912-1916)

Jimmy won only 63 games in his MLB career (all but six of them for the Cubs), but for one glorious day, he was unhittable. On August 31, 1915, he made his mark in history. Lavender pitched a no-hitter in the first game of a double-header in New York against the Giants. He walked one and struck out eight. With the victory, the Cubs got back to .500. Unfortunately, they lost the second game and fell back under. 1915 was the last season the Cubs played their home games at West Side Grounds, and it was a year of transition for the team. Among Lavender's teammates that season were the last two remaining members of the 1908 Champs (Wildfire Schulte & Heinie Zimmerman), and the man who would lead them to the World Series a few years later, pitcher Hippo Vaughn.

Historical note: On the day of the historic Eastland disaster in the Chicago River (1915), Jimmy was on the mound for the Cubs. He lost the game 1-0.

Vance Law 1956– (Cubs 1988-1989)

Vance Law's nickname (The long arm of the Law) was always a bit of a stretch, because Law didn't have the greatest range as an infielder, but he did have one crucial requirement for the nickname: his last name. Part of a baseball family, Law's father Verne starred in the majors himself. Law signed with the Cubs as a free agent for 1988, had a productive first half, and made the NL All-Star team. A bad back limited him in 1989, and he struck out in all three of his NLCS at-bats.

Matt Lawton 1971– (Cubs 2005)

The Cubs acquired the two-time All-Star at the trading deadline in 2005, thinking they were still in the pennant race. They unloaded him less than a month later when they realized they weren't. Lawton hit .244 in 19 games. Lawton had a very productive 12-year big league career with the Twins, Mets, Indians, Yankees, Pirates, and Mariners.

Tony Lazzeri 1903–2014 (Cubs 1938)

Poosh 'Em Up Tony got his nickname from being one of the best clutch hitters in baseball history. The Yankees could always count on him to push up the runners. Lazzeri's a Hall of Famer thanks to his contributions to those great Yankees teams of the 1920s and 1930s, but by the time the Cubs acquired him after the 1937 season, Tony Lazzeri was toast. For the Yankees, Lazzeri had over 100 RBI seven times. For the Cubs, he had 23. For the Yankees he had great speed, hitting over 10 triples in seven seasons, and stealing more than ten bases in eight seasons. For the Cubs he had zero triples and zero stolen bases. Lazzeri played in 54 games for the Cubs in '38 as a backup infielder and pinch hitter. He got two at-bats in the '38 World Series loss to his former team, striking out once. (By contrast, in the '32 World Series as a Yankee, he hit two home runs against the Cubs). The Cubs were swept in '38, and Lazzeri was let go after the season. He played one more season in New York with the Giants and Dodgers before retiring. Tragically, just a few years later, Tony slipped and fell at his home when no one else was there. He was found dead from the head injuries he sustained in the fall. He was only 42 years old.

Tommy Leach 1877–1969 (Cubs 1912-1914)

Leach arrived in Chicago in 1912 in exchange for two key members of the 1910 World Series Cubs team (King Cole & Solly Hofman). Leach was a renowned hitter — with a lifetime on-base percentage of .340. He had previously led the league in runs, triples, and homers with the Pittsburgh Pirates, and was part of their 1909 World Champion team. Tommy still had a few more good seasons in the tank. With the Cubs he led the league in runs again, stole more than 50 bases, and hit more than 90 extra base hits in two and half seasons.

Fred Lear 1894–1955 (Cubs 1918-1919)

When your last name is Lear, there's a good chance that even the semi-literate baseball crowd will nickname you King, and that's what happened to Fred. King Lear was a backup infielder during his two seasons in Chicago. He only had a cup of coffee with the 1918 pennant winners (two at-bats), but then got the most extensive playing time of his career the following year. The Cubs traded him to the Giants in 1920.

Hal Leathers 1898–1977 (Cubs 1920)

Leathers was a scrappy little infielder (only 5'8 , 150 lbs.) who played in the minor leagues for seven seasons, but did get one brief cup of coffee with the Cubs in 1920. He backed up Charlie Hollocher and Zeb Terry for the last few weeks of the season, and hit .304. Unfortunately, he also committed seven errors in only nine games, and that was it for Hal. He never got another chance in the big leagues.

Jack Leathersich 1990– (Cubs 2017)

Jack got into exactly one game in a Cubs uniform and it didn't go well for the reliever. He faced seven batters and five of them reached base — four of them via walks. The Cubs released him shortly thereafter and he signed with the Pirates.

Bill Lee 1909–1977 (Cubs 1934-1943)

Lee was a great pitcher for the Cubs, winning 130 games, and having a few dominant seasons including the World Series years of 1935 and 1938. His teammates nicknamed him after the Confederate general from the Civil War because of his last name (they called him General), but also because he truly was a Southern gentleman. He was the ace of the staff during the 1930s, but in 1940, Lee developed eye problems and had difficulty seeing the catcher's signs. He eventually got thick glasses, which helped a bit, but he was never the same. After he retired, he underwent delicate surgery for two detached retinas and eventually lost his sight.

Historical note: On the day the Social Security Act was passed establishing Social Security (1935), Lee was on the mound for the Cubs. He couldn't get out of the first inning, as the Cubs lost to the Dodgers 9-5.

Derrek Lee 1975– (Cubs 2004-2010)

D-Lee was one of the most popular Cubs during his time in Chicago. Cubs fans quickly forgot that he had gotten the big

hit during the Bartman game as a member of the Marlins in 2003. In 2005, Lee had a career season. He won the batting title, led the league in hits and doubles, finished second in homers (46), seventh in RBI, and third in the MVP voting. He also won a Gold Glove and a Silver Slugger award. In his stellar 15-year career, Derrek was a two-time All-Star (both times with the Cubs), a three-time Gold Glover (twice with the Cubs), and hit 331 homers (189 with the Cubs). His father Leon was a professional baseball player in Japan (where Derrek grew up), and his uncle Leron played in the big leagues for four teams before also going to Japan.

Don Lee 1934– (Cubs 1966)

He pitched in 16 games for the Cubs and went 2-1 with a 7.11 ERA. That was a very bad team. In fact, it still has the worst record in Cubs history (103 losses). Lee's stint in Chicago marked the end of his big league career. He finished up with 40 wins in nine big league seasons with the Tigers, Senators, Twins, Angels, Astros, and Cubs. His father Thornton also pitched in the Major Leagues (mostly for the White Sox). Ted Williams hit a homer off both father (1939) and son (1960).

Historical note: On the day the US started bombing raids in Vietnam (1966), Lee picked up the win for the Cubs against the Braves in Atlanta.

Tom Lee 1862– (White Stockings 1884)

Lee was a pitcher and shortstop with the Cubs (then known as the White Stockings). He appeared in only six games before jumping leagues to play in Baltimore. It was his only year in big league baseball.

Jim Lefebrve 1942– (Cubs manager 1992-1993)

He was a Rookie of the Year, All-Star, and World Series champ with the Dodgers, and was brought aboard by Cubs GM Larry Himes to bring a "winning attitude" to the Cubs. Lefebrve managed for two full seasons and finished with a .500 record — which makes him one of the best managers in Cubs history.

Craig Lefferts 1957– (Cubs 1983)

Lefferts was a promising young rookie left-handed reliever with one good season under his belt when the Cubs included him in the trade that brought Scott Sanderson to the Cubs.

Lefferts ended up in San Diego in that three-way trade, and had a very good career with the Padres as a reliever. Ironically, the highlight of his career was probably the 1984 NLCS against his old team, the Cubs. Craig appeared in three of those games and was the winning pitcher in both games that crushed the hearts and spirits of Cubs fans — the Garvey game (Game 4) and the Leon game (Game 5). He later also pitched against the Cubs in the 1989 NLCS for the San Francisco Giants. Lefferts saved over a hundred games in his twelve-year big league career.

Hank Leiber 1911 – (Cubs 1939-1941)
Leiber starred for the Giants before coming to Chicago, appearing in two World Series, and one All-Star game. He also set an unofficial record in the 1936 World Series for hitting one of the longest fly outs in history. His 490 ft. blast was the final out in the World Series that year. (The Polo Grounds had a huge outfield). With the Cubs, the outfielder hit over .300 and made the All-Star team again. Unfortunately for Hank, he played in the pre-helmet era. He suffered a few horrible beanings in his career (including one from fireballer Bob Feller), and another during the 1941 season with the Cubs. He retired in 1942.

Jon Leicester 1979 – (Cubs 2004-2005)
Jon was a right-handed reliever for the Cubs for a few seasons during the Dusty Baker era, appearing in 38 games with limited success. He last pitched in the big leagues in 2007 (for the Orioles), but has since pitched in both Japan and China.

Lefty Leifield 1883 – 1970 (Cubs 1912-1913)
One of the great names in baseball history, Lefty was a 20-game winner with the Pirates before coming to the Cubs. He was known as a pitcher who didn't have good stuff, but managed to keep hitters off balance by throwing it where they couldn't hit it; the prototypical soft-tossing lefty. In parts of two seasons, he won seven games with the Cubs. Lefty coached for the Browns, Tigers, and Red Sox after his playing career ended.

DJ LeMahieu 1988 – (Cubs 2011)
DJ was one of several LSU infielders to play for the Cubs. He was a highly rated prospect (2nd round draft choice), but didn't play much for the Cubs. They included him in the trade for Rockies third baseman Ian Stewart; a bad trade in retrospect. LeMahieu became their everyday second baseman; a .300 hitter and a Gold Glover. Stewart didn't work out in Chicago and was gone the following year.

Dick LeMay 1938 – (Cubs 1963)
The lefty reliever pitched in nine games for the Cubs and was hit hard. In just over 15 innings pitched, he gave up 26 hits, and never pitched in the big leagues again. LeMay won over a hundred games in his minor league career. He later managed for the Cubs in the minors.

Dave Lemonds 1949 – (Cubs 1969)
Lemonds was the first overall pick of the 1968 Amateur draft by the Cubs, a left-handed pitching star from the University of North Carolina (ahead of fellow first round picks Bart Johnson and Steve Garvey). He came up briefly in 1969 with the Cubs, but during their pennant chase wasn't considered reliable enough for manager Leo Durocher. He started one game in June and was quickly sent back down to the minors. Lemonds never made it back to the big leagues for the Cubs. He later got a cup of coffee with the 1972 White Sox.

Bob Lennon 1928 – 2004 Cubs 1957)
Lennon once hit 64 homers in a season in the minor leagues, but he only hit one in the big leagues, and it came for the Cubs against his favorite boyhood team, the Brooklyn Dodgers. Lennon was injured frequently (arm, ankle), and never really got a chance at a regular big league job. Unfortunately, he couldn't adjust to the pinch-hitting role, and hit only .165. He later played in Venezuela and Puerto Rico. His nickname was Archie.

Ed Lennox 1883 – 1939 (Cubs 1912)
Eggie, as he was known by his teammates, was a slick-fielding backup third baseman (to Heinie Zimmerman) on the Cubs for one season. That was a season in transition for the Cubs — the last season that saw Tinker, Evers, and Chance on the field at the same time. Eggie also played for Philadelphia, Brooklyn, and Pittsburgh of the Federal League. While he was with Pittsburgh, he hit for the cycle.

Dutch Leonard 1909−1983 (Cubs 1949-1953)

Dutch was one of the oldest players to ever suit up for the Cubs, and the oldest player in all of baseball during his time with the Cubs. Dutch was already 40 when the Cubs acquired the four-time All-Star (with the Senators during the war years) in 1949. They switched the knuckleballer to the bullpen, and in 1951, Dutch Leonard made the All-Star team a fifth time, at the tender age of 42. Dutch Leonard's impressive 20-year big league career ended in 1953. He was 44 years old at the time. After his retirement, Dutch became the Cubs pitching coach for three seasons.

Roy Leslie 1894−1972 (Cubs 1917)

Leslie was a first baseman who got limited playing opportunities backing up Fred Merkle. He later got a cup of coffee with the 1919 Cardinals and 1922 Phillies, but Roy was mostly a career minor leaguer. He had over 5000 plate appearances in 17 minor league seasons.

Jon Lester 1984−(Cubs 2015-present)

The three-time All-Star and two-time World Series champ became the highest paid pitcher in Cubs history before the 2015 season began. He was brought in to be one of the final pieces of the puzzle and help lead the Cubs to the promised land. The contract seemed outlandish at the time, but it has turned into an incredible investment for the Cubs. He has led them to the playoffs every year. What seemed like a pipe dream the day he signed the contract has become reality.

Lester posted a very respectable 3.34 ERA in his first Cubs season in 2015, but in 2016 he had a tremendous year — winning 19 games, finishing in second in the Cy Young voting, and serving as the ace of the Cubs during their World Series run. He was the MVP of the NLCS, won the crucial Game 5 of the World Series in Chicago, and even pitched a few innings in relief in Game 7. By comparison, his follow-up season in 2017 was mostly a disappointment. Lester had to be shut down for a while because of a dead arm, and finished the year with a 13-8 record and a 4.33 ERA. He was pulled in the 5th inning of Game 2 in the NLCS after walking five batters and throwing more than a hundred pitches. But in his fourth year with the Cubs, Lester bounced back to lead the club with 18 wins, post a sterling 3.32 ERA, and start the only playoff game. The Cubs lost that game, but

not because of Lester. The game went 13 innings before the Rockies squeaked out a victory.

Darren Lewis 1967−(Cubs 2002)

Lewis was a speedy Gold Glove-winning outfielder for the Giants, and had a few good years with Boston, but by the time he came to the Cubs in 2002, he was 34 years old. He hit .241 in 91 plate appearances. Darren had 247 career stolen bases, but only one of those was with the Cubs. Chicago was the last stop of his big league career.

Carlos Lezcano 1955− (Cubs 1980-1981)

The Puerto Rican center fielder got a cup of coffee with the Cubs in the early 1980s. Unfortunately, he was a bit overmatched by big league pitching, and posted a .186 average. That was his only stint in the majors. After his playing career he went into coaching with the San Diego Padres farm system.

Cubs players have had some great nicknames over the years. Among players starting with the letter L, you'll find nicknames like Dad, Dummy, Dutch, General, Goober, Human Icicle, King, Lefty, Link, Little Eva, Poosh 'Em Up, Peanuts, Porky, Red, Slim, Turk, and Whitey.

Jon Lieber 1970−(Cubs 1999-2003, 2008)

When the Cubs acquired Lieber from the Pirates for Brant Brown, it was one of the best deals they ever made. Lieber anchored the rotation, winning 10, 12, and 20 games in his first three seasons. No Cubs pitcher won 20 games again until Jake Arrieta did it in 2015. One day during a rain delay in Lieber's fourth season with the Cubs, Jon volunteered to come back out again when the game resumed. He did, but he was never the same after that. He eventually missed the entire 2003 season recovering from arm surgery. Lieber did come back and pitch a few more seasons for the Yankees and Phillies before finishing his career on the north side in 2008.

Gene Lillard 1913−1991 (Cubs 1936, 1939)

Gene was an infielder when he first came up to the Cubs in 1936 for limited duty. After the season he was converted into a pitcher, and made it back up to the big leagues a few years later on the defending NL Champs in 1939. Needless to say, they did not repeat. Gene pitched as a starter and a reliever, and appeared in twenty games. Lillard played in the minor leagues until 1954, shifting back and forth from pitcher to infielder to player/manager.

Brent Lillibridge 1983 – (Cubs 2013)

The former White Sox utility man made the Cubs during spring training of 2013 when the Cubs suffered a few injuries. Unfortunately for Lillibridge, he didn't exactly make the best of his opportunity. In 24 at-bats he got exactly one hit (an .042 average), and struck out nine times. By June he was in the Yankees organization.

Ted Lilly 1976 – (Cubs 2007-2010)

Ted Lilly was a fan favorite during his time with the Cubs. His full name is Theodore Roosevelt Lilly, and yes, he was named after the president. Lilly didn't really walk softly and carry a big stick. He was simply a reliable pitcher, something all too rare on the North Side of Chicago. Ted was an All-Star (2009), pitched in the playoffs (2007), and won 45 games in his 3 ½ years with the Cubs. He retired after the 2013 season after a stellar 15-year big league career. In 2015 he was charged with vehicle insurance fraud, and had to perform 250 hours of community service.

Chang-Yong Lim 1976 – (Cubs 2013)

Lim had a brief stint in the Cubs bullpen during September of 2013. He pitched well enough, but after the season he returned to his native South Korea.

Freddie Lindstrom 1905 – 1981 (Cubs 1935)

Lindstrom was a big star in New York for the Giants. In his rookie season of 1924, he came up late in the year and led the Giants to the World Series. Freddie had many great seasons in New York, especially 1928, when he finished 2nd in the MVP voting, but the Chicago boy (Lane Tech grad) must have been thrilled when he became a Chicago Cub in 1935. Not only did the Cubs go to the World Series that year, they set a record that still stands today by winning 21 games in a row. That turned out to be Lindstrom's only season in Chicago. He played one more season in the big leagues, but retired after the 1936 season at the age of 31. Fred settled back in his hometown after his career was over, where he got to see his son make the big leagues with the White Sox in 1958. The senior Lindstrom was inducted into the Hall of Fame by the veterans committee in 1976. He passed away in 1981, and is buried in All Saints Cemetery in Des Plaines.

Cole Liniak 1976 – (Cubs 1999-2000)

Liniak was a highly regarded prospect with the Red Sox and Cubs who never quite made it in the big leagues. He played twelve seasons in the minors but only got into fifteen games in the bigs, all with the Cubs. He was a third baseman. The Cubs acquired him in the trade that sent Rod Beck to Boston.

Dick Littlefield 1926 – 1997 (Cubs 1957)

Littlefield was the very definition of the well-travelled journeyman pitcher. Before coming to the Cubs, he pitched for the Browns, White Sox, Tigers, Orioles, Pirates, Cardinals, and Giants. His best season in the big leagues was probably 1954, when he won ten games for the Pirates. With the Cubs he was used almost strictly in relief. He saved four games, but also struggled with his control (a career-long issue) and the long ball. In his only Cubs season he gave up 12 homers in only 68 innings. Littlefield's claim to fame is probably the fact that he was the only person ever traded for Jackie Robinson. The Giants traded him to the Dodgers for Robinson, but Jackie refused to report and retired instead.

Jack Littrell 1929 – 2009 (Cubs 1957)

Future Cubs shortstop Jack Littrell got a few cups of coffee with the Athletics before coming to the Cubs in 1957. Even though he was backing up a future MVP that season (Ernie Banks), Jack got the most extensive playing time of his career in 1957. He also got a little time at second base and third, and did a very respectable job with his glove. Unfortunately, Jack never quite got the hang of big league pitching. His lifetime batting average was .204. 1957 turned out to be his last year in the big leagues. After he retired, he worked for the railroad, all the live long day.

Mickey Livingston 1914 – 1983 (Cubs 1943-1947)

The Cubs acquired Mickey from the Phillies in exchange for our one-time pitching ace Bill Lee. Mickey was slated to be the Cubs starting catcher after Clyde McCullough was drafted into the military, but Mickey's draft board decided to reclassify his medical status at the last second, and drafted him too. After enduring boot camp, the Army discovered that their initial ruling was correct. He was experiencing horrible headaches because of a previous concussion. So, Mickey was reclassified once again, and reported for duty with the Cubs instead. He was very lucky. His Army company fought in the Battle of the Bulge. Only 300 of the 5000 men in his company survived. Mickey had a pretty good year for the Cubs in 1945 as their primary catcher. He only struck out six times in over 200 at-bats. He also hit .364 and drove in four runs in the World Series. Livingston played with the Cubs until 1947, and in the big leagues until 1951.

Vince Lloyd 1917–2003 (Cubs announcer 1954-1986)

Vince was part of the Cubs broadcast team in four decades — mostly paired with his good friend Lou Boudreau. He became the main radio play-by-play man after the death of Jack Quinlan in 1965, and remained in that role for many years. He also broadcast games for the White Sox (and interviewed President Kennedy during one game), the Bears, and the Bulls. Vince died in 2003 of stomach cancer.

Hans Lobert 1881–1968 (Cubs 1905)

Hans played briefly with the Cubs in 1905, but the bulk of his 14-year big league career was spent with the Reds and the Phillies. He hit .300 or better in three different seasons with those clubs. A near riot broke out on Opening Day in 1908, thanks to Hans. He was the Reds third baseman at the time, and went into the stands, in the rowdy section known as "Rooter's Row," to spit at a heckler. After the game, he went into the stands to beat up a different heckler, landed a few punches, and was suspended.

Locked Up Cubs... Cubs are cuddly and lovable, but they have also spent some time in jail. Among the jailbirds...Red Downs (robbery), Uel Eubanks (possession of alcohol during Prohibition), Mark Grace (DUI), Mel Hall (aggravated sexual assault of a child and indecency), Jerry Martin (attempting to purchase cocaine), Don Prince (murder for hire), and Willie Wilson (attempting to purchase cocaine).

Bob Locker 1938– (Cubs 1973, 1975)

The Cubs traded one of their rare home-grown position players (Billy North) to get Bob Locker before the 1973 season. North was a speedy leadoff hitter that ignited the lineup of the World Champion Oakland A's, and Locker was a 35-year-old reliever. Admittedly, Locker wasn't bad in 1973. He won ten games and saved another 18, but he was sent back to Oakland in 1974, where he sat out the year recovering from arm surgery. For some reason, the Cubs traded for him again in 1975. That time it only cost them Hall of Famer Billy Williams. Locker was toast. In his last big league season he appeared in 22 games and posted an ERA just shy of five.

Whitey Lockman 1926–2009 (Cubs manager 1972-1973)

Whitey got his nickname when he was a kid. For his hair color, not his skin color. His real name was Caroll Walter Lockman, and he had been an All-Star player for the New York Giants team that Leo Durocher took to the championship. But Whitey Lockman also replaced Leo Durocher as the Cubs manager in 1972. Under Whitey's tutelage, the Cubs went south fast. In his one full season (1973), they finished in fifth place.

Kameron Loe 1981– (Cubs 2013)

Loe pitched in the big leagues nine seasons for the Rangers, Brewers, and Mariners before arriving in Chicago during the 2013 season. A starter earlier in his career, Loe was strictly a reliever for the Cubs. He appeared in seven games and posted a 5.40 ERA. The Cubs let him go and he signed with Atlanta for the rest of the year. Loe was hard to miss on the mound. He is 6'8" tall.

Kenny Lofton 1967– (Cubs 2003)

Lofton is a local kid, born in East Chicago. He wasn't on the Cubs for long, just half a season (2003), but he might have been the key acquisition that propelled the Cubs into the NLCS. Lofton was the leadoff man and center fielder for the Cubs after Corey Patterson was hurt, and gave them something they haven't had before or since: a true leadoff man with a great on-base percentage, the ability to steal a base, score some runs, and disrupt a pitcher's game plan. In the NLDS against the Braves, Lofton stole three bases against his former team. In the NLCS against the Marlins, he certainly did his part too, hitting .323 in the seven game series. Unfortunately, the Cubs opted not to re-sign him before the 2004 season. Management reasoned that Lofton was nearing the end of his career, but while the Cubs were watching the playoffs at home the next few seasons, Lofton was playing in the postseason three of the next four years with the Yankees, Dodgers, and Indians.

Tom Loftus 1856–1910 (Cubs manager 1900-1901)

Loftus managed the Cubs, then known as the Orphans, for the first two years of the 20th century. He was brought in to replace Tom Burns, and while his roster may have had a few Hall of Famers (Roger Bresnahan, Frank Chance, and Clark Griffith), Bresnahan and Chance were just kids, and Griffith was 30 years old. Loftus couldn't lead this team of youngsters and oldsters to the promised land. In his two seasons the Cubs finished sixth both years. Loftus was replaced after the 1901 season by Hall of Famer Frank Selee.

Bob Logan 1910–1978 (Cubs 1937-1938)

Bob Logan was a pitcher with a bit of a wild streak. He walked 17 batters in 22 innings for the Cubs. He also pitched briefly with Detroit, Cincinnati, and Brooklyn, but during the war he got his one extended shot with the Boston Braves. After not starting a single game in his previous big league career, he went 7-11 as a member of Boston's rotation. Logan was a left-handed pitcher, so naturally, his nickname was Lefty.

Bill Long 1960–(Cubs 1990)

Long was acquired from the White Sox, and pitched one season for the Cubs out of the bullpen. He went 6-1 with a 4.37 ERA. Long is the only Cubs player in history to be born on Leap Day.

Dale Long 1926–1991 (Cubs 1957-1959)

Dale Long had a pretty good career as a Cubs first baseman, but one game is probably remembered more than any other.

On August 20, 1958, Cubs catcher Moe Thacker was in the hospital. The Cubs started that game with only two catchers on the roster; Cal Neeman and Sammy Taylor. Taylor was pinch hit for, and Neeman came in to take his place. But Neeman was ejected from the game…meaning the Cubs didn't have a catcher in uniform to take his place. So, Cubs manager Bob Scheffing sent the ever-reliable Dale Long in to take over. When he entered the game he became the first left-handed catcher in baseball in more than 50 years. (The last before that was in 1906). He did it again a month later on September 11, 1958. There wasn't another left-handed catcher until 1980 (Mike Squires with the White Sox in a similar emergency role). Benny DiStefano of the Pittsburgh Pirates also did it in 1989. That makes it a grand total of three men in more than one hundred years of Major League baseball; and Dale Long of the Chicago Cubs is the charter member of that exclusive club. Long hit 55 homers in his three years with the Cubs.

Davey Lopes 1945–(Cubs 1984-1986)

He was thought to be on the descent of his career when the Cubs acquired Davey late in 1984 to provide bench help during the pennant run, but the following season Lopes proved he still had quite a bit left in the tank. At the age of 40, he switched positions and learned to play outfield. When Cubs regulars like Bobby Dernier were hurt, Lopes filled in. He took advantage of this second chance and stole 46 bases during the 1985 season. Davey was traded the following year for Frank DiPino, and helped the Astros make the postseason too. He retired after the 1987 season with more than 550 career stolen bases. He has been coaching in the big leagues ever since.

Rafael Lopez 1987– (Cubs 2014)

The rookie catcher was 26 years old when he was called up in September of 2014. He appeared in only seven games and hit .182. He has gone on to play for Cincinnati, Toronto, and San Diego.

Rodrigo Lopez 1975–(Cubs 2011-2012)

The Mexican-born Lopez was a two-time 15-game winner for the Orioles, but by the time he came to the Cubs, he was getting by on fumes. In 30 appearances over two seasons his

ERA was over six, and he allowed 18 homers. Chicago was the last stop of his big league career.

Historical note: On the day the Occupy Wall Street protest began in New York (2011), Lopez was on the mound for the Cubs and pitched one of his best games in a Cubs uniform, defeating the Astros 2-1 at Wrigley Field.

Andrew Lorraine 1972 – (Cubs 1999-2000)

Lorraine was a highly regarded prospect who had been traded for Jim Abbott and Danny Tartabull before arriving on the Cubs doorstep as a free agent. By then he had pitched for four big league teams with limited success. His time with the Cubs was about the same. He started 16 games over two seasons, and his ERA was over six. The left-hander later also pitched for Cleveland and Milwaukee.

Andy Lotshaw 1880 – 1953 (Cubs trainer 1922-1952)

Andy was the Cubs trainer for thirty years and also served in the same capacity for the Chicago Bears. Andy actually played an important role in the career of Cubs pitching great Guy Bush. During his Cubs years Bush pitched an amazing 2201 innings and completed 127 games. The rest of the league wanted to know what his secret was, but Guy Bush would never reveal it. There was a very good reason for that — he didn't know what it was. Cubs trainer Andy Lotshaw applied a secret dark liniment to Guy's arm, and Guy was convinced that liniment was what kept his arm loose. Andy wouldn't even tell Guy what it was. It wasn't until the Cubs traded Bush to the Pirates in 1935 that Lotshaw finally admitted the ingredients of the secret dark liniment to the pitcher. It was Coca-Cola.

Jay Loviglio 1956 – (Cubs 1983)

Jay only played in one game for the Cubs, on July 26, 1983. He pinch hit for Warren Brusstar in the 7th inning against the Dodgers and struck out against Fernando Valenzuela. Mel Hall struck out right after him and threw a tantrum and was tossed out of the game. Fernando and the Dodgers beat the Cubs at Wrigley Field, 5-2. Jay became a minor league coach after his playing days.

Grover Cleveland Lowdermilk 1885 – 1968 (Cubs 1912)

When your real name is a mouthful like Grover Cleveland Lowdermilk, you're bound to get tagged with a nickname. He was tall (6'4) and lanky (190 lbs.), so his Cubs teammates dubbed him Slim. Slim was born just a few months before President Cleveland officially took office. He didn't fare so well with the Cubs. His ERA was 9.69. Grover was later a member of the 1919 Black Sox (but wasn't implicated in their cheating). His brother Lou played for the Cardinals.

Bobby Lowe 1865 – 1951 (Cubs 1902-1903)

Lowe had a very impressive 18-year big league career, mostly for Boston and Detroit, but he also played two seasons in Chicago with the Cubs. He was their starting second baseman in 1902. Bobby was nicknamed Link, which was a catchy way of saying he turned a double play nicely. Unfortunately for Bobby, his replacement (future Hall of Famer) Johnny Evers did it a little bit better. Evers was later immortalized by the poet's pen (Franklin Adams), but it could have just as easily have been Tinker to Lowe to Chance.

Terrell Lowery 1970 – (Cubs 1997-1998)

Lowery was a Rule V draft pick out of the Mets system. The center fielder got into 32 games with the Cubs over two seasons. He later played for Tampa Bay and San Francisco. In college Terrell played basketball at Loyola Marymount with Hank Gathers and Bo Kimble. Lowery was the player who fed Gathers for his last basket. Gathers died on the court just a few moments later.

Turk Lown 1924 – 2016 (Cubs 1951-1958)

His real name was Omar Joseph Lown, but everyone called him Turk because he loved to eat turkey. The Cubs thought he was a starter, but after his 16-27 record as a starter — with an ERA over five, they moved him to the bullpen once and for all in 1956. Turk went to the White Sox a few years later and pitched on their pennant-winning team of 1959. He led the American League in saves that year.

Peanuts Lowrey 1917 – 1986 (Cubs 1942-1949)

There are two stories about where he got his nickname. The first story is that it came from his grandfather, who described him as "no bigger than a peanut." Peanuts was also a child actor, playing bit parts in silent films. The second story about his nickname origin is that actress Thelma Todd got him to perform with promises to buy him peanuts. Whatever the truth is, Peanuts played with the Cubs from 1942-1949, and was a starter on the 1945 World Series team. While the public and press called him Peanuts, his teammates gave him another nickname. They also called him Goober. Lowrey was a key member of the team in the 1940s. He played every position except first base, catcher, and pitcher, and made the All-Star team in 1946. Lowrey's Cubs playing career ended in 1949 when he was traded to the Reds for Hank Sauer; one of the best trades in Cubs history. (Sauer won an MVP as a Cub.) After his playing days ended Lowrey returned to the Cubs as a coach in the 1970s. Peanuts never totally lost the acting bug either. He had a speaking part in *The Winning Team*, which starred Ronald Reagan as Grover Cleveland Alexander. (He plays a pitcher that beans Ronald Reagan.) The man he was traded for (Hank Sauer) also appeared in that movie.

Pat Luby 1869–1899 (Colts 1890-1892)

In his rookie season of 1890, Luby won 18 straight games for the Cubs (then known as the Colts). That was a strange year in baseball history because there were three professional leagues, including a Player's League (featuring many former Chicago players). After that season Luby only won 20 more games in his career. He died of tuberculosis at age 30.

Historical note: On the day Arthur Conan Doyle's character Sherlock Holmes made his debut in Strand Magazine (1891), Luby beat Cincinnati 4-2.

Fred Luderus 1885–1961 (Cubs 1909-1910)

Luderus was a rugged German-American first baseman who backed up Hall of Famer Frank Chance during his first two seasons in the big leagues. He only hit one homer for the Cubs, and it was an inside-the-park shot against the team he played for the rest of his career, the Philadelphia Phillies. Chance traded Luderus to the Phillies in the middle of the 1910 season because catcher Jimmy Archer could handle first base too. Unfortunately for the Cubs, Fred became a big run producer for Philadelphia, finishing in the top ten in homers in eight of the ten seasons in that decade. In 1915, he became the first Phillies player to hit a homer in the World Series. Luderus started at first base for Philadelphia until 1920. The player the Cubs got in return for him (pitcher Bill Foxen) was out of baseball by 1911.

Mike Lum 1945– (Cubs 1981)

Lum had a very solid 15-year big league career, played mostly with the Braves (11 years) and the Reds (3 years). One of his most memorable days actually happened at Wrigley Field on July 28, 1977. He was one of the nine players to hit homers that day in a 16-15 Cubs win over the Reds. His last season in the big leagues was spent with the Cubs. He hit two homers and knocked in seven runs in limited action during the strike year of 1981. After his playing career ended, Lum became a well-respected hitting coach.

Carl Lundgren 1880–1934 (Cubs 1902-1909)

Lundgren pitched for three Cubs pennant winners (1906, 1907, and 1908). Even though he was a great pitcher, he never pitched in the World Series during those pennant-winning seasons because there were even better pitchers on the team (like Mordecai Brown, Orval Overall, and big Ed Reulbach). Lundgren was especially effective early in the season in cold weather, which led to his nickname "The Human Icicle." He won 17 games for the '06 pennant winners and 18 games for the '07 champs (with an unbelievable ERA of only 1.17 for the season), but slumped in '08 and managed to only win 6 games. After the next season his career was over. Lundgren's teammates didn't just think of him of as their fifth or (sometimes) sixth starter. He was a shrewd baseball man; just as valuable on the bench as he was on the field. Lundgren later went on to succeed Branch Rickey as the baseball coach at the University of Michigan, before ending his career in his dream job, as the coach of his alma mater, the University of Illinois.

Historical note: On the day that the Meat Inspection Act was passed (1906) ordering meat to be inspected for the first time in American history, Lundgren was on the mound for the Cubs. He tossed a two-hitter to defeat the Reds at West Side Grounds.

Tom Lundstedt 1949 (Cubs 1973-1974)

The local boy (Prospect High School in Mt. Prospect) was a first round pick of the Cubs in 1970 after a stellar career at the University of Michigan. His high school classmate was Dave Kingman (who went in the same 1970 draft), and his college roommate was Rudy Tomjanovich. He made it to the big leagues in September of 1973 and got to play alongside some of players he grew up watching like Billy Williams and Ron Santo. Lundstedt got a little more playing time as the backup catcher in 1974, and the Cubs traded him after the season to the Minnesota Twins. After his baseball career he moved to Wisconsin and became a motivational speaker.

Dummy Lynch 1926–1978 (Cubs 1948)

Dummy Lynch was a war hero — a paratrooper in World War II. He only got a few at-bats on the very bad 1948 Cubs team, but in his first big league game, he hit a homer against future Hall of Famer Warren Spahn. That makes Lynch one of only 26 players since 1908 to hit a homer in his first career game and never hit another one in his career. Despite the less-than-flattering nickname, Lynch was no dummy. After his baseball career, he became a practicing attorney in Texas.

Ed Lynch 1956– (Cubs 1986-1987, Cubs GM 1994-2000)

Lynch was a journeyman starter for the Mets in his seventh big league season when the Cubs acquired him in June of 1986. The Mets would go on to the win the World Series without Ed, while the Cubs finished in 5th place. After a year and a half with the Cubs, Lynch retired. He worked in management with the Padres for a while before being named the General Manager of the Cubs in 1994 by team president Andy McPhail. He made some good trades (acquiring Henry Rodriguez) and some bad trades (trading Jon Garland for Matt Karchner), but he was mainly let go because the Cubs only reached the postseason one time during Lynch's years at the helm. He became a scout after that, working for the Toronto Blue Jays.

Historical note: On the day President Reagan answered questions about the Iran Contra Affair (1987), Lynch was getting rocked by the Phillies in Philadelphia. He entered in a 7-7 tie, and left with the Cubs down 13-7. Juan Samuel hit a grand slam.

Henry Lynch 1866–1925 (Colts 1893)

Lynch was a part-time right fielder for the worst 19th century team Chicago ever put on the field. They finished in ninth place that season. Lynch didn't help much. He hit only .214 in limited playing time — his only stint in the major leagues. After the season, he went back to his native Massachusetts, where he lived the rest of his life.

Mike Lynch 1875–1947 (Orphans 1902)

Mike was a little center fielder who started the season with the 1902 Cubs (then known as the Orphans). Unfortunately he couldn't even hit his weight…and he only weighed 155 pounds. His .143 batting average didn't cut it in the big leagues, and he was released in May of that year. He played 13 more seasons in the minors.

Thomas Lynch 1863–1903 (White Stockings 1884)

Lynch was born in Southern Illinois during the Civil War. If you'd like to go back in time to see him play baseball, you need to set your wayback machine to August 5, 1884. That's the day the 21-year-old got his one and only start in the big leagues. He pitched seven innings and gave up two earned runs against Cleveland, as the Cubs (then known as the White Stockings) lost 8-5 in their home field, Lakefront Park. Thomas was known as Dummy, because he was a deaf-mute. The 1880s were not a politically correct time.

Red Lynn 1913–1977 (Cubs 1944)

Red was a 20-game winner for the Cubs minor league team in Los Angeles, but when he was brought up to the big leagues in 1944, he struggled with command. He pitched a total of 22 games for the Cubs, including seven starts, and posted a 4.06 ERA. He pitched in the minor leagues until 1956 and won 244 games.

Dad Lytle 1862–1950 (Colts 1890)

They called him "Dad" and "Pops" because he was a 28-year-old rookie when he arrived in the big leagues. The outfielder played exactly one game for the Cubs (then known as the Colts) on August 11, 1890. He went 0 for 4 in a 6-4 loss in Pittsburgh.

Additional Entries... If you check out the Every Cub Ever feature at www. justonebadcentury.com, you'll find several additional entries, including celebrity Cubs fans, writers, and bloggers. Under the letter L, you'll discover the first baseball commissioner Judge Kennesaw Mountain Landis (a huge Cubs fan), Cubs songwriter and Radio Hall of Famer John Records Landecker, and even Martin Luther, who believe it or not, had a tangential relationship to the Cubs.

CHAPTER THIRTEEN

M

The starting lineup for your Chicago Cubs starting with the letter M...

C – Keith Moreland, Zonk
1B – Fred Merkle, Boner
2B – Mickey Morandini, Unassisted Triple Play
SS – Rabbit Maranville, Hall of Famer
3B – Bill Madlock, Batting Champ
LF – Gary Mathews, Sarge
CF – Rick Monday, Flag Saver
RF – Bobby Murcer, Golden Boy
Bench – Les Mann, Olympic Pioneer
Bench – Fred McGriff, Crime Dog
Bench – Lennie Merullo, 1945 Cub
SP – Greg Maddux, Best Pitcher of All-Time
SP – Pat Malone, the 20-Game-Winning Drunk
RP – Randy Myers, the Closer

John Mabry 1970 – (Cubs 2006)

Mabry had his most productive seasons with the Cardinals early in his career, but he held on in the big leagues for 14 seasons. His second-to-last year was with the Cubs. In over 200 at-bats, Mabry hit only .205 for the Cubs. He played in the 2004 World Series that ended the Red Sox curse. Unfortunately for John, he was on the losing side (the Cardinals).

Robert Machado 1973 – (Cubs 2001-2002)

Machado had a very respectable nine-year big league career as a backup catcher, including two seasons with the Cubs (2001-2002). He backed up Todd Hundley and Joe Girardi. Machado also played for the White Sox, Expos, Mariners, Brewers, and Orioles.

Jose Macias 1972 – (Cubs 2004-2005)

The Panamanian was a utility man (every position except first base, catcher, and pitcher) who was a favorite of manager Dusty Baker during his two seasons with the Cubs. He played for the Tigers and Expos before coming to Chicago. After his Cubs days he played briefly in Japan, before moving on to Mexico. He still coaches in Mexico.

Bill Mack 1885 – 1971 (Cubs 1908)

The college boy from Syracuse may have only pitched in two big league games (both for the Cubs), but he achieved something that most Cubs cannot claim to achieve. He was part of a Cubs World Series championship team. If you want to see him pitch, set the wayback machine to July 14th and July 21st in 1908. When Mack died in 1971, he was the last of the 1908 Cubs to leave this earth.

Ray Mack 1916 – 1969 (Cubs 1947)

Mack had a chance to play in Wrigley Field years before he joined the Cubs because he was drafted by the Chicago Bears in 1938. He opted for baseball instead, and joined the Cleveland Indians organization. The second baseman saved Bob Feller's Opening Day no-hitter with an incredible lunging catch in 1940 and made the All-Star team that season, but he was 30 when he joined the Cubs in September of 1947. It was the last gasp of his playing career. His son Tom chose football instead of baseball — and the Los Angeles Rams lineman made it into Pro Football's Hall of Fame. Unfortunately Ray didn't live to see it. He died of cancer at the age of 52.

Steve Macko 1954 – 1982 (Cubs 1979-1980)

His story is one of the most tragic tales in Cubs history. His father was a coach with the Cubs, and Steve was one of their hot young phenoms. He was a middle infielder, and made it to the majors in 1979. In August of 1980, he was injured in a collision at second base. During the physical examination after the injury, the doctors discovered that Macko had cancer. He never played with the Cubs again. In his final season he hit .300 and had a 1.000 fielding percentage. He died just two years later, at the age of 27, on November 15, 1982.

Andy MacPhail 1953 – (Cubs President 1994-2006)

The Wunderkind who led the Twins to two World Series titles

had no such luck during his twelve years in Chicago. The Cubs finished 3rd, 4th, 5th, 2nd, 6th, 6th, 3rd, 5th, 1st, 3rd, 4th, and 6th during his years. They finished in last place twice as many times (4) as they made the playoffs (twice), and never made the World Series.

Len Madden 1890–1949 (Cubs 1912)

Madden was a left-handed pitcher, so naturally his teammates called him Lefty. The Cubs were the only team he pitched for in the big leagues, and it wasn't exactly a lengthy stay. He pitched in six games and was hit pretty hard. He gave up 16 hits and walked nine men in only twelve innings of work. If you ever want to travel back in time to watch him, set the wayback machine to August 31, 1912. You'll only need to stay in the past until September 19th, and you can witness his entire big league career.

Clarence Maddern 1921–1986 (Cubs 1946-1949)

Maddern was an outfielder in the Cubs system before the war, but didn't make it up to the big leagues until after the war. He hit with power in the minor leagues, but in his only real chance at a big league job (1948), he managed only 4 homers in over 200 plate appearances. Those weren't the kind of numbers the Cubs were looking for out of their corner outfielders. Clarence played in the minor leagues until 1957.

Joe Maddon 1954–(Cubs manager 2015-present)

The day Joe Maddon appeared at the press conference announcing his hiring, Chicago was instantly smitten. Maddon bought the entire press corps a beer, and said that he expected the Cubs to compete for the World Series title (after five years in a row in last place). Maddon's low-key approach really connected with the young Cubs and he led the team to 97 wins and two playoff series victories in his first year. In 2016 he brought the Cubs to the promised land — the World Series championship. He will forever be remembered for that accomplishment. Maddon also led the Cubs to a third consecutive NLCS in 2017, and a Wild Card spot in 2018. He previously managed the young Tampa Rays to the World Series in 2008.

Greg Maddux 1966–(Cubs 1986-1994, 2004-2006)

Early in his Cubs career, Greg Maddux acquired one of the best baseball nicknames, Mad Dog. Maddux's nickname is a combination of truth and irony. His looks are deceiving: a slightly-built boyish-looking player with a soft and unassuming voice. He hardly looked like a Mad Dog. He was, however a tenacious Mad Dog on the mound who mercilessly used every flaw he could find in an opponent. Maddux was not all warm and cuddly. He was quite simply the best pitcher to ever come out of the Cubs farm system (no one else is even close), and is in the Hall of Fame for his 350+ wins, 3000+ strikeouts, and 4 Cy Young awards. He won 133 of those games and that first Cy Young with the Cubs ('92). But to Cubs fans, Mad Dog also symbolizes what is wrong with the Cubs. They let him go in free agency for a petty amount of money, and he had his greatest years with the Braves, winning three Cy Youngs and a World Series. In fairness to the Cubs, they realized they made a mistake by letting him go. They tried to atone by bringing him back at the end of his career, and retiring his uniform number when he left the game. His #31 flies from the flagpole in Wrigley Field. They also hired Maddux in the front office as a special assistant to the general manager. Their genuine regret seems to have been taken as an apology by Greg. When it came time to choose which cap he would wear in the Hall of Fame, he opted not to wear the Braves cap even though he probably should have. He said his years in Chicago meant too much to him to snub the Cubs. Oddly enough, Maddux only holds one Cubs career record. He balked more times (22) than any other pitcher in Cubs history.

Historical note: On the day that Oprah Winfrey gave out 300 cars to her studio audience (2004), Maddux was pitching at Wrigley Field for the Cubs. He won his 14th game of the season by throwing seven shutout innings.

Bill Madlock 1951–(Cubs 1974-1976)

Bill Madlock was an All-Star and won two batting titles during his years with the Cubs. He also was known for his competitive nature. He was fined by the league in 1975 for arguing about a third strike. In 1976 he charged the mound against the Giants and started a brawl. The same year he got mad at his own pitchers for not protecting him from brushback pitches. He was the anti-Ernie, the kind of player that owner P.K. Wrigley just didn't like. There was no way he was going to pay him a big raise after his second batting title, and that's the main reason he was shipped out after the 1976 season. Bill Madlock still has the highest career Cubs batting average of all time (.336). After he left the Cubs, he had his biggest success in Pittsburgh. He won two more batting titles, appeared in two All-Star games, and won the World Series (1979). Madlock played 15 years in the big leagues and retired with a lifetime batting average of .305.

Sal Madrid 1920–1977 (Cubs 1947)

Sal got his only big league cup of coffee with the Cubs in the September of 1947. The shortstop didn't take advantage of the opportunity. He played in eight games and only managed three hits. In his last game on September 28, 1947 (a 3-0 win against the Cardinals), Cubs pitcher Johnny Schmitz had a better batting average than Sal. He was a big leaguer for eleven days. He was in the minors from 1937-1949.

Dave Magadan 1962–(Cubs 1996)

Magadan was a professional hitter. In nine of his sixteen big league seasons he hit .280 or better, including a .328 season in 1990, good for 3rd in the league. His career on-base percentage was also outstanding. At .390, it's the 101st best in baseball history. But when he was with the Cubs, Magadan wasn't anywhere near that level. He hit only .254 as a part-time third baseman. After his playing career ended, Mags (as he was called by his teammates) went into coaching. His cousin (and godfather) was also a famous coach/manager. Perhaps you've heard of him: Lou Piniella.

Lee Magee 1889–1966 (Cubs 1919)

His real name was Leo Hoernschemeyer. Magee was the first player in big league history to get five hits in a row. He came to the Cubs after stints with St. Louis (Cardinals and Browns), Brooklyn, New York (Yankees), and Cincinnati. He was also a player/manager in the Federal League. The Cubs were his last stop. He hit .292 and stole 14 bases, while playing every position except for pitcher, catcher, and first base. Lee was quietly banned for life in 1920 by Commissioner Landis for allegedly fixing games.

George Magoon 1875–1943 (Orphans 1899)

George was a shortstop on the Cubs (then known as the Orphans) in 1899, and hit .228 in 59 games. He was called "Maggie" and "Topsy" by his teammates. He also played for Baltimore, Cincinnati, Brooklyn, and the White Sox.

Freddie Maguire 1899–1961 (Cubs 1928)

Freddie was the starting second baseman for the Cubs in 1928, but he couldn't have been too disappointed to be replaced the following season. The man who took his place was none other than Hall of Famer Rogers Hornsby. In fact, Freddie was part of the five-man trade package needed to get Hornsby from the Braves. Freddie started at second base the next three seasons for the Boston Braves.

Ron Mahay 1971–(Cubs 2001-2002)

The journeyman reliever pitched 14 seasons in the big leagues, including two with the Cubs. He pitched fairly well out of the bullpen in 2001, but then followed that up with a terrible 2002. Mahay also pitched for the Red Sox, A's, Marlins, Rangers, Braves, Royals, and Twins.

Paul Maholm 1982–(Cubs 2012)

Maholm had a good half-season with the Cubs as a member of their starting rotation, but he was traded (along with Reed Johnson) to Atlanta for prospects, including fire-balling Arodys Vizcaino. Maholm won 9 games in his four-month-long Cubs career. One of his claims to fame was pitching to comedian Billy Crystal during spring training 2008 (while with the Pirates). He struck him out. Maholm had a ten-year big league career.

Pat Mahomes 1970–(Cubs 2001)

Mahomes was a well-traveled journeyman pitcher who lasted eleven seasons in the big leagues. He pitched for the Twins, Red Sox, Mets, Rangers, Pirates, and Cubs. His lifetime ERA was over five, and he never registered double-digits in either wins or saves, but he pitched in over 300 big league games. With the Cubs, Mahomes was 1-1, with a 3.86 ERA.

Mike Mahoney 1972–(Cubs 2000, 2002)

Mike made his big league debut with the Cubs as a 27-year-old in 2000. The backup catcher was a September call-up and only got into a handful of games. He spent the entire 2001 season in the minor leagues, but got another shot with the Cubs in 2002. Again, he only played in a handful of games.

In all, Mike caught 20 games for the Cubs. He later had a cup of coffee with the Cardinals.

Scott Maine 1985 – (Cubs 2010-2012)
Maine was a very effective closer in the minors (he saved 65 games), but big league hitters were not fooled. In 2011 he gave up four homers in only seven innings pitched. His lifetime ERA in the big leagues is 5.59.

Willard Mains 1868–1923 (White Stockings 1888)
His teammates nicknamed the youngster "Grasshopper" when he pitched for the Cubs (then known as the White Stockings) because he was only 20 years old. He went 1-1 in his two starts. His son Jim pitched in the big leagues as a 21-year-old in 1943. Needless to say, Willard was an older father. Father and son's big league debuts were 55 years apart.

Oswaldo Mairena 1975 – (Cubs 2000)
The Nicaraguan lefty pitched in two games for the Cubs in September of 2000. He was hit very hard, giving up seven hits (including a homer) and walking two in only two innings pitched. He later had a similarly brief cup of coffee with the Marlins in 2002. He later pitched in the Mexican League.

George Maisel 1892–1968 (Cubs 1921-1922)
Maisel had a very unusual big league career. He got his first shot with the St. Louis Browns way back in 1913, and had another cup of coffee with the Tigers in 1916, but then languished in the minor leagues until the Cubs gave him a shot in 1921. He responded with a very good season. George started in center field for the Cubs, and was among the best fielding outfielders in the league that year. He also hit over .300 and stole 17 bases. But the 29-year-old was replaced by Jigger Statz the following year, and was finished at age 30. George had a brother (Fritz) and a cousin (Charlie) who also played in the big leagues.

Mike Maksudian 1966–(Cubs 1994)
Mike was another backup catcher who spent some time in a Cubs uniform. When the Cubs got him in 1994, he was already known as the catcher who ate insects in the Blue Jays bullpen. He actually got the most at-bats of his career with Cubs. He batted 26 times, and got seven hits, including two doubles. He also walked 10 times, which means his OBP was .472. In his final at-bat he pinch hit for Dave Otto and grounded out to the pitcher. The next day, baseball players went on strike, and Maksudian never returned to the bigs. He was 28.

John Malarkey 1872–1949 (Orphans 1899)
Malarkey's nickname was not "Bunch Of" which is what we would have called him. His teammates nicknamed him Liz. He only pitched one game for Chicago, but it was a complete game. He gave up 19 hits and 13 earned runs on September 13, 1899. The Cubs (then known as the Orphans) lost to the New York Giants 13-2. In 1902 Malarkey made baseball history while with Boston when he became the first pitcher to win a game by hitting a walk-off home run.

Candy Maldonado 1960–(Cubs 1993)
Candy Maldonado had several good seasons…none of them with the Cubs. He arrived in town during the offseason the Cubs got rid of two Hall of Famers: Greg Maddux and Andre Dawson. Maldonado was supposed to replace Dawson. He didn't. Candy hit .186 in 70 games and was traded to the Indians for GlenAllen Hill.

Fergy Malone 1844–1905 (White Stockings 1874)
Malone was born in Ireland and caught for the White Stockings a few years before the creation of the National League. (He later played in the very first NL game — as a member of the Philadelphia A's). He is one of only two Cubs players who were veterans of the Civil War.

Pat Malone 1902–1943 (Cubs 1928-1934)
Malone was a two-time 20-game winner with the Cubs and led the team to the 1929 and 1932 World Series, but he also hung out with Hack Wilson. When they weren't playing baseball, they were either drinking or brawling. The stories are legendary. In Malone's first season with the Cubs his roommate was Percy Jones. They didn't get along. Jones insisted on getting a new roommate after Malone trapped some pigeons on a hotel ledge and put them in Jones' bed as he slept. One night Malone and Wilson got into a huge fist fight in a hotel. They were walking down the hallway of their hotel, and Wilson laughed. Someone in a hotel room

mimicked his laugh. Wilson and Malone broke into the room and beat the hell out of four men, until all of them were out cold. One of the men was still standing and Malone kept punching. Wilson pointed out that he was already knocked out. "Move the lamp and he'll fall." Malone moved the lamp, and the man fell to the ground. It didn't end well for either man. Wilson was only 48 years old when he drank himself to death. Malone didn't even last as long as Hack. He was only 40 years old when he died in 1943.

Billy Maloney 1878 – 1960 (Cubs 1905)

Billy only played one season with the Cubs, but the converted catcher had a heck of a year in the outfield for the 1905 Cubs. He led the National League in stolen bases that year with 59. His season was good enough to draw the interest of other clubs. The Cubs coaxed Jimmy Sheckard out of Brooklyn for Maloney, and Sheckard became a key part of their championship-era team. Maloney lost his touch in Brooklyn. He led the league in strikeouts three seasons in a row, and couldn't get on base enough to make an impact with his speed.

Gus Mancuso 1905 – 1984 (Cubs 1939)

Blackie, as he was known, was a two-time All-Star with the Giants before he came to the Cubs. He shared catching duties with his manager, Gabby Hartnett. It was his only season with the Cubs. Mancuso played throughout the war for the Cardinals, Giants, and Phillies, but even he admitted those last four years he only logged big league time because so many players were at war. After his playing career, Gus became a pitching coach for the Reds, and then a broadcaster. In the early 50s, Mancuso worked alongside a little-known St. Louis Cardinals radio announcer named Harry Caray. Gus' brother Frank played for the Browns and Senators.

Hal Manders 1917 – 2010 (Cubs 1946)

Hal pitched for the Tigers before being drafted into military service during World War II. When he returned, he pitched briefly for them again before being sent off to the team they beat in the previous year's World Series. He got one start in September for the Cubs and was hit pretty hard. It was his last hurrah in baseball. In all, Manders pitched three seasons in the big leagues, which under normal circumstances would have given him bragging rights at family gatherings. Unfortunately for Hal, his cousin was Bob Feller.

Garth Mann 1915 – 1980 (Cubs 1944)

His nickname was Red, and Red appeared in exactly one major league game. On May 14, 1944, he came in to pinch run for Lou Novikoff, the Mad Russian. Mann later scored on an Andy Pafko single. The big Texan never got a chance to pitch (he was a pitcher) or hit in the big leagues. He played 11 seasons of minor league ball.

Les Mann 1892 – 1962 (Cubs 1916-1919)

Mann was nicknamed Major after the World War 1 flying ace, Major Harry Mann. He was an outfielder for the Cubs in their inaugural season at the ballpark now known as Wrigley Field, but had also played there the year before, with the Federal League Whales. He actually became famous for a few things he did off the field, more than his career on the field (which was pretty good). Mann headed an unsuccessful player revolt for better shares in the 1918 World Series as a member of the pennant-winning Cubs. Late in his career he turned in a former 1918 Cubs teammate, Giant pitcher Phil Douglas, for writing him a letter inviting a bribe in 1922. In 1936, after his playing days were over, he convinced the World Olympic Committee to add baseball as an exhibition event, and brought two teams over to play in Nazi Germany for the 1936 Olympics. They drew a larger crowd in Berlin than had ever attended a World Series game in America.

Dick Manville 1926 – (Cubs 1952)

The tall right-handed reliever appeared in 11 games for the 1952 Cubs — the best Cubs team of the decade (which isn't saying much). He had a rough go of it, however, posting an ERA of nearly eight. He never made it back to the big leagues again. On the other hand, the Yale man had a fairly good education to fall back on.

Dillon Maples 1992 – (Cubs 2017-present)

The flame-throwing Cubs farmhand made his debut late in the 2017 season and got a handful of opportunities to show what he could do. While he managed to strike out eleven batters in only 5 1/3 innings of work, he also walked six and finished with an ERA over 10. In 2018, the results were almost identical — except his ERA was over 11.

Rabbit Maranville 1891–1954 (Cubs 1925)

His real name was Walter. Nicknamed for his speed and rabbit-like leaps, Rabbit Maranville was always a great fielder, but he was even better known for his partying. When he was with the Pirates he was known for playing with a flask in his pocket. One time (with the Cubs in spring training 1925) he was goofing around on the golf course with Charlie Grimm, who laid on his back and put a tee in his mouth with a ball on it, as a joke. Maranville hit the ball with a driver, scaring the hell out of Grimm. The first night after he became Cubs manager, he barged into the players' Pullman cars and threw cold water on their faces, saying "there will be no sleeping under Maranville management." That same night he got into a fight with a cab driver in New York after the Cubs arrived there over the cabbie grumbling about his tip. He had to be separated from the cabbie by the cops. After they separated him, he went after the cops and was arrested along with two of his players. He had no set rules for the team except that they couldn't go to bed before him. Another time he held the Cubs traveling secretary out of a hotel window by his feet. Yet another time, and as it turns out, the final incident, he ran through the train throwing the contents of a spittoon at his players. With Rabbit as manager, the Cubs finished in last place for the first time in franchise history. He was fired after eight weeks. Rabbit played for another ten years (with Brooklyn, St. Louis, and Boston), and was inducted into the Hall of Fame in 1954. That was just a few months after he died. Rabbit still holds the record for most hits of any MLB player born in Massachusetts.

Historical note: On the day the Scopes Monkey Trial ended, Rabbit and his buddy Charlie Grimm knocked in seven of the 15 runs in a Cubs victory.

Carlos Marmol 1982–(Cubs 2006-2013)

For several years in the mid-to-late '00s, Marmol was one of the most feared relief pitchers in the game. His slider was so nasty he made batters look absolutely foolish. It was largely on Carlos' arm that the Cubs dashed into the playoffs in 2007 and 2008, and it clearly wasn't his fault they were swept. Still, as nasty as Carlos could be, he also had a tendency to be very wild. It was not uncommon at all for Marmol to walk the

bases loaded before striking out the side. He saved over 100 games in a Cubs uniform, but it was a wild and bumpy ride. The Cubs finally had enough of the roller coaster in 2013, and shipped him off to the Dodgers. He finished his Cubs career with the third most saves in Cubs history, behind only Hall of Famers Lee Smith and Bruce Sutter.

Gonzalo Marquez 1946–1984 (Cubs 1973-1974)

Gonzalo was a star in his native Venezuela, leading his team to the Caribbean World Series in 1970. The big first baseman was never more than a fringe player in the big leagues, but he did show flashes of power with both Oakland and the Cubs. After his time in the majors was over, he went back to Venezuela and played there until his death. He was on his way home from a winter league game when he was killed in an automobile accident. Marquez was only 38 years old.

Luis Marquez 1925–1988 (Cubs 1954)

Luis got his start in baseball in the Negro Leagues, and played several seasons for New York, Baltimore, and Homestead before breaking into the big leagues. The Puerto Rican outfielder began the season with the Cubs in 1954. He didn't finish the year. He was traded in June to the Pirates for Hal Rice. During his time with the Cubs, Luis stole three bases and batted .083. He is still revered in his native Puerto Rico, where a stadium is named after him in Aguadilla. Unfortunately, his story doesn't have a happy ending. Marquez was killed in a domestic dispute in 1988.

Jason Marquis 1978–(Cubs 2007-2008)

For the first nine seasons of his big league career, Jason Marquis' teams were in the playoffs every year. The streak began in 2001 in his rookie season in Atlanta, and it ended when his 2010 Washington Nationals team didn't make the playoffs. He won the World Series with the Cardinals and made the All-Star team with the Rockies. His time with the Cubs was not exceptional, but he took the ball every five days during his two playoff seasons with the Cubs, and pitched more than 350 innings. He was also a strong hitter. He hit three homers and knocked in 14 runs during his Cubs tenure. Jason's last appearance with the Cubs was in the 2008 NLDS. He pitched one inning and gave up a homer to Dodgers catcher Russell Martin. In all, Marquis pitched for nine different teams in a solid 15-year big league career.

William Marriott 1893–1969 (Cubs 1917-1920)

Marriott was a utility man for the Cubs, playing a little everywhere including 2B, SS, 3B, and OF. The problem was he didn't play often. In parts of three seasons, he appeared in a total of 47 games. He later got a lot more playing time with Brooklyn and Boston.

Doc Marshall 1875–1959 (Cubs 1908)

He was a backup catcher and outfielder for the World Series champs. Marshall didn't play much. He came to the Cubs around Memorial Day, and played in only twelve games the rest of the season. He didn't even sniff the World Series that year, but Doc got a ring. He was a bit of a baseball vagabond, also playing with Philadelphia, Boston, New York, and Brooklyn in his five-year big league career. After his baseball career he really lived up to his nickname. He became a doctor.

Jim Marshall 1931– (Cubs 1958-1959, Cubs manager 1974-1976)

Marshall was both a player and a manager with the Cubs, although neither part of his career was particularly memorable. His best season as a player was in 1959. He got the most playing time of his career (331 AB) and hit 11 HR. As a manager, his 1975 and 1976 Cubs teams posted identical 75-87 seasons. Among his players on that team: Bill Madlock, Manny Trillo, Jose Cardenal, Rick Monday, Jerry Morales, Rick Reuschel, and Steve Stone.

Sean Marshall 1982– (Cubs 2006-2011)

Marshall had moments of brilliance as a starting pitcher in his first few years with the Cubs, but the 6'7 lefty really found his niche when he was moved to the bullpen. In his last two years in Chicago he appeared in 158 games, saved six, and posted a sparkling ERA in the mid-2s. He became one of the first players traded by the new Cubs brain trust before the 2012 season. The Cubs got Travis Wood in return.

Frank Martin 1878–1942 (Orphans 1898)

Martin played in exactly one game for Chicago. He started at second base, batted four times, and struck out three times. That may be why he never played in another game for the Cubs (then known as the Orphans). He also played briefly for Louisville and the New York Giants.

J.C. Martin 1936– (Cubs 1970-1972)

The veteran catcher was brought aboard as Randy Hundley's backup after his previous team (the 1969 Mets) won the World Series. Martin was known as a good handler of pitchers and a good defensive backstop, but he couldn't hit. His lifetime batting average over 14 big league seasons was only .222.

Jerry Martin 1949– (Cubs 1979-1981)

The Cubs acquired Martin in a big trade just before the 1979 season along with catcher Barry Foote and second baseman Ted Sizemore for Manny Trillo, Dave Rader, and Greg Gross. He had a couple of good years with the Cubs, hitting 19 and 23 homers in his first two years with the team. After he slumped in 1981, the Cubs traded him to the Giants. Martin will unfortunately always be known as one of the first active big league players to serve time in prison. When he was with the Royals in 1983, he and teammates Willie Wilson (a future Cub), Willie Aikens, and Vida Blue were sentenced to prison on cocaine charges. He later returned to the big leagues with the Mets, but wasn't nearly the same player.

Leonys Martin 1988– (Cubs 2017)

Projected to be a big star with Texas early in his career, Martin never quite lived up to the hype. The Cubs acquired the Cuban outfielder from the Mariners during the stretch run of the 2017 season for his defense and baserunning ability. He did manage to make the postseason roster in that capacity, and appeared in five playoff games. He was granted free agency after the season ended.

Mike Martin 1958– (Cubs 1986)

Martin played nine seasons in the minors and got only one brief taste of the big-time with the Cubs at the end of a disappointing 1986 season. He backed up Jody Davis and appeared in a grand total of eight games. In 13 at-bats, Martin got one hit. On the other hand, Mike has one memory he can always mention to impress people. On September 7, 1986, he caught the last pitch of Hall of Famer Greg Maddux's first-ever win.

Morrie Martin 1922–2010 (Cubs 1959)

Morrie was a lefty reliever, so naturally his nickname was Lefty. He was a World War II veteran who was badly wounded in Germany. He nearly had his leg amputated. But Martin worked his way back up to the big leagues. Lefty pitched for six clubs before coming to the Cubs in 1959 for his swan song. The song was off-key. He appeared in three games in April, and was released with an ERA of 19.29.

Speed Martin 1893–1983 (Cubs 1918-1922)

His real name was Elwood, but they called him Speed because he could get the ball up to the plate in a hurry. He was a member of the pennant-winning 1918 Cubs team, but only appeared in nine games for them that year, and didn't appear in the World Series. Speed became a bigger part of the team the next few years (winning 11 games in 1921), but he also started getting hit pretty hard. By 1922, his time in the big leagues was done. Speed ended his career with a losing record (29-42) and a high ERA for that era (3.78), but with one of the coolest nicknames in Cubs history.

Historical note: On the day Prohibition began, Speed and the Cubs beat the Reds 3-2 in 12 innings.

Stu Martin 1912–1997 (Cubs 1943)

Stu was an All-Star in his rookie season for the Cardinals in 1936 and led National League second basemen in fielding percentage in 1939, but by the time he came to the Cubs, Stu was strictly a backup. The infielder hit .220 in the last 64 games of his big league career.

Carmello Martinez 1960– (Cubs 1983)

Martinez showed plenty of promise during his rookie season of 1983. In only 96 plate appearances, he clubbed six homers and knocked in 16 runs. It appeared he would be a corner outfielder in Chicago for years to come. Instead, he was the centerpiece in the trade that helped the Cubs acquire starting pitcher Scott Sanderson. Martinez had a pretty good career in San Diego, hitting over a hundred career homers, but he didn't turn out to be the stud Cubs fans feared they were trading away. On the other hand, Martinez was able to do one thing with San Diego that he never would have been able to do with the Cubs. He played in the 1984 World Series.

Dave Martinez 1964– (Cubs 1986-1988, 2000)

Martinez came up through the Cubs system and debuted in the big leagues with the Cubs. At the time, he was only 21 years old. In 1987 he won the starting center field job. He hit .292 with 16 stolen bases. Why did the Cubs trade the youngster the following season for the much older Mitch Webster? There have been unsubstantiated rumors for years about this, but no one has ever confirmed or denied anything. Is it possible the Cubs traded a young outfielder with a very bright future for one who was near the end of his career for baseball reasons? Of course it is. The Cubs have done that countless times. Regardless of the reason, the Cubs clearly got the short end of that deal. Martinez went on to have a very good career. He played sixteen seasons in the big leagues with the Expos, Reds, Giants, White Sox, Blue Jays, Rays, Rangers, Braves, and the Cubs. Martinez won a ring with the Cubs in 2016, when he served as the right-hand man/bench coach for Joe Maddon. After the 2017 season he was hired to manage the Washington Nationals.

Ramon Martinez 1972– (Cubs 2003-2004)

Not to be confused with All-Star pitcher Ramon Martinez (Dodgers), this Ramon was a backup infielder for the Cubs during two pretty successful years. He backed up Grudzielanek at second base, Alex Gonzalez (and later Nomar) at shortstop, and Aramis Ramirez at third base. During his two years in Chicago he got a lot of playing time because of his reliable glove. That glove kept him in the big leagues for 12 years. Ramon's cousin later played for the Cubs too — Geovany Soto.

Sandy Martinez 1970– (Cubs 1998-1999)

Martinez was a backup catcher in the big leagues for eight seasons, but he will always be remembered for what he did on May 6, 1998, while wearing a Cubs uniform. Sandy was the catcher for Kerry Wood's famous 20-strikeout game. He also played for Toronto, Florida, Montreal, Cleveland, and Boston.

Joe Marty 1913–1984 (Cubs 1937-1939)

Marty was the fourth outfielder for the pennant-winning Cubs in 1938. He was the first Cub to ever homer in a night game (in Cincinnati), and had a great World Series, going 6 for 12 with a homer and 5 RBI. The Cubs traded him to the Phillies the following year. That turned out to be a good trade for the Cubs, because it brought Claude Passeau over to Chicago.

Historical note: On the day the Golden Gate Bridge was dedicated (1937), Marty had one of his best days as a Cub in a loss to the Reds at Wrigley Field.

Randy Martz 1956 – (Cubs 1980-1982)

Martz was a first round draft choice of the Cubs (12th overall) after he was the College Baseball MVP at the University of South Carolina. He had a few unimpressive seasons with some very bad Cubs teams before being sent to the White Sox as part of the trade that brought Steve Trout to the Cubs.

Mike Mason 1958 – (Cubs 1987)

Mason pitched most of his big league career with the Texas Rangers, but he did spend the bulk of the 1987 season with the Cubs. He won four games and posted an ERA of 5.68. The Cubs released him during spring training of 1988, and he finished his career with the Twins.

Gordon Massa 1935 – 2016 (Cubs 1957-1958)

He had two great nicknames ("Moose" and "Duke") and a lifetime batting average of .412, but not many people remember the Cubs career of Gordon Massa. Why is that? Probably because he only batted 21 times over a two-year period. Massa spent most of his career in the minors, where he hit only .257. Moose finally hung his spikes after the 1963 minor league season. He died just a few months before the Cubs finally ended their World Series drought.

Andy Masur 1967 – (Cubs announcer 2000-2007)

Masur was a local Chicago kid (Maine East High School, Bradley University) who got his big baseball break at WGN Radio when Pat Hughes decided he needed an inning break during the games. I interviewed Andy a few years ago (when he was the Padres radio play-by-play man), and he considers that Cubs experience his big break too: "I certainly do. I can remember when Dave Eanet the sports director at WGN radio asked me if I would mind doing a half inning of play by play in addition to my pre-game and post-game responsibilities, I'm not sure the entire question came out of his mouth before I said, I'LL DO IT! People may not realize how tough it was

though to do just 3 outs a game. It was difficult to get into a rhythm with anything, but hey I wasn't going to complain. It was such a pleasure to share the microphone with Pat and Ron. Imagine me, a kid growing up in Chicago, now in the booth as one of the announcers. It was amazing. The break certainly worked out in my favor and I can't thank everybody there enough."

Juan Mateo 1982 – (Cubs 2006)

Mateo was a starting pitcher from the Dominican Republic who threw the ball very hard. The Cubs gave him a shot in their rotation the last two months of the 2006 season, and he really struggled. His ERA was over five, he walked too many men, and he didn't pitch deep into games. He never got another chance in the big leagues. He pitched a few years in the minors, before moving to Mexico and pitching in the Mexican League.

Marcos Mateo 1984 – (Cubs 2010-2011)

He pitched parts of two seasons with the Cubs in 2010 and 2011 before requiring Tommy John surgery in 2012, and missing the entire season. The Diamondbacks drafted him as a Rule V pick, but returned him to the Cubs in spring training in March 2014. He got one last cup of coffee with the Padres in 2015.

Joe Mather 1982 – (Cubs 2012)

The former Cardinals utility man became a Cubs utility man in 2012. He played a little outfield, third base, first base, and even pitched once. Unfortunately, he also only hit .209. The Cubs allowed him to leave via free agency, and he never made it back up to the big leagues.

Nelson Mathews 1941 – (1960-1963)

Mathews was a center fielder with pop, but he couldn't break the Cubs lineup. He served as a backup for several seasons, getting his most extensive shot in 1963. The Cubs traded him to Kansas City after the season, and the A's gave him the starting center field position. He hit 14 homers, but led the league in strikeouts. That was his last shot at a starting position in the big leagues.

Gary Matthews 1950– (Cubs 1984-1987)

Gary Matthews earned the nickname Sarge for his dugout leadership, take-charge attitude, and competitive playing. He embraced the name, and beginning early in the '84 season, he would salute the legions of LF bleacher fans who would cheer his every appearance in the outfield. He was one of the most important players on the 1984 Cubs team that came within a few outs of the World Series. Sarge's on-base percentage was over .400, he hit 14 homers and stole 17 bases, and though he wasn't the fielder he was earlier in his career (with the Giants and Phillies), he played with toughness and grit. He played several seasons for the Cubs in the 1980s, but really only had one more good year (1986). He was getting up in age by that time. He later coached for the Cubs, and his son Gary Matthews Jr. began his major league career with the Cubs too.

Historical note: On the day President Nixon resigned the presidency (1974), Sarge hit a homer against the Cubs to help his Giants win 3-0 at Wrigley Field. Future Cub Dave Kingman hit a homer too.

Gary Matthews Jr. 1974–(Cubs 2000-2001)

Gary's dad was the reigning National League Rookie of the Year when Gary Jr. was born in 1974. He followed in his father's footsteps by becoming a big league ballplayer (and a Cub — just like his dad). His time in Chicago wasn't quite as successful as his father's. He got a fair amount of playing time with the Cubs, but had trouble hitting over .200. The Cubs released him in August of 2001. Turns out, he had a little more left in the tank. He played in the big leagues for the next ten seasons, including an All-Star season with the Angels in 2006. His legacy, however, was tarnished by being mentioned in George Mitchell's report about steroids.

Wid Matthews 1896–1965 (Cubs GM 1950-1956)

When Matthews came to the Cubs in 1950, he arrived with a sparkling reputation. Wid had been an assistant to Branch Rickey with the Dodgers, and he promised to return the Cubs to their glory days. He did do one thing that was long overdue before he left town; he signed the first two African-American players in Cubs history — Ernie Banks and Gene Baker. Unfortunately, this was seven full seasons after Jackie Robinson had broken the color line, and three full seasons after Matthews arrived in Chicago. It was far too little, and far too late. Wid Matthews had a knack for trades…that is, trades that helped the other team. He traded fan favorite Andy Pafko, All-Star pitcher Johnny Schmitz, and two other players to the Dodgers for catcher Bruce Edwards (who had a grand total of 250 at-bats as a Cub), Joe Hatten (a pitcher with an ERA over five), outfielder Gene Hermanski (who managed a total of 8 home runs as a Cub) and Eddie Miksis (the main player the Cubs wanted — a mediocre shortstop who never hit higher than .251 in his four Cubs seasons). That deal was so bad people in Chicago wondered if he was still on Branch Rickey's payroll. In 1952 he was holding a press conference before the season, predicting things were just about to turn around, when P.K. Wrigley walked into the press conference and ripped Matthews in front of the press, saying "I believe it's about time we stopped our daydreaming and wishful thinking and faced things as they are." When people starting hanging Matthews in effigy in 1956, Wrigley finally faced things as they were and got rid of him.

Bobby Mattick 1915–2004 (Cubs 1938-1940)

Bobby looked good in his rookie season with the Cubs, so they traded their shortstop Dick Bartell and gave Mattick the starting job in 1940. Unfortunately, big league pitchers figured him out, and Mattick only managed to hit .218. The Cubs traded him to the Reds after the season, the third straight off-season that they traded their starting shortstop.

Brian Matusz 1987–(Cubs 2016)

The Cubs were in the midst of a tremendous winning streak after the 2016 All-Star break but they needed a pitcher to come up for a spot start. The way the team was going, it appeared that just about anyone could have come up and pitched the team to victory. Not true. Matusz was rocked. He never got another chance to pitch for the Cubs. The former #1 draft pick of the Orioles ended the season in the minors. His Cubs ERA stands at 18.00.

Gene Mauch 1925–2005 (Cubs 1948-1949)

During his playing days, Gene Mauch was a backup second baseman and shortstop for the Cubs for two seasons (1948-1949). He was well-liked by his teammates, especially the guy playing ahead of him, shortstop Roy Smalley. Smalley eventually married Mauch's sister. Gene was never much of a hitter (5 career homers and a .239 lifetime batting average in nine ML seasons), and he played for some of the worst teams in history. Did his stint with the Cubs affect him as a manager? Judge for yourself. Despite having managed in more major league games than all but three other managers (at the time of his retirement), he never won a pennant. His 1964 Phillies probably had the most dramatic collapse in baseball history. Leading by 6 ½ games with two weeks to go, the Phillies blew it. Yes, I think it's safe to say…his stint with the Cubs did rub off on him.

Hal Mauck 1869–1921 (Colts 1893)

Hal was a Princeton boy…Princeton, Indiana. The right-hander was a starting pitcher for the Cubs (then known as the Colts) at West Side Grounds in 1893. He was 8-10 in 18 starts, but what might have been most remarkable about his season was his strikeout total. He pitched 143 innings that year and struck out only 23 batters. After he was released by Chicago he pitched in the minor leagues until 1900. One season in the minors, he struck out only ten batters.

Carmen Mauro 1926–2003 (Cubs 1948-1951)

Carmen was a local kid (Morton High School in Cicero) who got his first real chance to play in the big leagues with the 1950 Cubs. He served as the Cubs fourth outfielder that season, backing up Hank Sauer, Andy Pafko, and Bob Borkowski. Unfortunately for Carmen, he wasn't much of a hitter. He hit only .227 that season, and his lifetime batting average was only .231. He later also played for the Dodgers, Senators, and A's.

Jason Maxwell 1972–(Cubs 1998)

Maxwell was a September call-up during the Cubs Wild Card season of 1998. Because every game mattered, the infielder didn't get many opportunities. He was used as a pinch hitter, and did hit one homer in his three at-bats. It came in a 13-11 loss against the Brewers. Sammy Sosa hit his 59th homer in the same game. The Cubs cut Maxwell during spring training in 1999, and he later had a cup of coffee with the Minnesota Twins

Derrick May 1968–(Cubs 1990-1994)

Derrick was a first round Cubs draft choice in 1986, and made his big league debut in 1990. The son of big leaguer Dave May didn't really get regular playing time until 1992, but in his final three seasons with the Cubs he did show some promise. In '93 he had his best campaign, hitting 10 homers and driving in 77 while batting .295. After the 1994/1995 strike, May was permitted to leave as a free agent, and later played with the Brewers, Astros, Phillies, Expos, and Orioles.

Jakie May 1895–1970 (Cubs 1931-1932)

The little lefty (only 5'8) pitched 14 seasons in the big leagues, the last two of which were for the Cubs. He was used almost exclusively out of the bullpen. Jakie won 7 games and saved 3. He retired after the 1932 World Series loss to the Yankees, a few months shy of his 37th birthday. He had been rocked for seven runs in only two innings pitched in that series.

Scott May 1961–(Cubs 1991)

Scott was a September call-up at the end of the 1991 season and appeared in two games. The right-handed reliever gave up six hits and four earned runs in only two innings (an ERA of 18.00). It was his last chance at the big leagues. He previously had a cup of coffee with the Rangers.

Ed Mayer 1931–2005 (Cubs 1957-1958)

Mayer was a left-handed reliever for a few really bad Cubs teams. Over two seasons he appeared in 23 games, winning two and saving one. It was Mayer's only time in the majors. He pitched in the minor leagues for eight seasons.

Cory Mazzoni 1989–(Cubs 2018)

Cory got a cup of coffee with the Cubs in 2018 and pitched very well in limited action. In eight appearances he only gave up one run. After the season, he was allowed to become a free agent.

Bill McAfee 1907–1958 (Cubs 1930)

McAfee faced exactly ten batters while pitching in a Cubs uniform. Unfortunately for him, it was the year of the hitter, and five of those ten batters reached base. The right-hander later pitched for Washington, Boston, and the St. Louis

Browns. After his playing career, he was elected Mayor of his hometown of Albany, Georgia. He died in a plane crash in 1958.

Jim McAnany 1936–2015 (Cubs 1961-1962)

McAnany was a backup outfielder for five big league seasons, all of which were in Chicago. The first three were on the south side (including the '59 World Series season), and the last two were with the Cubs. Over two seasons with the Cubs, he got 18 plate appearances and managed to scrape out a total of three hits.

Bub McAtee 1845–1876 (White Stockings 1871)

Bub was the first baseman and lead-off man for the very first officially recognized professional team in Chicago. That makes Bub one of only a handful of players who played for Chicago before the Great Chicago Fire. He died the same year the National League was founded (1876). He was only 31 years old.

Ike McAuley 1891–1928 (Cubs 1925)

The Cubs inexplicably gave the starting shortstop job to McAuley at the beginning of the 1925 season even though he hadn't been in the big leagues for eight years, and hadn't really played much when he was. McAuley didn't play terribly. He hit .280 in the first 37 games, but he also made ten errors. The Cubs cut him loose in May. Ike passed away only three years later at the age of 36.

Algie McBride 1869–1956 (Colts 1896)

Algie (real first name Algeron) was thought to be the answer in left field for Cap Anson's 1896 Colts, but Cap grew weary of his light hitting, and sent him packing just a few weeks later. Algie later played for Cincinnati and the New York Giants.

Bill McCabe 1892–1966 (Cubs 1918-1920)

The local Chicago boy made it up to the big leagues during his hometown team's pennant-winning season of 1918. He was a utility man for the 1918 Cubs, logging a little time at all three outfield positions and second base. He even got into three games of that 1918 World Series as a defensive replacement. Unfortunately, Bill wasn't much of a hitter. His lifetime average was only .161.

Dutch McCall 1920–1996 (Cubs 1948)

McCall pitched one full season in the majors (1948) as a 27-year-old rookie, and was among the league leaders in several categories, most notably walks and losses. In fact, he set the Cubs record by recording 13 losses in a row. He also led the Cubs in home runs allowed, and the Cubs starters in highest ERA…and Dutch was their #3 starter. The Cubs finished 27 ½ games out of first place that year, in dead last.

Alex McCarthy 1889–1978 (Cubs 1915-1916)

Alex was acquired from the Pirates in 1915, which means he was on the roster when the Cubs played their last game at West Side Grounds, and their first game at Wrigley Field. In 107 at-bats in 1916, the infielder hit .243, with zero homers and only six RBI. The Cubs traded him back to Pittsburgh in the middle of the 1916 season.

Jack McCarthy 1869–1948 (Orphans 1900, Cubs 1903-1905)

Jack was a starting outfielder for the Cubs for a few seasons, but he wasn't considered anything special. He was part of the package that was offered to Brooklyn to acquire Jimmy Scheckard, who became one of the key members of the Cubs championship dynasty. Since 1900, no player has more at-bats without hitting a home run than Jack. McCarthy went 2736 at-bats without one after hitting his last homer in 1899.

Joe McCarthy 1887–1978 (Cubs manager 1926-1930)

Joe McCarthy was given the nickname of "Marse Joe" by sportswriters. "Marse" is a Southern English rendition of the word "master," and from the moment he took over the Cubs in 1926, Marse Joe let it be known that he was in charge. He led them to the National League pennant in 1929, and never had a losing season as Cubs manager, but they fired him after the 1930 season because they didn't think he had what it took to get to the next level. Unfortunately for the Cubs, they never got to that next level without him, and he got to the next level with the Yankees seven times. Two of those times he beat the Cubs in the World Series. Marse Joe is in baseball's Hall of Fame.

Jim McCauley 1863–1930 (White Stockings 1885)

McCauley was a catcher and outfielder for the Cubs (then

known as the White Stockings) in 1885 for a grand total of three games. He got one hit. Jim played small parts of three seasons in the big leagues, never quite catching on with Chicago, St. Louis, Providence, or Buffalo (both of whom were big league franchises at the time), but he must have loved the game because McCauley played in the minor leagues until 1897.

Harry McChesney 1880–1960 (Cubs 1904)

Harry had one of the great baseball nicknames. His teammates called him Pud. Pud had a very brief big league career. He backed up Kangaroo Davy Jones in the outfield, and got into 22 games for the Cubs. The rest of his baseball career (he played until 1915) was spent in the minor leagues. Pud was also one of the best football punters of his era.

Scott McClain 1972– (Cubs 2005)

Scott got a very brief call up with the Cubs in 2005 as a 33-year old 1B/3B. He hit .143 in 16 plate appearances. Scott had similar cups of coffee with the Tampa Rays and the San Francisco Giants.

Bill McClellan 1856–1929 (White Stockings 1878)

McClellan got to play for his hometown Cubs (then known as the White Stockings) in only their third season in the National League. He played second base and shortstop, and hit .224 in just over 200 plate appearances. It was his only season in Chicago. He retired to his hometown after stints with Providence, Philadelphia, Brooklyn, and Cleveland, and is buried in Rosehill Cemetery in Chicago.

Lloyd McClendon 1959– (Cubs 1989-1990)

Lloyd McClendon came up as a catcher, but he didn't play there much for the Cubs (only 5 games). During the 1989 season he platooned with Dwight Smith in left field, playing mostly against left-handed pitchers. He even started one game of the 1989 NLCS against the Giants, going 2 for 3. McClendon was traded to the Pirates at the end of the 1990 season. He has since become a big league manager and coach.

George McConnell 1877–1964 (Cubs 1914, 1916)

One of the last of the two-way players, McConnell both pitched and played outfield. He didn't have a tremendous amount of success doing either with the Cubs. He was 4-12 as a pitcher, and batted .158 as an outfielder. His best season in the big leagues was the year between his two years with the Cubs. That year (1915), the spitballer pitched for the Chicago Federals, and won a league-leading 25 games. The slender 6'3 pitcher was nicknamed Slats.

Barry McCormick 1874–1956 (Colts/Orphans 1895-1901)

Barry was a very valuable player for the Cubs (then known as the Colts, and then the Orphans). He was a middle infielder, but he started nearly the same number of games at second base, third base, and shortstop in his six years with Chicago. He jumped to the upstart American League for the last few years of his career, performing the same role for the St. Louis Browns and the Washington Senators. After his playing days he became a big league umpire.

Jim McCormick 1856–1918 (White Stockings 1885-1886)

In the early days of the National League, Jim McCormick was one of the first pitching stars. One season (1880), he won 45 games and pitched an astounding 657.2 innings (with 72 complete games). Obviously the rules were a little different in that era, but you can't take away his 265 career wins. In his two seasons with the Cubs (then known as the White Stockings), McCormick won 20 and 31 games. Chicago won the National League both years. After the 1886 season, Cubs owner Al Spalding sold McCormick (and several of his teammates) because he didn't approve of their hard-drinking lifestyle. Jim hailed from Scotland, and was the first MLB player born there.

<u>Historical note:</u> On the day President Cleveland got married in the White House, McCormick was on the mound for Chicago, and won the game 9-0.

Clyde McCullough 1917–1982 (Cubs 1940-1948, 1953-1956)

Clyde actually had three different stints with the Cubs. The pre-war stint (1940-1943), the post-war years after his military service (1945-1948), and the final stint at the end of his career (after spending a few years with Pittsburgh).

During the first one he was a young gun catcher with a great arm. The second stint began with one at-bat in the World Series (a strikeout) and ended with an All-Star appearance. The third stint featured yet another All-Star appearance. When he returned to the Cubs for that last stint, he was already 36 years old. His teammates didn't consider him one of the smarter players in the league. One anonymous teammate remarked in the book *Wrigleyville*: "We used to swear he had to put his head down to see how many fingers he was putting down." On the other hand, Clyde was behind the plate for the no-hitter tossed by Sam Jones.

Lindy McDaniel 1935–(Cubs 1962-1965)

The Cubs picked up Lindy McDaniel from the Cardinals in 1962, and he had a few very good years for the team, despite the fact that the Cubs were awful while he was there. In 1963 he even led the league in saves. That same year he might have had his best day in baseball. On June 6, 1963, he came in to save the game. The bases were loaded in the 10th inning of a tied game, and there was one out. McDaniel promptly picked Willie Mays off second base for the second out. Then he retired Ed Bailey for the third. Then, in the bottom of the tenth inning he came up to bat, and promptly hit a homer to win the game. That game obviously made an impression on the Giants, because they traded for McDaniel just a few years later. In return the Cubs got two prospects that became key members of their late 60s contenders: catcher Randy Hundley and pitcher Bill Hands.

Darnell McDonald 1978–(Cubs 2013)

Darnell was a first round draft choice of the Orioles who played parts of seven big league seasons, including the last few weeks of the 2013 season with the Cubs. The Cubs thought highly enough of him to ask him to stay in the organization as a coach after the season. Darnell's best season was with the 2010 Red Sox. He hit nine homers and batted .270 in over 300 at-bats.

Ed McDonald 1886–1946 (Cubs 1913)

Ed played in exactly one game for the Cubs on April 13, 1913 against the Pirates at West Side Grounds. He came in as a pinch runner, and didn't score. He never batted, and never fielded a ball. He did, however, previously play for the Boston Braves for two seasons as a third baseman. After leaving the Cubs he played another nine seasons in the minors. There's no record whether or not Ed McDonald had a farm. (E-I-E-I-O)

John McDonough 1953–(Cubs executive 1983-2007)

John served many roles with the Cubs, but is probably best remembered for his many innovative years as the team's marketing director. Under McDonough's direction Cubs attendance surged. Among his innovations — the creation of the Cubs Convention, and the guest conductor of the 7th inning stretch. In his final years he became the president of the club. Among his moves in that role — hiring Lou Piniella and signing Alfonso Soriano. He left the team to run the Chicago Blackhawks, and he has led that organization to three Stanley Cup titles.

Chuck McElroy 1967–(Cubs 1991-1993)

McElroy was acquired from the Phillies in the trade that sent Mitch Williams to Philadelphia. The Cubs used him a lot out of the bullpen. The lefty pitched in almost 200 games in his three seasons with the Cubs. In 1991 he finished fifth in the Rookie of the Year voting after posting a 1.95 ERA in 71 games. Over his three years with the Cubs, Chuck saved nine games and won 12. He was traded to the Reds after the 1993 season.

Monte McFarland 1872–1913 (Colts 1895-1896)

Monte started only five games over two season for the Cubs (then known as the Colts). The right-handed pitcher had a record of 2-4 with a 6.36 ERA. After his brief stint in the big leagues, he played minor league ball for another 14 seasons. Monte passed away in Peoria at the way too young age of 41. His brother Chappie later played for the Cardinals.

Casey McGehee 1982–(Cubs 2008)

Casey was a September call-up for a Cubs team that led the league in victories. He didn't get much playing time backing up Aramis Ramirez. The Cubs thought he wouldn't be needed, so they essentially gave him away to Milwaukee. McGehee (pronounced 'Mcgee') responded by starting at third base and hitting over 20 homers and driving in more than 100 runs for Milwaukee in 2010. He was eventually replaced in

Milwaukee by a free-agent signing…Aramis Ramirez.

Willie McGill 1873–1944 (Colts 1893-1894)

They called him "Kid" because he was only 16 when he came up to the big leagues in 1890 with Cleveland. By the time he pitched for the Cubs, McGill was a wise old man of 19. He won 17 games for the Cubs (then known as the Colts), but had a terrible year in 1894 and was cut loose. By the time he was 22 years old, Kid was finished. He pitched for six teams in his six year career. After his baseball career, McGill attended the University of Notre Dame.

Dan McGinn 1943– (Cubs 1972)

McGinn was hit pretty hard during his one season with the Cubs. He appeared in 42 games, but he posted an ERA of 5.89. He also pitched for the Reds and Expos during his big league career. McGinn will always be remembered in Montreal. He hit the first home run in Expos franchise history 4/8/69. The pitcher he victimized was Tom Seaver.

Gus McGinnis 1870–1904 (Colts 1893)

Gus went 2-5 with a 5.35 ERA in his half-season with the Cubs (then known as the Colts). He finished the season with Philadelphia, and won one last game. Gus never pitched in the big leagues again. Just eleven years after his final big league pitch, Gus was dead at the age of 33.

Lynn McGlothen 1950–1984 (Cubs 1978-1980)

Big Lynn was an All-Star with the Cardinals before coming to the Cubs. The Cubs got him from the Giants in exchange for third baseman Hector Cruz, and Lynn had a few good seasons in Chicago, winning 30 games for the Cubs. Unfortunately, he developed elbow problems, and was never the same after that. Lynn was only 32 years old when he was forced to retire. McGlothen's story ends tragically. He passed away in a mobile home fire in 1984. He was only 34 years old.

Fred McGriff 1963– (Cubs 2001-2002)

He was nicknamed the Crime Dog because of his last name's similarity to the "actual" crime dog McGruff. Our crime dog, it's safe to say, was at best a reluctant Cub. He refused to be traded to the Cubs at first, and then when he finally agreed to the trade, he seemed to be a bad luck charm as the surging Cubs faded out of contention shortly after he arrived in 2001. He had a great season in 2002 (30 HR, 103 RBI), but that team was headed nowhere. He played two more seasons after he left Chicago, and ended his career with 493 home runs. During his big league career he was one of the premier sluggers in the game.

Harry McIntire 1879–1949 (Cubs 1910-1912)

Harry pitched for the pennant-winning 1910 Cubs. He won 13 games that year, but ended his career 46 games under .500. That was mainly due to a disastrous few seasons in Brooklyn. He led the league in many categories while he pitched there, but none of them were the kind you want to lead the league in (namely hits allowed, and earned runs allowed). Harry also led the league three different times in hit batsmen. He hit nearly a hundred batters (96) in his nine-year big league career.

Jim McKnight 1936–1994 (Cubs 1960, 1962)

The Cubs got McKnight from the Cardinals in exchange for their slugging outfielder Moose Moryn. Moryn admittedly didn't have much left in the tank, but McKnight was not ready for prime time. The third baseman/outfielder spent the full 1962 season on the Cubs roster and was used mainly as a pinch hitter. He hit .224 and managed exactly one extra base hit (a triple). The Cubs traded him to the Giants after the season. McKnight was prototypical 4A player — pretty good in the minors (nine seasons with double-digit homers), but not quite good enough for the big leagues.

Polly McLarry 1891–1971 (Cubs 1915)

His real name was Howard, but everyone called him Polly. McLarry wasn't much of a major leaguer, but he was a minor league superstar. Polly was the best player on one of the best minor league teams in history (the 1921 Memphis Chicks). The first baseman led the team in hitting (.353) and the entire league in RBI and walks. His minor league numbers were staggering. He had an unbelievable 2723 hits in a 18-year minor league career, and his lifetime average was .317. It was a different story in the big leagues. Polly played for the White Sox briefly in 1912, and got one last shot with the Cubs three years later. That year he spent the entire season on the Cubs roster, but appeared in only 68 games, and hit .197.

When the Cubs started the 1916 season in their new ballpark (now Wrigley Field), Polly was back in the minor leagues. He would never return to the show.

Larry McLean 1881–1921 (Cubs 1903)

Larry had a 13-year big league career as a catcher and first baseman, but he only played one game for the Cubs in 1903, and went 0 for 4, with a walk. Granted, that walk came with the bases loaded, so he does have one RBI in a Cubs uniform. Larry later played for the Cardinals, Reds, and Giants, and became a pretty good defensive catcher. He was 6'5, which makes him the tallest catcher in big league history. Unfortunately, Larry was also known as a bit of a drinker and brawler. His career ended after he got into a fight with his Giants manager John McGraw, and his life ended when he got into a bar fight in 1921. A bartender in Boston shot him dead. Larry was 39.

Cal McLish 1925–2010 (Cubs 1949, 1951)

Calvin Coolidge was the president at the time of McLish's birth, and was widely regarded as the most boring man to ever serve in that capacity. Despite that, a young couple in Oklahoma named their son after him, and added a few more names for good measure. Not sure how they managed to fit it all on the birth certificate. The boy's name was Calvin Coolidge Julius Caesar Tuskahoma McLish. When he grew up, Cal McLish pitched for the Chicago Cubs (in 1949 and 1951). His time with the Cubs was nothing to write home about, but he blossomed a few years later. In 1958 he won 16 games for the Cleveland Indians. In 1959, he won 19, and was named to the All-Star team. McLish passed away in 2010 in his native Oklahoma. His nickname was Bus.

Jimmy McMath 1949–2010 (Cubs 1968)

Jimmy was the youngest player in the big leagues (19) when the Cubs called him up in 1968. He only managed 2 hits in 14 big league at-bats. In many ways, Jimmy's story was typical of Cubs draft choices from that era. He was a high school stud, drafted in the second round of the 1967 draft, and started off well in the low minors (hitting .388 for the Quincy Cubs). He worked his way all the way up to the big leagues in September of that year, but by the next spring began working his way back down the ladder. He went from AAA to Double-A,

and then back down to Quincy. After the 1971 season he was released, and his career was over at the age of 22. The draft is an inexact science, to be sure, but that 1967 draft was stocked with future big leaguers. Here are a few other players taken in that same round of that same draft, and all of them were taken after McMath: Vida Blue (A's), Jerry Reuss (Cardinals), and Don Baylor (Orioles).

Norm McMillan 1895–1969 (Cubs 1928-1929)

Called "Bub" because of his southern origins, Norm McMillan's most productive season came in 1929 with the Chicago Cubs when he hit .271 in 459 at-bats with 5 home runs and 55 runs batted in. He also had 13 stolen bases. That season Bub was involved in one of the stranger plays in baseball history. On Aug. 26, 1929, the Cubs and Reds were tied at 5-5 in the bottom of the eighth inning of a game at Wrigley Field, when McMillan hit an inside-the-park grand slam. The outfielder couldn't find the ball in the bullpen. After the game, Cubs reliever Ken Penner picked up his jacket in the bullpen and found the missing ball in his right sleeve. McMillan was a 33-year-old well-traveled utility man and surprised everyone by winning the starting 3B for the Cubs in 1929, but he only managed 2 hits in 20 at-bats in the World Series. The following year Woody English took McMillan's spot, and good ol' Bub never played in the majors again. Following his career in baseball, McMillan owned and ran a drug store in his native South Carolina.

Brian McNichol 1974–(Cubs 1999)

Brian's big league career lasted two games. His first big league game was a start against the Reds in the second game of a double-header. He was pounded for six runs in only four innings. Mike Cameron and Greg Vaughn both homered against him In a 10-3 loss. McNichol got his second (and last) start against the Phillies in Philadelphia. Mike Lieberthal took him deep, but Brian only gave up two runs on six hits in 5 innings. He still got the loss as the Cubs lost 2-1. He never got another shot in the majors.

Brian McRae 1967–(Cubs 1995-1997)

The son of big league standout Hal McRae had a very respectable ten-year Major League career. He was an outstanding defensive center fielder with power and speed.

One year with the Mets he was a 20/20 man. McRae was a valuable member of the team in his two years in Chicago. He hit .288 in '95 and scored 111 runs in '96, but he slipped to a .240 average in 1997 and was traded to the Mets along with Mel Rojas and Turk Wendell for Lance Johnson, Matt Clark, and Manny Alexander. In ten big league seasons he never made it to the postseason.

Cal McVey 1849–1926 (White Stockings 1876-1877)

McVey played for the Cubs (then known as the White Stockings) in the National League's very first season. Cal played every single position on the field, including pitcher, but he was best known for his hitting. McVey played in the big leagues for nine seasons and finished with a lifetime average of .346. After his playing career he endured tragedy after tragedy. His wife was seriously injured in the 1906 San Francisco earthquake. Cal worked as a miner and was crippled in a 30-foot fall. But in 1919 he was the guest of the Cincinnati Reds during the World Series. They were honoring the 50th anniversary of professional baseball that day. Little did they know the White Sox were cheating — throwing the series to eventual champion Cincinnati.

Historical note: On the last full day of Crazy Horse's life (1877), Cal was on the mound for Chicago. The White Stockings lost 7-1 to Hartford.

George Meakim 1865–1923 (Colts 1892)

George had the sort of pitching line that would give today's pitchers nightmares: 9 IP, 18 hits, 11 earned runs, 2 walks, and no strikeouts. Even in 1892 it was bad enough to ensure he would never get another start for the Cubs (then known as the Colts). He later pitched for Cincinnati and Louisville with similar results.

Yoervis Medina 1988–(Cubs 2015)

Medina was acquired by the Cubs in the trade that sent Wellington Castillo to the Mariners in 2015. He only got a cup of coffee with the Cubs, appearing in five games, all in relief. It didn't go so well for him. In nine innings of work, his ERA was 7.00.

Russ Meers 1918–1994 (Cubs 1941-1947)

World War II interrupted Meers' big league career. He was in the Navy for three years, serving in the South Pacific. In all, he pitched three seasons for the Cubs (1941, 1946, 1947), mostly as a middle reliever. Meers was nicknamed Babe.

Dave Meier 1959–(Cubs 1988)

Meier was a journeyman outfielder who played the final two games of his big league career with the Cubs. The outfielder/pinch hitter got two singles in five plate appearances. He had earlier played for Minnesota and Texas.

Sam Mejias 1952–(Cubs 1979)

The Dominican outfielder was a defensive specialist. With the Cubs he got into 31 games, but only batted fourteen times. Sam served a similar role for the Expos, Reds, and Cardinals. After his playing days, he went into coaching, and spent several years on the big league staffs of the Mariners and Orioles.

Jock Menefee 1868–1953 (Orphans/Cubs 1900-1903)

Jock had already pitched for Pittsburgh, Louisville, and New York before joining the Cubs (then known as the Orphans). His Cubs career was unspectacular (37-36 record in four seasons), but he does have the distinction of being the last National League pitcher to pull off a successful steal of home (7/15/1902).

Rudy Meoli 1951–(Cubs 1978)

The backup infielder for the Cubs in 1978 hit a whopping .103 for the season. His bat and glove weren't a big help, but his Cubs team got within sniffing distance of .500 (79-83). For that era in Cubs baseball, they were a juggernaut. Meoli also played for the Angels and Phillies.

Orlando Merced 1966–(Cubs 1998)

Merced had a few very good years with Pittsburgh in his 13-year big league career, and also played for Toronto, Minnesota, Boston, Montreal, and Houston. He was with the Cubs for less than one month in 1998. The Cubs acquired him to help with the playoff push that season, and he definitely made his presence felt. Orlando hit a dramatic game-winning homer in the closing days of the season. If he had been acquired a week earlier, the Cubs probably would have put him on the postseason roster, but because he arrived after September

1st, he was ineligible. Merced signed with Montreal as a free agent after the season.

Kent Mercker 1968 – (Cubs 2004)

Mercker was a good relief pitcher for the Cubs in 2004, appearing in 71 games as a left-handed specialist and registering a 2.55 ERA, but he is most remembered for his role in driving Steve Stone away from the Cubs broadcasting booth. On September 30, 2004, after the Cubs had choked away a nearly certain playoff spot, Steve Stone assessed the team on the air. He said the 2004 Cubs were: "(a) bunch of talented guys who want to look at all directions except where they should really look and kind of make excuses for what happened. … At the end of the day, boys, don't tell me how rough the water is, you bring in the ship." Kent Mercker was particularly vocal about what he considered a betrayal. Stone resigned after the season.

Ron Meridith 1956 – (Cubs 1984-1985)

Ron was brought up in September of their division-winning 1984 season but the lefty reliever didn't really contribute much to that team. The following season he pitched in 32 games for the Cubs and posted an ERA of 4.47. The Cubs traded him to the Rangers in 1986.

Fred Merkle 1888 – 1956 (Cubs 1917-1920)

Maybe the most unfairly maligned player in baseball history, Fred Merkle was known as "Boner" or "Bonehead" for nearly all of his major league career. Despite a very solid 16-year career in which he played in five World Series, Merkle will always be remembered for a baserunning error during his rookie season of 1908. On the play that should have provided the Giants with the game-winning run to clinch the 1908 pennant (over the Cubs), Merkle was the runner on first base. In a move that will haunt him for the rest of his life, he tried to escape the rioting Polo Grounds mob storming the field instead of touching second base (as he was technically required to do in those days). The Cubs noticed he didn't touch the base, got the ball back somehow, and, fighting their way through New York's rowdiest and drunkest fans, touched second base. Merkle was called out, the game was declared a tie, and it was ordered to be replayed at the end of the season by the president of the National League. The Cubs won the replayed game, and the pennant. Merkle was blamed by the NY fans for the rest of his life. His last name actually became a synonym for "a dumb mistake." Good ol' Bonehead later played four seasons with the Cubs (1917-1920) and was the starting first baseman for the 1918 pennant winners. Though he played in five World Series for three different teams, his team never won.

Historical note: On the day the Black Sox went on trial for throwing the World Series (1920), Merkle had a big day at the plate for the Cubs, hitting two doubles and a triple in a win against the Pirates.

Lloyd "Citation" Merriman 1924 – 2004 (Cubs 1955)

Though Merriman played five seasons in the big leagues, that was the least of his accomplishments. Lloyd Merriman was a genuine war hero in two different wars, World War II and the Korean War. Before he went to war, he was better known as a football star at Stanford. He was nicknamed Citation after the legendary horse because of his blinding speed on the football field. The Chicago Bears drafted him, but he chose service to his country instead. After World War II, he played three seasons of Major League baseball, before returning to the service to fly combat missions in Korea. He played two more seasons in the majors after his return from Korea, the last of which was for the Cubs in 1955. Merriman may not have been one of the best players to put on a Cubs uniform, but he was certainly among the most impressive.

Historical note: On the day that Albert Einstein died (1955), Merriman scored the winning run in the ninth inning to defeat the Cardinals 6-5 in St. Louis.

Bill Merritt 1870 – 1937 (Colts 1891)

Merritt began his career with the Cubs (then known as the Colts), and though he didn't get much playing time (11 games), the catcher/first baseman eventually played eight seasons in the big leagues with other teams, including Boston, Pittsburgh, and Cincinnati.

Sam Mertes 1872 – 1945 (Orphans 1898-1900)

Sandow, as he was called, was a utility man for the Cubs (then known as the Orphans) near the turn of last century. Sam played mostly second base and outfield, but he was ready to play whatever was needed. He literally played every single position in his big league career. With Chicago, he hit nearly .300 and was a very reliable RBI man. After he left the Cubs, he even led the league in that category. Mertes played in the big leagues for ten seasons.

Lennie Merullo 1917–2015 (Cubs 1941-1947)

Lennie was the starting shortstop for the Cubs in the 1940s, including the pennant-winning season of 1945. He wasn't known as a great fielder or hitter. In fact, Merullo averaged an error every three and half games or so (172 errors in 602 games, including four in one inning in 1942), a home run every 345 at-bats (a grand total of 6 in 2071 at-bats), and had a lifetime average of .240. But he was one of the team leaders. Lenny got into a couple of famous fights sticking up for his teammates. One time he fought former Cub Eddie Stanky, leading to a benches-clearing brawl. Another time, Lenny and Phil Cavarretta were attacked by Dixie Walker before the game, and had to be pulled off by the police. Merullo got an eight-game suspension. Lenny Merullo retired after the 1947 season. He became a scout after his playing days. Lenny's grandson Matt also played in the big leagues. When Lenny passed away at the age of 98, he was the last surviving member of the last Chicago Cubs World Series team. The Cubs won it again the year after Lennie's death.

Steve Mesner 1918–1981 (Cubs 1938-1939)

The third baseman was only 20 years old when he got the September call-up to play for the pennant-winning Cubs, but on a team stocked with talent, he didn't play much. He later got a full-time third base job for three full seasons during the war with the Cincinnati Reds. He also played 15 seasons in the minors, beginning at the age of 16.

Wayne Messmer 1950–(Cubs Singer/Public Address Announcer)

Wayne was a radio newsman for several stations in Chicago, but has been a part of the Cubs family in one way or another since 1985. For years he served as the public address announcer, but he is more known for his rousing version of the National Anthem. Wayne has performed it hundreds of times for Wrigley fans, but he also has performed it for the Blackhawks, White Sox, and Chicago Sting, as well as the Chicago Wolves, where he currently serves as senior executive vice president.

George Metkovich 1920–1995 (Cubs 1953)

His teammates called him Catfish. The clean-shaven outfielder/first baseman may be the only "catfish" who wasn't nicknamed for his whiskers. He was given the nickname by Casey Stengel when he injured himself trying to pull a hook from a catfish. Catfish played ten years in the big leagues for the Red Sox, White Sox, Indians, Pirates, Braves, and of course the Cubs. In his career he never hit ten homers and never hit .300, but he did have a little speed and was known as a good glove man in center field. He hit .234 in his season with the Cubs, the second-to-last season of his career ('53).

Charlie Metro 1918–2011 (Cubs manager 1962)

Charlie was one of the College of Coaches who got a shot at managing the team in 1962. He managed the last 100+ games that season, and led the Cubs to a 9th place finish. Believe it or not, he got another shot at managing in 1970 with the Royals and did even worse.

Roger Metzger 1947– (Cubs 1970)

Metzger only played in one game with the Cubs in June of 1970, and the former first rounder went 0 for 2 against Gaylord Perry in Candlestick Park in his big league debut. The following year the Cubs traded him to the Astros for Hector Torres in a straight shortstop for shortstop swap. Torres bombed out in Chicago. Metzger went on to become a Gold Glover and eight-year starter for the Astros. His career ended thanks to a freak accident. He accidentally sawed off the tips of four of his fingers with a table saw.

Alex Metzler 1903–1970 (Cubs 1925)

He was just a 22-year-old kid with the Cubs when he got some playing time at the end of the 1925 season, but he really blossomed after he left the team. In 1927 he was the best defensive center fielder in the league for the Chicago White Sox.

*Mexican Cubs...*Surprisingly few Cub players were born in Mexico...Hector Torres, Jessie Flores, Daniel Garibay, Rodrigo Lopez, Horacio Pina, Jaime Garcia, and Ismael Valdes.

Russ Meyer 1923–1997 (Cubs 1946-1948, 1956)

Not to be confused with the B-movie director who was obsessed with large breasts, this Russ Meyer was known as Mad Monk because he had a vicious temper and didn't take to coaching. One night he ran into an old girlfriend at a bar the players frequented. They began to argue and she got so mad at him that she bit off the tip of his nose. It was still hanging there, but he had to have it stitched back together. The next day he had to sneak into the clubhouse, but he couldn't hide his face forever. It was all bandaged up and he had two black eyes. The woman claimed she was retaliating for being bitten on the nose herself, and filed suit. It was quietly settled out of court near the end of the 1947 season. Shortly after that, Meyer was traded to Philadelphia (1948). Mad Monk frequently angered his teammates, opponents, and the umpires, often to his own detriment. He would lose his cool on the mound after a base hit or an infielder's error. Once, with the Phillies, after being knocked out of a game, he took off his spikes and hurled them into the shower ceiling, where they stuck. He won 17 games for the Phillies in 1949, and helped the Braves win the pennant in 1953. He returned to the Cubs only after he was washed up. While he was away from the Cubs he went 24-3 against them. Those 24 wins were almost one third of his 79 overall wins.

Levi Meyerle 1849–1921 (White Stockings 1874)

Levi was an infielder who played several seasons of pro ball, including one with the White Stockings organization that has become the Cubs. He won the batting title that year, hitting .394. Levi moved on to Philadelphia after the season and later also played for Cincinnati. Meyerle was one of the first Jewish professional baseball players.

Chad Meyers 1975–(Cubs 1999-2001)

Chad was a utility man for the Cubs, playing second base, third base, and all three outfield slots when he was needed. Unfortunately for Meyers, he wasn't a very strong hitter. In 212 lifetime big league at-bats, his batting average was only .208. Meyers finished his career with the Mariners.

Cubs players have had some great nicknames over the years. Among players starting with the letter M, you'll find nicknames like Babe, Blackie, Boner, Bub, Buns, Catfish, Citation, Crime Dog, Cowboy, Deacon, Doc, Grasshopper, Grump, Hack, Jock, Kid, Liz, Lefty, Mad Dog, Mad Monk, Mags, Major, Marse Joe, Moose, Ox, Polly, Prunes, Pud, Rabbit, Red, Sarge, Slats, Speed, Steam Engine in Boots, Stick, Topsy, Windy, and Zonk.

Gene Michael 1938–2017 (Cubs manager 1986-1987)

In his playing days Michael was a slick-fielding shortstop nicknamed "Stick" because he was so skinny. He was no longer quite so skinny when he came aboard to manage the Cubs after Dallas Green fired Jim Frey. That 1986 team was a mess, so no one was surprised that Michael couldn't turn them around. The following year he and Green feuded, and even though the Cubs had a 68-68 record, Green fired him. Michael was only 49 years old at the time, but he never managed again. He went back to the Yankees and took a front office job with them.

Ralph Michaels 1902–1988 (Cubs 1924-1926)

Michaels was a backup infielder (third and short) who played sparingly for the Cubs in the mid-20s. His most extensive playing time came in 1925, the first season the Cubs ever finished in last place. Ralph played twenty-two games for that dysfunctional outfit. He later played in the minor leagues until 1937. Ralph died just three days before the first night game at Wrigley.

Ed Mickelson 1926–(Cubs 1957)

Ed was mainly a career minor leaguer, but he did get three cups of coffee in the big leagues. His last one was with the Cubs in 1957. The first baseman was used mainly as a pinch hitter, and was 0 for 12. His most notable achievement in the big leagues occurred in 1953. He knocked in the final run in St. Louis Browns history. The team moved to Baltimore in 1954.

Matt Mieske 1968–(Cubs 1998)

He was a fourth outfielder for the Cubs in their Wild Card-winning season of 1998, and an important bat off the bench.

He hit nearly .300 in that capacity. The Cubs let him go after the season and he played another four years (for Seattle, Houston, and Arizona).

Pete Mikkelsen 1939–2006 (Cubs 1967-1968)

He came to the Cubs off waivers from the Pirates during the 1967 season, and was traded to the Cardinals in the middle of the 1968 season. Mikkelsen didn't pitch much. He appeared in ten total games for the Cubs, with an ERA north of six. In all, Pete pitched in the big leagues for nine seasons with the Yankees, Pirates, Cardinals, and Dodgers.

Hank Miklos 1910–2000 (Cubs 1944)

Hank was a Chicago-born and bred left-handed pitcher who had been out of baseball for five years when he tried out for the Cubs during the war. The Cubs gave the 33-year-old a shot, and he appeared in the only two games of his big league career. His ERA was 7.71.

Eddie Miksis 1926–2005 (Cubs 1951-1956)

Eddie was acquired from the Dodgers in the trade that sent Andy Pafko to Brooklyn. That was one of the most lopsided trades in Cubs history (and not in a good way). When the Cubs traded him to the Cardinals in 1956, that also was a lopsided trade (and not in a good way). During his Cubs years, the team broke the color barrier by bringing in Ernie Banks, Gene Baker, and Sam Jones. Eddie allegedly lent his glove to Ernie before Ernie's first game.

Aaron Miles 1976– (Cubs 2009)

He was coming off a good season with the Cardinals (.317 average) and appeared to be a good signing by the Cubs, but Aaron Miles never put it together in Chicago. By August the fed-up Cubs shipped him off in a trade to Oakland.

Bob Miller 1939–1993 (Cubs 1970-1971)

Miller might have seen the highest highs and lowest lows of any pitcher in big league history. He was on the incredibly bad 1962 expansion Mets, and lost 12 games in a row that year. (His one win was against the Cubs). He also played on three World Series winners, the '63 and '65 Dodgers and the '71 Pirates. Miller came to the Cubs at the tail end of the 1970 season to help shore up their bullpen. After only two

appearances the following year, the Cubs released him. He later became a pitching coach. Miller died in a car accident in 1993.

Damian Miller 1969– (Cubs 2003)

Miller was coming off an All-Star season in Arizona when the Cubs signed him to be their starting catcher in 2003. He handled the pitching rotation of Wood, Prior, Zambrano, and Clement quite well, but his lack of hitting (.233 average) left the Cubs searching for a replacement. In the 2003 postseason Miller was only 3 for 22. After the season ended he was traded for catcher Michael Barrett.

Doc Miller 1883–1938 (Cubs 1910)

The Canadian-born Miller got exactly one bat for the pennant-bound Cubs on May 4, 1910. He couldn't crack the Cubs lineup, and they needed pitching, so they traded him eight days later to Boston for pitcher Lew Ritchie. It turned out to be a good trade for both teams. Miller became the starting right fielder for Boston. He led the league in hits the following year and batted .333. Meanwhile Ritchie won 42 games over the next three seasons for the Cubs.

Dusty Miller 1876–1950 (Orphans 1902)

Miller played one season for the Cubs (then known as the Orphans), and it was his only season in the big leagues. The left-fielder hit .246 with ten stolen bases. The remainder of his career was spent in the minors. He retired the year of the Cubs World Series championship, 1908.

Hack Miller 1894–1971 (Cubs 1922-1925)

Hack got his nickname because he looked like a famous Russian wrestler of the era, Hackenschmidt. His real first name was Laurence. Miller was a short, squat guy, about 5'9", 200 pounds, but he was tough as nails and strong as can be. His father was a circus strongman (Sebastian the Strongman), and Miller used to entertain his teammates by bending iron bars, smashing large stones and hammering nails through 2-inch thick boards with his fist. After he retired from baseball, which happened pretty quickly — he was amazingly slow — he became a longshoreman. He only played six seasons in the majors, but his career batting average was .323.

Joe Miller 1850–1891 (White Stockings 1875)

Joe was born in Germany, but came to America as a young boy and learned how to play the game of baseball. The second baseman played 15 games in his final big league season, and hit a whopping .148. In over 100 career at-bats, Joe managed only one extra base hit (a double).

Kurt Miller 1972– (Cubs 1998-1999)

Miller was a right-handed reliever who got a taste of the big leagues with the Florida Marlins before joining the Cubs. He got into a handful of games in 1998, and then made the club at the beginning of the 1999 season. However, he had a rough outing at the end of April against his former team, and injured his rib cage. He rehabbed in the minors at Iowa, before signing a contract to pitch in Japan.

Ox Miller 1915–2007 (Cubs 1947)

His real name was John Anthony, and he was 6'1", 190 pounds, which by 1947 standards…was as big as an Ox. He finished his undistinguished (mostly wartime) career with the Cubs. Ox made 4 starts for the Cubs, went 1-2, and had an ERA of 10.13 (three of his four major league seasons he had ERA over 6.50). On the other hand, Ox actually hit pretty well for a pitcher. He hit a home run (a grand slam) for the Cubs and batted .429. Teammates on that 1947 Cubs team included both players who were shot by women during a season… Eddie Waitkus and Billy Jurges. (Waitkus wouldn't be shot for another two years). The 1947 Cubs were interesting, but they were bad. They finished in 6th place with a 69-85 record.

Wade Miller 1976– (Cubs 2006-2007)

The former 16-game winner (for the Astros) was coming off an arm injury when the Cubs gave him a chance to win the 5th starter job. Unfortunately for Miller, he was a shell of his former self. He started eight games for the Cubs over two seasons and didn't win a single game.

Ward Miller 1884–1958 (Cubs 1912-1913)

Miller had not one, but two great nicknames. He was called "Windy" and "Grump" by his teammates. Grump was a fourth outfielder for the Cubs, backing up Frank Schulte, Tommy Leach, and Jimmy Sheckard. He hit over .300 in his first season with the Cubs, but slumped to .236 the following year. After the 1913 season, he jumped to the Federal League.

Alec Mills 1991– (Cubs 2018)

The Cubs acquired Mills in a trade with the Royals before the 2018 season, but he didn't make his debut with the big league club until the closing months of the 2018 season. Mills came up as a spot starter, and pitched so well he stayed on the roster. In seven appearances he posted a 2.49 ERA.

George Milstead 1903–1977 (Cubs 1924-1926)

The Texas-born lefty was nicknamed "Cowboy" by his teammates. Cowboy pitched mainly out of the bullpen in his three seasons in Chicago — his only years in the big leagues. He won three games and registered a 4.16 ERA in 106 lifetime innings. Cowboy may have had a short big league career, but he pitched in the minor leagues for 25 years. Milstead was 47 years old when he finally retired after pitching in four different decades (20s, 30s, 40s, 50s).

Paul Minner 1923–2006 (1951-1957)

The big 6'4 pitcher was nicknamed Lefty, and he pitched for the Cubs for seven seasons. Just like every ballplayer named Lefty, Minner was a left-handed pitcher. He was big and strong, and had a couple of very respectable years for the Cubs, including 1952 when he was 14-9. It's true he was 17 games under .500 in his other six years, but those were some unbelievably lousy teams. His ERA was always respectable.

Fred Mitchell 1878–1970 (Cubs manager 1917-1920)

Mitchell led the 1918 Cubs to the National League pennant during the only war-shortened season in big league history. He was also the team president that year. However, the following year the Cubs got off to a slow start and Mitchell was relieved of his president title when owner William Wrigley promoted William Veeck Sr. The following year Mitchell was gone as manager too. He later managed the Boston Braves.

Mike Mitchell 1879–1961 (Cubs 1913)

The Cubs traded their Hall of Famer Joe Tinker to the Reds to get Mitchell. He was a speedy outfielder who hit tons of triples (88 in six seasons) and stole lots of bases (165 in six seasons) with the Reds. Not so much with the Cubs. He was cut loose by the Cubs before the season was over.

Sergio Mitre 1981 -(Cubs 2003-2005)

Sergio was one of the better starting pitchers in the Cubs organization at a time when they had a stacked pitching rotation. Luckily for him, the Cubs pitchers kept getting injured. He started 18 games over three seasons, and didn't have a tremendous amount of success, so the Cubs included him in the trade that landed Juan Pierre. Sergio stayed in the majors until 2011, and even pitched in the 2010 ALCS for the Yankees, but his lifetime record is 13-30.

George Mitterwald 1945—(Cubs 1974-1977)

While the Cubs were surging toward their 1945 National League pennant, future Cubs catcher George Mitterwald was born in California. Acquired in a trade for Randy Hundley in 1974, George hit 26 home runs for the Cubs. Granted, that was in four full seasons, but still. Mitterwald still holds the Cubs record for most total bases in a single game. He got 14 on April 17, 1974.

Bill Moisan 1925—2010 (Cubs 1953)

Moisan's Cubs career lasted exactly eight days. He made three appearances between September 17 and September 25, 1953. Even though he only pitched five innings and had a 5.40 ERA, it was the pinnacle of his long hard struggle. Moisan pitched ten long seasons in the minors. His roommate in the minors was future TV/movie star Chuck Connors.

José Molina 1975—(Cubs 1999)

Yes, that's right, the Cubs had a Molina. José was the middle brother of the big league catcher brother trio. He is a year younger than Bengie and seven years older than Yadier. José had a couple of career highlights, including winning a World Series with the Angels in 2002 and the Yankees in 2009, and hitting the last-ever homer at old Yankees Stadium. But he only had 21 plate appearances in a Cubs uniform, and was released by the team in 2000. The Cubs really called that one. He only played another 14 seasons in the big leagues.

Bob Molinaro 1950—(Cubs 1982)

He was a member of *Baseball Digest*'s all-rookie team with the White Sox in 1978, but by the time Bob Molinaro became a Cub in 1982 it was clear that he was merely a backup outfielder. In 66 at-bats for the Cubs he hit one home run, stole one base, drove in twelve runs, and hit a whopping .197.

Fritz Mollwitz 1890—1967 (Cubs 1913-1914, 1916)

Fritz was born in Germany and played in the big leagues during World War I — a time when Americans were being told that the Huns were eating babies. He certainly got his fair share of grief (you can't hide when your name is Fritz). Mollwitz was a backup first baseman for the Cubs. He didn't get a lot of playing time, but later had a very good season with the Pirates in 1918. His native country may have lost the war that year, but Fritz stole more than 20 bases as Pittsburgh's starting first baseman.

Historical note: On the day the Lusitania was sunk by a German U-boat killing nearly 1200 people, Fritz had one of his best days ever at the plate. He went 3 for 5 for the Reds and drove in four runs against Hippo Vaughn. The Cubs lost 9-2.

Rick Monday 1945—(Cubs 1972-1976)

Monday was a key member of the Cubs during the early-to-mid 70s. The former first overall pick in the draft cost the Cubs Kenny Holtzman to acquire him, but he was a rare combination of power and speed during his Cubs years, averaging over 20 homers a season out of the leadoff spot.

But that's not why he is remembered as a Cub. He's remembered for one particular day. He was patrolling center field for the Cubs against the Los Angeles Dodgers in Dodgers stadium on April 25, 1976 when two protesters came out on the field with an American flag, some lighter fluid, and some matches. Their plan was to set the American flag on fire. Their mistake was to do it within running distance of former United States Marine Reservist Rick Monday. While they were trying to set it on fire, Monday ran up to them and snatched the flag away just in time. Rick then ran it all the way over to the dugout to protect it. The crowd erupted into a spontaneous singing of the song "God Bless America," the protestors were arrested and escorted out of the ballpark, and the next time Monday came up to bat — and mind you this was in an opposing team's ballpark — the scoreboard flashed the following message to him: "Rick Monday...you made a great play." The following year the Dodgers acquired Monday in the trade that brought Bill Buckner and Iván de Jesus to the Cubs.

Craig Monroe 1977 – (Cubs 2007)

The Cubs acquired Monroe from the Tigers to help them down the stretch during their division-winning season of 2007. He had been a key contributor to the Tigers' World Series team the previous year, but he fizzled in Chicago, hitting only .204. Craig didn't make the postseason roster. Two bits of trivia about Monroe: his mother is named "Marilyn Monroe" (no relation to you know who), and his cousin is former Bears defensive back Nathan Vasher.

Luis Montanez 1981 – (Cubs 2011)

Montanez was the third overall pick in the 2000 draft, but he moved very slowly through the Cubs minor league system. So slowly that they eventually gave up on him. Montanez kept working at it, however, and finally made it to the big leagues in 2008 with the Baltimore Orioles. He was a reserve outfielder for them, and did well in limited action his rookie season, hitting .295. The Cubs eventually reacquired him before the 2011 season, and Montanez played his last big league season with the Cubs. Don't be too upset with the Cubs. 17 of the players picked in that first round never made it to the big leagues. Of course, a few of them that did (Adam Wainwright, Chase Utley, Rocco Baldelli) sure would have looked nice in a Cubs uniform.

Miguel Montero 1983 – (Cubs 2015-2017)

The Cubs signed the two-time All-Star catcher (with Arizona) as a free agent before the 2015 season. They brought the Venezuelan in because of his toughness, his renowned ability to frame pitches, and his left-handed bat. He served as the Cubs primary catcher and contributed 15 homers. His handling of the staff was excellent, but he also had trouble blocking low pitches in the playoffs, which led to a few crucial runs scoring against the Cubs in the NLCS in 2015. 2016 was a much rougher season for Miguel. He hit only .216 and lost his starting job to rookie Willson Contreras. On the other hand, Montero also clubbed one of the most dramatic homers in Cubs history — a grand slam in Game 1 of the NLCS. In 2017 Montero bristled at his diminishing role. When he blamed his lack of success at throwing out runners on Jake Arietta's slow delivery, the Cubs let him go. He finished the season with Toronto.

Mike Montgomery 1989 – (Cubs 2016-present)

The Cubs picked up Montgomery midseason from the Seattle Mariners to help fill a hole in the bullpen. They gave up a few good prospects for him too, including the highly-touted Dan Vogelbach. Mike wasn't thrilled about the trade at first, and his performance showed it. But in the home stretch of the season he went into the starting rotation and pitched well. In the playoffs he was one of the only relievers Joe Maddon trusted. When the Cubs finally won their first World Series in 108 years, Mike Montgomery was the pitcher on the mound. It was his first career save. In 2017 Montgomery was given a shot at the rotation when other pitchers (Lester, Hendricks) were injured. He responded very well in that role. Unfortunately, he didn't respond as well in the playoffs when he was back in his relief role. He gave up 14 hits (including 3 HRs) and walked four more in only 4 1/3 innings pitched. In 2018, Mike became a part of the starting rotation again after the injury to Darvish and the ineffectiveness of Chatwood. He performed quite well in that role, posting a 3.99 ERA in 19 starts.

Al Montreuil 1943 – 2008 (Cubs 1972)

The Louisiana native was a September call-up for the Cubs in 1972. He was 29 years old at the time, and it was his only chance at the big leagues. The second baseman got one hit in eleven at-bats. He played twelve seasons in the minors. After his playing career he retired to his native Louisiana and became a realtor.

George Moolic 1867 – 1915 (White Stockings 1886)

George had one of the greatest nicknames in Cubs history. His teammates called him Prunes. He was a 19-year-old backup catcher and outfielder for the 1886 National League champs, but he didn't make much of a contribution to the team. He hit only .143 in 56 at-bats. That was the full extent of his big league career. Prunes may not have lasted long, but he could always say that he played on one of the most star-studded teams in Major League history. Among his teammates: Hall of Famers Cap Anson, King Kelly, and John Clarkson, plus stars in their day like Ned Williamson, George Gore, Jimmy Ryan, and Silver Flint. Oh, and the most famous of them all, future evangelist Billy Sunday. Prunes got a bloody nose in 1915 at the age of 47. Doctors couldn't stop the bleeding, and after three weeks, he passed away. Official cause of death: nasal hemorrhage.

Charley Moore 1884–1970 (Cubs 1912)

The Indiana boy appeared in five games for the Cubs at West Side Grounds in 1912. That was the only taste of the big-time in his big league career. He went 2 for 9 with a triple, and played a little second, short, and third. After his playing days, he became a minor league manager.

Donnie Moore 1954–1989 (Cubs 1975, 1977-1979)

The Cubs traded him before he reached his prime. Donnie became an All-Star closer with the California Angels, but he also gave up the home run that knocked them out of the playoffs in 1986. That moment tormented him, and he was out of baseball just a few years later. The depressed Donnie took his own life in 1989. He was only 35 years old.

Historical note: On the day that Patty Hearst was captured (1975), Donnie got a rare start for the Cubs and lost to the Mets 7-5. Rusty Staub homered for the Mets.

Earl Moore 1877–1961 (Cubs 1913)

His Cubs career wasn't anything special, but his nickname might have been the best ever. They called him "Steam Engine in Boots". Moore was as cocky as they came — at the time many people believed that he came up with the nickname himself. Even if he didn't, he certainly embraced it. "Moore carries the title of 'Steam Engine in Boots,'" noted the Washington Post, "and after his name in the hotel registers always appears the letters 'S.E.I.B.'" S.E.I.B was a two-time twenty-game winner, and had 150 career wins under his belt by the time he came to Chicago in 1913, but he was also near the end of his career. He pitched in 7 games with the Cubs, won 1, and had a 4.45 ERA. The following year, he switched over to the Federal League for his final season of baseball. He died in 1961 at the age of 84.

Johnny Moore 1902–1991 (Cubs 1928-1932, 1945)

Johnny was the starting center fielder for the 1932 NL Champion Cubs, but went 0 for 7 in the World Series and was traded in the offseason to the Cincinnati Reds for Babe Herman. By 1938, Moore was in the minor leagues, playing in the sunshine of Southern California. He played eight full seasons there, and figured his big league career was over, but in September of 1945 as the Cubs were heading toward the World Series, the big club called him up for one last shot. Johnny Moore appeared as a pinch hitter six times, got one hit (a single), and then gave up baseball for good. He was 43 years old.

Scott Moore 1983– (Cubs 2006-2007)

Moore was a third baseman who played a bit for the Cubs at the end of the 2006 season, and was part of the trade package sent to the Orioles in 2007 for Steve Trachsel. Moore had a cup of coffee with the Orioles and Astros, and hung up his spikes after the Cardinals cut him during 2015 spring training.

Jake Mooty 1912–1970 (Cubs 1940-1943)

He actually pitched pretty well as a swingman. He won 6 games 1940, with a 2.92 ERA, and 8 games in 1941, with a 3.35 ERA. He also saved 6 games for the Cubs during his time with them. He went to the Tigers after his Cubs stint. His final season in the big leagues was 1944.

Jerry Morales 1949– (Cubs 1974-1977, 1981-1983)

Jerry was acquired in the trade with the Padres that cost the Cubs fan favorite Glenn Beckert, but Morales had a very respectable Cubs career. For parts of two decades his reliable glove patrolled all three outfield positions for the Cubs. His best season in a Cubs uniform was probably 1977. Morales was named to the All-Star team that year, and even scored a run in the 1977 All-Star Game. But to many of his Chicago fans, Jerry Morales will remembered for his most impressive off-the-field accomplishment. In the era of the bushy mustache, Jerry managed to grow the bushiest.

Historical note: On the day that Gerald Ford pardoned Richard Nixon (1974), Jerry hit a grand slam for the Cubs.

Bill Moran 1869–1916 (Colts 1895)

Moran was the third catcher on the 1895 Cubs (then known as the Colts). The Joliet native caught 15 games that year, and managed to only hit .164. That undoubtedly contributed to the end of his time in Chicago. After playing a few more seasons in the minors, Moran retired to his home in Joliet, where he passed away in 1916 at the age of 46.

Pat Moran 1876–1924 (Cubs 1906-1909)

Moran was a member of two championship teams, the 1907 and 1908 Cubs, as their backup catcher. He later managed in the big leagues, and led the Cincinnati Reds to the World Series championship in 1919. It's not Moran's fault that the Reds' opponent, the Chicago Black Sox, threw the series.

Mickey Morandini 1966– (Cubs 1998-1999)

The Cubs acquired the Indiana University graduate for Doug Glanville before the 1998 season, and Morandini stabilized the infield and the lineup for the Cubs team that made the playoffs that season. He reached career highs in homers, RBI, and average in 1998, and led the league's second basemen in fielding percentage. It was the dandy little glove man's best season in the big leagues, but he'll probably be more remembered for his time with the Phillies. He was the starting second baseman for the Phillies team that went to the World Series in 1993. As a Phillie he also pulled the rarest trick in baseball history…an unassisted triple play by a second baseman. It was only the second one in baseball history.

Historical note: On the day that Tupac was shot in Las Vegas (1996), Mickey (then a Phillie) had the game-winning hit to defeat the Cubs. The hit came off Cubs starter Steve Trachsel.

Seth Morehead 1934–2006 (Cubs 1959-1960)

Moe, as he was called by his teammates, was a lefty reliever for some pretty bad Cubs teams. His record reflects that. During his time with the Cubs, he was 2-10. He also pitched for the Phillies and Braves during his big league career. After he retired from baseball, he went into banking.

Ramon Morel 1974–(Cubs 1997)

Morel appeared in three games for the Cubs at the end of the 1997 season. The right-handed Dominican reliever must have liked the number three. In those three games he pitched three innings, gave up three hits, walked three batters, and struck out three more. Guess what number he wore with the Cubs? 33.

Keith Moreland 1954–(Cubs 1982-1987)

He was a tough former Texas football player with the given name of Bobby Keith Moreland, but to his Cubs teammates, he was simply known as Zonk. One of the many former Phillies on the Dallas Green-led Cubs of the mid-80s, Moreland was the Cubs' leading batter (.302) in 1983 and had his best season in 1985 (.307, 106 RBI). Moreland started as a catcher, but was a liability on defense, so they tried him all over the field. He eventually became a respectable right fielder, but not before some embarrassing growing pains. Steve Goodman famously references his defensive shortcomings in his song "A Dying Cubs Fan Last Request." The lyrics contain the line: "Keith Moreland drops a routine fly ball." The Cubs moved Zonk to third base in 1987 to replace Ron Cey, and he struggled defensively again. On the other hand, he hit a career-high 27 homers that season. The Cubs traded him to San Diego for Goose Gossage in 1988.

Bobby Morgan 1926–(Cubs 1957-1958)

Morgan was a big league infielder, who played for several teams as a backup (Dodgers, Phillies, Cardinals) before joining the Cubs in 1957. The Cubs gave him the starting second baseman job that year, and he responded by batting a whopping .207. After his playing career he became a minor league manager and scout.

Mike Morgan 1959 – (Cubs 1992-1995)

For a few years Mike Morgan shared the record for playing on the most big league teams (he pitched for 12 different teams) until it was broken by Octavio Dotel. He pitched 22 seasons in the majors, making his debut as an 18-year-old. Morgan was an All-Star with the Dodgers, but he probably had the best season of his career with the Cubs. He won 16 games in 1992 and posted a sterling 2.55 ERA. The following year he won another 10 games. In 1994, Morgan was minding his own business in his backyard, when he slipped on a boulder near his swimming pool and was hurt badly enough to miss the first month of the season. The Cubs got rid of him shortly after the strike ended in 1995. They had no way of knowing that he would pitch another seven seasons. In 2001, at the age of 41, he finally won the World Series as a member of the Arizona Diamondbacks.

Vern Morgan 1928–1975 (Cubs 1955-1956)

Morgan was a third baseman, but with Randy Jackson firmly entrenched at that position, Vern was used primarily as a pinch hitter. He batted .225 in 77 plate appearances over two seasons. Morgan spent most of his playing career in the minors. He had over 5000 minor league at-bats. Ironically, he spent most of his coaching career in the majors, with the Minnesota Twins. He coached until he died in 1975, after his body rejected a kidney transplant. Vern was only 47 years old.

Moe Morhardt 1937– (Cubs 1961-1962)

Moe played with the Cubs briefly during College of Coaches era as a first baseman and pinch hitter. He batted .206 in 34 career at-bats. That was his only time in the big leagues. He went into coaching after his playing career.

George Moriarty 1885–1964 (Cubs 1903-1904)

Moriarty was just a local Chicago kid from the Back of the Yards when he got a one-game tryout at the end of the 1903 season with the Cubs. He went 0 for 5 and was visibly nervous, but the Cubs invited him to join the team the following year. He played another four games in 1904 before being shipped out. After he left the Cubs, however, Moriarty made his mark in the big leagues. His best stint was with the Detroit Tigers. He was their third baseman for five seasons, and displayed a terrific glove, leading the league in fielding percentage and assists. George was a fierce competitor on the field…but he was known for his friendly personality off the field. His brother Bill played briefly for the Reds.

Jim Moroney 1883–1929 (Cubs 1912)

The left-handed pitcher got three very brief tastes of the big-time with three different teams, the last of which was the Cubs. He appeared in ten games for the Cubs in 1912, the final season of Tinker to Evers to Chance, and posted an ERA of 4.56. He previously pitched for the Phillies (1910) and Braves (1906).

Ed Morris 1899–1932 (Cubs 1922)

Big Ed got his first shot at the big leagues with the Cubs in 1922. He wasn't quite ready for prime-time, posting an ERA over eight. It took him six more years to get another shot, but when he did (for the 1928 Red Sox), big Ed was ready. He became a 19-game winner.

Frank Morrissey 1876–1968 (Cubs 1902)

Morrissey was nicknamed "The Deacon" and pitched for the Cubs the last few weeks of the 1902 season. His win-loss record was nothing special (he was 1-3), but Frank did set a record in his short time in Chicago. He is the shortest player to ever pitch in the big leagues. Frank stood 5'4 tall.

Brandon Morrow 1984– (Cubs 2018-present)

The Cubs signed the accomplished reliever and turned him into something he had never been in his career — a full-time closer. Brandon was lights out in that role, saving 22 games and posting a 1.47 ERA before getting hurt. His absence at the end of the season was a major contributor to the Cubs early playoff exit.

Moose Moryn 1926–1996 (Cubs 1956-1960)

His real name was Walter. He was a big boy, 6'2, 205 pounds, which undoubtedly led to his nickname. Moose had a few good power years, knocking in 88 runs in 1957 and hitting 26 home runs in 1958. In '58 he had three homers in one game (5/30/58) against the Dodgers. Moryn was never exactly an acrobat in the field, but his outstanding shoestring catch with two outs in the ninth saved Don Cardwell's no-hitter against the Cardinals in 1960. That was probably the highlight of his Cubs career. While Moose was a fan favorite, his teammate Jim Brosnan claimed Moose was never very happy with the Cubs. In the book *Wrigleyville*, Brosnan is quoted saying Moryn was constantly complaining that he was traded away from the Dodgers, because he always wanted to play on a pennant winner. Needless to say, he never did with the Cubs.

Paul Moskau 1953– (Cubs 1983)

Moskau was in his seventh big league season (after stints with the Reds and Pirates) when he joined the Cubs in 1983. The right-handed pitcher started the season in the rotation, but posted a 6.75 ERA and won only three of his eight starts. The Cubs sent him to the minors in May and he never made it back to the big leagues.

Jim Mosolf 1905–1979 (Cubs 1933)

Mosolf was a backup outfielder for the 1933 Cubs — a team that featured the likes of KiKi Cuyler, Babe Herman, and Riggs Stephenson. He was a pretty good pinch hitter, hitting

.268 with a homer and nine RBI. It was his last shot at the big leagues. He previously had played for Pittsburgh.

Mal Moss 1905–1983 (Cubs 1930)

Mal couldn't have picked a worse year to pitch in the big leagues. Many people thought the ball was juiced that season — several hitting records were set that year including Hack Wilson's 56 homers and 191 RBI. The college boy (from University of Chicago) didn't have much of a chance. He registered an ERA of 6.27 in twelve appearances out of the bullpen. Mal's final outing for the Cubs was a disaster. He faced seven batters, and retired only two of them. He gave up four walks and a hit, and every batter he allowed on base scored. The Cubs lost 15-5 to the Brooklyn Dodgers in front of a sold out crowd. (Hack Wilson hit his 40th homer of the season that game).

Jason Motte 1982– (Cubs 2015)

The Cubs signed Motte before the 2015 season to provide some veteran leadership in the bullpen. Motte was coming off serious arm troubles he suffered in 2013 with the Cardinals. Just a few years earlier he had been their closer in the World Series. For a brief stint during the summer of 2015 he served as the Cubs closer, but he soon developed more arm problems. For the season he was 8-1, with 6 saves. After the season, he was granted his free agency and signed with the Rockies.

Jamie Moyer 1962– (Cubs 1986-1988)

He was known mainly as Digger Phelps' son-in-law when he came up with the Cubs in 1986. The soft-tossing lefty had some good moments in a Cubs uniform. He was an innings-eater who pitched more than 200 innings twice with the Cubs, and he won 28 games over his three-year tenure. He still holds the team record for most strikeouts in a game by a left-handed pitcher. Unfortunately for Chicago, he was included in the trade that brought Mitch Williams to the Cubs. All Moyer did was pitch another 22 seasons in the big leagues and win 269 games. He also became an All-Star and a World Series champ.

Phil Mudrock 1937– (Cubs 1963)

If you want to go back in time to see Phil Mudrock pitch, set the wayback machine to April 19, 1963 and go to Candlestick

Park in San Francisco. Mudrock came in to relieve Cubs ace Larry Jackson in the 8th inning. He faced only five batters in his big league career, but listen to who those batters were: Jim Davenport, Willie Mays, Willie McCovey, Orlando Cepeda, and Felipe Alou…Three Hall of Famers in a row (Mays, McCovey, Cepeda). He gave up a double to Davenport and a single to McCovey (who he later balked to third), but Mudrock got out of the inning. He watched from the bench in the top of the 9th as his teammates Ron Santo, Ernie Banks, and Lou Brock hit against Juan Marichal…Three Hall of Famers in a row against another Hall of Famer. Phil Mudrock's career was only one inning long, but it sure must have been memorable.

Bill Mueller 1971– (Cubs 2001-2002)

Mueller was a steady if unspectacular third baseman in the big leagues for over a decade, first with the Giants, and then with the Cubs. He was saving his best for last, however. The year after he left the Cubs he won the batting title with the Boston Red Sox. In his second season in Boston he was a key contributor to the Red Sox team that ended the 86-year World Series drought. He returned to the Cubs as a hitting coach in 2014.

Terry Mulholland 1963– (Cubs 1997-1999)

He was a mediocre starting pitcher for the Cubs in 1997, but Mulholland was a key contributor out of the bullpen during their Wild Card season of 1998. He was the main lefty setup man, and when Rod Beck was resting his tired arm, Terry filled in for him. He finished 14 games and recorded three saves. He also made a few key starts for the Cubs when their starters were injured. After the Cubs got off to a slow start in 1999, he was traded to the Atlanta Braves for a few prospects who didn't pan out. Mulholland probably appreciated the change of scenery. The Braves went to the World Series. In 20 career seasons in the big leagues, Mulholland won 124 games for the Giants, Phillies, Mariners, Pirates, Dodgers, Indians, Twins, Diamondbacks, and Cubs.

Eddie Mulligan 1894–1982 (Cubs 1915-1916)

Mulligan got his start in the big leagues with the Cubs during their last season at West Side Grounds, and played his last season with them during their first year at Wrigley. He was predominantly a backup third baseman for Heinie

Zimmerman, but he also played a little shortstop. Eddie later played for the White Sox and Pirates.

Jerry Mumphrey 1952– (Cubs 1986-1988)

Mumphrey was an excellent hitter. His lifetime batting average (with nearly 5000 career at-bats) was .289. He also hit very well with the Cubs, posting averages of .304 and .333 in his first two seasons. But Jerry wasn't really an everyday player anymore at that point in his career. He was essentially a fourth outfielder. In retrospect, he probably wasn't worth the price the Cubs paid to get him: future World Series hero Billy Hatcher.

Bob Muncrief 1916–1996 (Cubs 1949)

When the Cubs acquired Muncrief in 1949, he had already pitched in an All-Star Game (1944) and two World Series (1944 with the St. Louis Browns and 1948 with the Cleveland Indians). With the Cubs he didn't do much. He went 5-6 in 34 games out of the bullpen. He later pitched for the Yankees in their 1951 World Series season.

Joe Munson 1899–1991 (Cubs 1925-1926)

Joe's middle name was Napoleon, but this little guy didn't quite rise to general status in the big leagues. He played parts of two seasons as an extra outfielder for the Cubs. He hit .287 with 3 homers in 42 games.

Bobby Murcer 1946–2008 (Cubs 1977-1979)

It's not like the Cubs went looking for Bobby Murcer. They had one thing in mind after their disastrous 1976 season, and that was getting rid of disgruntled two-time batting champion Bill Madlock. Madlock was going to cost too much money; therefore he had to be traded. The Giants were willing to take the best hitter in the National League off the Cubs hands. In exchange, they gave up one-time superstar Bobby Murcer and third baseman Steve Ontiveros. It's not that the Cubs fans didn't like Murcer, who had one good year in 1977 when the Cubs had a nice little run to the begin the season, it's just that he wasn't nearly the player he once was, and he was by no means a fair trade for Bill Madlock. In his heyday with the Yankees, Murcer had been a five-time All-Star — considered to be the second coming of Mickey Mantle. In Chicago his power disappeared, never to return.

After he hit a whopping nine homers in nearly 500 at-bats in 1978, the Cubs sent him back where he belonged in 1979 — to the New York Yankees for a minor leaguer named Paul Semall. That same season Bill Madlock was the starting third baseman for the World Series champion Pirates. Madlock later won two more batting titles.

Historical note: On the day Star Wars opened (1977), Bobby knocked in two runs to lead the Cubs to 7-3 win over the Expos.

Charles Murphy 1868–1931 (Cubs owner 1906-1914)

He bought the Cubs just as they were on the cusp of greatness, and managed to irritate, enrage, and dismantle the greatest dynasty Chicago baseball has ever known. After the Cubs went to the World Series for the fourth time in five years (1910), Charles Murphy began dismantling the team (beginning with a contract dispute with Johnny Kling). He later got rid of Frank Chance (while he was in the hospital for brain surgery), Johnny Evers (who went on to win another World Series with the Braves), and Joe Tinker (who returned after Murphy was gone). Murphy also ran off Mordecai Brown and Orval Overall in contract disputes. But maybe his worst sin was that he let West Side Grounds deteriorate so badly that fans feared for their lives in that wooden ballpark. The city threatened to condemn it, but Murphy stubbornly refused to lay out the money to improve it or build a new stadium. Murphy became so despised that his fellow National League owners ran him out of the game in 1914. Murphy's partner while he was the owner of the Cubs was the president's brother — Charles Taft—and though Taft was technically the owner between 1914-1916, Murphy still called the shots while he was technically no longer running things. It wasn't until Charles Weeghman took over in 1916 that Murphy was finally pushed out of the picture.

Daniel Murphy 1985–(Cubs 2018)

The Cubs acquired the three time All-Star from the Nationals after Washington fell out of the playoff race. Murphy started out strong but petered out at the end of the season. He never quite rediscovered the magic he had as a Cubs opponent in the 2015 NLCS when he almost single-handedly knocked the Cubs out of the playoffs.

Danny Murphy 1942 – (Cubs 1960-1962)

Murphy came up with the Cubs as an outfielder and was a little overmatched as a batter. He hit only .177. So, he went back down to the minors and became a pitcher. At the end of the 60s, he made it back up to the big leagues as a pitcher with the Chicago White Sox.

Donnie Murphy 1983 – (Cubs 2013)

The journeyman infielder had been bouncing around the big leagues off and on for nine years before he arrived in Chicago, when suddenly out of nowhere, he found his power stroke. In just 149 at-bats, Murphy hit 11 homers. During the following spring training, the Cubs released him. He had one more cup of coffee in 2014 with the Rangers.

Calvin Murray 1971 – (Cubs 2004)

Calvin was an outfielder who played for the Giants and Rangers before coming to the Cubs for the last gasp of his big league career. He appeared in only eleven games, mostly as a late inning defensive replacement. He was a great fielding center fielder (leading the league in range in 2001), but his lifetime batting average was only .231.

Jim Murray 1878 – 1945 (1902 Orphans)

Murray got 50 at-bats with Chicago in 1902, and then was stuck in the minors for years. He re-emerged with the St. Louis Browns in 1911. He was an outfielder.

Red Murray 1884 – 1958 (Cubs 1915)

Red played for the Cubs in their final season at West Side Grounds. By that time, he was just a backup outfielder. His glory days were with the Giants (1909-1914). During those years he was considered the best outfielder in baseball. The April 1924 issue of *Baseball Magazine* says: "His throwing arm was the best ever, his ground covering ability and sureness of eye were classic. Furthermore, he was remarkably fast as a baserunner, and a noted batter as well." Red was on the 1910 Giants team that lost to the Cubs and inspired the poem "Baseball's Sad Lexicon". His manager on the Cubs was former Giants teammate Roger Bresnahan.

Tony Murray 1904 – 1974 (Cubs 1923)

Murray was a local Chicago boy who played the last two games of the 1923 season for the Cubs at the tender age of 19. He went 1 for 4. In his first game he played right and left field, and got his only career hit against Cardinal pitcher Eddie Dyer. He filled in for starting center fielder Jigger Statz in the last game of the year, and made two catches in the outfield, but he went 0-2 at the plate against Johnny Stuart. The Cubs lost that game too. Even though he only played in those two games, he could always claim that he shared the field with a Hall of Famer (Gabby Hartnett). Murray became an attorney after his playing career ended. He died in 1974 at the age of 69, and is buried in the same cemetery as his old teammate Gabby Hartnett (All Saints Cemetery in Des Plaines).

Matt Murton 1981 – (Cubs 2005-2008)

Murton was acquired in the trade that also brought Nomar to the Cubs in 2004. He had a few pretty good seasons, hitting .321 and .297 in his first two years with the club. He didn't however, quite have the pop the Cubs were looking for from a corner infielder. Early in the 2008 season he was part of the package (along with future superstar Josh Donaldson) that was needed to acquire Rich Harden from the Oakland A's. Murton later went to Japan and starred there for six seasons. He came back to the Cubs and tried to make their roster in 2016, but was cut in spring training. He was hired by the Cubs front office in 2018. He still shares the Cubs record for most doubles in a game with four (2006).

Billy Myers 1910 – 1995 (Cubs 1941)

Myers had been the starting shortstop of the Reds for the previous six seasons before he joined the Cubs, and had just driven in the winning run in Game 7 of the 1940 World Series. But Billy couldn't crack the starting lineup in Chicago. In fact, he spent most of 1941 in the minors, and only appeared in 24 games with the Cubs.

Randy Myers 1962 – (Cubs 1993-1995)

Randy had a very good stretch with the Cubs in the 90s. He set the Cubs save record with 53 saves in 1993, and was an All-Star in both 1994 and 1995. Despite Randy's 100+ save career in Chicago, he's probably best remembered for two incidents. The first one was the day the Cubs staged Randy Myers Day. 10,000 Randy Myers posters were handed out to the fans as they arrived, and nearly all 10,000 of them came raining onto the field after Randy blew the save that day. The other incident happened during one of Randy's rare bad stretches. A fan came running onto the field to "fight" Randy for blowing a save. Randy clocked him with one punch. (That fan later sold the "It can happen" signs in 2008.)

Richie Myers 1930–2011 (Cubs 1956)
Myers was a local boy (Elk Grove High School) who made the big leagues thanks to his speed. The Cubs used him as a pinch runner during the first month of the 1956 season. He scored one run. After the Cubs released him, Richie hung up his spikes. He was 26 years old and had already logged several years in the minors (as a shortstop mainly).

*Additional Entries...*If you check out the Every Cub Ever feature at www. justonebadcentury.com, you'll find several additional entries, including celebrity Cubs fans, writers, and bloggers. Under the letter M, you'll discover the Marx Brothers, the Murray Brothers, actor Joe Mantegna, singer/ songwriter Michael McDermott (all big Cubs fans), plus "The Natural" author Bernard Malamud. There's also a great story about a Cubs minor leaguer Lee Meyers, who never made the big leagues, but did make his mark with the ladies in Hollywood.

CHAPTER FOURTEEN

N

The starting lineup for your Chicago Cubs starting with the letter N...

C—Tom Nagle, 19th Centurion
1B—Phil Nevin, #1 Pick in the Draft
2B—Hugh Nichol, Limey
SS—Paul Noce, Shawon-O-Backup
3B—Jose Nieves, '98 Cub
LF—Lou Novikoff, Mad Russian
CF—Bill North, World Series Champ
RF—Bill Nicholson, Feared Slugger
Bench—Xavier Nady, Big X
SP—Jamie Navarro, 15-game Winner
SP—Joe Niekro, the Other Niekro
SP—Fred Norman, World Series Champ
SP—Rich Nye, Slingin' Veterinarian
RP—Joe Nathan, Recovering Closer

Chris Nabholz 1967– (Cubs 1995)

Like many players, Nabholz finished his career with the Cubs, and he didn't go down in a blaze of glory. He had a 5.40 ERA in 34 appearances. Chris had a few good seasons with the Expos before he came to town. He also pitched for the Red Sox and Indians.

Xavier Nady 1978– (Cubs 2010)

The well-traveled veteran had played for the Padres, Mets, Yankees, and Pirates before coming to Chicago as a free agent signing in 2010. The Cubs hoped he could start at an outfield position or first base for them, but Nady was often hurt, and he never quite put it together. In over 300 at-bats, he managed to hit only six homers. The Cubs allowed him to leave after the season and he has since played for the Diamondbacks, Nationals, Giants, and Padres. His 2012 Giants team won the World Series.

Tom Nagle 1865–1946 (Colts 1890-1891)

Nagle Avenue on Chicago's Northwest Side is not named after Tom. He was a catcher/outfielder who played for the Cubs (then known as the Colts) for two seasons in the early 1890s. The Milwaukee native hit .249 in just under 50 games.

Buddy Napier 1889–1968 (Cubs 1918)

Napier was essentially a career minor leaguer (12 seasons) who got a few shots at the big leagues along the way. Buddy pitched in exactly one game in a Cubs uniform for the 1918 pennant winners. He came in relief early in the game and pitched the rest of the game (6.2 innings). Buddy gave up 10 hits and four runs in a Cubs loss. He later got a more extended chance in the big leagues with the Reds.

Joe Nathan 1974– (Cubs 2016)

Nathan was a six-time All-Star closer coming off an injury when the Cubs took a flyer on him during a period of bullpen injuries. Despite his advancing age (42), Nathan actually pitched well in his short stint with the Cubs. Unfortunately for him, when the injured players returned there wasn't a roster spot left for him, and the Cubs chose to release him. He finished the season with the Giants.

Joey Nation 1978– (Cubs 2000)

Nation was one of the prospects the Cubs got in return from the Atlanta Braves for Jose Hernandez and Terry Mulholland. Apparently the Cubs scouts weren't quite as sophisticated then as they are now. Nation may have been a second round draft choice of the Braves, but the left-handed pitcher never had a good season in the minors, let alone the big leagues. In his one taste of the big-time with the Cubs, he was lit up in two starts. The other prospects in that trade, Ruben Quevedo and Micah Bowie, were also lit up when they came to the big leagues.

*Native American Cubs...*The following Native-Americans have played for the Cubs... Virgil Cheeves, Ben Tincup, Vallie Eaves, and Cal McLish.

Dioner Navarro 1984– (Cubs 2013)

He only played one season with the Cubs as their backup catcher, but Navarro hit several dramatic game-winning home runs, and provided the only pop off the bench that season for the Cubs. One day he hit three homers in a game.

Efren Navarro 1986–(Cubs 2018)

Navarro came up ever so briefly in the summer of 2018 and got into two games as a first baseman when Rizzo was hurt. The Cubs released him in June.

Jaime Navarro 1967–(Cubs 1995-1996)

When the Cubs signed Navarro as a free agent, it was considered a very bad move by many of the scribes in Chicago. Navarro proved them wrong by posting two outstanding seasons (14 and 15 wins) before signing with the White Sox. That's where he imploded. Could it have worked out any better than that? Navarro's dad Julio was also a big league pitcher. Jaime went on to become the bullpen coach for the Seattle Mariners.

Historical note: On the day the U.S. Women's National Soccer Team won the 1999 World Cup. the Cubs beat the Sox and Jamie Navarro 10-2. Brandi Chastain tore off her shirt in celebration.

Thomas Neal 1987– (Cubs 2013)

Neal was an outfielder in the New York Yankees minor league system that had been released when the Cubs took a chance on him at the end of the 2013 season. He got four chances to hit for the Cubs, and got zero hits. The Cubs released him after the season. He has since become a hitting coach in the San Francisco Giants farm system.

Tom Needham 1879–1926 (Cubs 1909-1914)

Needham was born in Ireland and came to this country as a youngster. Deerfoot, as he was called, joined the Cubs in the midst of their historic run to be the backup catcher to Johnny Kling, and then Jimmy Archer. He even got to bat in the 1910 World Series against the A's. Deerfoot was known as a good defensive player, but never hit well (career average was .209). He played six seasons with the Cubs, but didn't quite last long enough to play in the new ballpark. In his last few years with the Cubs Needham was a player/coach. He later became the pitching coach for the White Sox.

Cal Neeman 1929–2015 (Cubs 1957-1960)

Cal was the starting catcher for the Cubs in 1957 and hit 10 homers, but he couldn't hold on to that spot and spent the rest of his career as a backup. In May of 1960 he was part of the trade that sent Tony Taylor to the Phillies in exchange for Don Cardwell and Ed Bouchee. He also played for the Indians and Senators in his seven-year big league career.

Art Nehf 1892–1960 (Cubs 1927-1929)

Nehf was a two-time 20-game winner and two-time World Series champ with the Giants before he came to the Cubs at the tail end of his career. He no longer had the stuff he had earlier in his career (he only struck out 79 batters in over 300 innings), but he did have a very good season in 1928, going 13-7 with a 2.65 ERA. He hung on for the 1929 season, and pitched (badly) in the World Series for the Cubs. Art was the pitcher who gave up the inside-the-park homer that Hack Wilson lost in the sun. That was his last hurrah in the big leagues.

Lynn Nelson 1905–1955 (Cubs 1930-1934)

Lynn was a pitcher who was known for his hitting — they called him "Line Drive" Nelson. Nelson had his best season as a pitcher with the Cubs in 1933, when he went 5-5 with a 3.21 ERA. His best season as a hitter came in 1937 (with the A's), when "Line Drive" hit four home runs. Unfortunately he was also prone to giving up the long ball. In 1939 he led the league with 27 homers allowed.

Dick Nen 1939–(Cubs 1968)

Nen backed up the aging Ernie Banks in 1968. Proving that age is relative, the younger Nen hit .181 with very little power (two homers), while Banks hit over 60 points higher with 32 homers. Nen also played for the Washington Senators and LA Dodgers in his six-year big league career. His son Rob later starred in the big leagues as a closer for the Marlins and Giants.

Phil Nevin 1971–(Cubs 2006)

Phil was a member of the Cubs for exactly two months, but during that time the former #1 overall pick in the draft did pretty well. He hit 12 homers filling in for the injured Derrek Lee. In his 12-year big league career he also played for the

Astros (who drafted him), Tigers, Angels, Padres, Rangers, and Twins. Phil hit over 200 career homers, and played every position on the field except shortstop, center field, and pitcher.

Joel Newkirk 1896–1966 (Cubs 1919-1920)

Sailor, as he was known by his teammates, was a right-handed pitcher who got an ever-so-brief sniff of the big leagues at the end of 1919 and beginning of 1920. He had three lifetime appearances and got lit up pretty heartily by the league. In 8.2 innings pitched, he allowed nineteen baserunners. After he gave up a homer to Cardinals pitcher Bill Sherdel, the Cubs sent Sailor back out to sea.

Charlie Newman 1868–1947 (Colts 1892)

The left fielder nicknamed "Decker" got a grand total of 62 plate appearances for the Cubs (then known as the Colts) in 1892, and never played in the big leagues again. Charlie played minor league ball in the Midwest for most of the 1890s. After that he became a police chief in Wisconsin, before settling out west in San Diego.

Ray Newman 1945–(Cubs 1971)

Newman was a big right-hander (6'5) who pitched for the Cubs in 1971. He got into thirty games and pitched respectably (3.52 ERA), but is remembered more for the way he got to work every day. He rode his bike. Leo Durocher thought he was nuts, but put up with it until Newman got into a bike accident on a day he supposed to pitch. He was shipped off to Milwaukee before the 1972 season

Bobo Newsom 1907–1962 (Cubs 1932)

His real name was Louis Norman Newsom but everyone called him Bobo…including himself. Bobo was one of the first players who constantly referred to himself in the third person. "I think I'm going to win this one for Bobo." He actually got his nickname Bobo because that was what he called most of his teammates. He was rarely around long enough to learn their names — Bobo played for eight different teams. He had a distinguished twenty-season major league career, was a four time All-Star, three-time 20-game winner, a World Series champion, and won more than 200 games in his career, but none of those came for the Cubs.

Bobo only pitched in one inning of one game for Chicago during the 1932 season. He didn't resurface in the majors until 1934 (with the St. Louis Browns), but then pitched in the big leagues until 1953.

> Cubs players have had some great nicknames over the years. Among players starting with the letter N, you'll find nicknames Like Bobo, Decker, Deerfoot, Line Drive, Mad Russian, Sailor, and Swish.

Art Nichols 1871–1945 (Orphans 1898-1900)

Nichols was a utility man for the Cubs (then known as the Orphans) for a few seasons, but he never really got extensive playing time. He played 39 games in three seasons as a catcher, first baseman, and outfielder. He later played with the Cardinals.

Dolan Nichols 1930–1989 (Cubs 1958)

Nick, as he was called by his teammates, was a reliever for the 1958 Cubs. In 24 appearances, he earned one save. The Cubs sent him back down to the minors by mid-season, and although he got another shot in September after the rosters were expanded, that was the extent of his big league career. Nichols pitched in the minors for a few more years before retiring at the age of 30.

Bill Nicholson 1914–1996 (Cubs 1939-1948)

Though he is known to history by his nickname Swish, Cubs fans didn't call him that. Brooklyn Dodgers fans did. The big left-handed hitter had a routine when he came up to bat. He would swing his bat across the plate several times after stepping in to face an opposing pitcher. Obnoxious Dodgers fans would yell, "Swish, swish, swish" in unison with each of his practice swings. He may have struck out a lot, but he was truly a feared slugger. One time he was even intentionally walked with the bases loaded. Swish led the league in homers in '43 and '44. Nicholson was also part of the '45 pennant team, but his power started to go that year. He wouldn't know it for a few more years, but he was losing his eyesight because he was diabetic. It's ironic Nicholson starred during the war years, because his lifelong dream was to serve as a naval officer. He was crushed when he was rejected for service because he was color-blind. He is one of only eight Cubs in history to hit more than 200 homers in a Cubs uniform.

George Nicol 1870–1924 (Colts 1891)

He came up with the St. Louis Browns the year before he joined the Cubs (then known as the Colts), and it's hard to imagine a better start to a career. In his first start, he threw a no-hitter. In his second start, he gave up one hit. But the 19-year-old was hit hard in his third start, and never came close to those dizzying heights again. With the Cubs he pitched in three games and didn't win any of them. His final lifetime ERA is north of seven.

Hugh Nicol 1858–1921 (White Stockings 1881-1882)

Hugh was born in the UK, and came to America as a youngster. He played two seasons for the Cubs (then known as the White Stockings) as an outfielder and a second baseman. He wasn't a very good hitter in Chicago (.204 and .199), but both of those teams won the championship. He later played for St. Louis and Cincinnati. After his playing career, Hugh became the head coach at Purdue.

Joe Niekro 1944–2006 (Cubs 1967-1969)

His brother Phil was already a star pitcher for the Braves when Joe Niekro was drafted in the third round by the Cubs in 1966. In his rookie season in Chicago (1967), Joe won 10 games. He won 14 games for the Cubs in 1968, but manager Leo Durocher, never very good with young players, seemed to lose faith in him. Leo wasn't alone in that assessment. Niekro's ERA was a little high (it was a pitchers era) at 4.32, he was far from overpowering (only 65 strikeouts in 177 innings), and his control was a little shaky. When the Cubs had a chance to get veteran Dick Selma early in the 1969 season, they didn't hesitate to include Joe Niekro in the deal. Selma won ten games for the Cubs that season, and really connected with the Bleacher Bums. It looked like the Cubs had made a pretty good deal, even though Selma was traded away the following season. Niekro bounced around the bullpens of Detroit and Atlanta for a while, never really making much of a name for himself. But while he was with the Braves, he finally perfected the knuckleball that had been the secret to his brother's success, and his career really took

off. The Astros put him in their rotation in 1977, and for the next eight seasons he averaged more than 15 wins a year, including back-to-back 20 win seasons in 1979 and 1980. By the time his career was over after the 1988 season, Joe Niekro had 221 career victories. Only 24 of those came for the team that drafted him and brought him to the majors: the Chicago Cubs.

Historical note: On the day actress Jayne Mansfield died in a car crash (1967), Niekro was on the mound for the Cubs. He beat the Pirates 4-3 at Wrigley Field.

Jose Nieves 1975– (Cubs 1998-2000)

Nieves was a backup infielder for three seasons, backing up Mickey Morandini and Eric Young at second base, Jose Hernandez and Ricky Gutierrez at shortstop, and Gary Gaetti and Willie Greene at third base. He later also played for the Angels.

> ***Nineteenth Century Cubs...*** Four of the top ten hits leaders in the 19th century played for Chicago, including the only one with more than 3000 hits – Cap Anson. Others on the list are Jimmy Ryan, Hugh Duffy, and George Van Haltren. Add Ross Barnes to the list of great hitters, he hit over .400 (and so did Cap Anson). No Cub has hit over .400 in the modern era (after 1900).

Al Nipper 1959– (Cubs 1988)

Sure the Cubs gave up a Hall of Fame relief pitcher (Lee Smith) to get him, and sure Al only had 2 wins and walked more batters than he struck out in 1988, but there's no getting around the fact that Nipper had a killer mustache. That's just a fact. The Cubs released him during spring training of 1989. Nipper pitched in the 1986 World Series for the Red Sox.

Paul Noce 1959– (Cubs 1987)

Noce was a middle infielder who was called into service in 1987 mainly because of an injury to shortstop Shawon Dunston. He got the most extensive playing time of his big league career (his only season with the Cubs), hitting .228 in nearly 200 plate appearances. He spent the next few seasons in the minors before reemerging briefly with the Reds in 1991. He became a college and minor league coach/manager after his playing days.

Dickie Noles 1956 – (Cubs 1982-1984, 1987)

Dickie was one of Dallas Green's favorites, and the Cubs got him from the Phillies along with Keith Moreland shortly after Green arrived in Chicago. Noles would have gotten along great with the 1930 Cubs, Hack Wilson and Pat Malone. He was a drinker and a brawler, and was arrested after doing both in Cincinnati in April 1983. Dickie not only got into a fight with another tavern patron, he fought the bouncer, and he fought the cop who came to arrest him. Noles had an obvious alcohol problem, but unlike the Cubs from the 30s, Noles got treatment. He served 14 days of his 30-day sentence in alcohol rehab. Green traded Dickie the next season for two minor leaguers who never made it to the majors, but Dallas always had a soft spot for the former Phillie. In 1987 he signed him again. In one of the most unusual moves in baseball history, Noles was traded later that same season to the Tigers for a player to be named later. That player turned out to be Dickie Noles himself. Dickie remains one of only three players in major league history to be traded for himself.

Pete Noonan 1881 – 1965 (Cubs 1906)

Pete played five games for the winningest team in baseball history (the 1906 Cubs) before being traded midseason for pitcher Jack Taylor. The catcher/first baseman played the rest of his career for the St. Louis Cardinals. With the Cubs he played only first base.

Wayne Nordhagen 1948 – (Cubs 1983)

Wayne had his biggest success on the south side of Chicago as a member of the White Sox. He hit over .300 for the South Side Hitmen and slugged 15 homers one year. By the time he came to the north side, he had made stops in Toronto and Pittsburgh and didn't have much left in the tank. His final big league at-bats came for the Cubs in 1983. He hit .143 in 35 at-bats before the Cubs released him. Nordhagen's nephew is former Red Sox first baseman Kevin Millar.

Irv Noren 1924 – (Cubs 1959-1960)

Noren had a good big league career that included an All-Star

appearance with the Yankees in 1954. By the time he came to the Cubs in 1959, Irv was mostly a backup outfielder. He hit over .300 in his first season in Chicago, but got off to a slow start in 1960 and was let go in May. He finished the year with the Dodgers and retired after the season. Irv was a three-time World Series champion as a player with the Yankees, and a two-time champ with Oakland A's as a coach.

Fred Norman 1942 – (Cubs 1964-1967)

Fred was one of their bright young prospects in the mid-60s, but the 5'8 screwball expert was traded to the Dodgers in 1967. Norman finally came into his own in the 1970s with the Cincinnati Reds. He was part of the rotation for two consecutive World Series champions (1975, 1976); the immortal Big Red Machine. In his big league career Fred Norman won 104 games. Zero of those came for the Chicago Cubs.

Bill North 1948 – (Cubs 1971-1972)

It isn't that difficult to understand what the Cubs were thinking on November 21, 1972. They were coming off four consecutive seasons where the pitching faltered at the end of the year. Cubs management believed that a better bullpen would save their starters, and in turn, preserve their chances to compete into September. Meanwhile, they had a speedster named Billy North just promoted from their minor league system and nowhere to play him. With Billy Williams entrenched in left field, Jose Cardenal in right, and former #1 draft choice Rick Monday in center field, the Cubs thought they could afford to give up their talented young center fielder Billy North. So they traded another potential superstar speedster. Unlike Lou Brock, who would torment the Cubs for a full decade, Billy North was traded somewhere he couldn't hurt them: Oakland. The only problem with this scenario, of course, is what they got in return. The Cubs traded one of their rare home-grown position players to the A's for Bob Locker, a soon-to-be washed up 35-year-old relief pitcher. North became the leadoff hitter for the World Series champs, igniting one of the best lineups in baseball history.

Ron Northey 1920 – 1971 (Cubs 1950, 1952)

Ron played 12 seasons in the big leagues and had a couple of very good seasons for the Phillies (before the war) and the Cardinals before joining the Cubs. The Cubs acquired him in June 1954 for Bob Scheffing. He played quite a bit of right field the second half of that season, splitting time with Bob Borkowski. Northey went into coaching after his playing days. He was on Danny Murtaugh's staff in Pittsburgh when he died unexpectedly in 1970 at the age of 50.

Phil Norton 1976–(Cubs 2000-2003)

Norton was a 10th round draft choice of the Cubs in 1996, who scratched and clawed his way up to the big leagues by the fall of 2000. He appeared in two games for the Cubs and was hit pretty hard. The following year he got hurt in the minors, and missed the entire following season because of an arm injury, but he returned to get one last cup of coffee with the Cubs in 2003. Phil still holds a Cubs record. On August 8th, 2000, Norton allowed four home runs in one inning against the Dodgers.

James Norwood 1993–(Cubs 2018)

Norwood came up as a 24-year-old rookie and got into eleven games for the Cubs. The right-handed reliever posted a 4.09 ERA, but struggled a bit. He allowed nearly two baserunners an inning and didn't make the postseason roster.

Don Nottebart 1936–2007 (Cubs 1969)

Don pitched for five teams and even had a no-hitter in 1963 for the Colt 45s, but Nottebart only got into 16 games with the Cubs in 1969. He tore a muscle in his arm, and his career was over. The last hitter he faced in his big league career was Roberto Clemente. After his playing career he owned a carpet and flooring business in Houston.

Lou Novikoff 1915–1970 (Cubs 1941-1944)

Lou was known as "The Mad Russian". He was born to Russian immigrant parents in Arizona, so the second half of his nickname is obvious. The "mad" part came from his eccentric proclivities. He had a colorful past before joining the Cubs, working as a harmonica player, a carnival strongman, and a striptease performer. The Mad Russian became a wartime Cubs fill-in (1941-1944) and an entertaining eccentric. He said he feared touching Wrigley's ivy-covered walls because he thought ivy was poisonous. He also claimed the foul lines were crooked. He once stole third with the bases loaded because, he said, "I got such a good jump on the pitcher." He had a pet Russian wolfhound, which he only fed caviar. Novikoff could hit (he hit .300 twice), but was a butcher in the outfield. The Phillies gave him one more shot in 1946, but that was it for his very colorful major league career.

Roberto Novoa 1979–(Cubs 2005-2006)

The Cubs acquired Roberto in the trade that sent Kyle Farnsworth to the Detroit Tigers. Novoa was a right-handed relief pitcher who was used pretty frequently by manager Dusty Baker in 2005 and 2006 (over 100 appearances). He was a big man with a lively arm, but he allowed too many baserunners to be effective in late inning situations. In his last season with the Cubs he also had trouble with the long ball. In 76 innings, he gave up 15 dingers. That turned out to be his last season in the big leagues as well. He hurt his shoulder in 2007.

Rube Novotney 1924–1987 (Cubs 1949)

Novotney was a University of Illinois product who got one short cup of coffee with the Cubs in 1949. He was a backup catcher who appeared in 22 games. He hit .269 in his limited appearances. Rube also played nine seasons in the minor leagues.

Jose Nunez 1964–(Cubs 1990)

Jose started his professional career in the American League with the Blue Jays, so he wasn't accustomed to batting. He was more than just a novice. He literally had no idea what he was doing. One time in spring training he forgot to take off his warmup jacket, then wore the helmet backwards like a catcher, and asked the catcher what pitch was coming. He got his first big league at-bat with the Cubs in 1990. It wasn't quite as embarrassing, but it certainly didn't lead to a hit. In his 15 big league at-bats, he got one hit and one walk. Of course, he was a pitcher, so he would forever be judged by his pitching performance. That didn't go much better. He appeared in 21 games for the Cubs, pitched 60.2 innings, and posted a whopping 6.53 ERA.

Rich Nye 1944–(Cubs 1966-1969)

The tall (6'4) right-hander's best season was 1967. He won

13 games for the Cubs (including seven complete games) while posting an ERA of 3.20. He remained in the Cubs rotation in 1968, although he only won 7 games. By his last Cubs season (1969), he was mostly used as a reliever. He later pitched for the Cardinals and the Expos. Nye was always one of the brightest players in baseball, and proved it after his playing career was over. He initially worked as a civil engineer, before going back to college (University of Illinois) and becoming a veterinarian.

Historical note: On the day Robert F. Kennedy was assassinated in Los Angeles (1968), Rich Nye was on the mound for the Cubs. Tom Seaver and the Mets beat him 4-2 at Wrigley Field.

> ***Additional Entries...***If you check out the Every Cub Ever feature at www. justonebadcentury.com, you'll find several additional entries, including celebrity Cubs fans, writers, and bloggers. Under the letter N, you'll discover the great comedian and Cubs fan Bob Newhart.

The starting lineup for your Chicago Cubs beginning with the letter O...

C—Bob O'Farrell, MVP
1B—Reggie Otero, 1945 Cub
2B—Nate Oliver, 1969 Cub
SS—Augie Ojeda, Crowd Favorite
3B—Steve Ontiveros, 1970s Mustache
LF—Jose Ortiz, Weak Link in the Lineup
CF—Barney Olsen, Wartime Cub
RF—Troy O'Leary, Non-Irishman
SP—Orval Overall, 1908 Ace
SP—Vern Olsen, Pre-War Starter
RP—Will Ohman, Well-Traveled Lefty

Mike O'Berry 1954– (Cubs 1980)

O'Berry was one of the backup catchers for the Cubs in 1980. They acquired him from the Boston Red Sox for Ted Sizemore. After the season the Cubs traded him to the Reds for relief pitcher Jay Howell. That would have been a great trade if the Cubs had held on to Howell. He went on to become an All-Star closer for the A's and Dodgers. O'Berry played five more years in the big leagues with the Yankees, Reds, Angels, and Expos.

John O'Brien 1866–1913 (Colts 1893)

The Canadian-born second baseman had one of the great nicknames on the Cubs (then known as the Colts). He was known as "Chewing Gum." Unfortunately for Chewing Gum, he played during the years before chewing gum magnate William Wrigley bought the team. O'Brien's entire Colts career lasted four days. He also played for the Pirates, Orioles, and Louisville, all before the turn of the century.

Pete O'Brien 1867–1937 (Colts 1890)

Pete was a 23-year-old backup second baseman on the Cubs (then known as the Colts). He hit .283 and played a respectable second base, but never played in the big leagues again.

Johnny O'Connor 1891–1982 (Cubs 1916)

If his name sounds Irish, there's a good reason for that. Johnny O'Connor was born in Ireland. He came to America and attended the University of Illinois. The catcher got one shot in the big leagues, and it wasn't on offense. He came in as a defensive replacement on September 16, 1916, but was replaced by Art Wilson before he got a chance to bat. The game was in Philadelphia, and the Cubs lost to Grover Cleveland Alexander (his 29th win of the season) and the Phillies, 6-3.

Hank O'Day 1859–1935 (Cubs manager 1914)

He was the umpire who made the most controversial call in baseball history…the play that became known as "The Merkle Boner." The NY Giants never forgave him for favoring the Cubs on that play, and were especially suspicious of him because he was born and raised in Chicago (although he played for the Giants in his playing days). In 1914, that call looked even more suspicious when Hank O'Day was hired by the Cubs to manage their team. Not only did they hire O'Day, they hired him to replace beloved Cub Johnny Evers, who owner Charles Murphy had run out of town. Evers spent the 1914 season managing (and playing for) the Boston Braves. The Braves went to the World Series. The Cubs finished in fourth place, 16 ½ games behind the Braves. O'Day's managing career with the Cubs lasted exactly one season. He went back to his original job…National League umpire. He remained in that job until 1927. He was recently (2013) elected into baseball's Hall of Fame (as an umpire).

Ken O'Dea 1913–1985 (Cubs 1935-1938)

Ken was primarily Gabby Hartnett's backup during his tenure with the Cubs. The Cubs were very good during those years, and O'Dea played an important role. He got some playing time in both the 1935 and the 1938 World Series for the Cubs, and responded with key hits in each series, including a homer off Hall of Famer Red Ruffing in 1938. After that series, O'Dea was traded to the Giants along with Billy Jurges and Frank Demaree for Dick Bartell, Hank Leiber, and Gus Mancuso. He stayed in the big leagues until 1946, and won two World Series as a member of the St. Louis Cardinals (1942 and 1944).

Bob O'Farrell 1896–1988 (Cubs 1915-1925)

Bob was the starting catcher for the Cubs in the years before Gabby Hartnett took over the job. He was considered an outstanding defensive catcher, renowned for his toughness. One year O'Farrell suffered a skull fracture after wearing the wrong equipment and getting a foul ball to the face. By 1925 the Cubs thought his best days were behind him and they traded him to the Cardinals. All he did with St. Louis was win the MVP award and help lead them to their first World Series championship. The following year he was the player/manager and led the Cardinals to a second place finish. O'Farrell ended up playing 21 years in the big leagues.

Hal O'Hagan 1869–1913 (Orphans 1902)

Hal had a strange career. He had a cup of coffee in the big leagues with Washington in 1892, and then went back to the minor leagues for ten years. In 1902, he was suddenly in great demand by everyone in the big leagues again. He was a backup first baseman for several clubs, including the Cubs (then known as the Orphans). He started the season in Chicago, but also played for New York, Cleveland, and then New York again the same season. Hal hit only .184 that year. After his vagabond MLB travels in 1902, he went back to the minors for five more years. Just five years later, Hal passed away at the age of 43.

Troy O'Leary 1969– (Cubs 2003)

Troy played eleven seasons in the big leagues, and had a few very good seasons with the Boston Red Sox (over a hundred homers). The outfielder's final big league season came with the Cubs. He was one of the contributors to the division champion team of 2003, although he didn't make the final playoff roster.

Ryan O'Malley 1980– (Cubs 2006)

The downstate native (Springfield) pitched in the Cubs organization for most of the '00s, and although he was never exactly dominant in the minors, he did get one shot at glory in 2006. The 26-year-old got two starts in August and pitched fairly well. In his first start, things got emotional. Per Yahoo! News:

O'Malley is one of just eight pitchers since 2000 to throw at least eight innings with zero runs allowed in his major league debut. That is some rare air. "It was one of the better pitched games the Cubs had that year," Len Kasper said. "Just at the end, he hugged his dad and he had shaving cream all over his face, his dad had shaving cream on his face and he's crying. We got really emotional in the booth. Right when I signed off, Bob and I were basically crying. I've never ever experienced that before as a broadcaster and I don't know if I ever will again. That game, of the thousands I've called in my career, still stands out as one of my favorites." O'Malley spent the next two years in the minors before hanging up his spikes at the end of the 2008 season.

Emmett O'Neill 1918–1993 (Cubs 1946)

Not to be confused with Emmet O'Neal, the 34th governor of Alabama, the Cubs picked up the ballplayer Emmett O'Neill after the Red Sox dropped him in spring training. He made one scoreless appearance for the Cubs, but they released him shortly thereafter. The White Sox picked him up, and Emmett finished his career on the other side of Chicago.

Jack O'Neill 1873–1935 (Cubs 1904-1905)

Jack is part of the Irish-born O'Neill clan. Four brothers played in the big leagues, and Jack was the oldest brother. Jack was a catcher for the Cubs for two seasons, but also played for St. Louis and Boston. Jim played all over the field for the Senators, Mike pitched for the Cardinals, and Steve was a catcher for the Indians. Steve later went on to manage the Tigers in the 1945 World Series against the Cubs. Jack wasn't conflicted during that series. He had already been dead for ten years.

Cubs players have had some great nicknames over the years. Among players starting with the letter O, you'll find nicknames like Chewing Gum, Pee Wee, and Tiny.

Will Ohman 1977– (Cubs 2000-2007)

Ohman was a lefty reliever who experienced some severe arm troubles while he was a member of the Cubs. Those arm troubles caused him to undergo Tommy John surgery and miss the entire 2002-2004 seasons. When he finally returned to the big leagues as a situational lefty, he had some success. In 2005 Ohman appeared in 69 games for the Cubs and posted a 2.91 ERA. That was probably his best season in Chicago. He later also pitched for the Braves, Dodgers, Orioles, Marlins, and White Sox.

Augie Ojeda 1974– (Cubs 2000-2003)

Augie came up with the Cubs during the summer of 2000 and immediately became a hit with the fans who seemed naturally predisposed to root for the little guy. In Augie's case, that was a literal description. He was only 5'9 . Over his four seasons with the Cubs, Augie went up and down between the minors and the big leagues. He filled in at second base, shortstop, and third base, but hit a disappointing .196 in a Cubs uniform. Ojeda had a more successful run with the Diamondbacks after his Cubs days were over. His stint in Arizona included facing his former team in the 2007 playoffs. Augie hit .444 for the series.

Gene Oliver 1935–2007 (Cubs 1968-1969)

Gene was one of the veterans on that memorable 1969 Cubs team: a 34-year-old backup catcher. He didn't get to play much because Randy Hundley didn't like to take a day off, but Gene was an important presence in the dugout, and beloved by his teammates. He had a couple of very good seasons with the Milwaukee Braves in the mid-60s, and also caught for the Cardinals, Phillies, and Red Sox. 1969 was his last season in baseball.

Nate Oliver 1940– (Cubs 1969)

He was a diminutive infielder on a Dodgers team that recently had another diminutive infielder nicknamed Pee Wee (Reese), so Nate Oliver became known as Pee Wee too. In 1964 he was the starting second baseman for the Dodgers, but for the rest of his career Nate Oliver was strictly a role player. He was a bench player for the Dodgers team that won the 1965 World Series and the 1966 team that lost the series to the Orioles, but Nate only got in one game. He was standing on second base as a pinch runner when Lou Johnson flied out to the end the series. The Cubs got Pee Wee in a trade with the New York Yankees early in their memorable 1969 season (in exchange for future Cubs manager Lee Elia). Oliver didn't play too much, only 49 at-bats in 44 games, but he bonded well with his teammates and became a fan favorite. Along with reserve outfielder Willie Smith, he became part of the singing Cubs. Willie and Nate sang the song "Pennant Feeling" (a parody of the Righteous Brothers song "You've Lost That Lovin' Feeling"), and then along with reserve catcher Gene Oliver sang "Hey Hey Holy Mackerel." But as the Cubs faded late in 1969, Nate Oliver's Cubs career faded into the sunset. His final big league game was in a Cubs uniform: September 27, 1969. After his playing career was over, Nate transitioned into coaching, as an infield and batting instructor, and also manager, in the farm systems of the Angels, Cubs, and White Sox.

Barney Olsen 1919–1977 (Cubs 1941)

Barney was a Cub for the last two months of the 1941 season. They actually gave him a decent shot at playing at the end of the year. The 22-year-old center fielder hit .288, and played well. But he spent the entire 1942 season in the minors and then was drafted into the military. Olsen played in the minors again after the war, but never made it back up to the show.

Vern Olsen 1918–1989 (Cubs 1939-1946)

Olsen's big league career was interrupted by a three-year tour of duty in the military. He was a member of the Cubs starting rotation before the war, notching two seasons of double-digit wins. But while the Cubs were on their way to the World Series in 1945, Olsen was stationed in Hawaii. When he came back in 1946, he was a shell of his former self. The Cubs released him after the season.

Historical note: On the day Paris fell to the Germans (1940), Vern was on the mound for the Cubs. He lost to the Braves 4-2 in Boston.

Mike Olt 1988– (Cubs 2014-2015)

Olt was a first round pick (Rangers), but didn't develop as projected. The Cubs more or less gave him the starting third base job out of spring training in 2014, and while Olt showed tremendous power (12 homers in 187 ABs), he had a very difficult time making contact. He struck out 84 times and hit only .139. That led to a demotion to Iowa. He was likewise given the big league job in 2015, but after only a few games was replaced by a little-known rookie named Kris Bryant. After spending most of the season on the DL, Olt was waived in September.

Steve Ontiveros 1961– (Cubs 1977-1980)

The former minor league player of the year was acquired from the Giants in the Bill Madlock trade. He may not have been a good replacement for Madlock at third base, but Steve Ontiveros wasn't terrible. He came within one hit of batting .300 in 1977. He played parts of three other seasons with the Cubs and didn't do much before being released in the middle of the 1980 season. He went to Japan after the Cubs let him go, and starred there for another five seasons.

Rey Ordonez 1971– (Cubs 2004)

He was a slick-fielding shortstop, one of the very best glove men in the big leagues in his nine-year career. He won three Gold Gloves with the Mets. Unfortunately for Rey, he never did quite master the trick of hitting big league pitching. His lifetime average was only .246. The Cubs were the last team to give him a chance and he hit .164.

Kevin Orie 1972– (Cubs 1997-1998, 2002)

One of the many "next Ron Santo" to man the position, Orie was the starting third baseman as a rookie in 1997. He had a decent season, hitting 8 homers and 44 RBI. But he had a sophomore slump the following year and was shipped off the Marlins before the season was over in the trade that brought Felix Heredia to Chicago. Orie later came back to the Cubs for his final season in the big leagues.

Jose Ortiz 1947–2011 (Cubs 1971)

The Puerto Rican outfielder played with the Cubs in 1971. He and fellow speedster Brock Davis shared the center field position with limited success. The Cubs went out and got Rick Monday after the season, and Ortiz' time in the big leagues was over. He previously also played for the White Sox.

Ramon Ortiz 1973– (Cubs 2011)

Ortiz had a very promising start to his career with the Angels.

He won 15 games for them in 2002 and anchored the team's rotation. But by the time he came to the Cubs in 2011, Ortiz had compiled six straight seasons of ERAs over five. He appeared in 22 games for the Cubs in his one season in Chicago, and registered an ERA of 4.86.

Bob Osborn 1903–1960 (Cubs 1925-1930)

Osborn pitched for the Cubs during one of the big hitting eras in major league history. He got a cup of coffee with the team during their pennant-winning year, but his best season was 1930 — a notoriously tough year for pitchers. Osborn won 10 games that year for the Cubs.

Donovan Osborne 1969– (Cubs 2002)

The Cubs took a flyer on Osborne after he had major arm problems with the St. Louis Cardinals. The formerly effective starter had gone two full seasons without pitching a ball, and he just didn't have it anymore. He registered a 6.19 ERA in limited appearances out of the bullpen.

Tiny Osborne 1893–1969 (Cubs 1922-1924)

His real name was Ernest Osborne, but he came by his nickname much the same way Curly Howard came by his. He was the opposite of Tiny. He was 6'4" and weighed 215 pounds. Tiny wasn't much of a pitcher with the Cubs. He had a losing record in his three Cub seasons, but he did lead the league in one category in 1922: He hit 12 batters. We're guessing nobody charged the mound.

Historical note: On the day Alexander Graham Bell died in 1922, Tiny Osborne pitched ten innings in relief of Percy Jones. The Cubs and Phillies called it a tie after 15 innings, 7-7, because of darkness and rain.

Johnny Ostrowski 1917–1992 (Cubs 1943-1946)

On March 3rd, 1945, Johnny was one of only six Cubs players who bothered to gather at Chicago's Dearborn Train Station to board the train to spring training that year: pitcher Ed Hanyzewski, minor league pitcher George Hennessy, semi-pro pitcher Al Nusser, former Giants catcher Joe Stephenson, a young player that had virtually no chance of making the team — Virgil Garriot, and Johnny. It didn't seem to help the local Chicago boy too much. Ostrowski played in only seven games with the Cubs that season. He batted .300 in ten plate appearances, and didn't make the post-season roster. The third baseman later played for the White Sox and the Senators.

Reggie Otero 1915–1988 (Cubs 1945)

The Cuban-born first baseman was a rookie for the 1945 Cubs, but he was no spring chicken. When he made his major league debut he was just a few days shy of his 30th birthday. Otero spelled Phil Cavarretta for a few games in September, but that's the extent of his major league career. He may not have had much time in the bigs, but he did end up with a .391 average in his 23 at-bats. Not a bad lifetime average.

*Other Guy Cubs...*There have been some truly famous Cubs players over the years, and the following BIG names also played for the Cubs. It's just not the guy you think it is... Bill Bradley, Milton Bradley, William Brennan, Bob Collins, Phil Collins, George Frazier, Bob Gibson, John Glenn, Kevin Hart, John Houseman, Rick James, Don Johnson, Howard Johnson, Ted Kennedy, Andy Sommers, Jimmy Stewart, Frank Thomas, Ted Turner, Mike Tyson, and Jack Warner.

Billy Ott 1940–2015 (Cubs 1962, 1964)

No relation to Hall of Famer Mel Ott. Billy was an outfielder on two of the worst Cubs teams of all-time. He got 73 plate appearances over those two seasons and mustered a .164 batting average. Billy was the man who initially replaced Lou Brock in the outfield after Brock was traded to the Cardinals. He played five games, went 4 for 22, and was sent down to the minors. After leaving baseball Billy became a cop.

Dave Otto 1964– (Cubs 1994)

The local product (Elk Grove High School) is probably better known for his time as a fill-in announcer during Cubs broadcasts, but Dave Otto also got a cup of coffee with his hometown team. During the strike season of 1994, he appeared in 36 games and posted an ERA of 3.80. That was the last year of his nine-season big league career. Otto also pitched for the A's, Indians, and Pirates.

Orval Overall 1881–1947 (Cubs 1905-1913)

Orval was a key member of the Cubs dynasty of 1906-1910. He was a two-time 20-game winner, and led the league in shutouts (twice) and strikeouts. For 108 years his claim to fame was that he was the last pitcher in Cubs history to win a World Series-clinching game. He won the deciding game of the 1908 World Series. (That honor now goes to Aroldis Chapman, who ironically served up a homer to tie the game, but got the win in Game 7 of the 2016 World Series). Orval wasn't much like the other guys on the team — he was a college boy who attended the University of California at Berkeley, where he was also an All-American football player. Overall pitched some of the greatest games in Cubs history, including two wins in the 1908 World Series. In one of those games he struck out four men in one inning — something no one else has ever done in the World Series since. He also started Game 1 of the 1910 World Series before being chased away from baseball by Cubs owner Charles Murphy during a contract dispute. He eventually returned to the Cubs with hat in hand in 1913, but by then, his time had passed, and he only won 4 more games in his career. Orval and his rotation mates Mordecai Brown and Jack Pfiester remain the only three Cubs pitchers in history with career ERAs under two. Orval still holds a Cubs all-time record. Hitters hit only .212 against him throughout his Cubs career.

Ernie Ovitz 1885–1980 (Cubs 1911)

If you want to go back in time to watch Ernie Ovitz pitch, simply set the wayback machine to June 22, 1911 and go to West Side Grounds in Chicago. The Cubs were getting walloped that day by the Pirates and the University of Illinois product was brought in to pitch the last two innings. Among the players he faced: Hall of Famer Honus Wagner.

Historical note: Ernie's only day in the big leagues also just so happened to be the day that King George V of England was crowned at Westminster Abbey.

Dave Owen 1958– (Cubs 1983-1985)

Owen was a backup infielder for the Cubs three seasons in the mid-80s. He will always be remembered for getting the winning hit in the famous Ryne Sandberg game against the Cardinals in the summer of 1984. Sandberg may have tied the game with homers against Bruce Sutter in the 9th and 10th, but Owen was the one who knocked in the game winner. Dave later played for the Royals. His brother Spike was also a big leaguer.

Mickey Owen 1916–2005 (Cubs 1949-1951)

Mickey led a fascinating life in and out of baseball. He was a four-time All-Star with the Brooklyn Dodgers during early 40s, and though he set a fielding record as a catcher in 1941, he is best remembered for a fielding error he made in Game 4 of the World Series that season. He couldn't handle a pitch that would have been the last out of the game (and tied up the series), but the runner reached first base on Mickey's error. That led to a four-run rally and a Dodgers loss.

Owen didn't serve in the military during the war, he was called up AFTER the war, and missed the 1946 season. When he came back, he was one of the players who bolted to the Mexican league. This angered Commissioner Happy Chandler so much, he wanted to ban those players from the major leagues for life. Chandler eventually cooled off, and Owen was allowed to return in 1949. That's when he joined the Cubs. Mickey was the starting catcher for a few incredibly bad Cubs teams. After his playing days were over, he became a scout, then formed a baseball academy. Among the graduates of that academy...Michael Jordan, Joe Girardi, and Charlie Sheen. Mickey later ran for public office, and served as the sheriff of Greene County in Missouri for three terms.

*Additional Entries...*If you check out the Every Cub Ever feature at www. justonebadcentury.com, you'll find several additional entries, including celebrity Cubs fans, writers, and bloggers. Under the letter O, you'll discover Cubs fan and "Parks and Recreation" star Nick Offerman.

CHAPTER SIXTEEN

P

The starting lineup for your Chicago Cubs beginning with the letter P...

C—Babe Phelps, All-Star
1B—Joe Pepitone, Free Spirit
2B—Charlie Pick, 1918 Cub
SS—Paul Popovich, 1969 Cub
3B— Pinky Pittenger, Best Pinky Ever
LF—Andy Pafko, All-Star
CF—Dode Paskert, 1918 Cub
RF— Rafael Palmeiro, One Who Got Away
Bench—Corey Patterson, Can't Miss Prospect
Bench—Felix Pie, Can't Miss Prospect
SP—Milt Pappas, No-Hitter
SP—Claude Passeau, World Series One-Hitter
SP—Jack Pfiester, 1908 Cub
RP—Dan Plesac, Future Announcer

Gene Packard 1887–1959 (Cubs 1916-1917)

Packard was an important part of the pitching staff in the Cubs' first season at Wrigley Field. He won ten games as a combination starter/reliever, including a one-hitter against the Braves. The following year he was sold to the Cardinals. He also pitched for the Phillies and Reds. In the minor leagues, Packard threw a perfect game.

Andy Pafko 1929–2013 (Cubs 1943-1951)

Nicknamed "Handy Andy," because of his incredibly dependable hitting and fielding, Pafko was one of the most popular Cubs, and a star of the 1945 World Series team. Handy Andy was a five-time All-Star during his Cubs career, the first three times as an outfielder (although one of those times, 1945, they didn't play the All-Star game because of the

war). After legendary Cubs' third baseman Stan Hack retired after the 1947 season, Pafko replaced him on the hot corner long enough to be named an All-Star there too, making him one of the few people to achieve All-Star status in both the infield and outfield. His 1950 season can only be described as DiMaggio-esque. That year Andy Pafko knocked the ball out of National League ballparks 36 times while only striking out 32 times. Only 14 players have ever accomplished that feat. Naturally, Handy Andy was rewarded for that incredible season in true Cubs fashion. He was traded to the Brooklyn Dodgers. He was crushed when the Cubs traded him, and it was a trade that Chicago would forever regret. The players they got in return had almost no impact with the Cubs, while Pafko would go on to play in the 1952 World Series with the Dodgers and the 1957 and 1958 World Series with the Braves. He came back to his hometown of Chicago after his playing career was over, settling in the northwestern suburbs.

Angel Pagan 1981–(Cubs 2006-2007)

Pagan came up to the big leagues with the Cubs and served as their fourth outfielder during his two years in Chicago. He got sick in his second season in Chicago, and lost a lot of weight. Cubs GM Jim Hendry didn't think he would be able to contribute much, so he traded him before the 2008 season began. Bad move by the Cubs. They traded him to the Mets for two minor leaguers who never made it to the big club. Meanwhile, Pagan turned out to be a very solid big league outfielder. He has a lifetime batting average over .280, has stolen over 150 bases, and was a key contributor to the 2012 and 2014 World Series champion Giants.

Vance Page 1905–1951 (Cubs 1938-1941)

Page's Cubs career lasted exactly four seasons to the date. He debuted on August 6, 1938 (as a 32-year-old, after 13 minor league seasons) and made his final appearance on August 6, 1941. Page pitched in Game 4 of the 1938 World Series and gave up two runs and two hits, although there is no shame in giving up hits to Lou Gehrig and Joe DiMaggio. Vance's first two years he was mainly a spot starter, and his final two seasons he worked predominantly out of the bullpen. The late bloomer didn't have much time to appreciate his post playing days. Just ten years after his last pitch, he fell off a barn and died of the injuries he sustained in the fall. He was only 45.

Karl Pagel 1955 – (Cubs 1978-1979)

Pagel was the first round pick of the Cubs in 1976, and unlike several of their top picks of that decade, he did make it to the big leagues. He got exactly three at-bats for the Cubs, two in 1978, and one in 1979. He struck out all three times. In fairness to the Cubs, 1976 wasn't a particularly strong draft. Only one player chosen in the top two rounds got extensive playing time in the majors — and that was Hubie Brooks. Pagel was traded to the Indians for aging slugger Cliff Johnson in 1980, and later played a bit for the Indians (1981-1983). He hit his only career homer for the Indians in 1981.

*Palindrome Cubs...*Two Cubs in history have last names that were palindromes...Dave Otto and Dick Nen. One former Cubs announcer also qualifies: Dwayne Staats.

Don Pall 1962 – (Cubs 1994)

He grew up a Sox fan and pitched for them too, but he also pitched across town for the Cubs. His teammates called him The Pope. Pall had a respectable ten-year big league career as a reliever. His best seasons were with the White Sox, where he recorded all ten of his big league saves. He only appeared in two games for the Cubs during the strike-shortened 1994 season.

Rafael Palmeiro 1964 – (Cubs 1986-1988)

Two incredibly bright prospects came up to the Chicago Cubs around the same time. Unfortunately, both Mark Grace and Rafael Palmeiro played the same position (first base). To get both of their bats into the lineup, Palmeiro was moved out to left field. His 1988 Cubs season was stellar. Palmeiro batted .307, slugged 41 doubles, and was named to the All-Star team. Naturally, the Cubs traded him after the season. They decided that Grace had better potential to develop power. It didn't exactly turn out that way. Palmeiro was so upset he cried when he was traded along with another guy who wouldn't amount to anything, Jamie Moyer, for Mitch Williams, Paul Kilgus, Steve Wilson, Curtis Wilkerson, Luis Benitez, and Pablo Delgado. Palmeiro had a Hall of Fame-caliber career (granted, perhaps with the help of some illegal substances). He was a four-time All-Star, three-time Gold Glover, and hit 569 career homers. Jamie Moyer pitched in the majors another 22 years. Not a good trade for the Cubs.

*Panamanian Cubs...*The following Cubs were all born in Panama...Manny Corpas, Jose Macias, Adolfo Phillips, Fernando Ramsey, Ray Webster, and Julio Zuleta.

Erik Pappas 1966 – (Cubs 1991)

Pappas was a local boy (Mt. Carmel High School) who came up as a catcher, and got a cup of coffee with the Cubs in April of 1991. He later went to the Cardinals, and they moved him to the outfield. In 2004, he played in the Olympics for the Greek National team. Pappas later became a coach in the Cubs minor league system.

Milt Pappas 1939 – 2016 (Cubs 1970-1973)

Milt had some of his best seasons as a big league pitcher with the Cubs at the tail end of his career. In 1971 he became one of only ten pitchers in big league history to strike out the side on nine pitches. In 1972 he came just one out away from pitching a perfect game (and never forgave the umpire for calling ball four on the 27th batter). Milt never seemed satisfied with *just* pitching a no-hitter, which is what he pitched that day.

Though he was a two-time All-Star and won more than 200 games in his career, Pappas was often embroiled in controversy. While he was with the Orioles, he admitted to grooving one to Roger Maris during his quest for 61 homers. He was traded to the Reds for Frank Robinson — who went on to win the triple crown for the Orioles. Milt got into a fight with Reds teammate Joe Nuxhall and was traded to the Braves.

His Cubs career wasn't without controversy either. He was in the middle of the fight that may have led to Leo Durocher losing his team once and for all. The date was August 23, 1971. Leo Durocher tells the tale himself in his book *Nice Guys Finish Last*. Essentially, here is the story. The Cubs were in the clubhouse before a game against the Cincinnati Reds. They were 11 games over .500 and only 4 1/2 games behind the first place Pittsburgh Pirates, but Leo was still upset with

Milt. The previous game he had allowed the winning run in a 4-3 loss when Doug Radar hit an 0-2 pitch. He called a club meeting and ripped Pappas for his stupidity. After his little speech he opened the floor for comments. Joe Pepitone, Ken Holtzman, and Milt Pappas began ripping Durocher. That's when Leo lost it. He tore into every player on the team in a legendary expletive-filled tirade. Among those he ripped was team captain Ron Santo. Santo had to be physically restrained by his teammates. The Cubs somehow went out and won the game, but afterwards they spiraled into a deep losing streak. They lost 16 of their next 21 games. Durocher had lost the club forever.

Mark Parent 1961– (Cubs 1994-1995)

Parent was an excellent defensive catcher and parlayed that into a 13-year big league career. But because he couldn't hit very well (lifetime average .214), he never really claimed a starting position. He was a solid backup for the Padres, Rangers, Orioles, Pirates, Tigers, Phillies, and the Cubs. Both years he played with the Cubs were strike-shortened seasons. He hit six homers in 56 games. Parent went into politics in his native Canada after his playing career.

Blake Parker 1985– (Cubs 2012-2014)

Parker was a Cubs draft choice who got a lot of action of out the bullpen during the 2013 season. He appeared in 49 games for the Cubs that year and pitched fairly well, registering an ERA of 2.72. Unfortunately, the 2014 season didn't go nearly as well, and Parker spent a lot of time in the minors. The Cubs designated Blake for assignment in May of 2015. They might have given up on him a little too soon. Parker became the closer for the Angels in 2017/2018.

Doc Parker 1872–1941 (Colts 1893-1896)

Doc only appeared in 18 games for Chicago, but they were in three different seasons. He was a pitcher by trade, but he wasn't a particularly good one. His lifetime ERA was 5.90, and that was in the deadest of deadball eras. On the other hand, he was a pretty good hitting pitcher. His lifetime batting average was .274. The Cubs (then known as the Colts) even tried him in the outfield one game to take advantage of his bat. Doc later became a big league umpire.

Historical note: On the day Louis Pasteur died (1895),

Doc was on the mound for the Colts. They lost to the Reds 5-4 in a rain-shortened game.

Roy Parmelee 1907–1981 (Cubs 1937)

Parmelee came to the Cubs in the ill-considered trade that sent Lon Warneke to St. Louis in 1937. The '37 Cubs sure could have used Warneke. He finished with 18 wins for the Cardinals, and won 77 games for them over the next four years. Parmelee was gone the next year, and the other player the Cubs acquired (Rip Collins) lasted two years. Parmelee's final record for the Cubs was 7-8, with an ERA over five. On the other hand, he had a great nickname. Parmelee is one of three Cubs in history who were nicknamed Tarzan.

Jiggs Parrott 1871–1897 (Colts 1892-1895)

One of the great names in baseball history, Jiggs started at second base one year for the Cubs (then known as the Colts) and as a third baseman another year. Jiggs wasn't too popular with the fans because he was a bit of a butcher at second base. By the end of his time in Chicago, his manager only played him on the road so that the crowd didn't get upset. His brother Tom also played for the team. The Parrott brothers were professional musicians. Jiggs died of tuberculosis in 1897. He was only 26 years old.

Tom Parrott 1868–1932 (Colts 1893)

Tacky Tom, as he was known, got his big league start in Chicago pitching for the Cubs (then known as the Colts). His brother Jiggs was on the team already, so it seemed like a natural choice, but the Cincinnati Reds claimed they had the rights to him. He didn't fare too well in Chicago (0-3, with a 6.67 ERA) before being ruled to be Cincy property. Parrott then went to the Reds and performed much better, winning ten games for them that year. They called him Tacky Tom because he was a flake and a free spirit, often doing and saying outrageous things. In his spare time, he also played the cornet. He scheduled his gigs around the team's road trips.

Dode Paskert 1881–1959 (Cubs 1918-1920)

His real name was George Henry Paskert, but everyone called him Dode. No one knows for sure the origin of Paskert's nickname, but more than likely it was a dig at his perceived low intelligence. The English Dialect Dictionary, published in 1900, describes a dode as a "slow [witted] person," and a scattering of press accounts confirm that Paskert was considered stupid. He was a pretty good player for the Phillies when the Cubs acquired him in 1918, but he came at a high price. Cy Williams, who they traded for him, became a big star for Philadelphia — one of the best players of the era (he won three home run titles for Philly). Dode Paskert, on the other hand, didn't do much. He did start in center field and had a good year in 1918 — when the Cubs made it to the World Series. (Although he only hit .190 in that series.) But Dode didn't have much left in the tank after that. He retired after the 1920 season.

Claude Passeau 1909–2003 (Cubs 1939-1947)
Claude Passeau was the ace of the Cubs staff for several years. From 1940-1942 he pitched in the All-Star game every year. Just before the pennant-winning 1945 season started, Cubs doctors discovered that he had a chipped humerous from an old high school football injury. They told Claude that he'd be fine after four days of X-ray therapy, and boy were they right. He recovered nicely to have another very good year, tossing five shutouts, winning 17 games, and pitching the second greatest game in World Series history, a 1-hitter. Passeau toughed out one more 9-win season in 1946, but it was all over for him before the end of the 1947 season.

Bob Patterson 1959–(Cubs 1996-1998)
Patterson was a journeyman reliever who pitched for the Pirates, Rangers, and Angels before coming to the Cubs. He was 5-10 for the Cubs in his three seasons, and was released during July of his pretty dreadful 1998, when he had a seven-plus ERA. The Cubs won the Wild Card that season.

Corey Patterson 1979– (Cubs 2000-2005)
The third overall pick of the 1998 draft, Corey was a can't-miss 5-tool prospect. He had power, speed, and played an outstanding center field. He certainly had flashes of greatness in a Cubs uniform, including an Opening Day when he drove in eight runs, but he also disappeared for weeks at a time, and had a very hard time mastering the strike zone. In 2003, he was having an All-Star caliber season when he got hurt. His injury forced the Cubs to go out and acquire Kenny

Lofton — who arguably was the MVP of the Cubs the rest of that season. In 2004, Corey clubbed 24 homers and stole 32 bases, and it looked he had finally arrived. But in 2005, it all fell apart for him. Patterson hit a woeful .215 and had more strikeouts than hits. The Cubs shipped him off to Baltimore after the season for two minor leaguers who never made it to the big club. Patterson played another six seasons in the big leagues for the Orioles, Reds, Nationals, Brewers, Blue Jays, and Cardinals. His career numbers were very respectable (118 homers, 218 stolen bases, .252 average), but he never quite lived up to the lofty expectations. Corey's father Don played in the NFL for the Giants and Lions, and his brother Eric was also a big league baseball player.

Eric Patterson 1983–(Cubs 2007-2008)
Corey's little brother was a utility man who got a small taste of the big leagues with the Cubs at the end of 2007 and the beginning of 2008 before being shipped off to Oakland in the trade that brought Rich Harden to the Cubs. He has since played for the A's, Red Sox, and Padres.

Ken Patterson 1964–(Cubs 1992)
Patterson was a left-handed reliever acquired in the trade that brought Sammy Sosa to the Cubs (for George Bell). Unfortunately for Ken, his Cubs career wasn't quite as decorated as his fellow ex-White Sox teammate. He went 2-3, with a 3.89 ERA in 32 appearances. After the season he was granted free agency and finished his career with the Angels.

Reggie Patterson 1958–(Cubs 1983-1985)
Patterson was a highly touted pitching prospect the Cubs got from the White Sox, but he never quite could put it together in the big leagues. His big claim to fame was giving up the hit that allowed Pete Rose to tie Ty Cobb for the all-time hits record. It happened in Wrigley Field.

David Patton 1984–(Cubs 2009)
Patton was a Rule V draft choice, who pitched in the Cubs for part of the 2009 season. He made twenty appearances and won three games, but also registered an ERA of 6.83. He never made it back up to the big leagues.

Spencer Patton 1988 – (Cubs 2016)

The Urbana-born Patton, a former Texas Ranger, pitched out of the bullpen for a few different stints during the 2016 season. Unfortunately he couldn't find his control. In only 21 innings pitched, he walked 14 men, which sealed his fate. After the season the Cubs released him.

Josh Paul 1975 – (Cubs 2003)

The local product (Evanston) was released by the White Sox after a few years on the south side and was picked up by the Cubs. If you blinked, you missed his time with the Cubs. He had exactly six plate appearances that year and didn't get on base. He made his mark in history a few years later as the catcher of the Angels when he rolled the ball to the mound after a strikeout by White Sox hitter A.J. Pierzynski in the 2005 playoffs. The umpire incorrectly ruled the ball hit the dirt and allowed Pierzynski to run to first base. The Sox came back to win the game, and with the undeserved momentum they attained, never lost again in the playoffs. Without that bad call, the 2005 Sox probably wouldn't have won the World Series. Historians will forever put an asterisk next to that World Series title. Right?

Mike Paul 1945 – (Cubs 1973-1974)

The Cubs acquired Paul from the Texas Rangers for Larry Gura during the 1973 season. He pitched pretty well out of the bullpen at the end of the 1973 season, but the Cubs released him in April of the following season. Larry Gura, on the other hand, went on to become a two-time 18-game winner in the American League. Paul pitched in the Mexican League until 1982.

Dave Pavlas 1962 – (Cubs 1990-1991)

Pavlas was a 28-year-old rookie when he joined the Cubs in 1990. The 6'7 right-hander pitched out of the bullpen in 14 games for the Cubs over two seasons, and did a respectable job. It was a nice reward for his very long (15 years) minor league career. He later also pitched briefly for the Yankees, and even spent a short stint in Japan.

Ted Pawelek 1919 – 1964 (Cubs 1946)

They called him Porky, and the Chicago Heights native and former U.S. Marine played in exactly four games with the Cubs. The catcher's only career hit came in his last at-bat with the Cubs on September 26, 1946. Porky doubled off Pirates pitcher Jack Hallet in a 5-3 Cubs win at Wrigley Field. After his playing career he became a scout with the Detroit Tigers. He died in an automobile accident at the age of 44.

Charlie Pechous 1896 – 1980 (Cubs 1916-1917)

Charlie was a 19-year-old backup third baseman and shortstop for the Cubs in their first year at Wrigley Field, and stuck around to help a bit in 1917. He played his last game in the big leagues on September 30, 1917. Charlie stuck it out for six more seasons in the minors before hanging up his spikes at the ripe old age of 26.

Jorge Pedre 1966 – (Cubs 1992)

Jorge was a September call-up for the Cubs in 1992, and got a grand total of four at-bats. He didn't get a hit. Jorge was a catcher who played eight seasons in the minors, mostly in the Kansas City organization.

Chick Pedroes 1869 – 1927 (Orphans 1902)

His real name was Pedro, but the Americanized "Chick" was 32 years old when he played for Chicago for two games in 1902. He was born in Cuba, which would make him the first Latin-American player who ever played for the Cubs, and the first Cuban-born player to ever play in the big leagues. For some reason, he is not often acknowledged. Probably because he had exactly zero hits in six big league plate appearances.

Carlos Pena 1978 – (Cubs 2011)

Carlos was a former All-Star, Gold Glover, and Silver Slugger when he signed with the Cubs as a free agent in 2011. Both sides knew it would be a short-term arrangement. Pena held up his side of the bargain by hitting 28 homers and knocking in 80 runs. But he also hit only .225. When the season ended, the two sides agreed to part ways. Pena is also known for being an incredible humanitarian. He gave food and medical supplies after the Haiti earthquake in 2010, and was nominated for the Roberto Clemente Award. Carlos was forever immortalized in the film *Moneyball* starring Brad Pitt. Turns out, despite his great skills, Pena was the anti-*Moneyball* player.

Felix Pena 1990 – (Cubs 2016-2017)

The hard-throwing Dominican right-hander came up through the Cubs system and made his big league debut during their World Series championship season. He was recalled from Iowa in August and actually pitched some meaningful innings for the Cubs during the home stretch. Pena appeared in 25 games for the Cubs in 2017, but he struggled with his control (18 walks in just over 30 innings) and he gave up the long ball eight times. The Cubs traded him to the Angels after the season.

Roberto Pena 1937–1982 (Cubs 1965-1966)

Pena was a backup infielder with the Cubs, and even though he was a 27-year-old rookie, he was nicknamed Baby. Pena wasn't much of a hitter (.245 lifetime average), but his glove kept him in the big leagues until he was 34. He also played for the Phillies, Padres, A's, and Brewers. He died in his native Dominican Republic at the age of 45.

Ken Penner 1896–1959 (Cubs 1929)

When Penner joined the Cubs in 1929, he hadn't been in the big leagues since 1916, one of the longest such streaks in baseball history. He was a pitcher. Ken was essentially a minor league lifer. He pitched 27 seasons in the minor leagues, and didn't hang up his spikes until he was 47 years old. After that he became a scout in the Cardinals organization.

Joe Pepitone 1940 – (Cubs 1970-1973)

On July 29, 1970, the Cubs traded their top prospect, shortstop Roger Metzger (who went on to play a decade in Houston) to the Astros for a player that had just walked out on his team because they tried to give him a roommate on the road — Joe Pepitone. Pepitone was a great glove man with power, but he also had one of the worst attitudes in Cubs history. The fans loved him though, because he was flamboyant and showy, and everything else the Cubs had always lacked. He wore his hair long (wigs), wore his shirt open to show his hairy chest and gold chains, and was the first player in baseball to bring a hair dryer into a clubhouse. On his first day as a Cub he arrived in a limo. He was so deep in debt he owed the team half his salary before the year began. Pepitone bought a club on Division Street and called it "Joe Pepitone's Thing." He opened a hair salon and started selling Joe Pepitone wigs.

He parked his Harley inside Durocher's office so that kids wouldn't bother him after the game. One time, during pre-game warmups, he was thrown a foil packet full of joints by his fans in the bleachers. He hid them in the outfield ivy until after the game (according to an interview he gave to *Rolling Stone* magazine many years later).

And while things were going well for the Cubs, Joe Pepitone was not a problem. On the other hand, manager Leo Durocher — who recognized a young version of himself in Pepitone — knew it was just a matter of time. In his autobiography *Nice Guys Finish Last*, this is how he referred to him. "If you're thinking that Pepitone was sent to me in just retribution…I have to admit there were times that the thought crossed my mind."

When things starting going bad, Pepitone was always in the middle of it. He had a real problem with authority figures and he incited some of his teammates to feel likewise. The relationship with Durocher soured and became toxic. It all blew up in 1972. He walked out on the team on May 2, 1972 and asked to be put on the voluntary retirement list. He was sick of baseball and wanted to concentrate on his nightclub, but as usual, the money sent him crawling back. Unfortunately for Pepitone, being placed on the list made him ineligible for sixty days. He returned the very first day he legally could, but he was rusty and just couldn't hit anymore. A year later the Cubs sent him packing, trading him to the Atlanta Braves. After his playing days Joe was busted on drug charges, and spent four months in prison at Rikers Island.

Historical note: On the day the *New York Times* began the publication of the Pentagon Papers (1971), Joe hit a double and a homer for the Cubs but it wasn't enough to beat the Reds at Wrigley Field. Reds 4-Cubs 3.

Joel Peralta 1976 – (Cubs 2016)

The Cubs were looking for bullpen help during the summer of 2016, so when the 40-year-old Peralta was released by the Mariners, the Cubs gave him a chance. After giving up two homers in only four innings of work, the Peralta experiment ended. Peralta previously pitched for the Angels, Royals, Rockies, Nationals, Rays, and Dodgers during his 12-year big league career.

Mike Perez 1964–(Cubs 1995-1996)

Perez was a reliever who pitched very well for the Cardinals. He won 18 games and saved 19 in his three seasons with St. Louis before joining the Cubs. It didn't go quite as well in Chicago. He won two and saved three and was released. The Puerto-Rican right-hander got one more cup of coffee with Royals before calling it a career.

Neifi Perez 1973–(Cubs 2005-2006)

Perez was a journeyman infielder when he arrived in Chicago, but for some reason he became Dusty Baker's favorite player. Perez played a steady shortstop, but his on-base percentage was among the worst in the league. Despite having some promising rookies behind him (like Ronnie Cedeno), Perez got the bulk of the playing time. He was traded to the Tigers late in the 2006 season.

Yorkis Perez 1967–(Cubs 1991)

Part of the Perez family that also brought Melido, Pascual, and Carlos Perez to the majors, cousin Yorkis was a September call-up for the Cubs in 1991, but only appeared in three games. Despite pitching fairly well, the Cubs let him go after the season. It took Perez a few years to make it back up to the big leagues, but he eventually pitched eight more seasons for the Marlins, Mets, Phillies, Astros, and Orioles.

Harry Perkowski 1922–2016 (Cubs 1955)

Harry was acquired along with Ted Tappe and Jim Bolger for Johnny Klippstein after the 1954 season. Perkowski had had a few double-digit win seasons with the Reds before coming to Chicago, but he didn't have a great season with the Cubs. He won three games and saved two in 25 appearances. Harry passed away during the Cubs 2016 World Series season at the age of 93.

Jon Perlman 1956–(Cubs 1985)

Perlman made his big league debut for the Cubs in their injury-ravaged year of 1985. He didn't fare well. In six outings he allowed more than two runners an inning and posted an 11.42 ERA. He was 28 years old at the time. Perlman got a few more cups of coffee in his 30s with the Indians and the Giants.

Pat Perry 1959–(Cubs 1988-1989)

The Cubs got Perry in the trade that sent Leon Durham to the Reds. He was a member of the division champion 1989 Cubs team, but he was used sparingly out of the bullpen (19 appearances), and didn't make the post-season roster. They released him in December of that year. He did manage to win two games and save two games during his tenure with the Cubs.

Scott Perry 1891–1959 (Cubs 1916)

Scott was a right-handed pitcher, and part of the Cubs staff in the first season they played at Wrigley Field. He won 2 games toward the end of the season as a starter. The following year he was pitching in Cincinnati, with limited success. It wasn't until he joined the Philadelphia Athletics that Perry came into his own. In the war-shortened year of 1918, Scott Perry became a twenty-game winner.

John Peters 1850–1924 (White Stockings 1874-1877, 1879)

Peters was a second baseman/shortstop in the days before players even used gloves. He was the starting shortstop on the inaugural National League 1876 championship team and hit .351. In the field, he made quite a few errors (including a league-leading 71 in 1879), but have we mentioned this was a time before players even wore gloves? He also played for Milwaukee, Providence, Buffalo, and Pittsburgh.

Billy Petrick 1984–(Cubs 2007)

Petrick was a big right-hander (6'6, 240 pounds) from Kankakee who worked his way through the Cubs system after being drafted in 2002. He got his one chance at the show in June and July of 2007, but appeared a bit overmatched by big league hitters. In only nine innings pitched, he gave up three homers and had an ERA of 7.45. He pitched in the minor leagues until 2012.

Bob Pettit 1861–1910 (White Stockings 1887-1888)

Not to be confused with the NBA Hall of Famer, this Bob Pettit was a utility man for the Cubs (then known as the White Stockings). He played in the infield (second and third base) as well as the outfield in a backup role. His lifetime batting average was .240.

Jesse Petty 1894–1971 (Cubs 1930)

Jesse was known as "The Silver Fox" because he didn't really make it in the big leagues until his 30s. He was a 35-year-old reliever on the Cubs team that blew the pennant in the last few weeks of the 1930 season, costing Joe McCarthy his job. Don't blame Jesse for that. His ERA was a respectable 2.97 in a year that was very friendly to the hitter (the same year Hack Wilson got 191 RBI). Petty previously pitched for Pittsburgh, Brooklyn, and Cleveland. After his playing days he became a minor league manager.

Fred Pfeffer 1860–1932 (White Stockings 1883-1889, 1896-1897)

Fred was one of the premier sluggers in the league during his years with the Cubs (then known as the White Stockings), finishing in the top ten in homers every season during his first stint in Chicago. He played mostly second base, but he also played all other infield positions if needed, occasionally played in the outfield, and even pitched a few times (he saved two games). Pfeffer jumped to the Players' League (along with several of his teammates) after the 1889 season. He returned to play for the Cubs for the last two seasons of his career. He retired with 94 career homers (a very high total at the time), and 383 stolen bases. His nicknames were Fritz and Dandelion.

Big Jeff Pfeffer 1882–1954 (Cubs 1905, 1910)

Big Jeff was a college boy (from the University of Illinois) during a time very few MLB players went to college. The downstate native got his crack at the big leagues after he graduated, the year before the Cubs set the record for most wins in a season. The 1905 version of the team was just a few players short…they hadn't yet acquired Orval Overall, Harry Steinfeldt, or Jimmy Sheckard. Pfeffer was essentially an extra starting pitcher, and occasional reliever. Unfortunately for Big Jeff, he left the best team in baseball to pitch for the worst (the Boston Braves). He returned to Chicago for their pennant-winning 1910 season, and pitched almost exclusively out of the bullpen that year. If he had only been a bigger star, surely Jeff Pfeffer would have inspired a tongue twister. Here's mine: Jeff Pfeffer's Heifer Heather Left a Leather Sweater.

Jack Pfiester 1878–1953 (Cubs 1906-1911)

Jack was an important member of the starting rotation during the Cubs dynasty. The team went to the World Series four of his six seasons. He won 20 games for the 1906 team that won a record-setting 116 games before losing the World Series to the White Sox. He lost two games in that series. The following year, Jack led the league with an astounding 1.15 ERA, and won Game 2 of the World Series. The Cubs won it all that year. Pfiester started the 1908 season by injuring his thumb when he couldn't get it unstuck from a bowling ball, and had several other injuries during the season. He only managed to win 12 games that season, but a few of those wins came in crucial games against the arch rival New York Giants. That's why Pfiester was known as "Jack the Giant Killer." Success began to elude him at the end of that season, however. He had to be removed after 2/3 of an inning in the one-game playoff game against the Giants, and was the only Cubs pitcher to lose a World Series game in 1908. He also appeared in the 1910 World Series for the Cubs, but by then he was being used primarily in relief. His 1.86 career ERA is the second best in Cubs history, behind only his teammate Three Finger Brown.

Art Phelan 1887–1964 (Cubs 1913-1915)

Art was the starting third baseman for the Cubs in their last season at West Side Grounds, but when the season ended, and the rosters of the Cubs and the Federal League Whales were combined, Art was not invited to come along to the new ballpark on Addison and Clark.

Babe Phelps 1908–1992 (Cubs 1933-1934)

His real name was Ernest Phelps, but he was known as Babe throughout most of his big league career. He was also known as Blimp when he played for the Cubs — a tribute to the hefty 225 pounds he carried on his frame. Phelps was a rarely used backup catcher for the Cubs in the early 30s, biding his time on the bench behind Hall of Famer Gabby Hartnett. The Cubs didn't think they needed Blimp, so they released him after the 1934 season. The Brooklyn Dodgers snatched him up pretty quickly, and Blimp officially became the Babe. Babe Phelps went on to become a three-time All-Star catcher for the Dodgers. His .367 average in 1936 was the highest ever for a catcher who qualified for the batting title. Unfortunately for the Dodgers, he was also a hypochondriac and had a horrible fear of flying. Those two factors contributed to ending his major league baseball career prematurely. Phelps retired at age 34 with a lifetime batting average of .310.

Adolfo Phillips 1941 – (Cubs 1966-1969)

His nickname was the Panamanian Flash. The Cubs thought they were acquiring their next superstar when they got Panamanian outfielder Adolfo Phillips from the Phillies in 1966. That turned out to be true, but it was the pitcher that was thrown in on the deal, Ferguson Jenkins, who really sparkled in Chicago. Phillips showed flashes of greatness for the Cubs, but he never quite managed to put it together. He had one good season for the Cubs in 1967, when he hit 17 HR, knocked in 70 runs, and stole 24 bases, but manager Leo Durocher never quite thought he could trust him and rode him pretty hard. After a disappointing 1968, and a slow start in 1969, Phillips was traded to the Expos. Fergie later explained that Adolfo didn't respond well to the pressure from his manager and teammates, and developed ulcers. Phillips lasted parts of 8 seasons in the big leagues, and ended up hitting 46 of his 59 career home runs for the Cubs.

T-Bone Phillips 1933 – (Cubs 1958-1959)

He went by Taylor, but to his Cubs teammates, he was always known as T-bone. Phillips was a lefty starter for the '58 Cubs and while he won only 7 games that year, it was probably the best season of his career. Hard-throwing and wild (he was among the league leaders in wild pitches), Phillips ranks as the fourth worst-hitting pitcher (minimum 100 at-bats) in big league history, going 6-113 (.053). He was one of three Taylors on the '58 Cubs (Tony and Sammy). The Cubs traded him after a rocky start in 1959 for Seth Morehead. T-bone pitched a few more seasons for the Phillies and White Sox before retiring.

Tom Phoebus 1942 – (Cubs 1972)

Phoebus was a member of the very impressive Baltimore Orioles starting rotation of the late 60s. He was a star right out of the gate. He threw shutouts in his first two big league starts and was named *Sporting News* Rookie of the Year in 1967. He won 15 and 14 games the next two years as well, tossed a no-hitter against the Red Sox, and won a game in the 1970 World Series. By the time he came to the Cubs in 1972, however, he was primarily a relief pitcher. He struggled with his control in Chicago, and the Cubs traded him to the Braves after the season for a career minor leaguer named Tony LaRussa. Not sure what happened to that LaRussa kid.

Bill Phyle 1875 – 1953 (Orphans 1898-1899)

Phyle pitched a shutout in his major league debut for the Cubs (then known as the Orphans), but didn't quite live up to that the rest of his career. He only pitched in limited games for Chicago. His best season was in 1901 with the Giants when he won 7 games, and pitched 16 complete games. After his playing career, he became a minor league umpire.

> Cubs players have had some great nicknames over the years. Among players starting with the letter P, you'll find nicknames like Babe, Baby, Chick, Dandelion, Dode, Giant Killer, Grandmother, Handy Andy, Panamanian Flash, Pep, Pinky, Pop, Pope, Porky, Shadow, Silver Fox, T-Bone, Tacky Tom, Tarzan, Tot, Whitey, and Wild Bill.

Charlie Pick 1888 – 1954 (Cubs 1918-1919)

Charlie was the starting second baseman in the 1918 World Series for the Cubs. During the regular season he had split time at 2B with Rollie Zeider, but he played every game against the Boston Red Sox during the World Series. He batted sixth, and hit .389 for the series, including an impressive 2 for 2 against Babe Ruth in Game 4. The Cubs traded him the following season (along with Les Mann) to the Boston Braves for Buck Herzog.

Eddie Pick 1899 – 1967 (Cubs 1927)

Eddie was a third baseman and outfielder who got a few cups of coffee in the big leagues with the Reds, but his biggest opportunity came with the 1927 Cubs. That year he got 181 at-bats as the Cubs utility man, logging playing time at 2B, 3B, and right field. Unfortunately, he didn't take advantage of the opportunity, hitting only .171. Pick played another six seasons of minor league ball before retiring from the game at the age of 34.

Jeff Pico 1966 – (Cubs 1988-1990)

Pico pitched a shutout in his Major League debut, but won only 12 more games, all of them with the Cubs. He was a member of their 1989 division champion team. He went into coaching after his playing career, and logged some time as the pitching coach for the Cincinnati Reds.

Felix Pie 1985 – (Cubs 2007-2008)

Felix was supposed to be the next big star in Chicago, a five-tool outfielder with dazzling talent. Like Corey Patterson before him, Pie never quite put it together. The Cubs handed him in the starting center field job in 2008, but he lost it by May. Chicago signed Jim Edmonds and sent Felix back to the minors. One thing many male Cubs fans will never forget about Pie is an injury he suffered during his time with the Cubs. It was called "testicular torsion" or twisted testicle. Some of us still have nightmares. The Cubs traded Felix to the Orioles in 2009.

Pat Pieper 1886 – 1974 (Cubs P.A. announcer 1916-1974)

He was known for his trademark opener…"Tention! Attention Please! Get your pencils and scorecards ready and I will give you the correct lineups for today's game." As of 2018, the Cubs were still playing a recording of Pieper's voice before home games. Pat got the job in 1916 when the Cubs first started playing in what is now known as Wrigley Field. He kept the job until his death in 1974 — an incredible streak of 59 years. When he first began, he had to do his job with a gigantic megaphone (this was before a public address system had been invented.) He said the starting lineups to the crowd from third base, and then did the same thing on the other side of the field from first base. In 1932, the Cubs finally installed a public address system. Pieper was the PA for six World Series, but he also handled those chores for the twenty consecutive seasons the Cubs finished in the bottom half of the league (1946-1966). When he died shortly after the 1974 season (October 22nd), the Cubs had just finished their most successful stretch since the 1930s.

George Pierce 1888 – 1935 (Cubs 1912-1916)

Pierce pitched six years in the big leagues — five of those with the Cubs — including the team's first season in what is now known as Wrigley Field. By then his career was winding down. He twice won double-digit games when the Cubs still played at West Side Grounds (1913 & 1915). One game in 1915 he was ejected for throwing his bat at the opposing pitcher after George was hit by a pitch.

Ray Pierce 1897 – 1963 (Cubs 1924)

Pierce was a lefty pitcher who got his first taste of the big leagues with the Cubs in 1924. He got knocked around a bit, so the Cubs thought he needed a little more seasoning. The Phillies chose him in the Rule V draft and gave him another shot in 1925. It also didn't go well there. Pierce didn't really have a strikeout pitch (only 38 in 182 innings), and without that, he struggled mightily against big league pitching. His nickname was Lefty.

Andy Piercy 1854 – 1932 (White Stockings 1881)

Not to be confused with the former lead singer of After the Fire ("Der Kommissar") with the same name, this Andy Piercy appeared in only two games for the Cubs (then known as the White Stockings). He hit two singles in eight plate appearances. Andy was a second baseman/third baseman.

Bill Piercy 1896 – 1951 (Cubs 1926)

His nickname was Wild Bill. He was 30 years old by the time he got to the Cubs, and had been in the minors for a whole season. Wild Bill went 6-5 with a 4.48 ERA in 90 innings during the 1926 season. Among his teammates that year: future Hall of Famers Gabby Hartnett, Hack Wilson, and Grover Cleveland Alexander. He also played with Home Run Baker and Babe Ruth during his two brief stints with the Yankees.

Juan Pierre 1977 – (Cubs 2006)

He was named after Hall of Famer Juan Marichal, but this Juan also had a great career. Chicago fans knew him well before he played for them thanks to his impressive series against the Cubs in the 2003 NLCS. He hit .300, got ten hits, and scored five runs as the Marlins broke the hearts of Cubs fans everywhere. One of Pierre's trademarks was his incredible work ethic. He played all 162 games five seasons in a row, including his only season with the Cubs. That year he led the league in at-bats (699) and hits (204), stole 58 bases, and hit .292. On the other hand, because of his weak arm, Pierre had become a liability in the outfield, and he didn't walk enough for a leadoff man. After the season, he was allowed to leave via free agency. By the time his career ended, Pierre had 631 stolen bases, 2217 hits, and a lifetime batting average of .295. Yet he never played in a single All-Star game.

Carmen Pignatiello 1982 – (Cubs 2007-2008)

The left-handed reliever got two very brief cups of coffee with the Cubs, at the end of 2007 and the beginning of 2008. He appeared in only six games, and had an ERA of 6.75. Carmen was a local boy (Providence High School in New Lenox) who pitched in the minors for ten seasons. He hung up his spikes for good when the Twins released him from their Triple-A team early in 2009.

George Piktuzis 1932 – 1993 (Cubs 1956)

He was a local Chicago boy from Morgan Park High School, but served in the military at the height of his baseball career, and only pitched in two games for the Cubs. He was a left-handed reliever.

Horacio Pina 1945 – (Cubs 1974)

The Mexican-born Pina was acquired from the Oakland A's for Bob Locker in November of 1973. He was only two years removed from his most productive season in the big leagues, when he saved 15 games for the Rangers, and a month removed from contributing to the 1973 World Series Champion Oakland A's, but he was a total bust for the Cubs. In 59 innings pitched, he allowed an astounding 89 baserunners; not the kind of numbers you need from someone you expect to be a key member of your late inning bullpen. The Cubs traded him to the Angels by the end of July. After the season, Horacio went back to his native Mexico. He pitched a no-hitter there in 1975, and a perfect game in 1978.

Lou Piniella 1943 – (Cubs manager 2007-2010)

Piniella arrived in Chicago with one of the most impressive resumes of anyone who had ever managed the club. He won a World Series as the manager of the Reds, and had led the Seattle Mariners to multiple division titles — including one year they had one of the best records of all-time. In addition to that, Sweet Lou had fire in his belly in those previous jobs, starting fights with umpires and even his players. Surely if anyone could finally lead the Cubs to the promised land, it was Lou. Unfortunately, the Piniella who arrived in Chicago was almost twenty years older than the World Series champ, and age had mellowed him almost beyond recognition. The only fire in his belly was caused by indigestion. Lou did lead the Cubs to two division titles (2007-2008), but he won exactly as many playoff games as you did. By 2010, he was completely phoning it in. Towards the end of the year, Piniella resigned — saying that he just wanted to be closer to his family.

Ed Pinkham 1846 – 1906 (White Stockings 1871)

Ed was part of the very first official Chicago White Stockings team, the last team to play in Chicago before the Great Chicago Fire. He was mainly a third baseman and right fielder, but he was occasionally allowed to pitch. He pitched in three games. After the fire, while the city of Chicago was rebuilding, Ed returned to his native Brooklyn. He never played another game in the big leagues.

Marc Pisciotta 1970 – (Cubs 1997-1998)

As a 12-year-old, Pisciotta was a superstar. He led his team to the Little League World Series championship in 1983. In the big leagues he wasn't quite as overpowering. On the other hand, how many Little League stars never make it all the way to MLB? Marc was a right-handed reliever for the Cubs for a few seasons. He won four games over two seasons, and appeared in a Cubs uniform 67 times. He later pitched for the Kansas City Royals.

Pinky Pittenger 1899 – 1977 (Cubs 1925)

Pinky was a backup third baseman and shortstop for a Cubs team that made history — they were the first Cubs team to ever finish in last place. After that blip year of 1925, the Cubs didn't finish in last place again for another 23 years. Pinky's real name was Clark Alonzo Pittenger, and he was one of the most educated players on the team (he had gone to dental school at Ohio State University). Of course, that didn't stop him from getting involved in an altercation along with his manager (the instigator) Rabbit Maranville, after which both of them wound up in jail. Pinky only played with the Cubs for one season (1925), and he hit .312 in limited action, but the Cubs released him after that season. He played parts of seven seasons in the majors (three with the Red Sox, three with the Reds, and one with the Cubs) and in more than 1000 Major League plate appearances he managed to hit exactly one home run.

Juan Pizarro 1937– (Cubs 1970-1973)

Juan was a two-time All-Star for the White Sox (1963-1964), and came to the Cubs from the Angels in the middle of the 1970 season. Pizarro had periods of brilliance with the Cubs, and often those happened when Tom Seaver was on the mound for the Mets. In September of 1971 he shut out the Mets in Shea Stadium 1-0, and the one run came off the bat of Juan himself, a solo homer against Seaver. But those moments didn't happen too often. Pizarro was never really more than a spot-starter for the Cubs during his time with them, and never won more than seven games in a season.

Whitey Platt 1920–1970 (Cubs 1942-1943)

When your real first name is Mizell, you're bound to get a nickname. Platt's blonde hair gave him that nickname. He played for the US National Team under former Cub Les Mann, who was trying to make baseball an international sport. Whitey later was an outfielder who got a little bit of playing time with the Cubs in '42 and '43 before going into the Navy. When the war ended he played for the White Sox and St. Louis Browns. His best season was 1948, when he was the starting left fielder for the Browns and knocked in 82 runs. Platt was only 49 years old when he passed away in 1970.

Dan Plesac 1962– (Cubs 1993-1994)

Plesac was a very effective reliever with the Brewers (a three-time All-Star), and he was a workhorse out of the bullpen during his two seasons in his hometown of Chicago (he's actually from Crown Point, Indiana). After his playing career ended he became a broadcaster. For a few years (2005-2008) he was the studio analyst for Comcast in Chicago. He has been with the MLB network since 2009.

Bill Plummer 1947– (Cubs 1968)

Bill was a 21-year-old rookie catcher when he made the Cubs team in spring training of 1968 (as a Rule V pick), but he got almost no playing time during his month-long Cubs stay. He didn't resurface in the big leagues until two years later, with the Reds. He became Johnny Bench's backup there, and played in Cincinnati for eight seasons in that role. After retiring as a player, he became a manager. In 1992, he managed the Seattle Mariners, but the rest of his managing career (more than 20 years) was spent in the minor leagues and the Venezuelan Winter League.

Tom Poholsky 1929–2001 (Cubs 1957)

Poholsky pitched in the big leagues with the Cardinals for several seasons before the Cubs acquired him in 1957. He had a very bad year in Chicago, winning only one game and losing seven, with an ERA of nearly five. It was the last gasp of his time in the big leagues. For his career, Poholsky was more than 20 games under .500.

Howie Pollet 1921–1974 (Cubs 1953-1955)

The Cubs acquired Pollet in the trade that also brought Ralph Kiner and Joe Garagiola to Chicago. Pollet was a former 20-game winner (twice), All-Star (three times), and World Series champ (two times) but was toward the end of his career by the time the Cubs got him. He won 17 games in his three full seasons with the Cubs. His best years were with the Cardinals. He was later also a pitching coach with the Cardinals and won his third ring in 1964.

Elmer Ponder 1893–1974 (Cubs 1921)

Ponder was a pitcher for the 1921 Cubs. The right-hander didn't miss many bats. He gave up 117 hits and seven homers in only 89 innings. He was part of the package of players the Cubs gave up to get Jigger Statz. Ponder never pitched in the big leagues again. His wife Zelpha was a silent film organist.

Tom Poorman 1857–1905 (White Stockings 1880)

Poorman was part of the 1880 championship team. He played in right field for seven games, and hit .200. He was also an occasional pitcher, and won two games on the mound. Poorman later hit and pitched for Toledo, Boston, and Philadelphia.

Paul Popovich 1940 – (Cubs 1964-1967, 1969-1973)

Popovich was a key sub during the Cubs resurgence of the late 60s and early 70s. He was an infielder who backed up Beckert, Kessinger, and Santo. Paul wasn't a great hitter (only 14 homers and a .233 average in nearly 2000 career plate appearances), but he was such a steady glove man, he played eleven big league seasons. After he left the Cubs (in 1974), he even got a taste of postseason baseball with the Pittsburgh Pirates. He went 3 for 5 in the NLCS.

Bo Porter 1972 – (Cubs 1999)

Porter was mainly a minor league outfielder, but he did get a few cups of coffee in the big leagues, including 1999 with the Cubs. He got only 25 plate appearances and hit .192. He later got similar tastes with Texas and Oakland. After his playing career he went into coaching. For two seasons he managed the Houston Astros, and has also been on the big league coaching staffs for the Marlins, Diamondbacks, Nationals, and Braves.

Bob Porterfield 1923 – 1980 (Cubs 1959)

Porterfield was a former 20-game winner and All-Star with the Washington Senators, but he was at the tail end of his career when he signed with the Cubs after being released by the Pirates. He appeared in four games and was rocked. After the Cubs cut him loose, the Pirates picked him up again and gave him one last chance. He retired after the 1959 season.

Bill Powell 1885 – 1967 (Cubs 1912)

If you would like to travel back in time to watch Bill Powell pitch for the Cubs, you'll have to set the wayback machine to 1912. Big Bill, as he was known, pitched in exactly one game for them that season. He lasted two innings. Powell got one more taste of the big leagues after that, in April of 1913 with the Cincinnati Reds. He previously pitched for the Pirates.

Phil Powers 1854 – 1914 (White Stockings 1878)

Powers had one of the great nicknames in Cubs history. They called him Grandmother. He played for the Cubs (then known as the White Stockings) as a rookie in 1878. That was only the third season in National League history. Powers didn't do much for Chicago, hitting only .161 in 32 plate appearances. The catcher played another six seasons in the

big leagues after that, but never did quite master the art of hitting. His lifetime batting average was .180.

Willie Prall 1950 – (Cubs 1975)

Willie was a September call-up in 1975, and was absolutely pounded by the National League. In fourteen innings pitched he gave up 21 hits and 14 runs. He remained in the Cubs organization a few more years but never returned to the big leagues. Some Willie Prall trivia: In the television series *Prison Break*, one of the characters claimed that Willie Prall was his favorite player as a boy (in a flashback scene).

Johnny Pramesa 1925 – 1996 (Cubs 1952)

The Cubs sent Smoky Burgess to the Reds to acquire Pramesa in a catcher-for-catcher swap. Burgess became an All-Star and played in the big leagues for 16 more seasons. Johnny backed up starting catcher Toby Atwell in 1952, and only appeared in 22 games for the Cubs. It was his last year in the big leagues.

Andy Pratt 1979 – (Cubs 2004)

Andy was acquired in the trade that sent Juan Cruz to the Braves. Pratt pitched in four games for the Cubs in 2004, and didn't give up a hit. Good, right? Um, not so much. He walked seven men in 1.2 innings and finished his Cubs career with an ERA of 21.60.

Todd Pratt 1967 – (Cubs 1995)

Pratt was a catcher in the National League for fourteen seasons, but he couldn't have picked a worse one to be with the Cubs. The summer of 1995 is still considered the hottest summer in Chicago history. On July 13th and 14th, the two hottest days in the city's hottest summer (106 degrees and 102 degrees), Todd Pratt caught all nine innings of both games. The second one was a day game. The Cubs lost both games.

Mike Prendergast 1888 – 1967 (Cubs 1916-1917)

Mike was on the Chicago Federal Whales roster the day Wrigley Field opened. He pitched well in the two seasons that the Federal League was around — well enough to be asked to stay when the Cubs took over the ballpark in 1916. In two seasons in a Cubs uniform, Prendergast won 9 and lost 17, but his real value to the Cubs came in the trade market. Prendergast and teammate Pickles Dillhoefer were traded to the Phillies for Hall of Famer Grover Cleveland Alexander and his catcher Bill Killefer. His nickname was Iron Mike — forty-five years before another Iron Mike starred for the Bears.

> **Presidential Cubs...** President Taft's brother Charles once owned the Cubs, but several other presidents have also attended Cubs games, including Warren Harding (1920), Herbert Hoover (1929), Franklin Delano Roosevelt (1932), Ronald Reagan (1988), Bill Clinton (1999), and George W. Bush (2006). The entire 1888 Cubs team met with President Cleveland during a White House visit before a game against Washington. The 1889 team did the same with President Harrison after returning from an international barnstorming tour. And the 2016 team met with President Obama in the closing days of his presidency. There have also been Cubs named after presidents, including George Washington "Zip" Zabel, "Sparky" John Adams, Abraham Lincoln "Sweetbread" Bailey, Theodore Roosevelt "Ted" Lilly, and Calvin Coolidge Julius Caesar Tuskahoma "Cal" McLish.

Tot Pressnell 1906–2001 (Cubs 1941-1942)

His real name was Forest Charles Pressnell, but Forest's brothers were much older, and people around his hometown of Findlay, Ohio knew Forest as the "tot" who always tagged along with his siblings. The nickname stuck to him the remainder of his life. It was an ironic nickname in the majors, because Tot was a 31-year-old rookie for the Dodgers in 1938. In Brooklyn, Pressnell was a decent starting pitcher. He was traded to the Cubs before 1941, and turned into a reliever. Tot was a knuckleball pitcher, and like many knuckleballers, couldn't find his control. After the '42 season, at the age of 36, Tot went back to his crib in Ohio.

Historical note: On the day the Battle of Midway began in the Pacific (1942), Tot gave up an 11th inning homer to Willard Marshall, and the Cubs lost to the Giants 4-3 in Wrigley Field.

Ray Prim 1906–1995 (1945 Cubs)

Prim was nicknamed "Pop" by his Cubs teammates for good reason; he was nearly 39 years old when he pitched on the 1945 Cubs. Pop was a classic wartime player. He had been out of the big leagues for quite a while before the war began, and saw an opportunity to return when so many players were drafted into the military. He made the most of his opportunity. In 1945 he won 13 games and posted a sterling 2.40 ERA (best in the National League that season). Unfortunately, when all the big leaguers returned in 1946, Pop was put out to pasture. He passed away in 1995 at the age of 88.

Don Prince 1938–2017 (Cubs 1962)

Prince's entire big league career consisted of exactly one inning pitched. He did it for the Cubs on September 21, 1962. The Cubs were playing the Mets at the Polo Grounds. Don faced four batters. He walked one, hit another one, and then faced future Cub Jim Hickman. Hickman grounded into a double play. The last batter Prince faced was Sammy Drake. He was easily retired, and Prince escaped with a perfect lifetime 0.00 ERA. After his playing career, in his golden years, Prince was sent to prison for hiring a hitman to murder two people. It wasn't a hitman. It was an undercover cop.

Mark Prior 1980–(Cubs 2002-2006)

Prior was considered the franchise. He was the second overall pick of the draft, and he pitched like it initially. He finished in the top ten in Rookie of the Year voting in 2002, and then put it all together in 2003. He won 18 games, struck out 245, and looked virtually unbeatable. He was on the mound during the infamous Steve Bartman moment, five outs away from securing the Cubs a spot in the World Series. We all know what happened then. The next year Prior got hurt, and try as he might to rehab, other than occasional flashes of his old self, he became a middle-of-the-rotation starter. By 2006 his injuries were serious enough to require surgery, and Prior hasn't pitched in the big leagues since.

Historical note: On the day U.S. Forces in Iraq captured Baghdad (2003), Prior was on the mound for the Cubs. He struck out 12 and threw a four-hit shutout to beat the Expos 3-0 at Wrigley Field.

Prohibition Cubs...Prohibition lasted for 13 years, and during those years the Cubs led the league in drunks. Rabbit Maranville, the manager of the Cubs for part of the 1925 season, played with a flask of whiskey in his pants. He once got busted at a speakeasy with his teammate Pinky Pittenger. Pat Malone and Hack Wilson were wild partiers that were arrested after creating several disturbances. Both men died young thanks to the ravages of alcohol. Grover Cleveland Alexander actually passed out drunk in the Cubs dugout during a game. Catcher Rollie Hemsley was arrested for public drunkenness. Ironically, Prohibition didn't have much of an effect at Wrigley Field. The Cubs didn't sell beer at Wrigley before Prohibition. Some of their biggest seasons at the box office were during the Prohibition years. They drew more than a million fans during a few of those seasons, something unheard of in the pre-night game era. It wasn't until after Prohibition was repealed that they began selling beer. They may still sell a pint or two to this day.

Mike Proly 1950–(Cubs 1982-1983)

Proly pitched pretty well for some pretty bad Cubs teams. He won six games and saved two more in over 100 appearances with the Cubs. His ERA in 1982 was a very respectable 2.30. Proly also pitched for the White Sox, Phillies, and Cardinals.

Puerto Rican Cubs...The following Cubs were all born in Puerto Rico...Javy Baez, Hiram Bithorn (first-ever Puerto Rican MLB player), Victor Caratini, Hector Cruz, Iván de Jesus, Raul Gonzalez, Jose Guzman, Jose Hernandez, Ramon Hernandez, Willie Hernandez, Carlos Lezcano, Candy Maldonado, Carmello Martinez, José Molina, Lou Montanez, Jerry Morales, Jaime Navarro, Angel Pagan, Juan Pizarro, Luis Quinones, Rene Rivera, Roberto Rivera, Dave Rosello, Rey Sanchez, Benito Santiago, Geovany Soto, Pedro Valdes, and Hector Villanueva.

Ed Putman 1953–(Cubs 1976-1978)

Putnam was the third overall pick of the 1975 draft by the Cubs. It was a pretty weak draft. Of all the first rounders, only Bump Wills (chosen two picks later) had anything resembling a good big league career. Putman was a catcher/first baseman, and the USC product played in exactly 22 games for the Cubs over two seasons (1976, 1978). He later had a cup of coffee for the Detroit Tigers.

Zach Putnam 1987–(Cubs 2013)

Putnam pitched for four teams in the big leagues, including the Cubs in 2013. His stint with the Cubs is probably not on his highlight reel. In five games he registered an ERA of 18.90. He had a much better run on the south side of Chicago after leaving the Cubs.

John Pyecha 1931–(Cubs 1954)

If you want to go back in time to see John pitch, set your wayback machine for April 24, 1954 and go to Cincinnati's Crosley Field for his big league debut. He was brought in from the bullpen in the 7th inning with the Cubs down 3-2. The Cubs took the lead 5-3 and Pyecha was in line for his first career win. Unfortunately, the bottom of the ninth didn't quite go the way he envisioned it. With two outs in the bottom of the ninth and two runners on base, he gave up a walk-off three-run homer to Wally Post. He never pitched in the big leagues again.

Shadow Pyle 1861–1908 (White Stockings 1887)

One of the all-time great names — Shadow Pyle — only appeared in four games for the Cubs (then known as the White Stockings). Pyle only won one of his four starts, and had terrible command — walking 21 batters in 26 innings. Shadow Pyle never pitched in the big leagues again. He died two months after the Cubs won the World Series for the last time in 108 years. (As far as we know, Pyle is no relation to Gomer)

*Additional Entries...*If you check out the Every Cub Ever feature at www. justonebadcentury.com, you'll find several additional entries, including celebrity Cubs fans, writers, and bloggers. Under the letter P, you'll discover actors William Petersen and Jeremy Piven (both big Cubs fans), plus Cubs-fan/author Sara Paretsky, the Bleacher Preacher Jerry Pritikin, and Fox-Chicago broadcaster Dane Placko.

CHAPTER SEVENTEEN

Q

The starting lineup of your Chicago Cubs beginning with the letter Q...

C–Pitch back Machine with Strike Zone
1B–Wimpy Quinn, Pitcher/First Baseman
2B–Joe Quest, 3-Time Champ
SS–Luis Quinones, Mustachioed Glove Man
3B–Mike Quade, 3rd Base Coach with Glove
LF–Frank Quinn, 19th Centurion
CF–Jimmy Qualls, No-Hitter Breaker
RF–Paddy Quinn, 19th Centurion
SP–Jose Quintana, Playoff Hero/Goat
RP–-Ruben Quevedo, Sheffield/Waveland Ball-Hawk Fan

Mike Quade 1957–(Cubs manager 2010-2011)
Quade was a local kid (Prospect High School) who had been a minor league lifer, and had coached for the Cubs for years. When Lou Piniella announced he no longer felt like being the Cubs manager towards the end of the 2010 season, Quade was elevated to interim manager and led the Cubs to a winning record the rest of the season. The players seemed to respond to him. However, the next year they didn't, and by midseason, everyone was saying that Quade was in over his head. Theo Epstein was hired after the season, and to the surprise of no one, he quickly terminated the contract of his manager.

Jim Qualls 1946–(Cubs 1969)
Qualls was one of the many players that Leo Durocher trotted out to center field to solve their outfield problems in 1969 (with less than stellar results). Jim was a rookie, and he only hit .250, but he did have one magical moment that summer.

On July 9th, he came up to bat with two outs in the 9th, and ruined Tom Seaver's no-hitter. The Cubs traded him to the Expos the following year (for Garry Jestadt). Qualls only batted nine times in an Expos uniform before being shipped back down to the minors. He later had a cup of coffee with the White Sox in 1972.

Joe Quest 1852–1924 (White Stockings 1879-1882)
He was born during the Millard Filmore presidency. In his four seasons with the Cubs (then known as the White Stockings), Quest was the starting second baseman. Three of those years (1881-1883), they won the National League championship.

Ruben Quevedo 1979–(Cubs 2000)
He was supposed to be the hot pitching prospect the Cubs got in the Terry Mulholland and Jose Hernandez trade with the Braves. He went 3-10 with 7.70 ERA.

Cubs players have had some great nicknames over the years. Among players starting with the letter Q, you'll find nicknames like Paddy and Wimpy.

Quickest Cubs... Ranker.com recently listed the top 100 fastest MLB players of all time, and there were several Cubs on the list, including Lou Brock (#5), Kenny Lofton (#8), Willie Wilson (#15), Juan Pierre (#18), Delino Deshields (#22), Eric Young (#43), Dexter Fowler (#47), Tony Womack (#52), Austin Jackson (#59), Joey Gathright (#64), Bobby Bonds (#70), Alfonso Soriano (#83), and Tom Goodwin (#92). Of course most of those players came to the Cubs after their prime years.

Jack Quinlan 1927–1965 (Cubs announcer 1950s/early 1960s)
He was the radio play-by-play man for the Cubs for nearly a decade, starting in the mid-1950s. When he first began there

were several stations covering the Cubs, and he handled the honors for WIND-AM. Beginning in 1957, he moved over to what became the exclusive flagship station of the Cubs, WGN. Jack was at the microphone during both of Ernie Banks' MVP seasons, and was the first Cubs radio announcer to mention the names of future Hall of Famers Billy Williams, Lou Brock, and Ron Santo. Jack Quinlan was a master of painting a picture with his words, and when he died in a car crash after a golf outing during Spring Training 1965, the Cubs lost one of the best.

Frank Quinn 1876–1920 (Orphans 1899)

Quinn played second base and outfield for the Cubs (then known as the Orphans) in his only big league season. The backup utility man appeared in 12 games as a 22-year-old. He was only 43 years old when he passed away in 1920.

Paddy Quinn 1849–1909 (White Stockings 1877)

Paddy was 16 years old when the Civil War ended — living in his hometown of Chicago. He embarked on a baseball career by the time he was 20, and played for several teams before the National League was founded. Paddy was 27 when he played for the Cubs (then known as the White Stockings) for four games in 1877. Unfortunately, the outfielder only managed to get one hit in 15 plate appearances.

Wimpy Quinn 1918–1954 (Cubs 1941)

His real name was Wellington Hunt Quinn, and his teammates called him Wimpy. Wimpy's Cubs career was very short — he only pitched in three games — and he wore a different uniform number each time. It's safe to say they didn't call him Wimpy because of his size. Wimpy Quinn was 6'2", 190 pounds, a big man by 1941 standards. He more than likely acquired the nickname because his given name (Wellington) was the same as J. Wellington Wimpy, the comic book character from Popeye. In 1942 the Cubs demoted their Wimpy and his 7.20 ERA all the way to their B-league team in Madison to learn how to pitch (he had been a first baseman — they were trying to convert him). Wimpy had a pretty good minor league career as a hitter (he hit .302 and hit 121 homers), but he never developed into a pitcher. Wimpy Quinn died of cancer at the incredibly young age of 36.

Luis Quinones 1962– (Cubs 1987)

The Cubs acquired him when they traded Ron Cey to the A's. Luis played exactly one season for the Cubs (1987) as a utility infielder, and hit a whopping .218, but Quinones was a welcome addition to the Cubs bench because of his good glove. The Cubs traded him to Cincinnati after the season for pitcher Bill Landrum. Luis was part of the 1990 Reds team (led by Lou Piniella) that won the World Series.

Jose Quintana 1989– (Cubs 2017-present)

The Cubs acquired Jose in a blockbuster crosstown deal with the White Sox just before the trading deadline in 2017. The Sox got two of the Cubs best prospects (Eloy Jimenez and Dylan Cease) in the deal. Quintana pitched very well down the stretch (7-3 record, 98 Ks in 84 innings) and pitched a gem in the 2017 NLDS versus the Nationals. He was also the tough-luck loser in Game 1 of the NLCS, leaving the game with the lead. Unfortunately, in his final start of the playoffs he was ROCKED by the Dodgers in the game that ended the Cubs championship run. Jose had an up and down 2018 season. He finished the year 13-11 with a 4.03 ERA.

CHAPTER EIGHTEEN

R

The starting lineup of your Chicago Cubs beginning with the letter R...

C—David Ross, World Series Champ
1B—Anthony Rizzo, World Series Champ
2B—Lenny Randle, Manager Puncher
SS—Andre Rodgers, Cricket Player
3B—Aramis Ramirez, All-Star
LF—Henry Rodriguez, '98 Cub
CF—Jimmy Ryan, All-Time Triples Leader
RF—Carl Reynolds, 1938 World Series Starter
Bench—Addison Russell, World Series Champ
SP—Ed Reulbach, World Series One-Hitter
SP—Rick Reuschel, Big Daddy
SP—Charlie Root, Alleged Called-Shot Victim
SP—Robin Roberts, Hall of Famer
RP—Dick Radatz, the Monster
RP—Phil Regan, the Vulture
RP—Hector Rondon, World Series Champ

Dick Radatz 1937–2005 (Cubs 1967)

Dick Radatz was power-pitching reliever, and a former fireman of the year. His towering presence and 95-mile-per-hour fastball made him baseball's most dominant relief pitcher in the mid-1960s and earned him the unforgettable nickname of "The Monster" when he was with the Red Sox. He also pitched for Cleveland, but by the time the Indians sent him to the Cubs, he didn't have much left. He had lost the movement on his fastball, tried to become a finesse pitcher, and just couldn't do it. His ERA with the Cubs was 6.56. He pitched one season for Chicago in '67, and was released before the season in 1968.

Dave Rader 1948–(Cubs 1978)

Rader was a Cub for only one season (1978), and he hit only .203 that season. Rader also caught for the Giants, Cardinals, Phillies, and Red Sox in his big league career. While he was with the Giants (1975) he caught Ed Halicki's no-hitter.

Historical note: On the day the Congress voted to return the Panama Canal to Panama (1978), Rader drove in the game-winning run against the Expos in a 2-1 Cubs win.

Ken Raffensberger 1917–2002 (Cubs 1940-1941)

Ken was a versatile lefty for the Cubs in 1940, starting and relieving. He won 7 games and saved 3 more. The Cubs traded him to the Phillies during the war, and it was probably a miscalculation. Raffensberger became an All-Star and pitched another 13 seasons in the big leagues for the Phillies and Reds.

Pat Ragan 1885–1956 (Cubs 1909)

Ragan had a couple of good seasons as a starting pitcher in the National League, winning 15 games one year for the Dodgers, and 17 games for the Braves another. He spent just a fraction of one season with the Cubs. It was the second stop of his rookie season (he debuted with the Reds), and pitched in two games as a reliever.

Steve Rain 1975–(Cubs 1999-2000)

Rain pitched exclusively out of the bullpen for the Cubs in parts of two seasons — the entirety of his big league career. He won three games and posted an ERA of 5.46. He pitched in the minors for the Cubs and Brewers a few years after that but never made it back up to the show.

Chuck Rainey 1954–(Cubs 1983-1984)

Rainey was a 14-game winner for the Cubs in 1983, by far his best season in the big leagues. In August of that year he came within one out of pitching a no-hitter. Eddie Milner of the Reds hit a single in the ninth. Rainey won the 1-hitter 3-0. He started the 1984 season with the Cubs too, but was traded in mid-season to Oakland for Davey Lopes. It turned out to be Rainey's final season in the big leagues.

Brooks Raley 1988–(Cubs 2012-2013)

Raley came up through the Cubs system and got a cup of

coffee in parts of two seasons, but didn't have a lot of success. In 2012 he came up as a starter and was rocked. He gave up seven homers and 33 hits in only 26 innings. In 2013 he came up a reliever and didn't fare well in that role either. He later pitched in Korea.

Bob Ramazzotti 1917–2000 (1949-1953)

The Cubs got him from the Dodgers in the 1949 season, and the oft-injured hard-luck scrapper played the next few seasons in Chicago as a backup infielder. His best season with the Cubs was 1952, when he hit .284 in nearly two hundred plate appearances.

Aramis Ramirez 1978–(Cubs 2003-2011)

The Cubs acquired Ramirez during the playoff push of 2003, and he paid off in a big way that season. He hit 4 homers and knocked in ten runs during the playoffs. He also became the best third baseman the Cubs have had since Ron Santo. He was a two-time All-Star, won a Silver Slugger award, and hit more than 25 homers in seven of his seasons in Chicago. Unfortunately, he disappeared when the Cubs needed him most in the 2007 and 2008 playoffs. He was only 2 for 23 in those two series. He signed as a free agent with Milwaukee before the 2012 season. As of Opening Day 2019, Ramirez is number 6 on the Cubs all-time home run list with 239.

Historical note: On the day Barack Obama became the first-ever African-American presidential nominee (2008), Aramis hit a three-run homer in the bottom of the 8th to beat the Phillies at Wrigley Field, 6-5.

Neil Ramirez 1989–(Cubs 2014-2016)

Ramirez was one of four players acquired by the Cubs in the trade that sent Matt Garza to the Rangers (along with Justin Grimm, Mike Olt, and CJ Edwards). Initially, Ramirez was the best of the bunch. He had a breakout season in 2014, when he appeared in 50 games, struck out 53 batters, and posted an ERA of 1.44. He suffered through arm problems in 2015, however, and was never the same pitcher. The Cubs waived him in May of 2016. He pitched for the Brewers and Twins the rest of 2016.

Domingo Ramos 1958–(Cubs 1989-1990)

Domingo was a backup infielder for the Yankees, Blue Jays, Mariners, Indians, and Angels before coming to the Cubs in 1989. Ramos proved be an invaluable member of that division-winning Cubs team in 1989. He got the most extensive playing time of his career that year, hitting .263 while backing up Shawon Dunston at shortstop and Vance Law at third. He had another good year the following season, but the Cubs opted not to sign him for 1991, so Domingo retired.

Willie Ramsdell 1916–1969 (Cubs 1952)

He was known as "Willie the Knuck" because he threw a knuckleball. In fact, it was his only pitch. Everyone knew he would be throwing it, but he threw it well enough to pitch in the big leagues until he was 36 years old. The Cubs were his last team (after stints with the Dodgers and Reds), and they used him out of the bullpen. Willie the Knuck was released in mid-season and finished his career pitching in the minors in California.

Fernando Ramsey 1965– (Cubs 1992)

The Panamanian center fielder was a speedster in the Cubs system, stealing over 30 bases in four different seasons. Unfortunately, he couldn't steal first base. His lifetime minor league average of .262 was hardly inspiring. He got a cup of coffee with the Cubs in September of 1992 and hit only .120. Ramsey never got another shot at the big leagues.

Newt Randall 1890–1955 (Cubs 1907)

Newt had a very good minor league career, but didn't get his shot at the big leagues until 1907. He earned a shot by having a great spring training in New Orleans that year, and came north with the defending National League champs. He was the only rookie on the team. On June 20th of that year, he was traded to Boston in a pretty unusual way. The two managers decided to trade their right fielders as they exchanged lineup cards at home plate. Newt was sent to the Boston dugout, and Del Howard came over to the Cubs. Newt finished the season in Boston, his only season in the big leagues.

Lenny Randle 1949– (Cubs 1980)

Lenny was famous as the guy who had punched his manager (Frank Lucchesi) in the face before the Cubs acquired him. The Cubs knew they were taking a chance, but Randle had a pretty good season with an incredibly bad team in 1980, and never punched either Cubs manager (Preston Gomez or Joey Almalfitano). He signed with the Mariners as a free agent the following year, and that's where he did the other thing he is most remembered for — he got on his hands and knees and tried to blow a slow roller down the third base line into foul territory.

Historical note: At the moment of the famous New York City blackout in 1977, Lenny was up to bat against the Cubs as a member of the Mets. The game had to be completed at a later date.

Merritt Ranew 1938–2011 (Cubs 1963-1964)

In 1963 he had the best year in his career with the Cubs. He got over 150 at-bats backing up catcher Dick Bertell and responded by hitting an astounding .338, almost a hundred points above his lifetime average. Merritt hit over .400 as a pinch hitter that year. He returned to earth the following year, and never hit higher than .247 again. Ranew was traded to the Braves in 1964 for Len Gabrielson. His last sniff of the big leagues came with the expansion Seattle Pilots in 1969.

Cody Ransom 1976– (Cubs 2013)

Cody had played for the Giants, Astros, Yankees, Phillies, Diamondbacks, Brewers, and Padres before he came to the Cubs in 2013. He was the very definition of the well-traveled journeyman. Ransom had good few months in Chicago hitting nine homers in only 158 at-bats, before slumping and being released just before the season ended.

Clay Rapada 1981– (Cubs 2007)

Rapada made his major league debut with the Cubs on June 14, 2007. The Cubs were facing the Seattle Mariners in an interleague game at Wrigley Field. Rapada was called in from the pen in the top of the eighth inning to face Raul Ibanez. The Mariners were up 4-3 at the time and there were runners on first and second. Rapada induced a harmless lineout to the right fielder, and was pulled for Bobby Howry. Ibanez was the only batter Rapada ever faced in a Cubs uniform. He was sent back down to the minors after the game, and was traded to the Tigers later that season for Craig Monroe. He has since pitched for the Rangers, Orioles, Yankees, and Indians.

Dennis Rasmussen 1959– (Cubs 1992)

The 6'7 lefty pitched for five teams in his 12-year big league career, including one month with the Cubs in the middle of the 1992 season. The Cubs picked up Dennis after the Orioles waived him, and gave him a few appearances to see if he could work out his problems. He couldn't. His final Cubs ERA was over 10. Of course, left-handers aren't that easy to come by, so after the Cubs cut him, the Royals gave him a shot too. He had a 1.43 ERA the rest of that season and pitched two more seasons for KC.

Tommy Raub 1870–1949 (Cubs 1903)

The jack-of-all-trades utility man played some catcher, first base, third base, and outfield for the Cubs in 1903, backing up the likes of Frank Chance and Johnny Kling. He hit .228 in 36 games. Raub later played briefly for the Cardinals.

Bob Raudman 1942– (Cubs 1966-1967)

His Cubs teammates nicknamed him "Shorty" because Raudman was only 5'9. He may have been short, but he was powerful. He hit 20 homers in the minors in 1966, which is the reason the Cubs called him up in September that year. They let him start eight games alongside Billy Williams and Adolfo Phillips, and Raudman performed pretty well. He made the Opening Day roster in 1967, but was sent down to the minors before the end of April. He came back up in September of that season for his last shot at the big leagues. Shorty hit only .154, and never made it back to the Cubs again. Despite his power in the minor leagues, Bob Raudman never managed to hit one out of the park in the majors. He became a professional motorcycle racer after his baseball days.

Fred Raymer 1875– (Orphans 1901)

Raymer was a utility man for the Cubs (then known as the Orphans), but his one season in Chicago didn't yield such great results. Fred got lots of playing time, but didn't get lots of hits. When the season was over, he was hitting only .233. He later got a cup of coffee with Boston.

Ronald Reagan 1911–2004 (Cubs announcer 1930s)

Reagan didn't just grow up a Chicago Cubs fan. He owes much of his success to the team. Following college graduation,

Reagan landed a job as a radio announcer at WOC in Davenport, Iowa and later at WHO in Des Moines. Radio was a brand-new medium in those days and he discovered quickly that getting in on the ground floor was his ticket to the top. He began broadcasting Chicago Cubs baseball games he had never seen. His descriptions were largely improvised, and were based solely on telegraph accounts of games in progress. Despite working in Iowa, he was voted as one of the top ten most popular baseball announcers in America. In 1937 his radio station sent him out to California to cover the Cubs in spring training. At that time they trained at Catalina Island. Reagan parlayed that trip into a screen test…and the rest, as they say, is history. One of the starring roles in his film career was playing Cubs great Grover Cleveland Alexander in *The Winning Team*. Reagan made one last stop at Wrigley Field the last year of his presidency (1988). He threw out the first pitch and spent some time in the broadcast booth alongside Harry Caray.

Frank Reberger 1944 – (Cubs 1968)

The tall right-hander (6'5) was nicknamed "Crane" by his teammates. He only appeared in three games for the Cubs as a rookie. The Padres selected him in the expansion draft the following spring, and he later pitched for San Diego and the Giants. After his playing career he went into coaching, and managed in the Giants minor league system.

Anthony Recker 1983 – (Cubs 2012)

The Cubs acquired the catcher from Oakland at the end of 2012, but released him after the season. He only appeared in nine games as a Cub. Recker caught on with the Mets the following year, and has also played for Atlanta.

Jeff Reed 1962 – (Cubs 1999-2000)

Reed was a (primarily backup) catcher in the big leagues for 17 seasons, the last two of which were with the Cubs. During those two seasons he backed up Benito Santiago and Joe Girardi. He also caught for the Twins, Expos, Reds, Giants, and Rockies.

Phil Regan 1937 – (Cubs 1968-1972)

Phil Regan wasn't known as the vulture until he was converted to a reliever by the Dodgers in 1966. He was given his nickname by Sandy Koufax for picking up (cheap) wins in short relief. The vulture went 14-1 that year with a 1.62 ERA, with a National League leading 21 saves. That year he was named the Comeback Player of the Year and the Fireman of the Year. Regan became a Cub in April of 1968. They got Regan and Jim Hickman in exchange for Jim Ellis and Ted Savage, neither of whom ever did much for the Dodgers, while Hickman had the best seasons of his ML career as a Cub, and Regan led the league with 12 relief wins and 25 saves in 1968. The vulture was widely suspected of doctoring up the ball. In 1968 an umpire punished him for it, but Regan appealed to the league office, and the umpire was told that he shouldn't have kicked him out of the game without solid evidence. That led umpires and opposing managers to have him searched countless times over the next few years. They never found a thing. Regan had a decent 1969 for the Cubs, but tired toward the end of the season, blowing leads in several key games. He pitched for the Cubs a few more years, but by 1972, he was done.

Herman Reich 1917 – 2009 (Cubs 1949)

Herman was the starting first baseman for the Cubs in 1949, and it's safe to say they weren't happy with his offensive production. In over 100 games played, he hit only three homers and drove in 34 runs. It was his only season in the big leagues. Reich batted right handed, but threw left-handed.

Hal Reilly 1894 – 1957 (Cubs 1919)

Hal played exactly one game for the Cubs—on June 19, 1919. He played left field and batted seventh, going 0-3 against Brooklyn. Among his teammates that day; the infamous Fred Merkle, one of the greatest nicknames in the biz (Sweetbread Bailey), the pitcher accused of throwing a game (Claude Hendrix), and the goat of the 1918 World Series (Max Flack). The Dodgers team that day featured Hall of Famer Zach Wheat. Reilly may have only played one game in the big leagues, but he had stories for the rest of his life.

Josh Reilly 1868 – 1938 (Colts 1896)

When he arrived in Chicago in 1896 from San Francisco, the Sporting News provided a little background information about the 27-year-old rookie, saying he had been "traded for a horse when he played in California some years ago." Then, he created a new legend for himself right out of the box. In his first big league game he started a triple play. Though he started with a bang, he was more of a shooting star than anything. After eight games, Reilly contracted typhoid fever, and just like that, his big league career was over. He lived another forty-plus years, but he never played baseball again.

Laurie Reis 1858–1921 (White Stockings 1877-1878)

Laurie was short for Laurence. The native Chicagoan pitched eight games for the Cubs (then known as the White Stockings) over two seasons, and all eight of them were complete games. To say he pitched in a different era is an understatement. Laurie gave up 42 runs in those eight starts, but only 16 of them were earned.

Ken Reitz 1951–(Cubs 1981)

Ken Reitz was an All-Star third baseman and Gold Glover for the St. Louis Cardinals when the Cubs acquired him along with Leon Durham for future Hall of Famer Bruce Sutter before the 1981 season. After arriving in Chicago, Reitz promptly forgot how to hit (.215). The Cubs released him after only one season, and he was out of the big leagues altogether just one year later.

Mike Remlinger 1966– (Cubs 2003-2005)

Jim Hendry was big believer in signing veteran relievers, and Remlinger was one of the guys he brought in to help put that 2003 team over the top. He was in his eleventh season in the big leagues (having already pitched for Atlanta, Cincinnati, the Mets and the Giants) when he joined the Cubs. Remlinger had a decent year, but the Cubs bullpen overall was very shaky during an otherwise impressive year. The following year Remlinger was hurt while sitting in his La-Z-Boy chair. True story. Remlinger's other claim to fame may have been that he picked up (and kept) a portion of Sammy Sosa's infamous broken corked bat as a souvenir. Remlinger was traded to the Red Sox in 2005.

Jack Remsen 1851–1884 (White Stockings 1878-1879)

Remsen was an outfielder with the Cubs (then known as the White Stockings) who did whatever he could to get on base. One year he led the league in walks (with 17). At the time, pitchers were throwing it underhand and it took nine balls to get a walk.

Laddie Renfroe 1962 –(Cubs 1991)

Laddie was a 29-year-old rookie when he got his cup of coffee with the Cubs in 1991. He lasted exactly two weeks that summer (7/3/91 to 7/17/91). His ERA was 13.50, and he was 0-1. His son David played in the Boston Red Sox minor league system.

Steve Renko 1944–(Cubs 1976-1977)

The Cubs paid a high price indeed to acquire the Expos' two time 15-game winner Renko (and Larry Biittner). They gave up their slugging first baseman Andre Thornton. Thornton went on to become an All-Star, while Renko won 10 games over two seasons. He was traded to the White Sox in 1977.

Rick Renteria 1961–(Cubs manager 2014)

Renteria was brought aboard to manage the Cubs in 2014 because he was renowned for working well with young and Hispanic players and the Cubs had a roster full of them. He actually did a pretty good job for the Cubs, and got career years out of Anthony Rizzo and Starlin Castro, but it was his misfortune to be the manager when a better manager became available. The Cubs hired Joe Madden for the 2015 season, and said farewell to Ricky after only one year.

Michael Restovich 1979– (Cubs 2006)

He played six big league seasons (2002-2007), but only one year with the Cubs, and only got 12 at bats. After his stint with the Cubs, he got a cup of coffee with the Nationals, before going oversees to Japan.

Ed Reulbach 1882–1961 (Cubs 1905-1913)

Big Ed Reulbach was one of the best players on the Cubs during their dynasty in the first decade of the 20th century. He had double digit wins every season with the Cubs, including 24 wins in 1908. And he was clutch. Big Ed pitched a one-hitter in the 1906 World Series, and pitched two shutouts in one day Sept 26, 1908 (three days after the Merkle boner game). Some say he is one of the best pitchers of all-time not to make the Hall of Fame. (His career ERA was 2.28 in more than 2600 innings pitched). The Cubs eventually traded him in the middle of the 1913 season, and he retired in 1917. During his playing days, Reulbach was always overshadowed by the other great pitchers on the Cubs (like Mordecai Brown and Orval Overall), but he was also overshadowed in death. He died on the same day as Ty Cobb (July 17, 1961).

Historical note: On the day the first Indy 500 was staged in 1911, Ed and the Cubs lost 4-1 to the Pirates. The Indy winner was Ray Harroun, who immediately retired from racing.

Paul Reuschel 1947–(Cubs 1975-1977)

When he was called up to the Cubs in 1975, his little brother Rick was already the ace of the staff. Rick was a starting pitcher, but Paul was used almost exclusively out of the bullpen (he started two games for the Cubs in 1976). The highlight of his career was undoubtedly August 21, 1975, during his rookie season. Brother Rick pitched a shutout for 6 1/3 innings before tiring, and Paul was brought in to finish off the Dodgers. He pitched the last 2 and 2/3 innings, and also didn't allow a single run. The Cubs won the game 7-0. The Reuschel brothers remain the only siblings in Major League history to combine for a shutout.

Rick Reuschel 1949–(Cubs 1972-1981, 1983-1984)

His real name was Rick Reuschel, but to his teammates he was Big Daddy. The nickname obviously had nothing to do with the Adam Sandler movie (because it didn't come out until many years after he retired), and it had nothing to do with the Burl Ives character in the movie "Cat on a Hot Tin Roof" because that came out fourteen years before his Cubs debut in 1972. He was dubbed Big Daddy by teammate Mike Krukow, because at 6'3 , 235 pounds, he didn't much look like someone who could pass for a professional athlete, let alone be one. For the decade of the 1970s, Rick Reuschel was the best pitcher on the Cubs. He got 135 of his 214 career wins for Chicago, which is the second highest win total of any Cubs pitcher since World War II (behind only Fergie Jenkins). Big Daddy won 10 or more games for nine years in a row (1972-1980), and on August 21, 1975, he and his brother Paul became the first brothers to combine on a major league shutout. After an injury plagued stint with the Yankees, the Cubs re-signed him, and he pitched for them again in '83 and '84. Unfortunately, they let him go because

they thought he was done. He wasn't. He won 70 more games for the Pirates and Giants over the next seven seasons. Only one pitcher in Cubs history has started more games for the Cubs than Reuschel; Hall of Famer Fergie Jenkins.

Historical note: On the day John Dean admitted to Congress that the Nixon White House was covering up facts about Watergate (1973), Rick was on the mound for the Cubs. He didn't factor in the decision, but the Cubs beat the Mets 3-2 after scoring all three runs in the 9th inning against Tug McGraw.

Jose Reyes 1983–(Cubs 2006)

Not to be confused with the stud infielder Jose Reyes (Mets, Marlins, Blue Jays), this Jose Reyes was a catcher who got a cup of coffee with the Cubs at the end of the 2006 season. He batted five times and struck out three of those times. He also got 2 RBI with his only big league hit. He was signed by the Mets the following year but never made it up to their big league club.

Archie Reynolds 1946–(Cubs 1968-70)

Archie pitched in parts of three seasons for the Cubs, but didn't get significant time in any of those seasons. The Cubs traded him in July of 1970 to the Angels for Juan Pizarro. Archie also pitched briefly for the Brewers.

Carl Reynolds 1903–(Cubs 1937-1939)

Carl was a ten-year veteran of the big leagues (White Sox, Senators, Browns, Red Sox) when he joined the Cubs in 1937, and claimed a starting outfield spot on the 1938 pennant winners. But in the World Series he came up to bat thirteen times and only got on base once (via walk). He went back to being the fourth outfielder in 1939 — his last season in the big leagues.

Bob Rhoads 1879–1967 (Orphans 1902)

Like every other baseball player with the last name of Rhoads, Bob was nicknamed Dusty. He was a 22-year-old rookie with the Cubs (then known as the Orphans) and started 16 games for them in 1902. That team had six players who would eventually go on to win the World Series for the Cubs (Tinker, Evers, Chance, Slagle, Kling, and Lundgren). The Cubs traded Dusty to the Cardinals the following April and he pitched eight more seasons in the big leagues. His best years were with Cleveland, where he became a 20-game winner.

Tuffy Rhodes 1968 – (Cubs 1993-1995)

In 1994, the Cubs had a memorable home opener against the New York Mets. A little-known player named Tuffy Rhodes hit three homers that day to power the Cubs to a victory. Cubs fans had delusions of grandeur after that game, but Tuffy hit only five more homers the rest of the season. 1994 was also the year that Major League Baseball canceled the World Series because the players were on strike. Not that the Cubs would have had a shot at winning it. When the league shut it down for the year in August, the Cubs were 15 games under .500 and 16 1/2 games out of first place. Tuffy left the Cubs the following season. He eventually played in Japan, where he finally realized his full potential. In 2001 he tied the Japanese League record for most home runs in a season, a record held by the immortal Sadaharu Oh since 1964. Tuffy easily could have broken the record, but after he tied Oh, Japanese pitchers intentionally walked him the rest of the year.

> Cubs players have had some great nicknames over the years. Among players starting with the letter R, you'll find nicknames like Big Daddy, Big Ed, Chinski, Crane, Dutch (3 of them), Fuzzy, Grandpa, Hoot, Monster, Rip, Shorty, Tuffy, Twitch, Vulture, and Willie the Knuck.

Del Rice 1922 – 1983 (Cubs 1960)

Rice was a big league catcher for 17 seasons, including an All-Star season with the Cardinals in 1953, and two championship seasons (Cardinals 1946, Braves 1957). By the time he came to the Cubs he was strictly a backup. He hit .231 in limited opportunities. Rice went into coaching after his playing days were over, culminating in one season at the helm of the Angels in 1977.

Hal Rice 1924 – 1997 (Cubs 1954)

Hal's nickname was "Hoot" and he was an outfielder and pinch hitter for seven big league seasons, including his last one with the Cubs. He was probably best known as Stan Musial's backup in St. Louis, and as you might imagine, didn't get a lot of playing time in that capacity. The Cubs brought him aboard to pinch hit, but when you hit only .153, it's usually enough to end your career. That's what happened to "Hoot" in Chicago.

Len Rice 1918 – 1992 (Cubs 1944-1945)

Len was one of the backup catchers on the last Cubs team to win the pennant before the 2016 Cubs. He appeared in 32 games that season, and hit .232 in just over a hundred plate appearances. When the regulars came back from the war, Rice's time in the big leagues was up. He played another four years in the minors before retiring from baseball.

Clayton Richard 1983 – (Cubs 2015-2016)

The former White Sox wunderkind arrived from the Pirates during the summer of 2015. At first it was thought he could fill the fifth starter role, but he eventually emerged as an important left-hander out of the Cubs bullpen. He was a part of the postseason roster in 2015, and pitched in six postseason games without allowing a run. The Cubs re-signed him after the playoffs, but 2016 was not a good year for Clayton. He suffered an injury, struggled when he returned, and was released by the Cubs in August. He finished the 2016 season with the Padres. The Cubs finished that season by breaking a 108-year championship drought.

Fred Richards 1927 – 2016 (Cubs 1951)

His teammates called him Fuzzy. The 23-year-old first baseman played the last two weeks of the 1951 season and batted .296 with four RBI, but that was the extent of his big league career. He played in the minors for another eleven years. He died during spring training of the Cubs 2016 World Championship season.

Lance Richbourg 1897 – 1975 (Cubs 1932)

Richbourg was a backup outfielder on the 1932 pennant-winning Cubs. It was the last season of his eight-year big league career (spent mostly in Boston). He was 34 years old at the time, and backed up all three starting outfielders: Kiki Cuyler, Johnny Moore, and Riggs Stephenson.

Lew Richie 1883–1936 (Cubs 1910-1913)

Richie was a starting pitcher in the big leagues for eight seasons, but he had the best two seasons of his career with the Cubs. He won 15 games and 16 games in 1911 and 1912. He also pitched (one inning) in the 1910 World Series. Nine of his teammates were veterans of the 1908 Cubs world champs. In August of 1913 he was traded for Hippo Vaughn.

Beryl Richmond 1907–1980 (Cubs 1933)

Beryl was a left-hander who worked out of the bullpen for the 1933 Cubs. He was a 25-year-old rookie who gave up a lot of hits. He pitched briefly for the Reds the following season, and then finished up his career in the minor leagues. Some of his minor league seasons were legendarily bad. For instance in 1935, he won 3 games and lost 18.

Reggie Richter 1888–1934 (Cubs 1911)

Reggie (real first name — Emil) was born in Dusseldorf, Germany and came over to America around the turn of the century. Reggie was a pitcher who worked mostly out of the bullpen for one big league season. He pitched a few more years in the minors before hanging up his spikes at the age of 27. Richter passed away in Winfield, Illinois at the age of 45.

Marv Rickert 1926 –1978 (Cubs 1942-1947)

His teammates called him Twitch. Rickert began his career with the Cubs, served in the Coast Guard during the war for three years, and then came back to play two more seasons in Chicago. He later played with the Reds, Braves (including in the World Series), Pirates, and White Sox. Twitch had two memorable Cubs moments, one good and one not so good. In spring training in 1946, he tried to steal second base… with the bases loaded. He atoned for that miscue later that year when he and Eddie Waitkus hit back-to-back inside-the-park home runs.

The Ricketts Family (Cubs owner 2009-present)

When the billionaire Ricketts family (TD Ameritrade) bought the Cubs from the *Tribune* in 2009, they promised to refocus on the fans, rebuild the ballpark, and to once and for all bring a winner to Chicago. The main owner Tom grew up a Cubs fan, and met his future wife in the bleachers in the 1980s. He is a constant presence in the ballpark, and goes out of his way to speak to the fans. He also did the most important thing an owner can do — he opened up the purse strings and brought in the best management team in baseball. Thanks to the moves made by Theo Epstein and Jed Hoyer, the Cubs finally ended their 108-year drought in 2016. Tom's siblings Laura and Todd are also involved in the running of the team. (Todd was once on the show *Undercover Boss*). The Ricketts family is very active politically. Laura and Todd are both big fundraisers — for opposite parties. Their brother Joe is the Governor of Nebraska. Their father Joe, the founder of TD Ameritrade, is one of the biggest donors to the Republican Party.

Jim Riggleman 1952–(Cubs manager 1995-1999)

Riggleman came to the Cubs from San Diego, where he had led the hapless Padres to several last place finishes. The Cubs must have seen something in him despite that record, because they handed the managing reigns to him. In his 4+ seasons with the Cubs he had some bright spots (the 1998 Wild Card season), and some low-lows (the 0-14 start in 1997). He was fired in 1999 after the Cubs finished in last place yet again.

George Riley 1956–(Cubs 1979-1980)

The lefty came up with the Cubs but didn't pitch well. His ERA over two seasons was over five. He later pitched for the Giants and Expos. Riley won exactly one game in his big league career, and it wasn't for the Cubs.

Allen Ripley 1952–2014 (Cubs 1982)

Believe it or not, Ripley was a starting pitcher for a few seasons in the late 70s and early 80s. His last season in the big leagues was with the Cubs. The right-hander went 5-7 with a 4.26 ERA in 19 starts. He also pitched for the Red Sox and the Giants. His dad Walter was a big leaguer with the Red Sox.

Rene Rivera 1983–(Cubs 2017)

The Cubs picked up the veteran backstop in August when they needed some veteran help. He filled in admirably for the injured Willson Contreras. The 34-year-old also had some big hits, including a grand slam to win a game. After the season he was granted his free agency. He has also played for Seattle, Tampa, Minnesota, San Diego, New York, Los Angeles, and Atlanta.

Roberto Rivera 1969–(1995 Cubs)

Roberto was a September call-up for the Cubs, and the left-hander appeared in seven games — all in relief. Four years later he also pitched out of the bullpen for the Padres. His big league career didn't quite make into the new century. He pitched in Mexico and the Dominican Republic after his stint with the Padres.

Anthony Rizzo 1989–(Cubs 2012-present)

Rizzo was one of the first young studs acquired by new Cubs president Theo Epstein after taking over the Cubs, and they built their whole club around him. The very highly regarded prospect had been drafted by Epstein and company in Boston, and was acquired from Jed Hoyer's previous team San Diego for Cubs pitcher Andrew Cashner. Rizzo burst onto the scene in the middle of 2012 and hit 15 homers the last few months of the season. In 2014, Anthony really announced his arrival with an All-Star season, and has never looked back. Anthony's all-world 2015 led the Cubs to the NLCS. He slugged 31 homers and drove in 101, was named an All-Star, and finished fourth in the MVP voting. In 2016, Rizzo set career highs in average, homers, and RBI, won a Silver Slugger Award, and his first Gold Glove. In fact, he won the Platinum Glove award for being the best defensive player in the National League. But he did much more than that. He led the Cubs to a World Series championship. Who can forget the sight of Anthony putting that last-out ball in his back pocket as bedlam ensued in Cleveland?

That clearly wasn't the last act for Anthony. In 2017, Rizzo slugged 32 homers, drove in 109, scored 99, and walked more often than he struck out (91 BB, 90 K). But after leading the team in RBI in the NLDS, he was ineffective in the NLCS, going only 1 for 17. The Cubs regressed a bit in 2018, and only made it to the Wild Card game, but Rizzo was not the reason for that. He still knocked in over 100 runs, and won his second Gold Glove. During the 2019 season Anthony will surpass 200 homers in a Cubs uniform. Only eight other Cubs have ever done that.

Donn Roach 1989–(Cubs 2015)

Roach was called up on June 27, 2015 for an emergency start against the Cardinals in St. Louis. It didn't go well. He gave up eight hits in 3.1 innings and posted a 10.80 ERA. The Cubs sent him back down to Iowa after the game, and released him a few weeks later. He also had a cup of coffee with the Padres (before) and Mariners (after).

Mel Roach 1933–(Cubs 1961)

Roach played eight years in the big leagues, including part of the 1961 season with the Cubs. They acquired him from Milwaukee for Frank Thomas. He played a little first base and a little second base, and hit an incredibly underwhelming .128. Mel missed two full seasons of his prime baseball years (while with Milwaukee) because he was serving in the military.

Skel Roach 1871–1958 (Orphans 1899)

Roach was born in Germany, and if his name doesn't sound very German to you, there's a good reason for that. His given name was Rudolf Weichbrodt. His teammates in semi-pro baseball couldn't (or didn't want to) pronounce his name. His manager thought he was skinny, so he called him Skeleton (or Skel for short). Another teammate gave him his last name Roach. Thereafter he went by Skel Roach. He only pitched one big league game, filling in for injured HOFer Clark Griffith. He won the game, but couldn't come to contract terms with Chicago to stay with the team. He never got another chance.

Fred Roat 1867–1913 (Colts 1892)

Fred was such an obscure player for the Cubs (then known as the Colts), that there's not even a record of whether he batted right or left-handed. He played second base for eight games and hit .194. After his short stint in the big leagues, he played another eleven seasons in the minors.

Kevin Roberson 1968–(Cubs 1993-1995)

In his rookie year of 1993, Roberson was given a fair amount of playing time (180 at-bats) and did deliver some power (9 HR, 27 RBI), but his lifetime batting average was .197. The downstate Illinois native later played for the Mets. He was an outfielder.

Dave Roberts 1944–2009 (Cubs 1978)

Roberts got knocked around pretty good during his year with the Cubs (1978), but he also won a World Series championship the following year with the Pittsburgh Pirates. Roberts is in the top five of several career categories for Jewish pitchers, behind only the likes of Sandy Koufax, Ken Holtzman, and Steve Stone. His other claim to fame was giving up the very last hit and RBI of Hank Aaron's career.

Robin Roberts 1926–2010 (Cubs 1966)

He is a Hall of Famer, a seven-time All-Star, a six-time 20-game winner, a man that led his team to the pennant as a 23-year-old, made the cover of *Time Magazine*, and ended up with 286 career wins. Roberts led the league in wins four times, strikeouts twice, and complete games five times. Of course, none of that happened during his short stint with the Cubs. The Cubs thought they should give him one last chance. Unfortunately, he was the oldest player in the majors (39) when he was picked up by the Cubs in 1966, and he didn't have anything left in the tank. The head and heart were willing, but the arm was not. In his nine starts with the Cubs, his ERA was over six, and he gave up eight home runs. Those just added to his record-setting total. Roberts served up more home runs than any other pitcher in history. One of his teammates on the 1966 Cubs is now second place on the all-time home run list: Ferguson Jenkins. The Cubs released Roberts on October 4, 1966. He never pitched in the majors again.

Daryl Robertson 1936–2018 (Cubs 1962)

Daryl got a very brief trial with the Cubs in 1962 during the College of Coaches era. He came to Chicago in the Moe Drabowsky trade, and played in nine games in May of 1962. In 19 at-bats, he managed only two hits. That was his only shot at the big leagues. Daryl may not have had a long big league career, but he did play alongside four Hall of Famers: Ernie Banks, Ron Santo, Lou Brock, and Billy Williams.

Dave Robertson 1889–1970 (Cubs 1919-1921)

The Cubs got Robertson from the Giants in exchange for troubled starting pitcher Shufflin' Phil Douglas. Robertson became the Cubs starting left fielder in 1920, and hit .300 with 50 extra base hits and 17 stolen bases. For once, the Cubs sold high. They traded him to the Pirates the following season for Elmer Ponder. Robertson was out of baseball by 1923.

Don Robertson 1930– (Cubs 1954)

The local boy (Thornton High School in Harvey) played with the Cubs the first month of the 1954 season, along with fellow rookies Ernie Banks and Gene Baker. Unlike his two teammates, Don didn't last. He was used mainly as a pinch runner, appearing in 14 games. He played a grand total of nine innings in right field, and made one putout. He batted six times, and didn't get a hit. It was his only taste of the big leagues.

Jeff Robinson 1960– (Cubs 1992)

Jeff pitched nine years in the big leagues, mostly as a reliever, although he did occasionally start. His final season was with the Cubs. He won four games and saved another in 49 appearances. Robinson also pitched for the Giants, Pirates, Yankees, and Angels.

Andre Rodgers 1934–2004 (Cubs 1961-1964)

Andre was the first player from the Bahamas to play in the big leagues. He was a great cricket player in his homeland who heard about baseball and came to America to give it a shot. It took him a few years to make it, but the talented athlete eventually played for the Giants, Cubs, and Pirates over an 11-year career. With the Cubs he took over the shortstop job when Ernie Banks was moved to first base. He and Ken Hubbs made a great double play combination. In 1962 they set a record (along with 1B Ernie) for most double plays in a season. His best year with the bat was probably his final year in a Cubs uniform, when Andre hit 12 homers. The Cubs traded him to the Pirates after the season because they had another shortstop in the pipeline ready to take over — Don Kessinger.

Fernando Rodney 1977– (Cubs 2015)

The Cubs picked up the former All-Star closer from Seattle at the end of August to augment their bullpen for the playoff run. Though clearly on the downside of his career, Rodney did provide a few important bullpen innings for them, and posted a sterling 0.75 ERA in the last month of the season.

In the playoffs it didn't go quite as well. He was one of four Cubs pitchers to serve up a long ball to Daniel Murphy of the Mets in the NLCS.

Freddy Rodriguez 1924–2009 (Cubs 1958)

Poor Freddy. Somewhere along the way he got on Mike Royko's bad side. Every year in the 60s and 70s, Royko would print a Cubs Quiz making fun of some of the lesser Cubs of his lifetime, and Freddy was often featured. Royko liked to say that Freddy was undefeated as a rookie, which was true, but he followed that up with a notation that Freddy also didn't win a single game, which was also true. Freddy was a Cub in April and May of 1958. His ERA was bad (over seven), but he saved two games before the Cubs cut him loose. In fairness to Rodriguez, the Cuban right-hander was a 33-year-old rookie who had pitched 18 seasons in the minors. Surely the team didn't expect a lot from him.

Henry Rodriguez 1967– (Cubs 1998-2000)

Henry started in left field for the Cubs in 1998, 1999, and 2000, and became a fan favorite. The left field bleacher bums would throw Oh Henry bars at him when he returned to his position after hitting a homer. He hit 75 of them in his three seasons in Chicago. The Cubs traded him to the Marlins for Ross Gload.

Henry Rodriguez 1987– (Cubs 2013)

Not to be confused with the Henry Rodriguez who played left field for the Cubs in the late 90s, this Henry Rodriguez (no relation) was a pitcher with a dynamite fastball. Unfortunately, he couldn't control it. In his six big league seasons he had 36 wild pitches in only 150 innings pitched. He also pitched for the Marlins, A's, and Nationals.

Roberto Rodriguez 1941–2012 (Cubs 1970)

The Venezuelan was one of the relievers in a very shaky Cubs bullpen in 1970. He saved two games for the Cubs, but he was routinely rocked. His final ERA for the season was 5.82. The Cubs tried to convert him into a starter in the minors the next season, and he stayed in their system for the next four years. He never made it back to the big leagues. Roberto is in the Venezuelan Baseball Hall of Fame.

Billy Rogell 1904–2003 (Cubs 1940)

The local boy (Fenger High School) played thirteen big league seasons for the Red Sox and Tigers before he finally got his chance to play for his hometown Cubs. He had been the starting shortstop of the Tigers team that beat the Cubs in the 1935 World Series. Billy was known as a slick fielder — he led the league in assists, putouts, double plays, and fielding percentage in the American League. With the Cubs he was the backup to Billy Herman, Bobby Mattick, and Stan Hack. It was his final season in the big leagues. After baseball he went into politics in Michigan. He was on Detroit's City Council for 36 years.

Dan Rohn 1956– (Cubs 1983-1984)

He was a mostly used as a pinch hitter, and in his rookie season of 1983 he was a pretty good one, hitting .387. In his second season he hit .129. The Cubs shipped him off to Cleveland for relief pitcher Jay Baller. Rohn went into coaching after his playing career. He has managed in the Mariners and Giants minor league systems.

Mel Rojas 1966– (Cubs 1997)

The Cubs signed Mel to be their closer after back-to-back 30-save seasons for the Expos. Something must have happened to him on the flight from Montreal to Chicago because he was lit up as the Cubs closer. Rojas gave up 11 homers and contributed greatly to the 0-14 start that year. He was so bad that the Cubs traded him before the season was over to the Mets in a bad contract for bad contract trade. And they considered themselves lucky. Rojas is possibly the worst free agent signing in Cubs history.

Hector Rondon 1988– (Cubs 2013-2017)

The Venezuelan was a Rule V pick for the Cubs, and made their Opening Day roster in 2013. He pitched in 45 games for a team that people simply stopped watching. In 2014 he became the team's closer after Jose Veras couldn't handle the job and Hector saved 29 games. He followed that up with a 30-save season in 2015. Around the trade deadline in 2016, however, the Cubs thought they needed a bullpen upgrade, so they traded for Aroldis Chapman and moved Hector into the setup role. He never really thrived there. First he suffered an injury, and when he returned, he never could quite put it all together. Hector pitched in the World Series for the Cubs, but unfortunately surrendered a home run. Hector had a very uneven 2017, and by the time the playoffs arrived, his manager didn't have much faith in him. Rondon surrendered two homers in the NLCS. After the season the Cubs let him go. He signed with the Astros.

Rolando Roomes 1962 – (Cubs 1988)

Rolando was born and raised in Jamaica, and it took him quite a while before he got his cup of coffee (16 at-bats) with the 1988 Cubs. He was 26 years old at the time. The Cubs traded him to the Reds for Lloyd McClendon after the season. While McClendon was an important part of the 1989 division-winning Cubs, Roomes was out of baseball by 1990.

Charlie Root 1899 – 1970 (Cubs 1926-1941)

In 1969 Root was named the all-time greatest Cubs right-hander, but despite all his accomplishments, he'll always be most remembered for something that probably never happened…Babe Ruth's called shot during the 1932 World Series. Root always denied that Ruth really did it. "He was just saying he had one strike left," Root insisted. The man that gave up the supposed called shot had a reputation as a headhunter, which is why it's doubtful Ruth actually called the shot. How much of a headhunter was he? One time Charlie was hit in the elbow by another pitcher (Adolpho Lugue). When he got back to the mound, he knocked down all nine guys on Lugue's team. One after another, bang, bang, bang. He was going to keep going but the umpire finally stepped in after he got every guy once. How much of a headhunter was he? His nickname was "Chinski" because he wasn't afraid to throw the ball right at your chin. Root pitched in four different World Series for the Cubs, but never won a postseason game (0-3, 6.75 ERA in the WS). He did, however, win over 200 games for the Cubs (the only pitcher who ever did).

Historical note: On the day John Dillinger was shot and killed outside the Biograph Theater in Chicago, Charlie was on the mound for the Cubs, pitching against the Phillies in Philadelphia.

Randy Rosario 1994 – (Cubs 2018-present)

The Cubs claimed the young Dominican off waivers from the Minnesota Twins, and he became a key part of their bullpen during the 2018 season. The lefty appeared in 44 games and posted a 3.66 ERA.

Dave Rosello 1950 – (Cubs 1972-1977)

The Cubs really thought Dave Rosello was their shortstop of the future when they traded away fan favorite Don Kessinger to open the position for him. Unfortunately, Rosello didn't quite live up to expectations. His fielding left a lot to be desired (he made 12 errors in only 80 plus games), and he hit only .242 with no power at all. The Cubs had seen enough. The next season, they acquired Iván de Jesus to take his place.

David Ross 1977 – (Cubs 2015-2016)

Ross was in his 14th big league season when he was acquired by the Cubs. He had previously caught for the Dodgers, Pirates, Padres, Reds, Braves, and Red Sox. The Cubs mainly got him because of his relationship with their new ace pitcher Jon Lester. Ross had served as Lester's personal catcher in Boston. He didn't hit well for the Cubs, but he did provide an important veteran voice in the clubhouse and was one of the team's undisputed leaders. He even pitched in a few blowouts, posting a perfect ERA. In 2016, Grandpa Rossy, as he was known by his teammates, announced that it would be his last season. He made the most of it, slugging ten homers, catching a no-hitter (by Jake Arietta), and winning the World Series. His teammates seemed to dedicate that World Series win to Ross — easily the most popular player in the Cubs clubhouse.

Gary Ross 1947 – (Cubs 1968-1969)

Ross came up to the big leagues with the Cubs, and contributed as a member of the bullpen for parts of two seasons. He was traded to the Padres along with Joe Niekro in the Dick Selma trade, and pitched another eight seasons in the majors. Unfortunately for him, he pitched for some truly bad teams (Padres and Angels), and ended his career with a 25-47 record. One year with the Angels (1976), he pitched 225 innings with a 3.00 ERA, and finished with an 8-16 record.

Zac Rosscup 1985 – (Cubs 2013-2015, 2017)

Rosscup has had a couple of shots in the big leagues with the Cubs as a situational lefty. In 2013 it went pretty well in ten appearances. In 2014, not so much. He posted an ERA of nearly 10 in 18 appearances. The Cubs kept the lefty for the 2015 season, and used him a bit more often (33 games), and he responded with an ERA of 4.39. His last cup of coffee with the Cubs came in 2017 when he pitched 2/3 of an inning. The Cubs traded him to Colorado in June.

Jack Rowan 1886 – 1966 (Cubs 1911)

Rowan pitched in the big leagues for seven seasons, but only made one appearance for the Cubs in 1911. He gave up four runs in two innings and was released. Rowan's claim to fame is that he pitched nearly 700 innings in the big leagues and only gave up eight home runs.

Wade Rowdon 1960 – (Cubs 1987)

Rowdon was a backup third baseman who played only eleven games for the Cubs in 1987. He hit .226 in 34 plate appearances. Before being called up to the big league club, he hit homers in four consecutive at-bats for Iowa. He later played in Japan.

Dave Rowe 1854 – 1930 (White Stockings 1877)

Rowe eventually played seven years of big league baseball, but it all began with his stint in Chicago. He played in exactly two games in the outfield for the Cubs (then known as the White Stockings), and batted seven times (two singles). He also pitched one inning of one of those games. The 5'9 right-hander gave up two runs — for an ERA of 18. His brother Jack also played in the bigs, although never with Chicago.

Luther Roy 1902 – 1963 (Cubs 1927)

Roy was a reliever for the 1927 Cubs, and pitched pretty well in his limited appearances with the club. He also pitched for the Indians, Phillies, and Dodgers in his four-year big league career.

Vic Roznovsky 1938 – (Cubs 1964-1965)

Vic was a backup catcher for the Cubs for two seasons on two very bad teams. Just as they were showing signs of turning the corner, Vic was traded to the Orioles. Of course, Roznovsky wasn't complaining. His first year with Baltimore, they won the World Series. Among his teammates on that team: former Cub Moe Drabowsky and future Cub Davey Johnson.

Dutch Rudolph 1882 – 1967 (Cubs 1904)

Dutch played in exactly two games for the Cubs in July of 1904. He went 1 for 3, and played right field. His only other cup of coffee came the previous season with the Philadelphia Phillies.

Ken Rudolph 1946 – (Cubs 1969-1973)

Ken served as the backup catcher to Randy Hundley for several seasons, beginning with the memorable 1969 season. He was only 22 years old when he broke camp with the Cubs that year. His best season in a Cubs uniform was probably 1973. He appeared in 64 games for the Cubs that year, although he hit only .206. Ken was traded to the Giants during spring training of 1974. He later also played for the Cardinals and Orioles.

Dutch Ruether 1893 – 1970 (Cubs 1917)

He was just a rookie pitcher when the Cubs sold him to the Reds. How could they have known that he would go on to win over 130 major league games (three seasons were great — 21, 19, and 18 wins), and lead two teams to the World Series (1919 Reds and 1926 Yankees). He won a game in the 1919 World Series for the Reds, but then again, the White Sox threw that series. After his playing career ended, Dutch came back to the Cubs and worked for them as a scout. Among the players he signed: Peanuts Lowrey and Joey Amalfitano.

Justin Ruggiano 1982 – (Cubs 2014)

The idea was to platoon Ruggiano, because he hit left-handers much better than righties, but the Cubs didn't face many lefties. He only appeared in 81 games and hit six homers. The Cubs traded him to the Mariners after the season.

*Runs Scored...*The only stat that really matters in the end is runs scored. Your team must score the most runs. Cap Anson is the all-time Cubs leader in that category. Only eight players in big league history have scored more runs than Cap, and they are among the best players in history...Rickey Henderson, Ty Cobb, Barry Bonds, Hank Aaron, Babe Ruth, Pete Rose, Willie Mays, and Alex Rodriguez.

Glendon Rusch 1974–(Cubs 2004-2006)

The soft-tossing lefty found a spot in the Cubs rotation for a few seasons, including a nine-win '05 season, but he never really put more than an isolated streak together. In his final Cubs season he was 3-8, with a 7.46 ERA. He pitched in the World Series for the Mets in 2000 in the Subway Series versus the Yankees.

Bob Rush 1925–2011 (Cubs 1948-1957)

The big right-hander was a two-time All-Star for some pretty bad Cubs teams. He won over 100 games in a Cubs uniform, including a 17-win year in 1952, and four different seasons with 13 wins. The Cubs traded him to the World Champion Milwaukee Braves after the 1957 season, and the veteran finally got a chance to pitch for a winner. He won 10 games for the 1958 pennant winners, and started Game 3 of the 1958 World Series against the Yankees. He and the Braves lost the game 4-0.

Chris Rusin 1986–(Cubs 2012-2014)

Rusin started 20 games for the Cubs over three seasons as a fill-in/spot starter. He had a 4-9 record with an ERA of 4.97, and was released in late September of 2014.

Addison Russell 1994–(Cubs 2015-present)

The prized prospect was picked up in the Jeff Samardzija/Jason Hammel trade with Oakland. It was thought that he would be spending the 2015 season in Iowa, but the disappointing play of the big league second basemen forced an earlier call-up. When he took his first at-bat in April, Addison was the youngest player in all of baseball. Russell had a tremendous rookie season, eventually wrestling away the starting shortstop position from Starlin Castro. He hit 13 homers, knocked in 54 runs, and played a dazzling shortstop. It wasn't a coincidence that the Cubs didn't play as well in the NLCS when Russell was out with a strained hamstring. With a healthy Russell in 2016, the Cubs won it all. Addison was named the starting shortstop in the All-Star game, hit 21 homers, and knocked in 95 RBI in his first full season. In the 2016 playoffs he came up big again, hitting three homers and knocking in 14 runs — including 9 in the World Series. The 2017 season, on the other hand, was a disappointment. Addison struggled with injuries and was limited to less than 400 at-bats. He did manage to hit 12 homers in the regular season and another in the NLCS. The 2018 season was an unmitigated disaster. It ended quite badly for Russell. He was suspended by the league for domestic abuse.

Jack Russell 1905–1990 (Cubs 1938-1939)

Russell was a two-time saves leader and an All-Star with the Senators before coming to the Cubs. The reliever pitched pretty well for the Cubs during their 1938 World Series year. He even got into two games of the series and was one of the rare Cubs pitchers who performed well. In all he pitched 15 years in the big leagues, and was an incredible 56 games under .500 (85-141).

James Russell 1986–(Cubs 2010-2014, 2015)

A key left-handed arm out of the Cubs bullpen for several seasons, James was the son of former big league closer Jeff Russell. He was traded to Atlanta in 2014, but it didn't work out for him there. The Cubs reacquired him after he was released by the Braves in 2015, but he didn't pitch well. The situational lefty did appear in 49 games, but his ERA of 5.49 was ugly. After the season he was signed as a free agent by the Phillies.

Historical note: On the day Osama Bin Laden was killed by Seal Team 6 (2011), Russell got a rare start for the Cubs against the Dodgers in Los Angeles. The opposing pitcher was Clayton Kershaw. Cubs lost 5-2.

Rip Russell 1915–1976 (Cubs 1939-1942)

He real first name was Glen, but Rip Russell was known for being able to rip line drives. He also came to the Cubs just after another first baseman named Rip Collins played for the team, so it was only natural that his teammates started calling him Rip. Russell played for the Cubs for four seasons, but his best season was definitely his rookie year of 1939.

Filling in for the injured Phil Cavarretta on the defending NL champs, Rip knocked in 79 runs, good enough for second best on the team. He spent the rest of career as a bench player, first with the Cubs in 1940-42, then after a stint in the military, with the Boston Red Sox in 1946 and 1947. Rip died at the age of 61. R.I.P, Rip.

Dick Ruthven 1951 – (Cubs 1983-1986)

Dick was a Dallas Green favorite. He was a member of the 1980 World Series team managed by Green, and shortly after Green took over the Cubs, Ruthven was one of the first players he acquired. Unfortunately, Dick never really clicked with the Cubs. In 1984 he began the season as the Opening Day starter, but the time the season ended, he was #5 (behind Sutcliffe, Trout, Eckersley, and Sanderson), and he didn't pitch in that tragic NLCS against the Padres. Ruthven stayed with the Cubs another season and a half, but after posting similarly mediocre numbers, he was released in early 1986. It was the end of his baseball career.

Historical note: On the day the movie *The Natural* was released, Dick was on the mound for the Cubs, facing Nolan Ryan of the Astros. Guess who won? Astros 3-1.

Jimmy Ryan 1863 – 1923 (White Stockings/Colts/ Orphans 1885-1890, 1892-1900)

Jimmy played for the Cubs so long, the team was known by three different names during his time (although, ironically, not the Cubs). He was mainly an outfielder, but that's not what Jimmy was known for — he was known for hitting. His lifetime batting average was over .300, he led the league in hits, doubles, homers, and total bases. He also stole more than 400 bases in his career. Ryan was one of the players that left the Cubs to jump to the Players' League in 1890, but unlike most of his teammates, he returned to the Cubs the following year. In 1893 while the Columbian Exposition was showing in Chicago, Jimmy and his teammates were involved in a train crash. Jimmy was hurt the most profoundly of any of the players — jagged glass got stuck in his leg, and he had to miss the rest of the season. He recovered and played another seven seasons. He still holds the club record for most career triples (142). It's hard to imagine anyone ever breaking that record. His nickname was Pony.

Jae Kuk Ryu 1983 – (Cubs 2006)

Ryu pitched in ten games for the Cubs and got pounded pretty hard. His Cubs ERA was 8.10. He later pitched for the Rays too. But Ryu is probably best remembered for what he did in the minor leagues. He threw a ball at an osprey, a protected bird in Florida, and it died a few days after he hit it. Shortly after that incident Ryu returned to his native Korea.

*Additional Entries...*If you check out the Every Cub Ever feature at www. justonebadcentury.com, you'll find several additional entries, including celebrity Cubs fans, writers, and bloggers. Under the letter R, you'll discover notorious assassin Jack Ruby, former U.S. Defense Secretary Donald Rumsfeld, and legendary columnist Mike Royko, who were all big Cubs fans. You'll also find Cubs artist Norman Rockwell, Cubs author Randy Richardson, Cubs publisher George Rawlinson, Cubs reporter Jesse Rogers, Cubs fan/radio co-host Jennifer Roberts, and fictional Cubs character Henry Rowengartner

CHAPTER NINETEEN

S

The starting lineup of your Chicago Cubs beginning with the letter S...

C – Geovany Soto, Rookie of the Year
1B – Harry Steinfeldt, World Series Champ (playing out of position)
2B – Ryne Sandberg, Hall of Famer
SS – Roy Smalley, 1950s Cub
3B – Ron Santo, Hall of Famer
LF – Hank Sauer, MVP
CF – Wildfire Schulte, MVP
RF – Sammy Sosa, MVP
Bench – Jimmy Sheckard, World Series Champ
Bench – Kyle Schwarber, World Series Champ
Bench – Jimmy Slagle, World Series Champ
Bench – Alfonso Soriano, World Record Contract
SP – Albert Spaulding, Hall of Famer
SP – Rick Sutcliffe, Cy Young Winner
SP – Steve Stone, Cy Young Winner
SP – Johnny Schmitz, All-Star
RP – Big Lee Smith, Hall of Famer
RP – Bruce Sutter, Hall of Famer

Vic Saier 1891 – 1967 (Cubs 1911-1917)

Vic was one of the players who played in the last season at West Side Grounds, and the Cubs' first season at Wrigley. The first baseman had huge shoes to fill on the Cubs — he replaced the Peerless Leader, Frank Chance. When he was healthy, Saier was a beast — a combination of speed, power, and clutch hitting. In 1913 he hit 21 triples, drove in 92 runs, stole 26 bases, and hit .289. He hit a career high 18 dingers the following season, and had another solid year in 1915. But

that season he suffered a bad leg injury, and Vic was never the same. The injury robbed him of his speed — a key ingredient of his game. Saier was done by 1919 at the age of 28.

<u>Historical note:</u> On the day Archduke Ferdinand was killed in Sarajevo (1914), igniting World War I, Saier had one of his best days at the plate. He knocked in three runs during an 8-5 Cubs victory over the Cardinals.

Angel Salazar 1961 – (Cubs 1988)

Not to be confused with the actor who played Chi-Chi in *Scarface*, this Angel Salazar was the Venezuelan shortstop who played for the Royals and Expos before joining the Cubs as a backup in 1988. He backed up Shawon Dunston, Vance Law, and even Ryne Sandberg occasionally. That was the last year of his big league career.

Luis Salazar 1956 – (Cubs 1989-1992)

Luis played against the Cubs in the 1984 playoff series vs. the Padres, but by the time the Cubs were back in the playoffs in 1989, he was a key member of the Cubs. He hit .368 with a home run in the NLCS that year, and remained with the Cubs for three more seasons. He retired after the 1992 season.

Salty Saltwell 1924 – (Cubs GM 1976)

His actual name was E.R. Saltwell, but everyone called him Salty. In 1975, after the long reign of General Manager John Holland ended, P.K. Wrigley replaced Holland with the only logical choice on the payroll: the team's former concessions manager E.R. "Salty" Saltwell. P.K. was no longer just thinking outside of the box; he didn't even know where the box was anymore. Salty was the GM of the Cubs for only one season (1976) but he made his mark. Who could forget his fleecing of the Cardinals of Mick Kelleher? Or his stealing of Rick Stelmaszek from the Yankees? He also acquired big names like Mike Garman, Ramon Hernandez, Tim Ireland, Tom DeTorre, and reacquired the incredibly washed-up Randy Hundley. Salty's deft touch in the draft was something to behold as well. In 1976, the Cubs had two first round draft choices. They selected Herman Segelke with the 7th overall pick, and Karl Pagel with the 20th pick. Salty knew better than to waste his time with the other future stars selected in that same first round: Steve Trout (White Sox), Mike Scoscia (Dodgers), Leon Durham (Cardinals), and Bruce Hurst (Red

Sox). Salty's crowning moment as general manager, however, had to be when he unloaded future slugging All-Star Andre Thornton for reserve outfielder Larry Biittner (and Steve Renko). Renko won 10 games in his Cubs career, Biittner hit 12 homers in his Cubs career, and Andre Thornton hit more than 30 homers three times. In September 1976, Steve Stone informed Saltwell of his impending free agency and attempted to get a contract. Salty responded by telling Stone that Mr. Wrigley was in the middle of a divorce and he would have to get back to him. Salty was demoted shortly after that. To this day, Salty Saltwell remains the only general manager in baseball history to rise from concessions manager to general manager and then back again to Director of Park Operations.

Jeff Samardzija 1985– (Cubs 2008-2014)

Jeff was a star football receiver for Notre Dame during his college years. The Cubs drafted him hoping they could convince him to choose baseball over football, and they were successful. Jeff first made it to the big leagues as a reliever during their successful 2008 playoff season. He became a solid starter for the Cubs for a few seasons, but these were the very dark rebuilding years. His win/loss record was well under .500. Samardzija was the starting pitcher on Opening Day in 2014 when the Cubs celebrated the 100th anniversary of Wrigley Field, but was traded later that season to the A's in the deal that brought Addison Russell to Chicago. Samardzija has since pitched for the White Sox and Giants. With the Giants he faced the Cubs in the 2016 NLDS. The Cubs lit him up and he didn't make it out of the third inning. Jeff's nickname is the Shark.

Eduardo Sanchez 1989– (Cubs 2013)

The young Venezuelan got a cup of coffee with the Cubs in 2013, but he had control problems in his limited appearances. They let him go at the end of the season, and he signed with Detroit, but Eduardo never made it back up to the big leagues.

Felix Sanchez 1981– (Cubs 2003)

The young Dominican reliever was only 22 when he was called up to the big leagues in September of 2003. Unfortunately for Felix, the Cubs were in a pennant race, and couldn't afford to take too many chances. He pitched in three games, and had an ERA of over 10. That turned out to be his only shot at the big-time. The Cubs traded him to Detroit the following April, and he never made it up to the Tigers big league team.

Jesus Sanchez 1974– (Cubs 2002)

Sanchez pitched only eight games for the Cubs in 2002 and was lit up. He finished his Cubs career with a 12.96 ERA. He also pitched for the Marlins, Rockies, Reds, and in Korea and Taiwan.

Rey Sanchez 1967– (Cubs 1991-1997)

Sanchez was a slick-fielding infielder; probably one of the best in the game during his 15-year big league career. He started out with the Cubs and was a key contributor for most of the 90s. He didn't have much pop in his bat, and that limited his time in the lineup, but his glove kept him in the big leagues for a long time. Ironically, the most famous moment in his Cubs career involved an error. Sanchez dropped an easy pop up one day, leading Harry Caray to memorably retort that "you'd think a guy from Puerto Rico wouldn't have trouble with the sun."

Ryne Sandberg 1959– (Cubs 1982-1994, 1996-1997)

He was destined to have a great nickname because he was named after the famous Yankees relief pitcher "Blind Ryne" Duren. Ryno was just a throw in to the Iván de Jesus/Larry Bowa trade with the Phillies. The Phillies had two other second base prospects who were pretty good (Juan Samuel, Julio Franco), but needless to say, neither one of them had the career Ryno had. He is in the Hall of Fame. Nicknamed Ryno for obvious reasons (not his similarity to the horned beast), Sandberg held the record for home runs by a second baseman when he retired. He was an MVP (1984), a ten-time All-Star, nine-time Gold Glover, seven-time Silver Slugger, and the most popular Cubs player of his era. After his playing career, he went back to Single-A ball to manage, and worked his way up to Triple-A. When the Cubs didn't give him the big league manager job, he left the team to coach the Phillies. Ryno still holds the record for most hits by any player born in the state of Washington. He also scored more runs than any other Cubs player in the

20th century.

Historical note: On the day Geraldine Ferraro made history by being named the first female VP candidate (1984), Ryno won a game with a tenth inning homer against the Dodgers in Wrigley Field.

Scott Sanders 1969–(Cubs 1999)
Sanders was a journeyman who pitched for seven big league seasons with the Padres, Mariners, and Tigers before coming to Chicago. The Cubs were the last team to give him a shot. In 1999 he appeared in 67 games, but he was hit pretty hard. His ERA for the season was 5.52, and he gave up a whopping 19 dingers in just over a hundred innings. After his time with the Cubs, he pitched in Japan.

Scott Sanderson 1956–2019 (Cubs 1984-1989)
The local kid (Northbrook) was acquired by Dallas Green before the 1984 season in the trade that sent Craig Lefferts and Carmelo Martinez to San Diego. Sanderson pitched very well for the Cubs that year. He was the fourth starter behind Sutcliffe, Trout, and Eckersley. Although poor Harry Caray had a hard time differentiating him with Ryne Sandberg, often calling one Scott Sandberg and the other Ryne Sanderson. Sanderson's only problem during his time with the Cubs was his inability to stay healthy. He only started more than 30 games three times, but two of those times were during years the Cubs went to the playoffs (1984 and 1989). He was the starting pitcher in the infamous Steve Garvey game (Game 4) in 1984, and pitched in relief of starter Greg Maddux in Game 4 of the 1989 NLCS. The Cubs lost both games. Sanderson left via free agency following that game and had a few more excellent seasons with the A's and Yankees (including an All-Star season in 1991). He finished his career with 163 wins.

Benito Santiago 1965–(Cubs 1999)
Santiago was a four-time All-Star, three-time Gold Glover, a Rookie of the Year, and of course, none of that occurred during his time with the Cubs. He was signed to a one-year deal by the Cubs after a horrible automobile accident almost ended his career in 1998. It was considered a reasonable gamble because the price was right, and it was a short-term deal. The Cubs brass was right about one thing: Santiago still

had a few good seasons in that bat and arm. Unfortunately, it didn't happen with the Cubs. Three years after leaving Chicago he led the Giants to the World Series, and was named the NLCS MVP. His big league career lasted an impressive twenty seasons.

Ron Santo 1940–2010 (Cubs 1960-1973, Cubs announcer 1990-2010)
He was the captain of that ill-fated (but incredibly talented) 1969 Cubs team — the man who clicked his heels after each Cubs victory. Santo was also the one who had the black cat cross his path while he stood in the on-deck circle in New York. Ron Santo is a Hall of Famer, something he wanted to be more than anything else in the world. Unfortunately, he wasn't inducted until after his death. His credentials should never have been questioned. Santo was a nine-time All-Star and five-time Gold Glover at third base. He hit 342 homers, and was the dominant player at his position (in the National League) during his playing days. And he did it all despite suffering from diabetes.

After his playing career he joined the Cubs radio broadcast booth, teaming up with the great Pat Hughes. He lost both legs to diabetes during his broadcasting days, and made an even stronger bond with Cubs fans. He never complained about his medical misfortune, and he exhibited the same kind of raw emotion that Cubs fans experienced: incredible joy when they won, and pure agony when they lost. His number was retired in 2003 and a #10 flag now flies on the left field foul pole at Wrigley Field. Santo also holds the Cubs career record for grounding into the most double plays (240).

Historical note: On the day Neil Armstrong walked on the moon (1969), Santo hit a game-winning home run against the Phillies in Philadelphia.

Dave Sappelt 1987–(Cubs 2012-2013)
He was obtained in the Sean Marshall trade with Cincinnati but never really caught on as a fourth outfielder candidate for the Cubs. In two years and over 150 plate appearances, Sappelt hit a grand total of two home runs. Not exactly what you're looking for in a corner outfielder.

Ed Sauer 1919–1988 (Cubs 1943-1945)
Hank's little brother Ed was a member of the 1945 Cubs

World Series team. He was in the Opening Day starting lineup because of the holdout of Peanuts Lowrey and the injury to Frank Secory, and he remained on the roster all season. Ed even got two at-bats in the World Series. Unfortunately, he struck out both times.

Hank Sauer 1917–2001 (Cubs 1949-1955)

Hank had a great 15-year big league career, and he was wearing a Cubs uniform during his best seasons. In his seven years in Chicago, Sauer hit 198 homers, thrilling the Wrigley Field crowd. In 1952 he led the league in homers and RBI and was named the league's Most Valuable Player. Hank was known for the big wad of chew he had in his mouth. Every time he homered, the left field faithful would shower him with his favorite brand. Sauer was so popular during his days in Chicago, the press referred to him as "The Mayor of Wrigley Field." His teammates, however, called him "The Honker" because of his rather large schnoz. The Honker had a great Cubs career.

Historical note: On the day the Korean War began (1950), Hank clubbed two homers for the Cubs against the Phillies in an 11-8 win.

Ted Savage 1936–(Cubs 1967-1968)

Savage played for eight teams in the big leagues (Phillies, Pirates, Cardinals, Cubs, Dodgers, Reds, Brewers, and Royals). He was a fourth outfielder type, who never really claimed a full-time position. With the Cubs he hit .218 in 1967. They traded him early in 1968 and it turned out to be a great trade. In exchange for Savage and Jim Ellis, the Dodgers sent the Cubs Jim Hickman and Phil Regan. Both players were key contributors to the Cubs over the next few years. Savage worked in the St. Louis front office for many years after his playing days.

Carl Sawatski 1927–1991 (Cubs 1948-1953)

Swats or Swisher, as he was known by his teammates, was a backup catcher for the Cubs. His time in Chicago was interrupted by military service during the Korean War, so he really only played parts of three seasons with the Cubs. He later played for the White Sox, Phillies, and Cardinals (always as a backup), and was a member of the 1957 World Champion Milwaukee Braves. After his playing career he

became the president of the Texas League (minors).

Bobby Scales 1977–(Cubs 2009-2010)

Everyone was rooting for Bobby Scales when he came up to the Cubs in 2009. He was a 31-year-old rookie who had really paid his dues in the minors (14 seasons). He briefly played well in a part-time role in the big leagues, filling in at third base, second base, left and right field. He also had a few dramatic clutch hits that made the fans rally around him. Unfortunately for Bobby, he had maximized his potential. He made his last appearance as a big league player on the final day of the 2010 season. He played a few more seasons after that in Japan.

Bob Scanlan 1966–(Cubs 1991-1993)

The Cubs acquired the tall (6'7) right-hander from the Phillies in the deal that sent Mitch Williams to Philadelphia. The Beverly Hills native was a highly regarded prospect, who stuck around with the Cubs for several years. He filled just about every role on the pitching staff at one time or another, from starter to closer. In three seasons he won 14 games and saved 15 games. After the 1993 season he was traded to the Brewers. Scanlan pitched in the big leagues until 2001 with additional stops in Detroit, Kansas City, Houston, and Montreal. After his playing career he went into television, working as an analyst on San Diego Padres broadcasts.

Germany Schaeffer 1876–1919 (Orphans 1901-1902)

Schaeffer was born in a town that boasted nearly 25% German heritage — Chicago, Illinois — and his parents were fresh off the boat immigrants. So naturally, he got the nickname Germany. He began his big league career in his hometown, but really made a name for himself in Detroit. He was the starting second baseman for the Tigers in both of their World Series losses to the Cubs (1907 and 1908). Germany was known for his wackiness. He once stole second base to draw a throw from the catcher, potentially allowing a teammate to score from home. When the catcher didn't fall for it, Germany stole first base on the next pitch, so he could try it again. According to the book *The Glory of Their Times,* Germany once came up as a pinch hitter and called his shot — a game-winning home run. On his way around the bases he slid into every base, and then tipped his cap after he slid into home. Germany Schaefer died way too young, from a hemorrhage at the age of 42. He had only been retired for about a year.

Jimmie Schaffer 1936– (Cubs 1963-1964)

Schaffer was catcher Dick Bertell's backup in his two years with the Cubs. 1963 was his best season; Jimmie slugged seven homers in his limited role. He never hit more than two homers in any other season in his eight-year big league career. Jimmie became a coach after his playing career ended, and was on the staff of the 1985 World Champion Kansas City Royals.

Joe Schaffernoth 1937–2016 (Cubs 1959-1961)

Joe was a right-handed reliever for the Cubs over three seasons in the late 50s/early 60s. He won two games and saved three in over 50 appearances for the Cubs. He was sold to the Indians in the middle of the 1961 season, and finished his career there. He died just a few months before the Cubs ended their 108-year World Series drought.

Bob Scheffing 1913–1985 (Cubs player 1941-1950, Cubs manager 1957-1959)

Scheffing was a Cubs catcher in 1941 and 1942, but was drafted into the military before the 1943 season. Unfortunately for him, he had to listen to his teammates make the 1945 World Series from afar, because he didn't get out of the service until 1946. Bob remained with the Cubs until the 1950 season, starting most of the games during the 1947 and 1948 seasons. After he retired, he went into coaching, and eventually was named the manager of his old team in 1957. From 1957-1959, Scheffing managed the team to three sub .500 seasons, and during those years had plenty of reasons to live up to the nickname his players bestowed on him. They called him Grumpy.

Hank Schenz 1919–1988 (Cubs 1946-1949)

Hank was mainly a backup infielder during his time in Chicago, but he did get one shot at starting in 1948. That season, a really bad one for the team, Schenz hit .261 and played a serviceable second base. The Cubs traded him to the Dodgers the following year for Bob Ramazzotti. Hank's final big league at-bat came in the 1951 World Series, as a member of the New York Giants.

Morrie Schick 1892–1979 (Cubs 1917)

Schick was a local Chicago boy who could really pick it as an outfielder, but simply couldn't hit big league pitching. He was 24 when he played with the Cubs in 1917, and hit only .147. Morrie knocked around the minors for nine seasons after that but never made it back up to the big-time.

Nate Schierholtz 1984– (Cubs 2013-2014)

Nate was one of the budget free agent signings by the Epstein/Hoyer regime. He won a ring with the 2010 Giants, but he was never really given a chance to be a full-time player until he arrived in Chicago. In his first season with the Cubs he hit more than 20 homers and played a very strong right field. It all fell apart in 2014, however, and by the end of the year, he was gone.

Calvin Schiraldi 1962– (Cubs 1988-1989)

The Cubs acquired Schiraldi in a lopsided trade that cost them their great closer Lee Smith. Calvin had been the Red Sox closer who helped blow the 1986 World Series, but the Cubs saw him as a starter. It didn't go too well. He won only nine games in 1988, was moved back to the bullpen in 1989, and was shipped off to San Diego before the end of that year. Meanwhile, Lee Smith closed for another ten years and retired with the all-time saves record.

Larry Schlafly 1878–1919 (Orphans 1902)

Larry played only one month with the Cubs (then known as the Orphans) at the end of the 1902 season. He appeared in ten games — but he shared a spot in the infield each time with three future Hall of Famers: Tinker, Evers, and Chance. After leaving Chicago he became known as a fiery competitor who would do anything to get on base (he led the league in being hit by pitches). He was also one of the people who helped create the Federal League. Schlafly was considered the league's best recruiter. He was only 40 years old when he passed away in 1919 of spinal meningitis.

Brian Schlitter 1985– (Cubs 2010, 2014-2015)

The local boy from Maine South High School broke into the big leagues briefly with the Cubs in 2010, but didn't fare well.

After a few more seasons in the minors, he re-emerged in 2014 and became a key part of the bullpen. New Cubs manager Joe Maddon thought he would be a big part of the bullpen in 2015, but Schlitter was rocked hard early and often. In only ten appearances, his ERA was north of seven. He was known for his long floppy hair and 95 MPH fastball. After his time with the Cubs, he pitched in Japan.

Freddy Schmidt 1916–2012 (Cubs 1947)

Schmidt came up to the big leagues during the war, and pitched in the 1944 all-St. Louis World Series (Browns vs. Cardinals), but when the regular players came back from the service, Freddy had a much tougher time making rosters. His last stop in the big leagues was with the Chicago Cubs. He started exactly one game, on September 24, 1947 in Cincinnati's Crosley Field, and was roughed up pretty badly by the Reds. He gave up four hits and five walks in only three innings pitched. The Cubs lost the game 6-5, but Freddy wasn't charged with the loss. Cubs reliever Emil Kush threw exactly one pitch that game, and it was knocked over the fence in the bottom of the ninth by Grady Hatton for a walk-off home run.

Johnny Schmitz 1920–2011 (Cubs 1941-1951)

He was nicknamed Bear Tracks because of his lumbering shuffle to the mound. Schmitz was only twenty when he was called up to the majors, and pitched two seasons for the Cubs, but was drafted to serve in World War II in 1942. Bear Tracks was one of the rare players who returned from the war an even better player. He led the National League in strikeouts in 1946, and was named to the All-Star team. He had another great year two years later, finishing with a 2.64 ERA and an 18-13 record for a last place team. During his Cubs years he was known as a fierce competitor. How many pitchers have been ejected from a game for wearing illegal spikes? Only Bear Tracks Schmitz, who did it to further intimidate the batters. A noted Dodger-killer during his career (he beat them 18 times), he was later traded to the Dodgers in the deal that also put Andy Pafko in a Brooklyn uniform. By then he was no longer an All-Star caliber pitcher. He pitched for the Dodgers, the Senators, the Red Sox, and the Orioles before retiring after the 1956 season.

Historical note: On the day President Truman ordered troops to Korea in 1950, Schmitz had his worst day ever on the mound for the Cubs. He didn't record a single out as the Cubs lost big to the Reds in Cincinnati.

Ed Schorr 1892–1969 (Cubs 1915)

Ed only pitched in two games for the 1915 Cubs (in the last home stand of their final season at West Side Grounds), but one of them was in Grover Cleveland Alexander's 30th win of the season (for the Phillies). Schorr pitched the final two innings in relief of Cubs starter Karl Adams.

Paul Schramka 1928– (Cubs 1953)

Schramka was a speedy outfielder who played in the Cubs minor league system from 1949-1954 (other than a military stint during the Korean War), but he did get a cup of coffee with the big league team in April of 1953. He appeared in two games for the Cubs. He pinch ran for catcher Clyde McCullough one game, and replaced outfielder Gene Hermanski for one inning during another game. That was it. He was interviewed by the Baseball Biography Project in 2007 about his time in baseball, and recalled it this way: "The Cubs had seven outfielders at the time. I was number seven. I knew my place."

Hank Schreiber 1891-1968 (Cubs 1926)

Hank had one of the oddest careers in MLB history. He played for five teams in the big leagues — each of them for one season — but none of them in consecutive seasons. He played for the White Sox, Braves, Reds, and Giants before coming to the Cubs for his last taste of the big-time. Hank played in ten games for the 1926 Cubs as a backup 2B/SS/3B. He was 34 years old at the time.

Pop Schriver 1865–1932 (Colts 1891-1894)

Pop was a catcher and first baseman who got quite a bit of playing time with the Cubs (then known as the Colts). Cap Anson considered Pop his starting catcher during the 1892 season, but Schriver only hit .224. He played 14 seasons in the big leagues with Chicago, New York, Philadelphia, Pittsburgh, Cincinnati, and St. Louis.

Al Schroll 1932–1999 (Cubs 1960)

His nickname was "Bull", but don't confuse him with the

Bull who let a groundball through his legs in the 1984 NLCS. This Bull was a pitcher. The Cubs got the big Louisiana kid from the Red Sox for Bobby Thomson, but he didn't exactly turn out to be the pitcher they had hoped. His Cubs career lasted 2 2/3 innings, and in those innings he posted an ERA of 10.13. Schroll got one more cup of coffee with Twins the following season (1961), and during that season he made history along with fellow Twins pitcher Jack Kralik. For more than forty years it was the last time two pitchers on the same team hit a homer in the same game. Schroll hit his off Al Fowler, who later became Billy Martin's pitching coach with the World Champion Yankees. Bull Schroll passed away in Louisiana in 1999 at the age of 67.

Art Schult 1928–2014 (Cubs 1959-1960)

Art's heritage was German, so of course his teammates called him Dutch. He was mainly a pinch hitter and backup first baseman/outfielder in his five-year big league career, the last two of which were with the Cubs. He also played with the Senators, Yankees, and Reds.

Wildfire Schulte 1882–1949 (Cubs 1904-1916)

Wildfire (real name Frank) didn't get his nickname for his style of play (although he stole home 22 times), or his tendency to hit the town (although Frank Chance used to chide him for that in the press). He got it because he named his favorite pony after his favorite Broadway show *Wildfire* (starring Lillian Russell), and soon it became his nickname too. Schulte was known as a bit of a flake, but his teammates loved him for it. Joe Tinker once said: "I doubt whether a quainter or more original character ever existed in the National Pastime." One of his more bizarre eccentricities was that he had a thing for hairpins. He thought they were good luck, so he would search the streets for them. The bigger the hairpin, the better the luck. Wildfire wasn't just a character, he was also a great player for the Cubs from 1904-1916, an era that spanned four NL pennants. He had a 13-game hitting streak in the World Series (and hit .321 overall in 91 World Series at-bats). He was the MVP of the league in 1911. He led the league in homers, triples, and RBI. In short, he was a superstar. Many years later, when Ty Cobb was an old man, he was asked what he remembered about Wildfire Schulte, his opponent in the 1907 and 1908 World Series. He said simply, "Schulte was one of the all-time greats." Wildfire passed away in 1949 at the age of 67.

Johnny Schulte 1896–1978 (Cubs 1929)

Schulte was a backup catcher for the Cubs (and the Browns, Cardinals, Phillies, and Braves). His one season in Chicago just happened to be a pennant-winning year, although Johnny didn't get to play in the World Series against the A's. After his playing career he became a coach, and was on the staff of many World Series champions with the Yankees. He also worked as a scout for ten years.

Barney Schultz 1926–2015 (Cubs 1961-1963)

Barney had the misfortune of pitching for the Cubs during the College of Coaches era. He was not a young pup either. The journeyman who had never spent a full season in the majors was 34 years old in 1961. His teammates called him "Mr. Old Folks." The Cubs used him pretty extensively out of the bullpen that year (41 appearances), and even more the following year. The Cubs traded the knuckleballer to the Cardinals in 1963, and Barney went on to become a key member of the 1964 World Series champs (although he did give up a gargantuan homer to Mickey Mantle in his only pitch at Yankee Stadium). After his playing career ended, Schultz became a pitching coach for the Cardinals and the Cubs.

Bob Schultz 1923–1979 (Cubs 1951-1953)

Schultz was a spot starter and reliever for three seasons. He had a respectable 9-11 record, but he gave up a ton of baserunners. As a member of the Cubs, Schultz walked almost twice as many batters as he struck out (113 BB/61 Ks). He later pitched for the Pirates and the Tigers. His nickname was Bullet Bob, which sadly turned out to be ironic. He was shot and killed at a VFW hall during an argument with another veteran. He was 55 at the time.

Buddy Schultz 1950–(Cubs 1975-1976)

Buddy set a college record. He struck out 26 batters in a game for Miami of Ohio. That's about as good as it gets. Schultz was a left-handed reliever for the Cubs for parts of two seasons, but didn't have a tremendous amount of success. His ERA in his Cubs years was over six (although he did get two saves).

After the Cubs traded him to the Cardinals, he blossomed and had a few very good seasons with St. Louis.

Joe Schultz 1893–1941 (Cubs 1915)

Schultz's nickname was Germany, and the German-American played in the big leagues for eleven seasons, including briefly with the Cubs during their last season at West Side Grounds. He batted only eight times for Chicago, got two hits, and drove in two runs. Germany's appeal was that he was a jack of all trades. The utility man parlayed his versatility into stints with the Braves, Dodgers, Pirates, Cardinals, Phillies, and Reds (every National League team at the time, except for the Giants). After his playing career ended he became the farm director for the Pittsburgh Pirates. He died of hepatitis at the age of 47.

Don Schulze 1962–(Cubs 1983-1984)

Schulze was a local high school hero (Lake Park High School in Roselle) when he was drafted in the first round (11th overall pick) by the Cubs in 1980. (Future Cubs manager Ricky Renteria was picked later in that round, as were fellow future managers Terry Francona and John Gibbons, and Oakland A's GM Billy Beane.) The Cubs brought him up to the big leagues at the end of the 1983 season and it didn't go well. He started three games and was roughed up to the tune of an ERA over seven. The following season he got another start and was hit even harder (ERA over 12). That's probably why Dallas Green didn't mind including Schulze in the deal that brought Rick Sutcliffe to the Cubs. Schulze pitched for the Indians, Mets, Yankees, and Padres in his big league career, but never experienced prolonged success. His lifetime record is ten games below .500, and his lifetime ERA is over five. He later pitched three seasons in Japan, and became a pitching coach in the Oakland farm system.

Wayne Schurr 1937–(Cubs 1964)

The Cubs drafted Schurr out of the San Francisco Giants system as a Rule V draft choice, and Wayne pitched for the Cubs for a good portion of the 1964 season. The right-handed reliever appeared in 26 games and registered an ERA of 3.72. He retired from baseball after his eighth minor league season in 1966.

Bill Schuster 1912–1987 (Cubs 1942-1945)

The New York native was known as "Broadway Bill" to his teammates. Schuster was a second baseman and shortstop who got quite a bit of playing time his first few seasons in Chicago. By his last year, the pennant-winning year of 1945, he wasn't playing much. He did, however, get into two of the World Series games. He was a pinch runner, and scored the winning run in Game 6, in the bottom of the 12th inning at Wrigley Field. For 71 years he was the last player in Cubs history to score a game-winning run in a World Series game

Kyle Schwarber 1993–(Cubs 2015-present)

The Cubs top draft pick in 2014 wasn't supposed to make it to the majors this quickly, but he absolutely crushed minor league pitching and the Cubs couldn't resist bringing him up to the big leagues. They weren't disappointed. In only 273 ABs, Kyle slugged 16 homers — and none of them were cheapies. In the playoffs he added five more — setting an all-time Cubs postseason record in his very first season. One of them will remain a fixture in Cubs lore. Against the hated Cardinals, Schwarber put a homer ON TOP of the video board in right field. In his third game of the 2016 season, unfortunately, Schwarber severely injured his knee and was ruled out for the season. It appeared he wouldn't be able to participate in their World Series-winning season. But somehow, miraculously, he was activated right before the World Series began and served as the DH in Cleveland. Schwarber didn't just show up, he inspired his entire Cubs team. He hit over .400, knocked in two runs, and even stole a base in the decisive Game 7 victory. The Cubs convinced themselves that Kyle was a lead-off hitter, and that's where he began the 2017 season. He struggled so badly there, they had to send him back to the minors. Schwarber got his act together in Triple A and when he came back up he was a different player. He ended the season with 30 homers. His postseason magic, however, was no longer there. Schwarber hit less than .200, although one of his three hits was a homer. In 2018 he played the whole season with the big league club as the (more or less) regular left fielder. He hit .238 with 26 homers.

Historical note: On the day Hurricane Maria slammed Puerto Rico (2017), Schwarber hit the game-winning homer for the Cubs in a 2-1 victory over the Tampa Rays.

Rudy Schwenck 1884–1941 (Cubs 1909)

Schwenck was a lefty from Kentucky who got a brief taste of the big leagues during the 1909 season. He came to Chicago at the very end of the season when the Cubs were already out of it. It was the first year since 1905 they weren't playing in the World Series. Schwenck bounced around in the minors for a few years after that, before coming back home to Kentucky.

Dick Scott 1933–(Cubs 1964)

The Cubs traded a very good prospect (pitcher Jim Brewer) to get the 30-year-old lefty Scott in December of 1963. It's one of the biggest head-scratching deals in Cubs history. While Brewer went on to have a very productive big league career including an All-Star season with the Dodgers, Scott struggled mightily. He wasn't even pitching well in the minors when they brought him up to the big club in July. They couldn't possibly have been shocked when it didn't go well. Scott was rocked hard. He pitched four innings, and gave up ten hits, including two homers. His final Cubs ERA was 12.46.

Gary Scott 1968–(Cubs 1991-1992)

Gary was the Opening Day third baseman in 1991 as a 22-year-old rookie. The second round draft choice was billed simply as the best Cubs third baseman since Ron Santo. It didn't turn out that way. After less than a hundred at-bats, it was clear that Scott couldn't hit big league pitching. He hit .165. They gave him another shot in 1992, and Gary responded with a .156 average. After the season the Cubs traded him to Miami for left-handed starting pitcher Greg Hibbard. Hibbard won 15 games for the Cubs. Scott never played in the majors again.

Milt Scott 1861–1938 (White Stockings 1882)

Milt Scott was a 21-year-old kid when he was signed to play one game for the Cubs (then known as the White Stockings) on September 30, 1882. The team had already clinched the championship and Cap Anson didn't feel like playing the last game of the season against Buffalo, so Mikado Milt (as he was known) got a shot. He went 2 for 5 and scored a run. He never played another game with the Cubs.

Pete Scott 1897–1953 (Cubs 1926-1927)

Pete was a part-time first baseman/outfielder for the Cubs

for two seasons, but paid huge dividends for them. Scott and teammate Sparky Adams were traded to the Pirates for future Hall of Famer Kiki Cuyler. Scott only played one more season for Pittsburgh, while Cuyler led the Cubs to two World Series (1929 and 1932).

Rodney Scott 1953–(Cubs 1978)

The Cubs acquired Rodney (known as "Cool Breeze") during spring training of 1978 for pitcher Pete Broberg, and he did play an important role on that 1978 Cubs team. Rodney played second, third, short, and center, and provided some much-needed speed to the lineup. In only 78 games, Rodney stole 27 bases and batted .282 (with a .403 OBP). Why the Cubs traded him to the Expos (along with Jerry White) for Sam Mejias remains a mystery. Rodney had a few very good seasons with the Expos. One year he led the league in triples and stole 63 bases.

> **Seasonal Cubs...**Is there a Cub for every season? Almost. There was a Jack Spring, a Champ Summers, and a Bill Faul (close enough). But there was no one named Winter. On the other hand, Winter is the off-season.

Tom Seaton 1887–1940 (Cubs 1916-1917)

Seaton was part of the Cubs pitching staff during their first two seasons at what is now known as Wrigley Field. He was a holdover from the Federal League (Newark and Brooklyn), so he played in the ballpark even before the Cubs did. Seaton started and relieved, and only gave up three homers in almost 200 innings pitched. After he left the Cubs (in 1920) he was accused of suspicious behavior. He and a Pacific Coast League teammate (Luther Smith) were identified as being too close to gamblers, and were released. Neither played organized baseball again.

Historical note: On the day the first American soldiers arrived in Europe to fight in World War I (1917), Seaton was on the mound for the Cubs. He defeated the Cardinals 8-6.

Frank Secory 1912–1995 (Cubs 1944-1946)

Secory was a reserve outfielder for the last Cubs team of the 20th century to make the World Series. He was a friendly guy who was well-liked by his teammates. They didn't just like him because he was nice. They liked him because he had a habit of getting big hits in big games. He only got nine hits and six RBI for the 1945 Cubs, but a few of those managed to defeat the defending champion Cardinals. Frank got another cup of coffee with the Cubs in 1946, the last gasp of his big league career as a player. However, that was far from the end of his big league career. Frank became a big league umpire and had a very distinguished career. He umpired nine no-hitters, four World Series, and six All-Star games. He retired after the 1970 season.

Historical note: On the day the NBA was founded (1946), Secory hit a walk-off pinch-hit twelfth inning grand slam to defeat the Giants at Wrigley Field.

Herman Segelke 1958–(Cubs 1982)

In 1976, three future Cubs were drafted in the first round by other teams drafting after the Cubs (Steve Trout, Leon Durham, and Pat Tabler) while the Cubs picked Herman Segelke. If Herman hadn't been the seventh overall pick of the draft, he probably never would have gotten a cup of coffee in the big leagues. His lifetime minor league ERA was over five. Segelke pitched in three games for the 1982 Cubs and was lit up. He gave up six hits, six walks, a homer, and four runs in only four innings pitched.

Kurt Seibert 1955– (Cubs 1979)

Kurt was a third round draft choice of the Cubs who showed a lot of speed in the minors (one year he stole 37 bases), but the second baseman only made it up to the big leagues once — and that was as a September call-up. The Cubs used him mainly as a pinch runner that September. He appeared in seven games and scored two runs.

Frank Selee 1859–1909 (Cubs manager 1902-1905)

Selee was already a 5-time pennant-winning manager (with Boston) before he came to the Cubs, but the Hall of Famer really made his mark in his short time in Chicago. He was more than just the manager — he put the team together. Among his moves: acquiring Three Finger Brown, Joe Tinker, and Johnny Evers. Unfortunately for Frank, he got very ill after the 1905 season and had to give up baseball, just as his team was about to blossom. He was replaced by

his favorite player — Frank Chance — who led the Cubs to four pennants over the next five years. Selee died during that championship run at the far too young age of 49. He was inducted into baseball's Hall of Fame in 1999.

Dick Selma 1943–2001 (Cubs 1969)

He was nicknamed Mortimer Snerd by his teammates after Edgar Bergen's famous dummy. Selma was a key member of the 1969 Cubs. He won 10 games for them and led the staff in strikeouts per nine innings after being acquired from the Padres. Selma became a fan favorite almost instantly because he led the Bleacher Bums in cheers from the bullpen. But 1969 was his only year with the Cubs. He was a part of the trade that brought Johnny Callison to the Cubs. Selma passed away in 2001 at the age of 58.

Mike Sember 1953–(Cubs 1977-1978)

Sember was a local boy (Hammond, Indiana) who got a cup of coffee with the Cubs in the late 70s. He was mainly a defensive replacement at shortstop and third base. Sember had a grand total of seven career big league at-bats (all with the Cubs), and got two hits (both singles).

Manny Seoane 1955–(Cubs 1978)

Manny was mostly a career minor leaguer, but he did get a cup of coffee with the Cubs in 1978. He was a September call-up and pitched in seven games, mainly out of the bullpen. He was acquired from the Phillies for Cubs fan favorite Jose Cardenal, in a trade that appears to have been a salary dump. Manny's story doesn't end well. After his cup of coffee with the Cubs, he never pitched in the big leagues again, and was out of baseball entirely by 1982. That year he and fellow former big leaguer Mark Lemongello were arrested for the kidnapping and robbery of Lemongello's cousins. He was sentenced to seven years probation.

Dan Serafini 1974–(Cubs 1999)

Dan was a first round draft choice of the Twins, but the lefty had a rough go of it pitching in the big leagues (6.04 lifetime ERA, 1.71 lifetime WHIP). Somehow, he managed to hang on for parts of seven seasons with the Twins, Padres, Pirates, Rockies, Reds, and Cubs. He also pitched in Japan. He is not the same Dan Serafini who wrote the blog "Serafini Says."

That was a Cubs fan — no relation.

Bill Serena 1924–1996 (Cubs 1949-1954)

Serena played his entire major league career with the Cubs. In 1950 he finished fifth in the Rookie of the Year voting after starting all season at third base and hitting 17 homers. Unfortunately, Serena missed most of the 1951 season with an injury, and was moved to second base after he returned. He always had good pop for an infielder (48 homers in six big league seasons), but was eventually replaced by more talented players (Gene Baker and Randy Jackson).

Scott Servais 1967–(Cubs 1995-1998)

Born on the same day as the man he was traded for (Rick Wilkins), Servais immediately became the starting catcher for the Cubs. He had several good seasons as the Cubs backstop, especially 1995 and 1996 when he had double-digit home run totals. His last year with the Cubs ended with his only career playoff appearance. He went 2 for 3 in the 1998 NLDS against Atlanta. Servais signed with the Giants the following season, and later played with the Rockies and Astros. After his playing career, he took front office positions with the Texas Rangers and the Los Angeles Angels.

Tommy Sewell 1906–1956 (Cubs 1927)

Tommy had exactly one big league at-bat. It came on June 21, 1927 at Sportsman Park in St. Louis. Tommy pinch hit for Cubs pitcher Percy Jones in the seventh inning against Cardinals pitcher Flint Rehm. Unfortunately for Tommy, Flint was a 20-game winner that season. Sewell didn't get on base and never got another chance in the big leagues. After that he played in the minor leagues for another four years before hanging up his spikes. Tommy couldn't even brag about his big league experience when he came home to Alabama. His brother Joe was a Hall of Famer, another brother Luke also played in the big leagues, and so did his cousin Rip.

Orator Shafer 1851–1922 (White Stockings 1879)

His real first name was George, but he was pegged with the nickname Orator because he was a smooth and gifted speaker, and that's what everyone called him. Orator played 13 seasons in the big leagues, including the 1879 season for the Cubs (then known as the White Stockings). He was their starting right fielder and batted over .300. Shafer is considered one of the best fielding right fielders of the 19th century. He also played for Hartford, New York, Philadelphia, Louisville, Indianapolis, Cleveland, Buffalo, and St. Louis.

Art Shamsky 1941–(Cubs 1972)

Shamsky was part of the Miracle Mets team that kept the Cubs out of the playoffs in 1969, but just a few years later he was wearing a Cubs uniform. The outfielder/first baseman was used in only 15 games, almost exclusively as a pinch hitter. He hit only .125 in that role before being released. He is a member of the National Jewish Sports Hall of Fame.

Red Shannon 1897–1970 (Cubs 1926)

The bulk of Red's big league career was from 1915-1921 (with Boston, Philadelphia, and Washington), but he did re-emerge after five years in the minors to get in 60 more games with the Cubs in 1926. Red was mainly a defensive replacement for the Cubs infielders that season.

Bobby Shantz 1925– (Cubs 1964)

The three-time All-Star, eight-time Gold Glover, and former MVP and World Series champion pitcher was a big name, but the Cubs must have known he was a shell of his former self when they acquired him in the horrific Lou Brock trade with the Cardinals. He was strictly a reliever by then, and in twenty appearances he posted an ERA of 5.56. The Cubs sold him to the Phillies exactly two months after they acquired him.

Bob Shaw 1933–2010 (Cubs 1967)

Shaw was an important part of the Go-Go White Sox of 1959, winning 18 games and shutting out the Dodgers in the World Series, but by the time he came to the Cubs he was at the tail end of his career. Shaw won over 100 games in his big league career, but none of those came for the Cubs. He was released on September 11, 1967. After his playing career, he became a big league pitching coach.

Sam Shaw 1863–1947 (Colts 1893)

Sam was a little guy, only 5'5, 140 pounds, and the 30-year-old had bounced around the minors for several seasons before arriving in Chicago during the 1893 season. He started two games for the Cubs (then known as the Colts) in June of that year, and won one of them. He also walked thirteen batters in only sixteen innings, which wasn't good enough to cut it in the big-time. Shaw finished up his baseball career in the southern leagues, before hanging up his spikes for good after the 1896 season.

Marty Shay 1896–1951 (Cubs 1916)

Shay played for the Cubs during their first season at Wrigley. The young shortstop played in exactly two games and went 2 for 7 (both singles). He was only 20 at the time. By the time he returned to the majors with the Boston Braves, he was 28.

Al Shealy 1900–1967 (Cubs 1930)

Al pitched in 24 games for the 1930 Cubs, but this was the year of the batter, and Shealy got lit up for an 8.00 ERA. He had previously pitched for the 1928 World Series champion Yankees.

Dave Shean 1883–1963 (Cubs 1911)

The Cubs acquired Shean from Boston to fill in for Johnny Evers, who suffered a nervous breakdown during the 1911 season. Dave was known as a solid second base glove, and he shared the position with well-known defensive butcher Heinie Zimmerman. Zimmerman was a great hitter, however, so he got the bulk of the playing time. 1911 was Shean's only season in Chicago. The following year he went back to Boston.

Jimmy Sheckard 1878–1947 (Cubs 1906-1912)

Sheckard was one of the first players Frank Chance acquired when he took over the Cubs in 1905/06. He gave up four players and $2000 (a high price) to Brooklyn to acquire him — but he knew that Brooklyn was mad at Sheckard for playing in the American League one season, and he knew that Sheckard was a great outfielder. Sheckard was more than a good ballplayer. He was a character. Thanks in large part to the writings of Ring Lardner, who was a reporter covering the Cubs, Sheckard became well-known for his horseplay with Solly Hofman and pitcher Lew Ritchie, with whom he formed three-quarters of a barbershop quartet (Jimmy sang baritone). He was a member of all four pennant-winning teams during the Cubs dynasty (1906-1910), but his best season was probably 1911. He led the league in runs scored that year. Jimmy's game was speed. In his 17-year big league career, he stole 465 bases.

Historical note: On the day that Orville and Wilbur Wright received a patent for the airplane (1906), Sheckard went 3 for 4 against Giants stud Joe McGinnity in a losing cause. Giants 8-Cubs 2.

Tommy Shields 1964–(Cubs 1993)

Shields was a late season call-up for the Cubs in 1993. The backup infielder got 36 plate appearances to show the brass what he could do. Unfortunately for Tommy, he didn't show much. He struck out ten times and only got six hits. After his playing career, he went into coaching.

Clyde Shoun 1912–1968 (Cubs 1935-1937)

Clyde Shoun was called "Hardrock" because he threw one — a great fastball. Hardrock was a wild pitcher that was knocked around a bit when he was with the Cubs for parts of 1935 and 1936. He became a part of the rotation in 1937, and the league knocked him around even more. His ERA that season was 5.61. The Cubs didn't think they were losing too much when they traded him to the Cardinals as part of the famous Dizzy Dean trade, but they were wrong. The Cardinals turned him into a reliever, and Clyde led the league in appearances in 1939 and 1940, and tied for the league lead in saves. He even won nine more games for the Cardinals than Dean won for the Cubs. Hardrock had two more good seasons as a starter with Cincinnati (14 wins and 13 wins) during the war. On May 15, 1944 he pitched a no-hitter against the Boston Braves. His only blemish in that game was a walk to the opposing pitcher Jim Tobin.

Terry Shumpert 1966–(Cubs 1996)

Shumpert had a 14-year big league career with stops in Kansas City, Boston, Colorado, San Diego, Tampa, and of course, the Cubs. He didn't get a great deal of playing time with the Cubs. He appeared in 27 games and served as a backup infielder and pinch hitter. He really blossomed with Colorado after leaving Chicago. His best season in the big leagues was 1999. He hit 10 homers, stole 14 bases, and hit .347.

Cubs players have had some great nicknames over the years. Among players starting with the letter S, you'll find nicknames like Bear Tracks, Big Lee, Brat, Broadway Aleck, Broadway Bill, Bull (2 of them), Champ, Cool Breeze, Dixie Thrush, Dutch, Germany (2 of them), Grumpy, Hardrock, Honker, Human Mosquito, Iron Man, Jigger, Lefty, Mayor of Wrigley, Mortimer Snerd, Mr. Old Folks, Old Hoss, Old Reliable, Orator, Pop, Rabbit, Red, Red Baron, Riverboat, Ryno, Salty, Slappy, Spook, Swats, Swede, Swisher, Tarzan, Tuck, Tuffy, and Wildfire.

Ed Sicking 1897–1978 (Cubs 1916)

Ed was a member of the Cubs team that played their first season at Wrigley Field in 1916, but just barely. He was only 19 years old on August 26th when he got his one chance to hit. He was called on to pinch hit for relief pitcher Gene Packard, but Ed didn't reach base. The pitcher he faced was Lefty Tyler, who would become an important part of the pennant-winning Cubs of 1918. Sicking later played for the Giants, Phillies, Reds, and Pirates. The infielder had more than 650 plate appearances in the big leagues but never hit a home run.

Walter Signer 1910–1974 (Cubs 1943, 1945)

Walter was a minor leaguer in the 1930s, but when war broke out, and many big leaguers were drafted into the military, Walter made a comeback — hoping to finally make it to the Major Leagues. His plan worked. He got two very brief shots with the Cubs. He made ten appearances and posted an ERA of 3.00. In his 33 innings pitched, Walter only struck out five batters.

Carlos Silva 1979– (Cubs 2010)

Silva was picked up in a bad-contract-for-bad-contract trade with the Seattle Mariners. The Mariners took the troubled Milton Bradley, and the Cubs took Silva. It's safe to say the Cubs got the better of the deal, even if there were no real winners here. Silva won his first eight decisions with the Cubs before developing arm problems. The Cubs cut ties with him during spring training 2011.

Charlie Silvera 1924– (Cubs 1957)

Charlie (known as Swede) was a backup catcher in the big leagues for ten years, mostly with the Yankees. As the understudy to Yogi Berra, Swede didn't get a lot of playing time. He was in his 30s when he was traded to the Cubs. In his last season in the bigs, he played in only 26 games and hit .208.

Curt Simmons 1929– (Cubs 1966-1967)

Simmons was a three-time All-Star that led his team to a World Series title, but of course, that team was not the Cubs. Curt Simmons was only two seasons removed from taking the Cardinals to the 1964 World Series when the Cubs acquired him in 1966. They hoped they were getting the pitcher that started two games in that memorable '64 series against the Yankees, after winning 18 games in the regular season. They weren't. They were getting a 37-year-old pitcher at the end of a very nice career. Simmons won 193 games during his 20-year baseball career, but only seven of those came with the Cubs. He started 24 games for the Cubs in 1966 and 1967, but the man who had a 3.54 career ERA, never sniffed an ERA south of four for the Cubs. He also allowed 17 home runs in those starts, prompting the team to sell him to the Angels. He retired shortly thereafter.

Joe Simmons 1845–1901 (White Stockings 1871)

The outfielder/first baseman played in all but one of the games during the first official season of the Chicago professional franchise (in the National Association). He was the hardest player in the league to strike out that year. He also played with Cleveland and Keokuk (yes, that was a real team in 1875).

Randall Simon 1975– (Cubs 2003)

The Cubs acquired Simon from the Pirates to bolster their lineup during their division champion season of 2003. He shared the first base position with Eric Karros, and got several clutch hits during the pennant drive. He even hit well in the 2003 playoffs. In the two postseason series, he hit .333 with a homer and six RBI. After the season he signed up with Pittsburgh again. Simon will always be remembered for something that had nothing do with baseball. During the famous "sausage race" in Milwaukee, he once hit the Italian sausage with a bat and knocked her over.

Duke Simpson 1927– (Cubs 1953)

His real name was Tom Simpson, and he was a multi-sport star at Notre Dame (and in the army after he was drafted in '45). This is what *Who's Who Magazine* wrote about Simpson after his rookie season for the Cubs in 1953: "Right-handed — throws a slider and a hard-curveball. A highly-rated rookie, he came on in relief in 29 games in '53, was 1-2 W/L in 45 innings, striking out 21 batters, walked 25 but had a disappointing 8.00 ERA." You read that last part right. His ERA was eight. The Cubs had purchased his contract before the 1953 season after he had pitched a no-hitter in the minor leagues. "The Cubs, with their typical luck, got themselves a sore-armed pitcher," Simpson later said. He never made it back to the majors.

Harry Sinclair 1876–1956 (Cubs minority owner)

Sinclair was a wealthy industrialist, and one of the men who bankrolled the Federal League. When the league folded, Sinclair made $2 million on the deal, part of which was the merging of the Federal League and National League teams in Chicago. The Cubs began playing in the Federal League park (now known as Wrigley). Unfortunately for him, Harry is not most-remembered for his time in baseball. Harry was at the heart of Warren G. Harding's biggest scandal, Teapot Dome. In 1922, Albert B. Fall, U.S. Secretary of the Interior, leased, without competitive bidding, the Teapot Dome fields to Sinclair. When the Senate got wind of this, they investigated. It was found that in 1921, Sinclair also "loaned" Secretary Fall a large amount of money. Fall was indicted for conspiracy and accepting bribes. He was sentenced to a year in prison and fined $100,000. Sinclair was acquitted, but was subsequently sentenced to prison for contempt of the Senate and for employing detectives to shadow members of the jury. After he served his six months in prison, he simply resumed his life as a wealthy industrialist. He retired as the CEO of Sinclair Oil in 1949, and died in 1956.

Elmer Singleton 1918–1996 (Cubs 1957-1959)

Singleton was a pitcher who was nicknamed Smoky. He came to the Cubs from Cincinnati in the trade that also brought Don Hoak to Chicago. His best season with the Cubs was his last year in the big leagues, 1959. Smoky pitched in 21 games for the Cubs, and registered a 2.72 ERA. He previously pitched for the Braves, Pirates, and Senators.

Judd Sirott 1969– (Cubs announcer 2008-2014)

Longtime Chicago radio and television personality Bob Sirott's nephew Judd was the fill-in announcer for Pat Hughes during Cubs games (when Pat took his inning-long break) for several years, in addition to hosting the pre- and post-game shows on the radio. I interviewed him a few years ago, and he had this to say: "To work with Pat and Ron was incredible. To be able to do play by play for the Cubs — c'mon, that's beyond my wildest dreams…With Ronnie (Santo) in the past, it was a treat. He was so much fun to work with. That's what I've wanted to do since I was a kid." Sirott has since become a full-time hockey announcer.

Ted Sizemore 1945– (Cubs 1979)

He was the Rookie of the Year in 1969 with the Dodgers, and played a scrappy second base for the Cardinals and the Phillies after that, but his Cubs career was rather brief. In 1979 he played most of the year for the Cubs. On August 2nd of that year he was involved in a little altercation at a Montreal restaurant. Cubs management treated the players to dinner that night, but they put a limit of two bottles of wine per table. Sizemore was incensed at the limit, and stormed out of the restaurant. The Cubs traded him to the Boston Red Sox two weeks later. When Herman Franks resigned as Cubs manager at the end of the year, one of the reasons he said he quit was because of the whiny players, specifically naming Sizemore, Bill Buckner, Barry Foote, and Mike Vail.

Roe Skidmore 1945– (Cubs 1970)

He played in exactly one game for the Cubs in 1970, and his lifetime batting average is 1.000. Skidmore hit a Jerry Reuss pitch over third baseman Joe Torre's head for a clean single against the Cardinals. *The New York Times* wrote a piece in 1999 about him and other players who only made it into one game. At that time, the ball he hit was on his mantle. Skidmore lives in Decatur.

Jimmy Slagle 1873–1956 (Cubs 1902-1908)

One of the wily old veterans on the last Cubs team to win the World Series (1908) in the 20th century. Slagle was 35.

He was known as Rabbit (because of his speed), and Shorty (because of his height — 5'7"), but most of his teammates referred to him as the "Human Mosquito" because he was such a pest. Slagle was the starting center fielder for the entire Cubs dynasty. He took over the job in 1902, and was the first player in World Series history to accomplish a straight steal of home plate (1907), but by 1908, Jimmy was just hanging on. When the 1908 World Series began, Solly Hofman had claimed the starting job. Slagle played his last game for the Cubs on October 3, 1908. He retired from baseball after the last out was recorded in the 1908 World Series-clinching game. Slagle stayed in Chicago after his baseball career and lived there until his death in 1956.

Cy Slapnicka 1886–1979 (Cubs 1911)

Cy pitched pretty well for the Cubs, but went back to the minor leagues after the season, and didn't return to the big leagues until he got a cup of coffee with the Pittsburgh Pirates in 1918. But that was not the end of Slacknicka's baseball career by a long shot. He stayed in the game for fifty years, working mainly as a scout for the Cleveland Indians. Among the players he discovered and signed: Hall of Famers Bob Feller and Lou Boudreau. In both cases there were some shenanigans involved in the signing. Feller was only sixteen years old — and Slappy got called in to see Commissioner Landis about that. (The Indians had to pay a fine.) In Boudreau's case, his mom received a $100 a month allowance while Lou was playing at the University of Illinois. Boudreau was banned from college sports when the news got out, and had no choice but to sign with the Indians. Those two players signed by Slapnicka led the Indians to a World Series championship in 1948.

Sterling Slaughter 1941–(Cubs 1964)

One of the all-time great names in Cubs history, Slaughter was a 22-year-old rookie pitcher with the Cubs in 1964. In his first start he combined on a one-hitter with Lindy McDaniel. His second start was a six-hitter. Unfortunately, that turned out to be a tease, because the youngster didn't win another game in his entire big league career. He developed arm problems and his rookie season was also his last. He is a member of the Arizona State University Baseball Hall of Fame.

Lefty Sloat 1918–2003 (Cubs 1949)

Lefty was born just a few weeks after World War I ended, and his baseball career was interrupted by World War II. By the time Sloat made it to the big leagues, he was 30 years old. He appeared in five games for the Cubs, including one start. Lefty was knocked around. His ERA was seven, and he never appeared in the big leagues again.

Heathcliff Slocumb 1966–(Cubs 1991-1993)

Slocumb was an important part of the Cubs bullpen during his rookie season of 1991, appearing in more than fifty games. He tailed off a bit, however, the following season, so in early 1993, they traded him to the Indians for Jose Hernandez. Slocumb really blossomed a few years later. In 1995 the Phillies made him their closer, and he responded with an All-Star season. Over the next four years Slocumb closed for the Phillies, Red Sox, and Mariners. His trade to the Mariners is often cited as one of the reasons the Red Sox won the World Series. In return for Slocumb, the Red Sox got Derek Lowe and Jason Varitek.

Roy Smalley 1926–2011 (Cubs 1948-1953)

Roy had good pop for a shortstop, hitting 21 home runs one year, but his lifetime batting average was only .227, and he didn't draw many walks either. In his first season, his on-base percentage was .265. That's a pretty stunning total for a player with over 300 at-bats. As much as he swung and missed (he led the league in strikeouts one year), Roy Smalley was probably better known for his fielding (and not in a good way). His wild throws were legendary. Imagine Shawon Dunston's arm with Steve Sax's accuracy. In his first three seasons when he was still playing every day, he made 34, 39, and 51 errors. The running gag at Wrigley Field was the nickname of Cubs double play combination: Miksis to Smalley to Addison Street.

Cubs named Smith...There have been 17 Cubs named Smith over the years, enough to field an entire team. This is one possible starting lineup...

C—Aleck Smith
1B—Paul Smith
2B—Harry Smith
SS—Greg Smith
3B—Charley Smith
LF—Dwight Smith
CF—Earl Smith
RF—Willie Smith
SP—Bob Smith
RP—Lee Smith
RP—Dave Smith

Aleck Smith 1871–1919 (Cubs 1904)

They called the New Yorker "Broadway Aleck" and Broadway had been around before he joined the Cubs in 1904. He had played for Brooklyn, Baltimore, Boston, and the Giants. Smith only played in ten games for the Cubs, but in one of them he knocked in the game-winning run to lead the Cubs to a 1-0 victory. Aleck was mainly a catcher, but he also played a little outfield and first base.

Bob Smith 1895–1987 (Cubs 1931-1932)

One of three Bob Smiths to play for the Cubs, this one has the distinction of being the first. He had a very unusual career. After coming up with Boston as a shortstop, Smith was moved to pitcher in his third big league season. Smith then pitched in the big leagues for thirteen seasons, and posted double-digit wins six years in a row. His last time doing it was for the 1931 Cubs. In that tumultuous year (when star player Hack Wilson and his manager Rogers Hornsby were at war all season), Bob won 15 games. The following year he was moved to the bullpen, and pitched for the Cubs in that capacity in the 1932 World Series. The team traded him in 1933 as part of the package used to acquire slugger Babe Herman.

<u>Historical note:</u> On the day construction was completed on the Empire State Building (1931), Smith was on the mound for the Cubs. He gave up three runs in a loss to the Cardinals.

Bob Smith 1927–2003 (Cubs 1959)

This Bob Smith is differentiated from the others by his great nickname. They called him Riverboat because he grew up in Missouri, along the Mississippi River. He was acquired by the Cubs from the Boston Red Sox in exchange for future manager Chuck Tanner during spring training of 1959. With the Cubs, he stunk up the joint. Although in all fairness to Riverboat, he didn't get much of a chance. He pitched in exactly one game, faced nine batters, and gave up 5 hits, 2 walks, 6 ER, and a wild pitch in 2/3 of an inning. The Cubs traded him shortly after the game to Cleveland for former Cubs favorite Randy Jackson. Both players were toast. Riverboat finished out the season with Cleveland with a 5.22 ERA in 12 appearances. Jackson had the last 74 at-bats of his career, and hit one home run. Neither player played a single MLB game in the 1960s.

Bobby Smith 1934–2015 (Cubs 1962)

This Bob Smith was an outfielder who spent a few weeks with the very bad 1962 Chicago Cubs. How bad were they? The expansion Houston Colt 45s had a better record. The only team that was worse was the worst team in big league history — the 1962 New York Mets. Unfortunately for Bobby Smith, he also played for that team.

Bull Smith 1880–1928 (Cubs 1906)

Bull was a member of the winningest team in baseball history (the 1906 Cubs), but he only played in one game. He later became a minor league manager. He also played football — which is where he got his nickname. He was the halfback on the Canton Bulldogs.

Charley Smith 1937–1994 (Cubs 1969)

No relation to the Charlie Smith who played for the Cubs 50 years earlier, this Charley was a third baseman/shortstop who played in two games during the 1969 season. He was 0 for 2 in two pinch-hitting appearances in April. Charley had a pretty good big league career in the 60s. He had stints with the White Sox, Dodgers, Phillies, Mets, Cardinals, and Yankees before finishing his career with those two at-bats with the Cubs. The highlight of his career probably came in 1966, when the Cardinals traded him to the Yankees straight up for Roger Maris.

Charlie Smith 1880–1929 (Cubs 1911-1914)

Smith hooked up with the Cubs just as their dynasty was beginning to fall apart. Frank Chance would retire as a player during this era, Johnny Evers would suffer a nervous breakdown, and the once-proud Cubs team would not win the National League. Smith was a pitcher for the Cubs, pitching mainly out of the bullpen his first few years, before becoming a starter in 1913. He won seven games that season — his best season in the big leagues. Charlie went into the horse business after his baseball career and owned a livery stable when he died of pneumonia in 1929. His brother Fred also played big league baseball.

Dave Smith 1955–2008 (Cubs 1991-1992)

Dave was a great relief pitcher for the Houston Astros for ten years. He was a two-time All-Star, and is second on the all-time Astros team save list. He came to the Cubs at the end of his career, and quickly developed arm problems. He struggled through two seasons as the Cubs closer (1991-1992) before retiring. When Smith died unexpectedly in 2008 at the age of 53, his ex-teammates were crestfallen. "He was probably one of the most giving people I ever met," former Astros reliever Charlie Kerfeld told the *Houston Chronicle*.

Dwight Smith 1963– (Cubs 1989-1993)

Dwight made an immediate impact with the Cubs after he was called up in May of 1989, finishing second in the Rookie of the Year voting behind teammate Jerome Walton. Smith hit .324 that year. Unfortunately for the Cubs, he never really came close to repeating those numbers, and he was brutal in the outfield. He stayed with the Cubs through 1993, and had flashes of his rookie self, but for the rest of his career he was essentially a journeyman outfielder, occasional pinch hitter, and even (once) the singer of the National Anthem. Smith and his ex-Cubs teammate Greg Maddux later won the World Series with the 1995 Atlanta Braves.

Earl Smith 1891–1943 (Cubs 1916)

Earl got his cup of coffee with the Cubs in their first season at their current ballpark. During that 1916 season, the corner outfielder got only twenty-seven at-bats, all of them in the month of September. He did manage seven hits, including a double and a triple, but the Cubs released the 25-year-old after the season. He later resurfaced with the Browns and the Senators.

Greg Smith 1967– (Cubs 1989-1991)

Smith was one of those rub-some-dirt-in-it gritty infielders the Cubs hoped would develop into a starter. It just didn't quite work out. He got a taste of the big-time in September of 1989 at the tender age of 22, and then made the club out of spring training in 1990. Unfortunately he had some fielding problems that April, and they sent him back down to the minors. Smith was later traded to the Los Angeles Dodgers for Jose Vizcaino. After his playing career was over, he became a scout for the Indians and Rangers, and a special assistant to the Rangers' general manager.

Harry Smith 1856–1898 (White Stockings 1877)

Harry got into only 24 games with Chicago in their second National League season, before moving on mid-season to play with Cincinnati. He played second base, center field, and catcher in the era before players wore gloves. Among his teammates in Chicago were Hall of Famers Al Spalding and Cap Anson. He died before the turn of the century (in 1898) at the way-too-young age of 42.

Jason Smith 1977– (Cubs 2001)

Smith was an infielder who was drafted by the Cubs and came up through their system, but only got one at-bat in a Cubs uniform. He was part of the trade that brought Fred McGriff to Chicago. After leaving the Cubs, Smith was a backup infielder for the Rays, Tigers, Rockies, Blue Jays, Diamondbacks, Royals, and Astros.

Joe Smith 1984– (Cubs 2016)

The Cubs acquired the submariner at the trading deadline, but Smith never really clicked in Chicago. He appeared in 16 games and gave up four long balls. When the playoffs rolled around, it appeared pretty obvious that he would not be making the postseason roster. After the season, the Cubs granted him free agency.

Lee Smith 1957– (Cubs 1980-1987)

When Big Lee came up with the Cubs in 1980, he was a starting pitcher. They moved him to the closer role when they floundered in 1981 after the trade that sent Bruce Sutter to the Cardinals. Big Lee turned out to be one of the most consistent closers in Cubs history. From 1982-1987 he saved an average of 30 games a year. He led the league in 1982, was named to the All-Star team in 1983 and 1987, and led the Cubs to the playoffs in 1984 (although he did give up that heartbreaking homer to Steve Garvey that postseason). The Cubs traded Lee for Al Nipper and Calvin Schiraldi after the 1987 season. Smith saved 300 more games in his career... for other teams. In the next seventeen years, the Cubs had 15 different closers. Lee still holds the all-time Cubs saves record. In 2018, Lee was named to baseball's Hall of Fame.

Historical note: On the day five million people clasped hands for Hands Across America (1986), Big Lee blew the save in the ninth against the Houston Astros.

Paul Smith 1931 – (Cubs 1958)

Smith was acquired from the Pirates during the 1958 season, and got a cup of coffee with the Cubs. He was mainly used as a pinch hitter, although he did log some time at first base as well. Unfortunately for Paul, he didn't hit well (.150), and was sent to the minors in June. He stayed in the game another six years, but never returned to the big leagues.

Willie Smith 1939 – 2006 (Cubs 1968-1970)

Willie's greatest day as a Cub happened on April 8, 1969. He hit a pinch-hit 2-run walk-off home run to win the game on Opening Day. That began a year-long love affair between the Cubs and their fans. On September 4, 1969, with the Cubs still holding onto a 5-game lead over the Mets, Willie and teammate Nate Oliver released a parody of the Righteous Brothers hit "You've Lost that Lovin' Feeling." Unfortunately for Willie, Nate, and Cubs nation, they weren't "going, going, going, all the way" like the song predicted.

Steve Smyth 1978 – (Cubs 2002)

Steve was a highly regarded prospect in the Cubs farm system who was brought in as one of the desperate attempts at finding a fifth starter in 2002. He got seven starts and pitched a grand total of 26 innings. Do the math. He didn't even average four innings a start. It was his only shot at the big leagues. The Cubs traded him to Atlanta in 2004. Smyth pitched in the minor leagues for ten full seasons.

Brad Snyder 1982 – (Cubs 2010-2011)

Snyder was a first round pick of the Indians, so the Cubs gambled that his pedigree would pay off when they got him on waivers. It didn't. In parts of two seasons with the Cubs, the outfielder hit .167. He later played for the Rangers before moving on to Korea.

Miguel Socolovich 1986 – (Cubs 2012)

The Venezuelan right-hander appeared in only six games for the Cubs in 2012. He later pitched for the Cardinals and Braves. Miguel paid his dues in the minors, pitching for 12 seasons.

Jorge Soler 1992 – (Cubs 2014-2016)

Soler was signed after he defected from Cuba. He had a rough start in the minors and had trouble staying healthy, but he put it all together in 2014. At each step of the minors he dominated, until he was brought all the way up to the big leagues. In his first at-bat with the Cubs, Soler hit a homer (against Mat Latos). He finished the year as the club's starting right fielder. He battled through more injuries in 2015, but when the playoffs arrived, so did Jorge. He hit an astounding .474 in the postseason and slugged three homers. At one point he reached base a record nine consecutive times. The injury bug bit him again in 2016, and he missed quite a bit of time. He did hit 12 homers, but he was really a non-factor in the Cubs World Series run. Before the 2017 season, he was traded to the Royals for reliever Wade Davis.

Marcelino Solis 1930 – 2001 (Cubs 1958)

The Mexican-born left-hander was nearly 28 years old when he made his big league debut in 1958. He pitched the second half of the season for the Cubs that year, and registered an ERA of over six in fifteen appearances. He stayed in the farm system for a few seasons before returning to Mexico to finish his career in his homeland.

Eddie Solomon 1951 – 1986 (Cubs 1975)

The Cubs traded stud pitcher Burt Hooton to the Dodgers to get Eddie, but they found out pretty quickly he wasn't their type of guy. He was considered a bad apple by Cubs management, and they didn't waste any time getting rid of him. Eddie was with the Cubs for only two months, but he did manage to pitch in the big leagues until 1982 with the Cardinals, Braves, Pirates, and White Sox. Just four years after his last big league game, he died in a car accident in Macon, Georgia at the age of 34.

Andy Sommers 1865–1908 (White Stockings 1889)

Not to be confused with the lead guitarist of The Police, this Andy Sommers was a catcher/outfielder for the first half of the 1889 season with the Cubs (then known as the White Stockings). He got into twelve games and hit .222 before being released in July. Sommers also played for New York, Boston, Indy, and Cleveland.

Rudy Sommers 1887–1949 (Cubs 1912)

Sommers appeared in one game for the Cubs on September 8, 1912 against the Reds in Cincinnati. He gave up four hits and one run in three innings, and the Cubs lost the rain-shortened game 10-8.

Lary Sorensen 1955–(Cubs 1985)

Lary (spelled with one 'R') pitched for seven teams in an eleven-season big league career including the Cubs in 1985. He was an All-Star with Milwaukee when he won 18 games for them in the 1978 season, but by the time he came to Chicago he wasn't the same pitcher. With the Cubs, Sorenson was converted into a reliever, pitching in 46 games. He was 3-7 with a 4.26 ERA and was released after the year.

Alfonso Soriano 1976–(2007-2013 Cubs)

When he signed an eight-year contract with the Cubs, he was heralded as the savior. After all, he had a rare combination of power and speed (40 homers and 40 steals). Unfortunately, that speed left him pretty quickly after he joined the team, and it wasn't long before the $136 million man heard the boo birds. In fairness to Alfonso, he did lead the Cubs to the playoffs his first two years, and he was an All-Star both seasons. He also displayed the power they were looking for when they signed him (148 homers in six and half seasons). But boy did he strike out a lot (over 700 times), and boy was he a butcher in the outfield. Nevertheless, Soriano always kept a smile on his face, and by the time he left town, Cubs fans were almost sad to see him go.

Historical note: On the day Senator John McCain chose Sarah Palin as his running mate (2008), Soriano hit the game-winning homer at Wrigley Field to beat the Phillies 3-2.

Rafael Soriano 1979–(Cubs 2015)

The Cubs took a flyer on the former All-Star closer after he released by the Washington Nationals in July of 2015. Turns out the Nationals released him for a reason. In only five innings with the Cubs, Soriano gave up two long balls in crucial situations. The Cubs released him in September.

Sammy Sosa 1968–(Cubs 1992-2004)

Sammy was a phenomenon during his time with the Cubs. He holds the all-time record for homers hit in a Cubs uniform (545), and many of them were hit in dramatic fashion. His chase of the Roger Maris record (along with Mark McGwire) captivated the world in 1998. During that season, he may have been the most popular Cubs player of all time.

Sammy was an MVP, a seven-time All-Star, won two home run titles, two RBI titles, led the league in runs three times, and hit more than 60 homers in a season a record-setting three times (although he didn't win the HR title in any of the seasons he did so). The fans loved the way he ran to his right field spot, raising his hat in the air as a tribute to the bleacher fans each day. They loved his home run hop, his post-home run dugout routine done for the cameras, his ever-present smile, and they chanted his name when he came up to bat: SAMMY, SAMMY, SAMMY. He received a great reception around the rest of the league too; many of the NL fans saw Sammy as the entertainer he clearly felt he was. President Clinton even invited Sammy to attend the State of the Union message one year.

The fans didn't seem to notice or care that his teammates didn't seem to feel the same way. They dismissed the anonymous grumbling and the accusations of "me first-ism" as jealousy. That all began to change in the summer of 2003. In an inter-league game against the Tampa Bay Devil Rays, Sammy's bat exploded and Rays catcher Toby Hall picked up the portion of the bat that remained on the ground. He and the umpire immediately noticed the cork, and Sammy was tossed out of the game. In a post-game press conference he swore he accidentally grabbed the wrong bat. The league supposedly checked the other bats after the game (after Sammy and/or the Cubs had plenty of time to get rid of any suspicious bats) and found no evidence against him. That year he didn't make the All-Star team for the first time since 1998.

When Sammy hit .308 with two home runs in the 2003 NL Championship Series vs. the Marlins, Cubs fans seemed ready to forget all about that little corking incident. But it went downhill fast during the 2004 season. The league instituted new testing for steroids, and suddenly Sammy was doing his home run hops on balls barely hit to the warning track. During that summer, Sammy sneezed in the clubhouse and injured himself so badly he missed nearly a month of games. The Cubs fans didn't officially desert him, however, until the team collapsed the last week of the 2004 season. In the final game of the year, Sammy left in a huff before the game was over. His teammates took that opportunity to bash his boom box into pieces with a baseball bat, an ignominious end to his Cubs career.

The Cubs traded Sammy to Baltimore, and he got the last 35 home runs of his major league career with the Orioles and the Rangers. His 600th career home run came against the Cubs in an inter-league game, but the love affair with Chicago was long gone.

<u>Historical note:</u> On the day of the great Chicago Flood (in 1992), Sammy was batting second in the order and playing center field.

Geovany Soto 1983 – (Cubs 2005-2012)

Soto was the Rookie of the Year and an All-Star for the Cubs in 2008 when he hit 23 homers and knocked in 86 runs, but never even came close to living up to those numbers again. It all started going downhill for Geo when he tested positive for pot in the 2009 World Baseball Classic while playing for his native Puerto Rico. The Cubs traded him to the Rangers in 2012. He has since also played for the A's, Angels, and White Sox.

Albert Spalding 1850–1915 (White Stockings player 1876-1877, owner 1878-1891)

Spalding was already a four-time champion in Boston before he came to Chicago and convinced a few of his teammates to help stock the first National League team in Chicago. It was the beginning of a dynasty in Chicago. In Spalding's first

year with the White Stockings the pitcher won 47 games. But though Spalding was a great player, he was always a little ahead of his time. For instance, while he was still playing, he became the first "sissy" who insisted on wearing a glove. And he did it because he wanted to sell them at his sporting goods store. It worked. His business mind eventually took over, and he bought the team. There was simply more money to be made in ownership than in playing the game. He came up with several innovations (other than the glove), including spring training (in Hot Springs, Arkansas in 1886) and night baseball (which didn't catch on in 1883). Al also created the world's first league-wide salary cap, an idea that lives on today in many other sports, but ironically, not in baseball.

Spalding is a Hall of Famer and a visionary, but clearly he was not a popular man because of the horrible way he treated his players. During a barnstorming world tour, one of his best players Ned Williamson was hurt in London. Spalding not only left him there, he refused to pay for his medical bills or his return passage to America. After the 1886 season, a season in which they lost the 19th century version of the World Series, Spalding decided that he had identified the problem. Spalding believed that alcohol was evil, and felt that his team simply had too many drunks. The Cubs certainly did have their share of drunks, and none was more obvious than their biggest star King Kelly. Kelly was known to show up drunk, drink during the game, and then get drunker still after the game. So, to clean up the team, King Kelly was the first player Spalding jettisoned. Kelly was sold to Boston for an unheard-of sum of money…$10,000. But Spalding was just getting started. Next, he got rid of the rest of the outfield. George Gore, a perennial .300 hitter, was traded to New York. Abner Dalrymple, their leadoff man and left fielder for their many pennant winners, was traded to Pittsburgh, along with one of their best pitchers, 31-game winner Jim McCormick. Only one "drunk" remained on the team, a future Hall of Fame pitcher named John Clarkson. He was sent away the following off-season.

So how did the team fare after the drunks were moved out and the team was purified? They didn't sniff the pennant for another nineteen years. It got so bad that the entire team quit to form a new league in 1890 (other than three players… Anson, Burns, and Hutchison). That signaled to Spalding that it might be time to step away from the game, which he did shortly after that.

Historical note: On the last full day of General George Armstrong Custer's life (1876), Al Spalding was on the mound for a 16-2 Chicago win over New York.

Al Spangler 1933–(Cubs 1967-1971)

Spanky, as he was known by his teammates, had some clutch hits for the Cubs over his five seasons as a backup outfielder and pinch hitter, but Spangler never had the kind of power necessary to start in the big leagues. He got his most extended playing time during Chicago's ill-fated 1969 season. In over 200 plate appearances he hit four homers and knocked in 27 runs. He also, unfortunately, only hit .211. That was the beginning of the end of his 13-year big league career. He later went into coaching.

Bob Speake 1930–(Cubs 1955,1957)

His real name was Robert Speake, and he went by Bob, but his nickname was Spook. Spook was an outfielder/first baseman for the Cubs during the '55 and '57 seasons, and had decent pop in his bat (12 and 16 home runs), but his average was terrible (.218 and .232). The Cubs traded him to the Giants after the '57 season for Bobby Thompson, and Speake drifted away. He only hit three more homers in his career and was out of baseball after the '59 season.

Chris Speier 1950–(Cubs 1985-1986)

Long before he was arrested for DUI as a coach for the 2006 Cubs, Chris Speier was a very respectable backup infielder for the 1985 and 1986 Cubs. He backed up Sandberg at second, Dunston at shortstop, and Ron Cey at third, and in 1986 hit .284 for the year, the best he ever hit in a season during his 19-year major league career. He was a three-time All-Star shortstop early in his career with the San Francisco Giants.

Justin Speier 1973–(Cubs 1998)

Chris Speier's son was drafted by the Cubs and made his big league debut for them just a few years later. The right-handed reliever was included in the trade package that brought Felix Heredia to the Cubs in July of 1998. Heredia was a bust with the Cubs, but Speier went on to make 600 more big league relief appearances for the Marlins, Braves, Indians, Rockies, Blue Jays, and Angels over a stellar 12-year career.

Rob Sperring 1949–(Cubs 1974-1976)

The jack of all trades played every position with the Cubs except first base, catcher, and pitcher. He never hit much (career average of .211), but he was a valuable backup. Sperring was later included as a throw-in to the Bill Madlock for Bobby Murcer trade with the Giants.

Karl Spongberg 1884–1938 (Cubs 1908)

He pitched exactly one game in the big leagues, and it was for the last Cubs team to win a World Series title. On August 1, 1908, Spongeberg came in to relieve Carl Lundgren in the third inning. The Cubs were already behind 7-0 to Boston at the time. Karl finished the game for him, but he gave up another 7 runs. His final ERA was 9.00.

Jerry Spradlin 1967–(Cubs 2000)

Spradlin was a journeyman right-hander who lasted seven big league seasons, including his last one with the Cubs in 2000. He appeared in eight games and was rocked hard (15 ERs in 15 innings). The Cubs released him after the season, and he never pitched in the big leagues again. Spradlin's career highlight probably came on July 22, 1999 when he struck out four San Diego Padres in one inning (as a member of the Giants). He is one of only seventy pitchers in big league history to pull off that feat.

Charlie Sprague 1864–1912 (White Stockings 1887)

Charlie was a left-handed starting pitcher who started three games for the Cubs (then known as the White Stockings) in the summer of 1887. He completed two of those games, and posted a 4.91 ERA. He later also pitched for Cleveland and Toledo.

Jack Spring 1933–2015 (Cubs 1964)

Spring pitched for seven teams in his eight big league seasons, and for exactly one month that team was the Cubs. They acquired Jack in May of 1964 (ironically—still technically spring), and he pitched in seven games over the next few weeks. But then on June 15, 1964, Spring was called into the manager's office and told he had been traded again. This time he was the throw-in in the trade that sent Lou Brock to the Cardinals. In St. Louis, Spring won a ring (although he didn't make the postseason roster that year). Not sure what happened to that Brock character. One of the most miraculous stats of Jack's career is this little tidbit: He once went 19 consecutive outings without recording a strikeout. That's the longest streak since 1957.

DeWayne Staats 1952– (Cubs announcer 1985-1989)

Staats was part of the Cubs broadcast team during the mid-to-late 80s. Among his highlights during that time was broadcasting the first night game at Wrigley Field (in 1988) and their division-winning season of 1989. Since leaving the Cubs he has been the broadcaster for the Yankees and the Tampa Rays.

Eddie Stack 1887–1958 (Cubs 1913-1914)

Eddie pitched for Chicago two seasons while they were still at the old West Side Grounds ballpark. The right-hander appeared in eighteen games over those two seasons, and won 4. After he retired from baseball, Eddie settled in the Chicago area, and is buried at Mount Carmel Cemetery in Hillside.

Tuck Stainback 1911–1992 (Cubs 1934-1937)

His real name was George Tucker Stainback, so it seemed obvious to call him Tuck…but it also just happened to create one of the all-time great names. Say it out loud: Tuck Stainback. It's positively poetic. Stainback was a backup outfielder for the Cubs from 1934-1937. He's probably best known for his ejection from the Cub bench for riding umpire George Moriarty during the 1935 Chicago-Detroit World Series. His taunting led to the entire dugout being thrown out of the game, which came back to haunt the Cubs in the ninth inning. The pitcher had to bat in a tied game with the winning run on third base because no one was left to pinch hit. Needless to say, the Cubs lost. Tuck was later a throw-in in the Dizzy Dean trade, one of the Cubs' worst. After he retired, he helped organize Major League Baseball's first pension for players in 1947.

Matt Stairs 1968– (Cubs 2001)

Stairs was brought in to play first base for the Cubs, even though he had previously only played a handful of games at that position. It didn't work out. The Cubs traded for Fred McGriff at the trading deadline to take his place. Nevertheless, Stairs did hit 16 homers in a Cubs uniform, and got several clutch hits during that 2001 season. It was his only year in Chicago, but he did play ten more seasons in the big leagues, and won a ring with the Phillies in 2008.

Gale Staley 1899–1989 (Cubs 1925)

The second greatest Gale to ever play in Wrigley (the other one played football) played at the tail end of the '25 season (Sept/Oct). That was the first year the Cubs ever finished in last place. In his first at-bat, Staley lined a single and drove in a run in the bottom of the 9th inning. A week later he got his first start at second base and batted seventh in the lineup, between Charlie Grimm and Gabby Hartnett. He went 2 for 3, and started a few double plays. He played there the rest of the season, including Pete Alexander's last start. By his fourth game he was batting second in the lineup behind Sparky Adams (who had shifted over to SS to replace Rabbit Maranville). Staley got at least one hit in every game he played, but he spent the rest of his career in the minor leagues.

Pete Standridge 1892–1963 (Cubs 1915)

Pete pitched for the Cubs in 1915 during the last season of the rickety old West Side Grounds. He went 4-1 in 29 appearances with a 3.61 ERA. He would never make it back to the bigs, despite being only 23 years old at the time. He pitched in the minor leagues until 1920, and later managed in Canada.

Eddie Stanky 1916–1999 (Cubs 1943-1944)

They called him the brat because he was a professional irritant. Leo Durocher pegged him with his nickname when he said: "Look at Mel Ott over there [in the Giant's dugout]. He's a nice guy, and he finishes second. Now look at The Brat (Stanky). He can't hit, can't run, can't field. He's no nice guy, but all the little SOB can do is win." Branch Rickey described Stanky the same way: "He can't hit, he can't run, he can't field, he can't throw, he can't do a goddamn thing…but beat you."

The ultimate rub-some-dirt-in-it gritty second baseman started out as a Cub (1943), but was traded to the Dodgers halfway through his second season for a journeyman pitcher named Bob Chipman. The Cubs thought they had a better second baseman to replace him: Don Johnson. Johnson did start at 2B for the Cubs World Series team in 1945, but Stanky went on to play in three World Series, was named to three All-Star teams, led the league in on-base percentage twice, and most famously started the ninth-inning rally that culminated in Bobby Thomson's pennant-winning home run.

After his playing career was over he managed the White Sox (in '66 and '67 — while Durocher was managing the Cubs), and for one game in 1977, the Texas Rangers. He quit after one day because he couldn't stand the modern ballplayers.

Joe Stanley 1881–1967 (Cubs 1909)

Stanley was only 16 years old when he got his first taste of the big leagues with the Washington Senators in 1897 and struck out in his only at-bat. But he hung in there and eventually played for the Boston Braves for several seasons. Stanley came to the Cubs in his final year in the big leagues as a grizzled 28-year-old veteran. He hit .135 in limited time in the Cubs outfield that year, but played alongside the stars that comprised the Cubs dynasty.

Tom Stanton 1874–1957 (Cubs 1904)

Stanton played in exactly one game for the Cubs. It happened on April 19, 1904. The catcher went 0 for 3 with a strikeout, while catching future World Series champ Carl Lundgren. The Cubs lost 9-3 in St. Louis.

Ray Starr 1906–1963 (Cubs 1945)

Ray Starr earned the nickname Iron Man by pitching both ends of more than 40 minor league double-headers during his 20-year career. One of his memorable quirks? Each season he pitched fastballs and curves for two hours on the first day of spring training. (Modern day pitching coaches faint at the mention of this ritual.) As a wartime pitcher with the Reds, Starr won 15 games in 1942 and made the All-Star team. But that was really his only good year. The Cubs picked him up from the Pirates during their pennant-winning 1945 season, but Iron Man didn't exactly pitch well. His ERA was 7.42. Starr gave up 17 hits and 7 walks in just 13 innings with the pennant-winning Cubs. He retired after the 1945 season.

Joe Start 1842–1927 (White Stockings 1878)

Joe was known as Old Reliable. He was 35 years old when he started at first base for the 1878 Cubs (then known as the White Stockings). He was the meat in the Cubs first baseman Hall of Fame sandwich. The man who started there the year before was Al Spalding, and the man who started there the year after was Cap Anson. Of course both Spalding and Anson were still part of that 1878 team (Spalding as owner, Anson as outfielder), but Old Reliable hit incredibly well for the White Stockings that year. He led the team in hitting with a .351 average. Start played in the big leagues another eight seasons (mainly for Providence) and didn't retire until he was 43 years old.

Jigger Statz 1897–1988 (Cub 1922-1925)

His real name was Arnold John Statz, and he was a local boy — born in Waukegan, around the same time as Jack Benny. When he was little the folks called him "chigger bug" because he was so small. That was spelled incorrectly by his parents, and voila, the name stuck. For many years Jigger held the all-time record for professional baseball games played, although most of his (18 years) were played in the minors in Wrigley Field (the one in Los Angeles). He did play 8 seasons in the big leagues, and was the starting center fielder for the Cubs in the early 20s (1922-1925). Only eight players have more than 4000 career hits in professional baseball. Jigger Statz is one of them. He played in the minors until he was 44 years old. Because he was located in Los Angeles, Jigger also got into the movie business. He played himself in *Fast Company* in 1929, and served as technical advisor on the Grover Cleveland Alexander story *The Winning Team* in 1952.

Historical note: On the day that Leopold & Loeb committed a horrible thrill killing in Chicago in 1924, Statz was the hitting star for the Cubs in a 8-6 win over the Phillies. Alexander was on the mound for the Cubs.

Ed Stauffer 1898–1979 (Cubs 1923)

Stauffer pitched in only one game for the Cubs on April 26, 1923. Ed pitched two innings and gave up five hits and three earned runs in a 7-5 loss to the Pirates. His final ERA in the NL is 13.50. Among the Pirates he faced that day: future Cub Charlie Grimm, and future Hall of Famers Rabbit Maranville and Pie Traynor. Stauffer later got a little longer shot with the 1925 St. Louis Browns (20 games).

John Stedronsky 1850–1924 (White Stockings 1879)

Stedronsky was an unlikely big league ballplayer. He was born in Czechoslovakia, and didn't pick up baseball until later in life. John was a 29-year-old rookie third baseman who got into the last four games of the 1879 season. He got exactly one hit, which in fairness to Stedronsky is one more big league hit than you or I ever tallied.

Kennie Steenstra 1970–(Cubs 1998)

Kennie pitched for the Cubs for two weeks at the end of May/ beginning of June in 1998. It didn't go too well for him. In four appearances covering 3.1 innings, he gave up two homers and posted an ERA north of 10. He pitched eleven seasons in the minor leagues, but this was his only taste of the big-time.

Morrie Steevens 1940–(Cubs 1962)

The lefty reliever made the Cubs out of spring training in 1962, and debuted against his favorite childhood team the Cardinals in April. Steevens gave up a two-run double to Bill White. He was only 21 years old at the time. He pitched a few more times before the Cubs sent him down to the minors. They didn't bring him back up until September. All told, the rookie appeared in twelve games and had a respectable ERA of 2.40. That was it for his Cubs career. He later also pitched for the Phillies.

Ed Stein 1869–1928 (Colts 1890-1891)

Ed was a starting pitcher for the Cubs (then known as the Colts) and had a few fairly good seasons, but it wasn't until he got to Brooklyn that Stein really showed what he could do. He won 27 games and 26 games in two different seasons for Brooklyn.

Historical note: Ed was on the mound for the Colts the day Vincent Van Gogh died (1890). He beat Philadelphia 8-6.

Randy Stein 1953–2011 (Cubs 1982)

Randy pitched for the Brewers and Mariners before finishing up his career with the Cubs. He went out in style, however. In his last big league appearance on September 22, 1982, he pitched three scoreless innings against the Mets in Wrigley Field. He didn't have many appearances like that. His career ERA was 5.72. Randy died after a long battle with Alzheimer's disease.

Harry Steinfeldt 1877–1914 (Cubs 1906-1910)

Harry was the forgotten man in the Cubs infield that also included Hall of Famers Tinker, Evers, and Chance, but he was every bit as important to that Cubs dynasty as any of them. If only his last name were a little more poetic — Franklin Adams may have included him in his famous poem. (In fairness to Adams, *you* try rhyming Steinfeldt.) Frank Chance considered Harry the final piece to the puzzle when he acquired him before the 1906 season, and boy was he right. Harry led the team in hits and RBI and batted .327 as the Cubs posted the best record in baseball history. The following year, Steinfeldt was the star of the 1907 World Series. He hit .471 to lead the Cubs to their first World Series championship. He was also the starting third baseman for the Cubs in the 1908 and 1910 World Series. Harry played briefly the next season with Boston, but his skills were obviously waning. After not being able to cut it in the minor leagues, he admitted defeat and retired. Harry Steinfeldt passed away of a cerebral hemorrhage in 1914 at the age of 36.

Rick Stelmaszek 1948–2017 (Cubs 1974)

The local Chicago boy (Mendel Catholic High) played his final season in the big leagues with the Cubs, serving as one of the team's backup catchers. His claim to fame with the Cubs was allowing a third strike to drop, which enabled an Expos runner to reach base. Pitcher Bill Bonham struck out four batters that innings thanks to Rick's error. After his playing career, he went into coaching for the Minnesota Twins, and was on the staff of two World Series winners.

Jake Stenzel 1867–1919 (Colts 1890)

Jake was an exile from the Players' League when Cap Anson convinced him to play a few games for the Cubs (then known as the Colts). Even though Anson couldn't convince Stenzel to stay in Chicago, it was obvious that he had a good eye for talent. Stenzel later played for Pittsburgh, Baltimore, St. Louis, and Cincinnati and finished his nine-year big league career with a .338 lifetime average. He opened a bar after his playing days, and sold it during World War I, just before Prohibition kicked in.

Earl Stephenson 1947–(Cubs 1971)

Earl made his big league debut with the Cubs in April of

1971 and made sixteen appearances before returning to the minors. He won a game and saved a game during his brief stint with the Cubs. He also had a cup of coffee with the Brewers and the Orioles, but spent most of his 11-year baseball career in the minor leagues.

Joe Stephenson 1921–2001 (Cubs 1944)

Joe languished in the minor leagues for ten years, but did get a few very brief tastes of the big-time during World War II, including his very short stint with the Cubs. The catcher appeared in only four games and managed to get one hit in eight plate appearances. Stephenson's baseball career is more notable for what he did after he retired as a player. He worked as a scout for the Red Sox and discovered the likes of Fred Lynn, Rick Burleson, Dwight Evans, and Bill "Spaceman" Lee.

John Stephenson 1941– (Cubs 1967-1968)

When you're a decent defensive catcher, they'll find a place for you in the majors. Stephenson was Randy Hundley's backup for two seasons, which means that he didn't get a lot of playing time. He also served as a backup catcher for the Mets, Giants, and Angels in a ten-year big league career. One of his claims to fame: making the final out in Jim Bunning's perfect game in 1964.

Phil Stephenson 1960– (Cubs 1989)

Phil played his college ball at Wichita State and set a hitting streak record (47 games) that was later broken by Robin Ventura. Stephenson came up with the Cubs as a 28-year-old rookie in 1989, but the left-handed first baseman/outfielder didn't get a lot of playing time before being sent to San Diego as the player to be named later in the Darrin Jackson/Calvin Schiraldi for Marvell Wynne/Luis Salazar trade. He got a lot more playing time with the Padres in 1990, but didn't respond well, hitting only .209 for the season. Phil later became a college coach in Kansas.

Riggs Stephenson 1898–1985 (Cubs 1926-1934)

Stephenson was a former All-American football player, and his nickname Old Hoss fit his build. Old Hoss was a great hitter, one of the best in Cubs history. He still holds the Cubs record for hitters with more than 2000 ABs, with a .336

lifetime average. In the Cubs' 1929 pennant-winning year, he combined with Hall of Famers Hack Wilson and Kiki Cuyler to form the only outfield in National League history with 100 RBI players at each spot. (Stephenson 110, Wilson 159, Cuyler 102). He had his problems in the outfield, however. Old Hoss threw like an Old Hoss thanks to an old football injury. He had major arm problems which hampered him, and eventually shortened his career.

Historical note: On the day Clarence Birdsong was granted a patent for frozen food (1930), Riggs got the game-winning hit in the bottom of the 11th at Wrigley Field to defeat Brooklyn.

Walter Stephenson 1911–1993 (Cubs 1935-1936)

Stephenson was from a small North Carolina mountain town, and he only played in twenty-two games for the Cubs in 1935 and 1936. Nicknamed Tarzan for his impressive physique (He was about 6', 180 pounds), he didn't get to play much because he was a backup catcher to Cubs ironman catcher Gabby Hartnett. Tarzan was a memorable character though, known for his toughness and temper. In 1935, he and Billy Jurges got into a fist-fight in the dugout at Forbes Field because Jurges made a crack about the South losing the Civil War (Jurges was from Brooklyn). Tarzan Stephenson later played ten more games for the Philadelphia Phillies before drifting off into the minors.

Dave Stevens 1970– (Cubs 1997-1998)

Stevens pitched for the Twins, Indians, and Braves in addition to the Cubs. With the Cubs he pitched strictly out of the bullpen. He posted a 9.64 ERA in 1997, and then did a bit better during the Wild Card season of 1998 (4.74 ERA). The Cubs released him after that season.

Jeff Stevens 1983– (Cubs 2009-2011)

Stevens got three shots to show his stuff with the Cubs, but never quite managed to seize the opportunity. In 33 appearances over three seasons, he posted an ERA of 6.27. In only 37 innings, he gave up 25 walks and seven homers.

Ace Stewart 1869–1912 (Colts 1895)

Ace wasn't given that nickname because of his stellar play, his real first name was Asa, and Ace was just a shortened way of saying that. The Indiana native (Terre Haute) was a second baseman for Chicago in his only big league season, and was a bit of a butcher in the field. He made 52 errors. Even though he never made it back to the bigs, he did play professional baseball in the minor leagues until 1907. Oh, and he also had a tremendous mustache.

Ian Stewart 1985 – (Cubs 2012-2013)

Stewart was one of the first players Theo Epstein acquired after being named Cubs president. Stewart cost the Cubs Tyler Colvin and D.J. LeMahieu, but Epstein figured that Ian had the talent to become the Cubs starting third baseman. Unfortunately, Stewart's wrist never seemed to heal, robbing him of his best attribute — his power. Without the power, his low batting average was a major liability. Still, Stewart wasn't officially let go by the Cubs until he posted some critical tweets. That's what sealed his fate.

Jimmy Stewart 1939 – 2012 (Cubs 1963-1967)

Not to be confused with the movie star of the same name, this Jimmy Stewart was a utility man who played every position for the Cubs except first base, catcher, and pitcher. His biggest shot came in 1964, when he played a lot of second base after the shocking death of Ken Hubbs, and hit .253 in over 400 plate appearances. Unfortunately for him, he slumped badly the following year, and was used less and less by new manager Leo Durocher. Stewart later played for the White Sox, Reds, and Astros.

Mack Stewart 1914 – 1960 (Cubs 1944-1945)

Mack Stewart got into eight games in the summer of 1944, and pitched fairly well. He also started the 1945 season with the Cubs, but wasn't very effective, so they sent him down to their single-A team in Nashville at the end of June. He had a couple more solid seasons in Double-A, but never made it back up to the big leagues. Stewart was already in his 30s when the season began and more than likely never would have made it on the Cubs if their team hadn't been so badly depleted during the war.

Tuffy Stewart 1883 – 1934 (Cubs 1913-1914)

The second most popular Tuffy in Cubs history was a local boy who wasn't really a boy anymore when he made his big league debut for his hometown Cubs. He was 30. In parts of two seasons he played in eleven games and got only one big league hit (a double that drove in two runs). Most of his appearances came as a late-inning defensive replacement in the outfield.

Tim Stoddard 1953 – (Cubs 1984)

In college he played in a national championship game in both basketball and baseball for North Carolina State University. He was basketball teammates with superstar David Thompson, and had to cover Bill Walton in their Final Four game. But he chose baseball over basketball and never looked back. Tim had a very successful 13-year big league career, including two seasons as the closer in Baltimore. Stoddard only pitched one season for the Cubs, but it just happened to be their division-winning season of 1984. He was the primary setup man for Lee Smith that year, saving seven games and winning ten in 58 appearances. After the season he was granted his free agency, and signed with the team that beat the Cubs in the playoffs, the San Diego Padres. The Cubs got a first round pick as compensation and selected Rafael Palmeiro.

Steve Stone 1947 – (Cubs 1974-1976)

Of course we all remember Steve Stone's long run as the TV color man for the Cubs, but he also pitched for them three seasons in the mid-70s ('74-'76). The Cubs acquired him from the White Sox (along with catcher Steve Swisher) for Ron Santo, who toiled away painfully on the South Side in his last big league season. Stone's best season with the Cubs was 1975 when he won 12 games. He became a free agent after the 1976 season and had two more good seasons (winning 15 games with the South Side Hitmen White Sox in 1977, and the Cy Young award with the Baltimore Orioles in 1980.) He became a broadcaster shortly thereafter, and still broadcasts baseball games somewhere. (It's too painful to say where). Stone still shares a spot in the Cubs record books. On July 9, 1974, he allowed five homers in one game.

Historical note: On the day President Nixon's impeachment hearings began in Congress (1974), Stone beat the Braves 3-2 at Wrigley Field. Billy Williams knocked in two of three Cubs runs.

Bill Stoneman 1944–(Cubs 1967-1968)

Stoneman was a local Chicago-area boy (Oak Park) the Cubs drafted in 1966. By July of '67 he was up with the big club, and pitched pretty well out of the bullpen. He saved four games and nearly struck out a man an inning. The following year the Cubs sent him to the minors to become a starter. Unfortunately, they left him unprotected in the expansion draft of 1968, and the Expos nabbed him. All Stoneman did for the Expos was throw two no-hitters (against the Phillies in April of 1969, and against the Mets in October of 1972) and pitch in the All-Star game (1972). After his playing career, he became the general manager of the Angels.

Dan Straily 1988–(Cubs 2014)

Straily was acquired in the trade that sent Jeff Samardzija and Jason Hammel to Oakland. He appeared in only seven games for the Cubs in 2014 and was hit pretty hard (11.25 ERA). He won 10 games for the A's in 2013.

Joe Strain 1954–(Cubs 1981)

Joe was one of the second basemen on the truly awful 1981 Cubs team. He arrived via the San Francisco Giants in the Jerry Martin trade. Strain didn't get a lot of playing time, and hit a mere .189. The Cubs pulled the plug on him on June 2nd of that year. He stuck it out in the minors for a few more seasons before hanging up his spikes for good.

Sammy Strang 1876–1932 (Orphans 1900, 1902)

Strang had one of the best nicknames of all time. They called him the Dixie Thrush. The native of Tennessee was a backup middle infielder for the 1900 Cubs (then known as the Orphans). He jumped to the upstart American League in 1902 (with the White Sox), although he did finish up that season with the Cubs. His best years came with the Giants, including the 1906 season when he led baseball with a .423 on-base percentage. He is the rarest of Cubs…a veteran of the Spanish-American War.

Doug Strange 1964–(Cubs 1991-1992)

Strange was a backup infielder for the Cubs for two seasons, and hit under .200 in about one hundred at-bats. Still, Doug managed to have a nine-year big league career. He also played for the Tigers, Mariners, Expos, and Pirates.

Scott Stratton 1869–1939 (Colts 1894-1895)

Stratton was a two-way player. He was mainly a pitcher, but his hitting was so good, he often played in the outfield on days he didn't pitch. By the time he came to the Cubs (then known as the Colts) he was getting hit pretty hard. He won 10 games in two seasons, but he also posted ERAs of 5.89 and 9.60. That was the last hurrah of his big league career.

Lou Stringer 1917–2008 (Cubs 1941-1942, 1946)

Lou became the starting second baseman after the Cubs made the ill-advised Billy Herman trade in 1941, and started there in 1942 too. He was known more for his glove (a decent double play man) than his bat, although he did have two pretty good offensive seasons with the Cubs before being drafted into the military. He missed three seasons of his big league career serving in the Army Air Corp. When he came back from the war he had another cup of coffee with the Cubs before they traded him to the Boston Red Sox. He finished his career in Boston in 1950.

Pedro Strop 1985–(Cubs 2013-present)

Strop was acquired along with Jake Arrieta in the trade that sent Scott Feldman and Steve Clevenger to the Orioles. The Dominican reliever has pitched well out of the bullpen for the Cubs since they acquired him. In 2015 he was the primary setup man to Hector Rondon and posted a sterling 2.91 ERA in 68 appearances, striking out 81 batters and saving three games. He had another pretty good season in 2016 (2.85 ERA), but he was hurt in September, and Maddon was hesitant to use him in his old role during the playoffs. He did pitch in every playoff series, and pitched well in three World Series appearances, but during crucial moments, his manager didn't call Strop's number. In 2017 Pedro was once again effective during the regular season (2.83 ERA), but this time Maddon did use him in the playoffs. He was one of the rare Cubs pitchers who performed well in the postseason. His 2018 season was probably his best in a Cubs uniform. Pedro became the closer after Morrow's injury and saved 13 games with a 2.26 ERA. His late-season injury greatly contributed to the Cubs 2018 late-season collapse.

George Stueland 1899–1964 (Cubs 1921-1925)

Stueland's best season was 1922, when he won 9 games. But

he wasn't fooling anyone. His career ERA with the Cubs (his entire big league career) was 5.73.

Historical note: On the day the Lincoln Memorial was dedicated in Washington by Supreme Court Chief Justice Taft and Lincoln's son Robert Todd Lincoln in 1922, Stueland beat the Cardinals at Cubs Park (Wrigley). He threw a 4-hitter and won the game 4-1.

Bobby Sturgeon 1919–2007 (Cubs 1940-1947)

Legend has it that Cubs manager Gabby Hartnett wanted his management to get him a young shortstop. The Cubs checked with the Dodgers about Pee Wee Reese, and thought they were asking for too much in return, so they asked the Cardinals. St. Louis offered them a choice between Marty Marion (a future MVP and seven-time All-Star) or Bobby Sturgeon. The Cubs picked Sturgeon. Bobby was given the starting job as a 21-year-old in 1941, and while he did an admirable job in the field, his batting was never very good. He didn't hit for power or average, and he didn't have a lot speed. 1941 was his only season as a starter. The rest of Bobby's career was spent on the bench.

Tanyon Sturtze 1970– (Cubs 1995-1996)

The 6'5 Sturtze came up with the Cubs, but only pitched in eight games over two seasons. He went on to have a pretty solid big league career, pitching for the Rangers, White Sox, Rays, Yankees, and Dodgers over twelve big league seasons.

Jim St. Vrain 1871–1937 (Orphans 1902)

St. Vrain had a fair amount of success on the mound for the Cubs (then known as the Orphans), but he is probably best remembered for running to the wrong base during an at-bat that season. Cubs manager Frank Selee convinced him to bat left-handed instead of right-handed, and when he hit the ball, he got confused and ran to third base instead of first. Needless to say, he was out.

Chris Stynes 1973– (Cubs 2002)

He had a couple of good seasons as a third baseman for the Reds before coming to Chicago, but with the Cubs he hit only .241. Before he came to the Cubs, as a member of the Royals, he stole second, third, and home on three consecutive pitches. No one has done that in the American League since.

Bill Sullivan 1853–1884 (White Stockings 1878)

Sullivan was an Irish immigrant who played in only a two games for the Cubs (then known as the White Stockings) on August 9 and August 10 in 1878. He got one hit. Not much is known about him. There is no record of whether he batted right-handed or left-handed, only that he played left field. He died at the age of 31.

John Sullivan 1890–1966 (Cubs 1921)

Sullivan was an outfielder for the Cubs in 1921, and he had a very good season as a bench player, hitting .329 in 250 at-bats. But after the season was over, Sullivan was shipped off to the Pacific Coast League so that the Cubs could acquire West Coast minor league star, Jigger Statz. Sullivan played another five years of minor league ball, but never made it back to the big leagues.

Marty Sullivan 1862–1894 (White Stockings 1887-1888)

Marty had a great rookie season with the Cubs (then known as the White Stockings) in 1887. The left fielder drove in 77 runs and batted .284. But Sullivan was also a bit temperamental. He got into a fight during a game in 1888 that had to be broken up by the police. He was arrested and charged with disturbing the peace. Although Marty played another four seasons in the big leagues with various different clubs, he never really approached the numbers of his rookie season again. In January of 1894, only two years after he played his last big league game, Marty passed away at the age of 31.

Mike Sullivan 1866–1906 (Colts 1890)

Big Mike, as he was called, pitched for the Cubs (then known as the Colts) early in his career. He went on to pitch in the big leagues for ten seasons for Washington, Philadelphia, New York, Cleveland, and Boston. In his one season in Chicago, he was 5-6 with a 4.59 ERA. Mike died only a few years after he retired, at the way-too-young age of 39.

Champ Summers 1946–2012 (Cubs 1975-1976)

Summers received his nickname "Champ" from his father: "Dad took one look at me when I was born and said, He looks like he's just gone 10 rounds with Joe Louis.'" His real name was John Junior Summers, and he played two of his eleven major league seasons with the Cubs. He didn't make it to the majors until he was 28 because he had served in Vietnam. Champ was a backup corner outfielder and first baseman with no power and a batting average in the low .200s with the Cubs, but he later had a couple of good seasons for the Detroit Tigers (hitting 20 and 17 home runs). The last at-bat of his career was in the World Series with the San Diego Padres, who had just knocked the 1984 Chicago Cubs out of the playoffs.

Billy Sunday 1862–1935 (White Stockings 1883-1887)

Sunday is one of the most famous players in Chicago baseball history. The story of his fame began in the summer of 1886. Sunday was out carousing in Chicago with his fellow players Mike King Kelly, Ned Williamson, and Silver Flint on Van Buren Street, nearby the many famous decadent State Street saloons (in the Levee section of town). They were totally drunk, sitting in a gutter, and the sun was coming up. While they tried to rouse themselves, a gospel wagon drove up and conducted a service. Sunday recognized the songs from his childhood in Ames, Iowa and saw the light at that moment. He said to his buddies: "Boys, it's all off; we have come to where the roads part." He swore off booze forever and dedicated himself to God. He still played baseball a little longer, but he now was playing with God on his shoulder. He often would tell the story of the day God helped him. He claimed the crowd overflowed onto the field one day, and as he was chasing a fly ball he prayed for the Lord's help, and screamed for everyone to get out of the way. They parted like the Red Sea, and Billy made the catch.

After he quit baseball he toured the country as an evangelist — using incredible theatrics to get his point across. He drew huge crowds wherever he spoke. Sunday was one of the leading voices in favor of Prohibition, and became one of the most famous people in the whole country. He hobnobbed with presidents. The song "Chicago Chicago" includes a line about him: "The town that Billy Sunday could not shut down."

But it all began with a bunch of ballplayers sitting in a Chicago gutter in 1886.

Jim Sundberg 1951– (1987-1988)

Sundberg was the backup catcher for the Cubs in 1987,

catching 57 games behind Jody Davis. He hit only .201. He was 36 at the time. Jim also played with the Cubs in 1988 for a few months. But that doesn't begin to tell the Jim Sundberg story. Before he came to Chicago Sundberg was a six-time Gold Glover, three-time All-Star, and caught a Hall of Famer's no-hitter in 1977 (Bert Blyleven). He also won a World Series as a member of the 1985 Kansas City Royals.

Rick Sutcliffe 1952–(Cubs 1984-1991)

The nickname "The Red Baron" was given to Rick Sutcliffe by Harry Caray, because of his intimidating presence (he was 6'7) and red beard. 82 of his 171 career wins came with the Cubs, including 16 in his Cy Young-winning season of 1984. He was almost unhittable that year as he led the Cubs to the NL East Division Championship. In 150 innings with the Cubs he struck out 155, walked only 39, had a 2.69 ERA, seven complete games and three shut outs. Among his wins: the division clincher, and Game 1 of the NLCS. After his great season in '84, he struggled through arm problems the next few years before bouncing back from '87-'89. In '87 he made the All-Star team, led the league in wins, and finished second in the Cy Young voting. In '89, he made another All-Star appearance and helped lead the Cubs back to the playoffs. He finished his career with the Orioles and Cardinals, and won 32 more games, but he was doing it on guile alone by then. Among his many accomplishments, the Red Baron holds the record for the most times facing Barry Bonds without letting up a home run.

Historical note: On the day the movie *Field of Dreams* was released, Sutcliffe was on the mound for the Cubs. He beat the Mets 8-4 at Shea Stadium.

Sy Sutcliffe 1862–1893 (White Stockings 1884-1885)

He's the other Sutcliffe in Cubs history. When Sy played for the Cubs they were known as the White Stockings, and they were a powerhouse. Sy played catcher and outfield in Chicago, although he was just a part-time player. He later got more playing time for St. Louis, Dayton (yes, Dayton), Cleveland, Washington, and Baltimore. Unfortunately for Sy, he lived in a time when high blood pressure wasn't fully understood. He died at the age of 30 from Bright's Disease, which is now basically known as kidney failure, brought on by hypertension.

Bruce Sutter 1953 – (Cubs 1976-1980)

Bruce Sutter is a Hall of Famer, but of course, he's not wearing a Cubs hat even though he had his best and most dominating seasons on the north side of Chicago. Sutter was a six-time All-Star including four times with the Cubs. He won the Cy Young Award in 1979 for a very mediocre Cubs team. He led the league in saves five times. And he won the World Series with the 1982 St. Louis Cardinals. Bruce Sutter was inducted into the Hall of Fame in 2006; his 13th season on the ballot. Bruce is still #2 on the all-time Cubs save list, behind only Lee Smith.

Historical note: On the day that Mt. St. Helens erupted (1980), Bruce gave up the game-winning hit to another Hall of Famer, Dave Winfield, in a Cubs loss to the Padres.

Dale Sveum 1963 – (Cubs manager 2012-2013)

Dale was the first manager hired by Theo Epstein and Jed Hoyer after they took over the club. He introduced the team to various statistical analyses they hadn't previously used, and implemented drastic infield shifts for certain hitters. In both seasons he was at the helm, the Cubs finished at the bottom of the division, but he probably would have remained on the job if young stars like Starlin Castro and Anthony Rizzo had responded to him. Both phenoms regressed under Sveum's tutelage. He was let go after the 2013 season.

Dave Swartzbaugh 1968 – (Cubs 1995-1997)

The Cubs used Dave as a spot starter his last two seasons, but it didn't turn out so well. He started seven games and didn't win a single one of them.

Bill Sweeney 1886–1948 (Cubs 1907, 1914)

Sweeney played the first season and the last season of his big league career with the Cubs, and his timing couldn't have been worse. When he came to the big leagues he was part of the best team in baseball. The Cubs were on their way to their first World Series title. Sweeney filled in for Joe Tinker when the shortstop was hurt, but he didn't exactly take advantage of the opportunity. He played in three games and made six errors. He also hit .100. So the Cubs traded him to Boston. He went from the best team in baseball to the worst team. Boston finished an average of 50 games a season behind the Cubs over the next few years. But Sweeney played well for Boston

and claimed their starting job at second base. By 1912 he was one of the best players in their lineup. Sweeney hit .344 and drove in a hundred runs. But just as Boston was getting good, he was traded back to the Cubs for Johnny Evers in 1914. Evers led the Braves to the title, while Sweeney played for a lousy Cubs team. He retired after the season at the age of 29, and moved back to Boston, where he ran a successful insurance company.

Ryan Sweeney 1985 – (Cubs 2013-2014)

Sweeney was a high draft pick of the White Sox, but he didn't remain with the team long. The Sox traded him to the A's as part of the Nick Swisher deal, then the A's traded him to the Red Sox in the Josh Reddick deal. The Cubs signed him as a free agent just before the 2013 season. He probably would have started the whole season in center field, but he was injured. The Cubs signed him to a two-year deal before the 2014 season, but released him after spring training 2015. He never played in the big leagues again.

Les Sweetland 1901–1974 (Cubs 1931)

Les was a starting pitcher for the Cubs in 1931. In that hitter-friendly year he won 8 games, completed 9, and posted an ERA of 5.04. That was his last taste of the big leagues. He previously pitched for the Philadelphia Phillies for four seasons.

Steve Swisher 1951 – (Cubs 1974-1977)

Swisher was acquired by the Cubs from the White Sox in the trade that sent Ron Santo over to the south side of the city. For most of his time with the Cubs, Swisher shared the catcher job with George Mitterwald. But in 1976, he had his best season in a Cubs uniform and was named an All-Star. That All-Star selection, however, may be more of a statement about the 1976 Cubs than an endorsement of Swisher. He hit only .236 that season. It was just that nobody else on the Cubs was worthy of making the team. Swisher was an outstanding defensive catcher, who played in the big leagues for nine seasons. His son Nick is a big leaguer too. Both father and son were first round draft picks.

Matt Szczur 1989 – (Cubs 2014-2017)

Szczur (pronounced "Caesar") got his first crack at the big

leagues in 2014. The former Villanova football star was a backup outfielder and pinch hitter for the Cubs, and got a few short shots in the big leagues during the 2014 and 2015 seasons. In 2016, he spent the entire season with the big league club and was an important bat off the bench. He hit 5 homers and knocked in 24 runs in 107 games, and picked up a World Series ring. Unfortunately for Matt, a roster crunch in 2017 forced the Cubs to let him go. Szczur finished the season as a starting outfielder in San Diego.

*Additional Entries...*If you check out the Every Cub Ever feature at www. justonebadcentury.com, you'll find several additional entries, including celebrity Cubs fans, writers, and bloggers. Under the letter S, you'll discover Cubs fans like game show host Pat Sajack, actor Gary Sinese, movie executive George Spoor, Supreme Court Justice John Paul Stevens, and the Sianis family of Billy Goat fame, plus Cubs authors Scott Simon, Becky Sarwate-Maxwell and Stuart Shea, and radio legends (and big Cubs fans) Bob Sirott and Bobby Skafish.

CHAPTER TWENTY

T

The starting lineup of your Chicago Cubs beginning with the letter T...

C—Sammy Taylor, Two-Balls-in-Play
1B—Andre Thornton, All-Star
2B—Manny Trillo, Gold Glover
SS—Joe Tinker, Hall of Famer
3B—Frank Thomas, Not the Big Hurt
LF—Lee Thomas, Future GM
CF—Bobby Thomson, the Flying Scotsman
RF—Scot Thompson, Rookie Sensation
Bench— Tony Taylor, Telstar Tony
Bench— Ryan Theriot, The Riot
SP—Jack Taylor, Complete Game Monster
SP—Lefty Tyler, 1918 World Series Starter
SP—Steve Trout, 1984 Playoff Hero
SP—Kevin Tapani, 1998 Stud
RP—Dick Tidrow, Dirt
RP— Julian Tavarez, World Series Champ

Jerry Tabb 1952–(Cubs 1976)

Tabb was a first round draft pick by the Cubs in 1973 and displayed tremendous power in the minor leagues, but could never do the same in the big leagues. He got one shot with the Cubs at the end of the 1976 season and in his twenty four at-bats, didn't get a single extra base hit. The Cubs sold him to the A's before the 1977 season.

Pat Tabler 1958– (Cubs 1981-1982)

Tabler was a #1 draft choice by the Yankees and the Cubs were enamored with his potential. So much so, they sent two future All-Star closers (that's right *two* — Bill Caudill and Jay Howell) to get him. In a way the Cubs were right about him. Tabler became an All-Star and a World Series champ. It just wasn't with the Cubs. After two years of limited duty

and averages south of .235, the Cubs included the 2B/3B in a January 1983 deal with the White Sox to get Steve Trout. The Sox traded him to the Indians before the 1983 season started (for future playoff goat Jerry Dybzinski). Tabler ended up playing in the big leagues for 12 seasons, and won a ring with the 1992 Blue Jays. His nickname was Mr. Clutch.

So Taguchi 1969–(Cubs 2009)

Taguchi was a ten-year veteran of the Japanese League when he came to America to play for the Cardinals in 2002. He never claimed a starting outfield position with the club, but he was a key contributor to two World Series teams in St. Louis. His time in Chicago was not nearly as glorious. He played six games for the Cubs, and decided to return to Japan to finish out his career in his homeland.

Hisanori Takahashi 1975–(Cubs 2013)

His name in Japanese is spelled this way: (   ). He earned a spot on the opening day roster in 2013, but by mid-April he was traded to the Rockies. Takahashi only pitched in three games for the Cubs. His best year in the big leagues was probably his first season with the Mets (2010) when he won ten games.

Bob Talbot 1927–2017 (Cubs 1953-1954)

Talbot was a good center fielder and a scrappy hitter who was tough to strike out, and was given the starting job during the 1954 season. Unfortunately for him, the Cubs converted Eddie Miksis into a center fielder the following year, and Talbot didn't have the power to justify a spot as a corner outfielder in the big leagues. He continued to play in the minors until 1960.

Chuck Tanner 1928–2011 (Cubs 1957-1959)

Chuck Tanner played in the big leagues for parts of eight different seasons. His career started with a bang — a home run in his very first big league at-bat for the Milwaukee Braves in 1955. They released him near the beginning of the 1957 season, and the Cubs grabbed him immediately. Tanner didn't have a lot of power or speed, but he was steady, and the Cubs weren't exactly scaring the National League with their outfield of Lee Walls, Bob Speake, and Moose Moryn. Tanner got more at-bats with the 1957 Cubs than he did for the rest of his career combined. He hit .286 that year and belted seven homers, but even on a team as pathetic as that 1957 Cubs team, that didn't cut it. By 1958, he was back on the bench, and by 1959, he was shipped off to Boston. Tanner later got a cup of coffee with the Indians and the Angels, but the enthusiastic and sharp-minded outfielder found his calling elsewhere. He went on to manage the 1979 Pittsburgh Pirates to the World Series title.

Kevin Tapani 1964–(Cubs 1997-2001)

Tapani was coming off seven consecutive double-digit-win seasons in the American League (and a World Series championship in Minnesota) when he joined the Cubs before the 1997 season. He didn't realize it at the time, but he was walking into a buzz saw. That '97 Cubs team lost their first 14 games on the way to a humiliating last place finish. On the other hand, Tapani was a key contributor the following season when the Cubs made it to the playoffs. He won 19 games during the regular season, and was leading the Braves 1-0 in the bottom of the ninth inning in Game 2 of the NLDS when Ryan Klesko touched him for a game-tying homer. The Cubs lost it in the 10th. Tapani lost it the following year, and never put up those kind of numbers again.

El Tappe 1927–1998 (Cubs 1954-1962)

El was a backup catcher with the Cubs in the mid-50s, but he is most remembered for being a faculty member in P.K. Wrigley's infamous College of Coaches. The plan called for this baseball college faculty to be rotated from the low minors all the way to the majors and back again, taking turns as "head coach." Like any well-respected college faculty, they had hoity-toity professorial names: El, Goldie, Harry, Verlon, Rip, Vedie, Charlie, and Bobby. In El's turn as head coach in 1961, the Cubs won 42 games and lost 54.

Ted Tappe 1931–2004 (Cubs 1955)

He was part of the ill-fated Johnny Klippstein trade with the Reds. Tappe played the first few months of the 1955 season before being sent down to the minors by the Cubs. He never returned. His Cubs career consisted of 50 at-bats. Ted played in the minors four more years before hanging up his spikes for good after the 1961 season.

Bennie Tate 1901–1973 (Cubs 1934)

Bennie was in his tenth big league season when the Cubs brought him in to back up Gabby Hartnett in 1934. Bennie had never been a starter for his previous teams (Senators, White Sox, and Red Sox), although he did get extensive playing time, including the 1924 World Series (with the Senators). Not so much with the Cubs. He appeared in 11 games and was released before the year was over. It was the last stop of his big league career.

Ramon Tatis 1973–(Cubs 1997)

Ramon was a rookie reliever on that incredibly bad '97 Cubs team that started the season 0-14. He appeared in 56 games for them and posted a horrific 5.34 ERA as a situational lefty. He also gave up 13 homers. He had one more cup of coffee with Tampa before moving on Japan.

Julian Tavarez 1973–(Cubs 2001)

Tavarez was part of the Cubs rotation during the 2001 season, and for a while, actually pitched quite well. He tailed off at the end of the year but still finished with 10 wins. After the season he was part of the package of players sent to the Marlins (along with Dontrelle Willis) to acquire starter Matt Clement and closer Antonio Alfonseca. Tavarez pitched in the big leagues for 17 seasons (for the Indians, Giants, Rockies, Marlins, Cardinals, Red Sox, Brewers, Braves, and Nationals), and won a World Series ring with the 2007 Boston Red Sox (although he didn't pitch in that series). He did pitch in two other World Series (one with the Indians, and another with the Cardinals).

C.L. "Chink" Taylor 1898–1980 (Cubs 1925)

Chink was a speedy little outfielder who was used primarily as a pinch runner by the Cubs during the first month of the 1925 season. In his first game he appeared as a pinch hitter in a 20-5 loss to the Cardinals. Future Cub Les Bell pounded the Cubs with two homers and six RBI in one of the most brutal losses of the century. Chink only got into eight games total as a Cub, and was sent down to the minors in May. He never made it back to the big leagues.

Danny Taylor 1900–1972 (Cubs 1929-1932)

Danny was a backup outfielder for the Cubs for a few seasons for a few very good teams. That 1930/1931 team had a loaded outfield (two Hall of Famers — Wilson and Cuyler), but Taylor got quite a bit of playing time anyway, and he responded well. He hit .283 and .300 filling in for the oft-injured Riggs Stephenson. In early 1932, Taylor was sold to Brooklyn.

Harry Taylor 1907–1969 (Cubs 1932)
The first baseman was 24 years old when he got his only taste of the big leagues on a simply loaded Cubs team. The 1932 Cubs team featured four Hall of Famers (Gabby Hartnett, Billy Herman, Kiki Cuyler, and Burleigh Grimes), and oddly enough, three guys with the last name of Taylor, including Harry (the other two were Zach and Danny).

Jack Taylor 1874 (Orphans 1898-1903/Cubs 1906-1907)
He was known as the Brakeman by his teammates. The brakeman was the person who would walk the length of a train atop the cars while the train was in motion and turn the brake wheel on each car to apply the train's brakes. That's the role Brakeman Jack Taylor had on the Cubs pitching staff early in his career — he would put the brakes on Cubs losing streaks. Taylor is most remembered for a record that will never be broken. From June 20, 1901 until August 9, 1906, The Brakeman threw 187 consecutive complete games, along with 15 additional relief appearances without being removed from a game — giving him 202 straight appearances without being removed. This stretch included occasions where he pitched both ends of a double-header, an 18-inning game, and two 14-inning games. The Cubs traded him to the Cardinals for one of the greatest Cubs players of all-time, Mordecai Brown, because Cubs owner James Hart was convinced that Taylor had fixed an exhibition game against the White Sox. Although Taylor came back to the Cubs in 1906 (under a new owner), and pitched for the winningest team of all-time (the 1906 Cubs), and the 1907 champs, they never really trusted him again and wouldn't let him pitch in either World Series — just in case. He was 34 when he retired just before the Cubs 1908 World Series Championship season.

Sammy Taylor 1933– (Cubs 1958-1962)
Taylor was a catcher for the Cubs in the late 50s and early 60s. His best season with the bat was 1959, when he clubbed 13 homers. But he also had a very rough time of it behind the plate, leading the league stolen bases allowed.

Taylor was also a key participant in the strangest play in Cubs history on June 30, 1959, when two balls ended up in play at the same time. It started when a missed strike three got away from him. Taylor, thinking it was a foul ball, didn't go after the ball. The bat boy, also thinking it was a foul ball, picked it up and tossed it to field announcer Pat Pieper. Pieper saw that the batter was running to first base, so he realized it was a live ball, and let it drop at his feet. Third baseman Alvin Dark ran over to grab it. Meanwhile, the umpire gave Sammy Taylor a new ball out of habit. In the confusion, the runner on first base, Stan Musial, made a run for second base. Cubs pitcher Bob Anderson took the ball out of Sammy Taylor's catcher's mitt and fired it to second base at the same time that third baseman Alvin Dark threw his ball to second base. Ernie Banks was covering second and caught one of the balls heading his way, while the other ball escaped into center field. Ernie tagged out Musial with one ball, while center fielder Bobby Thomson lobbed the other ball into the dugout. Thinking that the "real" ball had been tossed into the dugout, Musial kept on running and scored. The umpires had a very long discussion about this play on the field before finally ruling that Musial was out because Ernie tagged him. The Cardinals were enraged by the call on the field and lodged an official protest. The protest wasn't necessary. The Cardinals won the game anyway, 4-1.

Tony Taylor 1935– (Cubs 1958-1960)
Tony was the starting second baseman for the Cubs in 1958 and 1959, and was really starting to become a star. In 1959 he was in top ten in the league in runs, hits, doubles, and triples. He and MVP Ernie Banks made a great double play combination. Unfortunately, the Cubs brought in Don Zimmer and had nowhere to play him, so they traded Tony to the Philadelphia Phillies in 1960 for Don Cardwell to open a spot for Zimmer. Needless to say, this trade didn't work out. Cardwell pitched well (including a no-hitter) for a season or two, but Tony became an All-Star and played in the big leagues for another sixteen years with the Phillies and the Tigers. When he retired after the 1976 season he was the oldest player in baseball (40 years old). Don Zimmer was the manager of the Boston Red Sox at the time.

Zack Taylor 1898–1974 (Cubs 1929-1933)

Taylor was a backup catcher to Gabby Hartnett, which meant that he didn't get a lot of playing time. His best year with the Cubs was their World Series year of 1929. With Hartnett injured, Taylor was the starting catcher for that series, and hit .176. He later went on to manage the St. Louis Browns.

Bud Teachout 1904–1985 (Cubs 1930-1931)

Bud had a good rookie season in 1930, winning 11 games with a 4.06 ERA, quite an accomplishment considering 1930 was a season for hitters. Many hitting records were set that year, including Hack Wilson's 191 RBI. Bud's Cubs team, however, choked a big lead down the stretch, and just missed repeating as NL Champs. Teachout was traded in 1931 along with Hack Wilson in the trade that brought Burleigh Grimes to Chicago.

Taylor Teagarden 1983–(Cubs 2015)

Teagarden was a highly regarded prospect for the Rangers (he also played for the Orioles and Mets) who never quite figured out how to hit big league pitching. But his catching skills kept him in the big leagues, including a stint for the Cubs in 2015. He appeared in eight games and hit .200 (.002 below his lifetime average).

Patsy Tebeau 1864–1918 (White Stockings 1887)

Patsy was born just a few weeks after Abraham Lincoln's re-election in the closing days of the Civil War in the slave state of Missouri — a state that was claimed by both the Confederacy and the United States. (They sent representatives to both Congresses). Patsy was a 22-year-old rookie third baseman on the Cubs (then known as the White Stockings) in 1887, and didn't fare too well. He hit .162 in 20 games. He later enjoyed much more success with Cleveland. His big league career lasted 13 years. Patsy's brother George also played in the big leagues. Patsy later managed in the big leagues and was considered a powder keg. After his baseball career ended, Patsy was unhappy in life. After his wife left him, Tebeau killed himself.

Amaury Telemaco 1974–(Cubs 1996-1998)

Telemaco did manage to pitch in the big leagues for nine seasons, but if you look at his stats, you have to wonder how he pulled it off. His lifetime ERA is 4.94. In 64 career starts, he had one complete game. With the Cubs in his rookie season he gave up 20 homers in less than one hundred innings pitched. Telemaco's best year was 1998, when he won seven games and posted an ERA under four. After his playing days, he took a coaching job in the Red Sox farm system.

Historical note: On the day a bomb went off during the 1996 Summer Olympics in Atlanta, Amaury was on the mound for the Cubs in Colorado. He was rocked for six runs in a 10-5 loss.

*Ten Years (Or More) Cubs...*This list is like a Who's Who of Cubs history...

- **Cap Anson (1876-1897),**
- **Ernie Banks (1953-1971),**
- **Mordecai Brown (1904-1912, 1916),**
- **Guy Bush (1923-1934),**
- **Frank Chance (1898-1912),**
- **Johnny Evers (1902-1913),**
- **Silver Flint (1879-1889),**
- **Mark Grace (1988-2000),**
- **Charlie Grimm (1925-1936),**
- **Stan Hack (1932-1947),**
- **Gabby Hartnett (1922-1940),**
- **Solly Hofman (1904-1912, 1916),**
- **Randy Hundley (1966-1973, 1976-1977),**
- **Fergie Jenkins (1966-1973, 1982-1983),**
- **Billy Jurges (1931-1938, 1946-1947),**
- **Johnny Kling (1900-1911),**
- **Bill Lee (1934-1943, 1947),**
- **Greg Maddux (1986-1992, 2004-2006),**
- **Bob O'Farrell (1915-1925, 1934),**
- **Fred Pfeffer (1883-1889, 1891, 1896-1897),**
- **Charlie Root (1926-1941),**
- **Bob Rush (1948-1957),**
- **Jimmy Ryan (1885-1889, 1891-1900),**
- **Ryne Sandberg (1982-1997),**

- **Ron Santo (1960-1973),**
- **Bob Scheffing (1941-1950),**
- **Johnny Schmitz (1941-1951),**
- **Sammy Sosa (1992-2004),**
- **Joe Tinker (1902-1912, 1916),**
- **Lon Warneke (1930-1936, 1942-1945),**
- **Billy Williams (1959-1974),**
- **Ned Williamson (1879-1889), and**
- **Kerry Wood (1998-2008, 2010-2012).**

John Tener 1863–1946 (White Stockings 1888-1889)

The Irish-born Tener was a pitcher for the Cubs (then known as the White Stockings) while they were being managed by Cap Anson. In 1889 he had a good season, winning 15 games, and eating up 287 innings. He only pitched one more year in the big leagues after that. After his baseball career, however, Tener went into politics. He served in the U.S. House of Representatives from Pennsylvania, before becoming the 26th Governor of Pennsylvania. After his political career he became the President of the National League, and had to rule in a case involving his former team—a dispute between Cubs owner Charles Murphy and Cubs second baseman Johnny Evers.

Historical note: On the day Jack the Ripper claimed his first victim in London (1888), Tener was rocked in a 14-0 loss to the last place Hoosiers.

Adonis Terry 1864–1914 (Colts 1894-1897)

His real first name was William, but he went by Adonis. Terry was a fairly good pitcher. He won 197 games in his 14-year big league career (including 21 with the Cubs, then known as the Colts, in 1895). But Adonis also lost 196 games, and he was never what you'd call a dominant pitcher. He gave up 76 homers in an era of virtually no homers, and he walked almost as many men as he struck out. After his playing career ended, he became an umpire.

Zeb Terry 1891–1988 (Cubs 1920-1922)

Zebulon was the starting second baseman for the Cubs for three seasons. He was known as a reliable glove man and got his fair share of clutch hits. Terry averaged more than 50 RBI a season with the Cubs, but he had almost no power. In more than 2600 career plate appearances, he hit only two home runs. After the 1922 season ended, he retired to his native California at the age of 31.

Wayne Terwilliger 1925 – (Cubs 1949-1951)

Twig, as he was known by his teammates, made his big league debut for the Cubs on August 6, 1949. He made enough of an impression on the team to earn the starting second base job in 1950. He hit 10 homers for them that year. The following season he was traded to Brooklyn along with Andy Pafko, Johnny Schmitz, and Rube Walker in one of the worst trades in Cubs history. Twig later also played for the Senators, Athletics, and Giants.

Bob Tewksbury 1960 – (Cubs 1987-1988)

The Cubs saw some promise in the young right-hander when they acquired him from the Yankees in exchange for Steve Trout. They were right, but it didn't work out for Tewksbury in Chicago. He suffered through some health issues and didn't pitch much over his two seasons with the Cubs. After he signed with the Cardinals, he blossomed. Tewksbury had five double-digit-win seasons in a row for St. Louis, including an All-Star season, when he won 17 games.

Moe Thacker 1934–1997 (Cubs 1958-1962)

Moe was also a backup catcher during the era El Tappe played and managed the Cubs. His best season was probably 1962 when he got over a hundred plate appearances. Unfortunately, Moe was really just a defensive catcher. In over 300 plate appearances, he hit only two homers, and hit a woeful .177 lifetime.

Ryan Theriot 1979 – (Cubs 2005-2010)

Someone along the line noticed that if you split up the letters in Ryan Theriot's last name, it spells "The Riot." Cubs broadcasters started calling him that shortly after he was named starting shortstop, and it caught on. In his first two seasons as a starter, the Riot managed to do something that hadn't been done since Joe Tinker did it exactly one hundred years earlier. He started at shortstop for a Cubs playoff team in consecutive years. Theriot was a fan favorite because of his scrappy play, a media favorite because of his constant accessibility, and will always be remembered for his great nickname. After leaving the Cubs he won a World Series ring with the 2011 Cardinals and the 2012 Giants.

Frank Thomas 1929 – (Cubs 1960-1961, 1966)

Not to be confused with the Big Hurt, the White Sox Hall of Famer, this Frank Thomas was a third baseman, first baseman, and outfielder. He also had a memorable nickname. His teammates called him The Big Donkey. Frank was a three-time All-Star with the Pirates in the 50s before joining the Cubs. He hit 21 homers in his one full season in Chicago, but the team had a few superstars and budding superstars at his best positions (Santo, Banks, and Williams), so they traded him to the Braves for Mel Roach in early 1961. Thomas later returned to finish his career with the Cubs in 1966. His final stint with the team lasted only a few weeks. When he was released on June 4, 1966, his big league career was over. He hit 286 career home runs.

Lee Thomas 1936 – (Cubs 1966-1967)

Thomas was a backup outfielder/first baseman for the Cubs toward the end of his playing career. He had been an All-Star with the Red Sox earlier in his nine year career. Thomas retired the year after his last Cubs season and went into management. He was one of the architects of the Whitey Herzog-era Cardinals in the 80s, and then became the GM of the Phillies and led them to the 1993 World Series. The ex-Cub watched his ex-Cub closer Mitch Williams give up the walk-off series-ending home run to the ex-Cub outfielder Joe Carter.

Historical note: On the same afternoon John Lennon held a press conference at the Astor Hotel in downtown Chicago apologizing for his famous "we're more popular than Jesus" remark (1966), Lee knocked in the winning run for the Cubs in the bottom of the 11th inning to beat the Astros .

Red Thomas 1898 – 1962 (Cubs 1921)

Thomas' entire big league career consisted of eight games played in September of 1921. The 23-year-old center fielder knocked in five runs and played a strong center field, but he never got another shot at the big leagues.

Scot Thompson 1955 – (Cubs 1978-1983)

Scot (with one "t") was the 7th overall pick of the 1974 draft, ahead of future stars Gary Templeton, Lance Parrish, Willie Wilson, and Rick Sutcliffe (all first rounders). At first Scot (with one "t") appeared to be one of the rare non-busts in the Cubs farm system. In his rookie year he hit .289 and finished third in the Rookie of the Year voting. Unfortunately for the Cubs, he never again approached that level of production.

Historical note: On the day that Spider Dan Goodwin climbed the Sears Tower (1981), Scot got the game-winning hit in a dramatic 11-inning game against the Pirates at Wrigley Field.

Bobby Thomson 1923 – 2010 (Cubs 1958-1960)

Bobby Thomson got his nickname ("The Flying Scot") the old fashioned way — -he was actually born in Scotland, and he was known for his diving catches in center field. Most famous for his dramatic home run that won the pennant for the Giants, Thomson was nowhere near that player by the time he arrived in Chicago in 1958. He did have a decent season, but his descent into mediocrity was well underway. By 1959 he was sharing the center field job, and by 1960 the Cubs traded him away. He retired after the 1960 season. In his two seasons with the Cubs Thomson hit a respectable total of 32 home runs, but the team finished in 5th place both years.

Andre Thornton 1949 (Cubs 1973-1976)

Andre was acquired from the Braves in the trade that sent Joe Pepitone out of Chicago. That turned out to be a good deal for the Cubs, because Andre turned into one of the top young sluggers in the National League. His nickname was "Thunder" and he hit 18 homers in his first full season as the Cubs first baseman (1975). Thunder seemed poised for even bigger things, but early in 1976 the Cubs traded him for Larry Biittner and Steve Renko. Andre went on to become a two-time All-Star. He hit 253 homers in 14 big league seasons, but only 30 of those were hit for the Cubs.

Historical note: On the day that Lynette "Squeaky" Fromme tried to assassinate President Ford (1975), Andre hit a homer off Hall of Famer Steve Carlton to win the game for the Cubs.

Walter Thornton 1875 – 1960 (Colts/Orphans 1895-1898)

He was an outfielder and a pitcher for Chicago (when that was still relatively commonplace), and had a few respectable seasons, but he will always be remembered most for what happened on August 21, 1898. He took the mound in the second game of a double-header against Brooklyn (then known as the Bridegrooms) and pitched a no-hitter. Chicago won the game 2-0. After the season he left baseball in a contract dispute (at the age of 23). He later became a devout follower of another ex-Chicago-ballplayer, Billy Sunday. In the last few years of his life (he lived until 1960), he roamed the city of Los Angeles as a street preacher, doing whatever he could to help the poor.

Historical note: On the day Teddy Roosevelt led his Rough Riders up San Juan Hill during the Spanish-American War (1898), Walter was on the mound for Chicago. Thornton lost the game 8-4 against the Giants in New York.

Bob Thorpe 1935 – 1960 (Cubs 1955)

Thorpe was a minor league phenom, winning 28 games in the lower minors in 1954. The Cubs brought him all the way up the big leagues the following season, and he pitched in a few games out of the bullpen at the beginning of 1955. He wore the now retired #26 (Billy Williams), before being relegated back down to the minors. Thorpe blew out his arm, and never returned to the big leagues. He retired from baseball in 1959, and took a job as an apprentice electrician. Thorpe was accidentally electrocuted a short time later, and died at the age of 24.

Cubs players have had some great nicknames over the years. Among players starting with the letter T, you'll find nicknames like Babe, Big Donkey, Bird Eye, Brakeman, Catfish, Chink, Dirt, Flying Scotsman, La Malita, Lefty, Mr. Clutch, Mumbles, The Riot, Slug, Stretch, and Thunder.

Dick Tidrow 1947 – (Cubs 1979-1982)

His teammates called him "Dirt". His odd nickname reflected his basic, simple approach to the game. His real name was Richard William Tidrow, and he was the setup man for the Cubs (for Bruce Sutter) in the late 70s and early 80s. The Cubs got him from the Yankees for Ray Burris, one of the rare trades they never regretted. Tidrow had two great years ('79 and '80), one terrible year ('81), and one average year ('82) for the Cubs, before he went to the White Sox in the Steve Trout trade, and pitched in the playoffs for the Sox that year. That turned out to be another good trade for the Cubs. Trout started for the Cubs the next five years (and won Game 2 of the '84 playoffs), and Tidrow was out of baseball after the '84 season. The Cubs should have signed him *after* his playing career ended. He went into scouting, eventually becoming the Scouting Director for the San Francisco Giants. Among the pitchers he nurtured through their farm system: Tim Lincecum and Matt Cain.

Bobby Tiefenauer 1929 – 2000 (Cubs 1968)

Bobby pitched ten years in the big leagues despite never really having one outstanding breakthrough season. His lifetime record was 9-25. By the time he came to the Cubs in 1968, he was the fourth oldest player in the league. He posted a 6.08 ERA in the last nine appearances of his big league career. In 39 career at-bats, the pitcher got only one hit.

Ozzie Timmons 1970 – (Cubs 1995-1996)

Timmons was the right-handed half of a platoon in left field during his two seasons in Chicago. He hit the ball pretty well (15 HRs and 44 RBI), but never really could claim the job full-time. The Cubs traded him to the Reds the following year. He also got cups of coffee with the Rays and the Mariners.

Ben Tincup 1893 – 1980 (Cubs 1928)

Tincup may be the only Native American player in the early 20th century who wasn't nicknamed Chief. He was a Cherokee. He was also a World War I veteran. His big league career began before the war (with the Phillies). After he served in the military, he pitched in the minor leagues with Louisville for eight years before he got his one last shot with the Cubs in 1928. Ben pitched out of the bullpen in the last month of the season. That was it for his return to the big-time. Tincup may have only won eight Major League games in parts of four seasons spread over fifteen years, but he was a legend in the minor leagues. In 23 seasons he won 233 games.

Joe Tinker 1880–1948 (Cubs 1902-1912, 1916, Cubs manager 1916)

Tinker was the shortstop for the Cubs dynasty of 1906-1910, and he had many dramatic hits along the way. He also served as the player/manager for the Cubs in their first season at Wrigley Field (after serving in the same capacity in the first two seasons at Wrigley — then with the Federal League Whales). Ironically, Tinker didn't get along with his double-play mate Johnny Evers. What caused this unfortunate rift? According to Tinker, Evers started it because he ditched Tinker once and got a cab without him…which was of course unforgivable. They didn't speak to each other for thirty years. After his playing days, Tinker became a wealthy businessman, but lost it all in the stock market crash. Then in 1938, Tinker and Evers were asked to broadcast the World Series together. Both later admitted being more nervous about seeing each other again, than they were about their maiden broadcasting voyage. But when they saw each other, they smiled and hugged. They enjoyed a tearful reunion, and after that became friends once again. In 1946, they were inducted into the Baseball Hall of Fame together (along with the deceased Frank Chance). Evers died the following year, and Tinker the year after that. In death they are always remembered together, but in life, they spent most of their time apart.

Bud Tinning 1906–1961 (Cubs 1932-1934)

Bud was a long reliever and spot starter on some very good Cubs teams. He was a key contributor to the 1932 pennant winners, and pitched well in the World Series that year. He even struck out Babe Ruth. Tinning was better in 1933, leading the league in winning percentage. After the 1934 season the Cubs traded him to the Cardinals. Unfortunately for Bud, he hurt his arm in 1935, ending his baseball career.

Al Todd 1902–1985 (Cubs 1940-1941, 1943)

Al was 38 when he joined the Cubs, but he was the starting catcher for them in 1940. He previously caught for the Phillies, Pirates, and Dodgers. Among his teammates during his big league career: Hall of Famers Chuck Klein, Lloyd and Paul Waner, Dizzy Dean, and Leo Durocher. After his playing days he became a coach, manager, and scout.

Jim Todd 1947– (Cubs 1974, 1977)

Todd was drafted by the Cubs and made his debut with them in 1974. He didn't pitch badly, but the Cubs traded him to Oakland for Champ Summers. Todd pitched well for the A's, saving 12 games in '75 and four more in '76. The Cubs liked what they saw so they reacquired him, figuring he could strengthen their bullpen. It didn't work out that way. Todd was rocked hard his second time around in a Cubs uniform. He allowed 68 baserunners in only 30 innings, and posted an ERA over nine. He was traded to the Mariners for Pete Broberg after the 1977 season.

Chick Tolson 1898–1965 (1926-1930)

Chick was a backup first baseman and pinch hitter for the Cubs in the late 1920s. His teammates called him "Slug" for his less-than-speedy wheels. Slug played four seasons for the Cubs, and had his best season in 1929, when the Cubs won the pennant. He had a career high 109 at-bats that season, and even got one chance in the 1929 World Series. He struck out. In 1930, however, he did something that must have caused his teammates to hoot and howl. Slug stole the only base of his career.

Ron Tompkins 1944– (Cubs 1971)

The 6'4 reliever was naturally nicknamed Stretch. He appeared in 35 games exclusively out of the bullpen for a pretty good Cubs team in 1971. Among his teammates that year, Hall of Famers Ernie Banks (in his final season), Billy Williams, Ron Santo, and Cy Young Winner Fergie Jenkins. The Cubs finished in third place, behind the Cardinals and the World Series champion Pittsburgh Pirates. That was the last season of Tompkins' big league career. He pitched two more seasons in the minors before hanging up his spikes.

Fred Toney 1888–1953 (Cubs 1911-1913)

Toney got his big league start with the Cubs when they played at West Side Grounds, but didn't really blossom as a pitcher until he went to the Reds. He was a 24-game winner for the Reds in 1917, and pitched what may have been the greatest game in big league history. Toney faced off against

Cubs pitcher Hippo Vaughn in the famous double no-hitter. Toney's Reds eventually beat Vaughn's Cubs in extra innings.

Hector Torres 1945 – (Cubs 1971)

The Cubs acquired Torres in a straight shortstop for shortstop swap with the Houston Astros. The Astros got Roger Metzger in return. Torres hit .224 backing up Don Kessinger and Glenn Beckert in 1971. It was the Mexico native's only season with the Cubs. Metzger, meanwhile, was the Astros starting shortstop for the next seven years, and won a Gold Glove. Torres was nicknamed La Malita.

Paul Toth 1935 – 1999 (Cubs 1962-1964)

Toth is probably one of the most obscure pieces of the infamous Lou Brock trade. He went to the Cardinals along with Brock and Jack Spring. He never pitched in the big leagues for the Cardinals. His best year with the Cubs was 1962, when he won five games with a 3.10 ERA for an incredibly bad team.

Hal Totten 1902 – 1985 (Cubs announcer 1924-1939)

On April 23, 1924, the home opener became the very first Cubs game broadcast on the radio. The radio station was WMAQ. The announcer was Hal Totten. He broadcast from a small table on the roof. (The upper deck had not yet been built). Totten saw some pretty exciting years at Wrigley Field, including four World Series. One of those was the famous Babe Ruth 1932 series. Jerome Holtzman quoted Hal when he insisted that Babe Ruth didn't point before his called shot. From the Chicago Tribune in 1992: *Said Ruth to Totten: "Hell, no, I didn't point. Only a damned fool would do a thing like that. . . . I never really knew anybody who could tell you ahead of time where he was going to hit a baseball. When I get to be that kind of fool, they'll put me in a booby hatch."* In his career Totten also called one of the most famous boxing matches in Chicago history — the Jack Dempsey/Gene Tunney bout in 1927. He was also the original radio voice for the All-Star game on NBC.

Steve Trachsel 1970 – (Cubs 1993-1999,2007)

Trachsel had a couple of very good seasons for the Cubs. He was an All-Star in 1996, and won 16 games for them in 1998. He also pitched in a very historic game in a Cubs uniform.

On July 13th, 1995, the Cubs hosted the Cincinnati Reds at Wrigley Field. Although the game didn't start until 7:05 that night, the game-time temperature was still 103 degrees. It was the hottest night in Chicago history. Trachsel didn't make it out of the second inning. Barry Larkin torched the Cubs for three hits (including a triple and a homer), and three RBI, and former Cub Jerome Walton knocked in two more as the eventual Division-champion Reds won the game 11-5.

In 1998, there were two more historic games. The one moment he will probably be most remembered for is the home run he gave up to Mark McGwire. It was McGwire's 62nd homer of the year, surpassing the record held by Roger Maris. Trachsel appeared to be the only person in the stadium who was upset. Cubs first baseman Mark Grace patted McGwire on the bottom as he ran by, and Sammy Sosa charged in from right field to give him a hug. Later that same season, Trachsel pitched the 163rd game of the year…the one-game playoff versus the San Francisco Giants to determine that year's Wild Card team. Trachsel and the Cubs won the game.

Historical note: On the day that Kurt Cobain was found dead (1994), Trachsel was on the mound for the Cubs. He and his Cubs teammates beat Hall of Famer Pedro Martinez and the Expos.

Chad Tracy 1980 – (Cubs 2010)

Tracy only played a portion of 2010 with the Cubs. He hit .250 in limited at-bats filling in for Aramis Ramirez at 3B. The Cubs released him on July 1st of that year.

Jim Tracy 1955 – (Cubs 1980-1981)

Jim was a part-time outfielder and pinch hitter for the Cubs in his only two big league seasons. He didn't quite have enough power to claim a full-time corner outfielder job, and he didn't quite have the range to play center, so he took his services to Japan. After his playing career, Tracy went into coaching and achieved considerable success. He has since managed the Rockies, Pirates, and Dodgers. In 2009 he was named the National League's manager of the year, after taking the Colorado Rockies to the playoffs.

Bill Traffley 1859 – 1908 (White Stockings 1878)

Traffley was a backup catcher who appeared in two games for the Cubs (then known as the White Stockings) in 1878.

In nine plate appearances, Bill managed to get one hit, and drive in one run. He later played for both Cincinnati and Baltimore. Traffley died in the summer of 1908 as the Cubs were storming toward their World Series championship.

Fred Treacey 1847–? (White Stockings 1871, 1874)
Fred has the distinction of being Chicago's very first official home run champion. He led the league in 1871, the first official year of the Chicago franchise. He hit four. Fred bounced around baseball for the next few years, including another stop in Chicago in 1874. He also played in New York and Philadelphia. Fred was a great hitter, but he was also known as a bit of shady character who liked to hang around with gamblers. When his baseball career ended in 1876, he more or less disappeared. Despite repeated searches for him, no one is quite sure what happened to him. His brother Pete also played on Fred's last New York Mutuals team.

Tom Trebelhorn 1948– (Cubs manager 1994)
Trebelhorn managed the Cubs during the strike-shortened season of 1994. After a horrendous start, he famously went over to the firehouse across the street and held an impromptu press conference there — quoting Frank Sinatra's song "That's Life." The lyrics were "riding high in April, shot down in May." The Cubs finished in 5th place, 15 games under .500. Trebelhorn hasn't managed in the big leagues ever since.

Bill Tremel 1929–2013 (Cubs 1954-1956)
One of the all-time great nicknames — his teammates called him Mumbles. Mumbles was a reliever for the Cubs in the mid-50s and did manage six saves over three seasons. He had some control issues, however, and the Cubs sent him down to the minors in 1956. He never made it back to the big leagues. Mumbles hung his spikes for good in 1959.

Manny Trillo 1950– (Cubs 1975-1978, 1986-1988)
Trillo was a prospect acquired from Oakland in the trade that sent Billy Williams to the A's, and immediately became the team's starting second baseman. He had a few very good years for the Cubs, finishing third in the Rookie of the Year voting in 1975, and making the All-Star team in 1977, but the Cubs sent him to the Phillies after the 1978 season in a blockbuster trade. It turned out to be a bad deal for the Cubs. The players they acquired (Jerry Martin, Barry Foote, Ted Sizemore) didn't do much for Chicago, while Trillo went on to be a three-time Gold Glover, three-time All-Star, two-time Silver Slugger, and the NLCS MVP for the Phillies. Manny returned to the Cubs towards the end of his career, but by then he was a part-timer.

Coaker Triplett 1911–1992 (Cubs 1938)
Coaker's real first name was Herman, but everyone referred to him by his middle name. He was on the big league roster as a rookie at the beginning of the 1938 season, but that '38 Cubs team was loaded with veteran talent, and the backup outfielder didn't get a lot of playing time. He later reemerged in the big leagues in 1941 with the Cardinals and played through the war years with St. Louis and Philadelphia. Triplett was on the 1942 Cardinals World Series champion team.

Steve Trout 1957– (Cubs 1983-1987)
Steve Trout was nicknamed Rainbow by his high school teammates for obvious reasons…the Rainbow Trout. He was a flaky lefty who probably would have been nicknamed Dizzy if not for his father who already laid claim to the nickname. (Dizzy Trout pitched for the Detroit Tigers and actually beat the Cubs in the 1945 World Series.) Steve displayed a little "dizziness" of his own when he pitched for the Cubs, developing a reputation for his offbeat personality. On road trips to San Diego he was known to challenge teammates to burrito-eating contests at local Mexican restaurants. Rainbow never quite lived up to the status of his 2-time All-Star father, but he had a very respectable career, and was a big part of the 1984 Division champion Cubs team. The fan favorite went 13-7 in 1984 and won his LCS start against San Diego. The Cubs rewarded him with a big salary, but he developed elbow troubles over the next few seasons. When he showed signs he was returning to form in 1987, Trout was dealt to the Yankees. He also later pitched for the Seattle Mariners. His record with the Cubs was 43-28.

Harry Truby 1868–1953 (Colts 1895-1896)
Harry's nickname was one of the all-time greats. His teammates called him Bird Eye. Bird Eye was the backup

second baseman in 1895 and 1896 for Ace Stewart. The first year he hit .336. The second year his average dropped more than a hundred points to .234, and he was shipped off to the Pirates on July 4th. After finishing the year with Pittsburgh, Harry never made it back up to the big leagues again.

Jen-Ho Tseng 1994 – (Cubs 2017-present)

After spending most of the 2017 season in Triple A, Tseng got his chance to start for the Cubs during the closing days of the season. The Taiwanese hurler didn't fare too well, but at 22 years of age, he had gotten a taste of the show. In 2018, he got one more start with the Cubs. It only lasted two innings. His nickname is Catfish.

Michael Tucker 1971 – (Cubs 2001)

The Cubs acquired Tucker for the playoff push in 2001 along with Fred McGriff. Tucker was a valuable member of the team the rest of the way, but the Cubs fell a little short that season. They finished the year 14 games over .500, but in third place and out of the playoffs. Tucker left as a free agent after the season. In all he played 12 years in the big leagues with the Braves, Reds, Royals, Giants, Phillies, and Mets. One of his claims to fame was hitting the first ever homer in Turner Field in Atlanta (off Cubs pitcher Kevin Foster).

Pete Turgeon 1897 – 1977 (Cubs 1923)

He played for the Cubs at the very end of the 1923 season and managed to get into three games and come up to bat six times. Four of those at-bats came in the final game of the season when he started at shortstop for the Cubs. He got a single and scored a run in 6-3 loss to the Cardinals. He was back in the minors the following year and never made it back up for another taste of the big leagues.

Jacob Turner 1991 – (Cubs 2014)

Turner was the ninth overall pick of the draft in 2009 (Tigers), but by the time he came to the Cubs via trade in 2014, he was considered a disappointment. In six starts with the Cubs in 2014, he posted an ERA of 6.49. He has since pitched for the White Sox, Nationals, Marlins, and Tigers.

Ted Turner 1892 – 1956 (Cubs 1920)

That's right, Ted Turner played for the Cubs. Obviously we don't mean the thin-mustachioed media mogul. This Ted Turner was a pitcher. On April 20, 1920, Ted came in during the second inning after the Cubs starter Chippy Gaw had been tagged for 5 hits and 2 runs. He didn't do much better. He lasted one and a third innings, and gave up two earned runs. He faced only six batters, but one of them was the greatest right-handed hitter in history, Rogers Hornsby. The Cubs lost 10-3. It was the only appearance of Ted Turner's big league career.

Babe Twombly 1896 – 1974 (Cubs 1920-1921)

The Cubs have had lots of players nicknamed "Babe" over the years, but unfortunately none of their last names were Ruth. Babe Twombly played for the Cubs for two seasons and hit over .300 in a part-time role, but he never managed to secure a full-time slot. He probably got the nickname "Babe" because his big brother "Silent George" Twombly was already a big leaguer when Babe came to the Cubs.

Lefty Tyler 1889 – 1953 (Cubs 1918-1921)

His real name was George, but everyone called him Lefty. He was in his 8th major league season when he came to the Cubs (from the Boston Braves). Lefty had one great season for the Cubs, going 19-8 in 1918, and pitched well in the World Series that year, but developed a strange shoulder injury the next year. He was sent to Minnesota by the Cubs to get it examined at the Mayo Clinic. The experts there said there was nothing wrong with his shoulder…that his problems were caused by unusually bad teeth. They extracted almost all of his teeth to cure his shoulder injury, which amazingly, didn't do the trick. He was never the same after that. Lefty's brother Fred also briefly played in the big leagues with the Braves.

Historical note: On the day Czar Nicholas and his family were executed in Russia by the Bolsheviks (1918), Lefty threw a 21-inning complete game (that's right) victory against the Phillies.

Earl Tyree 1890 – 1954 (Cubs 1914)

The Cubs brought him up for the final game of the 1914 season and had him catch for Cubs pitcher Zip Zabel. He went 0 for 4 with a run scored in a 4-3 Cubs victory over the Cardinals in St. Louis. It was his only game in the big leagues.

Jim Tyrone 1949 – (Cubs 1972-1975)

The outfielder saw limited playing time with the Cubs during three different seasons. His brother Wayne also played in the Cubs organization at the same time, but somehow never played on the same team as Jim.

Wayne Tyrone 1950 – (Cubs 1976)

Tyrone had a nine-year minor league career, but he did get one brief cup of coffee with the Cubs in 1976. Wayne's power in the minors didn't really translate to the big leagues. He homered only once in his two-month stint with the team. He arrived in Chicago just a year after his brother left.

Mike Tyson 1950 – (Cubs 1980-1981)

Not to be confused with the former heavyweight boxing champion, this Mike Tyson was a middle infielder who played ten years in the big leagues. The first eight were with the Cardinals. The second baseman didn't have the greatest Cubs career (he hit .238 and .185), and he cost the Cubs a prized relief pitcher named Donnie Moore to acquire him.

Historical note: On the day the movie *Airplane!* was released (1980), Tyson knocked in the only run for the Cubs in a 3-1 loss to the Mets at Shea Stadium.

---

*Additional Entries...*If you check out the Every Cub Ever feature at www. justonebadcentury.com, you'll find several additional entries, including celebrity Cubs fans, writers, and bloggers. Under the letter T, you'll discover best-selling author Scott Turow (a huge Cubs fan), and Cubs blogger Brett Taylor.

CHAPTER
TWENTY ONE

U

The starting lineup for your Chicago Cubs beginning with the letter U....

Playing catch in the outfield...
Long toss pitcher – Koji Uehara, World Series Champ
Long toss pitcher – Duane Underwood, the Kid
Long toss outfielder – John Upham, the Converted Pitcher
Long toss outfielder – Bob Usher, the Pinch Hitter

Koji Uehara 1975 – (Cubs 2017)

The 42-year-old reliever was far from his prime when he joined the Cubs after a successful stint with the World Series champion Boston Red Sox. Nevertheless, he managed to appear in more than 40 games, posted a sub four ERA (3.98), and even saved 2 games for the Cubs.

Duane Underwood 1994 – (Cubs 2018-present)

Duane was the second round pick of the Cubs the first year of the Epstein/Hoyer era. He got his first taste of big league action in a June 2018 spot start. He pitched well, though he lasted only four innings and took the loss. His only blemish was giving up a homer to KiKi Hernandez of the Dodgers.

John Upham 1941 – (Cubs 1967-1968)

Upham pitched and played outfield for the Cubs in two brief big league trials. As a pitcher, he was a decent hitter. As an outfielder, he was a decent pitcher. His lifetime ERA in the big leagues was 5.40, and he never got an extra base hit. In fairness to Upham, he did bat .293 over his nine-year minor league career.

Bob Usher 1925 – 2014 (Cubs 1952)

Bob was one of the players acquired in the Smoky Burgess trade in the winter of 1951. He got exactly one plate appearance for the Cubs. On April 26, 1952, he pinch hit for Cubs starter Turk Lown and walked. After that, they shipped him out to the minors. It took Usher five years to return, and when he did, it wasn't for the Cubs. He probably had the best year of his career for the 1957 Washington Senators.

*Utility Cubs...*The following players played every position (including pitcher) during their big league careers (not necessarily all with the Cubs)...Cap Anson, Bernie Friberg, Peaches Graham, Frank Isbell, King Kelly, Sam Mertes, and Deacon White.

CHAPTER
TWENTY TWO

V

The starting lineup of your Chicago Cubs beginning with the letter V...

C—Hector Villanueva, Crowd Favorite
1B—Josh Vitters, Can't Miss Prospect
2B—Emil Verban, Society Inspiration
SS—Luis Vizcaino, Well-Traveled Infielder
3B—Luis Valbuena, All-Or-Nothing Luis
LF—George Van Haltren, Lead Off Man
CF—Otto Vogel, Babe Ruth of the Big Ten
RF—Mike Vail, .300 Hitter
Bench—Tom Veryzer, All-Rookie Team
SP—Johnny Van Der Meer, Back-to-Back No-Hitters
SP—Hippo Vaughn, No-Hitter Loser
SP—Ismael Valdes, The Rocket
RP—Hy Vandenberg, 1945 World Series Reliever
RP—Arodys Vizcaino, the Closer

Mike Vail 1951 – (Cubs 1978-1980)

He was already in his fourth big league season when the Cubs acquired Vail in the trade that sent Tarzan Wallis to the Indians. Vail was a talented hitter who hit well over .300 in his time with the Cubs, but he didn't have a lot of power, didn't walk a lot, and his play in the outfield was considered below average. In short, he was a bit of a one-dimensional player. After the 1980 season he was traded to the Reds for third baseman Hector Cruz. He also played for the Giants, Dodgers, Expos, and Mets in his ten-year career.

Chris Valaika 1985 – (Cubs 2014)

The unheralded infielder had cups of coffee with the Reds and Marlins before the Cubs took a chance on him in 2014.

He played quite a bit down the stretch after Anthony Rizzo was injured. Valaika played all four infield positions for the Cubs and hit .231. After spending the entire 2015 season in the minors, Chris hung up his spikes shortly before his 30th birthday.

Luis Valbuena 1985 – 2018 (Cubs 2012-2014)

Valbuena was picked up by the Cubs after the Blue Jays released him at the end of spring training in 2012, and was a pleasant surprise. The well-traveled Venezuelan infielder always had a good glove, but he also discovered a power stroke in Chicago. He hit 16 homers in 2014. The Cubs traded Luis to the Astros in January 2015 for Dexter Fowler, a trade that worked out for both teams. Luis got his only sniff at postseason play with the Astros in 2015 (and hit a homer). Fowler was a key member of the 2016 World Champion Cubs. Valbuena had two 20+ homer seasons after leaving Cubs, and still had quite a bit left in the tank when he tragically passed away in a car accident in Venezuela in December 2018. He was only 33 years old.

Pedro Valdes 1973 – (Cubs 1996, 1998)

Pedro got two brief shots with the Cubs at the big league level after turning in some pretty strong numbers in the minors. The slugger hit over 300 homers in the minors, Mexican league, and Japanese league (combined), but in his two stints with the Cubs, the first baseman didn't hit a single one. He finally got his first (and only) big league homer for the Rangers in 2000. He last played for the silver medal-winning Puerto Rican team in the 2013 World Games.

Ismael Valdes 1973 – (Cubs 2000)

He was known as "The Rocket" like another famous Ismael, football's Rocket Ismael. The Cubs acquired the former 15-game winner along with Eric Young, and immediately placed him in the starting rotation. Unfortunately for the Cubs, Valdez developed blister problems and had a hard time staying healthy. He won a grand total of two games in Chicago. Before the season was over, they traded him back to the Dodgers. He later pitched for the Angels, Rangers, Mariners, Padres, and Marlins. Valdez won 104 big league games, but he also lost 105. He does, however, have his name in the Cubs record books. Ismael shares the record for most homers allowed in one game. He served up five.

Vito Valentinetti 1928 – (Cubs 1956-1957)

Vito's big league career was delayed because he was serving in the military during the Korean War. When he returned he got a cup of coffee with the White Sox before moving to the other side of town. Vito was a right-handed reliever, and he had a fairly good season for the Cubs in 1956. He won six games and saved another with the Cubs, but was traded to the Dodgers for Don Elston the following May. That turned out to be a good trade for the Cubs. Elston became a key pitcher for the Cubs over the next seven years, and appeared in two All-Star games. Vito pitched for the Indians, Tigers, and Senators, but by 1960, his big league career was over.

Jermaine Van Buren 1980 – (Cubs 2005)

Jermaine was a right-handed reliever who pitched 11 seasons in the minors, but he did get a brief cup of coffee with the Cubs in 2005. He pitched in six games, but had trouble harnessing his command. The Cubs sold him to the Red Sox after the season, and he had one more (even less successful) chance with Boston the following year. In 19 big league innings, he walked 25 batters.

George Van Haltren 1866 – 1945 (White Stockings 1887-1889)

George was a pitcher his first few seasons, but when he was moved to left field in 1889, he really started to shine. He became one of the best leadoff men of his era. Unfortunately, he was also one of the players that left Chicago in the player revolt of 1890 to join the Players' League. He returned to the National League after the league folded, but not to Chicago. Van Haltren hit over .300 nine seasons in a row (for Pittsburgh and the New York Giants). He was 37 years old when his career ended in 1902 after he suffered a terrible ankle injury. "Rip" as he was called, received some Hall of Fame votes when the hall was created in 1936, but never enough to be enshrined.

Todd Van Poppel 1971 – (Cubs 2000-2001)

The former first rounder hadn't really put it together in his previous stops in Oakland, Detroit, Texas, or Pittsburgh. In fact, he had spent the entire previous season in the minors

with the Pirates. But Van Poppel turned himself into a pretty good relief pitcher in his stint with the Cubs. Todd appeared in over 100 games, winning eight and saving two, with a very respectable ERA. In fact, he parlayed that Cubs stint into a big free agent contract with the Rangers. His two seasons with the Cubs were probably the best of his career.

Ben VanRyn 1971 – (Cubs 1998)

Ben was a top prospect — a member of the U18 U.S. National Team, and a first round draft choice by the Expos, but he never quite put it together at baseball's top level. His first taste of the big leagues was a cup of coffee with the Angels, and that was six years after he was drafted. When he joined the 1998 Cubs, he was a 27-year-old journeyman. After only nine appearances, the left-handed reliever was traded to the San Diego Padres for Don Wengert. He pitched for four teams in the big leagues, including the Angels and the Blue Jays.

Ike Van Zandt 1876 – 1908 (Cubs 1904)

Van Zandt played three seasons in the big leagues, the middle of which was with the Cubs in 1904. The power-packed team didn't have a lot of room for him. He played in only three games. After his big league career he was playing in the minors in Albany, and was involved in a game-fixing scandal. When the details were about to be revealed, he committed suicide by shooting himself in the chest. The day he killed himself was exactly one month before his former teammates won the 1908 World Series. Van Zandt was only 32 years old.

Hy Vandenberg 1906 – 1994 (Cubs 1944-1945)

Vandenberg had been a fringe big league pitcher in the years before the war, pitching mainly in September for teams out of the pennant chase. He got a cup of coffee in 1935 with the Boston Red Sox (and was pounded), and then 1937-1940 with the Giants (and was pounded in each season). With the wartime Cubs of 1944, however, Vandenberg won seven games and pitched quite well in relief. He had another good season in 1945, and pitched brilliantly in relief during the World Series (3 appearances, 6 innings, only one hit allowed). When the big names returned to the game after the war, Hy stuck it out one more year in the minors, but it was clear he wouldn't get another chance. The 40-year-old hung up his spikes.

Johnny Vander Meer 1914—1997 (Cubs 1950-1951)

Johnny was a four-time All-Star, three-time strikeout king, and was world famous for throwing back-to-back no-hitters. (The last out in that second no-hitter? Leo Durocher). His record of 21 straight hitless innings will probably never be beaten. Johnny also struck out six batters in the 1943 All-Star Game.

As you might have guessed, all of that happened before he arrived in Chicago. By the time he joined the Cubs in 1950, he was toast. The Cubs tried him as a starter, and he couldn't do it anymore, so they used him as a closer — asking him to finish 17 games. Unfortunately, he walked more men than he struck out, gave up ten home runs in only 73 innings, and managed to record only one save. The Cubs released him in April of 1951.

Andy Varga 1930—1992 (Cubs 1950-1951)

Andy was a Chicago boy (Lane Tech High School) who made it to the big leagues at the tender age of 19. The left-hander only got into a few games over two September call-ups with the Cubs, and had command issues. By the time he turned 23, he was out of baseball.

Gary Varsho 1961—(Cubs 1988-1990)

Varsho came up through the Cubs system and got limited playing time as a backup outfielder in parts of three seasons. He had a little more success with his next team, the Pittsburgh Pirates, and hit his first career homer for them against the Cubs in Wrigley Field. After his playing days, he went into coaching and was very briefly (two games), the interim manager of the Pittsburgh Pirates. He also coached for the Angels organization.

Hippo Vaughn 1888—1966 (Cubs 1913-1921)

Hippo Vaughn got his nickname because of his size (he was about the same size as Rick Reuschel). He is quite simply one of the best pitchers in Cubs history. He arrived in Chicago as a struggling big leaguer. He hadn't quite been able to put it together during his years in New York and Washington (1908-1912), but he blossomed with the Cubs. He announced his arrival with a two-hitter in one of his first starts at the end of the 1913 season. By the following year, he was a 20-game winner. He followed that up with three more 20-win seasons

over the next four. One of those wins was the last-ever win at West Side Grounds. In 1917, Hippo was part of the famous double no-hitter game. Vaughn pitched a no-hitter for nine innings but lost the game in the tenth inning to another pitcher throwing a no-hitter, Fred Toney of the Reds. Jim Thorpe (yes, THAT Jim Thorpe) knocked in the winning run.

The following season was Hippo's masterpiece. He won pitching's Triple Crown (wins, ERA, strikeouts) and led the Cubs to the World Series. The 1919 Black Sox may have believed the 1918 Cubs threw that World Series, but if they did, no one suspected Hippo Vaughn was part of it. He started three games in that series, and although he was only 1-2, his ERA was 1.00 and he struck out 17 batters.

Hippo won the ERA title the following year too, and became a 20-game winner a fifth time, but after another 19-win season in 1920, one of the best pitchers in Cubs history had his career derailed by a Cubs Hall of Famer. In 1921 manager Johnny Evers suspended him for thirty days for insubordination. Hippo signed a contract with a semi-pro team to stay in shape, but Commissioner Landis suspended him indefinitely for that. It was technically against the rules because he was already under contract to the Cubs. (Vaughn was also stabbed by his father-in-law the same year…not a good year for Hippo.) Commissioner Landis was known as a bit of a hardliner, and he held the line against Vaughn for eight long years. He wasn't reinstated until 1930. By then Hippo was 43 years old. He did try to make the team in spring training in 1931, but he didn't have it anymore. There's little doubt Hippo Vaughn would have been a Hall of Famer if his last years of productivity weren't taken from him.

If there was a Cubs Hall of Fame, he'd be in it. Hippo is still in second place in Cubs career history with 35 shutouts. He's one of only eight Cubs pitchers with 150+ career wins for Chicago, and he's eighth on the all-time Cubs strikeout list.

<u>Historical note:</u> On the day American women won the right to vote in 1919, Hippo Vaughn and the Cubs lost a 1-0 heartbreaker in the tenth inning to the Pirates.

Bill Veeck Sr. 1876—1933 (Cubs president 1917-1933)

William Veeck Sr. was a sportswriter for *Chicago American* writing under the pseudonym Bill Bailey when new Cubs owner William Wrigley invited him over for dinner one night in 1917. Wrigley was a fan — he had read Bailey's articles and thought that he had some baseball insight. Veeck was very blunt with Wrigley, to which Wrigley replied: "If you're so smart, why don't you run the club?"

Veeck agreed. He was hired as vice president in 1917, and was promoted to president in 1918.
Veeck ran the Cubs every year of William Wrigley's ownership, and he brought the team to three National League pennants (1918, 1929, 1932). The trick to that was simple. He acquired talent, including some of the biggest names in Cubs history: Hack Wilson, Charlie Grimm, Kiki Cuyler, Riggs Stephenson, Charlie Root, and Guy Bush. But he also did something that sustained the Cubs for many many years. He made them into a popular attraction. Veeck was the one that urged Wrigley to broadcast the games on the radio, a pioneering move that turned out to be brilliant. The league was against the idea and tried to stop it, but Wrigley and Veeck insisted — and the league finally relented. The first broadcast was in 1924. By 1925, the Cubs owned Chicago once again.

When William Wrigley died in 1932, that was a big blow to the team, but it was an even bigger blow to the Cubs when Veeck Sr. died the following year (of leukemia). With a great nucleus of players (a nucleus strong enough to win pennants in 1935 and 1938), his eye for talent, and knack for promotion, Veeck's continued presence would have done wonders during the early reign of William Wrigley's inexperienced son P.K. Wrigley. By the late 30s as Veeck's players aged, the Cubs began to get ripped off by every team in the league. The 1941 Dodgers won the pennant with seven ex-Cubs. The Cardinals won the pennant several times with the players they acquired in the Dizzy Dean trade. And the Cubs? Well, suffice it to say they could have used the continued guiding hand of William Veeck Sr.

Bill Veeck Jr. 1914–1986 (Cubs front office/fan)
His father (Bill Veeck Sr.) was the President of the Chicago Cubs, and Bill Jr. idolized his dad. The elder Veeck was probably the greatest innovator of his time, but he was later surpassed by his son. At the age of 11, young Bill started helping out his dad at the ballpark. He worked on the grounds crew, as an office boy, and a vendor. As a fifteen-year-old kid, he was taking care of the Ladies' Day passes at Wrigley Field by day, and was tagging along with baseball hero Hack Wilson to the speakeasies in Cicero by night. "With a father who ran a ball club, my boyhood was the kind most kids dream about," Veeck says in his autobiography.

It's no wonder that Wrigley Field meant so much to him. Young Bill wasn't only hanging out with famous ballplayers like Wilson, Grover Cleveland Alexander, and Charlie Grimm, he really felt like he was part of the team. After his father died in 1933, Veeck quit college to work for the Cubs full-time. He eventually rose to the job of treasurer, but when he wasn't given the job of president a few years later, he moved on (in 1941). His most lasting accomplishment at Wrigley Field is something that still draws fans into the ballpark seventy years later…the ivy on the walls. Veeck was the one that planted the ivy in 1937.

In his final years, after a Hall of Fame career as a trailblazing and innovative owner, Veeck re-adopted the Chicago Cubs. He was a frequent sight at Wrigley Field, often found sitting in the bleachers without a shirt. He owned several different teams in his long baseball career (The Browns, the White Sox, the Indians, and the Brewers), but when he could go to any ballpark in the big leagues in any town in America, there was only one ballpark he came to again and again as a fan. He came home to his favorite place, the place of his childhood dreams. He came to Wrigley Field.

*Venezuelan Cubs…*All of the following Cubs players originally hailed from Venezuela… Jose Ascanio, J.C. Boscan, Henry Blanco, Miguel Cairo, Ronny Cedeno, Willson Contreras, Felix Doubrant, Rich Garces, Alberto Gonzalez, Geremi Gonzalez, Angel Guzman, Cesar Izturis, Robert Machado, Miguel Montero, Jose Nieves, Ruben Quevedo, Miguel Rojas, Hector Rondon, Luis Salazar, Carlos Silva, Miguel Socolovich, Manny Trillo, Luis Valbuena, Carlos Zambrano, and Eduardo Zambrano.

Jose Veras 1980–(Cubs 2014)
After a successful stint as a closer for the Astros, the Cubs signed Veras to be their closer in 2014. It became obvious early on that he couldn't handle the job. In 12 appearances

his ERA was over eight. Then he got hurt. When it was time to return to the roster, the Cubs cut him loose. Veras pitched for eight teams in his nine-year big league career.

Emil Verban 1915–1989 (Cubs 1948-1950)

Verban was a second baseman for the Cubs. They called him the Antelope because of his speed early in his career, but by the time Verban played in Chicago, he wasn't exactly tearing up the base paths. In his three seasons with the Cubs he stole a total of seven bases. To say that Verban wasn't exactly known for his power would be an understatement. The Antelope had 2911 career at-bats, and hit exactly one home run. It came while he was wearing a Cubs uniform, and he hit it against Johnny Vander Meer (the man who once threw consecutive no-hitters) on September 6th, 1948. Verban's name lives on thanks to the Emil Verban Society, formed in 1975 by a group of Washington-based Cubs fans. Among the original six members: Chief of Staff for President Gerald Ford, Dick Cheney. Later members included President Ronald Reagan and First Lady Hillary Clinton. The Antelope passed away during the Cubs playoff season of 1989. He was 72.

Dave Veres 1966– (Cubs 2003)

Veres was an excellent reliever with the Cardinals. He saved 60 games over a two-year period. But by the time he came to the Cubs, he was clearly a shell of his former self. In the seventh inning of Game 7 of the NLCS against the Marlins, the Cubs were only down by a run. Matt Clement was available in the pen, but Dusty Baker opted to bring in Veres, despite the fact that Veres had been routinely rocked the last few months of the season. Veres immediately gave up a two-run double, and the Marlins broke open the game. It was the last appearance of his big league career.

Randy Veres 1965–2016 (Cubs 1994)

Randy wasn't with the Cubs very long, but still makes it on the all-embarrassing Cubs injuries list. He hurt his hand pounding on the wall of his hotel room, trying to get the people next door to make less noise. He pitched in ten games for the Cubs in the strike season of 1994 and posted an ERA of 5.59. He also pitched for Milwaukee, Florida, Detroit, and Kansas City.

Joe Vernon 1889–1955 (Cubs 1912)

If you want to go back in time to see Joe Vernon pitch, set the wayback machine for July 20, 1912 and go to West Side Grounds in Chicago. He pitched the final four innings of a humiliating blowout to the Philadelphia Phillies. Grover Cleveland Alexander and the Phillies won the game 14-2. Joe gave up five of those runs. It was Vernon's only appearance in a Cubs uniform. He later got one more cup of coffee with Brooklyn in 1914.

Tom Veryzer 1953–2014 (Cubs 1983-1984)

In many ways Veryzer was the prototypical journeyman infielder, but he did have a few career highlights. He broke up a Ken Holtzman no-hitter with two outs in the ninth inning (when Kenny was with the A's), and was named to the All-Rookie team as a Detroit Tiger in 1975. With the Cubs he was a backup to both Ryne Sandberg and Larry Bowa during their ill-fated 1984 season. He made the post-season roster and got into a few of the games as a late-game defensive replacement. That was his last hurrah in the big leagues.

Cubs players have had some great nicknames over the years. Among players starting with the letter V, you'll find nicknames like Antelope, Babe Ruth of the Big Ten, Hippo, Rip, Rocket, and Vinegar Tom.

Tom Vickery 1867–1921 (Colts 1891)

Vinegar Tom, as he was known, pitched in Chicago for one year and went 6-5 in 14 appearances. He threw complete games in 7 of his 12 starts, but had a 4.07 ERA. In the deadball era, those were not great numbers. There's no record of why Vickery was saddled with the nickname (other than his first name perhaps?), but Vinegar Tom was a demon that looked like a cross between a cat and a greyhound dog, according to writings going back to the 17th century.

*Vietnam War Veteran Cubs...*The following Cubs players all served in the military during the Vietnam War...Matt Alexander, Larry Biittner, Bill Campbell, Larry French, George

Mitterwald, Bobby Murcer, Jimmy Qualls, and Champ Summers.

Carlos Villanueva 1983 – (Cubs 2013-2014)

Carlos was signed as a free agent after pitching seven big league seasons in Milwaukee and Toronto. He was a very valuable pitcher for the Cubs for two seasons, filling every conceivable role. Carlos started 20 games, finished 20 games, won 12, and saved two. He also sported the best mustache on the club — it was Rollie Fingers-esque. The Cubs allowed him to leave via free agency after the 2014 season. In all, his big league career lasted eleven years, and he pitched for Milwaukee, Toronto, St. Louis, and San Diego in addition to the Cubs.

Hector Villanueva 1964 – (Cubs 1990-1992)

Unlike most .230-hitting bad-fielding catchers, Hector managed to become a crowd favorite at Wrigley Field. Many fans saw themselves in Hector's Ruthian physique. Others appreciated his "swing for the fences on every swing" approach to hitting. Still others liked the way he flopped after wild pitches, his mammoth body sending plumes of dust into the air every time he made contact with the ground. The big Puerto Rican clubbed 22 homers in his three seasons with the Cubs. He also played briefly for the Cardinals.

Josh Vitters 1989 – (Cubs 2012)

Vitters was the third overall pick in the 2007 draft, behind only David Price and Mike Moustakas, so naturally, the expectations were very high for him. When you get picked ahead of the likes of Matt Wieters, Madison Bumgarner, Jason Heyward, Devin Mesoraco (all chosen in the next few picks), that's to be expected. Vitters' progress was agonizingly slow, however. He didn't make it to the big leagues until 2012, and when he did, it was clear that despite a good season at AAA, he wasn't quite ready for the big-time. He hit only .121 in over a hundred plate appearances, and hasn't been back up to the big leagues since.

Arodys Vizcaino 1990 – (Cubs 2014)

Vizcaino was damaged goods when the Cubs acquired him in the trade that sent Reed Johnson and Paul Maholm to the Braves in 2012. He was coming off Tommy John surgery. Arodys rehabbed for two full seasons before coming back in 2014. He spent most of the season in the Cubs minor league system, but was brought up for a cup of coffee in September of 2014. In that small taste, he showed flashes of why the Cubs brain trust went after him in the first place. His stuff was electric. Needless to say, it was a surprise when they traded him back to the Braves the following season. The Cubs did get catcher Victor Caratini in return, but the Braves got a closer. Arodys saved 30 games for them over the next three seasons.

Jose Vizcaino 1968 – (Cubs 1991-1993)

Jose had a long and impressive big league career. For most of his 18 seasons he was a valuable backup infielder, but with the Cubs he got a shot as a starter. In 1993 he spent the year as the Cubs starting shortstop, and posted some of the best numbers of his career. Jose hit .287, knocked in 54 runs, and stole 12 bases. After the season the Cubs traded him to the New York Mets for Anthony Young. Jose played for nine teams in the big leagues, and two of them made the World Series. His 2000 Yankees team beat the Mets, and his 2005 Astros team lost to the White Sox.

Historical note: On the day Hurricane Andrew hit the shores of Florida (1992), Jose got the game-winning hit for the Cubs in Los Angeles to defeat the Dodgers.

Luis Vizcaino 1974 – (Cubs 2009)

The Cubs got Vizcaino from the Rockies for Jason Marquis before the 2009 season, but Luis barely made it to May. The right-handed reliever appeared in four games for Cubs (and actually pitched pretty well — 0.00 ERA), but was released on May 3. He finished that season — the last of his 11 big league seasons — with the Indians.

Otto Vogel 1899–1969 (Cubs 1923-1924)

Otto was a star in college at the University of Illinois, and was known as the Babe Ruth of the Big Ten. (He also starred in football.) The Cubs sent him right to the big leagues, where he didn't quite live up to the Babe Ruth name. He fell just 713 homers short of Ruth. His one homer was hit in July of 1923. After his playing career he became the head coach at the University of Iowa. He held that job for 39 years.

Bill Voiselle 1919–2005 (Cubs 1950)

The Cubs got the former All-Star fireballer from the Braves in the trade that sent Gene Mauch to Boston. Unfortunately, Voiselle was a shell of his former All-Star self. He went 0-4, with a 5.79 ERA in 19 games.

Chris Volstad 1986–(Cubs 2012)

Volstad was acquired in exchange for clubhouse cancer Carlos Zambrano. The new regime led by Theo Epstein didn't want Zambrano's attitude (and contract) around, so it seemed like a good deal at the time. Volstad had been a first round draft choice and 12-game winner for the Marlins. But he was legendarily awful with the Cubs. His record (3-12) and ERA (6.31) don't even tell the story of how bad he was for the Cubs. He also allowed sixteen homers (in just over a hundred innings), walked almost as many as he struck out, and gave up 137 hits. After the season the Cubs let him go.

John Vukovich 1947–2007 (Cubs manager 1986)

Vukovich had a ten-year career in the big leagues as a backup infielder (mostly for the Phillies), but he also became a Cubs coach after his playing career ended. For two days he was even the manager of the team. After Dallas Green fired Jim Frey and before Gene Michael took over, Vukovich was the interim manager for two days. The Cubs won one and lost one.

---

*Additional Entries…*If you check out the Every Cub Ever feature at www.justonebadcentury.com, you'll find several additional entries, including celebrity Cubs fans, writers, and bloggers. Under the letter V, you'll discover Cubs fans like actor Vince Vaughn and musician Eddie Vedder, not to mention super fan Ronnie "Woo Woo" Vickers.

W

The starting lineup of your Chicago Cubs beginning with the letter W...

C – Deacon White, Hall of Famer
1B – Eddie Waitkus, Shooting Victim
2B – Todd Walker, .300 Hitter
SS – Rabbit Warstler, Hit Stealer
3B – Ned Williamson, 19th Century Home Run Hero
LF – Billy Williams, Hall of Famer
CF – Hack Wilson, RBI Champ
RF – Cy Williams, Home Run Champ
Bench – Jerome Walton, Rookie of the Year
Bench – Rick Wilkins, 30 Homer Fluke
SP – Rube Waddell, Hall of Famer
SP – Lon Warneke, 3-Time World Series
SP – Kerry Wood, 20-Strikeout Game
SP – Hank Wyse, 1945 All-Star
RP – Hoyt Wilhelm, Hall of Famer
RP – Mitch Williams, Original Wild Thing
RP – Turk Wendell, Quirky Oddball

Tsuyoshi Wada 1981 – (Cubs 2014-2015)

He was a 33-year-old rookie when he came up to the big leagues after an impressive season in Iowa, but Wada had lots of experience in his native Japan. Dr. K, as he is known, pitched well for the Cubs in 13 starts. In 2015 he hurt his arm and only appeared in eight games. After the Cubs released him, Wada returned to his native Japan.

Jason Waddell 1981 – (Cubs 2009)

After languishing for eight seasons in the San Francisco minor league system, Waddell finally got his shot at the big leagues with the Cubs in 2009 at the age of 28. He appeared in a grand total of three games, and registered a 5.40 ERA in 1.2 innings before being sent back down to the minors. 2011 was his last season in organized baseball.

Rube Waddell 1876 – 1914 (Orphans 1901)

Rube was a common nickname for hayseeds and farm boys, and Rube Waddell was definitely that. He only pitched one season for the Cubs (before they were even called that) in 1901, and was only a .500 pitcher that season, but he blossomed as a pitcher the next season when he moved over to the upstart American League. He won 20 games or more four years in a row and was the most dominating strikeout pitcher of his era. He led the league in strikeouts for six years in a row. His best season was probably 1904. While pitching for the Philadelphia A's, he struck out 349 batters in 383 innings pitched.

Despite his Hall of Fame career (he was inducted to the hall in 1946), Rube was known even more for his off-the-field antics, which were considered completely bizarre. For instance, he had a bad habit of leaving the dugout in the middle of games to follow passing fire trucks to fires. He also performed as an alligator wrestler in the off-season. And sadly, he had a horrible alcohol problem. Waddell reportedly spent his entire first signing bonus on a drinking binge. As you might expect, his odd behavior and excessive drinking led to constant battles with his managers and teammates. His A's teammates hated him so much, they forced management to trade him to St. Louis in early 1908, even though he was the by far the best pitcher on the staff. Modern day historians believe Waddell was on the autism spectrum. Rube was only 37 years old when he passed away in 1914.

Ben Wade 1922 – 2002 (Cubs 1948)

Ben made his big league debut as a Cub, but only appeared in two games for Chicago. He got more time pitching for Brooklyn in the early 50s, and also had cups of coffee with the Cardinals and Pirates. Wade pitched 16 seasons in the minor leagues. After his playing career, Ben became a scout for the Dodgers. He was part of the scouting staff that continually stocked the Dodgers with great prospects, and turned them into the best franchise in the National League during the 60s and 70s.

Gale Wade 1929 – (Cubs 1955-1956)

Wade was a backup center fielder for the Cubs in the mid-50s. He didn't get a lot of opportunities, playing in only 19 games over two seasons. Wade's game was speed — he was known as the Greyhound during his time playing winter ball in Venezuela. When your lifetime average in the big leagues is only .133, however, it's difficult to utilize your speed. Gale played 15 years in the minor leagues.

Eddie Waitkus 1919–1972 (Cubs 1941-1948)

Eddie Waitkus was a fresh-faced young first baseman for the Cubs who joined the Cubs briefly in 1941 before being drafted into the military. He returned for the 1946 season as a highly decorated military hero (four battle stars) and promptly took over the starting job, batting over .300 that year. Waitkus was known for his great defense, his smoking line-drives, and his left-handed bat. The pinnacle of his Cubs career came in 1948, when he made the All-Star team.

After the 1948 season the Cubs decided they needed to boost their pitching staff, so they traded the popular Waitkus to the Phillies for two aging starting pitchers (Dutch Leonard and Monk Dubiel). Many people in Chicago were very upset by that trade, but nobody was more upset than young Ruth Ann Steinhagen, who had pined for Waitkus since the 1941 season, when she was only 11 years old. She attended games whenever she could and kept an encyclopedic scrapbook of pictures and clippings of Waitkus. How obsessed was she? She heard that Eddie was Lithuanian, so she studied the language. Needless to say, 18-year-old Ruth Ann's world was shattered when Waitkus was traded. Eddie had no idea who Ruth Ann was, but he would find out soon enough. He was hitting over .300 for Philadelphia, and was leading all NL first basemen in All-Star game balloting when the Phillies came to Chicago on June 14, 1949 to play the Cubs at Wrigley Field. He must have felt vindicated when his Phillies trounced the team that traded him, 9-2. He had a celebratory dinner that night with his teammate Russ Meyer and Meyer's parents and fiancé.

Nothing seemed out of the ordinary when they returned to the Edgewater Beach hotel around 11:00 that night. There was a note waiting for Eddie there, from a "Ruth Ann Burns," a girl Eddie had been dating. The note simply said that Ruth Ann was staying in room 1297. Excited to see her, Eddie quickly went to room 1297 and knocked on the door. Instead of Ruth Ann Burns, however, another girl was waiting for him there. She claimed to be Ruth Ann's friend. Thinking it was perfectly conceivable, Eddie took her up on the offer. He was sitting in a chair in room 1297 when Ruth Ann Steinhagen emerged from the closet holding a 22-caliber rifle, and said…"If I can't have you, nobody can." Then she shot him in the chest. As Eddie slumped to the ground in agony, Ruth Ann Steinhagen calmly picked up the phone and told the front desk that she had just shot Eddie Waitkus. That phone call probably saved his life. The bullet narrowly missed his heart, and miraculously missed all of his other major organs, but he surely would have bled to death. As it was, it took several hours in the operating room to successfully remove the bullet. When it came time to punish Ruth Ann Steinhagen, Eddie refused to push for a harsh sentence. He did not attend the trial, and never saw her again. When asked about her, he simply replied: "She had the coldest-looking face I've ever seen."

This shooting, which was a huge nationwide story, surely influenced author Bernhard Malamud, who published his novel *The Natural* only three years later. Eddie, by the way, returned to the big leagues, and played until 1955. Ruth Ann was institutionalized for a few years, but was then declared sane and released, and lived in Chicago until her death in 2012.

Charlie Waitt 1853–1912 (White Stockings 1877)

Charlie was considered one of the first baseball players to use a glove. He was mocked for it at the time. Charlie was a backup outfielder for the Cubs (then known as the White Stockings) in their second season in the National League. He managed only four hits in 41 plate appearances. That .098 batting average wasn't quite enough to keep him in Chicago. He later played for Baltimore and Philadelphia.

Matt Walbeck 1969 – (Cubs 1993)

The catcher was an eighth round draft pick by the Cubs. He eventually made it up to the big leagues in Chicago, although he didn't get a lot of playing time. He started the 1993 season with the Cubs as the their backup catcher, but was sent down to the minors after only appearing in 11 games. After the season the Cubs traded Walbeck to Minnesota for Willie Banks. Matt caught for six big league teams in eleven seasons. He became a minor league manager after his playing days were over.

Chico Walker 1958– (Cubs 1985-1987, 1991)

Chico was strictly a backup in his first stint with the Cubs, mainly in the outfield. When he returned to the team in 1991, he had reinvented himself as a super-utility man. He played 2B, 3B, and all three outfield positions and got the most extensive playing time of his 11-year big league career. Chico hit .257 and stole 13 bases.

Harry Walker 1916–1999 (Cubs 1949)

Harry was an All-Star with the Cardinals before the war, and came to the Cubs a few years after the war ended. The Cubs got him in a trade for their former crowd favorite Bill Nicholson. Harry didn't work out in Chicago, but he did provide the team an invaluable trade bait. He had only hit one homer and was hitting .264 as a corner outfielder for the Cubs when they traded him to the Reds for Frank Baumholtz and Hank Sauer. Those two players were key members of the Cubs for years. The former anchored Wrigley's center field, and the latter became an MVP for the Cubs. Walker's brother Dixie also played in the big leagues, and is most remembered as the player who most vehemently protested Jackie Robinson's promotion to the Dodgers in 1947.

Mike Walker 1966– (Cubs 1995)

Walker was born in Chicago and eventually played for the Cubs as part of his major league journey. After washing out as a starter with the Indians, he was a reliever for the Cubs. In 42 games, he won one game, saved another, and posted a respectable 3.22 ERA. He later also pitched for Detroit.

Roy Walker 1893–1962 (Cubs 1917-1918)

Roy was on the same pitching staff as Claude Hendrix. He started and relieved for the pennant-winning 1918 Cubs, although he didn't see any action in postseason. Walker probably had his best season in the big leagues with the Cardinals in 1921, when he won 11 games. He also pitched for Cleveland.

Rube Walker 1926–1992 (Cubs 1948-1951)

May 23, 1948 was supposed to be Rube Walker's big break. The young catcher had played in a few games as a late inning defensive replacement, including the day Jackie Robinson stole home against the Cubs at Wrigley (right in front of Rube), but he had never started a game for the Cubs before. The Cubs were in the midst of a miserable season, and they were playing a double-header against the Boston Braves (in Boston). After losing the first game 8-5, Cubs manager Charlie Grimm penciled in Walker to start the second game; his first-ever start. In the top of the first, Walker even got a chance to bat. He dug in, waited for the pitch from Braves pitcher Vern Bickford, and boom! The pitch hit him right in the noggin. He went down and remained down. Remember, this was in the era before batting helmets. Walker had to be carried off the field on a stretcher and was hospitalized with a concussion…before he even got to catch one pitch as a starting catcher. Walker did manage to return to the majors that same season. He went on to have an eleven-year major league career as a backup catcher, and even got a chance to play in the World Series for the 1956 Brooklyn Dodgers. After he retired, Rube became a pitching coach for the New York Mets. You might remember that young Mets staff he coached, beginning in 1968. Not sure if they ever amounted to anything.

Todd Walker 1973– (Cubs 2004-2006)

Walker was a playoff star with the Boston Red Sox in 2003. He hit 5 homers in the ALCS that the Red Sox lost in seven games to the Yankees. The Cubs signed him as a free agent after that performance, and Walker had a few solid years with the Cubs. He hit 15 homers in his first year in Chicago, and followed that up with a .305 average the following year. In the midst of a horrible 2006 season (for the Cubs, not Walker), the team traded him to the Padres. Walker played for seven teams in his twelve-year big league career.

William Walker (Cubs president 1934)

After William Wrigley and Bill Veeck Sr. passed away (in '32 and '33), the Cubs were suddenly rudderless. New owner Phillip Wrigley knew that he didn't know anything about baseball, so he opted not to take over the team himself. Instead, he looked to one of the minority owners of the team, William Walker. The outspoken Walker hadn't been allowed to contribute to any baseball decisions during the Wrigley/Veeck era, and was chomping at the bit to take over. There was only one problem. He wasn't a baseball man. He was the owner of a wholesale seafood business. Walker didn't last the year. It didn't take long for the word to get out that the Cubs had a neophyte running their organization. One of his first trades is still known as one the worst trades in Cubs history. He traded slugger Dolph Camilli to the Phillies for Don Hurst. Camilli went on to hit over 200 home runs, made two All-Star teams, and led the 1941 Brooklyn Dodgers to the World Series. He won the MVP that year too. Don Hurst, on the other hand, hit .199 and retired after the season. Walker was such a terrible team president that P.K. Wrigley was forced to buy him out just to get him to stop destroying the team. The man who succeeded Walker as team president, however, remains the worst team president in Cubs history. P.K. Wrigley himself. He remained in the job until the year he died (1977).

Jack Wallace 1890–1960 (Cubs 1915)

Wallace caught exactly two games for the Cubs in their last season at West Side Grounds. Both appearances came at the very end of the season, and both of them were games pitched by a man who had thrown a no-hitter earlier in his career. In the first game Wallace caught Jimmy Lavender's 10th win of the season, and drove in a run. In his last game, he caught Lavender again — although this time it was a loss. He returned to his native Louisiana after the season, and finished out his playing days in the minor leagues down south.

Ty Waller 1957–(Cubs 1981-1982)

Waller arrived in Chicago as part of the Bruce Sutter/Leon Durham trade, along with fellow third baseman Ken Reitz. He started the '81 season in the minors, but was called up in June to help an incredibly bad Cubs team. Waller became a pretty good pinch hitter and bench player the rest of the way. He got three homers and 13 RBI in limited at-bats. The Cubs traded him to the White Sox in 1982 for pitcher Reggie Patterson, and Ty didn't make it back up to the big leagues again until he got a limited shot with the 1987 Astros. He retired from baseball following that season.

Joe Wallis 1952–(Cubs 1975-1979)

Joe Wallis earned the nickname "Tarzan" because he was fond of cliff diving. He played parts of four seasons with the Cubs, playing all three outfield positions, but predominantly a very shallow center field. Tarzan didn't hit much for average (lifetime .244), or power (16 career homers), and he didn't have a lot of speed (7 stolen bases in 5 big league seasons), but he did have one thing that many of his teammates desired for themselves…a great nickname.

<u>Historical note:</u> On the day Viking I landed on Mars (1976), Wallis led the Cubs to a 3-2 win over the Giants in San Francisco. He knocked in two runs with a bases-loaded single in the 8th.

Lee Walls 1933–1993 (Cubs 1957-1959)

The Cubs acquired him (and Dale Long) from the Pirates for Gene Baker and Dee Fondy, and Walls had a couple of good years for the Cubs. In 1957 he hit for the cycle in a game against the Reds. In 1958 he had his best big league season and was named to the All-Star team. In 1959, he was part of the package used to acquire Frank Thomas from the Reds. In all, Walls played in the big leagues for ten years.

Les Walrond 1976– (Cubs 2006)

Les got a cup of coffee with the Cubs in 2006. He appeared in ten games, and because he couldn't find his command (12 walks in 17 innings), he gave up a lot of runs. His earned run average with the Cubs was over six. He also had a cup of coffee with the Royals (2003) and Phillies (2008).

Tom Walsh 1885–1963 (Cubs 1906)

Walsh was a member of the winningest team in MLB history, the 1906 Cubs, but just barely. Tom was a catcher, and got into exactly two games (one in August, and one in September). He was also given only one opportunity to hit. (He struck out.) Despite being only 21 years old, Walsh never played another game in the big leagues. According to Baseball Reference, he never played a game in the minor leagues either.

Jerome Walton 1965–(Cubs 1989-1992)

Jerome burst onto the scene as a rookie in 1989 and immediately made his mark. The Cubs leadoff man stole 24 bases, hit .291, had a 30-game hitting streak, and was named the Rookie of the Year. He also led his team to the playoffs and hit .364 in the 1989 NLCS. Unfortunately, Jerome could never follow up that incredible opening act. The next year his average dipped, and then he started having injury problems.

By 1992, the Cubs let Walton leave as a free agent. He played sparingly for the Angels, Reds, Braves, Orioles, and Rays before calling it a career.

Chris Ward 1949– (Cubs 1972-1974)

Ward only got one at-bat in 1972, on September 10th. He pinch hit for Milt Pappas in the sixth inning of a game against the Phillies. He was retired by former Cubs fan favorite Dick Selma. (The Cubs won 5-3). In 1974 Ward got a much better chance. He got 137 at-bats as a backup left fielder/first baseman, but only hit .204.

Daryle Ward 1975– (Cubs 2007-2008)

Ward was the most important pinch hitter on two consecutive playoff teams for the Cubs. He also played a little first base and left field, but when the chips were on the line, manager Lou Piniella looked down his bench for Daryle. He got a RBI pinch hit in both playoff series.

Dick Ward 1909–1966 (Cubs 1934)

He pitched three games in relief during May of the 1934 season for the Cubs. In six innings, he gave up nine hits, two walks, and two earned runs. He later had a cup of coffee with the Cardinals. Ward died in 1966 at the age of 57. At the time of his death, another Ward was famous for portraying Batman's sidekick Robin. Burt Ward's character name was even Dick (Grayson).

Preston Ward 1927–2013 (Cubs 1950, 1953)

Ward was Cubs property for four seasons, but he was serving in the military during two of them (1951-1952). He was a first baseman for the Cubs in 1950, and was known as a pretty good glove man, but he didn't hit like a first baseman. Ward was not blessed with a lot of power. In nine big league seasons, he hit a total of 50 homers. Respectable, yes. But not what you'd expect from your corner infielder. Ward's best season in the big leagues was probably 1958, when he batted .284 and clubbed ten homers for the Indians and Athletics.

Lon Warneke 1909–1976 (Cubs 1930-1936, 1942-1945)

His nickname, "The Arkansas Hummingbird", was given to him by sportswriter Roy Stockton because of his "sizzling fast and darting form of delivery." And, of course, because he hailed from Arkansas. He wasn't just the owner of a great nickname, he was also a great pitcher — the best pitcher on the Cubs from 1930-1936, especially during the '32 and '35 pennant seasons. Unfortunately, he was traded for first baseman Ripper Collins in 1937 — even though the Cubs already had star 1B Phil Cavaretta on the roster. That will go down as one of their worst trades ever. Collins played two seasons for the Cubs, but Warneke averaged 15 wins a season over the next five years with the hated St. Louis Cardinals, and appeared in two All-Star games. The Arkansas Hummingbird came back to the Cubs during the war (1942-1943, 1945), but wasn't the same pitcher anymore. After his playing career ended, Lon Warneke became a Major League umpire.

Historical note: On the day Clark Gable was filming the famous "I don't give a damn" scene in *Gone with the Wind* (1939), Warneke was beating his former teammates the Cubs 5-2 in St. Louis.

Hooks Warner 1894–1947 (Cubs 1921)

You'd think with a nickname like Hooks that he had to be a pitcher, but he wasn't at all. Hooks was a third baseman. He hit .211 in 38 at-bats for the Cubs. He had previously played for the Pirates.

Jack Warner 1940– (Cubs 1962-1965)

No relation to the Jack Warner who founded Warner Brothers, this Jack Warner was a right-handed reliever for the Cubs in parts of four different seasons in the 1960s. He never appeared in more than 11 games (1965), and had limited success. His lifetime ERA in the big leagues (all with the Cubs) was 5.10. He had exactly one career hit as a batter, and it came against former Cubs teammate Don Cardwell.

Adam Warren 1987– (Cubs 2016)

The Cubs acquired the right-hander in the trade that sent Starlin Castro to the Yankees. The swingman started 17 games for the Yanks in 2015 and pitched well, winning seven games and posting an ERA of 3.29. The Cubs used him mainly out of the bullpen and he didn't fare as well. In 35 innings pitched he walked 19 batters and gave up seven homers. The Cubs sent him to the minors, before including him in a trade back to the Yankees. He was part of the deal that brought Aroldis Chapman to the Cubs.

Rabbit Warstler 1903–1964 (Cubs 1940)

His real name was Harold Burton Warstler, but they called him Rabbit because of his quickness in the field. He was a backup infielder for 11 seasons, and his last team was the Cubs in 1940. When Rabbit was in the American League, Connie Mack called him "the best defensive infielder in the American League." Babe Ruth complained that Warstler played so deep and had such a strong arm that he stole hits from him. But Rabbit could never hit much, and that's why he never claimed a starting job. And though he was nicknamed Rabbit because of his quickness, he never stole more than nine bases in a season.

Carl Warwick 1937–(Cubs 1966)

Warwick was an outfielder for six big league seasons. He was the starting center fielder for the expansion Houston Colt 45s in 1962, and a World Series champ in 1964 (with the Cardinals), but by the time he came to Cubs in 1966 he was clearly a backup. Carl got his final twenty-two at-bats in the majors (hitting .227) with Chicago. He earlier played for the Orioles, Cardinals, and Dodgers. During the 1964 World Series Carl set a record by reaching base his first four plate appearances…all as a pinch hitter.

Fred Waterman 1845–1899 (White Stockings 1875)

Fred played a grand total of five games for Chicago, his last five games in the league. He hit .300 in 20 at-bats. He was a third baseman.

Logan Watkins 1989–(Cubs 2013-2014)

Logan got his first taste of the big leagues at the end of the 2013 season. The infielder hit .211 with one extra base hit in 27 games. He also got into a handful of games in 2014, when the Cubs suffered injuries, illnesses, or personal issues. Those were his only two shots at the big leagues, however. Watkins played nine years in the minors.

Doc Watson 1885–1949 (Cubs 1913)

Watson pitched for the Cubs very briefly during the 1913 season, then jumped over to play in the Federal League for Chicago, which means he got to play in what is now known as Wrigley Field before any of his Cubs teammates. Why was he called Doc? It's elementary, my dear Watson. He was nicknamed after the famous sidekick of Sherlock Holmes.

Eddie Watt 1941–(Cubs 1975)

Watt had a stellar career as a reliever in the late 60s and early 70s, mostly with the Baltimore Orioles. He was a key member of the bullpen for three pennant winners, and pitched in three World Series for the Orioles. The Cubs picked him off the waiver wire in 1975 and Eddie didn't have much left in the tank. In six games he registered an ERA of 16.50.

David Weathers 1969– (Cubs 2001)

Weathers came to the Cubs in a trading deadline deal in 2001, and was supposed to shore up their bullpen and lead them to the playoffs. Unfortunately the team fizzled in the closing weeks of the season. It wasn't Weathers' fault. He fulfilled his part of the deal, posting a 3.18 ERA in a Cubs uniform. He left as a free agent after the season. Weathers pitched 19 years in the big leagues for nine different teams (Marlins, Yankees, Blue Jays, Indians, Reds, Brewers, Mets, Astros, and Cubs).

Harry Weaver 1892–1983 (Cubs 1917-1919)

Harry pitched for the Cubs during their early years in the new ballpark on Clark and Addison. He won three games in three big league seasons, but pitched fairly well in his limited opportunities. In the middle of his Cubs years, he also played with another team — the United States military. Harry served during World War I. Weaver pitched in the minors until 1924.

Jim Weaver 1903–1983 (Cubs 1934)

Big Jim was a starting pitcher for the Cubs in 1934, but he also pitched for Pittsburgh, Washington, New York (Yankees), St. Louis (Browns), and Cincinnati in his big league career. He won 11 games as the fifth starter for a stacked Cubs rotation featuring four ace-caliber starters Lon Warneke, Pat Malone, Guy Bush, and Bill Lee. Those five starters combined for 78 wins, but the Cubs only finished in 3rd place, 8 games behind the Gashouse Gang St. Louis Cardinals. Weaver was on the mound the day that John Dillinger attended his final Cubs game, a few days before he was shot dead outside the Biograph Theater.

Orlie Weaver 1886–1970 (Cubs 1910-1911)

Orlie was brought in during the final month of the Cubs 1910 pennant-winning season, and pitched in seven games. The following season he stuck with the big club, and was pitching quite well (2.06 ERA) when he was traded to Boston (along with Johnny Kling) in exchange for a handful of players including Peaches Graham. It all fell apart for Orlie with the Boston Braves. He lost twelve of his fifteen decisions and never pitched in the big leagues again.

Earl Webb 1897–1965 (Cubs 1927-1928)

Webb played a solid right field for the Cubs in 1927, but was a backup to KiKi Cuyler the next year. He also worked in one of William Wrigley's mines in California in the offseason. His best years came with the Red Sox. He still holds the all-time record for doubles in a season (67) which he did with the Red Sox in 1931. After his playing career ended, he went back to work in the coal mines.

Allen Webster 1990–(Cubs 2018)

The Cubs brought up Webster for the last few weeks of the 2018 season and the reliever appeared in three games. After the season he was released. Webster previously pitched for the Red Sox and the Diamondbacks, and also pitched a season in Korea.

Mitch Webster 1959–(Cubs 1988-1989)

Webster was a member of the Expos in 1987 when Bill Murray filled in for Harry Caray on the Cubs broadcast (after Harry's stroke). At one point during the game, Murray leaned out and taunted Mitch. The next season Mitch was on the Cubs, acquired in a trade for Dave Martinez. Webster played all three outfield positions, and was a contributor to the division-winning Boys of Zimmer in 1989. He spent 13 years in the big leagues.

Ramon Webster 1942–(Cubs 1971)

The Cubs were the last stop on Webster's five-year big league tour. The Panamanian outfielder/first baseman hit .313 in limited duty. His best season was probably his rookie year with the A's (1967) when he slugged eleven homers.

Charles Weeghman 1874–1938 (Cubs owner 1916-1918)

The ballpark we now known as Wrigley Field opened on April 23, 1914. The name of the stadium at the time was Weeghman Park, named after the man who built it — restauranteur Charlie Weeghman. Though he later owned the Cubs, and brought them to his ballpark to play, the Cubs weren't the home team the day the park opened. That team was the Chicago Federal League team, the Whales. The opposition was the Kansas City Packers. Weeghman's key executive was Charles G. Williams. Williams, and owner Weeghman, had a pretty ingenious plan to attract fans. They went after an audience that heretofore hadn't been so openly courted. They went after the ladies. According to the Chicago Tribune, they were there from Day One: *"The significant part of the affair to the new owners was the large number of women present."* Because Cubs owner Charles Murphy was so hated by the other National League owners (and most Chicagoans) and West Side Grounds had become a public hazard, Weeghman was recruited to buy the Cubs. The timing was right — the Federal League was folding — so Weeghman bought the Cubs, merged his two teams, and the Cubs now had a brand-new home. Unfortunately the purchase stretched Weeghman's finances beyond repair, and he eventually had to sell the team to one of the minority owners — William Wrigley. The ballpark was renamed Wrigley Field in the 1920s.

Jake Weimer 1873–1928 (Cubs 1903-1905)

Tornado Jake Weimer was a pitcher who had three very good years with the Cubs (1903-1905). He won 20, 20, and 18 games respectively in those years, but Tornado Jake may have served the Cubs even better by being traded to the Cincinnati Reds. The man the Cubs got back in that trade was the final piece to their championship puzzle: the trivia question answer, Harry Steinfeldt, the "other" man in the Cubs' Tinkers-to-Evers-to-Chance infield. Weimer won 20 games for the '06 Reds, but then faded, while the Cubs won the next three pennants with Steinfeldt at third.

Historical note: On the day Albert Einstein published his paper on the theory of special relativity (1905), Weimer lost a heartbreaker to Brooklyn, 1-0.

Lefty Weinert 1902–1973 (Cubs 1927-1928)

Weinert was a (wait for it) lefty pitcher. He came to the Cubs after pitching for the Phillies for six seasons, and pitched mainly out of the bullpen. He ended his career with the Yankees. When he came up to the big leagues with the Phillies in 1919, he was only 17 years old.

Butch Weis 1901–1997 (Cubs 1922-1925)

Butch was a backup outfielder, and not related to the gangster Hymie Weis, who was gunned down in front of Holy Name Cathedral during Butch's time on the Cubs. Butch's best season was his last one (1925). He hit the only two homers of his career that season. The Cubs were his only big league team.

Johnny Welch 1906–1940 (Cubs 1926-1928, 1931)

Welch was a left-handed pitcher who was on the Cubs for parts of four different seasons, but didn't get a tremendous amount action in any of them. He appeared in a total of 15 games, 3 of which were starts. After leaving the Cubs he went to the Red Sox and had much more success in Boston. He had two seasons of double-digit wins.

Todd Wellemeyer 1978–(Cubs 2003-2005)

Wellemeyer was one of the many fireballers that came up through Cubs farm system in the first decade of the 21st century. He was tall and imposing and had a blazing fastball, which led to quite a few strikeouts (92 Ks in 84 innings). But he also had control problems (61 BB in 84 innings), and that was his undoing in Chicago. The Cubs traded him before the 2006 season and he later pitched for the Marlins, Cardinals, Royals, and Giants.

Randy Wells 1982–(Cubs 2008-2012)

Wells had a tremendous rookie season with the Cubs in 2009, winning 12 games and posting a sparkling 3.05 ERA. He remained in the starting rotation the following season, although his win total slipped to 8, and his ERA climbed to 4.26. Wells had a few flashes the next two years, but never really reclaimed the magic from his rookie year. The Cubs released him at the end of 2012, and he retired in April of 2013, while with the Texas Rangers.

Turk Wendell 1967–(Cubs 1993-1997)

His real name was Steven John Wendell, but everyone called him Turk. His nickname came from his grandfather after he watched the three-year-old Steven repeatedly hurl himself into a snow mound out of the window of his western Massachusetts home. Turk was known for his eccentricities more than his pitching, which was really just so-so for the Cubs. Among his strange rituals…He wore a necklace made of claws and teeth of animals he killed. He chewed Brach's black licorice on the mound. He brushed his teeth between innings. He talked to the baseball. He drew crosses in the dirt on the mound. He leaped over the foul lines coming in and out of the game. Before he threw his first pitch he waved to the center fielder and wouldn't continue until the outfielder waved back. Oh, and of course, he wore #13. Turk had his best season with the Cubs in 1996 (getting 18 saves), but he later pitched in the playoffs and World Series for the New York Mets.

Don Wengert 1969–(Cubs 1998)

Wengert was acquired in May of 1998 from the Padres and was a spot starter and reliever for the Cubs the rest of that season. In 21 appearances he posted a 5.07 ERA. After the season he left the Cubs and signed with Kansas City. He also pitched for Atlanta, Pittsburgh, and Oakland.

Rip Wheeler 1898–1968 (1923-1924)

One of the rare pitchers to be dubbed "Rip", Wheeler pitched for the Cubs for two seasons in the 1920s. His best season was probably the year the Tribune Tower was built (1924). He appeared in 29 games as a spot starter and reliever, and registered a 3.91 ERA. He also pitched for the Pirates.

Pete Whisenant 1929–1996 (Cubs 1956)

Pete was the starting center fielder for most of his season with the Cubs, and he hit 11 homers. Unfortunately, he also only hit .239. It was his last shot at starting, but he did stay in the league for eight seasons. The Cubs traded him to the Reds in 1957. He hosted a baseball clinic after his playing days and brought in former teammates like Johnny Bench and Mickey Mantle as instructors.

Historical note: On the day the Interstate Highway System was approved (1956), Pete had one of his best days with the Cubs. He homered off Braves stud starter Lew Burdette and led the Cubs to an 8-4 victory at Wrigley Field.

> ***White and Brown Cubs...*** You could field an entire lineup of White and Brown Cubs. It might look a little something like this... Lew Brown–C , Joe Brown–1B, Deacon White–2B, Tommy Brown–SS, Warren White–3B, (Backup–Elder White–IF), Brant Brown–LF, Rondell White–CF, Roosevelt Brown–RF. (Backups–Jerry White–OF, Derrick White–OF/1B), Mordecai Brown–SP, Ray Brown–RP, Jophery Brown–RP, Jumbo Brown–RP.

Deacon White 1847–1939 (White Stockings 1876)

White was just recently (2013) inducted into baseball's Hall of Fame, 166 years after his birth. Deacon was one of the biggest stars in the first decade of professional baseball. He was one of the ringers brought in by Al Spalding, and only played one season for the Cubs (then known as the White Stockings), but it was an important one — the first season of the National League (1876). White led the league that year in RBI. He also played for Buffalo, Dayton, Cleveland, Pittsburgh, and Boston in his 20-year career. He played every single position on the field, including pitcher. They called him Deacon because he was a devoted religious man. White vehemently believed the world was flat.

Derrick White 1969– (Cubs 1998)

White got called up during the summer of 1998 (their Wild Card season). He got ten plate appearances in a Cubs uniform and struck out five of those times. He also played for the Rockies, Expos, and Tigers in his big league career. He was an outfielder and first baseman.

Elder White 1933–2010 (Cubs 1962)

Whitey, as he was known, was a backup infielder for the Cubs during the College of Coaches era. He appeared in 23 games and hit .151. It was his only taste of the big-time.

Jerry White 1952– (Cubs 1978)

White was an excellent outfielder for the Expos. The Cubs traded Woody Fryman to acquire him during the 1978 season, and then traded him back to the Expos after the season was over. In eleven big league seasons he stole nearly 150 bases.

Historical note: On the day President Carter signed the Middle East Peace Accord with Begin & Sadat (1978), Jerry White had three hits for the Cubs in a rain-shortened 4-2 win over the Cardinals.

Rondell White 1972– (Cubs 2000-2001)

The Cubs got White at the trading deadline in 2000, and he was considered a key addition to their lineup, providing protection for Sammy Sosa and Mark Grace. When he was healthy he played well for the Cubs, hitting over .300 and playing a very solid outfield. Unfortunately, he wasn't healthy often, and the Cubs let him leave after the 2001 season. White played 15 seasons in the big leagues, and was an All-Star in 2003 for the San Diego Padres. (He also played for the Expos, Yankees, Royals, Tigers, and Twins.)

Warren White 1844–1890 (White Stockings 1875)

Warren was a 32-year-old when he came to Chicago. He had already played for four different teams in the Washington/ Baltimore area. He might have been old for that era, but the third baseman/shortstop could still play. He didn't hit for power (zero career homers), but he played nearly every day. It was last season in the big leagues for a while. White obviously missed baseball, however, because he made a comeback almost ten years later in 1884 with Washington. That didn't work out quite as well. Warren only got one more hit.

Earl Whitehill 1899–1954 (Cubs 1939)

Whitehill won more than 200 games in the big leagues, but only four of those came for the Cubs, in his last big league season. He holds the record for the worst ERA of any 200-game winner in history (4.36). Earl's career really spans a few different eras. Early in his career, his player/manager on the Tigers was Ty Cobb. Ten years later, he almost ended Lou Gehrig's Iron Man streak when he beaned him on April 23, 1933, knocking him unconscious. Gehrig finished the game. By the time he joined the Cubs he was 40 years old

Eli Whiteside 1979–(Cubs 2014)

The 34-year-old catcher appeared in only eight games for the Cubs. He had previously caught for the Giants and Orioles. After the season, he signed with the Braves.

Robert Whitlow 1918–1997 (Cubs athletic director 1963-1964)

During the Cubs notoriously embarrassing College of Coaches phase, Phillip K. Wrigley was really in an experimenting mood. One of the things he decided his team needed was an athletic director. This would be someone to lead the program, much like an athletic director would lead a college's athletic department. Through his brother-in-law, Wrigley met someone who fit the bill. He hired Colonel Robert Whitlow in January of 1963. Whitlow was the athletic director of the Air Force Academy at the time. Like Wrigley's very early foray into sports psychology in 1930s, it's not that this was a terrible idea. It's just that it came at a time when everyone in the organization was already pretty certain the College of Coaches experiment was a fiasco, so this just sounded like another one of his crackpot schemes. Whitlow actually suggested some things that became common place a few decades later, like using computers to spot trends and position players, and focusing on diet and conditioning. Unfortunately for him, Whitlow was Wrigley's guy, and therefore wasn't respected by the players, the coaches, or the front office of the Cubs. GM John Holland ignored him. "Head Coach" Bob Kennedy ignored him. And, of course, the players ignored him too. After only two years on the job he resigned in January of 1965.

> Cubs players have had some great nicknames over the years. Among players starting with the letter W, you'll find nicknames like Arkansas Hummingbird, Bump, Butch, Deacon, Doc, Dr. K, Hack, Hooks (2 of them), Kettle, Kid K, Lefty, Pop, Rabbit, Rip, Rube (2 of them), Sweet Swingin Billy from Whistler, Tarzan, Tornado Jake, Turk, Whispering Joe, Whitey (2 of them), Wild Thing, and Woody (2 of them).

Bob Wicker 1878–1955 (Cubs 1903-1906)

Wicker was an outstanding starting pitcher for the Cubs in the years just before their dynasty. He won 20 games in his first season in Chicago, and another 30 games over the following two seasons, but started off slow in 1906. The Cubs traded him to the Reds for fellow starter Orval Overall. Orval became a vital part of the World Series champion Cubs, while Wicker never pitched in the big leagues again after the 1906 season.

Charlie Wiedemeyer 1914–1979 (Cubs 1934)

Charlie was also only 20 when he pitched for his hometown Cubs. It didn't go well (9.72 ERA). On the other hand, he had four Hall of Famers (Hartnett, Herman, Cuyler, and Klein) as teammates, which must have given the Chicagoan a lifetime of stories. He pitched in the minors until 1938.

Milt Wilcox 1950– (Cubs 1975)

Milt had a very successful 16-year career, but only made a brief stop to the north side of Chicago. The Cubs traded future closer Dave LaRoche and speedy outfielder Brock Davis to get him, but when Milt didn't make the club in 1976, they sold him to the Detroit Tigers. With the Tigers, Wilcox recorded double-digit wins seven seasons in row. He was a member of the 1984 World Series championship team.

Hoyt Wilhelm 1923–2002 (Cubs 1970)

The future Hall of Famer was 47 years old when the Cubs got him in 1970. He will be remembered for his great knuckleball, and his outstanding career as a reliever. When he retired he held the record for most games and wins in relief, and was the first relief pitcher to be named to the Hall of Fame. He won't, however, be remembered for his days with the Cubs. He pitched in three games, amassed a very impressive ERA of 9.82, and was traded after the season to the Braves. He is still the oldest player ever to play for the Cubs. Here's a little bit of trivia about Hoyt: He hit a home run in his first major league at-bat, and never hit another one in 21 major league seasons.

Harry Wilke 1900–1991 (Cubs 1927)

Wilke's entire big league career consisted of three games, May 12, 13, and 14 of 1927. He was brought up to fill in for

Sparky Adams at third base for a few days, but after getting exactly zero hits in his nine trips to the plate, he was cut loose again. Wilke played seven years of minor league ball.

Curt Wilkerson 1961–(Cubs 1989-1990)

The Cubs acquired Wilkerson in the trade that sent Rafael Palmeiro and Jamie Moyer to the Rangers and brought Mitch Williams to Chicago. He was a key bench player on the 1989 division winner, backing up Ryne Sandberg, Shawon Dunston, and Vance Law. He played in three of the five playoff games against the Giants that postseason. The Cubs let him go after the following season, and he later played for the Pirates and Royals.

Dean Wilkins 1966–(Cubs 1989-1990)

Wilkins was born in the south suburbs of Chicago (Blue Island), but grew up in California. He came to the Cubs in the trade that sent Steve Trout to the Yankees. Wilkins got into eleven games during the Cubs playoff year of 1989, although he didn't make the postseason roster. The following season, the right-handed reliever's time in the big leagues was far less successful. He was rocked hard, and lost his command in seven appearances. He was sent to the Astros after the season.

Rick Wilkins 1967–(Cubs 1991-1995)

Wilkins came out of nowhere to hit 30 homers for the Cubs in 1993. He had previously never hit more than 17 homers in a season, and that was in the low minor leagues. Unfortunately for the Cubs, the following season the prince turned back into a frog. He never again approached those heights, and was traded to the Astros in 1995 for future slugger Luis Gonzalez and fellow catcher Scott Servais.

Bob Will 1931–2011 (Cubs 1957-1963)

Butch, as his teammates called him, was an outfielder and pinch hitter for the Cubs for several seasons. He was a local boy from Berwyn, who attended Northwestern University. Butch got his most extensive playing time as the team's starting right fielder in 1960. Unfortunately, he didn't display a lot of power. Will only hit six homers and knocked in 53 runs, and by the beginning of the 1961 season the Cubs had corner outfielders with a little more pop (George Altman and Billy Williams). Butch Will remained in the Chicago area

after retiring from baseball, and passed away in Woodstock, Illinois in 2011.

Art Williams 1877–1941 (Orphans 1902)

Williams was a backup outfielder/first baseman for the Cubs (then known as the Orphans) in his only big league season. He wasn't much of a hitter, batting only .228 in 49 games.

Billy Williams 1938–(Cubs 1959-1974)

Billy Williams got his nickname ("Sweet Swingin' Billy from Whistler") because of his nearly perfect swing and his hometown: Whistler, Alabama. He played for the Cubs from 1959-1974 and is simply one of the greatest players to ever wear a Cubs uniform. Sweet Swingin' Billy was a six-time All-Star (and hit a homer in the '64 game), a batting champion, was named the MLB player of the year, finished second in the MVP balloting in two different years, hit more than 400 career home runs, and was inducted into baseball's Hall of Fame in 1987. Ernie Banks may have been Mr. Cub, but during the years he shared the field with Billy Williams, he may have only been the second best player on the team. Billy Williams manned left field for the Cubs for twelve years (other than a few years in the mid-60s when they switched him over to right). Near the end of the 1973 season, however, manager Whitey Lockman had the brilliant idea of moving the life-long outfielder to first base. After setting a NL record for most consecutive games played (1117), and establishing a reputation as an iron man outfielder, it only took a few games at first base for Billy to get spiked. He missed twice as many games in 1974 as he missed the previous twelve seasons combined. He finished his career with the Oakland A's, where Billy finally got a chance to play in the postseason.

<u>Historical note</u>: On the day the hotline was installed between the Kremlin and the White House (1963), Billy hit two homers against his former teammate Dick Drott in a 5-0 win over Houston in Wrigley Field.

Brian Williams 1969–(Cubs 2000)

Williams showed some promise early in his big league career with the Astros, finishing in the top ten in the Rookie of the Year voting that season, but the pitcher really struggled after that. The Cubs were desperate when they signed him in January of 2000. It didn't work out. He pitched in 22 games and his ERA was a staggering 9.62. The Cubs released him at the end of May.

Cy Williams 1887—1974 (Cubs 1912-1917)

The Cubs center fielder was the NL home run champ in 1916 with a whopping 12 homers. He also has the distinction of scoring the winning run in the first game the Cubs ever played at Wrigley Field. After the 1917 season, the Cubs traded Cy to the Phillies for a soon-to-be washed up Dode Paskert, center fielder for center fielder. Williams had been pretty good for the Cubs, but after the trade to the Phillies he blossomed into a superstar. He hit 217 of his 251 career home runs for the Phillies, and by the time he retired in 1930, he was one of only three players in major league history with over 250 career home runs (the other two were Babe Ruth and Rogers Hornsby). Paskert had two good years with the Cubs (although he helped them win the pennant in 1918), but his speed, which had been a key part of his game, was nearly gone. After the 1920 season he was released.

Dewey Williams 1916—2000 (Cubs 1944-1948)

Dewey was a member of the 1945 pennant-winning Cubs team as the backup catcher, and even played in two of the 1945 World Series games. He struck out as a pinch hitter in Game 5 at Wrigley Field, and came in to catch in extra innings during Game 6, the last World Series game the Cubs won before 2016.

Jerome Williams 1981—(Cubs 2005-2006)

The Cubs got him the trade that sent Latroy Hawkins to San Francisco. They gave the former Giant a shot at being in their rotation, and Williams responded with a decent season. In 18 starts, he won 6 and posted a 3.91 ERA. The following season, however, he was pounded. The Cubs sent him to the minors, and then waived him. Williams later pitched for the Nationals, Rangers, Astros, Angels, and Phillies.

Mitch Williams 1964— (Cubs 1989-1990)

Cubs fans would sing the rock song "Wild Thing" when Mitch Williams emerged from the Chicago bullpen in 1989, in reference to his explosive but uncontrollable fastball (and yes, he got that nickname before the movie *Major Leagues* came out). The Cubs got him in a trade in exchange for Rafael Palmeiro and Jamie Moyer, which in retrospect is a really, really, geez, legendarily bad trade. (Although Mitch did lead the Cubs to the playoffs in 1989, and pitched well in the playoffs, too. His ERA that series was 0.00 in 2 games.) Wild Thing saved 52 games in his two Cubs seasons, and eventually went to the World Series with the Phillies, losing the '93 Series by giving up Joe Carter's home run. In fairness to Mitch he did win two games and save the other two wins in the NLCS for Philly, but he'll always be remembered for that home run…and his World Series ERA of 20.25.

Otto Williams 1877—1937 (Cubs 1903-1904)

Otto was a slick-fielding utility man who backed up three Hall of Famers — Tinker, Evers, and Chance. He didn't hit well (just over .200), but he did get plenty of opportunities during his two seasons with the Cubs. He also played for the Cardinals and Senators.

Pop Williams 1874—1959 (Orphans/Cubs 1902-1903)

Williams was 11-16 with a 2.49 ERA, and 27 complete games in his first season with Chicago. The team wanted him back the next year, but he was coaching the Bowdoin College baseball team. He decided to give it one more shot, but it only lasted one game. He started a game, and decided Chicago was no longer the place for him. He later pitched for the Phillies and the Braves.

Wash Williams ?—? (White Stockings 1885)

Very little is known about Wash. We don't know his birthday or his year of birth. We don't know if he was right-handed or left-handed. We just know that he played exactly one game with the Cubs (then known as the White Stockings) on June 8, 1885. He started the game as the pitcher (and gave up five walks and five runs) and was moved to the outfield in the third inning. He did manage to get one hit in a Chicago uniform. After that, his trail disappears.

Ned Williamson 1857 —1894 (White Stockings 1879-1889)

Williamson was Chicago's star shortstop/third baseman during the 1880s. He thrilled the fans with his home runs, and was arguably the game's first home run hero. In 1884 he hit 27 in one 112-game season. That was the record for 35 years. It wasn't broken until 1919 by a little known slugger/pitcher named Babe Ruth. Of course, Ned's record came with an asterisk. During the 19th century the ground rules were made by each home team. Ned's manager Cap Anson declared that balls hit over a certain part of his field were to be declared homers. That just happened to be where Ned hit 25 of his 27 homers that season. The next season the team moved to West Side Grounds and Ned's power suddenly disappeared. On the other hand, Ned was no fluke. He also set the record for doubles with 49 in 1883, and was a key member of the Chicago team that won five championships that decade. His baseball career was still going strong until Albert Spalding organized a world tour to promote the game in 1889. While the team played in Paris, Ned injured his knee. He was never the same after that. Just four years after his playing career ended, Williamson contracted tuberculosis and died at age 36. He is buried in an unmarked grave in Rosehill Cemetery in Chicago.

Scott Williamson 1976 – (Cubs 2005-2006)
The former Rookie of the Year, All-Star, and World Series champ was coming off arm problems when the Cubs took a flyer on him in early 2005. He was supposed to be the team's closer, but Ryan Dempster took over that role instead, and Williamson struggled to regain his velocity. The Cubs traded him the following season to the Padres.

Jim Willis 1927 – (Cubs 1953-1954)
Willis spent his entire big league career in a Cubs uniform, but it didn't last long. The reliever had trouble with his command. In his final season with the Cubs he pitched twenty-three innings and walked eighteen men. Jim pitched in the minors until 1957 before hanging up his spikes at the age of 30.

Bump Wills 1952 – (Cubs 1982)
His real name is Elliot Taylor Wills. When he was a boy his big brother Barry called him "Bumpy" and it was later shortened to "Bump". Bump is the son of legendary Dodgers shortstop Maury Wills, and never quite managed to escape his father's shadow. In fact, throughout his baseball career, Bump tended to be known more for the circumstances surrounding him than his baseball ability (which was, in all fairness, pretty

solid). It began in his rookie season with the Rangers. He replaced Lenny Randle at second base, which led to Lenny punching manager Frank Lucchesi in the face. (Both of them later ended up with the Cubs.) Wills came to the Cubs in 1982 and was their starting second baseman that year. He hit a home run in his first at-bat, hit .272 for the season, and stole ten bases, but once again, he won't be remembered for that. He'll be remembered for who replaced him at second base the following spring: a youngster by the name of Ryne Sandberg. The player who took his number a few seasons later (#17) also became a well-known Cub: Mark Grace. (It's now Kris Bryant's number.) Wills' lone season with the Cubs turned out to be his last season in the big leagues. That 1982 Cubs team, by the way, had three future Hall of Famers (Fergie Jenkins, Ryne Sandberg, and Lee Smith), a future Cy Young winner (Willie Hernandez), and great players like Bill Buckner, Larry Bowa, and Leon Durham. They finished in 5th place.

Walt Wilmot 1863 – 1929 (Colts 1890-1895)
Walt was a good left fielder, but he was best known for hitting. A rare switch-hitter for his era, Wilmot led the league in homers and triples, and knocked in 130 runs in 1894. He settled in Chicago after his playing days were over. Wilmot still holds a Cubs record. He walked six times in a game in 1891, a feat that hasn't been accomplished since.

Art Wilson 1885 – 1960 (Cubs 1916-1917)
Wilson was a backup catcher for 14 big league seasons, including the first year of Wrigley Field (as a member of the Chicago Whales), and the first season the Cubs played at Wrigley Field (in 1916). He was also a member of three pennant-winning New York Giants teams, all of which lost the World Series. The highlight of his Cubs years was probably May 2, 1917. Wilson caught all ten innings of the double no-hitter game featuring Hippo Vaughn and Fred Toney.

Bert Wilson 1911 – 1955 (Cubs announcer 1944-1955)
Bert Wilson was a Cubs announcer during the first few seasons that Ernie Banks played for the team. In Spring Training of 1955, he interviewed the youngster, who was still shy and reserved at the time. The tape of that interview can found at www.justonebadcentury.com.

Enrique Wilson 1973–(Cubs 2005)

Wilson played nine seasons in the big leagues, mostly as a backup infielder. After stints with Cleveland, Pittsburgh, and the Yankees, he finished his career with the Cubs. In 25 plate appearances, he batted .136. How's this for a fluke statistic? In his career, Wilson batted over .400 against Hall of Famer Pedro Martinez. He faced him 25 times.

Hack Wilson 1900–1948 (Cubs 1926-1931)

Hack is still remembered for his record 1930 season when he drove in 191 runs, but during his Cubs days he was known for more than just slugging the baseball. He was known as a notorious hellraiser. Wilson had several run-ins with the law, his teammates, opposing players, and even fans. He was arrested for violating the Prohibition Act in 1926, but he was just getting started. Hack and his drinking buddy/teammate Pat Malone got into a fistfight in a hotel because they thought somebody was laughing at them. In 1928, he was fined after charging into the stands to fight with a heckler. Gabby Hartnett and Joe Kelly had to physically remove him off the fan — and thousands of fans swarmed the field. Hack once charged into the opposing dugout to punch a Reds pitcher…after Hack hit the ball. He was tagged out in the dugout. That same night he punched another Reds pitcher in the team train. A famous story, which may or may not be a legend, involved Cubs manager Joe McCarthy and Hack. To show Hack the dangers of drinking, Joe took a worm and dropped it in a glass of whiskey. The worm quickly died. "Now what does that prove?" asked Joe. Wilson thought about it for a while and replied, "It proves that if you drink whiskey, you won't get worms!"

Through it all, Hack was the most feared hitter in the National League. Hack still holds Cubs career records for best on-base percentage (.492), slugging percentage (.590), and OPS (1.002). He led the league in homers four years in a row, in walks and RBI twice, and led the Cubs to the World Series in 1929. For many years he held the single season home run record (56), and he still has the single season RBI record (191). But in 1931, things started to go south. Hack and player/manager Hall of Famer Rogers Hornsby didn't get along and were constantly at odds. It got so bad that the Cubs traded Hack to the Dodgers for Burleigh Grimes. Hack had one more good year with the Dodgers, but the end was near.

He retired after the 1934 season.

Near the end of his Wilson's life he appeared on a network radio show where he spoke about the effects of "Demon Rum." This was just a few months before his death on November 23, 1948. He was only 48. His body was unclaimed for three days before National League president Ford Frick paid for the funeral. The veterans committee named Hack to baseball's Hall of Fame in 1979.

Whispering Joe Wilson (Cubs announcer 1946-1952)

In the first televised Cubs game, the National League pennant flag was raised. The date was April 20, 1946, and WBKB-TV broadcast that first game with Whispering Joe Wilson behind the microphone. The Cubs lost 2-0. Joe was much more famous as a bowling announcer, but he did do Cubs baseball for a few years. In 1949, there were three television stations covering the Cubs. Whispering Joe Wilson on WBKB-TV, Jack Brickhouse on WGN, and Rogers Hornsby on WENR. (WGN didn't get exclusive rights until 1952). There were afternoons when those stations were the only three television stations on the air in Chicago, and the Cubs were broadcast on all three.

Jimmy Wilson 1900–1947 (Cubs manager 1941-1944)

Wilson was the primary manager for the Cubs during the war years. He had been a tough catcher with the Phillies, and served as their player/manager for several years in the 1930s. He also had a horrendous record in that role, compiling a .370 winning percentage. But 1940 was a different story. He was the catcher for the World Series-winning Reds in his last season as a player, so the Cubs thought they were bringing in a winner. Wilson never clicked with the Cubs. His best season as manager was 1943, when the team finished five games under .500. After getting off to a 1-9 start in 1944, Wilson was fired and replaced by Charlie Grimm.

Justin Wilson 1987–(Cubs 2017-2018)

When the Cubs acquired the fireballing lefty from the Tigers, they thought he was the final piece to their bullpen puzzle. Wilson had been tearing it up for Detroit as their closer (13 saves, 2.60 ERA), and the Cubs merely wanted him to be the setup man for Wade Davis. Something must have happened on the flight to Chicago because Wilson simply couldn't throw strikes. In 17 innings pitched, he walked 19 batters, and by the time the playoffs arrived, Wilson was on the very end of the Cubs bullpen bench. His 2018 season was much better, but the Cubs never quite felt like they could trust him, and let him go when his contract ran out.

Steve Wilson 1964–(Cubs 1989-1991)

Wilson was acquired along with Mitch Williams in the trade that sent Rafael Palmeiro and Jamie Moyer to the Rangers. During the Cubs division-winning season of 1989, he was a key arm in the bullpen. The lefty logged 54 appearances, winning six games and saving two more. On the other hand, he had a bit of a rough go in the playoffs that year. He only pitched three innings, and he gave up two homers. In 1991 the Cubs traded him to the Dodgers.

Willie Wilson 1955–(Cubs 1992)

Willie Wilson was one of the most dynamic players in baseball during the 1980s. Unfortunately, he wasn't on the Cubs during those years. He was one of the all-time great leadoff hitters, a two-time All-Star and Silver Slugger, and a batting champion, but it was his speed that made him truly special. Wilson led the league in runs, hits, singles (four times), triples (five times), and stolen bases, and was the leadoff hitter for the 1985 World Series Champion Kansas City Royals. He still has the most inside-the-park home runs since 1950 (with 13). The Cubs brought him aboard as a free agent during one of their many, many transition years. They got rid of dead weight like Greg Maddux and Rick Sutcliffe and brought aboard people like Jose Guzman (bust), Candy Maldonado (BUST!!!), and Willie Wilson. How did Willie do with the Cubs? Well, let's put it this way. In his career he stole 668 bases, but only eight of those came with the Cubs. He was 38 years old when he joined the team and his speed — which had always been his greatest asset — was gone.

Ed Winceniak 1929–(Cubs 1956-1957)

Ed was a local Chicago boy (Bowen High School), and a utility infielder during his time with the Cubs (his only time in the big leagues). He was used as a defensive replacement, pinch hitter, and pinch runner. His lifetime average was .209, and he hit one homer. The pitcher who served it up was former Cub Hal Jeffcoat.

Kettle Wirts 1897–1968 (Cubs 1922)

Wirts joined the team in 1922. The Cubs had three catchers on the roster: starter Bob O'Farrell and two young backups with awesome nicknames, Gabby Hartnett and Kettle Wirts. Wirts and Hartnett both caught 27 games that season for the Cubs, but their careers would go in very different directions. Hartnett would develop into such a force that the Cubs would find O'Farrell expendable. (They traded him to the St. Louis Cardinals, and he led them to their first World Series title in 1926.) Wirts, on the other hand, drifted off into obscurity. He played his last major league game in 1924. In parts of four big league seasons, Elwood Vernon Wirts managed to get only 86 at-bats. Although he accumulated a total of only three extra base hits (two doubles and one home run) in those at-bats, he also acquired a great nickname. Unfortunately, the origin of that nickname has disappeared into the ether like Kettle himself. Wirts died in Sacramento, California in 1968 at the age of 71.

Casey Wise 1932–2007 (Cubs 1957)

Wise came up to the big leagues with the Cubs in 1957. The second baseman/shortstop got the most extensive playing time of his big league career that season, appearing in 43 games and hitting .256. The Cubs traded him to the Milwaukee Braves after the season for pitcher Ben Johnson and outfielder Chick King. After his playing career ended, Wise became a dentist.

Harry Wolfe 1888–1971 (Cubs 1917)

Whitey, as he was known, played a little shortstop but was mostly a pinch runner and pinch hitter in the nine games he played with the Cubs in 1917. It was his only big league season, although he also played for Pittsburgh briefly that season. Harry played seven minor league seasons.

Harry Wolter 1884–1970 (Cubs 1917)

Wolter played six seasons in the big leagues before he came to the Cubs, including a stint playing for former Cubs manager Frank Chance in New York. The Cubs loved his smart approach to the game, calling him the brainiest outfielder in baseball. He went back to his native California during the war years and played in the minors there instead of accepting a cut in pay. He never returned to the big leagues.

Kathy Wolter-Mondelli (Cubs ball girl 1986-1987)

Lifelong Cubs fan Kathy replaced Marla Collins after she was fired midway through the 1986 season for posing nude in Playboy. For a season and a half she filled the same role, before the Cubs decided to go in a different direction. "I asked why they decided not to bring back the ball girls, and the Cubs told me they were going to use the batboys instead." Wolter-Mondelli remains in Chicago and remains a big fan of the team. In the book *Cubsessions* she says that the last out of the World Series win was a bittersweet moment because of the many people who never got to see it, including her father and grandfather.

Harry Wolverton 1873−1937 (Orphans 1898-1900)

As a rookie third baseman, Wolverton was the number three hitter in the Cubs (then known as the Orphans) lineup. He was known for his grit and determination — resulting in more than an occasional trip to the hospital. He was hit in the face with a ball, fractured his skull looking out of a train window and smashing into a pole, broke his collarbone and more. They nicknamed him "Fighting Harry." After leaving Chicago, Wolverton played most of his career with Philadelphia.

Tony Womack 1969−(Cubs 2003, 2006)

Womack had tremendous speed. He stole more than 20 bases in seven different seasons, and led the league three years in a row. The infielder was a late season pickup by the Cubs during their five-outs-away-from-the-World Series 2003 season. He hit only .235 in just over 50 plate appearances and didn't make the postseason roster. He later returned to the Cubs for his final stint in a big league uniform in 2006. Womack ended his career with 363 stolen bases.

Jimmy Wood 1843−1927 (White Stockings 1871)

Jimmy was a member of the first official Chicago professional team (in the National Association) in 1871. He was the best fielding second baseman in the league, and also hit .378 for the season. He later played for Troy, Brooklyn, and Philadelphia, but when the National League was founded in 1876, Jimmy's pro career was over. Unlike a lot of his contemporaries, Jimmy lived a long and healthy life. He was 83 when he died in 1927.

Kerry Wood 1977− (Cubs 1998-2008, 2011-2012)

He wasn't even 21 years old when he came up to the majors in May of 1998, but he made his mark right away. On May 6, 1998, he took the mound on a very cold and wet day in Wrigley Field and pitched one of the best games in Major League history. Before he was through, he had struck out 20 Houston Astros batters, allowed only one infield hit, and electrified an entire city. By the end of the day, he was forever branded Kid K. Wood won the Rookie of the Year award that season after striking out 233 batters in only 166 innings, and leading the Cubs to the playoffs.

Though Kid K. had his injuries during his Cubs career (he missed the entire 1999 season and long stretches of two other seasons), he was also on the mound for some of the greatest triumphs in Chicago Cubs history after a very long drought. In 2003 he was the winning pitcher in the game that gave the Cubs their first playoff series victory since 1908. He also pitched magnificently in the NLCS that year, though his luck ran out in Game 7. In 2008, he was the closer during that magical season (which, sadly, ended so disappointingly). Wood came back in 2011 to end his career in his adopted hometown. He was taken out of the game after striking out a batter — a perfect way to end his career.

When Wood retired he had the highest strikeouts-to-nine-innings rate in Cubs history, was third overall on the Cubs all-time strikeout list (behind Jenkins and Zambrano), and second on the all-time hit-by-pitches list (behind only the Old Fox, Clark Griffith).

Travis Wood 1987−(Cubs 2012-2016)

The Cubs got Wood in the Sean Marshall trade with Cincinnati, and he became one of their most reliable starters for a few years. In 2013, he started the season with nine straight quality starts, becoming the first pitcher since Three Finger Mordecai Brown in 1906. His greatest day as a Cub probably came when he hit a grand slam homer against the arch-rival White Sox. Wood was named to his first All-Star game just a few days later. Unfortunately, his 2014 season was a major step backwards.

The Cubs moved him into the bullpen in 2015, and he thrived in that role, appearing in 54 games. He saved four, won five, and struck out 118 batters in 100 innings pitched. In 2016, he was a workhorse, appearing in 77 games. In one memorable game, Joe Maddon moved him to the outfield when a right-hander was up so that he could bring him back to the mound for the next lefty. Wood made a great catch on a ball hit to the vines. Travis was part of the postseason roster and won a game in the NLDS, but he will probably be most remembered for what he did at the Cubs World Series parade. He wore camouflage at first, and eventually took off his shirt. Asked about his teammate's odd behavior, Jon Lester replied, "He's from Arkansas." After the 2016 season he signed with Kansas City.

Brad Woodall 1969–(Cubs 1999)

Woodall logged ten long years in the minor leagues, but he did get a few cups of coffee in the big leagues. His only full season in the majors was with the Brewers in 1998. His final appearance came in a Cubs uniform the following year. He started three games and registered a 5.63 ERA.

Gary Woods 1954–2015 (Cubs 1982-1985)

Woods was a backup outfielder for the Cubs in the early to mid-80s, and hit in the .240s during his stay on the North Side, which included the division-winning season of 1984. He also played for Oakland, Toronto, and Houston.

Jim Woods 1939–(Cubs 1957)

Woody, as he was known, was only 18 years old when he made his big league debut for his hometown Cubs. The recent Lane Tech grad didn't get a chance to bat, but he appeared in two games as a pinch runner (for catcher Gordon Massa), and scored a run. Neither of those appearances were in front of his hometown fans. They were in Busch Stadium in St. Louis. Just a few years later he was part of the trade that brought Hall of Famer Richie Ashburn to the Cubs. Woods had a brief cup of coffee with the Phillies in 1960-1961, and hit three homers.

Walt Woods 1875–1951 (Orphans 1898)

Walt was in the rotation for the Cubs (then known as the Orphans) in 1898 and started 22 games. To say he didn't have a strikeout pitch would be an understatement. In 214 innings pitched, he struck out only 26 men. Woods later pitched for Louisville and Pittsburgh.

World War II Veteran Cubs....24 Chicago Cubs served in the military during World War II, but Larry French was the only one to actively take part in the D-Day invasion. French was an active player until joining the Navy, but realizing his baseball career was essentially over, he decided to make the military his career. French stayed in the navy for 27 years (22 on active duty) before retiring in 1969 as a captain. Hoyt Wilhelm fought and was wounded in the Battle of the Bulge. He became a big leaguer after the war. Eddie Waitkus won four battle stars. Hal Rice fought in the South Pacific, and is the only Cub other than Civil War veteran Oscar Bielaski buried at Arlington National Cemetery.

Tim Worrell 1967–(Cubs 2000)

Worrell had a very productive 14-year big league career that featured a few very good seasons. He appeared in 678 games for the Padres, Tigers, Indians, A's, Orioles, Giants, Phillies, Diamondbacks, and Cubs. He won three and saved three games for the Cubs during his half-season in Chicago. After the season the Cubs traded him to the Giants for Bill Mueller. Tim's brother Todd was also a big leaguer.

Chuck Wortman 1892–1977 (Cubs 1916-1918)

He was a backup infielder for the Cubs for a few years, and even got an at-bat in the 1918 World Series. Wortman was a Cub during the first three seasons they played at Wrigley Field. Ironically, they didn't play the World Series there in 1918. Comiskey Park held more fans, so the Cubs played their home games there.

Bob Wright 1891–1993 (Cubs 1915)

If you want to go back in time to see Bob Wright pitch, set your wayback machine to either September 21st or September 24th in 1915. In his big league debut on the 21st, Wright came to pitch the final inning for Hippo Vaughn at West Side Grounds in a 5-4 loss to the Giants. He only gave up one hit. In his final big league game on the 24th, he pitched the final three innings for Zip Zabel of a 6-0 loss the Phillies. He got lit up in that one. Although he was only 23 years old, Bob wasn't asked to stay with the team when they moved across town the following season — for their first season at Wrigley Field. Bob's greatest accomplishment, however, didn't happen on the baseball field. When he died in 1993, he was 101 years old. At the time, he was the oldest living ballplayer.

Dave Wright 1875–1946 (Colts 1897)

Wright pitched exactly one game for the Cubs (then known as the Colts). It was on September 28, 1897, and he had a pitching line that simply isn't possible today. He pitched seven innings, gave up 17 hits and 14 runs…and won the game.

Mel Wright 1928–1983 (Cubs 1960-1961)

Mel didn't have a lot of success as a big league pitcher. He was already in his 30s when he came to the Cubs and was knocked around pretty well (7.68 ERA). However, after his pitching career ended, he went into coaching. He was part of the ridiculous College of Coaches experiment, served as a pitching coach for the Cubs and the Pirates, and was on the coaching staffs of the Yankees, Astros, and Expos.

Pat Wright 1868–1943 (Colts 1890)

Wright was a second baseman who played 14 seasons in the minor leagues, and exactly one game in the big leagues. On July 11th, 1890, just a week after his 22nd birthday, Wright started at second base for the Cubs (then known as the Colts). He went 0 for 2 with a walk. Chicago lost the game 6-0 in Boston.

Wesley Wright 1985– (Cubs 2014)

Wright signed as a free agent in 2014 and provided a good left-handed arm out of the bullpen. He appeared in 58 games and posted an ERA of 3.17. He became a free agent after the season. In his eight-year big league career, Wright pitched for five teams (Astros, Rays, Cubs, Orioles, Angels).

P.K. Wrigley 1894–1977 (Cubs owner 1932-1977)

He was 38 years old when he inherited the Chicago Cubs. At his father's deathbed in 1932, Wrigley promised he would never sell the team. Unfortunately for the Cubs, he lived up to that promise. Not only didn't he have the passion for baseball that his father William Wrigley Jr. had, he was completely indifferent to it. He didn't even attend the World Series in 1932, 1935, 1938, and 1945, even though his team was playing. Those teams from the 30s were essentially built by his father and his father's handpicked executives. The '45 team was a wartime fluke. After '45, we really saw the P.K. Wrigley effect. He owned the team from 1932-1977, during which time the most powerful team in the National League became the laughing stock of baseball. For twenty years in a row, under P.K. Wrigley, the Cubs never finished higher than 5th place (1947-1966). Charlie Grimm, a man who managed for him three different times, explained Wrigley's helping hand this way: "Whatever we said in the meetings, he'd always say, 'No that ain't right, let's do it this way.' He was absolutely wrong about everything." Then again, it's not fair to blame the whole bad century on this one man. He's only responsible for 45 years.

William Wrigley Jr. 1861–1932 (Cubs owner 1918-1932)

William Wrigley LOVED baseball. He didn't buy the Cubs as an investment. He bought the team because he loved the game, and had since he was a boy in Philadelphia. It killed him that his dad made him work at a young age, because every day he walked by the ballpark and heard the cheers, he wished he could go in and watch. He would tell his father that the relatives of his boyhood chums had died so that he could play hooky and go to the ballgame. He resolved that if he ever got a chance, he would own a baseball team one day.

Wrigley made his fortune in the chewing gum business, itself an act of accidental success. He started his business in Chicago selling his father's Wrigley's Scouring Soap. One day in 1892, he got the idea of offering two packages of chewing gum as an added incentive. The chewing gum was so popular he realized that he should concentrate on that, and he did. He began marketing it under his own name, and by 1893 Wrigley's Juicy Fruit gum and Wrigley's Spearmint gum were huge hits, and William Wrigley was a millionaire. By 1918 he was one of the most prominent citizens of Chicago, and had become an investor in the Cubs. When owner Charlie Weeghman couldn't sustain his finances, Wrigley took over as the majority owner, and finally realized his boyhood dream. He hired Bill Veeck Sr. that year, and with baseball lovers Wrigley and Veeck at the helm, the Cubs returned to their former glory. They won the pennant in both 1918 and 1929, and laid the groundwork for a team that would dominate the National League in the 1930s. Sadly, Wrigley wasn't around to see it. He died in 1932 before the Cubs made the World Series that year. On his deathbed he made his son Phillip promise never to sell the team. Even though Phillip didn't much care about baseball, he honored his father's wish and held on to the team until his death in 1977. Under the son, the Cubs atrophied and became the worst team in baseball, but they still played, and continue to play in the stadium that is named after his father, baseball lover William Wrigley.

Rick Wrona 1963 – (Cubs 1988-1990)

One of three young catchers on the 1989 Division Champion team (along with Joe Girardi and Damon Berryhill), Wrona got the least playing time of three. He lasted three seasons in Chicago as the team's third string catcher. He later also played for the Reds.

Michael Wuertz 1978 – (Cubs 2004-2008)

Michael was a reliever who appeared in 265 games for the Cubs, including two games in the 2007 playoffs against the Diamondbacks. He had moments of dominance and moments of struggling with his control. His best season was probably 2006, when he posted a 2.66 ERA. The Cubs traded him to Oakland after the 2008 season.

Marvell Wynne 1959 – (Cubs 1989-1990)

The local Chicago kid (Hirsh High School) finally got his chance to play for his hometown Cubs when he was no longer a kid. He was 29 when the Cubs picked him up to provide some veteran presence down the stretch of the 1989 division race. Marvell played all three outfield positions for that team, and got a taste of the postseason for the first and only time of his career. He previously played for the Pirates and the Padres. After the 1990 season, he finished his career in Japan. Marvell's son (Marvell Jr.) plays professional soccer.

Hank Wyse 1918 – 2000 (Cubs 1942-1947)

They called him Hooks because his best pitch was a devastating curveball. Hank Wyse was an important part of the Cubs starting rotation during the war years. In 1944 he won 16 games for the Cubs. But Wyse had his best season in the Cubs pennant-winning year of 1945. He won 22 games, posted a 2.68 ERA, and was named to the All-Star team. His results in the World Series, however, did not quite live up to the rest of his outstanding year. He lost the game he started (Game 2), and relieved in two other losses. For 71 years Hank Wyse was the last Cubs player to throw a pitch in the Fall Classic. He recorded the final Detroit Tigers out in the top of the 9th inning in Game 7 at Wrigley Field. Unlike many war players that never duplicated their success after all the stars returned, Wyse did have one more good year, but in 1947 his famous curveball lost its bite, and Wyse lost his spot in the Cubs rotation.

Additional Entries... If you check out the Every Cub Ever feature at www. justonebadcentury.com, you'll find several additional entries, including celebrity Cubs fans, writers, and bloggers. Under the letter W, you'll discover conservative commentator (and huge Cubs fan) George Will, and singer Hank Williams Jr, who is also a Cubs fan.

Y

The starting lineup of your Chicago Cubs beginning with the letter Y...

C – George Yantz, Cup of Coffee
1B – Pitchers Hand Out
2B – Eric Young, Basestealing Champ
SS – Steve Yerkes, World Series Champ
(playing out of position)
3B – Tony York, Wartime Cub
LF – Eric Yelding, Cool Breeze
CF – Don Young, 1969 Cub
RF – Automatic Out
Bench – Elmer Yoter, Cup of Coffee
SP – Carroll Yerkes, World Series Champ
SP – Anthony Young, Record Losing Streak
RP – Lefty York, 1920s Cub

George Yantz 1886 – 1967 (Cubs 1912)

Yantz got exactly one big league at-bat, and it came on September 30, 1912. He singled in that at-bat, leaving his batting average a perfect 1.000. Before and after his mini-taste of the big-time, he was a minor league catcher for ten years.

Eric Yelding 1965 – (Cubs 1993)

His teammates called him Cool Breeze. Yelding was an infielder/outfielder who was known for his blazing speed. One year with the Astros (before he came to the Cubs) he stole 64 bases, which was good for second in the league (1990). Unfortunately, he was also caught stealing 25 times. Yelding was a utility man for the Cubs in 1993, but was injured and missed most of the season. He hit only .204 and stole three bases in his limited time. He never played in the big leagues again.

Carroll Yerkes 1903 – 1950 (Cubs 1932-1933)

The lefty pitcher (nicknamed "Lefty" of course) was a member of the 1929 A's team that beat the Cubs in the World Series, but fell on hard times after that season, and didn't reemerge until the 1932 Cubs pennant-winning season. He only appeared in two games for the Cubs that year, and in one more the following season. That was the end of his big league career.

Steve Yerkes 1888 – 1971 (Cubs 1916)

Yerkes was a World Series hero immortalized in a poem by writer Grantland Rice, but that was before he came to the Cubs. He was a slick-fielding second baseman and clutch hitter for the Boston Red Sox in the American League, and then played in the Federal League and starred there as well. When Cubs manager Joe Tinker acquired him for the team's inaugural season at Wrigley, he figured he had something special. But Yerkes didn't do much for the Cubs and his big league career ended at the age of 28. The rest of his life was a struggle. His son died in childhood. His brother (another former big leaguer) killed himself. Yerkes stayed in baseball in the minor leagues, coaching and managing, finally ending his career as the freshman coach at Yale.

> Cubs players have had some great nicknames over the years. Among players starting with the letter Y, Cool Breeze, EY, and Lefty (2 of them).

Lefty York 1892 – 1961 (Cubs 1921)

Lefty got into quite a few games for the Cubs during his one season in Chicago. In 40 games, he went 5-9, with a 4.73 ERA. He was lucky it was that low. Lefty allowed 233 baserunners in only 139 innings pitched. He never pitched in the big leagues again

Tony York 1912 – 1970 (Cubs 1944)

Tony was a wartime player for the Cubs. At age 31 he made his big league debut and backed up shortstop Lenny Merullo and third baseman Stan Hack. Other than that one season, Tony was a career minor leaguer. He played 23 seasons in the minors, from 1933 to 1956.

Gus Yost (Colts 1893)

This is how obscure Gus Yost is. It is unknown when he was born or when he died. It is unknown if he was right-handed or left-handed. His hometown is unknown. The only thing we do know is that Yost pitched one game for the Cubs (then known as the Colts) in 1893 and gave up four earned runs in 2.2 innings pitched. He also walked eight men.

Elmer Yoter 1903–1966 (Cubs 1927-1928)

Yoter was primarily a career minor leaguer (19 seasons), but he did get a cup of coffee with the Cubs in 1927 and 1928. He got 31 plates appearances and knocked in five runs as a backup third baseman. After his playing days he worked for the Red Sox farm system as a coach and scout.

> ***Youngest Cubs to Homer....***Phil Cavaretta and Danny Murphy were only 18 years old when they hit their first homer for the Cubs. Harry Chiti, Ken Hubbs, Ted Tappe, and Don Young were 19.

Anthony Young 1966–2017 (Cubs 1994-95)

Anthony will always be remembered for his 0-fer streak. From May 6, 1992-July 24, 1993 (while with the Mets), Anthony went 27 consecutive starts without a win. He eventually won seven games for the Cubs over two seasons. Anthony passed away in 2017, the victim of an inoperable brain tumor. He was only 51 years old.

Danny Young 1971– (Cubs 2000)

The big left-hander broke camp with the Cubs in 2000, but had a very rough go of it. In only three innings pitched, he gave up six walks and five hits (including a grand slam homer). The Cubs sent him back down to the minors in early April and he never returned. The 83rd round draft pick is the lowest picked draft choice to ever make it to the big leagues.

Don Young 1945– (Cubs 1965, 1969)

Young remains infamous in Cubs history for a dropped fly ball in 1969. His teammate Ron Santo called him out in a postgame rant to the press, and many people think it damaged the kid's psyche and team unity. Santo apologized the next day, but Young was never the same after that. 1969 was his last season in the big leagues.

Eric Young 1967– (Cubs 2000-2001)

EY was acquired from the Dodgers in 2000 in a very good trade for the Cubs. The Cubs got a starting second baseman and a starting pitcher (Ismael Valdes) in exchange for a relief pitcher (Terry Adams). Young was a dynamic leadoff man. In 2000, he hit .297 and stole 54 bases. His totals went down a bit the following season, and the Cubs let him go in free agency. EY can now be seen on ESPN's Baseball Tonight and his son Eric Young Jr. followed in his big league footsteps. EY still shares a Cubs record (with Cliff Heathcote) for reaching base seven times in a single game.

> ***Additional Entries...***If you check out the Every Cub Ever feature at www.justonebadcentury.com, you'll find several additional entries, including celebrity Cubs fans, writers, and bloggers. Under the letter Y, you'll discover Cubs blogger Al Yellon.

CHAPTER
TWENTY FIVE

Z

The starting lineup of your Chicago Cubs beginning with the letter Z...

C—Todd Zeile, Well-Traveled Slugger
1B—Julio Zuleta, Panamanian Slugger
2B—Don Zimmer, Popeye
SS—Rollie Zeider, Bunions
3B—Heinie Zimmerman, Triple Crown
LF—Mark Zagunis, .400 Hitter
CF—Dutch Zwilling, Last Cub Listed
RF— Ben Zobrist, World Series MVP
Bench— Edwardo Zambrano, the Other Big Z
SP—Carlos Zambrano, Big Z
SP—Geoff Zahn, the Last Laugh
RP—Zip Zabel, Record-Setting Reliever
RP—Rob Zastryzny, World Series Champ
RP—Oscar Zamora, Cuban Closer

Zip Zabel 1891–1970 (Cubs 1913-1915)

When the Zabels had their little boy in Kansas around the time of George Washington's birthday, they thought it was only appropriate to name him George Washington Zabel. But no one ever called him George. His teammates called him Zip. Zabel pitched for the Cubs during their last three seasons at the rickety firetrap known as West Side Grounds (1913-1915). On June 17, 1915 he set a record there that will never be broken. He came in to spell Cubs starter Bert Humphries in the first inning, and went on to pitch the next 18 and 1/3 innings in relief. He faced 78 batters in those innings, and only gave up two runs. The Cubs finally won the game 4-3 in the bottom of the 19th.

Mark Zagunis 1993– (Cubs 2017-present)

Zagunis came up at the end of June in 2017 as a rookie and got a taste of the big leagues. Unfortunately for him, he didn't have a lot of success. In 18 plate appearances he reached base only four times (all walks). He did, however, manage to steal a couple of bases before the Cubs sent him back to the minors. In 2018 he got another brief (very brief) call-up. He hit .400 for the Cubs, but unfortunately for Mark that came in only five at-bats.

Geoff Zahn 1945–(Cubs 1975-1976)

Zahn was one of two pitchers acquired for Burt Hooton from the Dodgers after the 1974 season. The Cubs gave the left-hander ten starts in 1975 to see what he could do, and while he didn't have terrible numbers (4.45 ERA), his 2-7 record was pretty bad. He spent most of the 1976 season in the minors. The Cubs were so unimpressed by him they released him January of 1977. Zahn had the last laugh. He went to the American League and pitched in the regular rotation of the Angels and Twins over the next 8 seasons. He averaged nearly 200 innings pitched and 13 wins a seasons.

Zach Zaidman (Cubs broadcaster 2018-present)

After a 14-year stint as the sideline reporter for Chicago Bears broadcasts, Zaidman switched jobs with Mark Grote before the 2018 baseball season. He hosts the pre and post-game shows for the Cubs on the Score (670 AM), and does an inning of play-by-play when Pat Hughes takes a break during the game.

Carlos Zambrano 1981–(Cubs 2001-2011)

For all the controversy he stirred in his Cubs career, Carlos was a very good starting pitcher for a decade. He was a three-time All-Star, twice finished in the top five in Cy Young voting, won 13 or more games six seasons in a row, won three Silver Slugger awards (as the league's best hitting pitcher), and threw a no-hitter in 2008. He also started games for the Cubs in four different playoff series. Unfortunately for the Cubs, he didn't win any of his five playoff starts. Carlos will always be remembered in Chicago not for his pitching or hitting ability, but for his temper. He punched his teammate Michael Barrett in the face, got into a shouting match in the dugout with his teammate Derrek Lee, and stormed out of the locker room after a game saying he was quitting baseball. That last one led to a suspension. He later changed his mind and apologized, but it was too late. His Cubs career was over. Zambrano is #2 on the Cubs all-time strikeouts list behind only Fergie Jenkins (1542).

Eduardo Zambrano 1966–(Cubs 1993-1994)

Eduardo had some pop in his bat, but by the time the Cubs gave him a break, the Venezuelan outfielder was already 27 years old. During the strike-shortened 1994 season, Zambrano hit six homers in only 116 at-bats. His nephew Rougned Odor is a big leaguer too.

Oscar Zamora 1944–(Cubs 1974-1976)

Zamora pitched a perfect game in the minors on the same day that Milt Pappas almost pitched one for the big league club (9/2/72). Oscar became one of the Cubs closers in the mid-70s before the arrival of Bruce Sutter. He saved ten games in consecutive seasons (1974-1975), but the first year went considerably better than the second. In 1975, Zamora was hit hard. The Cuban reliever gave up 17 homers in only 71 innings. When the next season went similarly, the Cubs sent him back to the minors.

Rob Zastryzny 1992–(Cubs 2016-present)

The Canadian-born Zastryzny came up at the end of the year and pitched in some important games for the Cubs. He pitched so well (1.13 ERA in eight appearances, 17 Ks in 16 IP), that the Cubs named the lefty to the postseason roster for the NLCS against the Dodgers. He didn't appear in any of the games. Zastryzny spent nearly the entire 2017 and 2018 seasons in the minors. He was called back up ever so briefly both years, but didn't have much success

Rollie Zeider 1883–1967 (Cubs 1916-1918)

He remains one of only two men to have played for three different professional teams in Chicago (he played with the Cubs, the Sox, and the Federal League Whales). His last three seasons in the big leagues were spent with the Cubs, serving as their utility man. Zeider played every position on the field except catcher, pitcher, and center field. Rollie's time with the Cubs coincided with the first three years the team played at what is now known as Wrigley Field (1916-1918). Once

called "Hook" because of his beak-like nose, Zeider later became known as "Bunions" when he contracted blood poisoning after a Ty Cobb spiking sliced into his bunion.

Historical note: On the day Ernest Hemingway was wounded in World War I (1918), Rollie was the hitting star for the Cubs in 6-3 win over the Giants. He scored twice and drove in three runs.

Todd Zeile 1965–(Cubs 1995)

Zeile had a stellar 16-year career as a third baseman, catcher, and first baseman, but only half of one season was with the Cubs. The Cubs acquired him in 1995 for pitcher Mike Morgan, but Zeile was a free agent at the end of the year, and signed with the Phillies. He also played for the Cardinals, Dodgers, Orioles, Marlins, Rangers, Mets, Rockies, Yankees, and Expos. In his career he hit over 250 homers. Nine of those were with the Cubs. He may have been a good power hitter, but Zeile was a bit of a butcher in the field. He had more errors in the 1990s than any other player in baseball.

George Zettlein 1844–1905 (White Stockings 1871, 1874-1875)

George was the first pitcher in team history. In his day, pitchers pitched every day, and George was no exception. He pitched all 28 games of the 1871 season (winning 18 and leading the league in ERA). He pitched in 57 of the 59 games in 1874 (winning 27, leading the league with seven shutouts). In his last year in Chicago, he pitched in 31 of the first 35 games. He later pitched for Philadelphia, including the first year of the National League. George is one of the few players to play for Chicago before and after the Great Chicago Fire.

Historical note: On the day Mary Todd Lincoln was ruled insane (1875) in a hearing led by her own son, George Zettlein and the White Stockings beat St. Louis 9-4.

> Cubs players have had some great nicknames over the years. Among players starting with the letter Z, Big Z, Bunions, Dutch, Popeye, Zip, and Zorilla.

Bob Zick 1927–2017 (Cubs 1954)

Zick had a cup of coffee with the Cubs during the 1954

season. He was on the roster multiple times that year (he came up in May and September), but Bob didn't get many chances to show his stuff on the mound. He pitched in eight games and was knocked around (8.27 ERA) by big league hitters. It was his only stint in the majors, and he was 27 years old. The University of Illinois grad pitched one more year in the minors before hanging up his spikes.

Don Zimmer 1931–2014 (Cubs 1960-1961)

Most modern day Cubs fans know the tale of his managing days in Chicago, but not many know about his interesting stint as a Cubs player. In April of 1960, the Cubs made a trade with the reigning World Champion Dodgers to acquire one of their backup infielders. That backup infielder's name was Don Zimmer. It was one of those moves that caused everyone in the league to scratch their heads. Although Zimmer was a competent enough player (he managed to stay in the majors for twelve seasons), he was coming off a season in which he hit only .165 in nearly 250 at-bats. He had very little power, very little range in the infield, and his best days were behind him. Plus, the Dodgers didn't really have a place to play the 29-year-old Zimmer. He clearly wasn't going to crack the lineup in 1960. They had All-Star infielders like Charlie Neal (2B), Maury Wills (SS), and Junior Gilliam (3B). Nevertheless, the Cubs traded promising young minor league pitcher Ron Perranoski (and two other players) to get him. The Cubs said they acquired Zimmer to play him at 3B — but they already had a rookie phenom poised to take over the position…a youngster by the name of Ron Santo. Santo was furious when the trade was announced, and threatened to quit. Rather than upset the youngster, the Cubs put Zimmer at second base, and traded their fine young second baseman Tony Taylor to the Phillies.

How did this trade work out for the Cubs? Perranoski ended up becoming one of the premier relief pitchers in baseball for the next decade. He pitched in two league championship series, and three World Series, winning two rings with the 1963 and 1965 Dodgers. He also led the league in saves twice, and saved a total 179 games between 1961 and 1971. Tony Taylor, who was only 24 years old at the time of the trade, played another sixteen years in the majors with the Phillies and the Tigers. When he retired after the 1976 season he was the oldest player in baseball (40 years old). Don Zimmer was

the manager of the Boston Red Sox at the time.

Zimmer's Cubs career is probably best remembered for his very public criticism of the ridiculous "College of Coaches" system, which he claimed was stunting the growth of budding superstars Ron Santo, Billy Williams, and Lou Brock. His candor was rewarded with being left unprotected in the expansion draft of 1962. He was drafted by the New York Mets, and played on the worst team in baseball history.

Historical note: On the day East Germany began building the Berlin Wall (1961), Don Zimmer clubbed a homer for the Cubs in a losing cause against the Milwaukee Braves at County Stadium.

Heinie Zimmerman 1887–1969 (Cubs 1907-1916)

Heinie saw some of the biggest moments in Cubs history, including both of their World Series championships of the 20th century, their last-ever game at West Side Grounds, and their first-ever game at Weeghman Park (now known as Wrigley Field). He was a great hitter — he nearly won the Triple Crown in 1912 — but he was a butcher in the field (making four errors in a game several times) and a troublemaker in the clubhouse. In 1908 he threw bottle of ammonia at a teammate's face (Jimmy Sheckard), and nearly blinded him. He was suspected of being a game-fixer later in his career (in New York) and was kicked off the team. He later worked in a speakeasy with the notorious gangster Dutch Schultz. In 1935 he was indicted for tax evasion. Heinie may not have had the best judgement or temperament, but he still shares the Cubs single game record with 9 RBIs (on June 11, 1911)

Ben Zobrist 1981 – (Cubs 2016-present)

The Cubs signed the two-time All-Star veteran fresh off his World Series win with the Kansas City Royals. Zobrist had the best years of his very good career when Joe Maddon was his manager in Tampa Bay. The super-utility man led the Rays to the World Series in 2008. His acquisition was the reason the Cubs traded Starlin Castro to the Yankees. In his first season in Chicago, Zobrist did not disappoint. He was named the All-Star game starter (at 2nd base), hit 18 homers, and drove in 76 runs, while playing all over the field. By the time the playoffs began, Javy Baez had claimed the full-time second base job and Zobrist was in left field. He saved his greatest moments for the biggest stage, winning the World Series MVP award after hitting .357 and delivering big hits in crucial moments, including the game-winning RBI in Game 7. Zobrist was injured most of 2017, but played through those nagging injuries. It affected him at the plate (particularly from the right side). He hit 12 homers and drove in 50, but batted only .232. His postseason magic didn't return either. Zobrist was hitless in the NLCS. In 2018, Zobrist bounced back. He flirted with the batting title most of the season, finishing at .305. His power numbers were down a bit (only 9 homers), but he was probably the club's most consistent player.

> Zodiac Cubs...is there any significance to the Zodiac sign in relation to performance? Judge for yourself. Here are a few Cubs All-Time Greats...Bruce Sutter is a Capricorn. Ernie Banks was an Aquarius. Ron Santo was a Pisces. Greg Maddux is an Aries. Rogers Hornsby was a Taurus. Billy Williams is a Gemini. John Clarkson was a Cancer. Joe Tinker was a Leo. Ryne Sandberg is a Virgo. Three Finger Brown was a Libra. Sammy Sosa is a Scorpio. Fergie Jenkins is a Sagittarius.

Julio Zuleta 1975–(Cubs 2000-2001)

The Panamanian slugger had obvious power, but he couldn't claim a starting spot with the Cubs. He was big (6'5) and bright (he could speak five languages: Spanish, Portuguese, French, English, and Japanese), but he isn't really remembered for either thing in Chicago. He's remembered for the funny spells he would cast on the bats in the dugout, trying to coax more hits out of them. Zuleta later starred in Japan.

Dutch Zwilling 1888–1978 (Cubs 1916)

Until 2015, if you went to the Baseball Encyclopedia and looked at the last name listed there, you would have found Dutch Zwilling. (Now it is non-Cub Tony Zych). Dutch was born in St. Louis, and only lasted four big league seasons, but the center fielder might have seen more historic Chicago baseball history than any other player. His career started in 1910 with the Chicago White Sox. If that year doesn't instantly ring a bell, it should. It was the first season the White Sox played in their brand new Comiskey Park. After that year he kicked around the minors for a few seasons, but re-emerged in the newly formed Federal League in 1914. If that year doesn't sound familiar, it should. It was the opening season of the ballpark now known as Wrigley Field. Dutch played both seasons for the Feds, and led the league in homers one season and RBI the next. When his owner bought the Chicago Cubs the following year, he made sure that he brought his boy Dutch to play for the Cubs. That was 1916, the first season the Cubs played in Wrigley Field. Dutch Zwilling may be the second-to-last man listed in the Baseball Encyclopedia, but he saw things in his playing days that most of us would only dream of seeing. He and his buddy Rollie "Bunions" Zeider remain, and will always remain, the only two players to have played major league baseball for three different Chicago teams.

> ***Additional Entries...*** If you check out the Every Cub Ever feature at www. justonebadcentury.com, you'll find several additional entries, including celebrity Cubs fans, writers, and bloggers. Under the letter Z, you'll discover actor/Cubs fan Adrien Zmed.

ACKNOWLEDGEMENTS

There are so many people to thank for the hard work that went into this book. First let me thank the team that helped me create the Cubs website justonebadcentury.com. Mike Davis was my web guru and Dale Stebbins did the design work for the original site in 2008, and I'll forever be grateful. David Stern handled the merchandise, and other than the gleeful cackling he did when the Cubs collapsed in 2008 (he's a Sox fan), he did a pretty good job of being a professional about it.

During those first few years of Just One Bad Century, I also made the media rounds, and without the help of John Records Landecker (I appeared on his radio show weekly on WLS in 2008 talking about the Cubs and the site), *Chicago Sun Times* writer Elliot Harris (he featured us many times that year), WFLD-Channel 32's Dane Placko (who recorded videos for my site that were noticed by ESPN and used for their Bartman special), and WBBM-TV's Kristin Hartman (who did a feature on me during the 2008 playoffs), people simply wouldn't have known where to find us. That same year I also met a few fellow Cubs fans/writers who propelled me further into Cub-world. Editor Donald G. Evans discovered my site and asked me to be a part of *Cubbie Blues: 100 years of waiting for next year*. Writing for that book and promoting it introduced me to Randy Richardson, who has since written two Cubs books for my publishing company, and publisher George Rawlinson, who knows more about the Cubs than anyone I've ever met. There are so many more people I've met thanks to this site, and I'm thankful for meeting all of them. I'd also like to thank all of the fans of the website who have checked it out all these years. In particular I'd like to thank Kel Kissamis and Bob Skelly — two die-hard fans who noticed my mistakes and tactfully and helpfully led me to correct them.

Without the prodding of my podcast (Minutia Men) and publishing (Eckhartz Press) partner David Stern, I know I never would have gotten around to turning this into a book. Through his insults when I reported on Cubs minutia ("Have you ever kissed a girl?"), and his exasperation when we were putting our publishing schedule together ("You've ALREADY WRITTEN ABOUT EVERY G-D CUB — make it a book, dummy!"), he prodded me to get this done. Thanks also to my great designer Vasil Nazar for making it pretty, and my proofreader/editor Lauren Schultz for catching the last batch of mistakes. I'm sure there are some that we missed — but hell — you try to tackle a project like this without breaking a few eggs. Also, most importantly, thanks to the Chicago Cubs for finally winning the World Series again so that this book is not a pathetic compendium of failure. Nobody would have bought that book.

ABOUT THE AUTHOR

In addition to being the editor-in-chief of Just One Bad Century (justonebadcentury.com), **Rick Kaempfer** is the co-founder and publisher of Eckhartz Press, a boutique Chicago publishing company dedicated to serving the brave new 21st century publishing world. Eckhartz Press focuses on Chicago authors and Chicago stories, and hyper-focuses their marketing in this tiny little community of eight million people. As of March 2019, Eckhartz Press has released fifty titles, including the memoirs of local celebrities like television news anchors Joel Daly and Rich King, radio personalities John Landecker, Chet Coppock, Bobby Skafish, and Mitch Michaels, and Chicago writing institutions like Chicago Literary Hall of Fame founder Donald G. Evans, and Chicago Writer's Association president Randy Richardson.

Rick is also the author of four Eckhartz Press releases himself, *Father Knows Nothing, Records Truly Is My Middle Name* (with John Records Landecker), *The Living Wills* (with Brendan Sullivan), and now *EveryCubEver*. In addition, he has been twice published by New York publishers (including a novel *$everance* and a how-to-book about radio called *The Radio Producer's Handbook*). Before founding Eckhartz Press in 2011, Rick was also a member of the Chicago media for more than twenty years as the executive producer of two Hall of Fame radio shows (Steve Dahl & Garry Meier and John Records Landecker), and still covers the industry as the media critic for the Illinois Entertainer. Rick and co-publisher David Stern host a weekly podcast on the Radio Misfits Podcast Network called Minutia Men. One of their frequent topics of conversation is the Chicago Cubs.

Rick lives in suburban Chicago along with his wife Bridget, and their three sons.

Rick and his oldest son Tommy 1996

Rick's son Sean and Fergie Jenkins

Rick in the Cubs radio booth with Ron Coomer, Bobby Skafish, Zach Zaidman

Rick and Sean after Jason Heyward grand slam walk-off

Rick's son Johnny at Wrigley 2008

Lee Smith and Fergie Jenkins high-five over Rick's son Sean

Rick's son Johnny at Wrigley 2018

Rick and Sean at Wrigley

Rick and Sean in the dugout

Rick and Sean 2016

Wrigley Ivy with Sean

Wrigley birthday Rick

everycubever

is available at:
www.eckhartzpress.com

**ECKHARTZ
PRESS**

OTHER GREAT BOOK from Eckhartz Press:

- **Cubsessions – 2019 Edition,** Becky Sarwate & Randy Richardson
- **Your Dime, My Dance Floor: Chet Coppock in Pursuit of Chet Coppock,** by Chet Coppock
- **Back in the Game,** by Rich King
- **Best Seat in the House: Diary of a Wrigley Field Usher,** by Bruce Bohrer
- **Lost in the Ivy,** by Randy Richardson
- **Grace and Friends: A Burn Prevention/Fire Safety Activity Book,** by Ken Korber
- **Nose Over Toes,** by Janet Sutherland
- **Death of the Angels,** by Alex Burkholder
- **An Off-White Christmas,** by Donald G. Evans
- **Monkey in the Middle,** by Dobie Maxwell
- **Protecting Children: Bettering the World One Child at a Time,** by Michael Ian Bender
- **1001 Train Rides in Chicago,** by Richard Reeder
- **Father Knows Nothing,** by Rick Kaempfer
- **The Living Wills,** by Brendan Sullivan and Rick Kaempfer
- **The Scar Dance,** by William Mansfield
- **Cameo,** by Beth Jacobellis
- **Chasing the Lost City,** by Tom Weinberg
- **Records Truly is My Middle Name,** by John Records Landecker

- **The Daly News,** by Joel Daly
- **We Have Company: Four Decades of Rock and Roll Encounters,** by Bobby Skafish
- **Safe Inside,** by Lee Kingsmill
- **Ranting of a Bitter Childless Woman,** by Jeanne Bellezzo
- **Life Behind the Camera,** by Chuck Quinzio
- **Doin' the Cruise,** by Mitch Michaels with Ken Churilla
- **Everything I Know I Learned from Rock Stars,** by Bill Paige
- **Brandwidth,** by Kipper McGee
- **GelStrong,** by Mark Gelinas
- **Out the Door!** by M.L. Collins
- **In Small Boxes,** by Ann Wilson
- **Truffle Hunt,** by Brent Petersen
- **Cheeseland,** by Randy Richardson
- **Hugh Hefner's First Funeral and Other Tales of Love and Death in Chicago,** by Pat Colander
- **Down at the Golden Coin,** by Kim Strickland
- **Chug-A-Chug,** by Scott Redman

And more